Lecture Notes in Computer Science 1140

Edited by G. Goos, J. Hartmanis and J. van Leeuwen

Springer
Berlin
Heidelberg
New York
Barcelona
Budapest
Hong Kong
London
Milan
Paris
Santa Clara
Singapore
Tokyo

Herbert Kuchen   S. Doaitse Swierstra   (Eds.)

Programming Languages: Implementations, Logics, and Programs

8th International Symposium, PLILP '96
Aachen, Germany, September 24-27, 1996
Proceedings

 Springer

Series Editors

Gerhard Goos, Karlsruhe University, Germany

Juris Hartmanis, Cornell University, NY, USA

Jan van Leeuwen, Utrecht University, The Netherlands

Volume Editors

Herbert Kuchen
Lehrstuhl für Informatik I/II, RWTH Aachen
D-52056 Aachen, Germany
E-mail: herbert@demeter.informatik.rwth-aachen.de

S. Doaitse Swierstra
Department of Computer Science, Utrecht University
Padualaan 14, 3508 TB Utrecht, The Netherlands
E-mail: doaitse@cs.ruu.nl

Cataloging-in-Publication data applied for

Die Deutsche Bibliothek - CIP-Einheitsaufnahme

Programming languages: implementations, logics and programs
: 8th international symposium ; proceedings / PLILP '96,
Aachen, Germany, September 24 - 27, 1996. Herbert R. Kuchen
; S. Doaitse Swierstra (ed.). - Berlin ; Heidelberg ; New York ;
Barcelona ; Budapest ; Hong Kong ; London ; Milan ; Paris ;
Santa Clara ; Singapore ; Tokyo : Springer, 1996
  (Lecture notes in computer science ; Vol. 1140)
  ISBN 3-540-61756-6
NE: Kuchen, Herbert [Hrsg.]; PLILP <8, 1996, Aachen>; GT

CR Subject Classification (1991): D.1.1, D.1.6, D.3.1, D.3.4,F.3.3, F.4.1-3,
I.1.3, I.2.1

ISSN 0302-9743
ISBN 3-540-61756-6 Springer-Verlag Berlin Heidelberg New York

© Springer-Verlag Berlin Heidelberg 1996
Printed in Germany

Typesetting: Camera-ready by author
SPIN 10513615   06/3142 – 5 4 3 2 1 0   Printed on acid-free paper

Preface

This volume contains the proceedings of the *Eighth International Symposium on Programming Languages, Implementations, Logics, and Programs*, PLILP'96, held in Aachen, Germany, in conjunction with the *Fifth International Conference on Algebraic and Logic Programming*, ALP'96, and the *Third International Static Analysis Symposium*, SAS'96. The previous PLILP meetings took place in Orléans, France (1988), Linköping, Sweden (1990), Passau, Germany (1991), Leuven, Belgium (1992), Tallinn, Estonia (1993), Madrid, Spain (1994), and Utrecht, The Netherlands (1995). All proceedings have been published by Springer Verlag as Lecture Notes in Computer Science, volumes 348, 456, 528, 631, 714, 844, and 982.

This PLILP symposium aims at stimulating research on declarative programming languages, and seeks to disseminate insights in the relation between implementation techniques, the logics of those languages, and the use of these languages in constructing real programs. Topics of interest included implementation of declarative concepts, integration of paradigms, compiler specification and construction, program analysis and transformation, programming environments, executable specifications, reasoning about language constructs, experiences in constructing applications, and typing and structuring systems.

The cooperation with ALP and SAS has strengthened the attractiveness of the overall event and – as a consequence – the quality of the presentations. The quality and (still increasing) number of submitted papers serves as an indication of the success of this approach. The program committee selected 30 out of 97 papers (31%), as well as a couple of poster and system demonstrations.

All communication in organising the symposium was done electronically: submitting papers, distributing papers to reviewers, transmitting and discussing reviews among the program committee members, and giving feedback to the authors. The smooth exchange of opinions improved the quality of the refereeing process and helped both to reduce the costs of organising the symposium and to keep the time between the deadline for submissions and the conference short.

In addition to the selected contributions, an invited talk was given by Lambert Meertens. Thanks to the collaboration with ALP and SAS, four additional invited speakers, namely Flemming Nielson, Andrew Aiken, Bernhard Steffen, and Claude Kirchner, could be presented at the joint conference.

On behalf of the program committee, the program chairmen would like to thank all those who submitted papers, posters, and system demonstrations and all the referees for their careful work in the reviewing and selection process. The support of several sponsors, listed in this book, is also gratefully acknowledged. Finally, we would like to thank the members of the organizing committees for their invaluable support throughout the preparation and organization of the conference and the composition of the proceedings.

Aachen

Utrecht

July 1996

Herbert Kuchen

Doaitse Swierstra

Program Committee Chairmen

Program Committee

María Alpuente	Universitat Politècnica de València, Spain
Patrick Cousot	École Normale Supérieure Paris, France
Yike Guo	Imperial College London, UK
Maurizio Gabbrielli	Università di Pisa, Italy
Fritz Henglein	University of Copenhagen, Denmark
Tetsuo Ida	University of Tsukuba, Japan
Gerda Janssens	KU Leuven, Belgium
Thomas Johnsson	Chalmers University of Technology, Sweden
Herbert Kuchen	RWTH Aachen, Germany, co-chair
Daniel Le Métayer	IRISA Rennes, France
Alexander Letichevsky	Ukrainian Academy of Sciences Kiev, Ukraine
Rita Loogen	Philipps-Universität Marburg, Germany
Jan Małuszyński	Linköping University, Sweden
Erik Meijer	Universiteit Utrecht, The Netherlands
Dale Miller	University of Pennsylvania, USA
Masaki Murakami	Okayama University, Japan
Rinus Plasmeijer	KU Nijmegen, The Netherlands
Laurence Puel	CNRS Université Paris Sud, France
Gert Smolka	DFKI Saarbrücken, Germany
Doaitse Swierstra	Universiteit Utrecht, Netherlands, co-chair
Pascal Van Hentenryck	Brown University, USA

Organizing Committee

Olaf Chitil
Arnd Gehrmann
Michael Hanus
Herbert Kuchen
Markus Mohnen
Ursula Oebel
Frank Zartmann

Sponsors

The Assocation of Logic Programming
Esprit Compulog-Net
RWTH Aachen
SUN Microsystems

List of Referees

The following referees helped the program committee in evaluating the papers. Their assistance is gratefully acknowledged.

Mina Abdiche, Peter Achten, Kenichi Asai, Lex Augusteijn, Roberto Bagnara, Anindya Banerjee, Eddy Bevers, Madhu Bhabuta, Helmut Boll, Urban Boquist, George Botorog, Dmitri Boulanger, Hilbrand Bouwkamp, Johan Boye, Silvia Breitinger, Maurice Bruynooghe, J.H. Canós, Magnus Carlsson, M. Carro, Manuel Chakravarty, Wei-Ngan Chin, Olaf Chitil, A. Ciepielewski, K.C. Claessen, Evelyne Contejean, Justin Cormack, Marc-Michel Corsini, Régis Cridlig, Saumya Debray, Bart Demoen, Eelco Dijkstra, Rémi Douence, W. Drabent, D. Duchier, Martin Elsman, Emmanuel Engel, Sandro Etalle, Moreno Falaschi, Pascal Fradet, Ulrich Fröhlings, L. Geijtenbeek, Giorgio Ghelli, V. Gisbert, Robert Glück, Thomas Hallgren, Lars Hallnäs, Makoto Hamana, John Hannan, Frank Hartenstein, Matthijs Havik, Morten Heine Sørensen, Martin Henz, H. Hommersom, Kenji Horiuchi, Luke Hornof, Arjan Houtman, John Hughes, Sebastian Hunt, Klaus Indermark, Florent Jacquemard, Johan Jeuring, Jean Jourdan, Jesper Jørgensen, Tadashi Kanamori, Tadashi Kawamura, Delia Kesner, Martin Köhler, Dennis Kokkeel, Millo Korving, Matthijs Kuiper, Julia Lawall, Y.H. Lee, Francesca Levi, Qiang Li, Hendrik Lock, Salvador Lucas, Claude Marché, E. Marchiori, Andrea Masini, Laurent Mauborgne, Lambert Meertens, Michael Mehl, Torben Mogensen, Markus Mohnen, Bruno Monsuez, Lidia Moreno, Christian Mossin, Martin Müller, Tobias Müller, Kaninda Musumbu, Koji Nakagawa, Hiroshi Nakashima, Vishaka Nanayakkara, Phuong Lan Nguyen, Joachim Niehren, Henrik Nilsson, Ulf Nilsson, Tomoyuki Nishioka, Shin-ya Nishizaki, Thomas Noll, Johan Nordlander, Jacques Noye, Hitoshi Ohsaki, Javier Oliver, Hans Olsen, Yolanda Ortega-Mallén, Jukka Paakki, Ricardo Peña, Marco Pil, Javier Piris, Konstantin Popov, D. Pretolani, Laurence Puel, María José Ramírez, I. Ramos, Jakob Rehof, L. Ricci, Olivier Ridoux, Mads Rosendahl, Francesca Rossi, Eric Rutten, M. Sakai, Juan Sanchez Díaz, David Sands, Ralf Scheidhauer, Stéphane Schoenig, Christian Schulte, Francesca Scozzari, Pascal Serrarens, Sjaak Smetsers, J.C. Soepenberg, Mathijs Sterk, Taro Suzuki, Kazuko Takahashi, Peter Thiemann, Hing Wing To, Bo-Ming Tong, Ralf Treinen, Naoshi Uchihira, Kristof Van Belleghem, Joost van Dijk, Marko van Eekelen, Rik van Geldrop-van Eijk, Peter Van Roy, Henk Vandecasteele, Arnaud Venet, Thijs Vermoolen, Germán Vidal, Tanja Vos, Dag Wedelin, Martin Weichert, Carsten Weise, Bernhard Westfechtel, Ronny Wichers Schreur, J. Würtz, Toshiyuki Yamada, Shoji Yuen, A. Zibouh.

Table of Contents

Calculate Polytypically!

Lambert Meertens

lambert@cwi.nl

Department of Algorithmics and Architecture, CWI, Amsterdam, and
Department of Computing Science, Utrecht University, The Netherlands

Abstract. A polytypic function definition is a function definition that
is parametrised with a datatype. It embraces a *class* of algorithms. As
an example we define a simple polytypic "crush" combinator that can be
used to calculate polytypically. The ability to define functions polytypically adds another level of flexibility in the reusability of programming
idioms and in the design of libraries of interoperable components.

1 Introduction

Which is more exciting: to find yet another algorithm, or to discover that two
familiar algorithms are instances of one more abstract algorithm?

It is the latter that sparks new insight and opens the way for finding further
connections, that makes it possible to organise and systematise our knowledge
and eventually set as routine exercises problems that once were feats of scientific
discovery. Mathematics likewise gets its leverage from abstraction, by going from
the specific to the general. Essential to the expression of abstraction is the ability
to parametrise.

John Hughes argues in [15] that the ability to name and reuse — i.e., to
parametrise — is at the heart of the functional languages' power. Standard combinators (higher-order functions) like map and foldr capture very general programming idioms that are useful in almost any context. Polymorphic typing
enables us to use the same programming idiom to manipulate data of different
types.

The next step is the ability to *parametrise a function definition with a type*. A
function thus parametrised is called *polytypic*. The "derived" functions of Haskell
are all polytypic, as are catamorphisms and friends [24] [29] [31]. The standard
foldr combinator is just the instantiation of the cata combinator for the datatype
constructor *List*.

While a polymorphic function stands for one algorithm that happens to be
insensitive to what type the values in some structure are, a polytypic function
embraces a *class* of algorithms.

The ability to define functions polytypically adds another level of flexibility
in the reusability of programming idioms and in the design of libraries of interoperable components. This, I claim, is of tremendous importance. Yet the greatest
gain, I believe, is to come from the ability to *reason* polytypically in the process
of deriving programs, in particular by calculational methods.

2   So what is polytypy?

Here are a few datatype constructor definitions[1]:

> **data** *List a* $=$ cons a (*List a*) $|$ nil
>
> **data** *Maybe a* $=$ one a $|$ none
>
> **data** *Bin a* $=$ join (*Bin a*) (*Bin a*) $|$ tip a
>
> **data** *Rose a* $=$ fork a (*List*(*Rose a*))

Each of these types has its own map combinator, for which we only give the typings:

> map_{List} $\in$ $(List\ a \leftarrow List\ b) \leftarrow (a \leftarrow b)$
> map_{Maybe} $\in$ $(Maybe\ a \leftarrow Maybe\ b) \leftarrow (a \leftarrow b)$
> map_{Bin} $\in$ $(Bin\ a \leftarrow Bin\ b) \leftarrow (a \leftarrow b)$
> map_{Rose} $\in$ $(Rose\ a \leftarrow Rose\ b) \leftarrow (a \leftarrow b)$

Here are functions to test if a given value occurs in a data structure of one of these types.

> $e \in_{List}$ cons $u\ x$ $=$ eq $e\ u$ $\vee$ $e \in_{List} x$
> $e \in_{List}$ nil $=$ false
>
> $e \in_{Maybe}$ one u $=$ eq $e\ u$
> $e \in_{Maybe}$ none $=$ false
>
> $e \in_{Bin}$ join $x\ y$ $=$ $e \in_{Bin} x$ $\vee$ $e \in_{Bin} y$
> $e \in_{Bin}$ tip u $=$ eq $e\ u$
>
> $e \in_{Rose}$ fork $u\ xs$ $=$ eq $e\ u$ $\vee$ any $(e \in_{Rose})\ xs$

And here are functions to sum the elements in one of these structures — assuming they are numbers.

> sum_{List} (cons $u\ x$) $=$ u $+$ $\text{sum}_{List} x$
> sum_{List} nil $=$ 0
>
> sum_{Maybe} (one u) $=$ u
> sum_{Maybe} none $=$ 0

---

[1] Examples are in a pidgin based on functional languages like Haskell and Gofer. In particular the lexemic restrictions on constructor functions of these languages are not adhered to. To indicate the typing of a function, I write $f \in a \leftarrow b$ instead of $f : b \rightarrow a$. The advantage of this convention is that this matches the "backwardness" of composition, making it easier to assess the function typing of a composition.

$$\mathsf{sum}_{Bin} \quad (\mathsf{join}\ x\ y) \quad = \quad \mathsf{sum}_{Bin}\ x \ + \ \mathsf{sum}_{Bin}\ y$$
$$\mathsf{sum}_{Bin} \quad (\mathsf{tip}\ u) \quad = \quad u$$

$$\mathsf{sum}_{Rose} \quad (\mathsf{fork}\ u\ xs) \quad = \quad u \ + \ \mathsf{sum}_{List}\ (\mathsf{map}_{List}\ \mathsf{sum}_{Rose}\ xs)$$

Polytypy, now, allows us to replace all these definitions by a single definition for map_F, a single definition for $\in_F$ and a single definition for sum_F, each of which can be specialised to any of the above datatype constructors and many more by taking F to be *List*, *Maybe*, *Bin*, and so on.

Polytypy is orthogonal to polymorphism. The polytypic function map_F is truly polymorphic — that is, each of its instantiations is. The polytypic functions $\in_F$ and sum_F are as polymorphic as **eq** and $+$ are, which is, respectively, somewhat and hardly. However, **eq** is — or can be defined as — a polytypic function; see e.g. Sheard [34].

Other terms that have been used for the same concept are "structural polymorphism" (Ruehr [33]), "generic programming" (de Moor [5], Bird, de Moor and Hoogendijk [4]) and "type parametric programming" (Sheard [34]).

3 Some historical remarks

In what I'll refer to as "classic BMF" [28] [2], a.k.a. "Squiggol", the focus was on lists, with particular emphasis on a symmetric view in which lists are built up from the empty-list constructor [], the singleton-list constructor [_], and an associative constructor $+\!\!+$. Catamorphisms on these symmetric lists were written, in the most general case, in the form $\oplus/\cdot f*$ (a "reduce" after a "map"), which requires $\oplus$ to be an associative operator with some neutral element $\nu_\oplus$. In other words, $(\oplus, \nu_\oplus)$ constitutes a monoid, just like $(+\!\!+, [])$ does. The meaning is then inductively defined by:

$$\oplus/\cdot f* \ = h \ \textbf{where}$$
$$h\ (x+\!\!+y) = h\ x \ \oplus \ h\ y$$
$$h\ [u] \quad = f\ u$$
$$h\ [] \quad = \nu_\oplus$$

It is possible to leave $\nu_\oplus$ implicit since neutral elements — if they exist — are unique.

These notations were devised with one purpose only: to facilitate the derivation of programs by *calculation*. In spite of the focus on lists, the intention, from the start, has been to contribute to the development of "constructive algorithmics" as a discipline for calculational program construction encompassing much more than the theory of lists, however fertile by itself.

Malcolm [24] [25] [26] showed how to generalise essential parts of the theory to other initial datatypes, based on a categorical approach (Manes and Arbib [27], Hagino [13]). Fokkinga [7] [8] [11] honed the categorically-inspired calculational techniques to a fine edge.

While the theory developed by Malcolm and Fokkinga gave the basic tools needed for polytypic definitions, its application to deriving actual programs by calculation was initially largely confined to instantiations for, each time, one specific datatype.

The first calculational derivation of an actual polytypic algorithm that I saw, and an elegant one at that, was the one in Bird, de Moor and Hoogendijk [4]. Earlier work by Bird and de Moor on solving a variety of optimisation problems by calculation was polytypically unified by de Moor in [5]. Several further examples of polytypic calculations can be found in Bird and de Moor [3].

The most impressive polytypic algorithms today are those developed by Jeuring and his group, such as Jeuring's polytypic pattern-matching algorithm [21]. Jansson [17] presents a polytypic unification algorithm (see also Jansson and Jeuring [19]). Although not derived calculationally, these algorithms provide strong evidence of the potential of polytypic definitions.

Huisman [16] defines a polytypic function **unparser** — rather like polytypic flatten but with extra "hooks" for plugging in concrete syntax — and calculates a polytypic parser from it by function inversion. By defining a suitable intermediate abstract data type, the textual representation of a structured document can be changed by a composition **unparser · parser**.

4 Notation and terminology

The notation $(x :: e)$, in which the expression e may depend on the dummy x, denotes the same as the lambda form $(\lambda x \mapsto e)$. For any e, e^κ denotes the constant function that maps all arguments to e. Function id_a is the identity function restricted to type a. The datatype 1 stands for some one-element type, like that defined by:

data $1 = $ **blob**

Functor. An n-ary *functor*[2] F is a combinator that maps an n-tuple of functions $f_0, \ldots, f_{n-1}$ to a function $F f_0 \cdots f_{n-1}$ in such a way that composition and identities are respected:

$$F (f_0 \cdot g_0) \cdots (f_{n-1} \cdot g_{n-1}) = F f_0 \cdots f_{n-1} \cdot F g_0 \cdots g_{n-1}$$
provided that $f_i \in a_i \leftarrow b_i$ and $g_i \in b_i \leftarrow c_i$

$$F \text{ id } \cdots \text{ id } = \text{ id}$$

The clause concerning the typing serves to ensure the definedness of the compositions.

An example are the functions map_F, since they satisfy the functional identities $\mathsf{map}_F (f \cdot g) = \mathsf{map}_F f \cdot \mathsf{map}_F g$ and $\mathsf{map}_F \text{ id } = \text{ id}$. So they are unary functors. As is easily verified, $\mathrm{id}_a{}^\kappa$ is also a functor. It is n-ary for all n. Further, each extraction combinator

---

[2] The terminology is borrowed from category theory, but no knowledge of category theory is needed to follow the exposition here. Gentle introductions to category theory that are inspired by its use for program calculation can be found in [9] and [30].

$$\mathsf{Ex}_i^n \ f_0 \ \cdots \ f_{n-1} \ = \ f_i, \ i \ = \ 0, \ldots, n-1$$

is an n-ary functor. We write Id for the unary functor Ex_0^1, and Exl and Exr for the binary functors Ex_0^2 and Ex_1^2.

An n-ary functor induces a mapping on n-tuples of types. Let, for $f_i \in a_i \leftarrow b_i$, $i \ = \ 0, \ldots, n-1$, the (most general) typing of $F \ f_0 \ \cdots \ f_{n-1}$ be given by

$$F \ f_0 \ \cdots \ f_{n-1} \in A \leftarrow B$$

Then we denote these types A and B by

$$F \ a_0 \ \cdots \ a_{n-1} \ = \ A$$
$$F \ b_0 \ \cdots \ b_{n-1} \ = \ B$$

So for unary functor F we have

$$F \ f \in F \ a \leftarrow F \ b \ \Leftarrow \ f \in a \leftarrow b$$

Looking at the typing of map_F:

$$\mathsf{map}_F \ f \in F \ a \leftarrow F \ b \ \Leftarrow \ f \in a \leftarrow b$$

we see that the type mapping induced is F, i.e., $(a :: F \ a)$. We shall from here on use the *same* notation for the combinator and for its induced type mapping. Moreover, when applicable, we use the name of the type mapping for that. So, from here on, for function f, we write $List \ f$ rather than $\mathsf{map}_{List} \ f$. Likewise, we write a^κ instead of $\mathsf{id}_a{}^\kappa$.

To introduce polytypic definitions, we need to abstract from the constructor function names. Here are some basic functors that will be helpful, together with some auxiliary functions.

The sum functor. The binary sum functor $+$ is given by:

> **data** $a + b \ = \ \mathsf{inl} \ a \ | \ \mathsf{inr} \ b$
>
> $f + g \ = \ h \ \textbf{where}$
> $\qquad h(\mathsf{inl} \ u) \ = \ \mathsf{inl}(f \ u)$
> $\qquad h(\mathsf{inr} \ v) \ = \ \mathsf{inl}(g \ v)$
> $f \triangledown g \ = \ h \ \textbf{where}$
> $\qquad h(\mathsf{inl} \ u) \ = \ f \ u$
> $\qquad h(\mathsf{inr} \ v) \ = \ g \ v$

The following typing rule will be used:

$$f \triangledown g \in c \leftarrow a + b \ \Leftarrow \ f \in c \leftarrow a \ \wedge \ g \in c \leftarrow b$$

The product functor. The binary product functor $\times$ is given by:

> **data** $a \times b = $ **pair** $a\ b$

> $f \times g = h$ **where**
> $\qquad\qquad h(\text{pair } u\ v) = \text{pair } (f\ u)\ (g\ v)$
> $\text{exl}(\text{pair } u\ v) = u$
> $\text{exr}(\text{pair } u\ v) = v$

The following typing rules will be used:

> $\text{exl} \in a \leftarrow a \times b$
> $\text{exr} \in b \leftarrow a \times b$

Functor composition. If F is a k-ary functor, and $G_0, \ldots, G_{k-1}$ are all n-ary functors, their composition $F^\vartriangle G_0 \cdots G_{k-1}$ is an n-ary functor that maps an n-tuple z to $F\ (G_0\ z) \cdots (G_{k-1}\ z)$. Instead of $+^\vartriangle F\ G$ we write $F + G$, and likewise for $\times$.

From k-ary F we can make a unary functor $F^\star$ by defining $F^\star = F^\vartriangle \text{Id} \cdots \text{Id}$. So $F^\star z = F\ z \cdots z$, with k "z"s. When F is unary, $F^\star = F$. Furthermore we have a distribution property:

$$(F^\vartriangle G_0 \cdots G_{k-1})^\star = F^\vartriangle G_0{}^\star \cdots G_{k-1}{}^\star$$

In the expression $(a^\kappa)^\star$ the value of k is not determined, but since it is immaterial to the result this shouldn't be a problem.

5 Catamorphisms

We first look at a simple inductively defined datatype, that of the Peano naturals:

> **data** $Nat = $ **succ** $Nat\ |\ $ **zero**

There is only one number zero, which we can make explicit by:

> **data** $Nat = $ **succ** $Nat\ |\ $ **zero** 1

Instead of fancy constructor function names like **succ** and **zero** we now employ boring standard ones:

> **data** $Nat = $ **inl** $Nat\ |\ $ **inr** 1

The choice here is that afforded by sum, so we obtain, finally,

> **data** $Nat = $ **in**$(Nat + 1)$

in which there is one explicit constructor function left.

Now define the unary functor N by

> $N\ z = z + 1$

Using the notations introduced earlier, this functor can also be expressed as $N = \mathsf{Id} + 1^{\kappa}$. The functor N captures the pattern of the inductive formation of the Peano naturals. The point is that we can use this to rewrite the definition of *Nat* to

> **data** *Nat* $=$ $\mathsf{in}(N\ Nat)$

Apparently, the pattern functor N uniquely determines the datatype *Nat*. A functor built only from constants, extractions, sums, products and composition is called a *polynomial* functor. Whenever F is a unary polynomial functor, a definition of the form **data** $Z = \mathsf{in}(F\ Z)$ uniquely determines Z. We need a notation to denote the datatype Z that is obtained, and write $Z = \mu F$. So $Nat = \mu N$. Replacing Z by μF in the datatype definition, and adding a subscript to the single constructor function in in order to disambiguate it, we obtain:

> **data** $\mu F = \mathsf{in}_F(F\ \mu F)$

Now in_F is a polytypic function, with typing

> $\mathsf{in}_F \in \mu F \leftarrow F\ \mu F$

Each datatype μF has its cata combinator, which we denote with Malcolm's banana brackets:

> $(\!\lvert f \rvert\!)_F \in a \leftarrow \mu F \quad \Leftarrow \quad f \in a \leftarrow F\ a$

It is defined by:

> $(\!\lvert f \rvert\!)_F = h$ **where**
> $\qquad h\ (\mathsf{in}_F\ xs) = f\ ((F\ h)\ xs)$

In words, when catamorphism $(\!\lvert f \rvert\!)_F$ is applied to a structure of type μF, this means it is applied recursively to the components of the structure, and the results are combined by applying its "body" f. The importance of catamorphisms is that they embody a closed expression for a familiar inductive definition technique ("canned induction") and thereby allow the polytypic expression of important program calculation rules, among which this fusion law (Malcolm):

> $h \cdot (\!\lvert f \rvert\!)_F = (\!\lvert g \rvert\!)_F \quad \Leftarrow \quad h \cdot f = g \cdot F\ h$

6 Type functors

Playing the same game on the definition of *List* gives us:

> **data** *List* $a = \mathsf{in}((a \times List\ a) + 1)$

Replacing the datatype being defined, *List* a, systematically by z, we obtain the "equation"

> **data** $z = \mathsf{in}((a \times z) + 1)$

Thus, we see that the pattern functor here is $(z :: (a \times z) + 1)$. It has a parameter a, which we make explicit by putting

$$L\,a \;=\; (z :: (a \times z) + 1)$$

Abstracting from a and z, we can write: $L \;=\; (\times) + 1^{\kappa}$. Now $List\,a \;=\; \mu(L\,a)$, or, abstracting from a:

$$List \;=\; (a :: \mu(L\,a))$$

In general, a parametrised functor $F\,a$ gives rise to a new functor, like here $List$. Such functors are called *type functors*. We introduce a notation:

$$\tau F \;=\; (a :: \mu(F\,a))$$

so $List \;=\; \tau L$, with L as above. The parameter a may actually be an n-tuple if functor F is $(n + 1)$-ary, and then τF is an n-ary functor. The "map" part of a unary type functor can be expressed as a cata:

$$\tau F\, f \;=\; (\!\!|\,\mathrm{in}_{F\,a} \cdot F\,f\,\mathrm{id}\,|\!\!)_{F\,b} \quad \text{for } f \in a \leftarrow b$$

Repeating this game for $Rose$, we find for its pattern functor $R\,a\,z \;=\; a \times List\,z$, or $R \;=\; \mathsf{Exl} \times List^{\triangle}\,\mathsf{Exr}$. This is not a polynomial functor, because of the appearance of the type functor $List$. Yet τR is well defined. Incorporating type functors into the ways of constructing functors extends the class of polynomial functors to the class of regular functors.

7 Regular functors

The definition of Fokkinga [10] will be followed, with one minor modification. A functor built only from constants, extractions, sums, products, composition and τ is called a *regular* functor. A formal grammar for the n-ary regular functors is:

$$
\begin{array}{lll}
F^{(n)} ::= & t^{\kappa} & n\text{-ary constant functor, for each type } t \\
\mid & \mathsf{Ex}_i^n & n\text{-ary extraction, } i = 0,\ldots,n-1 \\
\mid & + \mid \times \quad (\text{only if } n = 2) & \text{binary sum and product functor} \\
\mid & F^{(k)\triangle}\,F_0^{(n)} \cdots F_{k-1}^{(n)} & \text{functor composition} \\
\mid & \tau F^{(n+1)} & \text{the type functor induced by } F^{(n+1)}
\end{array}
$$

The minor modification, now, is that in the constant functors we do not allow any type t, but consider only the constant functor 1^{κ}. This has a technical background that we cannot go into for space limitations.

Here is how the functor $Rose$ is produced by this grammar:

$$Rose \;=\; \tau(\times^{\triangle}\,\mathsf{Ex}_0^2\,((\tau(+^{\triangle}\,(\times)\,1^{\kappa}))^{\triangle}\,\mathsf{Ex}_1^2))$$

Daunting as this may look, it was obtained by purely mechanical unfolding of earlier definitions. The embedded τ corresponds to the type functor $List$.

8 Polytypic crush

The key to polytypic type definitions (given the present state of the art — no *Polyps From Outer Space* yet but see Freyd [12], Meijer and Hutton [32], Sheard and Fegaras [35] and Fegaras and Sheard [6] for possible extensions) is the formal grammar for regular functions. The class of regular functors is itself like (and can be modelled by) an inductive datatype, and so polytypic functions can be defined by induction on the formation of a regular functor.

Let us see how we can define a polytypic crush combinator that, applied to a suitable "body", results in a function $r[F]$ with typing $a \leftarrow F^\star a$ for all regular F. We write $r[F]$ here rather than r_F because, in this definition, F is the main parameter. In the process we shall see what ingredients are needed for its "body". We shall make a concerted effort to minimise the number of ingredients that need to be supplied to the combinator, and — also to stay as polymorphic as possible — we let ourselves be guided by typing considerations to take whatever will do when available "for free".

So we consider all cases corresponding to the production rules of the grammar. The inductive hypothesis is that we already have

$$r[F] \in a \leftarrow F^\star a$$

for sufficiently simple F. For the case τF we assume, for the sake of simplicity, that F is binary. We postpone the case 1^κ to the last.

Case Ex_i^n: the requirement is $r[\mathsf{Ex}_i^n] \in a \leftarrow a$.
(Recall that $\mathsf{Ex}_i^n{}^\star a = \mathsf{Ex}_i^n \, a \cdots a = a$). The choice is obvious: $r[\mathsf{Ex}_i^n] = \mathsf{id}$. So this need not be supplied.

Case $+$: the requirement is $r[+] \in a \leftarrow a + a$.
Here there is one (and only one) polymorphic function that will do, namely $\mathsf{id} \triangledown \mathsf{id}$.

Case $\times$: the requirement is $r[\times] \in a \leftarrow a \times a$.
There are polymorphic possibilities, namely exl and exr, but fixing any choice from these here would constitute an unacceptable discrimination against either the Left or the Right. So some ingredient $\oplus \in a \leftarrow a \times a$ will have to be supplied.

Case $F^\triangle \, G_0 \, \cdots \, G_{k-1}$: the requirement is
$$r[F^\triangle \, G_0 \, \cdots \, G_{k-1}] \in a \leftarrow F \, (G_0{}^\star a) \, \cdots \, (G_{k-1}{}^\star a).$$
(The typing uses $(F^\triangle \, G_0 \, \cdots \, G_{k-1})^\star = F^\triangle \, G_0{}^\star \, \cdots \, G_{k-1}{}^\star$.) By the inductive hypothesis we have

$$r[F] \in a \leftarrow F^\star a$$

as well as $r[G_i] \in a \leftarrow G_i{}^\star a$, so that, using the typing of functors,

$$F \, r[G_0] \, \cdots \, r[G_{k-1}] \in F^\star a \leftarrow F \, (G_0{}^\star a) \, \cdots \, (G_{k-1}{}^\star a)$$

By composing these two we obtain for free

$$r[F] \cdot F\, r[G_0] \cdots r[G_{k-1}]$$

as having the required typing.

Case τF: the requirement is $r[\tau F] \in a \leftarrow \tau F\, a$.
Using $\tau F\, a = \mu(F\, a)$, and pattern matching against

$$(\!(f)\!)_G \in a \leftarrow \mu G \;\;\Leftarrow\;\; f \in a \leftarrow G\, a$$

(replace here G by $F\, a$) we see that we can use a catamorphism

$$(\!(f)\!)_{Fa} \in a \leftarrow \mu(F\, a)$$

which has the required typing if

$$f \in a \leftarrow F^{\star} a$$

The latter requirement is solved by $f = r[F]$. The free solution is therefore $r[\tau F] = (\!(r[F])\!)_{Fa}$.

Case 1^{κ}: the requirement is $r[1^{\kappa}] \in a \leftarrow 1$.
We need some value of type a. We solve this by imposing the requirement on the ingredient $\oplus$ (needed for the case $\times$) that it have a neutral element $\nu_{\oplus}$, and take that.
□

So, in summary, we only need to supply one ingredient: a binary operation $\oplus \in a \leftarrow a \times a$ that has a neutral element. We introduce the notation

$$\langle\!\langle \oplus \rangle\!\rangle_F \in a \leftarrow F^{\star} a$$

for this polytypic crush.

More flexibility. We make our crush more flexible by allowing an optional second parameter $f \in a \leftarrow b$ and defining

$$\langle\!\langle \oplus, f \rangle\!\rangle_F \in a \leftarrow F^{\star} b$$
$$\langle\!\langle \oplus, f \rangle\!\rangle_F = \langle\!\langle \oplus \rangle\!\rangle_F \cdot F^{\star} f$$

which generalises the one-parameter form since $\langle\!\langle \oplus \rangle\!\rangle = \langle\!\langle \oplus, \mathsf{id} \rangle\!\rangle$.

We also define a variant crush, actually just a useful abbreviation, designed for duty under bad weather conditions. What if $\oplus$ has no neutral element, like, for example, the operation $\downarrow$ selecting the lesser of two naturals? This was dealt with in classic BMF by introducing so-called "fictitious values". Here is a precise way of handling this. Given $\oplus \in a \leftarrow a \times a$ we construct a new operator $\oplus^{M} \in Maybe\, a \leftarrow Maybe\, a \times Maybe\, a$ which behaves like $\oplus$ on the range of one, preserves associativity and symmetry, if any, also on the extended domain and has none as a neutral element:

$$\text{one } u \oplus^M \text{one } v = \text{one}(u \oplus v)$$
$$\text{one } u \oplus^M \text{none} = \text{one } u$$
$$\text{none } \oplus^M \text{one } v = \text{one } v$$
$$\text{none } \oplus^M \text{none} = \text{none}$$

We use this now to define the variant. To distinguish it from the normal one we prepend a superscript M. With $\oplus$ and f typed as before,

$$^M\langle\!\langle\oplus, f\rangle\!\rangle_F \in \textit{Maybe } a \leftarrow F^\star b$$
$$^M\langle\!\langle\oplus, f\rangle\!\rangle = \langle\!\langle\oplus^M, \text{one} \cdot f\rangle\!\rangle$$

As for the normal crush we may omit the f-parameter when it is id.

9 Crush compared to cata

So isn't this crush a cata? No, it is not. For one thing, we saw that every type functor can be written as a catamorphism. Simple typing considerations show that in general type functors can not be expressed in the form of a crush. In that sense the crush combinator is less general. It is more general in the polytypic sense that crushes apply to source type $F^\star a$ for any functor F, while catamorphisms are only defined on source types of the form μG. (However, if $G = F\, a$, then μG is $\tau F\, a$, and the crush for τF is indeed a catamorphism.)

An interesting connection to classic BMF is

$$\langle\!\langle\oplus, f\rangle\!\rangle_{List} = \oplus/ \cdot f*$$

when $\oplus$ is the operator of a monoid. So we see that the catamorphism combinator $(\!(\_)\!)$ introduced by Malcolm [24] [25] [26] and the present $\langle\!\langle\_\rangle\!\rangle$ are different, incomparable, generalisations of Classic Cata™.

The most telling difference is the following. While $(\!(\_)\!)$ *itself* is a polytypic combinator, its *application* to a body does in general not result in a polytypic function. In contrast, the application of $\langle\!\langle\_\rangle\!\rangle$ always gives a polytypic function.

10 Some examples of polytypic crush

Function sum from Section 2 can be defined polytypically as a crush:

$$\text{sum} = \langle\!\langle+\rangle\!\rangle$$

in which "+" is addition on numbers. Using the flexibility afforded by the optional parameter, we can modify this to define polytypic size, a function for counting the number of elements in a structure:

$$\text{size} = \langle\!\langle+, 1^\kappa\rangle\!\rangle$$

Polytypic membership is obtained by

$$e \in = \langle\!\langle\vee, \text{eq } e\rangle\!\rangle$$

Here is polytypic flatten:

$$\text{flatten}_F \in \text{List } a \leftarrow F^\star a$$
$$\text{flatten} = \langle\!\langle +\!\!+, [\_] \rangle\!\rangle$$

Polytypic first returns the first element of its argument (first in in-order depth-first traversal). Since there may be no first element, we use the weatherproof variant:

$$\text{first}_F \in \text{Maybe } a \leftarrow F^\star a$$
$$\text{first} = {}^M\!\langle\!\langle \ll \rangle\!\rangle \text{ where } u \ll v = u$$

In all these examples the crush has the form $\langle\!\langle \oplus, f \rangle\!\rangle$ in which $\oplus$ is associative. This is not a coincidence. Although not required for the well-definedness, the associativity of the operation is suggested by the fact that modelling n-tuples with pairs can be done from the left or from the right, corresponding to the isomorphy of types $(a \times b) \times c$ and $a \times (b \times c)$. Since the choice is arbitrary, it makes sense to require $\oplus$ to be associative.

Why, then, not *require* it to be associative? Well, here are some interesting applications with a non-associative operator.

Polytypic depth (or height, if you prefer), returns the depth of the deepest element, if any:

$$\text{depth} = {}^M\!\langle\!\langle \odot, 0^\kappa \rangle\!\rangle \text{ where } m \odot n = (m \uparrow n) + 1$$

Function binned returns a $\text{Maybe}^\triangle \text{Bin}$ value preserving the tree shape (if any) while converting type $F^\star a$ to $\text{Bin } a$:

$$\text{binned}_F \in \text{Maybe}(\text{Bin } a) \leftarrow F^\star a$$
$$\text{binned} = {}^M\!\langle\!\langle \text{join}, \text{tip} \rangle\!\rangle$$

11 Calculating with polytypic functions

Polytypic crush captures one particular — although rather common — pattern of polytypic definition. For instantiations to specific datatypes, the calculation rules are well known. For example, if $h = \langle\!\langle \oplus, f \rangle\!\rangle_{Bin}$,

$$h \cdot \text{join} = \oplus \cdot h \times h$$
$$h \cdot \text{tip} = f$$

But we can go further. Not only can "canned" polytypy be put to good use to save a lot of work in writing polytypic programs, it can also be used to "calculate polytypically", giving identities that are polytypically valid.

As an illustration, we give, without proof, a polytypic fusion law for crushes, analogous to the fusion law for catamorphisms.

Crush fusion. *If the following three equations are satisfied:*

$$h \cdot \oplus = \otimes \cdot h \times h$$
$$h \ \nu_\oplus = \nu_\otimes$$
$$h \cdot f = g$$

then

$$h \cdot \langle\!\langle \oplus, f \rangle\!\rangle = \langle\!\langle \otimes, g \rangle\!\rangle$$

□

This is basically the "free theorem" (Wadler [37]) for polytypic crush, but a bit of fudging with the type is needed to handle the neutral elements. Jeuring and Jansson [22] show how to derive these for polytypic functions in general.

We can use this fusion law to find a condition under which

$$\langle\!\langle \oplus, f \rangle\!\rangle_{List} \cdot \mathsf{flatten} = \langle\!\langle \oplus, f \rangle\!\rangle$$

Using $\mathsf{flatten} = \langle\!\langle +\!\!+, [\_] \rangle\!\rangle$ and putting $h = \langle\!\langle \oplus, f \rangle\!\rangle_{List}$, crush fusion gives the conditions:

$$h \cdot +\!\!+ = \oplus \cdot h \times h$$
$$h \ [] = \nu_\oplus$$
$$h \cdot [\_] = f$$

From the theory of lists [2] we know that these are satisfied when $h = \oplus / \cdot f*$, that is, when $\oplus$ is associative. This shows that for associative $\oplus$ the crush $\langle\!\langle \oplus \rangle\!\rangle$ disregards any tree structure of the argument; it might as well have been a linear list.

For bad weather we have:

Corollary. *If the following two equations are satisfied:*

$$h \cdot \oplus = \otimes \cdot h \times h$$
$$h \cdot f = g$$

then

$$Maybe \ h \cdot {}^{\mathsf{M}}\langle\!\langle \oplus, f \rangle\!\rangle = {}^{\mathsf{M}}\langle\!\langle \otimes, g \rangle\!\rangle$$

□

An application is:

$$Maybe \ \langle\!\langle \oplus, f \rangle\!\rangle_{Bin} \cdot \mathsf{binned}_F = {}^{\mathsf{M}}\langle\!\langle \oplus, f \rangle\!\rangle_F$$

12 Some futuristic remarks

Suppose we need a function to swap two naturals, with the typing swap $\in$ $Nat \times Nat \leftarrow Nat \times Nat$. That is not a hard task, but somehow it is in the nature of programming that it consists of easy tasks, only there are so many of them. The hard thing is to combine all the easy solutions to the little easy tasks in the right way, and anything helpful in that is helpful in programming. A good typing discipline is helpful. No decent functional programmer would define swap specialised to the naturals, but instead use a polymorphic function

$$swap \in a \times b \leftarrow b \times a$$

In fact, giving this typing, you just can't get it wrong or else the type checking will tell you.

Similarly, even when — for all we know — a function may be needed for only one specific datatype, it may be helpful to define it polytypically. The possibilities to get it wrong but type correct are, if not crushed, then at least definitely reduced. Hindley-Milner style type inference for polytypic functions is described by Jansson and Jeuring [20]. Also, the polytypic version may be genuinely simpler. Just compare the polytypic definitions of $e\in$ and sum with the versions specialised for *Rose* from Section 2.

I started the Introduction with a question. Finding a new algorithm may be exciting, but coding yet another specialisation of a generic algorithm is not. Polytypy may prove to be the key to the level of flexibility needed to achieve interoperability by structural (as opposed to *ad hoc*) techniques. To facilitate polymorphic definition, we need elementary polytypic building blocks. Backhouse, Doornbos and Hoogendijk define, in a relational setting, a doubly polytypic and polymorphic zip. Jeuring [21] and Jeuring and Jansson [22] give many examples of further building blocks. More research is needed on "canned" polytypy, obviating the need of explicit induction on the formation of a regular functor. The crush combinator defined above is just a start.

References

1. Roland Backhouse, Henk Doornbos and Paul Hoogendijk. A Class of Commuting Relators. Unpublished, Eindhoven University of Technology, 1992. WWW ftp://ftp.win.tue.nl/pub/math.prog.construction/zip.dvi.Z.

2. Richard S. Bird. An introduction to the theory of lists. In M. Broy, editor, *Logic of Programming and Calculi of Discrete Design*, volume F36 of *NATO ASI Series*, pages 5–42. Springer-Verlag, 1987.

3. Richard Bird and Oege de Moor. *Algebra of Programming*. To appear, Prentice Hall, 1996.

4. Richard Bird, Oege de Moor and Paul Hoogendijk. Generic functional programming with types and relations. *J. of Functional Programming*, 6(1):1–28, 1996.

5. Oege de Moor. A Generic Program for Sequential Decision Processes. In Manuel Hermenegildo and S. Doaitse Swierstra, editors, *PLILP'95: Programming Languages: Implementations, Logics and Programs*, volume 982 of *LNCS*, pages 1–23. Springer Verlag, 1995.

6. Leonidas Fegaras and Tim Sheard. Revisiting catamorphisms over datatypes with embedded functions. In *Proceedings Principles of Programming Languages, POPL '96*, 1996.

7. Maarten M. Fokkinga. *Law and Order in Algorithmics*. PhD thesis, University of Twente, Dept INF, Enschede, The Netherlands, 1992.

8. Maarten M. Fokkinga. Calculate categorically! *Formal Aspects of Computing*, 4(4):673–692, 1992.

9. Maarten M. Fokkinga. A gentle introduction to category theory — the calculational approach. In *Lecture Notes of the STOP 1992 Summerschool on Constructive Algorithmics*, pages 1–72 of Part 1. Utrecht University, 1992.

10. Maarten M. Fokkinga. Monadic maps and folds for arbitrary datatypes. Memoranda Informatica 94-28, University of Twente, 1994.

11. Maarten M. Fokkinga. Datatype laws without signatures. *Mathematical Structures in Computer Science*, 6:1–32, 1996.

12. Peter Freyd. Recursive types reduced to inductive types. In *Proceedings Logic in Computer Science, LICS '90*, pages 498–507, 1990.

13. Tatsuya Hagino. *Category Theoretic Approach to Data Types*. PhD thesis, University of Edinburgh, 1987.

14. Paul F. Hoogendijk. Generators, Destructors and Natural Transformations. Unpublished, Eindhoven University of Technology, 1993. WWW ftp://ftp.win.tue.nl/pub/math.prog.construction/gendes.dvi.Z .

15. John Hughes. The Design of a Pretty-printing Library. In Johan Jeuring and Erik Meijer, editors, *Advanced Functional Programming*, LNCS 925, pages 53–96. Springer Verlag, 1995.

16. Marieke Huisman. *The Calculation of a Polytypic Parser*. Master's thesis, Utrecht University, Dept. of Computing Science, 1996.

17. Patrik Jansson. *Polytypism and Polytypic Unification*. Master's thesis, Chalmers University of Technology and University of Göteborg, 1995. WWW file:// ftp.cs.chalmers.se/pub/users/patrikj/papers/masters/thesis.ps.Z .

18. Patrik Jansson and Johan Jeuring. Polyp — a polytypic programming language. Submitted for publication, 1996. WWW http://www.cs.chalmers.se/~johanj/ polytypism/polyp.ps .

19. Patrik Jansson and Johan Jeuring. Polytypic unification — implementing polytypic functions with constructor classes. Submitted for publication, 1996. WWW http://www.cs.chalmers.se/ johanj/polytypism/unify.ps .

20. Patrik Jansson and Johan Jeuring. Type inference for polytypic functions. In preparation, 1996.

21. Johan Jeuring. Polytypic pattern matching. In S. Peyton Jones, editor, *Conference Record of FPCA '95, SIGPLAN-SIGARCH-WG2.8 Conference on Functional Programming Languages and Computer Architecture*, pages 238–248, 1995. WWW http://www.cs.chalmers.se/~johanj/ppm.dvi .

22. Johan Jeuring and Patrik Jansson. Polytypic programming. To appear in *Proceedings of the Second International Summer School on Advanced Functional Programming Techniques*, LNCS, Springer Verlag, 1996. WWW http://www.cs.chalmers.se/~johanj/polytypism/notes.ps .

23. Mark P. Jones. Functional Programming with Overloading and Higher-Order Polymorphism. In Johan Jeuring and Erik Meijer, editors, *Advanced Functional Programming*, LNCS 925, pages 97–136. Springer Verlag, 1995.

24. Grant Malcolm. Homomorphisms and promotability. In J.L.A. van de Snepscheut, editor, *Mathematics of Program Construction*, LNCS 375, pages 335–347. Springer Verlag, 1989.

25. Grant Malcolm. *Algebraic Data Types and Program Transformation.* PhD thesis, University of Groningen, 1990.

26. Grant Malcolm. Data structures and program transformation. *Science of Computer Programming*, 14(2–3):255–280, 1990.

27. Ernest G. Manes and Michael A. Arbib. Algebraic Approaches to Program Semantics. Text and Monographs in Computer Science. Springer Verlag, 1986.

28. Lambert Meertens. Algorithmics—towards programming as a mathematical activity. In J.W. de Bakker, M. Hazewinkel, and J.K. Lenstra, editors, *Proceedings of the CWI Symposium on Mathematics and Computer Science*, volume 1 of *CWI Monographs*, pages 289–334. North–Holland, 1986.

29. Lambert Meertens. Paramorphisms. *Formal Aspects of Computing*, 4(5):413–425, 1992.

30. Lambert Meertens. Category Theory for Program Construction by Calculation. *Lecture Notes for ESSLLI'95*, 1995. WWW http://www.cwi.nl/~lambert/e95.ps.Z .

31. Erik Meijer, Maarten M. Fokkinga and Ross Paterson. Functional programming with bananas, lenses, envelopes and barbed wire. In *FPCA91: Functional Programming Languages and Computer Architecture*, LNCS 523, pages 124–144. Springer Verlag, 1991.

32. Erik Meijer and Graham Hutton. Bananas in space: extending fold and unfold to exponential types. In S. Peyton Jones, editor, *Conference Record of FPCA '95, SIGPLAN-SIGARCH-WG2.8 Conference on Functional Programming Languages and Computer Architecture*, pages 324–333, 1995.

33. Fritz Ruehr. *Analytical and Structural Polymorphism Expressed Using Patterns Over Types.* PhD thesis, University of Michigan, 1992.

34. Tim Sheard. Type parametric programming with compile-time reflection. Oregon Graduate Institute of Science and Technology, 1993.

35. Tim Sheard and Leonidas Fegaras. A Fold for All Seasons. In *FPCA'93, Conference on Functional Programming Languages and Computer Architecture*, pages 233–242. ACM Press, 1993. WWW ftp://cse.ogi.edu/pub/crml/fpca93.ps.Z .

36. Daniël Tuijnman. *A Categorical Approach to Functional Programming.* PhD thesis, Universität Ulm, Fakultät für Informatik, Abteilung Programmiermethodik und Compilerbau, 1995.

37. Phil Wadler. Theorems for free! In *Functional Programming Languages and Computer Architecture, FPCA '89*, pages 347–359. ACM Press, 1989.

Limits of ML-Definability

Stefan Kahrs

University of Edinburgh
Laboratory for Foundations of Computer Science
King's Buildings,
Edinburgh EH9 3JZ
United Kingdom
email: smk@dcs.ed.ac.uk

Abstract. It is well-known that the type system of ML is overly restrictive in its handling of recursion: certain intuitively sound *terms* do not pass ML's type-check. We formalise this intuition and show that the restriction is semantical: there are computable (semantical) *functions* which cannot be expressed by well-typed (syntactical) terms.

Keywords: definability, polymorphism, recursion, ML, completeness

1 Introduction and Outline

Are all computable functions definable in ML? One should think so, after all ML supports general recursion and it is easy to define natural numbers with all their primitive operations using ML's datatypes.

But what about computable functions on other types, for example function types and inductive datatypes? Is ML "complete" w.r.t. to those types as well? Can we invert Milner's slogan "well-typed programs don't go wrong" and type-check programs that always go right? Before we address this specific question we shall define a general notion of completeness in a more abstract context.

1.1 Type Systems for Labelled Transition Systems

We first look at a general notion of type system for labelled transition systems. This is explored at greater depth in [5]. The idea is to view the operational semantics of a programming language as a labelled transition system and define an appropriate notion of completeness on this abstract level. Moreover, imposing a type system on a programming language can be viewed as an operation on transition systems.

Definition 1.1. A *transition system* is a structure (Sta, Lab, Tra) where

- Sta is a set of *states*,
- Lab is a set of *labels*, and
- Tra $\subset$ Sta $\times$ Lab $\times$ Sta is the *transition relation*.

A transition system is called *pointed* if there is a distinguished initial state ι.

As usual, we write $s \xrightarrow{l} s'$ for $(s, l, s') \in \text{Tra}$; also, $s \xrightarrow{w} s'$ with $w \in \text{Lab}^*$ is shorthand for: there exist states $s_0, \ldots, s_n$ and labels $l_1, \ldots, l_n$ with $s = s_0$, $s' = s_n$, $w = l_1 \cdots l_n$ and $s_{i-1} \xrightarrow{l_i} s_i$. If $s \xrightarrow{w} s'$ then s' is *reachable from* s; a state is *reachable* iff it is reachable from the initial state ι. We write $s \twoheadrightarrow s'$ for the reachability relation $\exists w \in \text{Lab}^*. s \xrightarrow{w} s'$.

Definition 1.2. Given a transition system, a relation $\precsim$ on states is a *simulation* if the following holds: If $s_1 \precsim s_2$ then

$$\forall l \in \text{Lab}, s_1' \in \text{Sta}. (s_1 \xrightarrow{l} s_1' \supset \exists s_2' \in \text{Sta}. (s_2 \xrightarrow{l} s_2' \wedge s_1' \precsim s_2')).$$

A *bisimulation* is a simulation $\precsim$ such that $\succsim$ is a simulation as well.

Here are a few useful observations on simulations and bisimulations: simulations are closed under (arbitrary) union and composition, hence the transitive closure of a simulation is a simulation and there is always a largest simulation. We write $\precsim$ for the largest simulation in a TS (which is necessarily a preorder) and $\approx$ for the largest bisimulation (which is necessarily an equivalence). The reflexive transitive closure of a simulation is also a simulation, since the identity relation obviously is one. Bisimulations are also closed under inversion and hence under equivalence closure or partial equivalence closure. The symmetric interior of a simulation is a bisimulation whenever the TS is deterministic.

For pointed transition systems, one could say that they are complete iff every state is reachable. However, this tends to be a stronger condition than we are really interested in: we only want to reach states up to bisimilarity:

Definition 1.3. A state s is called *complete* iff $\forall s_1 \in \text{Sta}. \exists s_1' \in \text{Sta}. (s \twoheadrightarrow s_1' \wedge s_1 \precsim s_1')$. It is called *bicomplete* iff $\forall s_1 \in \text{Sta}. \exists s_1' \in \text{Sta}. (s \twoheadrightarrow s_1' \wedge s_1 \approx s_1')$. A pointed TS is (bi-) complete iff its initial state ι is (bi-) complete.

For a corresponding notion of soundness we could declare a subset of states as error states with the idea of declaring a TS as sound if no error state is reachable and a state s as sound if no error state is reachable from s. In the presence of error states, the notion of completeness should be modified, i.e. we are only interested to reach each *sound* state (up to bisimilarity).

Definition 1.4. A *typed transition system* (short: TTS) is a structure $(A, B, :)$ such that A and B are pointed transition systems and $: \subseteq \text{Lab}_A \times \text{Lab}_B$. Given a TTS $(A, B, :)$ we define the associated *untyped transition system* $A : B$ as the pointed TS given as:

- the set of states $\text{Sta}_A \times \text{Sta}_B$,
- the set of labels $\text{Lab}_A \times \text{Lab}_B$,
- the initial state (ι_A, ι_B),
- the transition relation:
  $$(X, Y) \xrightarrow{(x, y)} (X', Y') \iff x : y \wedge X \xrightarrow{x} X' \wedge Y \xrightarrow{y} Y'.$$

It is beyond the scope of this paper to motivate the definition of TTS in depth [5]. However, the reader may observe in the course of this paper how the general definition neatly specialises to type systems for functional programming.

1.2 Completeness and ML

Traditionally [6], the operational semantics of ML is defined through a ternary relation $E \vdash e \to v$, meaning that the expression e evaluates in the environment E to the value v. We can turn this into a transition system M by taking environments as states and defining transitions as follows:

$$E \xrightarrow{(e,x)} E[x \mapsto v] \iff E \vdash e \to v$$

In other words, we can evaluate an expression and bind the resulting value to a variable. This corresponds very closely to the behaviour of an SML interpreter which (on top-level) evaluates *declarations* rather than expressions. We can turn M into a pointed TS by choosing the empty environment as initial state.

The structure of a type system for ML is similar: we have a similar ternary relation, with type environments instead of environments and types instead of values. The labels (e, x) are exactly the same. We can therefore turn a type system into a corresponding pointed transition system T and form a TTS $(M, T, :)$ where ":" is the equality relation. While M can be seen as the underlying untyped language, $M : T$ is the typed one in which we only evaluate well-typed expressions: each state in $M : T$ is a pair of a type environment and a (value) environment, and in each reachable state the types and values "fit" in a certain sense. One can identify various primitive error scenarios in ML which should not occur on run-time, e.g. using a number as a function. We can add corresponding transitions to error states whenever these scenarios occur — by the soundness of ML's type system these error states are unreachable. The completeness question is whether there are unreachable states in which the types and values still fit (i.e. the state is sound), but which cannot be simulated by reachable ones.

ML's type system limits the way a recursive function can be used in its own definition; although the function is polymorphic, the recursive calls cannot exploit this polymorphism.

    fun f x = f f

This function declaration does not type-check in SML, although f is perfectly sound (for type $\alpha \to \beta$): it is the totally undefined function; moreover, the declaration would type-check in an extension of ML's type system that guarantees soundness [4]. But the example only shows that certain sound *function declarations* do not type-check. The corresponding value is still ML-definable:

    fun g x = g x

which does type-check such that the value of g is equivalent to the value of f w.r.t. all function types, i.e. replacing one by the other in some environment E results in a bisimilar E' and thus this example does not show incompleteness.

Let us have a look at another example that makes use of these features and is limited by ML's approach to recursion in a more substantial way:

```
datatype 'a lift = One | An of 'a
(*  unlift: ('a lift) list -> 'a list *)
fun unlift [] = []
  | unlift (An x::xs) = x::unlift xs
  | unlift (One::xs) = unlift xs

datatype 'a lam =
    Var of 'a | App of 'a lam * 'a lam | Lam of ('a lift) lam
(*  fvars: 'a lam -> 'a list *)
fun fvars (Var x) = [x]
  | fvars (App (t,u)) = fvars t @ fvars u
  | fvars (Lam t) = unlift (fvars t)
```

The idea of the example is that the type `'a lam` is the type of λ-calculus terms with de Bruijn indices [2], where we leave the control over increasing and decreasing indices to the type system. For example, the named λ-term $\lambda x.\lambda y.x$ has a de Bruijn representation of $\lambda\lambda1$ which is expressed as `Lam(Lam(Var (An One)))`. The function `fvars` is supposed to compute the list of free variables of a term. We can observe that this function definition does not typecheck in SML, because the last recursive call uses `fvars` in the type instance $(\text{'a lift}) \text{lam} \rightarrow (\text{'a lift}) \text{list}$.

Thus we have a similar problem as in the earlier example, a sound function declaration that is rejected by ML's type system. The similarity ends here. This time there is no way to define an equivalent environment in SML and we shall later see why. The problem arises whenever we try to define a non-trivial recursive function on a recursive datatype with a non-regular recursive structure.

One could argue how useful these types are in practice, but this is not the kind of question I am concerned with in this paper. It is my opinion that completeness is a desirable property from a language design point of view. Completeness for ML can be achieved by either *extending* the type system of ML to support polymorphic recursion, or *restricting* it by banning non-regular recursive datatypes. Strictly speaking, the first part of this claim is a conjecture, since the standard argument to show completeness [5] does not go through for this language.

1.3   Sketch of Incompleteness Proof

How can we show there is no ML-function that implements `fvars`?

Given a term of type `'a lam` it is clear that any implementation of `fvars` has to "look at" all `Lam` constructors in its argument. "Looking at" a constructor means to match it through pattern matching, i.e. each `Lam` is matched by a corresponding pattern. Notice that nested occurrences of `Lam` have different types. ML type checking guarantees that we only match values of type t against patterns of type t, so how does a well-typed implementation of `fvars` find patterns of all these types? The answer is: it can't. One can eliminate ML polymorphism by making enough syntactic copies of the polymorphic bits, but this technique is doomed to fail for proper polymorphic recursion where "enough" means: arbitrarily many. Technically, the proof proceeds by showing that a certain relation between environments and type environments which holds for all reachable environments forbids an implementation of **fvars**; it is the same relation one would typically use for a soundness proof.

There is a connection with the pumping-lemma of formal language theory: if we view the type **'a lam** as an infinite tree in the style of [1] then we can observe that this tree is not regular, it has infinitely many different subtrees. ML functions can only fully recognise values of regular types.

2 Operational Semantics

To make the claims precise we present here the operational semantics for a small functional programming language with recursion and pattern matching.

$$
\begin{aligned}
e &::= x \mid b \mid c \mid (\lambda m) \mid \\
&\quad (e\ e') \mid (e, e') \mid \\
&\quad \mathbf{let}\ x = e'\ \mathbf{in}\ e \mid \\
&\quad \mathbf{fix}\ x = e'\ \mathbf{in}\ e \\
\\
m &::= p.e \mid p.e; m \\
\\
p &::= x \mid b \mid (c\ p) \mid (p, p')
\end{aligned}
\qquad
\begin{aligned}
v &::= b \mid c \mid c \cdot v \mid (v, v') \mid (E, m) \\
\\
w &::= v \mid \langle e \rangle \\
\\
E &::= \bullet \mid E[x \mapsto w] \\
\\
R &::= E \mid \square
\end{aligned}
$$

Table 1. Abstract Syntax

We consider expressions over the abstract syntax as shown in left-hand column of table 1, for which we assume the usual notational conventions for enriched λ-calculi, regarding the omission of parentheses etc. The metavariable e ranges over *expressions*, p over *patterns*, and m over *matches* (lists of pairs of patterns and expressions); x ranges over a set of variables and b and c over a set of constructors where b are thought to be nullary constructors. The set of variables is assumed to be countably infinite. In a match $p_1.e_1; \cdots ; p_n.e_n$ the variables in p_i bind variables in e_i. Expressions of the form $\mathbf{fix}\ x = e'\ \mathbf{in}\ e$ model recursive bindings, i.e. x is recursively defined by e'.

This language is in similar form included in most functional programming languages. However, it is significantly more complex than the simple expression languages usually considered in related research papers, for example [7]. The reason for this complication lies in the issues we want to address which are inextricably linked with both pattern matching and recursion.

To define an operational semantics for this language we need a notion of value and environment, as defined in the right column of table 1. The metavariable v

ranges over *values* which are either constructors, constructor applications, pairs of values, or closures; w ranges over *environment entries* which are either values or expressions, the latter being a special way of representing fixpoints. E ranges over *environments*, finite lists of pairs of variables and environment entries; R ranges over pattern matching results which are either environments or $\square$, where $\square$ indicates that matching has failed.

We now can define the mentioned ternary evaluation relation $E \vdash e \to v$. We also define two 4-place relations: $E, v \vdash p \to R$ meaning that the value v matches the pattern p giving rise to the matching result R; $E, v \vdash m \to v'$ meaning that the function denoted by m (with free identifiers determined by E) evaluates to v' when applied to the argument v.

2.1 Pattern Matching and Function Application

The rules for pattern matching can be given independently from the others, see table 2. The rules for pattern matching are straightforward and follow essentially the rules for SML [6] with $\square$ playing the rôle of FAIL. The only notable difference is that instead of returning the environment consisting of exactly the bindings caused by the pattern matching, we return the extension of the current environment with such bindings.

$$\frac{}{E, v \vdash x \to E[x \mapsto v]}$$

$$\frac{}{E, b \vdash b \to E} \qquad \frac{b \neq b'}{E, b' \vdash b \to \square} \qquad \frac{}{E, c \cdot v \vdash b \to \square}$$

$$\frac{E, v \vdash p \to E'}{E, c \cdot v \vdash (c\, p) \to E'} \qquad \frac{c \neq c'}{E, c' \cdot v \vdash (c\, p) \to \square} \qquad \frac{}{E, b \vdash (c\, p) \to \square}$$

$$\frac{E, v \vdash p \to E' \quad E', v' \vdash p' \to R}{E, (v, v') \vdash (p, p') \to R} \qquad \frac{E, v \vdash p \to \square}{E, (v, v') \vdash (p, p') \to \square}$$

Table 2. Pattern Matching

The rules for function application (table 3) and expression evaluation are mutually recursive. Function application is also defined very similar to [6], patterns are tried from left to right.

2.2 Expression Evaluation

The rules for expression evaluation in table 4 differ from SML's, because we have chosen a different and slightly more expressive method of unravelling recursion.

We have three rules for variable access: (i) we skip irrelevant environment entries, (ii) we access value entries, and (iii) we unravel recursive entries. The evaluation of constructors and λ-abstractions finishes instantly, as they are more

$$\frac{E, v \vdash p \to E' \quad E' \vdash e \to v'}{E, v \vdash p.e \to v'}$$

$$\frac{E, v \vdash p \to \square \quad E, v \vdash m \to v'}{E, v \vdash p.e; m \to v'} \qquad \frac{E, v \vdash p \to E' \quad E' \vdash e \to v'}{E, v \vdash p.e; m \to v'}$$

Table 3. Function Application

$$\frac{x \neq x' \quad E \vdash x \to v}{E[x' \mapsto w] \vdash x \to v} \qquad \frac{}{E[x \mapsto v] \vdash x \to v} \qquad \frac{E[x \mapsto \langle e \rangle] \vdash e \to v}{E[x \mapsto \langle e \rangle] \vdash x \to v}$$

$$\frac{}{E \vdash b \to b} \qquad \frac{}{E \vdash c \to c} \qquad \frac{}{E \vdash (\lambda m) \to (E, m)}$$

$$\frac{E \vdash e \to v \quad E \vdash e' \to v'}{E \vdash (e, e') \to (v, v')} \qquad \frac{E \vdash e \to c \quad E \vdash e' \to v}{E \vdash (e\, e') \to c \cdot v}$$

$$\frac{E \vdash e \to (E', m) \quad E \vdash e' \to v \quad E', v \vdash m \to v'}{E \vdash (e\, e') \to v'}$$

$$\frac{E \vdash e' \to v \quad E[x \mapsto v] \vdash e \to v'}{E \vdash \mathbf{let}\ x = e'\ \mathbf{in}\ e \to v'} \qquad \frac{E[x \mapsto \langle e' \rangle] \vdash e \to v}{E \vdash \mathbf{fix}\ x = e'\ \mathbf{in}\ e \to v}$$

Table 4. Expression Evaluation

or less considered values themselves. The rules for pairs and constructor application are self-explanatory. Closure applications are defined in terms of the judgement form $E, v \vdash m \to r$. The rule for **let** does what one would expect; **fix** is similar, but the binding is recursive and the evaluation is delayed until the recursive identifier is used. So one can use **fix** to simulate lazy evaluation.

2.3 Properties

As already mentioned we can define a pointed transition system based on the operational semantics.

Definition 2.1. The pointed transition system M is defined as follows: environments are states, the empty environment $\bullet$ is the initial state, transitions are defined as:

$$E \xrightarrow{(e, x)} E[x \mapsto v] \iff E \vdash e \to v$$

A transition of M can be viewed as evaluating a declaration in an ML interpreter, the states of M correspond closely to those states of an (untyped) ML interpreter the user can interact with.

Proposition 2.2. M *is deterministic; more specifically:*

1. Let $E \vdash e \to v$ and $E \vdash e \to v'$. Then $v = v'$.

2. Let $E, v \vdash m \to v'$ and $E, v \vdash m \to v''$. Then $v' = v''$.

3. Let $E, v \vdash p \to R$ and $E, v \vdash p \to R'$. Then $R = R'$.

Determinism simplifies the reasoning about programs significantly. In particular, bisimulation equivalence and trace equivalence coincide for deterministic transition systems; this means here that two environments are indistinguishable iff they evaluate the same sequences of expressions. One can sharpen that result: two environments are indistinguishable iff they evaluate the same expressions.

Since the bindings for program variables are purely syntactic, environments, values and expressions can be seen as terms over some many-sorted first-order signature and similarly the three judgement forms (plus the inequality of constructors and variables) as first-order predicate symbols. This allows the reading of our specification of the evaluation relation as a first-order logic program (a set of Horn clauses), which has exactly the desired meaning once we augment it with some symbols for the formation of constructors and program variables and the appropriate clauses for the inequality predicates for these sorts.

Consequences of this logic program are not only the judgements of the operational semantics but also certain open judgements, e.g. $E, b \vdash b \to E$ is not only derivable for any concrete E and b but also as an open judgement where E and b are meta-variables ranging over environments and constructors. Remark: we have notationally suppressed injections into coproducts. As always, derivable judgements are closed under substitutions (of meta-variables). For simplicity, we shall only consider meta-variables for values and not for other sorts.

Terms with meta-variables can be preordered by the subsumption preorder (see for instance [3]): $t \preceq u \iff \exists \theta. \widehat{\theta}(t) = u$. We write $\widehat{\theta}$ for the homomorphic extension of a substitution θ to a function on first-order terms.

Definition 2.3. Suppose J is a derivable judgement. A *principal judgement* for J is a derivable judgement J_0 such that $J_0 \preceq J$ and for all $J' \preceq J$ we have $J_0 \preceq J'$.

In other words, a principal judgement of J is an initial object in the preordered category of derivable judgements (with order $\preceq$) with terminal object J. We simply say that J is principal if it is a principal judgement of itself.

Proposition 2.4. *For any derivable judgement there is a principal judgement.*

One can show this proposition by constructing a principal judgement for a derivable judgement J: take its derivation tree, form the principal judgements of the premises and find the mgu for a unification problem that makes them fit the premises of the last applied rule. This is a well-defined construction because each derivable judgement (of this language) has a unique derivation tree.

Given an (open) judgement J, we say that a meta-variable x *occurs negatively* in J iff it occurs "left from $\vdash$", e.g. x occurs negatively in the application judgement $E, v \vdash m \to v'$ iff it occurs in either E or v or both.

Lemma 2.5. *Let J be a principal judgement. Then no meta-variable occurs more than once negatively in J.*

Proof. Sketch: by induction on the derivation tree, we simply replace shared by distinct meta-variables and obtain a more general derivable judgement. □

For lemma 2.5 it is vital that we have restricted ourself to meta-variables of value sort; meta-variables for constructors or program variables may well be shared negatively in principal judgements.

Lemma 2.6. *Let* $J = J'[c \cdot v/x]$ *be a principal judgement such that* x *occurs negatively in* J'. *Then the derivation tree of* J *contains a subtree with conclusion of the form* $E, c \cdot v \vdash (c\,p) \to E'$.

Proof. Sketch: the proof goes by induction on the height of the derivation tree of J. The argument is typically as in this example: let J be the judgement $E \vdash (e\,e') \to v'$. Unless e evaluates to some c' (a case we ignore here) it must have been derived from the premises $J_1 = E \vdash e \to (E', m)$, $J_2 = E \vdash e' \to v''$, and $J_3 = E', v'' \vdash m \to v'$ for some E', m, and v''. We can consider the principal judgements J_i' for the judgements J_i and observe that J is derived from the mgu of a system of equations (making the components of the J_i' fit to the schema of the closure-application rule) none of which mentioning the constructor c. This means that at least one of these principal judgements has a negative occurrence of some $c \cdot v_0$ (which is mapped by the mgu to $c \cdot v$): we can apply the induction hypothesis to the corresponding premise and obtain the desired result by applying the mgu to the derivation trees of the principal judgements. □

Lemma 2.6 says informally that when we need to read a constructor in order to get a result we have to do so by matching a constructor pattern against the value that has this constructor on top. This should hardly be surprising. The restriction to negative occurrences is necessary, because we can produce a constructor value in a positive occurrence by evaluating a constructor application.

Consider the values $v_n = \mathtt{Lam}^n(\mathtt{Var}(\mathtt{An}^n(v)))$ (we use superscript for iterating functions) and $v_n' = \mathtt{Lam}^n(\mathtt{Var}(\mathtt{An}^{n-1}(\mathtt{One})))$ of type $\mathtt{t\ lam}$ where $\mathtt{t}$ is the type of v. Clearly, v_n "contains a free variable" and v_n' does not. In other words:

Lemma 2.7. *Suppose* (E, m) *implements* $\mathtt{fvars}$.

1. *The judgements* $J = E, v_n \vdash m \to c \cdot (v, b)$ *and* $J' = E, v_n' \vdash m \to b$ *are derivable, where* b *is* $\mathtt{[]}$ *and* c *the list constructor* $\mathtt{::}$.
2. *The principal judgement of* J' *has the form* $E_1, v_n' \vdash m \to b$.

Proof. The first part is obvious as this is the required behaviour of $\mathtt{fvars}$. Suppose the principal judgements of J and J' are $E_0, v_0'' \vdash m \to v_c$ and $E_1, v_1'' \vdash m \to v_b$, respectively.

By assumption there are substitutions σ_i mapping E_i to E, also $\widehat{\sigma_1}(v_1'') = v_n'$ which implies $v_1'' \preceq v_n'$. By lemma 2.5 the meta-variables in v_1'' and E_1 are disjoint. If $v_1'' \prec v_n'$ then we also have $v_1'' \prec v_n$ and by the previous observation there is a substitution υ such that $\widehat{\upsilon}(v_1'') = v_n$ and $\widehat{\upsilon}(E_1) = E$. In particular, we can derive $E, v_n \vdash m \to \hat{v}(v_b)$. By determinism and the fact we can derive J we must have $\hat{v}(v_b) = c \cdot (v, b)$. We also have $\widehat{\sigma_1}(v_b) = b$. Since b and c are different constructors, v_b must be a meta-variable. By determinism and substitutivity of judgements v_b must occur in either E_1 or v_1''. It cannot occur in v_1'', because $b = \widehat{\sigma_1}(v_b)$ does not occur in v_n'; it cannot occur in E_1 either, because the substitutions v and σ_1 agree on E_1. Hence the assumption $v_1'' \prec v_n'$ leads to a contradiction and we must have $v_1'' = v_n'$ since v_n' is ground. $\qquad\Box$

Lemma 2.7 means that we can apply lemma 2.6 to *all* constructors in v_n', e.g. for each Lam there has to be a corresponding pattern match. Since this is true for the principal judgement it trivially follows for J' itself.

Corollary 2.8. *Consider the judgement J' of lemma 2.7 (for some given n). Its derivation tree contains pattern matching judgements of the form*
$$E_k, \mathtt{Lam}^k(\mathtt{Var}(\mathtt{An}^{n-1}(\mathtt{One}))) \vdash (\mathtt{Lam}\, p_k) \to E_k' \text{ for all } k, 0 \leq k \leq n.$$

Claim: For any occurrence of a pattern p (or: expression e', match m') in the derivation tree of $E \vdash e \to v$ (including v) there is a corresponding occurrence of p (or e', m', respectively) in either E or e; we make analogous claims for derivation trees of $E, v \vdash m \to v'$ and $E, v \vdash p \to E'$.

That any occurrence of a piece of syntax can be traced back to E or e is obvious from the shape of the rules: no rule uses "free" syntax in their premises. A pattern p may occur several times in E and/or e, but each occurrence of p in the derivation tree can be traced to a particular occurrence of p in either E or e, because no rule uses repeated patterns in its conclusion. One could make this tracing precise by giving patterns unique labels, similarly to labelling techniques for the λ-calculus used for the tracing of residuals of redexes.

2.4 let-expansion

The presence of let-expressions in the language only becomes significant once we type them in a special way; operationally, the expression let $x = e$ in e' is clearly equivalent to $(\lambda x.\, e')\, e$, but ML's typing rules differ. However, there is a different way of removing let-expressions that preserves well-typedness, it is expressed by the second-order rewrite rule let $x = e$ in $Z(x) \Rightarrow Z(e)$. This rule replaces all free occurrences of x in e' by e.

The rule is only correct if we prevent the free program variables of e to be bound by the substitution. This is automatically taken care of if we use higher-order abstract syntax for the programming language such that its binding constructs (**let**, **fix**, and λ) are all expressed in terms of the binding construct of the rewrite language. Alternatively, we can stick to first-order terms and first-order rewriting and explicitly rename bound program variables whenever necessary. We leave the details to the imagination of the reader and use $\Rightarrow$ for the pre-congruence closure of this rewrite relation.

Proposition 2.9. *The relation $\Rightarrow$ (on environments and values) is a subrelation of $\precsim$; also, $E \xrightarrow{(e,x)} E'$ and $e \Rightarrow e'$ imply $\exists E''.\, E \xrightarrow{(e',x)} E''$ and $E' \precsim E''$.*

Proposition 2.9 can be proved most easily for a first-order presentation of $\Rightarrow$. The statement is only in terms of $\precsim$ rather than $\approx$ since the expression e in **let** $x = e$ **in** e' needs to be evaluated for the evaluation of the whole expression but this might be avoided by the expansion, most notably if x does not occur at all in e'.

Proposition 2.10. *The relation* $\Rightarrow$ *is strongly normalising.*

As a consequence any environment has a normal form w.r.t. the relation $\Rightarrow$ which simulates it; the normal forms of $\Rightarrow$ do not contain **let**-expressions. Thus for any implementation (E, m) of **fvars** its **let**-free normal form (E', m') implements **fvars** as well.

3 Type System

We briefly repeat here the type system of SML [6] adapted to our little language. First we give an abstract syntax for types, type schemes and type environments. Types t are first-order terms over a signature with two distinguished binary function symbols "$\rightarrow$" and "$\times$". A type scheme σ has the form $\forall\alpha_1.\cdots.\alpha_k.t$ which we abbreviate as $\forall\alpha_k.\,t$. Type environments B associate (program) variables with type schemes, the notation is analogous to environments.

Type schemes can be seen as polymorphic types. The $\forall$ sign in $\forall\alpha.\,\sigma$ is a variable binder, i.e. $\mathrm{FV}(\forall\alpha.\,\sigma) = \mathrm{FV}(\sigma) \setminus \{\alpha\}$, and for types: $\mathrm{FV}(\alpha) = \{\alpha\}$ and $\mathrm{FV}(f(t_1,\dots,t_n)) = \bigcup_{1\leq i \leq n} \mathrm{FV}(t_i)$. Free variables for type environments are analogous to environments: $\mathrm{FV}(B[x \mapsto \sigma]) = \mathrm{FV}(\sigma) \cup \mathrm{FV}(B)$, $\mathrm{FV}(\bullet) = \emptyset$. We write $\sigma \rhd t$ iff for some type variables $\alpha_1, \dots, \alpha_k$ and some types $t', t_1, \dots, t_k$ we have $\sigma = \forall\alpha_1.\cdots.\forall\alpha_k.\,t'$ and $t'[t_1/\alpha_1, \dots, t_k/\alpha_k] = t$. We write $\mathrm{Clos}_B(t)$ for some type scheme $\forall\alpha_k.\,t$ such that $\{\alpha_1, \dots, \alpha_k\} = \mathrm{FV}(t) \setminus \mathrm{FV}(B)$.

In the following we will assume the existence of a function A that maps constructors to type schemes. Moreover, this function should have the following properties: $\forall b. \exists f, t_1, \dots, t_k. A(b) = \forall\alpha_n. f(t_1, \dots, t_k) \wedge f \notin \{\times, \rightarrow\}$ which is the assumption that there are no nullary constructors for function and product types and similarly for non-nullary constructors: $\forall c. \exists f, t, t_1, \dots, t_k. A(c) = \forall\alpha_n. (t \rightarrow f(t_1, \dots, t_k)) \wedge f \notin \{\times, \rightarrow\} \wedge \mathrm{FV}(t) \subseteq \bigcup_{1 \leq i \leq k} \mathrm{FV}(t_i)$. The condition on $\mathrm{FV}(t)$ ensures that the type checking equivalent of pattern matching is deterministic, i.e. whenever $B, t \vdash p : B_1$ and $B, t \vdash p : B_2$ then $B_1 = B_2$. This property is also crucial for the soundness of pattern matching.

Similar to the presentation of evaluation, the type system is given in three parts, rules for type checking abstractions of the form $B \vdash m : t$, rules for type-checking patterns of the form $B, t \vdash p : B'$ and rules for type-checking expressions of the form $B \vdash e : t$.

As one would expect, the rule that crucially restricts the interaction between recursion and polymorphism is the typing rule for the **fix** construct. By replacing the premise $B[x \mapsto t'] \vdash e' : t'$ in that rule by the two premises $B[x \mapsto \sigma] \vdash e' : t'$ and $\mathrm{Clos}_B(t') = \sigma$ we could transform the type system into one with full-blown polymorphic recursion.

$$\frac{B,t \vdash p : B' \quad B' \vdash e : t'}{B \vdash p.e : t \to t'} \qquad \frac{B \vdash p.e : t \quad B \vdash m : t}{B \vdash p.e;m : t}$$

$$\frac{}{B,t \vdash x : B[x \mapsto t]} \qquad \frac{B,t \vdash p : B' \quad B',t' \vdash p' : B''}{B,t \times t' \vdash (p,p') : B''}$$

$$\frac{B \vdash b : t}{B,t \vdash b : B} \qquad \frac{B \vdash c : (t' \to t) \quad B,t' \vdash p : B'}{B,t \vdash (c\,p) : B'}$$

$$\frac{A(b) \rhd t}{B \vdash b : t} \qquad \frac{A(c) \rhd t}{B \vdash c : t} \qquad \frac{B \vdash m : t}{B \vdash \lambda m : t}$$

$$\frac{\sigma \rhd t}{B[x \mapsto \sigma] \vdash x : t} \qquad \frac{x \neq x' \quad B \vdash x : t}{B[x' \mapsto \sigma] \vdash x : t}$$

$$\frac{B \vdash e : (t' \to t) \quad B \vdash e' : t'}{B \vdash (e\,e') : t} \qquad \frac{B \vdash e : t \quad B \vdash e' : t'}{B \vdash (e,e') : t \times t'}$$

$$\frac{B \vdash e' : t' \quad \sigma = \mathrm{Clos}_B(t') \quad B[x \mapsto \sigma] \vdash e : t}{B \vdash \mathbf{let}\ x = e'\ \mathbf{in}\ e : t}$$

$$\frac{B[x \mapsto t'] \vdash e' : t' \quad B[x \mapsto t'] \vdash e : t}{B \vdash \mathbf{fix}\ x = e'\ \mathbf{in}\ e : t}$$

Table 5. Type System

Definition 3.1. The pointed transition system T is defined as follows: type environments are states, the empty type environment $\bullet$ is the initial state, transitions are defined as:

$$B \xrightarrow{(e,x)} B[x \mapsto \sigma] \iff \exists t.\ B \vdash e : t \wedge \mathrm{Clos}_B(t) = \sigma$$

Although T is not deterministic (an expression can have many types), it is still the case that bisimulation and trace equivalence coincide and we also have a similar compression property as in the operational semantics, i.e. two type environments are equivalent iff they type-check the same expressions. More specifically, it is not difficult to see that two type environments are equivalent iff they have the same domain and are pointwise equivalent, where the equivalence of type schemes just means that they can instantiate to the same types. This equivalence is exactly the equality of type schemes and static environments in the static semantics of SML [6].

Proposition 2.9 carries over to the transition system T: judgements are substitutive and free syntactic type variables are just like meta-variables for types. The **let**-expansion then operates on types and type schemes like a β-reduction. As a consequence, the **let**-free normal form of any well-typed expression is well-typed (in the same type environment). Together with the original proposition 2.9 this means in particular that any well-typed implementation of **fvars** gives rise to a well-typed **let**-free implementation.

From M and T we can define the typed transition system $M : T$ determined by the relation $l : l' \iff l = l'$ between labels. The states and transitions of

$$\frac{v : \forall \alpha.\, t}{v : t[t'/\alpha]} \qquad \frac{v : \sigma}{v : \forall \alpha.\, \sigma}$$

$$\frac{v : t \quad v' : t'}{(v, v') : t \times t'} \qquad \frac{E : B \quad B \vdash m : t}{(E, m) : t}$$

$$\frac{\bullet \vdash b : t}{b : t} \qquad \frac{\bullet \vdash c : (t' \to t) \quad v : t'}{c \cdot v : t} \qquad \frac{\bullet \vdash c : t}{c : t}$$

$$\frac{}{\bullet : \bullet} \qquad \frac{v : \sigma \quad E : B}{E[x \mapsto v] : B[x \mapsto \sigma]} \qquad \frac{E : B \quad B[x \mapsto t] \vdash e : t}{E[x \mapsto \langle e \rangle] : B[x \mapsto t]}$$

Table 6. Types of Values and Environments

$M : T$ capture the states and evaluations of a typed ML interpreter: we only ever evaluate expressions which are well-typed in the current environment and the resulting value is asserted the type we obtained from this type-check. One can formalise and prove a subject reduction theorem for $M : T$ by defining a well-typedness predicate P for its states and showing that P is an invariant; the soundness of $M : T$ would additionally require that the initial state satisfies P.

There is another way of defining exactly the same transition system, simply by defining judgements like $(E, B) \vdash e \to (v, t)$ as the combination of $E \vdash e \to v$ and $B \vdash e : t$. By considering the various cases for e we can derive inference rules for this judgement form which are largely defined in terms of themselves. For example, for closure application we get the following derived rule:

$$\frac{(E, B) \vdash e \to ((E', m), t' \to t) \quad (E, B) \vdash e' \to (v', t') \quad E', v' \vdash m \to v}{(E, B) \vdash (e\ e') \to (v, t)}$$

In general, the application judgement $E', v' \vdash m \to v$ of this derived rule has no corresponding typing judgement. In order to get such a thing we need some assumptions about the relationship between E and B. Table 6 defines such a relation $E : B$, which intuitively means that E has "type" B. Notice that this typing judgement is decidable and consequently it is much more restrictive than a proper semantic notion of type inhabitance would be like. Claim: if $E \Rightarrow E'$ and $E : B$ then $E' : B$.

The relation $E : B$ is an invariant of the transition system $M : T$, i.e. states (E, B) satisfying $E : B$ have only transitions into other such states.

Proposition 3.2. *Let $E : B$ and $(E, B) \vdash e \to (v, t)$. Then $v : t$.*

Proof. Sketch: we make analogous claims for pattern matching and function application and prove the result by induction on the height of the derivation tree. The non-trivial cases are closure application and the unravelling of recursion.

Consider our derived rule for closure application: We can apply the induction hypothesis to the premise $(E, B) \vdash e \to ((E', m), t' \to t)$ which gives us $(E', m) : t' \to t$. By the rules for types of values this is the case iff there is a B' such $E' : B'$

and $B' \vdash m : t' \to t$. Thus we also have $(E', B'), (v', t') \vdash m \to (v, t)$. Moreover, $E' : B'$ as we have already seen and $v' : t'$ follows from the induction hypothesis of the second premise. Thus we can apply the induction hypothesis to this statement as well (its derivation height is equal to the height of $E', v' \vdash m \to v$) and get the result.

Unravelling recursion: Assume $E = E'[x \mapsto \langle e \rangle]$ with $(E, B) \vdash x \to (v, t)$ and $E : B$. The first condition means $B \vdash x : t$ and $E \vdash e \to v$; from the second condition we get $B = B'[x \mapsto t']$ and $B \vdash e : t'$. Thus $B'[x \mapsto t'] \vdash x : t$ which implies $t = t'$. Putting all of this together gives us $(E, B) \vdash e \to (v, t)$ and we can use the induction hypothesis.   □

Corollary 3.3. *For any reachable state (E, B) in $M : T$ we have $E : B$.*

Proposition 3.2 can be regarded as a subject reduction theorem of the typed language and its corollary as a (part of a) soundness statement. The subject reduction proof proves a bit more than just the proposition: from $E : B$ and $(E, B) \vdash e \to (v, t)$ it constructs a derivation tree in which all evaluation (application, pattern matching) steps are of such a guarded form.

Consider any pattern match $(E_0, B_0), (v_0, t_0) \vdash p \to (E_1, B_1)$ in the derivation tree of $(E, B) \vdash e \to (v, t)$ such that B contains only types (no proper type schemes) and E and e are let-free. As we mentioned earlier, the pattern p can be traced back to either E or e. In the former case, the judgement $B_0, t_0 \vdash p : B_1$ occurs in the derivation tree of $E : B$, in the latter case in the derivation tree of $B \vdash e : t$. This follows from the way these trees are constructed in the subject reduction proof. The absence of polymorphic bindings is vital: whenever an identifier x is accessed then we can create a proof that $v : t$ (its value v has type t) from the proof that $E : B$; if B is monomorphic then this derivation occurs as a subderivation of $E : B$. The further absence of let-expressions is necessary to maintain the absence of type schemes for the full attributed derivation tree.

Theorem 3.4. *No reachable state in $M : T$ contains an implementation of* **fvars**.

Proof. Suppose (E, B) were reachable and contained such an implementation (E_0, m_0). We know $E : B$ from corollary 3.3. From proposition 2.10 we know that E has a let-free normal form $E \Rightarrow^* E'$ and it is easy to see that $E' : B$. By proposition 2.9 we have $E \precsim E'$. In particular, if we have $E_0, v'_n \vdash m_0 \to b$ (v'_n and b as mentioned earlier) then we also have $E'_0, v'_n \vdash m'_0 \to b$ for the let-free normal form (E'_0, m'_0) with a corresponding typing judgement $B_0 \vdash m'_0 : t \to t'$. From corollary 2.8 we know for any n that the derivation tree of $E'_0, v'_n \vdash m'_0 \to b$ contains judgements of the form $E_k, \text{Lam}^k(\text{Var}(\text{An}^{n-1}(\text{One}))) \vdash (\text{Lam}\, p_k) \to E'_k$ (for any $0 \le k \le n$) each of which having a corresponding typing judgement $B_k, t_k \vdash (\text{Lam}\, p_k) \to B'_k$.

If B_0 is monomorphic then we know that these typing judgements occur in the proofs of either $E_0 : B_0$ or $B_0 \vdash m'_0 : t \to t'$. But this is impossible because each t_k is (must be) different and for sufficiently large n there simply are not enough types in these proofs. If B_0 is not monomorphic then we can transform

(B_0, m'_0, E'_0) into something equivalent but monomorphic by linearising (E'_0, m'_0) in its polymorphic program variables: if x is used in different type instances in the proofs of $E'_0 : B_0$ and $B_0 \vdash m'_0 : t \to t'$ then we introduce a fresh program variable $x_{t''}$ for every type instance t'' of x's type scheme that occurs in these proofs and replace each occurrence of x in m'_0 by the corresponding $x_{t''}$; we bind $x_{t''}$ to t'' and the old value of x, respectively. Notice that thunks $\langle e \rangle$ are never polymorphic, i.e. x must be bound to some v (never $\langle e \rangle$) in E'_0 if it is bound to a proper type scheme in B_0. $\qquad\square$

Corollary 3.5. *$M : T$ is incomplete.*

4 Final Remarks

We have shown that ML's type system is incomplete: there are values that can be soundly given a type t which cannot be expressed in ML, even modulo observational equivalence. One can show with a standard argument (see [5]) that ML's type system is complete for datatypes with a regular tree structure. Considering the extended (undecidable) type system of [4], it seems likely that it is complete as well but the mentioned standard argument does not apply here.

Acknowledgements

Thanks to Claudio Russo for carefully reading an earlier version of this paper. Also thanks to the PLILP referees for some helpful suggestions.

The research reported here was supported by SERC grant GR/J07303.

References

1. F. Cardone and M. Coppo. Two extensions of Curry's type inference system. In P. Odifreddi, editor, *Logic and Computer Science*, pages 19–76. Academic Press, 1990.
2. N. G. de Bruijn. Lambda calculus notation with nameless dummies, a tool for automatic formula manipulation. *Indagationes Mathematicae*, 34:381–392, 1972.
3. Nachum Dershowitz and Jean-Pierre Jouannaud. Rewrite systems. In Jan van Leeuwen, editor, *Handbook of Theoretical Computer Science*, volume B, chapter 6, pages 244–320. Elsevier, 1990.
4. Fritz Henglein. Type inference with polymorphic recursion. *ACM Transactions on Programming Languages and Systems*, 15(2):253–289, 1993.
5. Stefan Kahrs. About the completeness of type systems. In *Proceedings ESSLLI Workshop on Observational Equivalence and Logical Equivalence*, 1996. (to appear).
6. Robin Milner, Mads Tofte, and Robert Harper. *The Definition of Standard ML*. MIT Press, 1990.
7. Mads Tofte. *Operational Semantics and Polymorphic Type Inference*. PhD thesis, University of Edinburgh, 1988. CST-52-88.

Functorial ML

G. Bellè[2], C.B. Jay[1] and E. Moggi[2]

[1] SOCS - Univ. of Tech. Sydney, P.O. Box 123 Broadway, 2007, Australia
phone: ++612 330-1814, fax: ++612 330-1807, e-mail: cbj@socs.uts.edu.au
[2] DISI - Univ. di Genova, via Dodecaneso 35, 16146 Genova, Italy
phone: +39 10 353-6629, fax: +39 10 353-6699, e-mail: {gbelle,moggi}@disi.unige.it

Abstract. We present an extension of the Hindley-Milner type system
that supports a generous class of type constructors called functors, and
provide a parametrically polymorphic algorithm for their mapping, i.e.
for applying a function to each datum appearing in a value of constructed
type. The algorithm comes from shape theory, which provides a uniform
method for locating data within a shape. The resulting system is Church-
Rosser and strongly normalising, and supports type inference.

1 Introduction

The interplay between type theory, programming language semantics and category theory is now well established. Two of the strongest examples of this
interaction are the representation of function types as exponential objects in
a cartesian closed category [LS86] and the description of polymorphic terms as
natural transformations (e.g. [BFSS90]). For example, the operation of appending
lists can be represented as a natural transformation $L \times L \Rightarrow L$ where $L: \mathcal{D} \to \mathcal{D}$
is the list functor on some category $\mathcal{D}$. Of course, these natural transformations
must have associated functors for their domain and codomain. System F supports
a notion of *expressible functor*, i.e. a type constructor and a corresponding action on functions [RP90], but such encodings are rather unsatisfactory ([GLT89,
Section 15.1.1]). In particular, the action of a functor on morphism, its *mapping*,
must be defined anew for each choice of type constructor.

A better approach, primarily advocated by adherents of the Bird-Meertens
style (e.g. [MFP91, MH95, Jeu95]), is to give a combinator for mapping, whose
type can be expressed as:

$$\mathrm{map} \colon \forall F \colon 1. \forall X, Y. (X \to Y) \to FX \to FY \ .$$

That is, for any functor $F\colon 1$ (i.e. taking one argument), types X and Y, and any
morphism $f\colon X \to Y$ we have

$$\mathrm{map} \ F \ X \ Y \ f \colon FX \to FY$$

whose action is to take each datum of type X in FX and apply f to it. Unfortunately, the existence of this type does not solve the problem of realising this
high-level algorithm, since the question of how to *find* the data remains.

Naturally, one can use the functor to determine the algorithm. There are basically two ways to do this. One method is to have the user specify the mapping algorithm, say by instantiating a *constructor class* [Jon95]. In this particular case, the functor and type arguments are suppressed to obtain map f a, since the choice of functor can be inferred from the type of a. Unfortunately, it follows that if F and G are functors such that FX and GY are intended to be the same for some types X and Y then a dummy constructor must be introduced to distinguish them.

The other method is to generate the mapping algorithm automatically, from the structure of the functor. This results in a small loss of flexibility, but saves the user from supplying repetitive algorithms. Charity [CF92] encodes this directly. Jeuring [Jeu95] uses a pre-processor to determine the appropriate Haskell code for mapping and other *polytypic* operations. *Intensional polymorphism* [HM95] is a general technique for describing type-dependent operations in an extension of ML, designed to obtain more efficient compilation. Although in the same spirit as the other approaches, the lack of sum types makes it hard to make direct comparisons.

Perhaps surprisingly, there is a generous class of covariant functors for which it is possible to describe a mapping algorithm that is independent of the choice of functor, i.e. which support *parametric functorial polymorphism*. The first such algorithms for (polymorphic folding) were produced for a small experimental language **P2** [Jay95a]. Polymorphic mapping for an extension of the *covariant* type system [Jay96] was produced in [Jay]. This paper presents an extension of Hindley-Milner called Functorial ML, or FML, which supports parametric functorial polymorphism.

For example, it supports:

$$\text{map } f \text{ (cons } h \text{ } t) \rightarrow_* \text{cons } (f \text{ } h) \text{ (map } f \text{ } t)$$
$$\text{map } f \text{ (leaf } x) \rightarrow_* \text{leaf } (f \text{ } x)$$

where cons is the usual list constructor, and leaf is the leaf constructor for binary trees with labeled leaves. It is important to note that these evaluations are not achieved by pattern matching on primitive combinators, but that the constructors cons and leaf have internal structure, which is used in the reduction to find the data in a uniform way. We can also use mapping within a let-construct:

$$\text{let } g = \text{map } f \text{ in pair } (g \text{ (cons } h \text{ } t) \text{ } (g \text{ (leaf } x)))$$

where pair is the pairing for binary products. The polymorphic mapping allows us to support polymorphic folding, too, as will be shown in the body of the paper. Functors of many variables are also catered for. For example, we have

$$\text{map}_2 \text{ } f \text{ } g \text{ (in}_0 \text{ } t) \rightarrow \text{in}_0 \text{ } (f \text{ } t) \tag{1}$$
$$\text{map}_2 \text{ } f \text{ } g \text{ (pair } s \text{ } t) \rightarrow \text{pair } (f \text{ } s) \text{ } (g \text{ } t) \text{ .} \tag{2}$$

where in_0 is the left inclusion to a binary sum, Thus, map_2 f g is equally able to act on values whose type is a sum or product, etc.

Shape theory [Jay95b] provides the basis for these algorithms. It is a new approach to data types based on the idea of decomposing values into their shape (or data structure) and the data which is stored within them. The data structure corresponds to the type constructor, or functor, whose argument is the type of the data. Thus *shape polymorphism* is closely linked to functorial polymorphism, as distinct from the *data polymorphism* of operations like append. Thus, the data-shape decomposition supports uniform mechanisms for storing data within a shape, which are exploited by our mapping algorithm.

To see how this works, consider the projection functors $\Pi_i^m \colon \mathcal{D}^m \to \mathcal{D}$ which pick out the ith argument from m. It is tempting to identify $\Pi_0^2(X, X)$ and $\Pi_1^2(X, X)$ with X but this would obliterate the shape-data distinction. Rather, these types are "isomorphic", a situation captured by terms

$$\mathrm{pex}_{2,j} \colon X_j \to \Pi_j^2(X_0, X_1)$$

(for $j \in 2$) and their inverses. Now given $x \colon X$ we have the reductions:

$$\mathrm{map}_2 \; f \; g \; (\mathrm{pex}_{2,0} \; x) \to \mathrm{pex}_{2,0} \; (f \; x)$$
$$\mathrm{map}_2 \; f \; g \; (\mathrm{pex}_{2,1} \; x) \to \mathrm{pex}_{2,1} \; (g \; x) \; .$$

In other words, the isomorphisms are used to determine where to find the data associated to each argument of the functor. Similarly, we have isomorphisms to disambiguate composite functors, e.g.

$$\mathrm{dex}_{1,1} \colon F(G(X)) \to F\langle G \rangle^1(X) \; .$$

Its source is the functor F applied to $G(X)$ while its target is the composite functor $F\langle G \rangle^1$ applied to X. The corresponding reduction for map is:

$$\mathrm{map} \; f \; (\mathrm{dex}_{1,1} \; t) \to \mathrm{dex}_{1,1} \; (\mathrm{map} \; (\mathrm{map} \; f) \; t)$$

whose corresponding diagram is:

$$
\begin{array}{ccc}
F(G(X)) & \xrightarrow{\;\mathrm{dex}_{1,1}\;} & F\langle G \rangle^1(X) \\
\downarrow{\scriptstyle \mathrm{map}\,(\mathrm{map}\,f)} & & \downarrow{\scriptstyle \mathrm{map}\,f} \\
F(G(Y)) & \xrightarrow[\;\mathrm{dex}_{1,1}\;]{} & F\langle G \rangle^1(Y) \; .
\end{array}
$$

These isomorphisms may be viewed as a systematic method for resolving the ambiguities addressed by the dummy constructors mentioned above. The other approaches use implicit substitution to handle functor composition, making a uniform algorithm impossible.

The significance of these isomorphisms becomes particularly clear in certain application contexts. For instance, in distributed or parallel computing the shape-data distinction can be used to describe data distributions [Jay95c] in which case the isomorphisms represent redistributions of the data. Also, such isomorphisms between different composites are central to bicategories [Ben67].

The polymorphism of the mapping algorithm can be captured in a system that supports inference of functors as well as types. We work with an extension of the Hindley-Milner types which supports a syntactic class of functors, as well as those of types and type schema. Another possibility is to identify types and type schemes (so extending system F with functors). Such a system is used in the proof of strong normalisation. Again, one could identify types with functors of arity 0, at the cost of introducing another pair of isomorphisms. We emphasise the tri-partite division for reasons of clarity, and to obtain type inference.

In this paper we will consider only FML with untyped terms, i.e. à la Church (in the terminology of [Bar92]), because the main focus is on parametric functorial polymorphism. However, FML à la Curry is very important, too: it allows a more aggressive use of type information (as advocated in [HM95]) and it is more suitable for a semantic investigation.

The following sections of the paper are devoted to: the type system (functors, types and type schema); terms and type assignment, including the type inference algorithm; term reduction and its properties (subject reduction, Church-Rosser and strong normalization); examples, and conclusions and future work. For more technical details the reader can refer to [BJM96].

2   Functors, types and type schema

A *(covariant) functor* is a structure-preserving morphism of categories, i.e. it maps objects to objects and morphisms to morphisms, so as to preserve the sources and targets of the morphisms, the composition and identities. The symbols m and n will denote natural numbers throughout this paper. If $F: \mathcal{D}^m \to \mathcal{D}$ is a functor from the mth power of a category $\mathcal{D}$ to itself, then we may express this by saying F is of arity m and write it as $F: m$.

Here are some elementary examples and constructions. $+, \times: 2$ are binary functors representing sums and products, and $1: 0$ is the functor of no arguments that produces the terminal object, corresponding to the unit type. Let i range over $m = \{0, \ldots, m-1\}$. The ith projection functor of m arguments is $\Pi_i^m: m$. A sequence $G_i: n$ of functors may be written as $G_{i \in m}$ or even $\overline{G}$ when the choice of m is either clear from the context, or irrelevant. Similar notation will be used for other sequences below, of types, etc. If $F: m$ then

$$\mathcal{D}^n \xrightarrow{\langle \overline{G} \rangle} \mathcal{D}^m \xrightarrow{F} \mathcal{D}$$

is their *composite*. If $F: m + 1$ is a functor then $\mu^m F: m$ represents the functor whose action on the tuple $\overline{X}$ yields the initial $F(\overline{X}, -)$-algebra (e.g. [BW90])

$$F(\overline{X}, \mu^m F(\overline{X})) \to \mu^m F(\overline{X})$$

used to find minimal solutions of recursive domain equations.

These constructions motivate the choice of functors in the following description of the raw syntax for functors, types and type schema.

$$F, G ::= X \mid C \mid \Pi_i^m \mid F\langle\overline{G}\rangle^n \mid \mu^m F$$
$$\tau ::= X \mid F(\overline{\tau}) \mid \tau_1 \to \tau_2$$
$$\sigma ::= \tau \mid \forall X{:}\,T.\tau \mid \forall X{:}\,m.\sigma \ .$$

We adopt the following notational conventions throughout. X and Y range over functor and type variables. C ranges over functor constants, in particular we will consider $+, \times$, the binary functors representing sums and products, and 1, the functor of no arguments that produces the terminal object, corresponding to the unit type. F and G range over functors (though sometimes are used as functor variables), τ ranges over types, and σ ranges over type schema throughout the paper. A type τ may be distinguished from functors or type schema by giving it the fixed arity $\tau{:}\,T$. We write $\tau_1 \times \tau_2$ for $\times(\tau_1, \tau_2)$ and $\tau_1 + \tau_2$ for $+\langle\tau_1, \tau_2\rangle$ and 1 for the type $1()$.

The functor notation is as described above. The given types are variables, functor applications, and function types. The application of a functor to a tuple $\tau_{i\in m}$ of types represents the action of the categorical functor on objects. Note that all of the ancillary type constructors, such as products and sums, have been pushed into the declaration of the functors.

The type schema are types, universal quantification over type variables and universal quantification over functors of given arity. The former quantification is familiar from Hindley-Milner and is used to express data polymorphism; the latter quantification will allow us to express functorial polymorphism.

A *type context* (notation Δ) is a sequence of type variables with assigned arities (either $X{:}\,n$ or $X{:}\,T$) with no repetition of variables. We may identify Δ with a partial function from functor and type variables to arities, and write $\mathrm{DV}(\Delta)$ for its domain.

For each of the syntactic categories above we give rules to infer when a raw expression of that category is well-formed in a type context. The symbol i ranges over m. $\Delta \vdash$ means that Δ is a well-formed typed context.

$$(\text{empty}) \ \frac{}{\emptyset \vdash} \qquad (\text{functor}) \ \frac{\Delta \vdash}{\Delta, X{:}\,n \vdash} \ X \notin \mathrm{DV}(\Delta)$$

$$(\text{type}) \ \frac{\Delta \vdash}{\Delta, X{:}\,T \vdash} \ X \notin \mathrm{DV}(\Delta)$$

$\Delta \vdash F{:}\,n$ means that F is a functor of arity n in context Δ. The formation rules for functors express the constraints on arities implicit in the category theory.

$$(X) \ \frac{\Delta \vdash}{\Delta \vdash X{:}\,m} \ m = \Delta(X) \qquad (C) \ \frac{\Delta \vdash}{\Delta \vdash C{:}\,n_C}$$

$$(\text{FPi}) \ \frac{\Delta \vdash}{\Delta \vdash \Pi_i^m{:}\,m} \qquad (\text{Fcomp}) \ \frac{\Delta \vdash F{:}\,m \quad \Delta \vdash G_i{:}\,n}{\Delta \vdash F\langle G_{i\in m}\rangle^n{:}\,n}$$

$$(\text{Fmu}) \ \frac{\Delta \vdash F : m+1}{\Delta \vdash \mu^m F : m}$$

$\Delta \vdash \tau : \text{T}$ means that τ is a type in context Δ.

$$(X) \ \frac{\Delta \vdash}{\Delta \vdash X : \text{T}} \ \text{T} = \Delta(X) \qquad (\text{Fapp}) \ \frac{\Delta \vdash F : m \quad \Delta \vdash \tau_i : \text{T}}{\Delta \vdash F(\tau_{i \in m}) : \text{T}}$$

$$(\to) \ \frac{\Delta \vdash \tau_1, \tau_2 : \text{T}}{\Delta \vdash \tau_1 \to \tau_2 : \text{T}}$$

$\Delta \vdash \sigma$ means that σ is a type schema in context Δ.

$$(\tau) \ \frac{\Delta \vdash \tau : \text{T}}{\Delta \vdash \tau} \qquad (\forall_m) \ \frac{\Delta, Y : m \vdash \sigma\{Y/X\}}{\Delta \vdash \forall X : m.\sigma} \ Y \notin \text{DV}(\Delta)$$

$$(\forall) \ \frac{\Delta, Y : \text{T} \vdash \sigma\{Y/X\}}{\Delta \vdash \forall X : \text{T}.\sigma} \ Y \notin \text{DV}(\Delta)$$

The *free variables* of a functor are defined in the usual way, and the functors are defined to be equivalence classes of well-formed functor expressions under α-conversion. Types and schema are defined similarly. We denote with $\forall\Delta.\tau$ the following schema: τ, if $\Delta = \emptyset$, $\forall\Delta'.(\forall X : n.\tau)$ if $\Delta = \Delta', X : n$ and $\forall\Delta'.(\forall X : \text{T}.\tau)$ if $\Delta = \Gamma', X : \text{T}$.

Lemma 1. *1. Uniqueness of derivation: each judgement $\Delta \vdash J$ has at most one derivation (up to α-conversion).*
2. Uniqueness of arity: if $\Delta \vdash F : n_j$ is derivable for $j \in 2$ then $n_0 = n_1$.

Proof. For the first, use induction on the size of the derivation of $\Delta \vdash J$. For the second, use induction on the structure of F. □

A *substitution* is a partial function S from type variables to expressions for functors, types or schema. The action of a substitution is extended homomorphically to any expressions containing free type variables. If R is another substitution then their *composite* substitution $S \, R$ has action given by $(S \, R)X = S(RX)$. The notation $S : \Delta_1 \to \Delta_2$ means that Δ_i are well-formed contexts, $\text{DV}(\Delta_1)$ is included in the domain of S and for each $X \in \text{DV}(\Delta_1)$ we have

$$\Delta_2 \vdash SX : \Delta_1(X) .$$

S is a *renaming* if it is an injective function from variables to variables. Then define Δ_S by

$$\emptyset_S = \emptyset$$
$$(\Delta, X : a)_S = \Delta_S, S(X) : a .$$

Lemma 2.

1. *Renaming: let S be a renaming, then $\Delta \vdash J$ implies $\Delta_S \vdash S(J)$.*
2. *Thinning: $\Delta_1, \Delta_2 \vdash J$ implies $\Delta_1, X : a, \Delta_2 \vdash J$, provided $X \notin \mathrm{DV}(\Delta_1, \Delta_2)$ and a is either T or an arity m.*
3. *Substitution: let $S : \Delta_1 \to \Delta_2$ be a substitution, then $\Delta_1 \vdash J$ implies $\Delta_2 \vdash S(J)$.*

Proof. Each of the proofs is by induction on the derivation of the premise. The first two results are used to handle the $\forall$ rules in the latter proofs. $\qquad\square$

Let $\Delta \vdash J_j : a$ be well-formed functors or types having the same arity a for $j \in 2$. A *unifier* for (Δ, J_0, J_1) is a pair (Δ', S) such that $S : \Delta \to \Delta'$ is a substitution and $S(J_0) = S(J_1)$. Their *most general unifier* $\mathcal{U}(\Delta, J_0, J_1)$ is a unifier (Δ', S) such that if (Δ'', S') is any other unifier for them then there is a substitution $R : \Delta' \to \Delta''$ such that $S' = R\,S$ on $\mathrm{DV}(\Delta)$.

Lemma 3. *If (Δ, J_0, J_1) has a unifier then it has a most general unifier.*

Proof. Standard. Note that the introduction of functors does not lead to higher order unification since, for example, $\Pi_i^m(\overline{X})$ and X_i do not have a unifier. $\qquad\square$

3 Terms and type assignment

The Hindley-Milner type system may assign either type schema or types to terms [Tof88]). The former has separate rules for abstracting and instantiating type variables, whereas the latter combines these with the rules for typing variables and combinators, and the let-construct, respectively. Both type assignment systems can be extended easily to FML. Here, we consider only the latter, since it is closer to the type inference algorithm.

The untyped terms we will consider here are like those considered in Hindley-Milner, but with several additional constants and no fix-point combinator (since we wish to have strong normalisation):

$$t ::= x \mid c \mid \lambda x.t \mid t_1\, t_2 \mid \text{let } x = t_1 \text{ in } t_2 \ .$$

These terms are variables; constants; λ-abstractions and applications and a let-construct. The novelty, and power, of the system resides in the more powerful types assigned to these terms, and the choice of constants, which will be used to capture important properties of functors.

Their description uses the following notational conventions which will be maintained throughout this paper. x and y range over term variables, c ranges over combinators, and t ranges over terms. Γ ranges over *term contexts*, i.e. sequences of $x : \sigma$ with no repetitions of term variables x. The usual conventions of λ-calculus concerning grouping of declared and bound variables apply (see [Bar84]); $\mathrm{FV}(t)$ is the set of free variables of t; $e'\{e/x\}$ is the substitution of e for x in e'.

Here are the term formation rules. $\Delta; \Gamma \vdash$ means that $\Delta; \Gamma$ is a well-formed context.

$$(\text{empty}) \frac{\Delta \vdash}{\Delta; \emptyset \vdash} \qquad (\text{term}) \frac{\Delta; \Gamma \vdash \quad \Delta \vdash \sigma}{\Delta; \Gamma, x{:}\sigma \vdash} \; x \notin \mathrm{DV}(\Gamma)$$

$\Delta; \Gamma \vdash t{:}\tau$ means that t is a term of type τ in context $\Delta; \Gamma$ and hence that t is *typable* in this context.

$$(x) \frac{\Delta; \Gamma \vdash \quad S{:}\Delta' \to \Delta}{\Delta; \Gamma \vdash x{:}S(\tau)} \; \Gamma(x) = \forall \Delta'.\tau$$

$$(c) \frac{\Delta; \Gamma \vdash \quad S{:}\Delta' \to \Delta}{\Delta; \Gamma \vdash c{:}S(\tau)} \; (\forall \Delta'.\tau) = \sigma_c$$

$$(\lambda) \frac{\Delta; \Gamma, y{:}\tau_1 \vdash t\{y/x\}{:}\tau_2}{\Delta; \Gamma \vdash (\lambda x.t){:}\tau_1 \to \tau_2} \; y \notin \mathrm{DV}(\Gamma)$$

$$(\text{app}) \frac{\Delta; \Gamma \vdash t{:}\tau_1 \to \tau_2 \quad \Delta; \Gamma \vdash t_1{:}\tau_1}{\Delta; \Gamma \vdash (t\, t_1){:}\tau_2}$$

$$(\text{let}) \frac{\Delta, \Delta'; \Gamma \vdash t_1{:}\tau_1 \quad \Delta; \Gamma, y{:}(\forall \Delta'.\tau_1) \vdash t_2\{y/x\}{:}\tau_2}{\Delta; \Gamma \vdash (\text{let } x = t_1 \text{ in } t_2){:}\tau_2} \; y \notin \mathrm{DV}(\Gamma)$$

Let $\Delta_j; \Gamma_j$ be well-formed contexts for $j = 1, 2$. Define $S{:}\Delta_1; \Gamma_1 \to \Delta_2; \Gamma_2$ to mean that $S{:}\Delta_1 \to \Delta_2$ is a substitution, and $\mathrm{DV}(\Gamma_1)$ is included in the domain of S and that $\Delta_2, \Delta; \Gamma_2 \vdash S(x){:}S(\tau)$ whenever $\Gamma_1(x) = \forall \Delta.\tau$. Note that α-conversion is used to ensure that Δ_2 and Δ have no variables in common.

Lemma 4.

1. $\Delta; \Gamma \vdash$ implies $\Delta \vdash \Gamma(x)$ for any $x \in \mathrm{DV}(\Delta)$.
2. *Well-typing:* $\Delta; \Gamma \vdash t{:}\tau$ implies $\Delta \vdash \tau{:}\mathrm{T}$.
3. Let $S{:}\Delta_1 \to \Delta_2$ be a substitution; then $\Delta_1; \Gamma \vdash$ implies $\Delta_2; S(\Gamma) \vdash$.
4. *Type substitution:* let $S{:}\Delta_1 \to \Delta_2$ be a substitution; then $\Delta_1; \Gamma \vdash t{:}\tau$ implies $\Delta_2; S(\Gamma) \vdash t{:}S(\tau)$.
5. Let S be a renaming of Δ; then $\Delta; \Gamma \vdash J$ implies $\Delta_S; \Gamma_S \vdash S(J)$.
6. *Thinning:* $\Delta; \Gamma_1, \Gamma_2 \vdash J$ implies $\Delta; \Gamma_1, x{:}\sigma, \Gamma_2 \vdash J$ for any $x \notin \mathrm{DV}(\Gamma_1, \Gamma_2)$.
7. *Term substitution:* let $\Delta_1, \Delta; \Gamma_1 \vdash t{:}\tau$; then $\Delta_1, \Delta_2; \Gamma_1, x{:}(\forall \Delta.\tau), \Gamma_2 \vdash t'{:}\tau'$ implies $\Delta_1, \Delta_2; \Gamma_1, \Gamma_2 \vdash t'\{t/x\}{:}\tau'$.

Proof. Each statement is proved by induction on the structure of its premise, in some cases using earlier statements in the lemma. $\qquad \square$

The combinators are of two kinds. The first collection express properties of the functorial calculus. The others capture properties of the functor constants introduced to the basic system. The symbol i ranges over m and j ranges over 2. In the first group we have:

$$\mathrm{map}_m \ : \forall F\!:\! m.\forall X_{i\in m}, Y_{i\in m}\!:\! \mathrm{T}.(X_i \to Y_i) \to_{i\in m} F(\overline{X}) \to F(\overline{Y})$$
$$\mathrm{pex}_{m,i} \ : \forall X_{j\in m}\!:\! \mathrm{T}.X_i \to \Pi_i^m(\overline{X})$$
$$\mathrm{pin}_{m,i} \ : \forall X_{j\in m}\!:\! \mathrm{T}.\Pi_i^m(\overline{X}) \to X_i$$
$$\mathrm{dex}_{m,n} \ : \forall F\!:\! m.\forall G_{i\in m}\!:\! n.\forall X_{j\in n}\!:\! \mathrm{T}.F(G_i(\overline{X})_{i\in m}) \to F\langle\overline{G}\rangle^n(\overline{X})$$
$$\mathrm{din}_{m,n} \ : \forall F\!:\! m.\forall G_{i\in m}\!:\! n.\forall X_{j\in n}\!:\! \mathrm{T}.F\langle\overline{G}\rangle^n(\overline{X}) \to F(G_i(\overline{X})_{i\in m})$$
$$\mathrm{intro}_m \ : \forall F\!:\! m+1.\forall X_{i\in m}\!:\! \mathrm{T}.F(\overline{X}, \mu^m F(\overline{X})) \to \mu^m F(\overline{X})$$
$$\mathrm{fold}_m \ : \forall F\!:\! m+1.\forall X_{i\in m}, Y\!:\! \mathrm{T}.(F(\overline{X}, Y) \to Y) \to \mu^m F(\overline{X}) \to Y \ .$$

map_m expresses the action of functors of arity m on m-tuples of morphisms. The rest of the combinators in this group are linked to the various functor formation rules. The pairs of terms $\mathrm{pex}_{m,i}$ and $\mathrm{pin}_{m,i}$, and $\mathrm{dex}_{m,n}$ and $\mathrm{din}_{m,n}$ should be thought of as pairs of inverse isomorphisms. $\mathrm{pex}_{m,i}$ makes its argument the ith argument of m. It is used to store data in a uniform way, suitable for mapping. $\mathrm{dex}_{m,n}$ is an isomorphism between two different ways of associating a triple composition of functors. intro_m and fold_m are the introduction and elimination terms for the initial algebra functors. Recalling that initial algebras are defined for a functor, not just a type constructor, it should not be surprising to realise that once we have polymorphic mapping then we obtain polymorphic folding for free, as will be seen in the reduction rules below.

The second group of combinators are associated with the given constant functors $+$, $\times$ and 1. They are the familiar combinators for pairing, projection, inclusion, case analysis, and the canonical term of unit type.

$$\mathrm{pair} : \forall X_0, X_1\!:\! \mathrm{T}.X_0 \to X_1 \to X_0 \times X_1$$
$$\mathrm{pi}_j : \forall X_0, X_1\!:\! \mathrm{T}.X_0 \times X_1 \to X_j$$
$$\mathrm{in}_j : \forall X_0, X_1\!:\! \mathrm{T}.X_j \to X_0 + X_1$$
$$\mathrm{case} : \forall X_0, X_1, Y\!:\! \mathrm{T}.(X_0 \to Y) \to (X_1 \to Y) \to X_0 + X_1 \to Y$$
$$\mathrm{un} : 1 \ .$$

3.1 Type inference

A *typing* for a triple (Δ_1, Γ, t) consisting of a type context, a term context and a term is a triple (Δ_2, S, τ) such that $S\colon \Delta_1 \to \Delta_2$ is a substitution and

$$\Delta_2; S(\Gamma) \vdash t\!:\! \tau \ .$$

A *most general typing* for (Δ_1, Γ, t) is a typing as above such that if (Δ_2', S', τ') is any other typing for it then there is a substitution $R: \Delta_2 \to \Delta_2'$ such that $RS = S'$ and $R(\tau) = \tau'$.

Milner's algorithm W (see [Mil78, Tof88]) can be modified to produce a most general typing for our terms, whenever any typing exists. In the description of the algorithm we assume that bound variables are renamed to avoid clashes, and fresh variables are introduced whenever needed.

- $W(\Delta, \Gamma, x) = (\Delta\, \Delta_1, \mathrm{id}, \tau)$, where $\Gamma(x) = \forall \Delta_1.\tau$
- $W(\Delta, \Gamma, c) = (\Delta\, \Delta_1, \mathrm{id}, \tau)$, where $\sigma_c = \forall \Delta_1.\tau$
- $W(\Delta, \Gamma, \lambda x.t) = (\Delta_1, S, SX \to \tau_2)$, where

$$(\Delta_1, S, \tau_2) = W(\Delta\ X\!:\!\mathrm{T}, \Gamma\ x\!:\!X, t)$$

- $W(\Delta, \Gamma, t\ t_1) = (\Delta_3, U\ R\ S, UX)$, where

$$(\Delta_1, S, \tau) = W(\Delta, \Gamma, t)$$
$$(\Delta_2, R, \tau_1) = W(\Delta_1, S(\Gamma), t_1)$$
$$(\Delta_3, U) = \mathcal{U}(\Delta_2\ X\!:\!\mathrm{T}, R(\tau), \tau_1 \to X)$$

- $W(\Delta, \Gamma, \mathrm{let}\ x = t_1\ \mathrm{in}\ t_2) = (\Delta_4, R\ S, \tau_2)$, where

$$(\Delta_1, S, \tau_1) = W(\Delta, \Gamma, t_1)$$
$$\Delta_2 = \Delta_1 \lceil (\cup\{FV(SX) | X \in DV(\Delta)\})$$
$$\Delta_3 = \Delta_1 - \Delta_2$$
$$(\Delta_4, R, \tau_2) = W(\Delta_2, S(\Gamma)\ x\!:\!\forall \Delta_3.\tau_1, t_2)$$

By definition Δ_2 is the smallest sub-context of Δ_1 such that $S: \Delta \to \Delta_2$, so that we will obtain $R\ S: \Delta \to \Delta_4$ as required.

Theorem 5. *Let $\Delta_1; \Gamma$ be a well-formed context.*

1. *Soundness: if $W(\Delta_1, \Gamma, t) = (\Delta_2, S, \tau)$, then $S: \Delta_1 \to \Delta_2$ and $\Delta_2; S(\Gamma) \vdash t:\tau$.*

2. *Completeness: if $S': \Delta_1 \to \Delta_3$ and $\Delta_3; S'(\Gamma) \vdash t:\tau'$, then (W succeeds and) there exists a substitution $R: \Delta_2 \to \Delta_3$ such that $S' = R\ S$ on $DV(\Delta_1)$ and $\tau' = R(\tau)$.*

Proof. Both statements are proved by induction on the structure of t (see [Tof88]) and use type substitution (see Lemma 4) . $\qquad\square$

4 Term reduction and its properties

The reduction Fβ on terms of **FML** is defined as follows. Basic reductions (defined below) applied to a sub-term yields a one-step reduction. Then a reduction $t \to t'$ is a finite sequence of one-step reductions.

The basic reductions are given by the following rules, in which i ranges over m and j ranges over 2.

$$(\lambda x.t_2)\ t_1 > t_2\{t_1/x\}$$
$$\text{let } x = t_1 \text{ in } t_2 > t_2\{t_1/x\}$$
$$\text{pi}_j\ (\text{pair } t_0\ t_1) > t_j$$
$$\text{case } f_0\ f_1\ (\text{in}_j\ t) > f_j\ t$$
$$\text{fold}_m\ f\ (\text{intro}_m\ t) > f\ (\text{map}_{m+1}\ (\lambda x.x)_{i \in m}\ (\text{fold}_m\ f)\ t)$$
$$\text{pin}_{m,i}\ (\text{pex}_{m,i}\ t) > t$$
$$\text{din}_{m,n}\ (\text{dex}_{m,n}\ t) > t$$
$$\text{map}_m\ f_{k \in m}\ (\text{pex}_{m,i}\ t) > \text{pex}_{m,i}\ (f_i\ t)$$
$$\text{map}_n\ f_{k \in n}\ (\text{dex}_{m,n}\ t) > \text{dex}_{m,n}\ (\text{map}_m\ (\text{map}_n\ \overline{f})_{i \in m}\ t)$$
$$\text{map}_m\ f_{i \in m}\ (\text{intro}_m\ t) > \text{intro}_m\ (\text{map}_{m+1}\ \overline{f}\ (\text{map}_m\ \overline{f})\ t)$$
$$\text{map}_2\ f_0\ f_1\ (\text{pair } t_0\ t_1) > \text{pair}\ (f_0\ t_0)\ (f_1\ t_1)$$
$$\text{map}_2\ f_0\ f_1\ (\text{in}_j\ t) > \text{in}_j\ (f_j\ t)$$
$$\text{map}_0\ \text{un} > \text{un}$$

The reduction rules above can be classified as follows. The first two rules express β-reduction and its equivalent for let-terms. The next three rules express introduction-elimination rules for products, sums and initial algebras. The last of these may be unfamiliar. When $m = 0$ it is

$$\text{fold}_0\ f\ (\text{intro}_0\ t) > f\ (\text{map}_1\ (\text{fold}_0\ f)t)\ .$$

That is fold$_0$ f acts by recursively mapping itself across all of the substructures of intro$_0$ t and then applying f to the result:

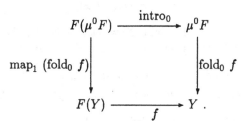

Without polymorphic mapping it would be necessary to expand this definition for each choice of functor. The next two rules reflect the status of pin$_{m,i}$ etc. as isomorphisms. The remaining rules describe the action of mapping. Most interesting is the first of these, which shows how a mapping locates its data. $\text{pex}_{m,i}$ identifies the datum t as being the ith argument of m so enabling the ith function argument f_i to be applied to it. Note that $\text{pex}_{m,i}$ still appears in the result, since now $f_i\, t$ is the ith argument. The rules for $\text{dex}_{m,n}$ and intro_m shows how to pass a mapping inside an outer functor argument. The last two rules are particular to the constant functors $+$ and $\times$ introduced to the system, and express their intended functoriality.

Theorem 6 SR. *Let $t \to t'$. If $\Delta; \Gamma \vdash t : \tau$ then $\Delta; \Gamma \vdash t' : \tau$.*

Proof. Without loss of generality, one can assume that the reduction is basic and perform the proof by case analysis. In each case one has to analyse only the last rules in the derivation of the premise, using Lemma 4 to handle term substitutions. □

Theorem 7 CR. *Fβ on untyped terms is Church-Rosser.*

Proof. Standard. The combinatory reductions rules for Fβ are left-linear and non overlapping, and one can apply the result in [Acz78] (see also [Klo80]). □

Corollary 8 CR. *Fβ on typable terms is Church-Rosser.*

Proof. Immediate from SR and CR on untyped terms. □

Theorem 9 SN. *If $\Delta; \Gamma \vdash t : \tau$, then t is strongly normalising.*

Proof. We prove SN for a system more powerful than FML, *functorial* F (briefly FF), which can type every term typable in FML (see Section 3), therefore SN for FF trivially implies SN for FML. The proof follows [Men91] and uses semantic techniques (reducibility candidates). The details are in [BJM96]. □

5 Examples

Define the polymorphic identity, and composition in the usual way, by

$$\text{id} = \lambda x.x$$
$$g \circ f = \lambda x.g\ (f\ x)\ .$$

Composition associates to the right. Now let us consider the list functor, $L = \mu^1 F$ where $F = +\langle 1\langle\rangle^2, \times\rangle$. Then for any type X we have the constructors

$$\text{nil} = (\text{intro}_1 \circ \text{dex}_{2,2} \circ \text{in}_0 \circ \text{dex}_{0,2})\ \text{un}: LX$$
$$\text{cons} = \lambda x.\lambda y.(\text{intro}_1 \circ \text{dex}_{2,2} \circ \text{in}_1)\ (\text{pair}\ x\ y): X \to LX \to LX\ .$$

The composite applied to un in defining nil is displayed as the top line of Figure 1. Let us see how the usual pattern-matching reductions for mapping and folding over lists can be recovered as composite reductions. Other inductive types are handled similarly. Let $f: X \to Y$ be a morphism. Then $\text{map}_1\ f$ nil reduces to nil by five map-reductions, as diagrammed in Figure 1, where $g = \text{map}_2\ f\ (\text{map}_1\ f)$. Similarly,

$$\text{map}_1\ f\ (\text{cons}\ h\ t) \to (\text{intro}_1 \circ \text{dex}_{2,2} \circ \text{in}_1)\ (\text{map}_2\ f\ (\text{map}_1\ f)\ (\text{pair}\ h\ t))$$
$$\to \text{cons}\ (f\ h)\ (\text{map}_1\ f\ t)\ .$$

For folding over a list, let $d\colon D$ and $g\colon X \times D \to D$ be terms. Then we can define

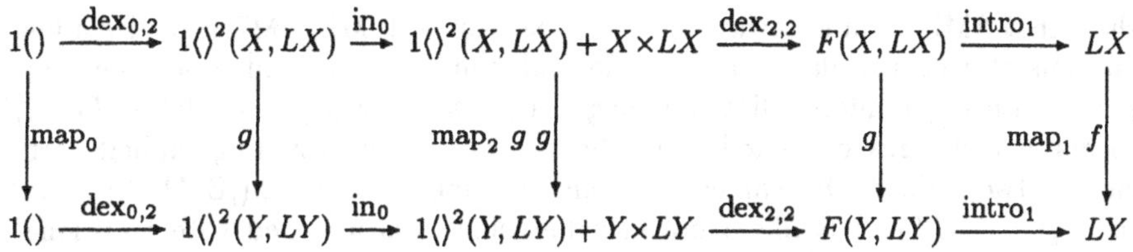

Fig. 1. $\text{map}_1 f$ nil

$$f = (\text{case}\ (\lambda x.d)\ g) \circ \text{din}_{2,2}\colon F(X, D) \to D\ .$$

Hence, given $h\colon X$ and $t\colon LX$ we have:

$$\text{fold}_1\ f\ \text{nil} \to f(\text{map}_2\ \text{id}\ (\text{fold}_1\ f)\ ((\text{dex}_{2,2} \circ \text{in}_0 \circ \text{dex}_{0,2})\ \text{un}))$$
$$\to f(\text{dex}_{2,2}(\text{in}_0(\text{dex}_{0,2}\ \text{un}))) \to d$$
$$\text{fold}_1\ f\ (\text{cons}\ h\ t) \to f\ (\text{map}_2\ \text{id}\ (\text{fold}_1\ f)\ ((\text{dex}_{2,2} \circ \text{in}_1\ (\text{pair}\ h\ t))))$$
$$\to f\ ((\text{dex}_{2,2} \circ \text{in}_1\ (\text{pair}\ h\ (\text{fold}_1\ f\ t))))$$
$$\to g(\text{pair}\ h\ (\text{fold}_1\ f\ t))\ .$$

6 Conclusions and future work

FML is an extension of the Hindley-Milner type system that supports parametric functorial polymorphism. That is, one can write algorithms (e.g. mapping and folding) which work uniformly for any functorial type constructor, unlike previous, ad hoc algorithms. The Hindley-Milner type inference algorithm extends smoothly to FML and reduction on well-formed terms is confluent and strongly normalising.

The functor syntax admits functors of many variables, and functor composition. Canonical isomorphisms are used to distinguish different orders of composition, which allow terms to express the shape-data, or functor-argument decomposition necessary to locate their data (this feature is essential for parametric algorithms).

Much remains to be done. We expect that the usual denotational models of system F can be extended to handle explicit functors. Also, the exact relationship between FML and Fω is not yet clear. Many of the subscripts on the combinators seem to be redundant. By introducing *form variables* [Jay95a] to represent sequences of types we may be able to infer many of them, just as we infer types. Another, basic shape polymorphic operation is that of extracting the data from the shape. This is fundamental to search operations, pattern-matching etc. and should be comfortably supported within the current system, as a new combinator.

FML should be considered as an intermediate language. Indeed, the examples show that FML is rather awkward in comparison with ML. FML provides a fine analysis of access to data via the canonical isomorphisms, and should be compared with other intermediate languages, e.g. those proposed in [PJ91, Ler92] to distinguish between boxed and unboxed values and providing explicit coercions between them. One can envisage an intensional semantics ([BJM96]) where $\text{pex}_{m,i}(t) \in \Pi_i^m(\overline{X})$ is like a boxed value, since t is wrapped with additional information about m and i, while $\text{dex}_{m,n}$ acts like data redistribution, here distinguishing between types and functors is crucial.

Finally, it remains to implement FML as an extension of an existing programming language, so that its merits can be tested by the community of programmers.

References

[Acz78]   P. Aczel. A general Church-Rosser theorem. Technical report, Univ. of Manchester, 1978.

[Bar84]   H.P. Barendregt. *The Lambda Calculus: Its Syntax and Semantics*. North Holland, 1984. revised edition.

[Bar92]   H.P. Barendregt. Lambda calculi with types. In *Handbook of Logic in Computer Science*. Oxford Univ. Press, 1992.

[Ben67]   J. Benabou. *Introduction to bicategories*, volume 47. Springer, 1967.

[BFSS90] E.S. Bainbridge, P.J. Freyd, A. Scedrov, and P.J. Scott. Functorial polymorphism. *Theoretical Computer Science*, 70:35–64, 1990.

[BJM96]   G. Bellè, C. B. Jay, and E. Moggi. Functorial ML. available from ftp://ftp.disi.unige.it/person/MoggiE/functorial_ml.dvi, 1996.

[BW90]   M. Barr and C. Wells. *Category Theory for Computing Science*. International Series in Computer Science. Prentice Hall, 1990.

[CF92]   J.R.B. Cockett and T. Fukushima. About **charity**. Technical Report 92/480/18, University of Calgary, 1992.

[GLT89]   J.-Y. Girard, Y. Lafont, and P. Taylor. *Proofs and Types*, volume 7. CUP, 1989.

[HM95]   R. Harper and G. Morrisett. Compiling polymorphism using intensional type analysis. In *Conference Record of POPL '95: 22nd ACM SIGPLAN-SIGACT Symposium on Principles of Programming Languages*, pages 130–141, San Francisco, California, January 1995.

[Jay]   C.B. Jay. Type-free term reduction for covariant types. Tech. report to appear.

[Jay95a] C.B. Jay. Polynomial polymorphism. In R. Kotagiri, editor, *Proceedings of the Eighteenth Australasian Computer Science Conference: Glenelg, South*

Australia 1-3 February, 1995, volume 17, pages 237–243. A.C.S. Communications, 1995.

[Jay95b] C.B. Jay. A semantics for shape. *Science of Computer Programming*, 25:251–283, 1995.

[Jay95c] C.B. Jay. Shape analysis for parallel computing. In *Parallel Computing Workshop '95 at Fujitsu Parallel Computing Centre, Imperial College*, 1995.

[Jay96] C.B. Jay. A fresh look at parametric polymorphism: covariant types. In *Proceedings of the 19th Australasian Computer Science Conference, Melbourne, Australia, January 31–February 2 1996.*, pages 525–533, 1996.

[Jeu95] J. Jeuring. Polytypic pattern matching. In *Conference on Functional Programming Languages and Computer Architecture*, pages 238–248, 1995.

[Jon95] M.P. Jones. A system of constructor classes: overloading and implicit higher-order polymorphism. *J. of Functional Programming*, 5(1), 1995.

[Klo80] J.W. Klop. *Combinatory Reduction Systems*. PhD thesis, Mathematical Center Amsterdam, 1980. Tracts 129.

[Ler92] X. Leroy. Unboxed objects and polymorphic typing. In *19th Symp. on Principle of Programming Languages*. ACM Press, 1992.

[LS86] J. Lambek and P.J. Scott. *Introduction to Higher-Order Categorical Logic*, volume 7 of *Cambridge Studies in Advanced Mathematics*. Cambridge University Press, 1986.

[Men91] N.P. Mendler. Inductive types and type constraints in the second-order lambda calculus. *Annals of Pure and Applied Logic*, 51, 1991.

[MFP91] E. Meijer, M. Fokkinga, and R. Paterson. Functional programming with bananas, lenses, envelopes and barbed wire. In J. Hughes, editor, *Procceding of the 5th ACM Conference on Functional Programming and Compter Architecture*, volume 523 of *LNCS*, pages 124–44. Springer Verlag, 1991.

[MH95] E. Meijer and G. Hutton. Bananas in space: extending fold and unfold to exponential types. In *Procedings 7th International Conference on Functional Programming and Computer Architecture, San Diego, California, June 1995*. ACM Press, 1995.

[Mil78] R. Milner. A theory of type polymorphism in programming. *JCSS*, 17, 1978.

[PJ91] S. Peyton Jones. Unboxed values as first-class citizens. In *Functional Programming and Computer Architecture*, volume 523 of *LNCS*, 1991.

[RP90] J. Reynolds and G.D. Plotkin. On functors expressible in polymorphic lambda-calculus. In G. Huet, editor, *Logical Foundations of Functional Programming*. Addison-Wesley, 1990.

[Tof88] M. Tofte. *Operational Semantics and Polymorphic Type Inference*. PhD thesis, University of Edinburgh, 1988. available as CST-52-88.

Parametric Polymorphism for Typed Prolog and λProlog

Pascale Louvet and Olivier Ridoux

IRISA, Campus Universitaire de Beaulieu, F-35042 RENNES Cedex, FRANCE
{louvet,ridoux}@irisa.fr

Abstract. Typed Prolog and λProlog are logic programming languages with a strict typing discipline which is based on simple types with variables. Experiments show that this discipline does not handle properly common logic programming practices used in Prolog. For instance, the usual transformation for computing the Clark completion of a Prolog program does not work well with some typed programs. We observe that the so-called head-condition is at the heart of these problems, and conclude that it should be enforced. We propose a second-order scheme which is compatible with usual practices. It allows quantifying types and terms, passing type and term parameters to goals and terms, and to express type guards for selecting goals. We give its syntax and deduction rules, and propose a solution to keep the concrete notation of programs close to the usual one.

Keywords: Logic programming, typing, polymorphism, second-order λ-Calculus.

1 Introduction

The work we describe here belongs to the prescriptive typing perspective. From this perspective, types are considered as properties of the formulas one wants to give a meaning to. This may eliminate programs that have a denotation in the untyped framework. The purpose is to bridge the gap between the intended semantics and the semantics of the actual program. The issues are to find structures in which properties can be checked before running the program, or structures for which one can synthesize the run-time checking of the intended property. In logic programming systems that follow this perspective (e.g., Gödel [9], Typed Prolog [12], λProlog [14, 15]) the agreement is that predicate symbols and term constructors have their types declared, while types of variables are inferred[1].

Variables are authorized in types to offer *generic polymorphism*. The ML programming language [16] is often considered as the paradigm for generic polymorphism. Its typing discipline has been transposed in logic programming as the Mycroft–O'Keefe discipline [17], and refined as Typed Prolog [12]. Polymorphism can also be modeled by the capability to pass types as parameters. This is known as *parametric polymorphism* and has only been marginally explored for logic programming. When applied to the λ-Calculus it yields the second-order λ-Calculus [6, 11, 1].

A notion that receives no common agreement is the notion of *head condition*. The issue is as follows. A predicate is generally defined as several clauses, and the question

---

[1] Note that λProlog has two types of variables: λ-variables, and logical variables.

is to choose whether the clauses obey the ML-like typing discipline independently, or whether there is a supplementary typing correlation between them. More precisely, the ML-like typing discipline states that the types of every occurrence of constants (including predicate constants in clause heads) are independent instances of their type scheme. The head condition adds that the types of all the occurrences of a given predicate symbol in clause heads must be the same (i.e., they are not independent instances). The head condition is implicit in the Mycroft–O'Keefe discipline [17]. It is explicitly enforced in the Gödel system [10] and in our implementation of λProlog [2]. It is not mentioned in the first writings on λProlog [14, 18], but it is rejected in further works [19]. An objective of this article is to give support to enforcing the head condition. The head condition makes the inference of the types of predicate constants non-decidable, but this will not be a problem here since we assume that all constants have their type declared.

Gödel and λProlog seem to be the first logic programming systems that incorporate a type discipline which is truly imposed[2], and with which one has experienced the programming of rather large applications. In this context, the impact of typing on software engineering becomes evident. On one side, the impact is positive: a lot of errors are spotted at compile-time, and types offer a minimal documentation. On the other side, the impact is negative: the typing discipline adds difficulties that are usually circumvented by unproductive tricks. In our developments, the difficulties have been of two kinds. First, the head condition tends to prevent the programming of polymorphic relations that are not generic (e.g., printing, reading, all operations in which the actual computation depends on the type of the arguments). To solve this problem, one must use non-transparent wrappers to map all types on a single one. For instance, a constant with type $(\alpha \to i)$ maps everything to a term of type i. However, it is not transparent since type variable α appears in the argument type, but not in the result type. This violates safety conditions that allow to prove a semantic soundness theorem [7, 8, 10]. Second, generic polymorphism does not fit well with meta-programming because a polymorphic object structure is degraded to a monomorphic type if no care is taken. Moreover, generic polymorphism and the head condition are not compatible with several useful program transformations.

We will present a parametric polymorphic typing discipline which solves the problems mentioned above and is compatible with common practice. We will develop in Section 2 the problems we met and how parametric polymorphism can solve them. Then we will present a variant of λProlog that incorporates parametric polymorphism (Section 3). In Sections 4 and 5, we present the theory of the new discipline, and we prove several identities that can be used for transforming programs. Finally, we observe that the formal notation used so far is cumbersome, and we present in Section 6 a concrete notation for programs that is close to a first-order typing language though it can be expanded into the formal second-order notation. We conclude and give hints for further works in Section 7.

We assume an elementary knowledge of the typed λ-Calculus and of typed logic programming. More specific concepts will be exposed briefly when necessary.

---

[2] Several logic programming systems have a type-checker, but it is not in the core of the language, and it can be switched off at will.

2 Motivations

We show that an important transformation of Prolog and λProlog programs requires the head condition when it is applied to typed programs. However, we also show that the head condition with generic polymorphism rejects legitimate programs that are accepted by the head condition with parametric polymorphism.

We also show a logically legal transformation of λProlog programs that breaks generic polymorphism, but is compatible with parametric polymorphism.

2.1 Program transformations

Program transformations are some of the promised advantages of using a declarative programming paradigm. The idea is that declarative languages lend themselves to logical identities (e.g., De Morgan identities) which can be oriented as transformation rules, and used for manipulating programs. We will study a transformation that is important because it produces an intermediate form for compilers, and because it is at the heart of the completion semantics for negation as failure [3]. This transformation applies both to Prolog and λProlog and only requires that there is some notion of clause. We will also study a transformation which is proper to λProlog and uses the ability to have an implication connective and a universal quantifier in clause bodies.

Predicate transformations for Prolog and λProlog. The common aspect of the languages of Prolog and λProlog is that there is a notion of clauses and goals. Clauses are universally quantified implications whose conclusion is an atomic formula (the *head*), and goals are conjunctions and disjunctions of formulas (the *body*). At this point, Typed Prolog and λProlog differs by the connectives that are admitted in body formulas. A program is a set of clauses.

The following identities are well-known logic programming identities[3].

Identity 1 $\forall \overline{v_A}(A \Leftarrow B) , \forall \overline{v_A}(A \Leftarrow C) \equiv \forall \overline{v_A}(A \Leftarrow B \vee C)$

Identity 2 $\forall \overline{v}(A[x \leftarrow t] \Leftarrow B) \equiv \forall \overline{v} x(A \Leftarrow x = t \wedge B)$, where $x \in \mathcal{FV}(A) \backslash \mathcal{FV}(B)$.

Example 1 *Because of Identity 2, program* { p 1 , p [1] } *is equivalent to program* { $\forall X(p\ X \Leftarrow X=1) , \forall X(p\ X \Leftarrow X=[1])$ }, *which is equivalent to program* { $\forall X(p\ X \Leftarrow X=1 \vee X=[1])$ } *by Identity 1.*

Predicate { *p 1 , p [1]* } stands for larger, and more important, predicates that are polymorphic, but not generic. They accept arguments of different types, but they have different definitions for the different types. This is the case for term readers and printers, general purpose meta-programs like tracers, and meta-predicates like (the extensional version of) *name/2*. Identities 1 and 2 are important because they are the rational for a normalization that is used for compiling and analyzing programs, and for building the Clark completion of a Prolog Program. The normalization rule is obtained by reading the identities left-to-right.

---

[3] In the following, $\overline{v_A}$ denotes a vector of all the variables that are free in A, $\mathcal{FV}(A)$ denotes a set of all the variables that are free in A, and $A[x \leftarrow t]$ denotes A where every free occurrence of a variable x is replaced by t.

Program transformations for λProlog. We now present program transformations that are proper to λProlog. The novelty of the formulas of λProlog is that implications and universal quantifications may occur in goal formulas. Formulas generated this way are called *hereditary Harrop formulas*.

The semantics of λProlog is usually given in proof-theoretic terms [15]. The deduction rules of the intuitionistic sequent calculus that correspond to connectives ∀ and ⇒ in goals are as follows:

$$\frac{P \vdash G[x \leftarrow c]}{P \vdash \forall x\, G} \;\; \forall \text{ in goals} \qquad \frac{P, D \vdash G}{P \vdash D \Rightarrow G} \;\; \Rightarrow \text{ in goals}$$

where P, G, and D are respectively a program, a goal, and a clause, and c does not occur free in P or G.

The rule for ⇒ in goals shows that clauses of the program can be moved in the goal. Miller suggests to use implication as a scoping device for modularity purposes [13]. In his scheme, clauses from the program are moved as the premise of the goals that need the clauses in their proofs. Similarly, the rule for ∀ in goals shows that symbols can be moved from the program to the goal. Using both connectives, one can write a fully abstract and modular *append* predicate.

Example 2 *A fully abstract and modular* append *predicate:*
$$\dots \Leftarrow \forall \text{append}(\quad \forall X(\text{ append } [] \; X \; X\;)$$
$$\Rightarrow \forall A \; X \; Y \; Z(\text{ append } [A\,|\,X] \; Y \; [A\,|\,Z] \Leftarrow \text{append } X \; Y \; Z\;)$$
$$\Rightarrow \dots)$$

The problem is that this version of *append* is not at all polymorphic because every occurrence of a universally quantified variable (here, *append*) must have the same type. This is to be contrasted with the *let* construct of ML, which introduces polymorphic variables. In short, and as far as polymorphism is concerned, a ∀ is more like a λ than like a *let*.

2.2 Typing problems

We show that Identity 1 requires the head condition, and that parametric polymorphism restores the head condition even when polymorphic relations are not generic.

Problems with the head condition. If the head condition is not assumed in the leftmost part of Identity 1, the two A's can be considered independently, and their predicate symbols and arguments may have different types. However, the rightmost formula can be well-typed only if the leftmost formula can be well-typed with the head condition. In Example 1, the first program is well-typed only without the head condition, but the last one is not well-typed at all because variable X needs to be assigned two incompatible types, *int* and *(list int)*.

Note that if the ∀-quantification had shown the type of the bound variable, Identity 1 could have been made more precise.

Identity 3 *(Identity 1 revisited)*
$$\forall \overline{v_A : \tau_A}(A \Leftarrow B) \,, \, \forall \overline{v_A : \tau_A}(A \Leftarrow C) \;\; \equiv \;\; \forall \overline{v_A : \tau_A}(A \Leftarrow B \vee C)$$

Identity 3 shows more precisely the range of its applicability than Identity 1, but it does not increase this range. Indeed, terms in similar positions in different heads must still have the same type.

Parametric polymorphism. We introduce types as parameters and their quantification. This allows for a parametric polymorphism capability, and it makes the head condition vacuously true because polymorphism is no more based on the instantiation of type schemes.

Identity 4 *(Identity 1 re-revisited)*
$$\forall \alpha : type \forall \overline{v_A : \tau_A}(A \Leftarrow B) , \forall \alpha : type \forall \overline{v_A : \tau_A}(A \Leftarrow C)$$
$$\equiv \ \forall \alpha : type \forall \overline{v_A : \tau_A}(A \Leftarrow B \vee C)$$
where the α's may occur in the τ_A's and in A, B, or C.

Using Identities 2 and 4, the problem of the above example is solved as follows.

Example 3 *Because of Identity 2, program { p int 1 , p (list int) [1] } is equivalent to program { $\forall$T:type$\forall$X:T(p T X $\Leftarrow$ T=int $\wedge$ X=1) , $\forall$T:type$\forall$X:T(p T X $\Leftarrow$ T=(list int) $\wedge$ X=[1]) }, which is equivalent to program { $\forall$T:type$\forall$X:T(p T X $\Leftarrow$ (T=int $\wedge$ X=1) $\vee$ (T=(list int) $\wedge$ X=[1])) } by Identity 4.*

With second-order typing, symbol p can be assigned a product type[4] $\Pi\alpha.\alpha \rightarrow o$ in both clauses. This restores the head condition though relation p is not generically polymorphic. Its implementation still depends on the actual type of its parameter.

In Example 3, Identity 2 is applied to a type as if it were a term. We introduce a special notation for type equalities, which yields a new version of Identity 2. The $s=t \rightarrow G$ construct acts as a typing guard. It binds together types s and t in the scope of goal G.

Identity 5 *Identity 2 revisited:*
$$\forall \overline{v : \alpha}.(A[x\leftarrow\tau] \Leftarrow B) \equiv \forall x : type \forall \overline{v : \alpha}(A \Leftarrow x=\tau \rightarrow B) \ \ where \ x \in \mathcal{FV}(A)\backslash\mathcal{FV}(B).$$

Example 4 *Because of Identity 5, program { p int 1 , p (list int) [1] } is equivalent to program { $\forall$T:type$\forall$X:T(p T X $\Leftarrow$ T=int $\rightarrow$ X=1) , $\forall$T:type$\forall$X:T(p T X $\Leftarrow$ T=(list int) $\rightarrow$ X=[1]) }, which is equivalent to program { $\forall$T:type$\forall$X:T(p T X $\Leftarrow$ T=int $\rightarrow$ X=1 $\vee$ T=(list int) $\rightarrow$ X=[1]) } by Identity 4.*

The introduction of parametric polymorphism also solves the problem with the fully abstract and modular rendering of predicate *append*.

Example 5 *A fully abstract and modular rendering of a polymorphic* append:
$$... \Leftarrow \forall append:\Pi\alpha.((list\ \alpha) \rightarrow (list\ \alpha) \rightarrow (list\ \alpha) \rightarrow o)($$
$$\forall T:type \ \forall X:T(\ append\ T\ [] \ X\ X\ )$$
$$\Rightarrow \forall T:type \ \forall A:T \ \forall X:(list\ T) \ \forall Y:(list\ T) \ \forall Z:(list\ T)($$
$$append\ T\ [A\,|\,X]\ Y\ [A\,|\,Z] \Leftarrow append\ T\ X\ Y\ Z)$$
$$\Rightarrow ...\ )$$

---

[4] Product types express how types are passed as parameters to functions, and how the types of term parameters depend on type parameters. A type like $\Pi\alpha.\alpha \rightarrow o$ expresses that a type is passed as a first argument, and that the second argument is a term of this type. To sum-up, a product type is an arrow type that expresses a type dependency.

In the sequel, we define an extension of λProlog, which we call λ_2Prolog, and we give a formal syntax for the new quantifications, type constructions, and term construction. We will give a typing discipline and a semantics to these programs. We will prove the new identities, and we will present a concrete syntax that avoids most of the unconveniences of the formal syntax.

3 Language design

The syntax of λ_2Prolog is presented in three parts: the types, the terms, and the formulas. We will present quantifiers for types, terms, and formulas. In every case, we assume that bound variables can be renamed apart by α-equivalence. In the grammars that follow we note as a superscript the set of variables that are allowed to have free occurrences in a structure. We note $(\_)^n$ the repetition of n items.

3.1 Types

Types are generated by the following grammar. Only one class of variables may occur in a type: type variables. So, the type non-terminals have one superscript for denoting the type variables that may occur free.

Grammar 1 $\mathcal{T}^A ::= \Pi\alpha.\mathcal{T}^{A\cup\{\alpha\}} \quad | \quad A \quad | \quad (\mathcal{K}_n \ (\mathcal{T}^A)^n) \quad | \quad (\mathcal{T}^A \to \mathcal{T}^A)$
where $\mathcal{K}_n$ denotes type constructors of arity n, (e.g., $\mathcal{K}_0 \supset \{\text{o, int, float}\}$, $\mathcal{K}_1 \supset \{\text{list}\}$).

Symbol $\to$ is the constructor of function types (a term of type $\sigma \to \sigma'$ can be interpreted as a function that returns a term of type σ' whenever it is passed a term of type σ). Parentheses are dropped in rightmost nested arrows; $(\sigma_1 \to (\sigma_2 \to \ldots))$ is written as $\sigma_1 \to \sigma_2 \to \ldots$. Π is the constructor of product types (a term of type $\Pi\sigma.\sigma'$ can be interpreted as a function that returns a term of type σ' when it is passed a type σ; σ' may depend on σ).

3.2 Terms

Terms are generated by the following grammar. Two classes of variables may occur in a term: type variables, and term variables. So, the term non-terminals have two superscripts: the first one for type variables, and the second one for term variables.

Grammar 2

$\mathbf{2}^{A,X}$	$::= \mathcal{C} \quad | \quad X$	(2.i)
$\mathbf{2}^{A,X}$	$::= \lambda \ x{:}\mathcal{T}^A.\mathbf{2}^{A,X\cup\{x\}} \quad | \quad (\mathbf{2}^{A,X} \ \mathbf{2}^{A,X})$	(2.ii)
$\mathbf{2}^{A,X}$	$::= \Lambda\alpha.\mathbf{2}^{A\cup\{\alpha\},X} \quad | \quad [\mathbf{2}^{A,X} \ \mathcal{T}^A \ ]$	(2.iii)

where $\mathcal{C}$ denotes the set of term constants, and X denotes the set of term variables that may have free occurrences.

Symbol λ denotes the abstraction of a term in a term: i.e., an ordinary λ-abstraction. Rule (2.ii) generates applications of a term to another. Parentheses will be dropped in leftmost nested applications: $((\ldots t_{n-1}) \ t_n)$ is written as

$(\ldots t_{n-1}\ t_n)$. Λ denotes the abstraction of a type in a term; this is where second-order comes in terms. Rule (2.iii) generates applications of a term to a type. Square brackets will be dropped in leftmost nested applications: $[[\ldots t_{n-1}]\ t_n]$ is written as $[\ldots t_{n-1}\ t_n]$.

Rules (2.i) and (2.ii) generate terms of λProlog. Rule (2.iii) is specific to λ_2Prolog.

3.3 Formulas

Formulas are generated by the following grammar. Two classes of variables may occur in a formula: type variables, and term variables. So, the term non-terminals have two superscripts: one for type variables, and the other for term variables.

Grammar 3

$$
\begin{array}{llll}
\mathcal{D}_{\mathbb{W}}^{A,X} & ::= \mathbb{W}\alpha.\mathcal{D}_{\mathbb{W}}^{A\cup\{\alpha\},X} \mid \mathcal{D}_{\mathbb{V}}^{A,X} & & (3.\text{i}) \\
\mathcal{D}_{\mathbb{V}}^{A,X} & ::= \forall x{:}\mathcal{T}^A.\mathcal{D}_{\mathbb{V}}^{A,X\cup\{x\}} \mid \mathcal{A}^{A,X} \Leftarrow \mathcal{G}^{A,X} \mid \mathcal{A}^{A,X} & & (3.\text{ii}) \\
\mathcal{G}^{A,X} & ::= \mathcal{G}^{A,X} \wedge \mathcal{G}^{A,X} \mid \mathcal{G}^{A,X} \vee \mathcal{G}^{A,X} \mid \mathcal{A}^{A,X} & & (3.\text{iii}) \\
\mathcal{G}^{A,X} & ::= \mathcal{D}_{\mathbb{W}}^{A,X} \Rightarrow \mathcal{G}^{A,X} \mid \forall x{:}\mathcal{T}^A.\ \mathcal{G}^{A,X\cup\{x\}} \mid \exists x{:}\mathcal{T}^A.\ \mathcal{G}^{A,X\cup\{x\}} & & (3.\text{iv}) \\
\mathcal{G}^{A,X} & ::= \exists\ \alpha.\ \mathcal{G}^{A\cup\{\alpha\},X} \mid \mathbb{W}\ \alpha.\ \mathcal{G}^{A\cup\{\alpha\},X} & & (3.\text{v}) \\
\mathcal{G}^{A,X} & ::= \mathcal{T}^A = \mathcal{T}^A \rightarrow \mathcal{G}^{A,X} & & (3.\text{vi}) \\
\mathcal{A}^{A,X} & ::= \mathbf{2}^{A,X} & & (3.\text{vii})
\end{array}
$$

The formulas are a refinement of the usual formulas built with definite clauses ($\mathcal{D}$), goals ($\mathcal{G}$), and atomic formulas ($\mathcal{A}$). The novelties are, first, universal quantifications of types at the clause level (rule (3.i)), and their existential and universal quantifications at the goal level (rule (3.v)), and, second, the introduction of type guards (rule (3.vi)). Atomic formulas are made of terms.

According to rules (3.i) and (3.ii), all clauses have the following form: $\mathbb{W}\alpha_1\ldots\mathbb{W}\alpha_n.\ \forall x_1{:}\tau_1\ldots\forall x_m{:}\tau_m.\ (A \Leftarrow G)$ where the type variables $\alpha_1, \ldots, \alpha_n$ can occur in the types $\tau_1, \ldots, \tau_m$, and in the sub-formulas A and G. This makes the quantification structure predictable and reconstructible.

Rules (3.ii), (3.iii), and (3.vii) generate Horn clauses (Prolog), and they generates hereditary Harrop formulas (λProlog) when rule (3.iv) is added. Rules (3.i), (3.v), and (3.vi) are specific to λ_2Prolog. The type guards make it possible to program polymorphic non-generic predicates.

Example 6 *(Ad hoc polymorphism made parametric)*

$$\mathbb{W}\alpha.\ \forall N_1{:}\alpha.\forall N_2{:}\alpha.\forall N_3{:}\alpha.($$
$$[\text{plus } \alpha]\ N_1\ N_2\ N_3 \Leftarrow (\ \alpha = \text{int} \rightarrow \text{plus\_int}\ N_1\ N_2\ N_3$$
$$\vee\ \alpha = \text{string} \rightarrow \text{append}\ N_1\ N_2\ N_3\ ))$$

expresses in a unique parametric clause

$$\forall N_1{:}\text{int}.\forall N_2{:}\text{int}.\forall N_3{:}\text{int}.($$
$$[\text{plus int}]\ N_1\ N_2\ N_3 \Leftarrow (\ \text{plus\_int}\ N_1\ N_2\ N_3\ ))$$
$$\forall\ N_1{:}\text{string}.\forall\ N_2{:}\text{string}.\forall\ N_3{:}\text{string}.($$
$$[\text{plus string}]\ N_1\ N_2\ N_3 \Leftarrow (\ \text{append}\ N_1\ N_2\ N_3\ ))$$

To sum-up this section, types are introduced as first-class citizens through the use of three quantifications (Π in types, Λ in terms, $\mathbb{W}$ in formulas), one application ($[\textit{term type}]$), and a type guard ($\textit{type}_1 = \textit{type}_2 \rightarrow \textit{goal}$).

4 Typing

We present a deductive type system that is based on second-order typed λ-Calculus, but also takes into account typing guards. Its theorems are sequents of the following form: $\Gamma \vdash_* t : \sigma$. Such a sequent reads "Given assumption Γ, term t has type σ". Assumptions are sets of pairs $a{:}\tau$ where a is either a constant or a variable, and τ is a type. There will be no proper rules for formula connectives. Indeed, they will be considered as term constructors and subject to the same rules. We assume that Γ always contains at least the signature $\Gamma_0 = \{\mathbb{W}, \exists : ((\Pi\alpha.o) \rightarrow o); \forall, \exists : \Pi\alpha.((\alpha \rightarrow o) \rightarrow o); \Leftarrow, \Rightarrow, \wedge, \vee : (o \rightarrow o \rightarrow o)\}$. So, simple connectives are no problems, and quantified formulas $\mathbb{W}\alpha.F$, $\exists\alpha.F$, $\forall x{:}\alpha.F$, $\exists x{:}\alpha.F$ will be considered as terms $(\mathbb{W} \, \Lambda\alpha.F)$, $(\exists \, \Lambda\alpha.F)$, $([\forall \, \alpha] \, \lambda x{:}\alpha.F)$, $([\exists \, \alpha] \, \lambda x{:}\alpha.F)$.

The deduction rules of the type system are as follows.

$$\overline{\Gamma \vdash_* x : \sigma} \qquad \textit{if } x : \sigma \in \Gamma \; (\textit{Axiom})$$

$$\frac{\Gamma \vdash_* t_1 : \sigma \rightarrow \tau \qquad \Gamma \vdash_* t_2 : \sigma'}{\Gamma \vdash_* (t_1 \, t_2) : \tau} \qquad \textit{if } \sigma =_\alpha \sigma' \;\; (\mathcal{E}_\rightarrow)$$

$$\frac{\Gamma \cup \{y : \sigma\} \vdash_* t[x \leftarrow y] : \tau}{\Gamma \vdash_* \lambda x : \sigma.t : \sigma \rightarrow \tau} \qquad \textit{if } y \notin \Gamma \;\; (\mathcal{I}_\rightarrow)$$

$$\frac{\Gamma \vdash_* t : \Pi\alpha.\sigma}{\Gamma \vdash_* [t \; \tau] : \sigma[\alpha \leftarrow \tau]} \; (\mathcal{E}_\Pi) \qquad \frac{\Gamma \vdash_* t : \sigma}{\Gamma \vdash_* \Lambda\alpha.t : \Pi\alpha.\sigma} \; (\mathcal{I}_\Pi)$$

$$\frac{\theta\Gamma \vdash_* \theta G : o}{\Gamma \vdash_* \sigma = \sigma' \rightarrow G : o} \qquad \textit{if } \theta = mgu(\{\sigma, \sigma'\}) \qquad (\mathcal{E}_{o,=\rightarrow})$$

They are all very classical, except for the last one. The idea is to hoist a type equality goal as a type assumption for a specific goal. This is why we have specialized these type equality goals into type guards. Rule $(\mathcal{E}_{o,=\rightarrow})$ is the only one that makes use of unification for binding type variables. Note that the bindings are local to the guarded goal. This should be contrasted with generic polymorphism in which instantiations of type scheme must be propagated throughout the expression.

Given signature Γ_0 and the above rules, one may derive typing rules $(\mathcal{E}_{o,\Leftarrow})$, $(\mathcal{E}_{o,\mathbb{W}})$, and $(\mathcal{E}_{o,\forall})$ as a shorthand.

Example 7 *The following type sequent is provable with the above rules:*
$$\Gamma_1 \vdash_* \mathbb{W}A.\forall X{:}A.([p \, A] \, X) \Leftarrow (A = int \rightarrow q \, X) \; : \; o$$

$$\cfrac{\cfrac{\cfrac{\cfrac{\Gamma_2 \vdash_* p : \Pi\alpha.\alpha \rightarrow o}{\Gamma_2 \vdash_* [p \, A] : A \rightarrow o}(\mathcal{E}_\Pi) \quad \Gamma_2 \vdash_* X{:}A}{\Gamma_2 \vdash_* ([p \, A] \, X) : o}(\mathcal{E}_\rightarrow) \quad \cfrac{\cfrac{\Gamma_3 \vdash_* q : int \rightarrow o \quad \Gamma_3 \vdash_* X : int}{\Gamma_3 \vdash_* (q \, X) : o}(\mathcal{E}_\rightarrow)}{\Gamma_2 \vdash_* (A = int \rightarrow q \, X) : o}(\mathcal{E}_{o,=\rightarrow})}{\Gamma_2 \vdash_* ([p \, A] \, X) \Leftarrow (A = int \rightarrow q \, X) \; : \; o}(\mathcal{E}_{o,\Leftarrow})}{\cfrac{\Gamma_1 \vdash_* \forall X{:}A.([p \, A] \, X) \Leftarrow (A = int \rightarrow q \, X) \; : \; o}{\Gamma_1 \vdash_* \mathbb{W}A.\forall X{:}A.([p \, A] \, X) \Leftarrow (A = int \rightarrow q \, X) \; : \; o}(\mathcal{E}_{o,\mathbb{W}})}(\mathcal{E}_{o,\forall})$$

with $\Gamma_1=\Gamma_0\cup\{$p$:\Pi\alpha.\alpha\rightarrow$o, q:int$\rightarrow$o$\}$, $\Gamma_2=\Gamma_1\cup\{$X:A$\}$, and $\Gamma_3=\Gamma_2[$A$\leftarrow$int$]$.

The type system forbids to quantify over a type variable when the typing rules show that this type variable should be bound to something else. Informally, the type system deems ill-typed any clause whose $\mathbb{W}$-quantifications do not correspond to actual polymorphism. If $\mathbb{W}$-quantifications are required, typing guards must be used for binding locally the type variables.

Example 8 *The following type sequent is not provable with the above rules:*
$$\Gamma_1 \vdash_* \mathbb{W}A.\forall X:A.([p\ A]\ X) \Leftarrow q\ X\ :\ o$$
Indeed, if it had a proof, it would start as the proof in Example 7, but, it would contain a proof of sequent $\Gamma_2 \vdash_* (q\ X):o$ instead of sequent $\Gamma_3 \vdash_* (q\ X):o$. However, sequent $\Gamma_2 \vdash_* (q\ X):o$ is not provable because it leads to sequent $\Gamma_1 \cup \{X:A\} \vdash_* X:int$ via rule $(\mathcal{E}_\rightarrow)$. This last sequent can only be the conclusion of rule Axiom, but it is not true that X:int is in $\Gamma_1 \cup \{X:A\}$.

5   Semantics

The semantics is given as a simple deductive system that is not realistic in two respects. First, it does not show the necessary goal-orientation of a programming paradigm. Second, quantifier elimination is done via instantiation of bound variables by closed terms; there are never any free variables in formulas.

The fix for the first problem is to replace all the left rules by a unique backchaining rule. We will present it in this article because it makes it easier to prove the identities of the motivation section. The fix for the second problem is to instantiate bound variables by new free variables, and to rely on unifiability rather than on equality for comparing atomic formulas. This will not be presented in this article.

5.1   A non-oriented and variable free deduction system

A sequent $P,\Gamma,K \vdash G$ must be read as "goal G is a consequence of program P in a context where term constants are in Γ, and type constants are in K".

Axiom

$$\frac{A =_{\alpha\beta\eta} A'}{P\cup\{A\},\Gamma,K \vdash A'} \qquad (\lambda-equivalence)$$

Left introductions

$$\frac{P,\Gamma,K \vdash G \qquad A =_{\alpha\beta\eta} A'}{P\cup\{A \Leftarrow G\},\Gamma,K \vdash A'} \qquad (\Leftarrow_D)$$

$$\frac{\Gamma \vdash_* t:\sigma \qquad P\cup\{D[x \leftarrow t]\},\Gamma,K \vdash A}{P\cup\{\forall x:\sigma.D\},\Gamma,K \vdash A} \qquad if\ t \in \mathbf{2}^{\emptyset,\emptyset}\ (\forall_D)$$

$$\frac{P\cup\{D[\alpha \leftarrow \sigma]\},\Gamma,K \vdash A}{P\cup\{\mathbb{W}\alpha.D\},\Gamma,K \vdash A} \qquad if\ \sigma \in \mathcal{T}^\emptyset\ (\mathbb{W}_D)$$

Right introductions

$$\frac{P,\Gamma,K \vdash G[\alpha \leftarrow \sigma]}{P,\Gamma,K \vdash \exists \alpha.G} \qquad \qquad if\ \sigma \in \mathcal{T}^{\emptyset} \quad (\exists_{\mathcal{G}})$$

$$\frac{P,\Gamma,K \cup \{\tau\} \vdash G[\alpha \leftarrow \tau]}{P,\Gamma,K \vdash \mathbb{W}\alpha.G} \qquad \qquad if\ \tau \in \mathcal{K}_0 \backslash K \quad (\mathbb{W}_{\mathcal{G}})$$

$$\frac{\Gamma \vdash_* t : \sigma \qquad P,\Gamma,K \vdash G[x \leftarrow t]}{P,\Gamma,K \vdash \exists x : \sigma.G} \qquad \qquad if\ t \in \mathbf{2}^{\emptyset,\emptyset} \quad (\exists_{\mathcal{G}})$$

$$\frac{P,\Gamma \cup \{t : \sigma\},K \vdash G[x \leftarrow t]}{P,\Gamma,K \vdash \forall x : \sigma.G} \qquad \qquad if\ t \in C \backslash \Gamma \quad (\forall_{\mathcal{G}})$$

$$\frac{P \cup \{D\},\Gamma,K \vdash G}{P,\Gamma,K \vdash D \Rightarrow G} \qquad \qquad (\Rightarrow_{\mathcal{G}})$$

$$\frac{P,\Gamma,K \vdash G}{P,\Gamma,K \vdash \sigma = \sigma \rightarrow G} \qquad \qquad (\rightarrow_{\mathcal{G}})$$

$$\frac{P,\Gamma,K \vdash G_1 \qquad P,\Gamma,K \vdash G_2}{P,\Gamma,K \vdash G_1 \wedge G_2} \qquad \qquad (\wedge_{\mathcal{G}})$$

$$\frac{P,\Gamma,K \vdash G_i}{P,\Gamma,K \vdash G_1 \vee G_2} \qquad \qquad if\ i \in \{1,2\} \quad (\vee_{\mathcal{G}})$$

Note that in rule $(\mathbb{W}_{\mathcal{G}})$ the type constants used for instantiating a $\mathbb{W}$-quantifier are taken in $\mathcal{K}_0$; they are types. In this way, the quantified goal can only compute terms that depend on types, i.e., second-order terms. If we had allowed to take type constants in $\mathcal{K}_i$ for $i > 0$, we would have opened the possibility to compute ω-order terms, that is terms that depend not only on types but also on type constructors.

The subsystem made of rules (λ-equivalence), $(\forall_{\mathcal{D}})$, $(\Leftarrow_{\mathcal{D}})$, $(\wedge_{\mathcal{G}})$, and $(\vee_{\mathcal{G}})$ is complete for Horn clause provability. When augmented with rules $(\Rightarrow_{\mathcal{G}})$, $(\forall_{\mathcal{G}})$, and $(\exists_{\mathcal{G}})$ it is complete for the provability of hereditary Harrop formulas. Finally, rules $(\exists_{\mathcal{G}})$, $(\mathbb{W}_{\mathcal{G}})$, $(\rightarrow_{\mathcal{G}})$, and $(\mathbb{W}_{\mathcal{D}})$ are required for our type dependent system.

Our system is a conservative extension of an intuitionistic deduction system for hereditary Harrop formulas. It makes more formulas provable, but the only new provable formulas are not hereditary Harrop formulas.

Theorem 1 *The deduction system is sound and complete for intuitionistic hereditary Harrop formulas.*
Proof scheme *A case analysis on each deduction rule.*

5.2 An oriented and variable free deduction system

We replace all the left-introduction rules by a unique backchaining rule.

$$\frac{P,\Gamma,K \vdash G}{P,\Gamma,K \vdash A} \;\; if \;\; \begin{cases} \exists k \geq 0, \exists n \geq 0, \\ \exists \, [\mathbb{W}\alpha_1 \ldots \mathbb{W}\alpha_k.\forall x_1 : \sigma_1 \ldots \forall x_n : \sigma_n.(A' \Leftarrow G')] \; \in \; P \\ \exists \tau_1 \ldots \tau_k \; \in \; \mathcal{T}^0 \; \exists t_1 \ldots t_n \; \in \; \mathbf{2}^{0,0}, \\ \qquad such\ that \\ \Gamma \vdash_* \; t_1 : \sigma_1[\alpha_1 \leftarrow \tau_1 \ldots \alpha_k \leftarrow \tau_k] \\ \quad \cdots \\ \Gamma \vdash_* \; t_n : \sigma_n[\alpha_1 \leftarrow \tau_1 \ldots \alpha_k \leftarrow \tau_k] \\ (\; G'[\alpha_1 \leftarrow \tau_1 \ldots \alpha_k \leftarrow \tau_k]\;)\; [x_1 \leftarrow t_1 \ldots x_n \leftarrow t_n] = G \\ (\; A'[\alpha_1 \leftarrow \tau_1 \ldots \alpha_k \leftarrow \tau_k]\;)\; [x_1 \leftarrow t_1 \ldots x_n \leftarrow t_n] =_{\alpha\beta\eta} A \end{cases}$$

Theorem 2 *The deduction system where the backchaining rule replaces all left-introduction rules is sound and complete with respect to the initial system.*
Proof scheme
Soundness: every instance of the backchaining rule can be emulated by some combination of the left-introduction rules.
Completeness: the backchaining rule sums-up sequences of left-introduction rules in uniform proofs.

5.3 Basic identities

We can now prove the identities that were informally presented in Section 2.

Theorem 3 *(Identity 4)*
$\quad \mathbb{W}\overline{\alpha}\forall\overline{x} : \overline{\sigma}.(A \Leftarrow G_1) \land \mathbb{W}\overline{\alpha}\forall\overline{x} : \overline{\sigma}.(A \Leftarrow G_2) \equiv \mathbb{W}\overline{\alpha}\forall\overline{x} : \overline{\sigma}.(A \Leftarrow G_1 \lor G_2)$
where variables (types or terms) that appears only in G_1 or G_2 are supposed existentially quantified in G_1 or G_2.
Proof scheme *The backchaining rule.*

Theorem 4 *(Identity 5)*
$\quad \mathbb{W}\overline{\alpha}\forall\overline{x} : \overline{\sigma}. \; (A[\beta{\leftarrow}\tau] \Leftarrow G) \equiv \mathbb{W}\overline{\alpha}\beta\forall\overline{x} : \overline{\sigma}. \; (A \Leftarrow \beta{=}\tau{\rightarrow}G),$
$\quad$*where $\beta \in \mathcal{FV}(A)\backslash\mathcal{FV}(G)$.*
Proof scheme *The backchaining rule.*

6 Notation

The fully explicit notation we have used so far for writing programs is almost unusable in practice because it is cluttered up with type notations. However, they are mostly redundant, and we show in this section that the usual, untyped notation, can be recovered in many cases.

Example 9 *The following presentation of the recursive clause of predicate* map *declared with type $\Pi\alpha\beta. \;((\alpha{\rightarrow}\beta){\rightarrow}(list\ \alpha){\rightarrow}(list\ \beta){\rightarrow}o)$ is hardly readable:*
$\quad \mathbb{W}\alpha_1\alpha_2. \; \forall F{:}\alpha_1{\rightarrow}\alpha_2 \; \forall X{:}\alpha_1 \; \forall L{:}(list\ \alpha_1) \; \forall FL{:}(list\ \alpha_2).$
$\qquad (\; [map\ \alpha_1\ \alpha_2]\ F\ [X\,|\,L]\ [(F\ X)\,|\,FL] \Leftarrow [map\ \alpha_1\ \alpha_2]\ F\ L\ FL\;)$
Given a few assumptions, the following notation will do as well.
$\quad$map $F\ [X\,|\,L]\ [(F\ X)\,|\,FL] \Leftarrow$ map $F\ L\ FL$

Note that what is at stake here is not "type reconstruction" in the usual sense (say, the ML sense). We prefer to call it "type completion". Given kind declarations for every type constant, and type declarations with possibly missing Π-quantifications for every term constant, and given formula with possibly missing type parameters and $\mathbb{W}$- and $\forall$-quantifications (the *implicit notation*), the problem is to make explicit all the type parameters and the type quantifications in the type declarations and the formulas.

6.1 Completion of quantifications in clauses

We adopt the convention that all outermost clause quantifications can be dropped. They can be reconstructed by using the lexical convention that is used in Prolog: "Identifiers of variables begin with a capital letter". With this convention alone, predicate *map* can be defined as

$([map\ A\ B]\ F\ [X\,|\,L]\ [(F\ X)\,|\,FL] \Leftarrow [map\ A\ B]\ F\ L\ FL\ )$

The selection of the actual quantifier ($\mathbb{W}$ or $\forall$) is deduced from the position of the variable. Variables A and B are recognized as type variables because they occur as the arguments of an application of a term to types. All other variables are term variables. It is the fact that the two kinds of applications are syntactically distinguished that helps in classifying the variables. When quantifying a term variable, one must know its type. For this purpose, the type-checker is turned into a type-inferencer for types of variables. This is an easy thing to do, because there is no polymorphism in variables, and the only equivalence relation considered on types is α-equivalence.

A further refinement is to complete a clause with existential quantifications ($\exists$ and $\exists\!\!\!\!-$) when a variable does not occur in the head. This makes the scheme relevant also for question goals.

6.2 Completion of quantifications in types

We adopt the convention that all outermost type quantifications can be dropped in declaration. All the free variables in a type declaration are assumed Π-quantified near the outermost level. Again, a lexical convention will help discriminating variable identifiers. There is a small subtlety in the placement of the implicit Π-quantifications. Though consecutive Π-quantifications commute, the implicit Π-quantifications must be placed *after* the already existing outermost Π-quantifications. The reason is that there may be application of terms to type in the implicit notation whose order is based on the explicit Π-quantifications.

For instance $\Pi\alpha_1.((list\ \alpha_1) \to (list\ \alpha_2) \to o)$ will be completed as $\Pi\alpha_1.\Pi\alpha_2.((list\ \alpha_1) \to (list\ \alpha_2) \to o)$, but not as $\Pi\alpha_2.\Pi\alpha_1.(\ldots)$.

So, the only Π-quantifications that cannot be made implicit are non-prenex Π-quantifications. For instance, in $\Pi\alpha_1.(\Pi\alpha_2.(\alpha_1 \to \alpha_2) \to \alpha_1 \to o)$ variable α_1 can be Π-quantified implicitly, but α_2 cannot. Non-prenex Π-quantifications is one of the problem of second-order type-inference; there is not a unique principal type. The fact that all constants are declared solves the problem: only programs that actually use non-prenex Π-quantifications will have to make Π-quantifications explicit.

According to this type completion rule, the declared type for *map* can be $((A{\to}B){\to}(list\ A){\to}(list\ B){\to}o)$.

6.3 Completion of applications of terms to types

Finally, some applications of terms to types can be omitted. Every time a term whose type is Π-quantified is applied to a term, an implicit application to some type is assumed. If the type contains type variables, they must be explicitly quantified also.

We present a deductive type system whose theorems are sequents of the following form: $\Gamma \vdash_{comp} t : \sigma : u$. Such a sequent reads "Given assumption Γ, implicit term t has type σ, and its explicit form is u". Most rules are derived from the type system of Section 4 by simply adding an extra field for the completed term.

$$\frac{\Gamma \vdash_* t : \sigma}{\Gamma \vdash_{comp} t : \sigma : t} \qquad\qquad (Axiom)$$

$$\frac{\Gamma \vdash_{comp} t_1 : \sigma \to \tau : u_1 \quad \Gamma \vdash_{comp} t_2 : \sigma' : u_2}{\Gamma \vdash_{comp} (t_1\ t_2) : \tau : (u_1\ u_2)} \qquad if\ \sigma =_\alpha \sigma' \qquad (\mathcal{E}_\to)$$

$$\frac{\Gamma \cup \{y : \sigma\} \vdash_{comp} t[x \leftarrow y] : \tau : u[x \leftarrow y]}{\Gamma \vdash_{comp} \lambda x : \sigma.t : \sigma \to \tau : \lambda x : \sigma.u} \qquad if\ y \notin \Gamma \qquad (\mathcal{I}_\to)$$

$$\frac{\Gamma \vdash_{comp} t : \sigma : u}{\Gamma \vdash_{comp} \Lambda \alpha.t : \Pi \alpha.\sigma : \Lambda \alpha.u} \qquad\qquad (\mathcal{I}_\Pi)$$

$$\frac{\theta \Gamma \vdash_{comp} G_1 : o : G_2}{\Gamma \vdash_{comp} \sigma = \sigma' \to G_1 : o : \sigma = \sigma' \to G_2} \qquad if\ \theta = mgu(\{\sigma, \sigma'\}) \quad (\mathcal{I}_{o,=\to})$$

Rules that are specific to the completion are as follows:

$$\frac{\Gamma \vdash_{comp} t : \Pi \alpha.\sigma : u}{\Gamma \vdash_{comp} [t\ \tau] : \sigma' : [u\ \tau]} \qquad if\ \begin{cases} \sigma' = \sigma[\alpha \leftarrow \tau] \\ \Gamma \vdash_* [t\ \tau] : \sigma' \end{cases} \qquad (\mathcal{E}_\Pi^{regular})$$

$$\frac{\Gamma \vdash_{comp} [t\ \tau] : \sigma : u}{\Gamma \vdash_{comp} t : \sigma : u} \qquad if\ \begin{cases} \sigma\ is\ not\ \Pi \alpha.\dots \\ \Gamma \vdash_* t : \Pi \alpha.\dots \end{cases} \qquad (\mathcal{E}_\Pi^{completion})$$

Rule $(\mathcal{E}_\Pi^{regular})$ is constructed like the other rules, but rule $(\mathcal{E}_\Pi^{completion})$ performs the completion by simply keeping track of the added type parameter.

A consequence of this system is that the term which is applied to inferred types must be well-typed (i.e., complete). So, the limitation that makes completion feasible is that when a term contains several nested type applications separated by other constructs, only one of them can be omitted. For instance, in $([[[f\ \sigma_1 \dots \sigma_s]\ s_1 \dots s_r)\ \tau_1 \dots \tau_m]\ t_1 \dots t_n)$, either the σ_i's or the τ_j's may be omitted but not both.

The three mechanisms for making explicit Π-quantifications, type applications, and $\mathbb{W}$-quantifications, must be used in this order. They make the usual writing of the definition of *map* sufficient.

7 Conclusion

We have presented motivations for imposing the head condition to prescriptively typed logic programs. It can be summed-up by the idea that typing must be robust to fundamental program transformations. This leads to the definition of a second-order type system for λProlog, which applies to Prolog as a fragment. With the system we have proved identities that can serve as safe grounds for applying two important program transformations to typed logic programs. The formalism is syntactically restricted in such a way that the form of the legal structures is predictable. This gives the basis for a type completion procedure that permits an almost type-free notation of programs.

The proposed type system can give a type to usual, but hard-to-type, predicates like *read*, *print* and *name*. Predicates *read* and *print* have type $\Pi A.A \to o$, and can be defined by a non-generic induction on the type. Predicate *name* has type $\Pi A.string \to A \to o$, and can be defined extensionally as follows:

[name $\Pi A.(list\ A)$] "nil" [] .

[name $\Pi A.A \to (list\ A) \to (list\ A)$] "." '.' .

[name $\Pi A.(list\ A) \to (list\ A) \to (list\ A) \to o$] "append" append .

. . .

Note that the explicit applications of constant *name* to types can be suppressed, since they can be easily completed.

One may object against parametric polymorphism because it suggests dynamic typing whereas generic polymorphism usually leads to static typing. In fact this is a matter of implementation, and we hope to be able to make static significant parts of the typing. Moreover, we have seen that non-transparent wrappers are often required. This breaks the safety conditions that make static typing possible. So, some dynamic typing is required, and our proposal gives a logical status to it.

The emphasis of this work is different than previous works on higher-order typing for logic programming [20, 4, 5], or polymorphic typing of higher-order logic program [8]. The first type of work insists more on the ability to reason in a full higher-order typed logic than we do. On the opposite, we are more concerned with the practical software engineering consequences of a type system. The second kind of work leaves open the question of the head condition, and concerns higher-order programming only because goals can be passed as parameters. We think that the head condition must be enforced, and our type scheme applies to the more ambitious kind of higher-order programming of λProlog. In the work of Nadathur and Pfenning on the typing of λProlog [19], the head condition is rejected. We have shown this is not compatible with useful program transformations.

Much remains to be done. First, a less naive elimination of quantifiers is required. It will amount to replacing bound variables by free variables, and to replace equality testing by unifiability. The expected result is a deduction system that is close to an interpreter. Second, our pragmatic emphasis does not tolerate an arbitrary usage of term that would make higher-order unification lead to a non-deterministic interleaving of type unification and term unification. We will have to find the conditions for a disciplined use of type, and the means for enforcing them. Finally, we will have to implement all this as a usable λ_2Prolog system.

References

1. H. Barendregt and K. Hemerik. Types in lambda calculi and programming languages. In N. Jones, editor, *European Symp. on Programming, LNCS 432*, pages 1–35, Springer-Verlag, 1990.

2. P. Brisset and O. Ridoux. The architecture of an implementation of λProlog: Prolog/Mali. In *Workshop on λProlog*, Philadelphia, PA, USA, 1992. ftp://ftp.irisa.fr/local/lande.

3. K.L. Clark. Negation as failure. In H. Gallaire and J. Minker, editors, *Logic and Data Bases*, pages 293–322, Plenum Press, New-York, USA, 1978.

4. C.M. Elliott. Higher-order unification with dependent function types. In N. Derschowitz, editor, *3rd Int. Conf. Rewriting Techniques and Applications, LNCS 355*, pages 121–136, Springer-Verlag, 1989.

5. C.M. Elliott and F. Pfenning. A semi-functional implementation of a higher-order logic programming language. In P. Lee, editor, *Topics in Advanced Language Implementation*, pages 289–325, MIT Press, 1991.

6. J.-Y. Girard. *Interprétation fonctionelle et élimination des coupures dans l'arithmétique d'ordre supérieur*. Thèse de doctorat d'état, Université de Paris VII, 1972.

7. M. Hanus. Horn clause programs with polymorphic types: semantics and resolution. In *TAPSOFT'89, LNCS 352*, pages 225–240, Springer-Verlag, 1989.

8. M. Hanus. Polymorphic higher-order programming in Prolog. In G. Levi and M. Martelli, editors, *6th Int. Conf. Logic Programming*, pages 382–397, MIT Press, 1989.

9. P.M. Hill and J.W. Lloyd. *The Gödel Programming Language*. MIT Press, 1994.

10. P.M. Hill and R.W. Topor. A semantics for typed logic programs. In F. Pfenning, editor, *Types in Logic Programming*, pages 1–62, MIT Press, 1992.

11. J. Reynolds. Towards a theory of type structure. In *Colloque sur la Programmation, LNCS 19*, pages 408–425, Springer-Verlag, 1974.

12. T.K. Lakshman and U.S. Reddy. Typed Prolog: a semantic reconstruction of the Mycroft-O'Keefe type system. In *Int. Logic Programming Symp.*, pages 202–217, 1991.

13. D.A. Miller. A logical analysis of modules in logic programming. *J. Logic Programming*, 6(1–2):79–108, 1989.

14. D.A. Miller and G. Nadathur. Higher-order logic programming. In E. Shapiro, editor, *3rd Int. Conf. Logic Programming, LNCS 225*, pages 448–462, Springer-Verlag, 1986.

15. D.A. Miller, G. Nadathur, F. Pfenning, and A. Scedrov. Uniform proofs as a foundation for logic programming. *Annals of Pure and Applied Logic*, 51:125–157, 1991.

16. R. Milner. A theory of type polymorphism in programming. *J. Computer and System Sciences*, 17:348–375, 1978.

17. A. Mycroft and R.A. O'Keefe. A polymorphic type system for Prolog. *Artificial Intelligence*, 23:295–307, 1984.

18. G. Nadathur. *A Higher-Order Logic as the Basis for Logic Programming*. Ph.D. Thesis, University of Pennsylvania, 1987.

19. G. Nadathur and F. Pfenning. The type system of a higher-order logic programming language. In F. Pfenning, editor, *Types in Logic Programming*, pages 245–283, MIT Press, 1992.

20. F. Pfenning. Partial polymorphic type inference and higher-order unification. In *ACM Conf. LISP and Functional Programming*, pages 153–163, ACM Press, 1988.

GOTA Algebras: A Specification Formalism for Inheritance and Object Hierarchies

Joaquín Mateos-Lago[*] and Mario Rodríguez-Artalejo[**]

Departamento de Informática y Automática. Universidad Complutense de Madrid
e-mail: {jmlago, mario}@eucmos.sim.ucm.es

Abstract. As a first step towards an integration of Object-Oriented Programming and Declarative Programming we present a purely algebraic framework for the specification of inheritance and object hierarchies, based on the known idea of representing records as order-sorted feature terms. Specifications in our formalism have an intended semantics which can be formally characterized as an initial algebra. We argue that the new formalism improves over some shortcomings of related approaches. In particular, we can express a novel mechanism called *genetic inheritance*, which allows to deal with multiple inheritance in a very flexible way.

1 Introduction

Object-Oriented Programming (OOP) looks like being here to stay. Increasingly more languages are incorporating object-oriented extensions, and declarative languages are not an exception. As a far reaching goal, we are looking towards a formal approach to build object-orientation inside the declarative paradigm. As a first step, the present paper aims at establishing a theoretical framework which covers the main static aspects of traditional OOP: *classes*, *inheritance*, and *state*, leaving the methods and the dynamic aspects for a later study. More precisely, we are particularly interested in the following static aspects of the object-oriented paradigm: explicit class hierarchies, description by attributes, multiple inheritance, and specialization of attributes. A simple example which illustrates these characteristics is the following.

Example 1. We are going to consider four classes: **Machine**, **Plane**, **Ship**, and **Seaplane**. Of these, **Plane** and **Ship** are *subclasses* of **Machine**, meaning that a plane, or a ship is also a machine. **Seaplane** is a subclass of both **Plane** and **Ship**, meaning that a seaplane is both a plane and a ship. These subclass relationships determine a *hierarchy* of classes. The classes are described by their *attributes*, this way **Machine** has an attribute *age*, **Plane** has attribute *engines*, and **Ship** has *draught*. Attributes are inherited from classes to subclasses, so **Plane** and **Ship** have attribute *age*, and **Seaplane** has attributes *age*, *engines* and *draught*. For **Seaplane**, attributes are multiple inherited from its superclasses **Plane** and **Ship**, having that seaplanes have *engines* and *draught*.

[*] This work is supported by both Spanish CICYT Project CPD (TIC95-0433-C03-01), and UCM Project PDPGO (UCM-5621).

[**] This work is supported by Spanish CICYT Project CPD (TIC95-0433-C03-01).

Furthermore, attributes can be redefined by subclasses to specially suit their needs. For instance, the class **Seaplane** might redefine the inherited attribute *age*, so that seaplanes ages may not be of the same sort as machines ages.

There are several known formalisms which enjoy a neat semantics and are able to represent object hierarchies like the one in Example 1. In order to motivate our own approach, let us recall three representative ones here. In each case, we will briefly discuss some inadequacies that we wish to improve.

Order-Sorted Algebra (OSA) [GM], [SNGM] is based on defining signatures with sort symbols which follow an inclusion relationship dictated by a partial order. This way, a representation of class hierarchies can be achieved with sorts acting as classes, and the existence of objects in the sorts/classes can be obtained by defining *constructor operations* which form terms for every sort/class. Inheritance of attributes from superclasses is obtained as a particular case of inheritance of operations from supersorts. OSA equational specifications have an initial semantics, which is indeed a good property. However, from our point of view, writing OSA specifications is a cumbersome way to model object-oriented hierarchies, mainly due to the necessity of introducing different explicit constructors for the different sorts/classes. Moreover, the idea of classes defined by their attributes is hidden because attributes are not apparent in constructor terms hence having that attributes and their values are separated.

Feature Trees (FT) [AKPS], [ST], [BS] show a quite different approach. A feature tree has sorts as labels for nodes, and features as labels for edges. This way, feature trees can be used to model objects with attributes (corresponding to the features). Feature trees can be described by constraints in a constraint system which enjoys nice computational properties. Though being an attribute-related way to express objects, FT lack an explicit class hierarchy, where attributes are related to classes. Besides, attributes do not have declarations, and in a feature tree, every node can have edges labelled with every existing feature. That means that sorts/classes have every attribute, which seems a little confusing from an OOP point of view. Finally, although we can define inclusions between sorts, there is no controlled inheritance of attributes[3], since attributes are not related to sorts/classes, and are sortworld-wide accessible.

Jumping from the specification-oriented approach of OSA to the description-oriented approach of FT we can find in the middle a certain equilibrium point. **Inheritance Hierarchies** (IH) [SAK] combines good properties from both OSA and FT. Classes are defined with an explicit hierarchy where attributes describe them. It is assumed that attributes are inherited from upper classes to lower classes (hence the name). Semantics of inheritance hierarchies can be achieved by means of a translation to an order-sorted specification which has initial semantics. This line comes quite close to our expectations but there is still some disagreement with our vision. The point is that semantics of inheritance hierarchies conceives objects to exist only in *terminal* classes, i.e. classes which stand at the bottom of the hierarchy. Intermediate classes behave just as the join of their subclasses without introducing any proper objects. In Example 1, the IH

---

[3] There is an inheritance of constraints, accomplished by extending the description of an "object" with more features. In this sense, the new object inherits the constraints from the original object.

approach would lead to have no proper objects in the classes **Machine, Plane** or **Ship**, other than seaplanes. In contrast to this, the idea underlying our own view of OOP is that *classes characterize collections of objects with a common behaviour*, given by the available attributes and methods. Therefore, any class should allow for proper objects corresponding to all the possible legal combinations of values for attributes of the class.

In this paper we present **GOTA Algebras**[4] as a new formalism for the specification of the static aspects of object-oriented hierarchies. Our aim is to improve over the above mentioned limitations of other approaches and to introduce a novel view of inheritance, so called *genetic inheritance*, which is more expressive than the usual inheritance mechanisms from OOP languages. The organization of the paper is as follows: after this Introduction, Section 2 presents signatures and feature terms for GOTA, and lays down the peculiarities of our approach, including genetic inheritance and the possibility to specify free Abstract Data Types. Section 3 goes into the semantics of GOTA signatures, defining GOTA algebras which have to satisfy some conditions in order to attain the desired object-oriented behaviour, and exposing the denotation for terms. Section 4 includes the results about the initial semantics of GOTA specifications, defining homomorphisms and proving the existence of initial algebras. Section 5 closes the paper with conclusions and indications of further research lines. A full version of the paper including more examples and proofs is available as technical report [MR].

2 Signatures

GOTA signatures will be defined from two disjoint sets of symbols, one for the *sorts* and one for the *attributes*. We start by defining *attribute declarations*.

Definition 1. An **attribute declaration** has the form $g : s \to w$ where g is an attribute symbol, and s and w are sort symbols. We say that sort s has a **proper** declaration of g.

With attribute declarations we can define GOTA signatures.

Definition 2. A **GOTA signature** Σ is a triple $(S, \leq, A)$, where S is a nonempty finite set of sort symbols, $\leq$ is a partial order over S, and A is a (possibly empty) finite set of attribute declarations with symbols of S and A, such that there are not two proper declarations of the same attribute for any sort.

GOTA signatures have the following interpretation: sorts represent object classes, where the partial order induces the class hierarchy, understood as inclusion; attributes values characterize the state of an object, which can be seen as a tuple or record; some sorts having no attributes can represent single values (constants); see Example 7 below. Therefore, a GOTA signature contains enough information to serve as specification of a static object-oriented class hierarchy.

Example 2. Considering the hierarchy of Example 1, a GOTA signature representing it would be:

---

[4] GOTA stands for the spanish *Géneros Ordenados y Términos de Atributos*, which means Ordered Sorts and Feature Terms.

```
sorts Nat OnetoThirty Machine Plane Ship Seaplane .
subsort OnetoThirty < Nat .
subsorts Plane Ship < Machine .
subsort Seaplane < Ship Plane .
att age: Machine -> Nat .
att engines: Plane -> Nat .
att draught: Ship -> Nat .
att age: Seaplane -> OnetoThirty .
```

where we use a notation akin to that of OBJ3 [GWMFJ]. The set A of attribute declarations consists of the declarations preceded by **att**. Note that, although there are two declarations of attribute **age** there is only one proper declaration for each sort, since one is for **Machine**, and the other for **Seaplane**.

If there is no ambiguity we will refer to GOTA signatures simply as signatures from now on. A sort will have proper and *inherited* declarations of attributes, the latter ones corresponding to proper declarations of supersorts. The next definition specifies which attribute declarations are regarded to be available *for* each particular sort.

Definition 3. Given a signature $\Sigma = (S, \leq, A)$ and a sort symbol $s \in S$, an attribute declaration, $g : s' \to w'$ is a **declaration of** g **for** s, if $s \leq s'$ and there is no other declaration, $g : s'' \to w''$ such that $s \leq s'' < s'$. We say that a sort s **has** an attribute g, if there exists at least one declaration of g for s.

The idea behind this definition is that objects in any class inherit attributes from the closest superclasses. The following proposition is easy to prove.

Proposition 4. *Given a signature* $\Sigma = (S, \leq, A)$ *if a sort* $s \in S$ *has attribute* g *then every sort* $w \leq s$ *has attribute* g.

Multiple attribute inheritance is allowed, as it is shown in the following example.

Example 3. We have a hierarchy which represents a classification of individuals in families. There are two classes and a third subclass which shares the behaviour of the former. Attributes are common in both superclasses, but with different declarations:

```
sorts Smiths Jones Smith-Jones .
subsorts Smith-Jones < Smiths Jones .
sorts Blue Green Black Brown Light Dark .
subsorts Blue Green < Light .
subsorts Black Brown < Dark .
sorts Small Rounded Pointed Big Human Weird .
subsorts Small Rounded < Human .
subsorts Pointed Big < Weird .
att eyes : Smiths -> Light .
att ears : Smiths -> Human .
att eyes : Jones -> Dark .
att ears : Jones -> Weird .
```

Attribute **eyes** has two different declarations for sort Smith-Jones, as well as attribute **ears**. This situation will lead to the concept of *genetic inheritance* that will be presented below.

Obviously, if a sort s has a proper declaration of an attribute g, then that is the only declaration of g for sort s. In general, we are interested in all the possible combinations of attributes a class may have. Those will be *complete sets of attributes* for a sort.

Definition 5. Given a signature $\Sigma = (S, \leq, A)$, and a sort $s \in S$, we define a **complete set of attributes of** s as a collection of attribute declarations $g_j : s_j \to w_j$ with $j = 1, \ldots, m$, such that the g_j are all the attributes that s has, and every declaration in the set is a declaration of attribute g_j for s.

Example 4. Going on with the hierarchy of Example 3, we have that sorts Smiths and Jones have just one complete set of attributes:

att eyes : Smiths −> Light .	att eyes : Jones −> Dark .
att ears : Smiths −> Human .	att ears : Jones −> Weird .

But sort Smith-Jones has *four* complete sets of attributes which represent all the combinations of features from the closest superclasses:

att eyes : Smiths −> Light .	att eyes : Jones −> Dark .
att ears : Smiths −> Human .	att ears : Jones −> Weird .
att eyes : Smiths −> Light .	att eyes : Jones −> Dark .
att ears : Jones −> Weird .	att ears : Smiths −> Human .

We continue by presenting terms of GOTA signatures. Given a signature $\Sigma = (S, \leq, A)$, we will have a set V including infinitely many variables x, y, z with *associated sort* s, for each s in S. We will write $s(x)$ to refer to the sort associated to variable x. Capital letters X, Y, Z will denote subsets of V.

Definition 6. Given a signature $\Sigma = (S, \leq, A)$ the set of Σ-**terms of sort** s is inductively defined as follows:

- $x \in V$ if the associated sort of x is $w \in S$ and $w \leq s$. In this case we will say that x is a Σ-variable of sort s.
- $w[g_1 \Rightarrow t_1, \ldots, g_m \Rightarrow t_m]$ if $w \in S$ is such that $w \leq s$, the attribute symbols g_j are different and there exist declarations $g_j : w_j \to s_j \in A$ for w, and every t_j is a Σ-term of sort s_j for $j = 1, \ldots, m$.

The second condition introduces *feature terms* [AKPS], [ST], [BS] which combine three important characteristics: explicit mention of the sort (class) of the term by the use of a *sort label* w; explicit mention of the features the represented values (objects) have to show by the use of a *description body* which is limited by brackets; the possibility of including in the description just some (not necessarily all) attributes of the sort, which corresponds to a *partial description*, and therefore representing *a set of possible* values (objects). It is also possible to include no attribute at all, such a term with an empty description will represent *all values* of the sort (all objects of the class).

Definition 7. Given a signature $\Sigma = (S, \leq, A)$, we say that t is a Σ-**term**, if t is a Σ-term of sort s for some $s \in S$.

We will use letters t, u, and v to denote the Σ-terms of a signature Σ. We will refer to Σ-terms as terms when the nature of Σ results clear from the context. For a term t that is of sort s we will also say that t admits sort s. The concept of class inclusion applies to terms in the expected way, as stated by the following proposition.

Proposition 8. *Given a signature* $\Sigma = (S, \leq, A)$, *if* t *is a term of sort* s, *and* $s \leq s'$, *then* t *is a term of sort* s'.

The set of variables that occur in a Σ-term t is denoted by $\mathbf{var}(t)$. A Σ-term t is *ground* if no variable occurs in it, this is, $\mathbf{var}(t) = \emptyset$. The set of Σ-terms formed with variables of a set X is denoted by $T_\Sigma(X)$. We will also use the notation $T_{\Sigma,s}(X)$ to refer to the set of terms of sort s formed with variables of $X \subseteq V$. In concrete examples we will declare variable sorts by using an OBJ3-like syntax.

Example 5. The following are well-formed terms of the signature of Example 2 for the variables declaration:

    var X : Seaplane .
    var One Two : Nat .
    var Three : OnetoThirty .

- Ship[age $\Rightarrow$ Two, draught $\Rightarrow$ Three] is a feature term of sorts Ship and Machine.
- Seaplane[age $\Rightarrow$ Three, engines $\Rightarrow$ Two, draught $\Rightarrow$ One] is a feature term of sorts Seaplane, Plane, Ship, and Machine.
- Ship[] is a feature term with an empty description, representing every ship.

2.1 Genetic Inheritance

Complete sets of attributes serve to view the declarations of attributes as genes existing in parents. Every declaration shows part of the behaviour of a parent class, and we would like them to be genetically combined in some objects. Therefore, objects in a class with inheritance collisions are not compelled to behave uniformly; rather, each one is "free" to choose its inheritance.

Example 6. We take the hierarchy of Example 3, a term of sort Smith-Jones could be: Smith-Jones[eyes $\Rightarrow$ Blue[], ears $\Rightarrow$ Pointed[]] which has ears from the Jones, and eyes from the Smiths. Other Smith-Jones individual is Smith-Jones[eyes = > Green[], ears $\Rightarrow$ Small[]] which has eyes and ears from the Smiths. Different objects in the class Smith-Jones may choose different complete sets of attributes to build their state.

This expressivity is not considered in object-oriented programming languages where a subclass is obliged to monolithically inherit from a preferential superclass. In the previous example, that would mean inheriting from only one parent, as long as every attribute of sort Smith-Jones has an inheritance conflict. It would result in having no Smith-Jones at all, since if they act as Smiths, or as Jones it makes no sense to distinguish. Naturally, there would be solutions in those languages which cope with this problem by defining different classes of Smith-Jones, one for each complete set of attributes. Our feeling is that this can be done from inside the theoretical framework as a natural property, and so are we going to do.

2.2 Abstract Data Types (with Free Constructors)

Without entering the controversy on "classes vs ADTs", our position is that it should be possible to specify both notions within a single formalism. Since we are not considering equations for the moment we will limit our discussion to ADTs with free constructors. Presumably, an adequate solution will be extensible to the more general case of equational ADT specifications. Free ADT constructors behave as injective mappings. Therefore, they have associated *selector* operations that map a free construction back to its arguments. Our idea to specify free ADTs in GOTA is simply to take a dual view, giving our attention to selectors and expressing them as attributes.

Example 7. Let's think of an order-sorted signature for the natural numbers, we will have under the OSA formalism the following declarations:

```
sorts Nat Pos .
subsort Pos < Nat .
op zero: —> Nat .
op suc: Nat —> Pos .
```

which proclaim the operations zero and suc constructors for the sort Nat[5]. With them we can obtain the terms which represent abstract values of natural numbers: zero, suc(zero), suc(suc(zero)), etc.. Within GOTA, we can use and attribute pre (for *predecessor*) and build the signature:

```
sorts Nat Pos Zero .
subsort Zero Pos < Nat .
att pre: Pos —> Nat .
```

With this signature we can "construct" terms representing the abstract values of the natural numbers: Zero[], Pos[pre ⇒ Zero[]], Pos[pre ⇒ Pos[pre ⇒ Zero[]]], etc..

Notice the role of the sort Zero, as we can not define constants in GOTA, certain sorts will serve as constants. These are sorts which have neither attributes nor subsorts, and its meaning has to be a single value. When defining ADTs with GOTA signatures, it is important not to include as attributes other operations the ADT might have. In [MR] the reader can find an example which clarifies this point, as well as a GOTA specification of the ADT for lists.

3 Algebras

Once the basic syntactic elements are laid down we are ready to define the algebras that give meaning to them. Sort inclusion, and attributes inheritance

---

[5] To be precise, suc is a constructor for sort Pos which is included in Nat.

and polymorphism are going to be solved just like for order-sorted signatures. In [SNGM] non-overloaded algebras are considered due to their advantages to obtain non-ambiguous meanings for terms without burdening the signatures with extra requirements as the *monotonicity condition* and *GJM-regularity*. We will accept those arguments for GOTA algebras on the basis of its similarity with the order-sorted case, thus discarding overloaded algebras for their need of additional conditions on signatures [GM].

But, how the GOTA algebras have to be? what elements must they have? Let's take a look to terms. A well-formed term from the signature in Example 3 is Smiths[eyes ⇒ Blue[], ears ⇒ Small[]], to give meaning to this term we will have to include in the algebra an abstract object having the same features, this is, blue eyes and small ears. To do this we need abstract objects and mappings to interpret attributes in algebras. Since this has to be done for every term of the signature, GOTA algebras must be required to include as many abstract objects as possible combinations of the values for the attributes in the description.

The question now is, may algebras have more than one abstract object sharing the same description? At first glance, it might not be considered a flaw, since we could accept some amount of junk in algebras, but that is not really true mainly due to our goal of representing ADTs. Remember that we have switched from constructors to selectors while defining GOTA signatures for ADTs. When giving meaning to a constructor term with suc we use a denotation for suc which is a mapping, that means that for every argument *there is only one result*. The analogy in GOTA algebras would be that for every combination of possible values for attributes, *there is only one abstract object* which behaves that way. Hence, we will demand for GOTA algebras that *only one object* with a given combination of values for its attributes must exist.

A particular situation arises with sorts that have no attributes and no subsorts. As we commented earlier, these sorts act as single values, constants of an order-sorted signature. GOTA algebras must guarantee that these sorts have denotations which are singletons. Let us formally introduce GOTA *algebras*.

Definition 9. Given a signature $\Sigma = (S, \leq, A)$, a Σ-**algebra** $\mathcal{A}$ consists of **denotations** for the sort symbols $s^{\mathcal{A}}$, and the attribute symbols $g^{\mathcal{A}}$ of Σ, such that the following six conditions hold:

1. For every $s \in S$, $s^{\mathcal{A}}$ is a set.
2. If $s \leq w$ then $s^{\mathcal{A}} \subseteq w^{\mathcal{A}}$.
3. If $s \in S$ has an empty complete set of attributes, and there are no sorts $s' < s$, then $s^{\mathcal{A}}$ is a singleton.
4. $\mathcal{C}_{\mathcal{A}} = \bigcup s^{\mathcal{A}}$ with $s \in S$, is the **carrier set** of $\mathcal{A}$.

We say that $b \in w^{\mathcal{A}}$ is **proper** if $b \notin s^{\mathcal{A}}$ for any $s < w$.

5. $g^{\mathcal{A}}$ is a mapping $\mathcal{D}_g^{\mathcal{A}} \to \mathcal{C}_{\mathcal{A}}$, with $\mathcal{D}_g^{\mathcal{A}} \subseteq \mathcal{C}_{\mathcal{A}}$, such that for every sort s with an attribute g, if $b \in s^{\mathcal{A}}$ then $b \in \mathcal{D}_g^{\mathcal{A}}$.
6. Given a sort s, for every complete set of attributes of s, $g_j : s_j \to w_j \in A$ with $j = 1, \ldots, m$, and any values $b_j \in w_j{}^{\mathcal{A}}$ for $j = 1, \ldots, m$, there exists a sole proper value $b \in s^{\mathcal{A}}$ such that $g_j^{\mathcal{A}}(b) = b_j$ for $j = 1, \ldots, m$.

Condition (6.) expresses the richness of GOTA algebras, as to represent every possible object of the hierarchy. For each sort s, and the attributes of every complete set, we consider every value that could fit to compound a description of an object. A sole proper element with that description has to be in the denotation of sort s. Let's see an example.

Example 8. We have the hierarchy of Example 3. An algebra $\mathcal{A}$ for this signature might have the following denotations for sorts:

$$\text{Smith-Jones}^{\mathcal{A}} = \{john, joseph, james, jeremy, jacob, julius, julian, joshua,$$
$$jane, jerome, jared, jill, jason, jonathan, jennifer, jackson\}$$

$$\text{Smiths}^{\mathcal{A}} = \{john, joseph, james, jeremy, jacob, julius, julian, joshua,$$
$$jane, jerome, jared, jill, jason, jonathan, jennifer, jackson,$$
$$ann, adam, alan, andrew\}$$

$$\text{Jones}^{\mathcal{A}} = \{john, joseph, james, jeremy, jacob, julius, julian, joshua,$$
$$jane, jerome, jared, jill, jason, jonathan, jennifer, jackson,$$
$$george, gordon, gerald, gena\}$$

$\text{Blue}^{\mathcal{A}} = \{blueye\}$	$\text{Green}^{\mathcal{A}} = \{greeye\}$	$\text{Light}^{\mathcal{A}} = \{blueye, greeye\}$
$\text{Black}^{\mathcal{A}} = \{blaeye\}$	$\text{Brown}^{\mathcal{A}} = \{broeye\}$	$\text{Dark}^{\mathcal{A}} = \{blaeye, broeye\}$
$\text{Small}^{\mathcal{A}} = \{smaear\}$	$\text{Rounded}^{\mathcal{A}} = \{rouear\}$	$\text{Human}^{\mathcal{A}} = \{smaear, rouear\}$
$\text{Pointed}^{\mathcal{A}} = \{poiear\}$	$\text{Big}^{\mathcal{A}} = \{bigear\}$	$\text{Weird}^{\mathcal{A}} = \{poiear, bigear\}$

Sort denotations for Blue, Green, Black, Brown, Small, Rounded, Pointed, and Big are singletons as condition (3.) says. Denotations for Light, Dark, Human, and Weird are no singletons, having no attributes though. This is because their subsorts denotations may have elements that, by condition (2.), are included in them.

Notice that we need 4 Smiths (*ann, adam, alan, andrew*), due to condition (6.) which requires that every possible combination of values for attributes in the (only) complete set of Smiths had an object, so there will be 2×2 objects. By the same reason there are 4 Jones (*george, gordon, gerald, gena*). However, we need 16 Smith-Jones due to the four complete sets this sort has. Denotations for attributes take care of assigning different behaviour to the proper objects of a class, in order to achieve condition (6.):

$$\text{eyes}^{\mathcal{A}} = \{(john, blueye), (joseph, greeye), (james, blaeye), (jeremy, broeye),$$
$$(jacob, blueye), (julius, greeye), (julian, blaeye), (joshua, broeye),$$
$$(jane, blueye), (jerome, greeye), (jared, blaeye), (jill, broeye),$$
$$(jason, blueye), (jonathan, greeye), (jennifer, blaeye), (ann, blueye),$$
$$(jackson, broeye), (adam, greeye), (alan, blueye), (andrew, greeye),$$
$$(george, blaeye), (gordon, broeye), (gerald, blaeye), (gena, broeye)\}$$

$$\text{ears}^{\mathcal{A}} = \{(john, smaear), (joseph, rouear), (james, poiear), (jeremy, bigear),$$
$$(jacob, rouear), (julius, poiear), (julian, bigear), (joshua, smaear),$$
$$(jane, poiear), (jerome, bigear), (jared, smaear), (ann, smaear),$$
$$(jason, bigear), (jonathan, smaear), (jennifer, rouear), (jill, rouear),$$
$$(jackson, poiear), (adam, smaear), (alan, rouear), (andrew, rouear),$$
$$(george, poiear), (gordon, smaear), (gerald, bigear), (gena, bigear)\}$$

where:

- *john, joseph, jacob, jonathan, ann, adam, alan,* and *andrew* have eyes and ears of the Smiths.
- *james, jeremy, julian, jackson, george, gordon, gerald,* and *gena* have eyes and ears of the Jones.
- *julius, jane, jerome,* and *jason* have eyes of the Smiths, and ears of the Jones.
- *joshua, jared, jill,* and *jennifer* have eyes of the Jones, and ears of the Smiths.

Definition 10. Given a signature Σ, we define the **class of Σ-algebras**[6] as the family $GOTAAlg_\Sigma = \{\mathcal{A} \mid \mathcal{A} \text{ is } \Sigma\text{-algebra}\}$.

Since variables of a sort may represent any element of that sort, it seems adequate to *assign* them a meaning in the denotation of the sort. But there is subtle point, which is that the denotation of a variable will be a *set* of values. If we admit that terms might represent more than one value, it seems reasonable that variables do the same. We will have *variable assignments* for GOTA signatures and algebras.

Definition 11. Given a signature Σ and a Σ-algebra $\mathcal{A}$, we define a variables assignment in $\mathcal{A}$, for the variables of a set $X \subseteq V$, which we will call $\mathcal{A}$-**assignment** for X, as any mapping $\alpha : X \to \mathcal{P}(\mathcal{C}_\mathcal{A})$ such that, for any variable $x \in X$, $\alpha(x)$ is a non-empty subset of $(\mathbf{s}(x))^\mathcal{A}$, i.e. $\emptyset \neq \alpha(x) \subseteq (\mathbf{s}(x))^\mathcal{A}$.

Now, we can go with *terms denotation* but bearing in mind that terms, even ground terms, may represent more than one value.

Definition 12. Given a signature Σ, a Σ-algebra $\mathcal{A}$, an $\mathcal{A}$-assignment for X α, and a term t of $T_\Sigma(X)$, the **denotation of t in $\mathcal{A}$ under** α, $[\![t]\!]^\mathcal{A}_\alpha$ is inductively defined as follows:

- If $t \equiv x$, then $[\![t]\!]^\mathcal{A}_\alpha = \alpha(x)$.
- If $t \equiv w[g_1 \Rightarrow t_1, \ldots, g_m \Rightarrow t_m]$, then $[\![t]\!]^\mathcal{A}_\alpha$ is the set $\{b \in w^\mathcal{A} \mid \forall j \in \{1, \ldots, m\}\ \ g_j^\mathcal{A}(b) \in [\![t_j]\!]^\mathcal{A}_\alpha\}$.

Proposition 13. *Let Σ be a signature, $t \in T_\Sigma(X)$ a term, and $\mathcal{A}$ a Σ-algebra. For every $\mathcal{A}$-assignment for X, α it holds that if t is of sort s then $[\![t]\!]^\mathcal{A}_\alpha$ is well-defined, and $[\![t]\!]^\mathcal{A}_\alpha \subseteq s^\mathcal{A}$.*

Proof. (Sketch) Demonstration is based on structural induction over Σ-terms t, where Definition 12 and condition (2.) of Definition 9 guarantee the result. $\square$

Please notice that if t is a feature term like $w[\,]$ then its denotation is $[\![t]\!]^\mathcal{A}_\alpha = w^\mathcal{A}$ because the quantification $\forall j \in \{1, \ldots, m\}$ of the definition ranges over an empty set and every $b \in w^\mathcal{A}$ verifies it.

4 Initial Semantics

We are interested in recognizing which algebras are closer to the abstract idea we intend for a signature. By analogy with the OSA approach, we try to characterize them as *initial algebras* [GM], [SNGM], for which we need the concept of *homomorphism* between algebras.

---

[6] This is not the "class" concept of object-orientation.

Definition 14. Given a signature $\Sigma = (S, \leq, A)$, and two Σ-algebras $\mathcal{A}$ and $\mathcal{B}$, we define a **homomorphism** between $\mathcal{A}$ and $\mathcal{B}$ noted by $h : \mathcal{A} \rightarrow \mathcal{B}$ as a mapping h between the carrier sets of $\mathcal{A}$ and $\mathcal{B}$, $h : \mathcal{C}_{\mathcal{A}} \rightarrow \mathcal{C}_{\mathcal{B}}$ such that:

1. $h(s^{\mathcal{A}}) \subseteq s^{\mathcal{B}}$ for every sort symbol $s \in S$.
2. $h(\mathcal{D}_g^{\mathcal{A}}) \subseteq \mathcal{D}_g^{\mathcal{B}}$ for every attribute symbol g of Σ.
3. $h(g^{\mathcal{A}}(b)) = g^{\mathcal{B}}(h(b))$ for every attribute symbol g of Σ, and every value $b \in \mathcal{D}_g^{\mathcal{A}}$.

We use the same definition of homomorphism of non-overloaded order-sorted algebras. With this concept we can define initiality in the usual way [GM], [SNGM].

Definition 15. Given a signature Σ, and a Σ-algebra $\mathcal{A}$, we say that $\mathcal{A}$ is a **initial algebra**, or just **initial**, if for any Σ-algebra $\mathcal{B}$, there exists a sole homomorphism h between $\mathcal{A}$ and $\mathcal{B}$.

By a well-known categorical argument initial GOTA algebras can be shown to be unique up to isomorphism [GM]. But, are there any initial algebras? We will answer to this question by building the *algebra of ground canonical terms* $\mathcal{T}_\Sigma$.

For many-sorted, and order-sorted signatures it is interesting to define the *ground term algebra*, since the ground constructor terms hold a relation with the abstract values we try to express. It is known that the ground term algebra is initial in the class of all order-sorted Σ-algebras [GM], [SNGM]. However, a direct analogon of the ground term algebra construction does not work for GOTA algebras. One problem is that values of some attributes cannot be defined for partial description feature terms. For instance, there is no natural way to define the value of attribute **ears** for the term Smiths[eyes $\Rightarrow$ Blue[]]. Another problem is that syntactically different terms may bear the same abstract information. This is the case for the two terms Smiths[eyes $\Rightarrow$ Blue[], ears $\Rightarrow$ Small[]] and Smiths[ears $\Rightarrow$ Small[], eyes $\Rightarrow$ Blue[]]. Our goal is to define a term algebra with just the necessary elements, so as to serve as initial algebra, for this we will use *canonical terms*.

Definition 16. Given a signature $\Sigma = (S, \leq, A)$ we define the set of **canonical Σ-terms of sort** s inductively as follows:

- $x \in V$ if the associated sort of x is $w \in S$ and $w \leq s$. In this case we will say that x is a Σ-variable of sort s.
- $w[\,]$ if $w \in S$ is $w \leq s$, w have an empty complete set of attributes, and there are no sorts $w' < w$.
- $w[g_1 \Rightarrow t_1, \ldots, g_m \Rightarrow t_m]$ if
  - $w \in S$ is $w \leq s$,
  - there exists a complete set of attributes of w formed by declarations, $g_j : w_j \rightarrow s_j \in A$ with $j = 1, \ldots, m$,
  - every t_j is a canonical term of sort s_j for $j = 1, \ldots, m$, and
  - $g_j <_a g_{j+1}$ for $j = 1, \ldots, m-1$, for some total order $<_a$ defined over the attribute symbols.

We are requiring canonical terms to be "under control", that is, every attribute of a complete set must appear in the description, and they must do it in a specific order. Notice that a term of a sort having neither attributes nor subsorts is always canonical.

Definition 17. Given a signature $\Sigma = (S, \leq, A)$, we say that t is a **canonical Σ-term** if t is a canonical Σ-term of sort s, for some sort $s \in S$.

We will refer to canonical Σ-terms as canonical terms when the nature of Σ results clear from the context. Canonical terms are terms, hence having any of their properties, and accepting any of the definitions which refer to terms. The set of ground canonical Σ-terms is denoted by TC_Σ. We will also use the notation $TC_{\Sigma,s}$ to refer to the set of ground canonical terms of sort s. We are going to define the algebra of ground canonical terms.

Definition 18. Given a signature $\Sigma = (S, \leq, A)$, and the set of ground canonical terms TC_Σ, we define the Σ-**algebra of ground canonical terms** $\mathcal{T}_\Sigma$ as follows:

- For every $s \in S$, $s^{\mathcal{T}_\Sigma} =_{def} \{t \in TC_\Sigma \mid t \text{ admits sort } s\}$ that is, $TC_{\Sigma,s}$.
- The carrier set is $\mathcal{C}_{\mathcal{T}_\Sigma} =_{def} TC_\Sigma$ the set of ground canonical terms.
- For every attribute symbol g,
  $\mathcal{D}_g^{\mathcal{T}_\Sigma} =_{def} \{w[g_1 \Rightarrow t_1, \ldots, g_m \Rightarrow t_m] \in TC_\Sigma \mid \exists j \in \{1, \ldots, m\}\ g \equiv g_j\}$.
- The denotations of attribute symbols are defined as $g^{\mathcal{T}_\Sigma}(w[g_1 \Rightarrow t_1, \ldots, g_m \Rightarrow t_m]) =_{def} t_j$ for the $j \in \{1, \ldots, m\}$ such that $g \equiv g_j$.

$\mathcal{T}_\Sigma$ so defined is an algebra for signature Σ as the following proposition states.

Proposition 19. *Given a signature* $\Sigma = (S, \leq, A)$, *the Σ-algebra of ground canonical terms* $\mathcal{T}_\Sigma$ *is an algebra for* Σ.

Proof. (Sketch) To prove that $\mathcal{T}_\Sigma$ is a Σ-algebra we have to show that the six conditions required in Definition 9 are fulfilled. This holds by the definition of $\mathcal{T}_\Sigma$ and its use of ground canonical terms, particularly, condition (6.) holds because there is only one ground canonical term with a particular sort label and attributes description. □

To show that the ground canonical term algebra is initial we will need to construct the homomorphism h whose existence and uniqueness is required by Definition 15. A crucial step is that a term, and its related homomorphic image must represent the same abstract object. The problem is that in GOTA algebras we can have different elements that share the same behaviour.

Example 9. Let's take the hierarchy of Example 3, and the algebra $\mathcal{A}$ of Example 8. Some elements which are different exhibit a partial similarity of their behaviour. For instance, *john* and *jacob* have the same eyes; as *joseph* and *julius*; as *james* and *julian*. Even more, some elements behave exactly: *ann* and *john* have the same eyes and ears; as *joseph* and *andrew*; as *jacob* and *alan*.

This situation arises from subsorts inheriting attributes, while permitting proper objects to exist in a supersort. For no problem to appear when defining h, we have to consider the information of which is the sort the elements properly belong to. This leads to the definition of the *proper denotation* of terms.

Definition 20. Given a signature Σ, a Σ-algebra $\mathcal{A}$, an $\mathcal{A}$-assignment for X α, and a term t of $T_\Sigma(X)$, the **proper denotation** of t in $\mathcal{A}$ under α, $(\![t]\!)_\alpha^{\mathcal{A}}$ is inductively defined as follows:

- If $t \equiv x$, then $(\!|t|\!)^{\mathcal{A}}_{\alpha} = \alpha(x)$.
- If $t \equiv w[g_1 \Rightarrow t_1, \ldots, g_m \Rightarrow t_m]$, then $(\!|t|\!)^{\mathcal{A}}_{\alpha}$ is the set $\{b \text{ proper of } w^{\mathcal{A}} \mid \forall j \in \{1, \ldots, m\} \ g_j^{\mathcal{A}}(b) \in (\!|t_j|\!)^{\mathcal{A}}_{\alpha}\}$.

It holds that the proper denotation is part of the denotation of a term.

Proposition 21. *Let Σ be a signature, $\mathcal{A}$ a Σ-algebra, and α an $\mathcal{A}$-assignment for X, it holds that $(\!|t|\!)^{\mathcal{A}}_{\alpha} \subseteq [\![t]\!]^{\mathcal{A}}_{\alpha}$ for any term t of $T_{\Sigma}(X)$.*

We say a term has *unitary denotation* if its denotation is a singleton.

Proposition 22. *Given a signature Σ, a Σ-algebra $\mathcal{A}$, every ground canonical term has unitary proper denotation.*

Proof. (Sketch) Condition (6.) of Definition 9 guarantees that any complete description corresponds to only one proper abstract value in any algebra. Canonical terms are precisely those with a complete description, hence by structural induction their proper denotations will have just one value. $\square$

To ease the notation, when dealing with the meaning of ground terms we will omit the variable assignment as it is not needed, thus writing $[\![t]\!]^{\mathcal{A}}$, or $(\!|t|\!)^{\mathcal{A}}$. Now we can show that the algebra of ground canonical terms is an initial Σ-algebra in the class of all Σ-algebras.

Proposition 23. *Given a signature $\Sigma = (S, \leq, A)$, the algebra of ground canonical terms $\mathcal{T}_{\Sigma}$ is initial in the class of all Σ-algebras $GOTAAlg_{\Sigma}$.*

Proof. We have to show that for any Σ-algebra $\mathcal{A}$, there exists a sole homomorphism $h : \mathcal{T}_{\Sigma} \to \mathcal{A}$. That means proving three statements:

(i) *There exists a mapping $h : TC_{\Sigma} \to \mathcal{C}_{\mathcal{A}}$.* For every $t \in TC_{\Sigma}$ we define $h(t)$ as the only value of the proper denotation of t in $\mathcal{A}$. That is, $h(t) =_{def} b$ where b is the only value of $(\!|t|\!)^{\mathcal{A}}$. By Proposition 22 this definition is correct, since ground canonical terms have unitary proper denotation.

(ii) *h is a homomorphism.* We have to show that the mapping h defined in point (i) fulfills the requirements of the definition of homomorphism:

    1. $h(s^{\mathcal{T}_{\Sigma}}) \subseteq s^{\mathcal{A}}$. We have to show that for every $t \in s^{\mathcal{T}_{\Sigma}}$ it holds that $h(t) \in s^{\mathcal{A}}$. By definition of $\mathcal{T}_{\Sigma}$ we have $s^{\mathcal{T}_{\Sigma}} = TC_{\Sigma,s}$, let t be a term of $TC_{\Sigma,s}$. By Proposition 13, and Proposition 21, since t is of sort s it holds $(\!|t|\!)^{\mathcal{A}} \subseteq [\![t]\!]^{\mathcal{A}} \subseteq s^{\mathcal{A}}$. Since we defined $h(t)$ as the only value of $(\!|t|\!)^{\mathcal{A}}$ we have $h(t) \in s^{\mathcal{A}}$, for every $t \in s^{\mathcal{T}_{\Sigma}}$ and so $h(s^{\mathcal{T}_{\Sigma}}) \subseteq s^{\mathcal{A}}$.

    2. $h(\mathcal{D}_g^{\mathcal{T}_{\Sigma}}) \subseteq \mathcal{D}_g^{\mathcal{A}}$ for every attribute symbol g of Σ. Let g be an attribute, and t be a value of $\mathcal{D}_g^{\mathcal{T}_{\Sigma}}$. By the definition of the domain of $g^{\mathcal{T}_{\Sigma}}$, t is a ground canonical term of a sort w such that, by Definition 16, has a complete set of attributes which includes a declaration of g. Now, by Proposition 13, and Proposition 21, $(\!|t|\!)^{\mathcal{A}} \subseteq [\![t]\!]^{\mathcal{A}} \subseteq w^{\mathcal{A}}$ and, by condition (5.) of Definition 9 of algebra, $(\!|t|\!)^{\mathcal{A}} \subseteq \mathcal{D}_g^{\mathcal{A}}$. Since we defined $h(t)$ as the only value of $(\!|t|\!)^{\mathcal{A}}$, it holds $h(t) \in \mathcal{D}_g^{\mathcal{A}}$. Thus, for any $t \in \mathcal{D}_g^{\mathcal{T}_{\Sigma}}$ it holds $h(t) \in \mathcal{D}_g^{\mathcal{A}}$, and $h(\mathcal{D}_g^{\mathcal{T}_{\Sigma}}) \subseteq \mathcal{D}_g^{\mathcal{A}}$ for every attribute symbol g of Σ.

3. $h(g^{\mathcal{T}_\Sigma}(t)) = g^{\mathcal{A}}(h(t))$ *for every attribute symbol g of Σ, and every value* $t \in \mathcal{D}_g^{\mathcal{T}_\Sigma}$. Let g be an attribute symbol, and t a value of $\mathcal{D}_g^{\mathcal{T}_\Sigma}$. By the definition of the domain of $g^{\mathcal{T}_\Sigma}$, t is a ground canonical term of the form $w[g_1 \Rightarrow t_1, \ldots, g_m \Rightarrow t_m]$ with $g \equiv g_k$ for certain $k \in \{1, \ldots, m\}$. Now, by definition of $\mathcal{T}_\Sigma$ it holds $g^{\mathcal{T}_\Sigma}(t) = t_k$, and by definition of h, it holds $h(g^{\mathcal{T}_\Sigma}(t)) = h(t_k)$ is the only value of $(\!|t_k|\!)^{\mathcal{A}}$. Besides, $h(t)$ is the only value b_0 of $(\!|t|\!)^{\mathcal{A}}$ which is a singleton by Proposition 22. Particularly, as $g \equiv g_k$ for certain $k \in \{1, \ldots, m\}$ it holds $g^{\mathcal{A}}(b_0) \in (\!|t_k|\!)^{\mathcal{A}}$, which is $g^{\mathcal{A}}(b_0) = h(t_k)$ since the $(\!|t_j|\!)^{\mathcal{A}}$ are singletons for $j = 1, \ldots, m$, by Proposition 22. Finally, from $g^{\mathcal{T}_\Sigma}(t) = t_k$, $g^{\mathcal{A}}(b_0) = h(t_k)$, and $h(t) = b_0$ it holds $h(g^{\mathcal{T}_\Sigma}(t)) = h(t_k) = g^{\mathcal{A}}(b_0) = g^{\mathcal{A}}(h(t))$. Thus, for every attribute g, and every $t \in \mathcal{D}_g^{\mathcal{T}_\Sigma}$ it holds $h(g^{\mathcal{T}_\Sigma}(t)) = g^{\mathcal{A}}(h(t))$.

(iii) *There is only one such h.* We will show that any other homomorphism h' : $\mathcal{T}_\Sigma \to \mathcal{A}$ coincides with h. We will prove $h'(t) = h(t)$ for every $t \in TC_\Sigma$ by structural induction over the form of t:

- If $t \equiv w[\,] \in TC_\Sigma$ that can only be if sort w has an empty complete set of attributes, and has no subsorts. By Definition 9, the denotation of w in any algebra is a singleton. Particularly, in $\mathcal{T}_\Sigma$ we have $w^{\mathcal{T}_\Sigma} = \{b \in TC_{\Sigma,w}\} = \{w[\,]\}$. By definition of h, we have that $h(w[\,])$ is the only value of $(\!|w[\,]|\!)^{\mathcal{A}}$, which is $\{b \in w^{\mathcal{A}}\} = w^{\mathcal{A}}$ a singleton by definition of algebra. Now, since h' is a homomorphism it holds $h'(w^{\mathcal{T}_\Sigma}) \subseteq w^{\mathcal{A}}$, and $h'(w[\,]) \in w^{\mathcal{A}}$ thus having $h'(t) = h(t)$.

- If $t \equiv w[g_1 \Rightarrow t_1, \ldots, g_m \Rightarrow t_m] \in TC_\Sigma$, that can only be if there exists a complete set of attributes of w with declarations for attributes g_j, $g_j : w_j \to s_j$ for $j = 1, \ldots, m$. Besides, it holds $t_j \in TC_{\Sigma,s_j}$, hence, by Definition 18, those are values of $s_j^{\mathcal{T}_\Sigma}$ with $j = 1, \ldots, m$. We also have $h'(t_j) \in s_j^{\mathcal{A}}$ since h' is a homomorphism. Now, by Definition 9, since w is a sort with a complete set of attributes with declarations $g_j : w_j \to s_j$ for $j = 1, \ldots, m$, and we have values $h'(t_j) \in s_j^{\mathcal{A}}$, there must exist a sole b proper of $w^{\mathcal{A}}$ such that $g_j^{\mathcal{A}}(b) = h'(t_j)$ for $j = 1, \ldots, m$. But,
  - ∗ by Definition 18 of algebra $\mathcal{T}_\Sigma$, the denotation of attributes g_j is $g_j^{\mathcal{T}_\Sigma}(t) = t_j$,
  - ∗ since h is a homomorphism it holds $h(g_j^{\mathcal{T}_\Sigma}(t)) = g_j^{\mathcal{A}}(h(t))$,
  - ∗ also, since h' is a homomorphism it holds $h'(g_j^{\mathcal{T}_\Sigma}(t)) = g_j^{\mathcal{A}}(h'(t))$,
  - ∗ by hypothesis of structural induction for the t_j it holds $h(t_j) = h'(t_j)$,

  for $j = 1, \ldots, m$, hence having

  $$g_j^{\mathcal{A}}(h'(t)) = h'(g_j^{\mathcal{T}_\Sigma}(t)) = h'(t_j) = h(t_j) = h(g_j^{\mathcal{T}_\Sigma}(t)) = g_j^{\mathcal{A}}(h(t))$$

  that is $g_j^{\mathcal{A}}(h'(t)) = h'(t_j) = g_j^{\mathcal{A}}(h(t))$ for $j = 1, \ldots, m$. Finally, as b is the only value that verifies $g_j^{\mathcal{A}}(b) = h'(t_j)$ it holds $h'(t) = b = h(t)$.

□

5 Conclusions

GOTA algebras permit the representation of the static aspects of OOP in a direct way, having interesting properties, both syntactic and semantic. Among the former, we can mention the possibility of representing ADTs with free constructors, and the possibility of naturally considering genetic inheritance. Regarding the latter, algebras represent the universe of possible states for objects under the hierarchy expressed by the signatures, showing an initial semantics.

Further research steps should go into the study of equational specifications which will be interesting for fully representing ADTs, and also the description of relations between attributes that may define certain object subclasses. In parallel, the concept of unification will be explored considering the unification with feature terms. A step beyond would be introducing dynamic concepts. Eventually, the resulting integration of OOP and Declarative Programming should be compared with existing proposals such as [AP], [Mese], [FHM], [HSW], [BDLM].

References

[AKPS] H. Aït-Kaci, A. Podelski, G. Smolka, A Feature-based Constraint System for Logic Programming with Entailment, *Theoretical Computer Science* 122 (1-2):263-283, Elsevier 1994.

[AP] J. M. Andreoli, R. Pareschi, Linear Objects: Logical Processes with built-in inheritance, *New Generation Computing* 9 (3-4):445-473, 1991.

[BS] R. Backofen, G. Smolka, A Complete and Recursive Feature Theory, *Theoretical Computer Science* 146 (1-2):243-268, Elsevier 1995.

[BDLM] M. Bugliesi, G. Delzamo, L. Liquori, M. Martelli, A Linear Logic Calculus of Objects, to appear in *Proceedings of JICSLP'96*, 1996.

[FHM] K. Fisher, F. Honsell, J.C. Mitchell, A Lambda Calculus of Objects and Method Specialization, *Nordic Journal of Computing* 1 (1):3-37, 1994.

[GM] J. Goguen, J. Meseguer, Order-sorted algebra I: equational deduction for multiple inheritance, overloading, exceptions and partial operations, *Theoretical Computer Science* 105:217-273, Elsevier 1992.

[GWMFJ] J. Goguen, T. Winkler, J. Meseguer, K. Futatsugi, J. P. Jouannaud, Introducing OBJ3, *Technical Report SRI-CSL-92-03*, SRI International, Computer Science Laboratory, 1993.

[HSW] M. Henz, G. Smolka, J. Würtz, Object-oriented concurrent constraint programming in Oz, in V. Saraswat and P. Van Henterick, eds., *Principles and Practice of Constraint Programming* Chap. 2:27-48, MIT Press, Cambridge, MA 1995.

[MR] J. Mateos-Lago, M. Rodríguez-Artalejo, GOTA Algebras, *Technical Report 26/96*, Departamento de Informática y Automática, Universidad Complutense de Madrid, 1996.

[Mese] J. Meseguer, A Logical Theory of Concurrent Objects and Its Realization in the Maude Language, in G. Agha, P. Wegner, A. Yonezawa, eds., *Research Directions in Concurrent Object-Oriented Programming*:315-390, MIT Press 1993.

[SAK] G. Smolka, H. Aït-Kaci, Inheritance Hierarchies: Semantics and Unification, *Journal of Symbolic Computation* 7:343-370, Academic Press 1989.

[SNGM] G. Smolka, W. Nutt, J. Goguen, J. Meseguer, Order-sorted equational computation, in M. Nivat, H. Aït-Kaci, eds., *Resolution of Equations in Algebraic Structures* :299-367, Academic Press 1989.

[ST] G. Smolka, R. Treinen, Records for Logic Programming, *Journal of Logic Programming* 18 (3):229-258, 1994.

Towards Independent And-Parallelism in CLP*

María García de la Banda[1], Francisco Bueno[2] and Manuel Hermenegildo[2]

[1] Monash University, Clayton 3168 VIC, Australia
[2] Universidad Politécnica de Madrid, 28660-Boadilla del Monte, Spain

Abstract. In this paper we propose a complete scheme for automatic exploitation of independent and-parallelism in CLP programs. We first discuss the new problems involved because of the different properties of the independence notions applicable to CLP. We then show how independence can be derived from a number of standard analysis domains for CLP. Finally, we perform a preliminary evaluation of the efficiency, accuracy, and effectiveness of the approach by implementing a parallelizing compiler for CLP based on the proposed ideas and applying it on a number of CLP benchmarks.

1   Introduction

Independent-and parallelism refers to the parallel execution of "independent" goals in the body of a clause. Its purpose is to achieve increased speed while maintaining correctness and efficiency w.r.t. sequential programs. Given the promising performance gains achieved using this type of parallelism in LP [11, 18, 2], it seems natural to explore the possibility of exploiting such parallelism in CLP programs. However, although both the and-parallel model and the notion of independence have already been extended to the CLP context [6], no practical parallelizing compilers have been reported so far. Even for concurrent constraint languages, designed for this purpose, to the best of our knowledge there have been no parallel implementations reported which perform real constraint solving.[3]

In this paper we study the new issues which need to be addressed in order to develop a parallelizing compiler for CLP programs. We first redefine the clause parallelization process for CLP programs, which as we show requires some significant modifications w.r.t. the traditional parallelization process used in LP. We then show how independence can be derived from the information inferred by a number of standard analysis domains for CLP. Finally, we provide empirical results from a prototype implementation of a parallelizing compiler based on two different notions of independence. It is important to note that the technology

* This work was funded in part by ESPRIT project 7195 "ACCLAIM" and by CICYT projects TIC93-0975-CE and TIC93-0737-C02-01 IPL-D. We thank M. Bruynooghe for comments on previous versions of this paper.

[3] Partial exceptions are Andorra-I [17] and AKL [14], but their constraint solving capabilities are comparatively limited, they are based on execution models which are quite different from the CLP scheme, and they rely to a large extent on run-time technology for detecting parallelism.

necessary for parallel LP has taken almost a decade to mature to the point of producing significant speedups. Therefore, our empirical results cannot be expected to match such maturity level. More realistic benchmarks, faster run-time independence tests, and a more robust and versatile CLP parallel system are still needed. However, we feel we do provide a major step forward in that direction.

2 The automatic parallelization process in LP

The aim of the parallelization process is to detect the program parts that can always be run in parallel (are independent), those that must be run sequentially (are dependent), and, for those parts whose parallelism depends on unknown characteristics of the input data, to introduce the fewest run-time checks possible. Among the several different approaches proposed for LP, a particularly effective one seems to be that defined in [2, 1]. In this section we briefly summarize this approach. Its extension to CLP will be discussed in the following sections.

The parallelization process is performed as follows. Firstly, if required by the user, the program is analyzed using one or more *global analyzers*, aimed at inferring useful information for detecting independence. Then, an *annotator* performs a source-to-source transformation of the program in which eligible clauses are annotated with parallel expressions. This source–to–source transformation is referred to as the *annotation process*.

The annotation process is in turn divided into three subtasks. The first one is to *identify the dependencies* between each two literals in a clause and to generate the conditions which ensure their independence (we will only consider parallelization at the literal level). The left-to-right precedence relation for the literals in each clause $h{:}{-}b_1 \cdots b_n$ is represented using a conditional, directed, acyclic graph (CDG) in which each node i represents the literal b_i, every two literals b_i, b_j, $i < j$, are connected by an edge e_{ij} from i to j, and each edge e_{ij} is adorned with a set of tests T_{ij}. The set T_{ij} is defined as $\{def(D_{ij}), ind(I_i, I_j)\}$, where $D_{ij} = vars(b_i) \cap vars(b_j)$ and $I_k = vars(b_k) \setminus D_{ij}, k \in [i, j]$; the test $def(D_{ij})$ is true when D_{ij} is definite, and the test $ind(I_i, I_j)$ is true when I_i and I_j are independent for the particular independence notion considered. We will assume that the independence notion is symmetric.

Example 1.
The following figure provides the CDG associated to the clause:
h(x,y,w):-p(x,y),q(x,z),s(z,w).
For readability, in an abuse of notation, the singleton $\{x\}$ is represented as the element x. □

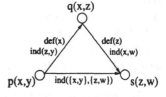

The run-time execution of the tests attached to the CDG edges can be expensive [2]. Therefore, the second task in the annotation process is to *simplify the dependencies*, reducing the sets of tests T_{ij} by means of the information inferred by the anayzers for the i-th program point. This improvement is based on identifying tests in T_{ij} which are ensured to either fail or succeed w.r.t. such information: if a test is guaranteed to succeed, it can be reduced to true; if a test is guaranteed to fail, the entire set of tests can be reduced to false.

As presented in [2], both the set of tests T_{ij} and the compile-time information associated to each program point i in each clause C, can be translated into a *domain of interpretation DI* for definiteness and independence: a subset of the propositional[4] logic theory, such that each element κ of DI defined over the variables in C is a set of formulae (interpreted as their conjunction) from a language suitable for expressing both the relevant information and the tests. The domain is augmented with axioms which hold for the notion of independence used, in such a way that the simplification task can be viewed as propositional theorem proving in this theory (although specific efficient algorithms can be used in practice). The accuracy and the size (the number of atomic formulae for simple facts) of each $\kappa \in DI$ depend on the kind of analysis performed.

Example 2. Consider the *strict independence* notion, in which terms b_1 and b_2 are said to be strictly independent for substitution θ iff vars$(b_1\theta) \cap$ vars$(b_2\theta) = \emptyset$. Let $ind(I_i, I_j)$ be satisfied for substitution θ iff I_i and I_j are strictly independent for θ. Let $def(D)$ be satisfied for substitution θ iff $vars(D\theta) = \emptyset$. It is easy to prove that, in strict independence, the sets $\{def(D), ind(I_i, I_j)\}$ and $\{def(x)|x \in D\} \cup \{ind(x,y)|x \in I_i, y \in I_j\}$ are equivalent. I.e., the conditions defined over sets of variables can be "split" into conditions on single variables. Therefore, the domain DI can be based on a language containing only predicates of the form $def(x)$ and $ind(y, z)$, $\{x, y, z\} \subseteq vars(C)$, with the following simple axioms:

$$\{def(x) \rightarrow ind(x,y)|\{x,y\} \subseteq vars(C)\} \cup \{ind(x,x) \rightarrow def(x)|x \in vars(C)\}.$$

Parallelization methods based on such "split" domains will be referred to as *split methods*. Consider the clause h(x,y,w) :- p(x,y),q(x,z),s(z,w) whose CDG was shown in the previous example. Assume that, according to the information provided by some global analyzer, x is definite when h(x,y,w) is called. Then, for all program points previous to the execution of q(x,z), the following information is available: {def(x), ¬def(z), ind(y,z)}. Thus, both tests labeling the edge from p(x,y) to q(x,z) are known to be true. Furthermore, at least one test labeling the edge from q(x,z) to s(z,w) is known to be false. Thus, the set can be simplified to *false*.

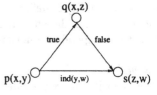

Finally, test ind({x,y},{z,w}) labeling the edge from p(x,y) to s(z,w) is split into {ind(x,z),ind(x,w),ind(y,z),ind(y,w)} and simplified to ind(y,w). □

As mentioned before, in the approach described, program parallelization is conceived as a source-to-source transformation into a suitable parallel language. The third and last task in the annotation process is concerned with expressing in such a language the conditional parallelism contained in the CDG. Consider a

---

[4] Although our syntax resembles first order formulae, clause variables can be regarded as constants, and a simple mapping into a propositional language can be done.

language in which parenthesized expressions are built using a fork / join operator, which is normally represented by "&/2", in addition to the sequential connective "," (such expressions are said to be *linear*). Then, the aim of this last task is to apply a particular strategy *to obtain a (quasi-)optimal linear parallel expression* among all the possibilities represented by the simplified CDG, hopefully further optimizing the number of tests. Many different strategies for obtaining a linear parallel expression from a CDG can be defined [1]. A strategy is correct if the resulting linear parallel expression ensures that if the two linear subexpressions E_1 and E_2 are executed in parallel in store π, then E_1 and E_2 are independent for π, for the particular notion of independence considered.

Example 3. Let $lit(E)$ represent the set of literals in the linear expression E. When considering strict independence, linear expressions E_1 and E_2 are independent w.r.t. θ if $\forall b_i \in lit(E_1)$ and $\forall b_j \in lit(E_2)$, the tests associated to the edge connecting b_i and b_j are true w.r.t. θ. This can easily be ensured at run–time by, for example, using an if–then–else expression. Consider the simplified CDG shown in the previous example. It is possible to build different correct linear parallel expressions such as:

```
h(x,y,w):- (p(x,y) & q(x,z)), s(z,w) and
h(x,y,w):- ind(y,w)->p(x,y)&(q(x,z),s(z,w));p(x,y),q(x,z),s(z,w) □
```

3 Independence in CLP

Independence refers to the conditions that the run-time behavior of the goals to be run in parallel must satisfy to guarantee correctness and efficiency w.r.t. the sequential execution. The above parallelization process has been proved correct, implemented, and evaluated for the particular case of strict independence in LP languages [2, 1]. However, correctness can in fact be proved for all independence notions which, as strict independence, are *a-priori*, i.e., tests exist that can be executed prior to the goals, and *grouping*, i.e., if goal g_1 is independent of goals g_2 and g_3 for store π, then g_1 is also independent of the goal (g_2, g_3) for π.

The most general a-priori notion in CLP is defined in [6] as follows. Let $def\_vars(c)$ denote the set of definite variables in the constraint c (i.e., the set of variables uniquely defined by c). Let $\bar{x}$ denote a sequence of distinct variables. $\exists_{-\bar{x}}\phi$ denotes the existential closure of the formula ϕ except for the variables $\bar{x}$. Goals $g_1(\bar{x})$ and $g_2(\bar{y})$ are *projection independent* for constraint store π iff $(\bar{x} \cap \bar{y} \subseteq def\_vars(\pi))$ and $(\exists_{-\bar{x}}\pi \wedge \exists_{-\bar{y}}\pi \rightarrow \exists_{-\bar{y}\cup\bar{x}}\pi)$. Intuitively, the notion states that all shared variables must be definite, and that any constraint c in π defined over variables of both $\bar{x}$ and $\bar{y}$ is "irrelevant".[5] The same definition can also be applied to terms and constraints without any change.

Example 4. The goals $p(x)$ and $q(z)$ are independent and can be executed in parallel if the state of the store just before their execution is $\pi \equiv \{x > y, z > y\}$ since $\exists_{\{x\}}\pi = \exists_{\{z\}}\pi = \exists_{\{x,z\}}\pi = true$. However, they would be dependent for $\pi \equiv \{x > y, y > z\}$ since $\exists_{\{x\}}\pi = \exists_{\{z\}}\pi = true$ but $\exists_{\{x,z\}}\pi = \{x > z\}$. □

---

[5] That is, it is entailed by the conjunction of the constraints over $\bar{x}$ and the constraints over $\bar{y}$. Note that $(\exists_{-\bar{x}}\pi \wedge \exists_{-\bar{y}}\pi \leftarrow \exists_{-\bar{y}\cup\bar{x}}\pi)$ is always satisfied.

Unfortunately, projection is an expensive operation. A pragmatic solution, proposed in [6], is to simplify the run-time tests by checking if the variables involved are "linked" through the constraints in the store, thus sacrificing accuracy in favor of simplicity. Let Π denote the sequence of constraints in the store, $link_\Pi(x, y)$ holds if $\exists c \in \Pi$ s.t. $\{x, y\} \subseteq (vars(c) \setminus def\_vars(\Pi))$. The relation $links_\Pi(x, y)$ is the transitive closure of $link_\Pi(x, y)$. Finally, $links$ is lifted to set of variables by defining $Links_\Pi(\bar{x}, \bar{y})$ iff $\exists x \in \bar{x}, y \in \bar{y}$ such that $links_\Pi(x, y)$ holds. We then have that $g_1(\bar{x})$ and $g_2(\bar{y})$ are link independent for Π if $\neg Links_\Pi(\bar{x}, \bar{y})$. Note that it is possible to further simplify $link_\Pi(x, y)$ by not taking knowledge of definite variables into account. This is simpler to detect for solvers which do not propagate definiteness. Run-time tests based on both this simpler version (*link independence*) and the original projection independence will be evaluated in our experiments. Note that while link independence is a grouping notion for any CLP language, projection independence is not.

Example 5. Consider goals p(x), q(y), and s(z), and equation $x = y + z$. While $ind(x, y)$ and $ind(x, z)$ hold for projection independence, $ind(x, \{y, z\})$ does not. Thus, p(x) is independent of q(y) and of s(z), but not of q(y),s(z). $\square$

4   The annotation process for non-grouping notions

Non-grouping independence notions considerably affect the annotation process. While the first subtask of the annotation process (identifying dependencies) is not affected, the other two subtasks become somewhat more complex.

The first problem appears during simplification of dependencies: the sets $\{ind(I_i, I_j)\}$ and $\{ind(x, y) | x \in I_i, y \in I_j\}$ are no longer equivalent. This happened in the previous example, where $\{ind(x, [y, z])\}$ was shown to be different from $\{ind(x, y), ind(x, z)\}$ since, for example, the latter succeeds but the former fails for the linear equation $x = y + z$. As a consequence, the domain DI becomes more involved: it is now based on the language containing predicates of the form $def(x)$ and $ind(I_1, I_2)$, $\{x\} \cup I_1 \cup I_2 \subseteq vars(C)$, with the following axioms:

1. $\{def(x) \rightarrow ind(x, vars(C)) \mid x \in vars(C)\}$
2. $\{ind(I_1, I_2) \rightarrow def(I) \mid I \in subseteq \in (I_1 \cap I_2), I_1 \cup I_2 \subseteq vars(C)\}$
3. $\{ind(I_1, I_2) \rightarrow ind(I_{11}, I_{21}) | I_{11} \subseteq I_1, I_{21} \subseteq I_2, I_1 \cup I_2 \subseteq vars(C)\}$
4. $\{ind(I, I_1 \cup I_2), ind(I_1, I_2) \rightarrow ind(I \cup I_1, I_2) \mid I \cup I_1 \cup I_2 \subseteq vars(C)\}$

The first and second axioms correspond to those defined for strict independence. The third states the independence of subsets of variables of an already proved independence test. The last one allows us to prove an independence test from the conjunction of other independence tests which are known to hold. In combination with the third axiom it can also be used as a heuristic: if $ind(I, I_1 \cup I_2)$ holds then $ind(I \cup I_1, I_2) \leftrightarrow ind(I_1, I_2)$, and we can replace $ind(I \cup I_1, I_2)$ by $ind(I_1, I_2)$. Definite and unconstrained variables can be eliminated using this heuristic. Parallelization methods based on this complex domain will be referred to as *non-split methods*. The parallel program obtained using a non-split method can always be executed using a grouping independence notion.

The non-grouping characteristics of the independence notion also affect the creation of the independence tests appearing in a linear parallel expression.

Example 6. Consider the clause $h(x,y,z) :- p(x),q(y),s(z)$ whose associated CDG is shown in the following figure. In strict independence, the three literals can be run in parallel in store π if all tests labeling the associated edges are satisfied in π. The following linear expression ensures this condition:
$(ind(x,y),ind(x,z),ind(y,z)) \rightarrow p(x)\& q(y)\& s(z)$; $p(x),q(y),s(z)$

Unfortunately, the above expression is not correct for non-grouping independence notions. Consider projection independence and the constraint store $\pi \equiv \{x = y + z\}$. Though all three tests are satisfied for π, $p(x)$ is not independent of $q(y)\&s(z)$ for π, as we saw in the previous example. Thus, they cannot be executed in parallel. □

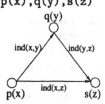

As illustrated above, for a non-grouping notion, the conjunction of the tests labeling the edges involved is not enough for ensuring correctness. The solution is to directly apply the correctness condition: a linear parallel expression is correct if for any subexpression of the form E_1 & E_2, the test $\{def(D), ind(I_1, I_2)\}$, where $D = vars(E_1) \cap vars(E_2)$ and $I_k = vars(E_k) \setminus D, k \in [1,2]$, is ensured to be satisfied immediately before their parallel execution.

Since the simplified tests are not used during the construction of the linear parallel expression, it is natural to question the usefulness of the simplification of dependencies subtask. Indeed, when considering non-grouping notions, the only aim of the second subtask is to detect edges whose label can be reduced to *false*. If so, the literals connected are known to be dependent and cannot be run in parallel. It is in the third subtask, after the parallel expression has been built, that the (full) simplification of dependencies should be performed.

Example 7. For the CDG in the above example, the independence test required to obtain a correct linear expression is $\{ind(x,\{y,z\}), ind(y,z)\}$. If the store $\pi \equiv \{x = y + z\}$ occurs in the program, and the compile-time analysis is able to infer that $\neg ind(x,\{y,z\})$ holds, then the condition is reduced to *false* and no attempt is made to construct a parallel expression with all three goals. Otherwise the tests will have to be executed at run-time to determine independence. □

5 Global Analysis-Based Test Simplification

Compile-time information is usually obtained via global analysis, generally based on the abstract interpretation technique [4, 13]. In this section we study how definiteness and independence can be inferred by some analysis domains proposed for CLP programs: the Def[6] [5], Free [7], and FD domains [5].

Def approximates *definiteness* information. An abstract constraint AC is of the form (D, R), where the set of variables D approximates the definite variables,

---

[6] This domain is a variant of the *Prop* domain [3] for CLP, with efficient abstract functions specific for the framework of the PLAI analyzer used in our experiments.

and each element $(x, SS) \in R$ approximates definite dependencies. In particular, the variable x is known to be definite if all variables in a set S of SS are also definite. Consider an abstract constraint $AC_i = (D, R) \in \mathsf{Def}$ for program point i of a clause C. The contents of the corresponding $\kappa_i \in DI$ are as follows:

- $def(D)$
- $def(S) \to def(x)$ if $(x, SS) \in R, S \in SS$
- $ind(x, S) \to def(x)$ if $(x, SS) \in R, S \in SS$

The first rule states that all variables in D are known be definite. The second rule represents the definiteness dependencies approximated by each $(x, SS) \in R$. The third rule states that the dependencies approximated by R are definite: x and S can only be independent if x is definite. This rule can be used to (a) execute $def(\{x\})$ at run-time instead of $ind(\{x\}, S)$ (definiteness tests are faster and, thanks to the above axiom, they are known to be equivalent) and (b) with the aid of non-definiteness information, obtain $\neg ind(\{x\}, S)$, confirming a dependency.

Example 8. Consider a clause C such that $vars(C) = \{x, y, z, v, w\}$ and an abstract constraint $AC = (\{x\}, \{(z, \{\{w, v\}\})\})$. The corresponding κ will be: $\{def(x), def(\{w, v\}) \to def(z), ind(z, \{w, v\}) \to def(z)\}$. $\square$

Free approximates *freeness* information. An abstract constraint AC is a set of set of variables approximating *possible* dependencies. In particular, if x does not appear in any element of AC, then x is known to be unconstrained; and if $\{x\}$ is not an element of AC, then x is possibly constrained but still free to take any value within its particular constraint type (referred to as *free* variables). Consider an abstract constraint $AC_i \in \mathsf{Free}$ for program point i of a clause C. Let $(AC_i)^*$ denote its closure under union. Then $\kappa_i \in DI$ contains:

- $\neg def(x)$ if $x \in vars(C), \{x\} \notin AC_i$
- $ind(I_1, I_2)$ if $\forall I_1' \subseteq I_1, I_1' \neq \emptyset, \forall I_2' \subseteq I_2, I_2' \neq \emptyset : (I_1' \cup I_2') \notin (AC_i)^*$

The first rule states that unconstrained and *free* variables cannot be definite. The second is an extension of Prop. 3.1 of [7] defining the conditions under which I_1 and I_2 ae independent w.r.t. AC_i.[7] Note that unconstrained variables are independent of any other set of variables.

Example 9. Consider a clause C such that $vars(C) = \{x, y, z, v, w\}$ and an abstract constraint $AC = \{\{x\}, \{z\}, \{v\}, \{z, w\}\}$. The corresponding κ will be: $\{\neg def(y), \neg def(w), ind(x, w), ind(v, w), ind(y, \{x, z, v, w\})\}$. $\square$

The aim of the **FD** domain is to improve the efficiency of the **Free** analyzer by explicitly separating the definite variables and specializing the abstract operations to make use of this particular information. The $\kappa \in DI$ corresponding to an abstract constraint in **FD** is obtained by conjoining the result of translating its definiteness and freeness components.

---

[7] The closure is needed due to the solved form in **Free** which eliminates any set in AC which can be obtained by the union of other sets in AC.

6   Experimental Results

Our experimental study evaluates (a) the efficiency and usefulness of the analyzers when parallelizing CLP programs, (b) the trade-off between the complexity and usefulness of the split and non-split methods (c) the efficiency and accuracy of the projection and link independence notions, and (d) the amount of a-priori and-parallelism detected by the method. To perform the evaluation we have implemented a parallelizing compiler based on the proposed ideas and incorporated it into the *CIAO* system [10]. The abstract machine includes native support for *attributed variables* [12] (used for implementating the constraint solvers), as well as for parallelism and concurrency (it is a derivation of the &-Prolog PWAM [11]). The system also includes the PLAI analysis framework [16] and several algorithms for obtaining the linear parallel expression associated to a given CDG. In the experiments we will use the **MEL** algorithm (see [1]).

Bench.	AgV	MV	Cl	Ls	Ps	Rec	Gs	Bench.	AgV	MV	Cl	Ls	Ps	Rec	Gs
ackerman	2.33	4	9	30	1	100	4	matmul1	2.50	5	6	5	3	100	3
amp, amp2	4.62	18	45	69	16	37	20	mg, mggnd	3.00	6	2	3	1	100	2
amp3	5.03	26	60	103	24	37	33	mg-extend	3.90	8	10	16	6	33	9
bridge	3.72	12	18	33	6	66	17	mining	2.63	18	43	78	21	52	27
circuit	3.39	10	18	25	8	62	10	nombre	2.62	11	64	91	10	0	15
dnf	2.34	7	32	40	3	100	14	ode2, ode3	3.67	7	6	9	5	20	5
fib	1.33	4	3	4	1	100	3	ode4	4.17	9	6	12	5	20	7
ladder	3.69	10	13	28	9	33	13	pic	5.71	9	7	23	7	0	9
laplace1	4.00	12	4	4	2	100	4	power	3.14	19	42	75	18	50	24
laplace3	4.75	15	4	7	2	100	3	rkf45a	7.30	26	97	236	41	24	63

Table 1. Benchmark Profile

6.1   Benchmarks

The set of benchmarks used includes programs in the set of examples of the clp($\Re$) distribution (fib, mg, dnf, and laplace), programs designed for PrologIII (nombre, mining, and power) which have been translated into clp($\Re$), and others designed for clp($\Re$) and used, for example, in the evaluation of several optimizations performed for the clp($\Re$) compiler. Table 1 provides information regarding the (reachable code of the) benchmarks, useful for interpreting the analysis and annotation performance results:[8] average (AgV) and maximum (MV) number of variables in each clause; total number of clauses (Cl), of body literals (Ls), and of predicates analyzed (Ps); percentage of predicates which are recursive (Rec), and total number of different goals solved in analyzing the program (Gs), i.e., of syntactically different calls. The benchmarks have not been normalized.

---

[8] Benchmarks in the same row refer to different queries with identical reachable code. Benchmarks with the same name in different rows refer to queries with different reachable code.

Benchmark	Analysis Times			Annotation Times							
				Split				Non-Split			
	Def	Free	FD	Lo	Def	Free	FD	Lo	Def	Free	FD
ackerman	0.04	0.12	0.10	0.03	0.05	0.05	0.05	0.04	0.05	0.06	0.06
amp	0.66	4.87	5.62	0.30	0.35	0.57	0.54	0.24	0.30	0.33	0.37
amp2	0.66	4.87	5.62	0.30	0.35	0.57	0.54	0.24	0.30	0.33	0.37
amp3	0.94	6.33	6.86	0.66	1.05	1.55	1.64	0.47	0.71	0.66	0.90
bridge	0.28	2.66	1.28	0.10	0.14	0.19	0.18	0.10	0.13	0.18	0.17
circuit	0.27	10.75	1.73	0.09	0.12	0.12	0.13	0.08	0.11	0.10	0.13
dnf	0.41	2.37	1.53	0.14	0.19	0.23	0.23	0.13	0.19	0.22	0.24
fib1	0.02	0.05	0.05	0.02	0.03	0.03	0.03	0.02	0.03	0.03	0.03
fib2	0.04	0.06	0.07	0.03	0.03	0.03	0.04	0.02	0.03	0.03	0.04
fib3	0.03	0.04	0.06	0.02	0.03	0.03	0.03	0.02	0.03	0.03	0.04
ladder	0.11	0.30	0.38	0.14	0.20	0.21	0.25	0.14	0.19	0.18	0.21
laplace1	0.03	0.00	0.05	0.02	0.02	0.00	0.03	0.02	0.02	0.00	0.02
laplace3	0.09	5.06	5.14	0.06	0.09	0.11	0.14	0.03	0.07	0.05	0.08
mmatrix	0.02	0.07	0.05	0.03	0.03	0.04	0.03	0.03	0.03	0.03	0.04
matmul1	0.03	0.08	0.12	0.03	0.03	0.03	0.03	0.03	0.03	0.03	0.03
mg-extend	0.98	0.31	1.77	0.06	0.09	0.11	0.10	0.06	0.08	0.10	0.10
mg	0.05	0.05	0.11	0.02	0.03	0.03	0.03	0.02	0.02	0.02	0.03
mggnd	0.01	0.05	0.03	0.02	0.02	0.03	0.02	0.02	0.02	0.02	0.02
mining	0.27	3.54	3.63	0.28	0.42	0.64	0.73	0.26	0.37	0.42	0.51
nombre	0.62	5.85	4.17	0.78	1.04	1.31	1.30	0.64	0.92	1.01	1.16
ode2	0.06	0.11	0.17	0.04	0.05	0.05	0.06	0.04	0.06	0.05	0.06
ode3	0.09	0.07	0.21	0.04	0.05	0.05	0.06	0.04	0.05	0.04	0.06
ode4	0.14	0.14	0.30	0.06	0.09	0.09	0.12	0.06	0.09	0.08	0.11
pic	0.04	0.12	0.11	0.22	0.16	0.23	0.18	0.17	0.16	0.17	0.17
power	0.45	5.43	1.99	0.39	0.62	0.83	0.94	0.29	0.47	0.50	0.69
rkf45a	335.14	61.00	482.69	2.06	27.81	3.45	22.15	1.20	15.19	1.52	17.76
Average 1	13.13	4.57	20.15	0.23	1.27	0.42	1.14	0.17	0.76	0.25	0.90
Average 2	0.25	2.22	1.65	0.16	0.21	0.30	0.30	0.13	0.18	0.20	0.23

Table 2. Compilation Efficiency Results

6.2 Efficiency

Table 2 presents the analysis and annotation times (for both the split and non-split methods) in seconds (SparcStation 10, one processor, SICStus 2.1 #5, native code). The times are the average out of ten executions. The last two rows show the average time for each analyzer and annotator with and without considering the results for rkf45a, respectively. The column Lo provides the results for the parallelization with information provided by a simple local analysis.

The analysis times are quite reasonable: 4-10 seconds for the bigger benchmarks. There are two exceptions: laplace1 and rkf45a. The analysis of rkf45a takes between 1 and 8 minutes, depending on the analyzer. In part, this is due to the high number of different calling patterns analyzed: 5 predicates have 10-15 different calling patterns, and one has 25. Even then, most analysis time is spent analyzing a single clause containing 12 atoms and 27 variables related by many definite and possible dependencies. In particular, the **Def** abstractions for this clause keep track of up to 593 sets of variables and 3166 variables, per abstraction. The other exception is the behavior of the **Free** analyzer for laplace1, which did not finish after one hour due to the high number of different calling patterns generated by the analysis. This is solved in laplace3 by performing a simple normalization which reduces the number of variables in the literal and thus the number of calling patterns. Thus, to be practical, the analyses should include a widening step (perhaps switching selectively to a special, compact definition of "top") and a tighter control of the number of calling patterns allowed.

Regarding the annotators, we observe that both methods are quite fast, the non-split method behaving almost consistently better, specially for the complex cases. This could seem surprising since, in the non-split method, further simplifications have to be performed for the final CGEs. However, the high number of tests obtained after splitting decreases the efficiency of the split method. We can conclude that, although conceptually more complex, the non-split method is usually faster.

6.3 Effectiveness: static tests

One way to measure the accuracy and effectiveness of the analysis information is to count the number of parallel expressions (or CGEs) annotated, the number of these which are unconditional (i.e., do not require run-time tests), and the number of definiteness and independence tests in the remaining CGEs. These numbers give an idea of the overhead introduced in the program. The results for the non-split method are shown in the upper part of Table 3. Then, the benchmarks for which the results obtained with the split method are different to those obtained with the non-split method are shown in the lower part of Table 3. For clarity, we only show those numbers which differ from the column corresponding to the annotation performed with the information provided by the FD analyzer, the rest appearing blank. Benchmarks that all analyzers determine to be sequential (mg, mggnd, ode2, ode3, and ode4) do not appear in the table.

In general, a lower number of CGEs and a higher number of unconditional CGEs indicate a better parallelization. It usually means that CGEs whose tests are going to fail have been detected and eliminated. This reasoning is valid for all benchmarks but ladder. In ladder the better information inferred by FD allows the annotator to change its strategy, obtaining better (because unconditional) parallel expressions. We can conclude that the higher information content provided by FD produces the best results, showing advantage in almost half of the benchmarks. Furthermore, many benchmarks present unconditional parallelism: the non-split method with the information provided by FD accurately detects that all a-priori and-parallelism in bridge, fib1, mmatrix, matmul1, laplace1, and mg-extend, is unconditional. Also, all analyzers successfully detect that mg, mgnd, ode2, ode3, and ode4 do not have any a-priori parallelism, FD being also capable of adding nombre to this list. Finally, though conceptually different, the non-split and split methods provide the same results for all but six benchmarks. In nombre the split method for **Free** is able to simplify 29 independence

Benchmark	CGEs: Tot/Unc				Conds: def/indep			
	Lo	Def	Free	FD	Lo	Def	Free	FD
ackerman				1/0	2/1		2/1	1/0
amp				3/0	2/	2/		1/3
amp2				3/0	2/	2/		1/3
amp3	6/	6/		5/0	5/21	5/	2/21	3/8
bridge	/0		/0	3/3	3/		3/	0/0
circuit	3/	3/		2/0	1/13	3/	0/9	2/1
dnf	/0		/0	14/12	/30		/30	0/2
fib1	/0	/0	/0	1/1	1/1	/1	1/	0/0
fib2				1/0				1/1
fib3				1/0	/1	/1		1/0
ladder	7/0	7/1	7/1	8/4	/34	5/8	/29	3/9
laplace1	/0			1/1	2/1			0/0
laplace3				1/0				2/1
mmatrix	/0	/0	/0	2/2	2/8	/2	2/2	0/0
matmul1	2/0	2/0	/0	1/1	2/8	1/1	1/1	0/0
mg-extend	/0		/0	1/1	/2		/2	0/0
mining	/0	/1	/0	4/2	5/8	/5	5/5	2/4
nombre	5/	5/	5/	0/0	/111	12/11	/65	0/0
pic	4/0	4/	/0	3/2	7/12	1/5	6/8	0/2
power				5/1	/46	/46		3/42
rkf45a	5/	5/		1/0	10/85	17/22		2/2
fib1	1/	1/	1/	0/0	1/1	/1	1/	0/0
fib2	1/	1/	1/	0/0	1/1	1/1	1/1	0/0
fib3	1/	1/	1/	0/0	1/1	1/1	1/	0/0
nombre	5/	5/	5/	0/0	/111	12/11	/47	0/0
power	5/	5/	5/	3/1	3/46	3/46	3/18	2/3
rkf45a	5/	5/		1/0	10/85	17/34		2/2

Table 3. Parallel Expressions / Conditional Checks

tests more than the non-split method. In fib1, fib2, fib3, and power, CGEs are eliminated for FD due to independence tests which are known to fail for any grouping notion (split method), but might succeed for a non-grouping one (non-split method). Finally, the results of the simplification function depend on the order in which the tests to be simplified are considered (the simplified set of tests is not always minimal). This only affects the parallelization of rkf45a with Def.

6.4 Link vs. Projection Independence

In this section we study the overhead created by the definiteness and independence tests, and compare the accuracy of the link and projection independence versions. Thus, we only consider benchmarks whose parallelized versions have tests. Unfortunately, we have not been able to execute some of these benchmarks (rkf45a, mining and power) in our parallel system, due to precision problems. For the rest, tables 4 and 5 show the results of the execution on one processor

Benchmark	Definite		Link Independence					Projection Independence				
	S	F	S	F	AS	AF	O	S	F	AS	AF	O
ackerman	0	1187	0	0	0	0	0.00	0	0	0	0	0.00
amp	0	1	10	3	1	0	0.62	10	3	1	0	4.77
amp2	0	1	10	5	1	0	0.67	11	4	1	0	5.87
amp3	0	7	48	98	0	1	0.17	48	98	0	1	0.63
circuit	0	14	1	7	0	0	0.12	1	7	0	0	3.40
dnf	0	0	115	0	1	0	0.33	115	0	1	0	3.00
fib1	0	0	0	609	0	1	0.39	609	0	1	0	0.71
fib2	0	1503	0	0	0	0	0.00	0	0	0	0	0.00
fib3	0	1503	0	0	0	0	0.00	0	0	0	0	0.00
ladder	0	154	50	0	2	0	0.00	50	0	2	0	0.00
laplace3	0	3	0	0	0	0	0.00	0	0	0	0	0.00
mmatrix	0	0	182	0	2	0	0.47	182	0	2	0	3.53
matmul1	0	25	5	0	1	0	0.00	5	0	1	0	0.00
nombre	0	448	0	0	0	0	0.00	0	0	0	0	0.00
pic	0	3	3	0	1	0	0.00	3	0	1	0	0.01

Table 4. Dynamic Results for Def

Benchmark	Definite		Link Independence					Projection Independence				
	S	F	S	F	AS	AF	O	S	F	AS	AF	O
ackerman	0	1187	0	0	0	0	0.00	0	0	0	0	0.00
amp	0	1	10	3	1	0	0.46	10	3	1	0	4.77
amp2	0	1	10	5	1	0	0.40	11	4	1	0	5.47
amp3	0	6	48	98	0	1	0.17	48	98	0	1	0.63
circuit	0	13	1	7	0	0	0.10	1	7	0	0	3.45
dnf	0	0	115	0	1	0	0.33	115	0	1	0	3.00
fib2	0	1503	0	0	0	0	0.00	0	0	0	0	0.00
fib3	0	1503	0	0	0	0	0.00	0	0	0	0	0.00
ladder	0	153	0	1	0	1	0.04	0	1	0	1	0.01
laplace3	0	3	0	0	0	0	0.00	0	0	0	0	0.00
pic	0	0	3	0	1	0	0.00	3	0	1	0	0.00

Table 5. Dynamic Results for FD

of the benchmarks parallelized with the non-split method, using the information provided by the Def and FD analyzers, respectively. The last ten columns in each table show the number of times that the tests have succeeded (S) and failed (F), the number of tests which have always succeeded (AS) and always failed (AF), and the overhead w.r.t. the execution of the original sequential program (TestTime/SeqTime), for the link and projection independence tests. For the definiteness tests only the number of successes and failures are shown, their overhead being negligible (it ranges from 0.0002 for ladder to 0.0028 for fib3).

Several conclusions can be extracted from the tables. First, although there exist cases, like fib1, in which projection independence detects parallelism which link independence fails to detect, this is not a common case. Second, as implemented, the independence tests introduce too much overhead, specially when using projection independence. The implementation of the tests is still very naive. In particular, the projection independence test can be improved significantly by, for example, performing a link test while doing the projection, so that success can be detected in an amount of time similar to that of the link test. In any case, significant effort must be devoted to implementing these tests efficiently.

Finally, given the cost of the independence tests and the number of them which always succeed or fail, we can conclude that more accurate information is needed. The domain (**LSign**) recently defined for CLP [15] approximates information about possible interaction between linear arithmetic constraints. A preliminary implementation performed at Monash University shows very promising accuracy, and will hopefully help in further simplifing the number of tests.

6.5 Effectiveness: speedup tests

The ultimate way of evaluating the effectiveness of the annotators is by measuring the speedup achieved, i.e., the ratio of the parallel execution time of the program to that of the sequential program. Since we are interested in the quality of the parallelization process, and not in the characteristics of a particular runtime system, this should ideally be done in a controlled environment. To this end, we have performed a number of preliminary experiments using the simulation tool IDRA [8], which was already shown to match actual speedups in several LP systems. This tool takes as input a real execution trace file of a parallel program run on the *CIAO* system (i.e., an encoded description of the events that occurred during such execution) and the time for its sequential execution, and computes the achievable speedup for any number of processors. The results presented in the following table show the speed-ups obtained parallelizing the benchmarks with the noi split method, using the information provided by the FD analyzer, and running the programs with the link independence tests. Only benchmarks with at least a parallel expression in the parallelized version have been considered. The column labeled "@2" provides the speedup on two processors and the column labeled "Max" the maximum possible speedup for the input data used.

Bench.	Max	@2
ackerman	1.00	1.00
fib2	0.99	0.99
fib3	0.99	0.99
laplace3	1.00	1.00

Bench.	Max	@2
bridge	1.02	1.02
fib1	80.84	1.99
laplace1	1.97	1.97
mmatrix	37.83	1.94
matmul1	3.53	1.71

Bench.	Max	@2
dnf	0.91	0.91
ladder	0.97	0.97
pic	1.97	1.50
dnf	0.94	0.94
ladder	1.16	1.16
pic	1.92	1.50

Bench.	Max	@2
amp	0.57	0.57
amp2	0.57	0.57
amp3	0.88	0.88
circuit	0.92	0.92
amp	0.97	0.97
amp2	0.97	0.97
amp3	1.00	1.00
circuit	1.00	1.00

The first four benchmarks are the only programs without a-priori parallelism whose parallelization actually contains conditional parallel expressions (mg, mg-gnd, nombre, ode2, ode3, and ode4 where already detected as sequential during the parallelization process). Even then, since the tests introduced by the parallelization are only definiteness tests, the overhead is negligible. In the next five benchmarks the compile-time information has been capable of determining for all tests whether they are going to succeed or fail, thus only obtaining unconditional parallelism. As a result, no slow-downs are obtained and most benchmarks get quite good speed-ups (which, as in many other benchmarks, depend on the size of the input data, which is generally small in the benchmarks used).

The next three benchmarks contain one or two conditional parallel expressions. The associated overhead in this case is higher (e.g., for dnf). This suggests perhaps eliminating those parallel expressions which contain tests. Since the overhead introduced by definiteness tests has proved negligible, only independence tests would need to be removed. The next three rows in the table show the results of applying this idea to the three previous benchmarks: although the achievable speed-up in pic is reduced w.r.t. the previous version it still has a speedup of 1.5, and the approach succeeds in eliminating the slow-down for the other two benchmarks.

The final four benchmarks have several independence tests which sometimes succeed and sometimes fail. The result is a considerable slow-down. However, after eliminating all parallel expressions containing independence tests, the results are shown in the last 4 rows of the table: no slow-downs occur, and since none of the benchmarks had very useful parallelism, the effect is quite satisfactory.

7 Conclusions and Future Work

We conclude from this preliminary evaluation that the parallelization process can be quite efficient (using widening) and relatively effective, specially considering the genericity of the domains used. Very often sequential programs and programs containing unconditional parallelism were statically identified as such. Surprisingly, the conceptually more complex non-split annotation method is faster in practice due to the reduced number of tests in the simplification. Regarding link and projection independence, although the latter can detect parallelism more accurately, it seems that in practice this rarely happens. While definiteness tests are very efficient our independence tests for these notions introduce significant overhead, which reduces the effectiveness of the parallelization. Overall, it appears best to use the non-split method, the most accurate domain, and, in order to avoid slow-downs while independence tests remain unoptimized, reduce such tests to false. Clearly, there is still quite a bit of room for improvement. The speedup results are significant when compared to standard compiler optimizations, but they are certainly not as good as those obtained for LP programs (e.g., [2]), and those obtained by or-parallelism for CLP programs which perform intensive search [9]. Identified avenues for future research include considering more realistic CLP benchmarks solving larger problems and combining both LP and CLP, studying better suited domains such as perhaps LSign [15], applying specialization, improving run-time test performance, controlling granularity, allowing the exploitation of a-posteriori parallelism, and parallelizing at finer grain levels than the goal level.

References

1. F. Bueno, M. García de la Banda, and M. Hermenegildo. A Comparative Study of Methods for Automatic Compile-time Parallelization of Logic Programs. In *Parallel Symbolic Computation*, pages 63–73. World Scientific Publishing, 1994.

2. F. Bueno, M. García de la Banda, and M. Hermenegildo. Effectiveness of Global Analysis in Strict Independence-Based Automatic Program Parallelization. In *International Logic Programming Symposium*, pages 320–336. MIT Press, 1994.

3. A. Cortesi, G. File, and W. Winsborough. Prop Revisited: Propositional Formulas as Abstract Domains for Groundness Analysis. In *Sixth IEEE Symposium on Logic in Computer Science*, pages 222–327, 1991. IEEE Computer Society.

4. P. Cousot and R. Cousot. Abstract Interpretation: a Unified Lattice Model for Static Analysis of Programs by Construction or Approximation of Fixpoints. In *ACM Symposium on Principles of Programming Languages*, pages 238–252, 1977.

5. M. García de la Banda and M. Hermenegildo. A Practical Approach to the Global Analysis of Constraint Logic Programs. In *International Logic Programming Symposium*, pages 437–455. MIT Press, 1993.

6. M. García de la Banda, M. Hermenegildo, and K. Marriott. Independence in Constraint Logic Programs. In *ILPS'93*, pages 130–146. MIT Press, 1993.

7. V. Dumortier, G. Janssens, M. Bruynooghe, and M. Codish. Freeness Analysis in the Presence of Numerical Constraints. In *Tenth International Conference on Logic Programming*, pages 100–115. MIT Press, 1993.

8. M.J. Fernández, M. Carro, and M. Hermenegildo. Idra (ideal resource allocation): Computing ideal speedups in parallel logic programming. In *Proceedings of EuroPar'96*, LNCS. Springer-Verlag, 1996.

9. P. Van Hentenryck. Parallel Constraint Satisfaction in Logic Programming. In *International Conference on Logic Programming*, pages 165–180. MIT Press, 1989.

10. M. Hermenegildo, F. Bueno, M. García de la Banda, and G. Puebla. The CIAO Multi-Dialect Compiler and System. In *Proc. of the ILPS'95 Workshop on Visions for the Future of Logic Programming*, 1995.

11. M. Hernenegildo and K. Greene. The &-Prolog System: Exploiting Independent And-Parallelism. *New Generation Computing*, 9(3,4):233–257, 1991.

12. C. Holzbaur. Metastructures vs. Attributed Variables in the Context of Extensible Unification. In *International Symposium on Programming Language Implementation and Logic Programming*, pages 260–268. LNCS631, Springer Verlag, 1992.

13. J. Jaffar and M.J. Maher. Constraint Logic Programming: A Survey. *Journal of Logic Programming*, 13/20:503–581, 1994.

14. S. Janson and S. Haridi. Programming Paradigms of the Andorra Kernel Language. In *Int'l Logic Programming Symp.*, pages 167–183. MIT Press, 1991.

15. K. Marriott and P. Stuckey. Approximating Interaction Between Linear Arithmetic Constraints. In *Int'l Logic Prog. Symp.*, pages 571–585. MIT Press, 1994.

16. K. Muthukumar and M. Hermenegildo. Compile-time Derivation of Variable Dependency Using Abstract Interpretation. *Journal of Logic Programming*, 13(2 and 3):315–347, 1992.

17. V. Santos-Costa, D.H.D. Warren, and R. Yang. Andorra-I: A Parallel Prolog System that Transparently Exploits both And- and Or-parallelism. In *ACM SIGPLAN Symp. on Principles and Practice of Parallel Programming*. ACM, 1990.

18. K. Shen. Exploiting Dependent And-Parallelism in Prolog: The Dynamic, Dependent And-Parallel Scheme. In *Joint Int'l. Conference and Symposium on Logic Programming* MIT Press, 1992.

Annotated Structure Shape Graphs for Abstract Analysis of Prolog

Geoffrey Weyer[1] and William Winsborough[2]

[1] Dept. of Comp. Sci. and Eng., Penn State, University Park, PA, weyer@cse.psu.edu
[2] Transarc Corp., Gulf Tower, 707 Grant St., Pittsburgh, PA, winsboro@transarc.com

Abstract. The paper presents an abstract interpretation of Prolog that derives information about the shape and sharing of structures to which variables are bound at runtime. The purpose is to support analysis of live structures, which in turn supports compile-time memory reuse. The abstract domain consists of graphs that use shared subgraphs to represent shared substructure in the heap. This sharing in the abstract representation is not new, though we are the first to use it in a context where unification must be modeled. The principal contribution is a system of annotations that increases the precision of the sharing information and the efficiency of the analysis.

Keywords Abstract Analysis, Structure Shape Graph, Unify Set, Compile-Time Garbage Collection, Update-In-Place, Type Graph, Aliasing, Sharing, Structure Sharing, Liveness.

1 Introduction

Abstract interpretation is a program analysis technique that simulates the execution of a program by manipulating abstract data elements in place of concrete elements. This is done to derive approximations of the concrete values to which variables can be bound when control reaches certain program points during execution. The binding information may be used in conjunction with liveness information to allow an optimizing compiler to generate specialized code.

The compiler optimizations that our analyzer supports include *compile-time garbage collection* (CTGC) [MJMB89] and *update-in-place* (UIP) [GW93]. These optimizations produce specialized code for sections of the program where storage cells are accessed for the last time. The specialized code reuses the dead storage cells, rather than relying on the garbage collector to reclaim them. Because all memory management is handled internally in Prolog, these optimizations can have a significant impact on performance [GW93]. They go a long way toward addressing a fundamental performance problem incurred by purely declarative languages, which eschew destructive assignment.

In order to detect reusable storage cells at compile time, it is necessary to identify heap cells that are reachable from more than one variable or via more than one path in the term structure. This sort of may-share or may-alias information is fundamental to determining whether a structure cell is live, and is the subject of our study and others, including [CBC93, LH88]. The program analysis presented in this paper uses an abstract domain that consists of annotated graphs referred to as *Structure Shape Graphs*, or SSGs. These graphs approximate heap states, capturing both structure shape and structure sharing.

Previous static analyses designed to infer structure liveness properties of Prolog programs have met with qualified success. An early analysis by Mulkers et al. [MWB90, MWB94] obtained impressive precision by using the structure-shape information provided by *type graph* analysis [JB92]. However, the analyzer also inherited serious efficiency problems: It runs out of memory on medium sized programs. This can be attributed at least in part to the fact that type graphs provide a separate representation for the structure to which each variable is bound. A second analysis that was designed to overcome this efficiency problem forgoes all structure shape information and as a result executes very quickly [BGW92]. For many programs, that analyzer successfully identifies opportunities to apply memory management optimizations.

Unfortunately, for many other programs, structure shape information is essential. In particular, when part of a structure is live and part dead (e.g., list elements and constructor cells, resp.) safety requires that the entire structure be marked live, preventing reclamation of the dead portions of the structure. As this scenario occurs frequently, we are motivated to explore abstract domains that provide some structure shape information while being efficient enough for practical use. To this end, we use a domain that consists of very compact graphs. The principal features of this domain are as follows.

1. Structure shape graphs are used to represent shape and sharing.

   (a) Shared structure in the heap is represented by shared structure in the SSG [JM81]. We present the first abstract interpretation that models unification over such a domain.

   (b) The number of nodes in an SSG is bounded by the number of constructor occurrences in the program [JM82, CWZ90]. We allocate one node in an SSG for each occurrence of each constructor in the program. [3]

       i. The number of constructor occurrences in a program determines an upper bound on the graph size.
       ii. The fixed node set eliminates the need for explicit graph-folding operations to limit the graph size.
       iii. The fixed node set simplifies several basic operations. Because nodes have identities, graph isomorphisms can be constructed quickly, expediting comparison of graphs done to determine when the analysis terminates. The fixed node set also simplifies graph union at clause exit.
       iv. The fixed node set need not be explicitly represented in each graph constructed by an analyzer.

---

[3] For example, the clause `P(X,Y) :- X=cons[_|_], Y=cons[_|_]` contains *two* constructor occurrences. Our SSG contains one node for each of these two occurrences.

(c) An SSG may be simpler to understand than type graphs because shared heap structures are represented by shared SSG structures. A set of pointers referencing the same cell is represented by a set of arcs pointing to the same node. Thus, SSGs provide a better visualization of sharing. In type-graph based models [MWB90, MWB94], structures that share in the heap are each represented by their *own* type graph structure (the nodes of which are linked by a binary may-share relation to indicate that they may represent the same heap cell).

2. Our SSGs have *sharing annotations* that identify when sharing in the graph represents sharing in the heap, and when it results from folding up the graph. (Sharing annotations are formalized as binary relations over arcs.) By distinguishing these cases, annotations improve the analyzer's precision and efficiency. Our system of annotations is an original technical contribution.

    (a) The annotations improve the expressiveness and precision of the analyzer output, identifying more places where sharing does *not exist* in the heap. This in turn identifies more dead structures.

    (b) The annotations improve the efficiency of the analyzer. By identifying places where sharing definitely occurs in the heap, we can eliminate unnecessary weak updates[4] to the graph. We can also reduce the amount of work done when simulating unification by identifying more pairs of arcs which should *not* be unified. This reduces the amount of work that needs to be done in both the current, and subsequent operations.

3. Unary *existence annotations* are applied to collections of (possibly) unified arcs. Existence annotations help reduce the number of those collections that the analysis must manipulate, again improving analyzer precision and performance. (Sharing annotations are also required to reduce that number.)

1.1 The role of sharing annotations

To ensure termination, program analyzers work with an approximation of the program's true behavior. The main motivation of our system of annotations is to limit the extent of this approximation while allowing efficient program analysis.

Graph based analyzers model heap structures by using nodes to represent heap cells, and directed arcs to represent pointers from parent cells to child cells. The representation can be formalized by a *recognition function*, which maps heap cells to graph nodes, preserving labels and parent/child relationships.

One problem concerning precision derives from the fact that an abstract node with multiple inarcs may recognize either several unshared cells or one shared cell. This is illustrated by Figure 1, which shows two heap environments and an SSG that recognizes them both. Suppose a program analysis were to construct that SSG to represent the heap state at some program point. Without further information, it is impossible to tell whether the actual heap is Heap 1, which has real sharing, or whether in fact it is Heap 2, with the apparent sharing merely

---

[4] A weak update to a graph is one in which arcs or nodes may be added, but not replaced, moved, or deleted [CWZ90].

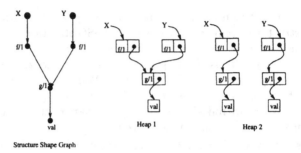

Fig. 1. An SSG that represents more than one possible heap state.

resulting from a folding operation on the SSG. The difference determines whether the structure-reuse optimization is safe. Suppose that liveness analysis were to determine that X is dead and Y, live at the given program point. The compiler would have to know that the actual heap is definitely Heap 2, and cannot be Heap 1, in order to reclaim safely the storage of the structure referenced by X. As mentioned in point (2.a) above, providing this kind of information is one of the goals of our system of annotations. The second problem addressed by our annotations is the efficiency of abstract unification, as mentioned in point (2.b) above and taken up in section 3 below.

1.2 Organization of Discussion

Section 2 introduces the abstract domain, presenting the sharing annotations on pairs of arcs. It also presents a simple axiomatization that assists in characterizing the system of annotations. Section 3 shows how the annotations support reducing the number of unify sets generated during a unification operation, improving the efficiency of unification and the precision of its outcome. It also describes the *existence* annotation on unify sets. Placement and maintenance of the sharing annotations is explained in section 4. Section 5 discusses our experience with the prototype implementation. Related work is described in section 6..

2 The Abstract Domain

An SSG denotes the set of heap states that it recognizes. A heap state consists of a set of cells, together with a set of pointers between those cells, where pointers are modeled as pairs of cells and are indexed by source cell and child number. Heap cells and SSG nodes are each labeled by a constructor, by a program variable, or by the special symbol V, which stands for an anonymous variable. Each SSG arc is labeled by a set of child numbers.

Recognition is formalized by a label-preserving mapping, $\mathcal{R}$, from heap cells to SSG nodes. $\mathcal{R}$ is required to map each pointer to an SSG arc that is labeled by a set containing the pointer's child number. That is, for each pointer *ptr* in the heap state, there must exist an arc a in the SSG such that $\mathcal{R}(src(ptr)) =$

$src(a)$ and $\mathcal{R}(dest(ptr)) = dest(a)$. In this case we extend $\mathcal{R}$ to pointers, writing $\mathcal{R}(ptr) = a$. Furthermore, the child number that indexes ptr is a member of the set of child numbers labeling a. Naturally, $\mathcal{R}$ is in general a many-one function. We denote the preimage of an arc as $C(a) = \{ptr|\mathcal{R}(ptr) = a\}$.

When $\mathcal{R}$ is many-one, we can think of the SSG as containing a folded image of the heap state. Folding is essential for finite representation of recursive data structures. However, it also introduces sharing of substructures in the SSG that does not represent substructure sharing in the heap. For instance, an SSG may contain cycles, although a heap state may not. This raises the problem of distinguishing sharing in the represented heap from sharing that was introduced in the SSG by folding. We address this problem by using a system of sharing annotations, which are formalized as binary relations that partition the cartesian product $arcs \times arcs$.

The annotations help to constrain the set of heap states recognized by an SSG. Below we refine the definition of $\mathcal{R}$ accordingly. The question of what annotations are correct can be discussed with reference to one or more particular heap states that the SSG is obliged to recognize. In the following discussion we refer to such a heap state as a *true heap state*.

A pair of arcs may be annotated *no-share* (i.e., in the *ns* relation) if no pair of pointers recognized by the pair of arcs share a destination. We assume that arcs with distinct destinations are implicitly annotated *ns*. A pair of arcs may be annotated *do-share* (i.e., in the *ds* relation) if (*i*) every pair of pointers that they recognize in a true heap state both point to the same cell, and (*ii*) either both arcs recognize at least one pointer, or neither does. Lastly, all other pairs of arcs are annotated *may-share* (i.e. in the *ms* relation). This annotation provides no additional useful information.

Definition 2.1 Sharing annotations. *Let a_1 and a_2 be (possibly identical) arcs in a given SSG and let C be the inverse of a recognition function $\mathcal{R}$ that demonstrates that the SSG recognizes a given heap state.*

$a_1\ ns\ a_2 \Rightarrow \forall ptr_1 \in C(a_1), \forall ptr_2 \in C(a_2),\ dest(ptr_1) \neq dest(ptr_2)$.

$a_1\ ds\ a_2 \Rightarrow \forall ptr_1 \in C(a_1), \forall ptr_2 \in C(a_2), dest(ptr_1) = dest(ptr_2)$ and
$\qquad C(a_1) = \{\} \iff C(a_2) = \{\}$.

$a_1\ ms\ a_2$ *is always true.*

It can be helpful to characterize the system of sharing annotations by a collection of axioms. The axioms we present are employed by the portion of the analyzer that places annotations in order to make those annotations more accurate. Axioms take the form of *annotation formulas*. Atomic annotation formulas have the form $a_1\ r\ a_2$ where $r \in \{ds, ns, ms\}$. Compound annotation formulas are formed by using the connectives $\vee, \wedge, \neg$, and $\Rightarrow$. The interpretation of these connectives is given below.

To facilitate the following definitions, we define an *unannotated* SSG as an SSG less its sharing component. Thus, an SSG may be expressed as a combination of an unannotated SSG, $\mathcal{US}$, and a sharing annotation, $\mathcal{S}$:

$$SS = \langle \mathcal{US}, \mathcal{S} \rangle$$
$$\mathcal{S} : Sharing = \mathcal{A} \times \mathcal{A} \rightarrow \{ds, ns, ms\}, \text{where } \mathcal{A} \text{ is the set of arcs in } \mathcal{US}.$$

Satisfaction of an annotation formula φ is defined inductively with respect to a fixed but arbitrary unannotated SSG, $\mathcal{US}$. Annotations determine which heap states may be recognized by a given SSG, and by which recognition function these heap states may be recognized. Thus, we define satisfaction of φ relative to a pair consisting of a heap state, $\mathcal{H}$, and a recognition function, $\mathcal{R}$.

For a fixed unannotated SSG, the annotation formulas allow us to discuss the semantic impact of how we annotate part of the SSG. This impact is seen in the heap states that are recognized, and in the corresponding recognition functions. For example, $\langle \mathcal{H}, \mathcal{R} \rangle \models_{us} (a_1 \; r \; a_2)$ indicates that there is an annotation for $\mathcal{US}$ that contains $(a_1 \; r \; a_2)$ and that permits $\mathcal{US}$ to recognize $\mathcal{H}$ via $\mathcal{R}$.

Definition 2.2 *Satisfaction of annotation formulas*

- $\langle \mathcal{H}, \mathcal{R} \rangle \models_{us} (a_1 \; r \; a_2)$ *if there exists an $\mathcal{S}$ in Sharing such that $\mathcal{S}(a_1, a_2) = r$ and $\langle \mathcal{US}, \mathcal{S} \rangle$ recognizes $\mathcal{H}$ via $\mathcal{R}$.*
- $\langle \mathcal{H}, \mathcal{R} \rangle \models_{us} \varphi_1 \Rightarrow \varphi_2$ *if $\langle \mathcal{H}, \mathcal{R} \rangle \models_{us} \varphi_1$ implies $\langle \mathcal{H}, \mathcal{R} \rangle \models_{us} \varphi_2$.*
- $\langle \mathcal{H}, \mathcal{R} \rangle \models_{us} \varphi_1 \vee \varphi_2$ *if $\langle \mathcal{H}, \mathcal{R} \rangle \models_{us} \varphi_1$ or $\langle \mathcal{H}, \mathcal{R} \rangle \models_{us} \varphi_2$.*
- $\langle \mathcal{H}, \mathcal{R} \rangle \models_{us} \varphi_1 \wedge \varphi_2$ *if $\langle \mathcal{H}, \mathcal{R} \rangle \models_{us} \varphi_1$ and $\langle \mathcal{H}, \mathcal{R} \rangle \models_{us} \varphi_2$.*
- $\langle \mathcal{H}, \mathcal{R} \rangle \models_{us} \neg \varphi_1$ *if $\langle \mathcal{H}, \mathcal{R} \rangle \models_{us} \varphi_1$ does not hold.*

The notation $\langle \mathcal{H}, \mathcal{R} \rangle \models_{us} \varphi$ means that φ is satisfied with respect to a given $\mathcal{US}$, $\mathcal{H}$ and $\mathcal{R}$. When the $\langle \mathcal{H}, \mathcal{R} \rangle$ component is dropped, the remaining $\models_{us} \varphi$ means that for all $\langle \mathcal{H}, \mathcal{R} \rangle$, φ is satisfied with respect to the fixed SSG $\mathcal{US}$. Finally, the notation $\models \varphi$ means that for all SSGs $\mathcal{US}$ which contain the arcs $a_1, \ldots, a_n$ referred to in φ, $\models_{us} \varphi$. That is, $\models \varphi$ is a tautology in the space of SSGs. We present several annotation formulas as axioms of the annotation system:

$$\models (a_1 \, ms \, a_2)$$
$$\models (a_1 \, ns \, a_2) \Rightarrow \neg (a_1 \, ds \, a_2)$$
$$\models (a_1 \, ds \, a_2) \Rightarrow \neg (a_1 \, ns \, a_2)$$
$$\models (a_1 \, ds \, a_2) \Rightarrow \neg (a_1 \, ns \, a_1) \wedge \neg (a_2 \, ns \, a_2)$$
$$\models (a_1 \; r \; a_2) \Rightarrow (a_2 \; r \; a_1), \quad r \in \{ds, ns, ms\}$$
$$\models (a_1 \, ds \, a_2) \wedge (a_2 \, ds \, a_3) \Rightarrow (a_1 \, ds \, a_3)$$

3 Modeling Unification

Concrete unification of terms can be modeled by constructing an equivalence relation over subterms that are required to be identical by the unification problem [PW78]. The equivalence classes induced by this relation provide a basis for stating the safety requirement of an abstract unification operation over SSGs.

When the equivalence classes are projected onto the SSG, their images are possibly overlapping sets of graph nodes, which we refer to as *unify* sets.[5]

Term unification is modeled in the SSG by constructing and propagating unify sets. The safety requirement is that abstract unification must construct a collection of unify sets that includes each equivalence class's image under the recognition function. When the recognition function maps an equivalence class (surjectively) onto a unify set, we say that the unify set recognizes the equivalence class, and also that the unify set is the image of the equivalence class (under the recognition function).

As with any abstract operation, approximation must be expected. In abstract unification, approximation enters when a unify set is introduced that is not the image of an equivalence class for a recognized term.

Once all necessary unify sets have been created, the SSG must be updated to reflect the fact that variables may become bound to nodes in the same unify set. Thus, unnecessary unify sets may lead to unnecessary (possible) bindings in the SSG, reducing the precision of the analysis.

Operationally, abstract unification employs two collections of unify sets called **candidates** and **members**, and two operations called **propagate** and **merge**. The set **members** constitutes the collection of unify sets that recognize equivalence classes in recognized term environments. **Candidates** acts as a filter to prevent incomplete or unnecessary sets from being included in **members**. Both of these sets grow monotonically, and termination occurs when no new sets are added by applying **propagate** nor by applying **merge**. The unification process begins with some initial unify sets in **candidates**. An application of **merge** examines the new additions to **candidates** and constructs the unions of appropriate combinations of sets in **candidates**, adding the unions to **members**. **Propagate** adds new sets to **candidates**. Each new set is derived from a unify set in **members** by including at least one successor arc for each unify-set element that has successor arcs. The process is iterated until neither **propagate** nor **merge** introduces a new set.

A naive definition of **merge** could be constructed by unioning all collections of unify sets that possibly recognize intersecting equivalence classes. This intuition can be made precise by viewing the unify sets as the nodes of a graph.

Definition 3.1 *Let $G = \langle V, E \rangle$ be the graph given by*

- V = candidates
- $E = \left\{ (u, u') \middle| \begin{array}{l} u, u' \in V \text{ and there exist } a \in u \text{ and } a' \in u' \text{ such that} \\ a \text{ and } a' \text{ have the same destination} \end{array} \right\}$

Definition 3.2 naivemerge(candidates) = $\{ \bigcup C \mid C \subseteq V$ *is a connected subgraph of $G \}$*

The drawback of such a simple approach is that **naivemerge** returns an excessively large set. At the end of the current section we present a definition of **merge**

---

[5] For technical reasons, our unify sets are actually sets of arcs whose destinations are those graph nodes.

that takes advantage of our annotations to improve significantly on naivemerge in terms of efficiency and precision. To show how these improvements are obtained, we study an example of how changing one sharing annotation in an SSG effects the efficiency and outcome of unification.

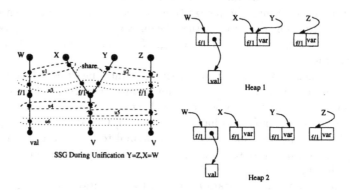

Fig. 2. An SSG with two heaps it can represent, depending on which sharing relation the label share is replaced with. Unify sets are shown on the SSG for the unification, Y=Z, X=W.

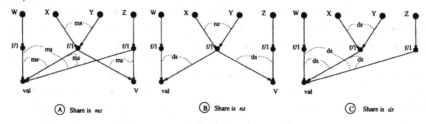

Fig. 3. Results of the unification pictured in Figure 2 showing the effect of replacing share with different sharing annotations.

Consider the SSG undergoing unification in Figure 2, and the two heap states, both of which must be recognized by the SSG, depending on which sharing relation the label share is replaced with. To simultaneously simulate the unification operations Y=Z and X=W, we initialize candidates to $\{u_1, u_2\}$, members to $\{\}$, and begin iterating the merge and propagate steps.

Referring to Figure 2, we see that u_1, u_2, and u_3 (which is $u_1 \cup u_2$) are all candidates for inclusion, as indicated by Definition 3.2. The set u_3 is needed to represent the unification in Heap 1, where the equivalence classes $\{\text{dest}(W),\text{dest}(X)\}$ and $\{\text{dest}(Y),\text{dest}(Z)\}$ intersect at the shared heap cell $\text{dest}(X) = \text{dest}(Y)$. The sets u_1 and u_2 also need to be included to represent the unification that takes place in Heap 2, where the corresponding equivalence classes do not intersect.

The annotation shown as share in Figure 2 can safely be ns when it is known that Heap 2 is the true heap, and not Heap 1. In terms of the graph, G, given in Definition 3.1, the edge between u_1 and u_2 is unnecessary, in that case. Thus, merge need *not* return u_3, reducing the number of unify sets in members. In general, an edge between sets u and u' does not need to be included in G's edge set E if, for all arcs $a \in u$ and $a' \in u'$, the sharing annotation between a and a' is *ns*.

The annotation share in Figure 2 may be *ds* when it is known that the true heap is Heap 1 and *not* Heap 2. In this case, merge would have the information that if there is a unify set u_1, there must be a unify set u_2 such that those two sets are unioned. More precisely, merge would take the union of u_1 and u_2, producing u_3, but would add u_3 to members, and *not* u_1 *or* u_2. Thus, the efficiency of the analysis would be increased because propagate would have to propagate only one unify set.

Let us continue the example. Applying propagate to u_1, u_2, and u_3, when they exist, adds u_4, u_5, and u_6, respectively, to candidates. Application of merge then promotes these sets to members, which brings the process to a fixed point. When share is *ms*, that fixpoint has members=$\{u_1, u_2, u_3, u_4, u_5, u_6\}$. The presence of unify sets u_4, u_5, and u_6 indicates that there are two possible results of concrete unification: there may be two variables, both bound to *val*, as would occur in Heap 1; or there may be three variables, one of which is bound to *val*, and the other two of which are bound together, as would occur in Heap 2. The SSG after unification in this case is shown in Figure 3, part Ⓐ. Thus, after the unification, we do not know which of X, Y, and Z is free or bound, nor which ones share. By contrast, when share is *ns*, members=$\{u_1, u_2, u_4, u_5\}$, and when share is *ds*, members=$\{u_3, u_6\}$. The SSGs after unification in each of these cases are shown in Figure 3, parts Ⓑ and Ⓒ, respectively. Note that the information is more precise than that obtained in part Ⓐ.

Naturally, we want to avoid including a combination of unify sets whenever possible. Intuitively, it is safe to omit a connected subgraph of G (i.e., a combination of unify sets) from members when the subgraph is incomplete in some sense. This can occur when a unify set, included as a node in the subgraph, contains an arc that definitely shares with some arc (possibly itself). A property of unify sets that aids in identifying cases where such exclusions are safe is the knowledge that a unify set recognizes some equivalence class in *every* recognized heap state. When our analyzer knows that a unify set has this property, it annotates the unify set *does-exist*. When the property can not be determined, the set must be labeled *may-exist*. These *existence annotations* are created inductively during unification. Initial unify sets placed at the beginning of the unification are annotated does-exist.

The does-exist annotation, together with the *ds* sharing annotation, allows some connected subgraphs to be treated as *inseparable* groups by merge. That is, if one node of an inseparable subgraph is included in a union, so are all nodes in the subgraph. The impact on the size of merge's output is as follows. For a connected component containing n nodes (unify sets) with g inseparable subgraphs that contain a total of m nodes ($m \geq g$), the number of combinations computed by merge decreases from 2^n to $2^{(n-m+g)}$.

Two unify sets should be inseparable only if they both definitely exist (DE).

If one of the unify sets definitely exists, the other may exist, and the two unify sets definitely share, then the ME set is said to *depend* on the DE set. Whenever the ME set is included in a grouping, the DE set must also be included; however, the converse does not necessarily hold. Inseparability is therefore equivalent to mutual dependence, as illustrated by the *ds* case of the previous example.

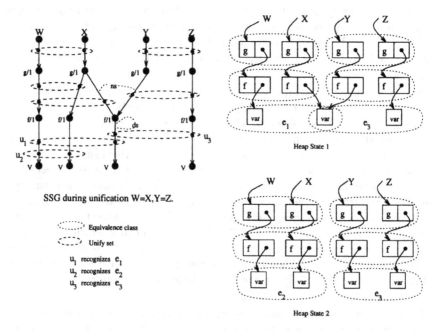

Fig. 4. Destructive merging of unify sets requires the does-exist annotation for safety.

Figure 4 provides an example of unify set dependence that is asymmetric. Our analyzer inductively annotates u_3 as definitely existing and u_1 as maybe existing. These annotations indicate that while u_3 recognizes an equivalence class (e_3) that exists in all recognized heaps, u_1 recognizes an equivalence class (e_1) that exists in some heaps, but not all. Note that the sets u_1 and u_3 both contain an arc whose sharing with itself is *ds*. Together, these (existence and sharing) facts indicate that u_1 depends on u_3. Because e_3 exists in all recognized heap states, when e_1 exists, it is definitely unioned with e_3. Consequently, whenever u_1 is included in a merge grouping, it is safe also to include u_3. In the case that e_1 does not exist, as in Heap State 2, e_3 is not unioned with anything. Thus, safety requires the inclusion of merge groupings that include u_3 while omitting u_1. This is why the dependence in this example goes one way, but not the other.

Definition 3.3 (connect)

– connect(u, u') = *strong if there exists* $a \in u$ *and* $a' \in u'$ *such that* a *ds* a'.

- connect(u, u') = *weak if there exists $a \in u$ and $a' \in u'$ such that a ms a' AND there* does not *exist $a \in u$ and $a' \in u'$ such that a ds a'.*
- connect(u, u') = *none if all $a \in u$ and $a' \in u'$ satisfy a ns a'.*

Definition 3.4 (merge) *Let* new $\subseteq$ candidates. *We define* merge(new, candidates) : $\wp(\bigcup \text{candidates})$ *to be the set of unions returned by step 8 of the following non-deterministic algorithm.*

1. *Let* included : $\wp(\wp(\text{Node}))$ *be a mutable variable.*
2. *Nondeterministically choose $u_0 \in$ new.*
3. included = $\{u_0\}$.
4. *If there is a pair $\langle u, u' \rangle$ with $u \in$ included and $u' \in$ (candidates − included) such that* connect(u, u') = *strong and u' is marked DE, then add u' to* included *and goto step 4; else continue.*
5. *Nondeterministically either go to step 8 or continue.*
6. *If there is a pair $\langle u, u' \rangle$ with $u \in$ included and $u' \in$ candidates − included such that* connect$(u, u') \in \{strong, weak\}$, *add u' to* included*; else goto step 8.*
7. *Goto step 4.*
8. *If there is a pair of distinct arcs $\langle a, a' \rangle$ with $(a$ ds $a')$ and some $u \in$ included has $a \in u$, but no $u' \in$ included has $a' \in u'$, then fail; else return $\bigcup$ included.*

4   Maintaining annotations

After merge and propagate have completed, variables are bound. If a DE unify set contains an arc a with a variable destination and an arc a' with a non-variable destination, binding of the variable is indicated by reassigning the destination of a to that of a'. In the case that all arcs in the unify set have variable destinations, some a' is selected from among them at random. In the case that the unify set has ME annotation, a new arc is added from the source of a to the destination of a', but a is not deleted, indicating a *possible* binding.

After variables have been bound, sharing annotations are updated. A pair of arcs must have its sharing annotation updated if one of the arcs recognizes either a pointer in newly allocated structure, or a pointer to a variable that has just been bound. For the most part, variables that have just been bound are easy to recognize because the corresponding SSG arc gets reassigned. However, there is one case that is not so obvious. It occurs when a single SSG arc recognizes several pointers to distinct free variables, and new sharing may be introduced among those variables. In this case, binding occurs in the heap structure, although no arcs are reassigned in the SSG.

An example of a unification that requires updates to the sharing annotations is shown in Figure 5. After the unification, the arc from the variable Z to the node labeled *cons* recognizes a pointer that represents a binding of a variable that was free before the unification. That is, no new pointers were added to the heap in this unification, but an existing pointer was reassigned.

In the example, the initial SSG represents a heap state where X and Y are bound to distinct constructor (cons) nodes, and Z is free. The *ns* annotation

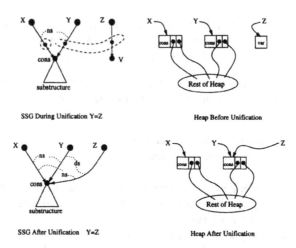

Fig. 5. A unification that binds a free variable.

indicates that X and Y do not share, thus the unification binds Z to what Y points to, but should not involve X. In the resulting SSG, the sharing annotations indicate that Y and Z share with one another, but that neither shares with X.

To facilitate the identification of arcs and nodes that recognize new pointers and cells, we employ additional *new-structure* annotations. We summarize the information that they provide.

– Annotations identify which arcs and nodes recognize new pointers and cells.
– When arcs recognize new pointers or pointers to freshly bound variables, the annotations indicate whether those pointers point to the same cell.
– When arcs recognize new pointers that point to the same cell, the annotations indicate whether that cell is new.

Tables 1 and 2 determine the appropriate new sharing annotations, based on the old sharing annotations and on a case analysis of the possible recognized heap structures. That case analysis is based

– on the unify sets computed by **propagate** and **merge**,
– on the new-structure annotations,
– on the fact that the *ds* relation is transitive, and
– in the case of pairs of distinct arcs (Table 2), on the new self-sharing annotations of the respective arcs, as determined by Table 1.

A complete discussion can be found in [Wey96].

5 Results

The annotations discussed in this paper are being incorporated in a prototype abstract analyzer for Prolog using the framework of [LV92, VCL94]. The sharing

	Old Sharing			
	a ds a	a ns a	a ms a	none
a recognizes one new pointer only.	NA	NA	NA	a ds a
a recognizes one new pointer that points to a new cell, and one old pointer that points to an old cell.	a ns a	NA	NA	NA
a recognizes one new pointer that points to a new cell, and possibly some old pointers.	a ms a	a ns a	a ms a	NA
a recognizes one new pointer that points to an old cell, and possibly some old pointers.	a ds a	a ms a	a ms a	NA

Table 1. How an arc's self-sharing annotation is updated. The conditions that label rows are identified by *new structure* annotations associated with the arc. *For brevity, arcs that represent newly bound variables are treated the same as arcs that recognize new pointers.* The column label "none" indicates that a did not exist prior to the current unification. "NA" (not applicable) indicates that the case is impossible.

	Old Sharing			
	a_1 ds a_2	a_1 ms a_2	a_1 ns a_2	none
a_1, a_2 both recognize only *new* pointers all of which have the same *new* cell as a destination.	NA	NA	NA	a_1 ds a_1
a_1, a_2 both recognize *new* pointers that have the same *new* cell as their destination, and a_1 or a_2 recognize an old pointers.	a_1 ms a_2	a_1 ms a_2	a_1 ms a_2	a_1 ms a_2
a_1, a_2 both recognize *new* pointers, all of which have the same *old* cell as a destination.	a_1 ds a_2	a_1 ms a_2	a_1 ms a_2	a_1 ms a_2
a_1 recognizes a *new* pointer with an *old* destination, a_2 recognizes only *old* pointers, and all unify sets that contain a_1 also contain a_2	a_1 ds a_2	a_1 ms a_2	a_1 ms a_2	a_1 ds a_2
a_1 and a_2 may both recognize *new* pointers, all of which point to distinct, *new* cells	a_1 ms a_2	a_1 ns a_2	a_1 ms a_2	a_1 ns a_2
all other cases:	a_1 ms a_2	a_1 ms a_2	a_1 ms a_2	a_1 ms a_2

Table 2. How a sharing annotation between distinct arcs a_1 and a_2 is updated. The conditions that label rows are identified by *new structure* annotations associated with the arcs, the self-sharing annotations on the arcs, and the presence of unify sets. (See also the caption of Table 1.)

annotations used for this implementation consist of the do-share, no-share, and may-share annotations presented here. The final analyzer will be incorporated into the SIVA project [GW93], which applies transformations to Prolog programs to obtain update-in-place memory reuse.

The unification operation has been implemented in 5000 lines of C code, and has been tested on short sequences of unifications that model simple programs. Initial results show that on average 23% fewer unify sets are created, as compared to the number of sets that are generated when all of the annotations are *ms*. In one extreme case, the analyzer running time was reduced by a ratio of 45:1.

Typical cases demonstrated more modest improvements of about 2:1.

The correctness of the abstract unification operation used in the implementation has been proven [Wey96]. The proof begins by defining a formal graphical model of heap states, which are referred to as *Term Environment Graphs*. Concrete unification is defined over these graphs. Abstract unification is then proven to model concrete unification in a manner that preserves recognition. Supporting proofs of the correctness of the operations that place new-structure annotations, and place and update sharing annotations are also given.

6 Related work

The analysis method presented in this paper uses graphs to capture structure shape and sharing information. Alternative analysis methods employ domains that capture structure shape information (e.g., [Hei92]) or sharing information (e.g., [Deu94]), but not both. Heintz's work has many attractive features, including elegance, modularity, and efficiency. However, the set constraint approach appears unable to approach the power of abstract interpretation to infer control-flow based information such as structure liveness. This appears to make it unsuitable for supporting update-in-place transformations. A promising line of investigation is presented in [Deu94]. It remains to be seen whether that approach is well suited to supporting structure liveness in the presence of the unification operation.

Abstract analysis methods that use SSGs have been proposed for imperative languages [CWZ90]. These methods may benefit from using the annotations proposed here by increasing the ratio of strong updates to weak updates.

In the logic programming context, previous graph-based analyses have used *type graphs* [JB92], rather than SSGs. Type graphs by themselves do not express structure sharing, making them unsuitable for supporting update-in-place transformations. Additional structure-sharing information can be layered on top of type graphs, as done in [MWB90, MWB94]. However, the resulting analysis is excessively costly, in large part because type graphs do not allow sufficient sharing of substructure in their own representations.

The related, but much simpler, problem of analyzing the ground subset of Prolog for the same application has been studied in [Klu88] and [Kag93].

Acknowledgement

William Winsborough was partially supported by NSF CCR-9210975.

References

[BGW92] B. Burton, G. Gudjonsson, and W. Winsborough. An algorithm for computing alternating closure. Technical Report CS-92-15, Penn State, June 1992.

[CBC93]   J.D. Choi, M.G. Burke, and P. Carini. Efficient flow-sensitive interproce-
          dural computation of pointer-induced aliases and side-effects. *POPL*, pages
          232–245, January 1993.

[CWZ90]   D.R. Chase, M. Wegman, and F.K. Zadeck. Analysis of pointers and struc-
          tures. *PLDI*, pages 20–22, June 1990.

[Deu94]   A. Deutsch. Interprocedural may-alias analysis for pointers: Beyond k-
          limiting. *PLDI*, pages 230–241, June 1994.

[GW93]   G. Gudjonsson and W. Winsborough. Update in place: Overview of the
          siva project. In Dale Miller, editor, *ILPS*, pages 94–113. MIT Press, 1993.

[Hei92]   N. Heintze. Practical aspects of set based analysis. In Krzysztok Apt,
          editor, *JICSLP*, pages 765–779. MIT Press, 1992.

[JB92]   G. Janssens and M. Bruynooghe. Deriving descriptions of possible values
          of program variables by means of abstract interpretation. *Journal of Logic
          Programming*, 13(2&3):205–258, July 1992.

[JM81]   N.D. Jones and S. Muchnick. Flow analysis and optimzation of lisp-like
          structures. In S. Muchnick and N.D. Jones, editors, *Program Flow Analysis:
          Theory and Applications*, pages 102–131. Prentice-Hall, 1981.

[JM82]   N.D. Jones and S. Muchnick. A flexible approach to interprocedural data
          flow analysis and programs with recursive data structures. *POPL*, pages
          66–74, 1982.

[Kag93]   A. Kagedal. Improvements in compile-time analysis for ground prolog. In
          M. Bruynooghe, J. Penjam, editors, *PLILP*. LNCS 714, Springer-Verlag,
          August 1993.

[Klu88]   F. Kluźniak. Compile-time garbage collection for ground Prolog. In R. A.
          Kowalski and K. A. Bowen, editors, *ICSLP*, pages 1490–1505. MIT Press,
          August 1988.

[LH88]   J. R. Larus and P. N. Hilfinger. Detecting conflicts between structure ac-
          cesses. *PLDI*, pages 21–34, July 1988.

[LV92]   B. Le Charlier and P. Van Hentenryck. Experimental evaluation of a generic
          abstract interpretation algorithm for prolog (extended abstract). *Fourth
          IEEE International Conference on Computer Languages*, April 1992.

[MJMB89] A. Marien, G. Janssens, A. Mulkers, and M. Bruynooghe. The impact of
          abstract interpretation: An experiment in code generation. In G. Levi and
          M. Martelli, editors, *ICLP*. MIT Press, 1989.

[MWB90]   A. Mulkers, W. Winsborough, and M. Bruynooghe. Analysis of shared
          data structures for compile-time garbage collection in logic programs. In
          D. H. D. Warren and P. Szeredi, editors, *ICLP*. MIT Press, 1990.

[MWB94]   A. Mulkers, W. Winsborough, and M. Bruynooghe. Live-structure data-
          flow analysis for Prolog. *TOPLAS*, 16, 1994.

[PW78]   M. S. Patterson and M. N. Wegman. Linear unification. *Journal of com-
          puter and system sciences*, 16:158–167, 1978.

[VCL94]   P. Van Hentenryck, A. Cortesi, and B. Le Charlier. Type analysis of prolog
          using type graphs. *PLDI*, 1994.

[Wey96]   G. Weyer. Structure shape graphs with explicit sharing for prolog-like lan-
          guages. Master's thesis, Dept of Computer Science and Engineering, Penn
          State, May 1996.

A Reactive Implementation of *Pos* Using ROBDDs

Roberto Bagnara

Dipartimento di Informatica, Università di Pisa, Corso Italia 40, 56125 Pisa, Italy
E-mail: bagnara@di.unipi.it.

Abstract. The subject of groundness analysis for (constraint) logic programs has been widely studied, and interesting domains have been proposed. *Pos* has been recognized as the most suitable domain for capturing the kind of dependencies arising in groundness analysis. Its (by now standard) implementation is based on *reduced ordered binary-decision diagrams* (ROBDDs), a well-known symbolic representation for Boolean functions. Even though several authors have reported positive experiences using ROBDDs for groundness analysis, in the literature there is no reference to the problem of the efficient detection of those variable which are deemed to be ground in the context of a ROBDD. This is not surprising, since most currently implemented analyzers need to derive this information only *at the end* of the analysis and only for presentation purposes. Things are much different when this information is required *during* the analysis. This need arises when dealing with languages which employ some sort of *delay mechanism*, which are typically based on groundness conditions. In these cases, the *naïf* approaches are too inefficient, since the abstract interpreter must quickly (and often) decide whether a constraint is delayed or not. Fast access to ground variables is also necessary when aliasing analysis is performed using a domain not keeping track of ground dependencies. In this paper we introduce and study the problem, proposing two possible solutions. The second one, besides making possible the quick detection of ground variables, has also the effect of keeping the ROBDDs as small as possible, improving the efficiency of groundness analysis in itself.

1 Introduction

The task of *groundness analysis* (or *definiteness* analysis as it is also referred to) is to derive, for all the program points of interest, whether a certain variable is bound to a unique value (or *ground*). This kind of information is very important: it allows substantial optimizations to be performed at compile-time, and is also crucial for most semantics-based program manipulation tools. Moreover, many other analysis are made much more precise by the availability of groundness information. For these reasons, the subject of groundness analysis for (constraint) logic programs has been widely studied. After the early attempts, some classes of Boolean functions have been recognized as constituting good abstract domains for groundness analysis [7, 16, 1, 19]. In particular, the set of *positive Boolean functions*, (namely, those functions which assume the true value under the valuation assigning true to all variables), which is denoted by *Pos*, has been recognized as the most precise domain for capturing the kind of dependencies arising in groundness analysis.

The standard implementation of *Pos* is based on *reduced ordered binary-decision diagrams* (ROBDDs), a well-known symbolic representation for Boolean functions. Indeed, ROBDDs are general enough to represent *all* Boolean functions. However, nobody has succeeded, to date, in exploiting the (seemingly very small) peculiarities of positive functions in order to obtain a more efficient implementation. Several authors have reported positive experiences using ROBDDs for groundness analysis (see, e.g., [16, 1]). However, in the literature there is no reference to the problem of detecting, as efficiently as possible, those variables which are deemed to be ground in the context of a ROBDD. This is not surprising, since most currently implemented analyzers need to derive this information only *at the end* of the analysis and only for presentation purposes. In these cases efficiency is not a problem and the simple approaches are good enough. Things are much different when this information is required *during* the analysis. This need arises when dealing with languages which employ some sort of *delay mechanism*, which are typically based on groundness conditions. One of these languages is CLP($\mathcal{R}$) [14], where non-linear constraints are delayed until they become linear; only then they are sent to the constraint solver. In the context of our work on data-flow analysis for CLP($\mathcal{R}$) we were thus facing the following problem: in programs with many non-linear constraints, the abstract interpreter was spending a lot of time deciding whether a constraint is delayed or not. In the early implementations of the CHINA analyzer this kind of information (which is needed quite often) was derived using the ROBDD package itself (see Sect. 5). This had the advantage of making possible the use of untouched, readily-available ROBDD software, while having the big disadvantage of inefficiency.

In this paper we introduce and study the problem of quick detection of ground variables using ROBDDs. We first propose an easy, even though not completely satisfactory, solution. We then take a different approach where we represent *Pos* functions in a hybrid way: ground variables are represented explicitly, while ROBDDs come into play only for dependency and disjunctive information. This solution uses the more efficient representation for each kind of information: "surely ground variables" are best represented by means of sets (bit-vectors, at the implementation level), whereas ROBDDs are used only for "conditional" and "disjunctive" information. In such a way, besides making the information about ground variables readily available, we can keep the ROBDDs generated during the analysis as small as possible. This promises to be a win, given that most real programs (together with their typical call-patterns) exhibit a high percentage of variables which are ground at the program points of interest. Notice that Boolean functions are used in the more general context of *dependency analysis*, including *finiteness analysis* for deductive database languages and *suspension analysis* for concurrent (constraint) logic programming languages [1]. The techniques we propose might be useful also in these contexts. However, this is something we have not studied yet. In Sect. 2 we briefly review the usage of Boolean functions for groundness analysis of (constraint) logic programs (even though we assume familiarity on this subject). Sect. 3 presents the main motivations of this work. Binary-decision trees and diagrams, and the problem of extracting *sure groundness information* from them are introduced in Sects. 4 and 5. In Sect. 6 we show a first non-trivial solution to the problem, while Sect. 7 introduces the hybrid domain. The results of the experimental evaluation are reported in Sect. 8. Sect. 9 concludes with some final remarks.

2   Boolean Functions for Groundness Analysis

After the early approaches to groundness analysis [17, 15], which suffered from serious precision drawbacks, using Boolean functions has become customary in the field. The reason is that Boolean functions allow to capture in a very precise way the *groundness dependencies* which are implicit in unification constraints such as $z = f(g(x), y)$: the corresponding Boolean function is $(x \wedge y) \leftrightarrow z$, meaning that z is ground if and only if x and y are so. They also capture dependencies arising from other constraint domains: for instance, $x + 2y + z = 4$ can be abstracted as $((x \wedge y) \to z) \wedge ((x \wedge z) \to y) \wedge ((y \wedge z) \to x)$. We now introduce Boolean valuations and functions in a way which is suitable for what follows. *Vars* is a fixed denumerable set of variable's symbols.

Definition 1 (Boolean valuations.) *The set of* Boolean valuations over *Vars is given by* $\mathcal{A} \stackrel{\text{def}}{=} \textit{Vars} \to \{0, 1\}$. *For each* $a \in \mathcal{A}$, *each* $x \in \textit{Vars}$, *and each* $c \in \{0, 1\}$ *the valuation* $a[c/x] \in \mathcal{A}$ *is given, for each* $y \in \textit{Vars}$, *by*

$$a[c/x](y) \stackrel{\text{def}}{=} \begin{cases} c, & \text{if } x = y; \\ a(y), & \text{otherwise.} \end{cases}$$

For $X = \{x_1, x_2, \dots\} \subseteq \textit{Vars}$, *we write* $a[c/X]$ *for* $a[c/x_1][c/x_2] \cdots$.

Definition 2 (Boolean functions.) *The set of* Boolean function over *Vars is* $\mathcal{F} \stackrel{\text{def}}{=} \mathcal{A} \to \{0, 1\}$. *The distinguished elements* $\top, \bot \in \mathcal{F}$ *are the functions defined by* $\top \stackrel{\text{def}}{=} \lambda a \in \mathcal{A} . 1$ *and* $\bot \stackrel{\text{def}}{=} \lambda a \in \mathcal{A} . 0$. *For* $f \in \mathcal{F}$, $x \in \textit{Vars}$, *and* $c \in \{0, 1\}$, *the function* $f[c/x] \in \mathcal{F}$ *is given, for each* $a \in \mathcal{A}$, *by* $f[c/x](a) \stackrel{\text{def}}{=} f(a[c/x])$. *When* $X \subseteq \textit{Vars}$, $f[c/X]$ *is defined in the obvious way.*

The question whether a Boolean function f forces a particular variable x to be true (which is what, in the context of groundness analysis, we call *sure groundness information*) is equivalent to the question whether $f \to x$ is a tautology (namely, $f \to x = \top$). In the sequel we will also need the notion of *dependent variables* of a function.

Definition 3 (Dependent and true variables.) *For* $f \in \mathcal{F}$, *the set of variables on which* f *depends and the set of variables necessarily true for* f *are given, respectively, by*

$$\textit{vars}(f) \stackrel{\text{def}}{=} \{ x \in \textit{Vars} \mid \exists a \in \mathcal{A} . f(a[0/x]) \neq f(a[1/x]) \},$$
$$\textit{true}(f) \stackrel{\text{def}}{=} \{ x \in \textit{vars}(f) \mid \forall a \in \mathcal{A} : f(a) = 1 \implies a(x) = 1 \}.$$

Two classes of Boolean functions which are suitable for groundness analysis are known under the names of *Def* and *Pos* (see [1] for details). *Pos* consists precisely of those functions assuming the true value under the *everything-is-true* assignment (i.e., $f \in Pos$ iff $f \in \mathcal{F}$ and $f[1/Vars] = \top$). *Pos* is strictly more precise than *Def* for groundness analysis [1]. The reason is that the elements of *Pos* allow to maintain disjunctive information which is, instead, lost in *Def*.

3 Combination of Domains and Reactivity

It is well known that different data-flow analyses can be combined together. In the framework of abstract interpretation this can be achieved by means of standard constructions such as reduced product and down-set completion [10, 11]. The key point is that the combined analysis can be more precise than each of the component ones for they can mutually improve each other. However, the degree of cross-fertilization is highly dependent on the degree and quality of interaction taking place among the component domains. For the limited purpose of this paper, when we talk about *combination of domains* we refer to the following situation: we have several distinct (both conceptually and at the implementation level) analysis' domains and, for the sake of ensuring correctness or improving precision, there must be a flow of information between them. This can be formalized in different ways. A methodology for the combination of abstract domains has been proposed in [9]. It is based onto low level actions such as *tests* and *queries*. Basically, the component domains have the ability of querying other domains for some kind of information. Of course, they must also be able to respond to queries from other domains. For instance, the operations of a domain for numerical information might ask a domain for groundness whether a certain variable is guaranteed to be ground or not. Another way of describing this kind of interaction is the one proposed in [3]. Here the interaction among domains is asynchronous in that it can occur at any time, or, in other words, it is not synchronized with the domain's operations. This is achieved by considering so called *ask-and-tell constraint systems* built over *product constraint systems*. These constraint systems allow to express communication among domains in a very simple way. They also inherit all the semantic elegance of concurrent constraint programming languages [18], which provide the basis for their construction. We will now see, staying on an intuitive level and following the approach of [3] for simplicity, examples of how these combinations look like.

In the CLP($\mathcal{R}$) system [14] non-linear constraints (like $X = Y * Z$) are delayed (i.e., not treated by the constraint solver) until they become linear (e.g., until either Y or Z are constrained to take a single value). Obviously, this cannot be forgotten in abstract constraint systems intended to formalize correct data-flow analyses of CLP($\mathcal{R}$). When the abstract constraint system is able to extract information from non-linear constraints (such as the one proposed in [4]), you cannot simply let $X = Y * Z$, or better, its abstraction $\alpha(X = Y * Z)$ stand by itself. By doing this you would incur the risk of *overshooting* the concrete constraint system (thus loosing soundness), which is unable to deduce anything from non-linear constraints. The right thing to do is to combine the numeric abstract constraint system with one for groundness and using, instead of the abstraction $\alpha(X = Y * Z)$, the agent

$$A \stackrel{\text{def}}{=} \text{ask}(ground(Y); ground(Z)) \rightarrow \alpha(X = Y * Z).$$

The intuitive reading is that the abstract constraint system is not allowed to do anything with $X = Y * Z$ until Y *or* (this is the intuitive reading of the semicolon) Z are ground. In this way, all the abstractions of non-linear constraints are "disabled" until their wake-up conditions are met (in the abstract, which, given a sound groundness analysis, implies that these conditions are met also at the concrete level). The need for interaction between groundness and numerical domains does not end here. Consider again the constraint $X = Y * Z$: clearly X is definite if Y and Z are so. But we cannot conclude that the groundness of Y follows from the one of X and Z, as we need also the condition $Z \neq 0$. Similarly, we would like to conclude that X is definite if Y or Z have a zero value. Thus we need approximations of the concrete values of variables (i.e., bounds analysis), something which is not captured by common groundness analyses while being crucial when dealing with non-linear constraints. In the approach of [3] $X = Y * Z$ would be *abstractly compiled* into an agent of the form[1]

$$A \parallel \text{ask}(ground(Y) \wedge ground(Z)) \rightarrow \text{tell}(ground(X))$$
$$\parallel \text{ask}(Y = 0; Z = 0) \rightarrow \text{tell}(ground(X))$$
$$\parallel \text{ask}(ground(X) \wedge ground(Z) \wedge Z \neq 0) \rightarrow \text{tell}(ground(Y))$$
$$\parallel \text{ask}(ground(X) \wedge ground(Y) \wedge Y \neq 0) \rightarrow \text{tell}(ground(Z)).$$

Of course, this is much more precise than the *Pos* formula $X \leftarrow Y \wedge Z$, which is all you can say about the groundness dependencies of $X = Y * Z$ if you do not have any numerical information. It is clear from these examples that, when analyzing CLP($\mathcal{R}$) programs there is a bidirectional flow of information: groundness information is required for a correct handling of delayed constraints and thus for deriving more precise numerical patterns which, in turn, are used to provide more precise groundness information. Indeed, we are requiring a quite complicated interaction between domains.

Another application of groundness analysis with fast access to ground variables is for *aliasing analysis*. The most popular domain for this kind of analysis is *Sharing* [13]. Without going into details, its strength over the previous approaches [15, 12] comes from the fact that it keeps track of groundness dependencies. In fact, *Sharing* has, as far as groundness information is concerned, the same power of *Def*. When *Pos* is used for groundness, using *Sharing* for aliasing at the same time is a waste: *Sharing* spends time and space for keeping track of groundness, which is already done, and more precisely, by *Pos*. A possible solution is to adopt

---

[1] We choose this form of presentation for clarity. It is clear that this agent will be itself compiled to something different. For instance, the second agent of the parallel composition will "live" in the groundness component, if the latter is able to capture the indicated dependency.

a variation of the domains proposed in [15, 12] (which are much less computationally expensive than *Sharing*) and to combine it with *Pos*. We are currently working along this line. This, however, is beyond the scope of this paper.

Whatever conceptual methodology you follow to realize the combination of any domain with one for groundness, a key component for the efficiency is that the implementation of the latter must be *reactive*. By this we mean that: (a) it must react quickly to external queries about the groundness of variables; and, (b) it must absorb quickly groundness notifications coming from other domains.

4 Binary Decision Trees and Diagrams

Binary decision trees (BDTs) and diagrams (BDDs) are well-known abstract representations of Boolean functions [5, 6]. Binary decision trees, such as the ones presented in Fig. 1 are binary trees where non-terminal nodes are labeled

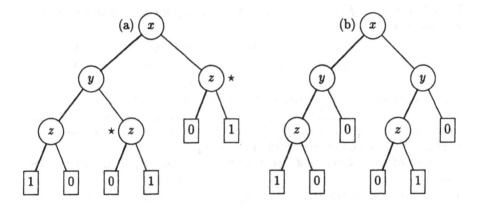

Fig. 1. OBDTs for $(x \land y) \leftrightarrow z$ (a) and $(x \leftrightarrow z) \land y$ (b).

with variable names, while terminal nodes are labeled with the Boolean constants 0 or 1. The value of the represented function, for a given assignment of Boolean values to variables, can be recovered by following a particular path from the root: at any non-terminal node labeled with a variable v, the thick branch is taken if v is assigned to 1, otherwise the thin branch is taken. The terminal node reached by this walk on the tree is the function value. For a non-terminal node n, we will call the node connected to n by means of the thick (resp. thin) edge the *true* (resp. *false*) *successor of n*. A BDD is a directed acyclic graph which can be thought of as obtained from a BDT by collapsing identical subtrees. With reference to Fig. 1 (a), the subtrees marked with '$\star$' can be collapsed, as well as all the terminal nodes having the same label. The action of collapsing identical subtrees does not change the represented function. Given a total ordering on the variable symbols, an *ordered binary decision tree* (OBDT) is a BDT where the sequence of variables (associated to non-terminals) encountered in any path from the root is strictly increasing. The trees depicted in Fig. 1 are indeed OBDTs where the ordering is such that $x \prec y \prec z$. Applying the very same restriction to BDDs we obtain the notion of *ordered binary decision diagram*, or OBDD.

Definition 4 (BDTs and OBDTs.) *A binary decision tree is any string generated by the grammar*

$$\text{BDT} ::= \mathbf{0} \mid \mathbf{1} \mid \text{ite}(v, \text{BDT}, \text{BDT})$$

where $v \in Vars$. The set of all BDTs is denoted by $\mathcal{B}$. The semantics of BDTs is expressed by the function $[\![\cdot]\!] : \mathcal{B} \to \mathcal{F}$, defined as follows:

$$[\![\mathbf{0}]\!] \stackrel{\text{def}}{=} \bot, \qquad [\![\mathbf{1}]\!] \stackrel{\text{def}}{=} \top, \qquad [\![\text{ite}(v, b_1, b_0)]\!] \stackrel{\text{def}}{=} ite(v, [\![b_1]\!], [\![b_0]\!]),$$

where for each $w \in Vars$, $f_1, f_0 \in \mathcal{F}$, and each $a \in \mathcal{A}$,

$$ite(w, f_1, f_0)(a) \stackrel{\text{def}}{=} \begin{cases} f_1(a), & \text{if } a(w) = 1; \\ f_0(a), & \text{if } a(w) = 0. \end{cases}$$

The subset $\mathcal{B}_o \subseteq \mathcal{B}$ of ordered BDTs (OBDTs) is defined be the following recurrent equation:

$$\mathcal{B}_o \stackrel{\text{def}}{=} \{0, 1\} \cup \left\{ \text{ite}(v, b_1, b_0) \left| \begin{array}{l} \forall i = 0, 1 : b_i \in \mathcal{B}_o \wedge \\ \exists w \in Vars . \exists b_1', b_0' \in \mathcal{B}_o . \\ b_i = \text{ite}(w, b_1', b_0') \Rightarrow v \prec w \end{array} \right. \right\}.$$

In the sequel we will deliberately confuse a BDT with the boolean function it represents. In particular, for $b \in \mathcal{B}$, when we write $vars(b)$ or $true(b)$ what we really mean is $vars([\![b]\!])$ or $true([\![b]\!])$. This convention of referring to the semantics simplifies the presentation and should not cause problems.

A *reduced ordered binary decision diagram*, or ROBDD, is an OBDD such that:

1. there are no duplicate terminal nodes;
2. there are no duplicate non-terminal nodes (i.e., nodes having the same label and the same true and false successors);
3. there are no redundant tests, that is each non-terminal node has distinct true and false successors.

Any OBDD can be converted into a ROBDD by repeatedly applying the reduction rules corresponding to the above properties: collapsing all the duplicate nodes into one and removing all the redundant tests, redirecting edges in the obvious way. Application of these rules does not change the represented functions. ROBDDs have one very important property: they are *canonical*. This means that, for each fixed variables' ordering, two ROBDDs represent the same function if and only if they are identical.

The nice computational features of ROBDDs make them suitable for implementing *Pos* (see, e.g., [16, 1]), even though ROBDDs are clearly able to represent any Boolean function. In this paper we deal formally only with OBDTs, since our results do not need all the properties of ROBDDs. Indeed, since every OBDT is an OBDD and the reduction rules do not change the represented Boolean function, everything we say about OBDTs is true also for ROBDDs.

5   Is x Ground?

Capturing dependency and disjunctive information is essential for precise ground-ness analysis. However, this kind of information is only needed for maintaining precise intermediate results *during* the analysis. Instead, the only information which is relevant for the user of the analysis' results is whether a certain vari-able is guaranteed to be ground at a certain point or not. When combinations of domains are considered, as explained in Sect. 3, it is vital to recover the set of ground variables quickly even *inside* the analysis. The problem of deriving this sure groundness information from ROBDDS has not been tackled in previous works [7, 16, 1]. Basically we know about five ways of doing that:

1. Given $x \in$ *Vars* and a ROBDD representation b of a boolean function f, use the ROBDD package to test whether $f \to x$ is a tautology, that is, whether $f \to x$ is equivalent to $\top$. This test can be performed in $O(|b|)$ time. The main advantage of this solution is that it does not require any change to the ROBDD package. One of the drawbacks is that the reduction of $f \to x$ causes the creation and disposal of "spurious" nodes.

2. Given $x \in$ *Vars* and a ROBDD representation b of a boolean function f, the information whether x is forced to 1 by f is obtained by visiting b. The answer is affirmative if (a) there is at least one node in b labeled with x; and, (b) each node in b labeled with x has its false branch equal to 0. This method has still linear complexity, requires the incorporation of the visit into the ROBDD package, and does not involve the creation of any node.

3. Another possibility is to visit the ROBDD representation b to derive, in one shot, the set G of *all* the variables which are forced to 1. We will see how this can be done in Sect. 6.

4. A variation of the previous method consists in avoiding visiting b, while obtaining exactly the same information, by modifying ROBDD's nodes so that every node records the set of variables which are forced to true by the boolean function it represents. Sect. 6 explains how this method of keeping explicit the information about true variables can be easily implemented.

5. The last method is based on a quite radical, though very simple, solution. Intuitively, it is based on the idea of keeping the information about true vari-ables totally separate from dependency and disjunctive information. True variables are represented naturally by means of sets whereas only the depen-dency and disjunctive information is maintained by means of ROBDDs. This will be explained in Sect. 7.

6   Extracting Sure Groundness from ROBDDs

Here is the only property of OBDTs (and thus of ROBDDs) we need.

Definition 5 (Weak normal form.) *A BDT $b \in \mathcal{B}$ is said to be in weak normal form if and only if either $b = 0$ or $b = 1$, or there exist $b_1, b_0 \in \mathcal{B}$ such that $b = \mathrm{ite}(v, b_1, b_0)$, $v \notin vars(b_1) \cup vars(b_0)$, and both b_1 and b_0 are in weak normal form.*

Proposition 6 *Each OBDT* $b \in B_o$ *is in weak normal form.*

This is indeed the distinctive property of "free BDDs" or "1-time branching programs", where no ordering is required but each path from the root is allowed to test a variable only once [6].

Theorem 7 *Let* $b = \text{ite}(v, b_1, b_0)$ *be in weak normal form. Then we have*

$$
true(b) = \begin{cases} true(b_0), & \text{if } b_1 = 0; \\ \{v\} \cup true(b_1), & \text{if } b_1 \neq 0 \text{ and } b_0 = 0; \\ true(b_1) \cap true(b_0), & \text{otherwise.} \end{cases}
$$

This theorem gives us at least two ways of deriving sure groundness information from ROBDDs. One is by implementing a post-order visit, collecting true variables as indicated. Another one, which is more in the spirit of a reactive implementation, is based on a modification of the node structure which is used to represent ROBDDs. In standard implementations, a non-terminal node n has one field $n.V$ which holds the test variable, plus two fields $n.T$ and $n.F$ which are references to the nodes which are the roots of the true and false branch, respectively. All the nodes are created by means of a function $create(v, @n_1, @n_0)$, taking a variable's symbol and two references to (already created) nodes, and returning a reference to the newly created node. We can modify this state of things by adding to the node structure a field $n.G$, containing the set of true variables for the function represented by the ROBDD rooted at n, and by modifying the creation function to initialize $n.G$ as indicated by Theorem 7.

7 A New, Hybrid Implementation for *Pos*

The observation of many constraint logic programs shows that the percentage of variables which are found to be ground during the analysis, for typical invocations, is as high as 80%. This suggests that representing *Pos* elements simply by means of ROBDDs, as in [16, 1], is probably not the best thing we can do. Here we propose a hybrid implementation where each *Pos* element is represented by a pair: the first component is the set of true variables (just as in the domain used in early groundness analyzers [17, 15]); the second component is a ROBDD. In each element of this new representation there is no redundancy: the ROBDD component does not contain any information about true variables. In fact, as we will see, the hybrid representation has the property that ROBDDs are used only in what they are good for: keeping track of dependencies and disjunctive information. True variables, instead are more efficiently represented by means of sets. The hybrid representation has two major advantages: (a) it is *reactive* in the sense of Sect. 3; and, (b) it allows for keeping the ROBDDs small, during the analysis, when many variables come out to be true, as it is often the case. Consider Fig. 1 (b): the information about y being a true variable (besides not being readily available) requires two nodes. In more involved cases, the information about trueness of a variable coming late in the ordering can be scattered over a large number of nodes. Notice that, while having many true variables, in a straight ROBDD implementation, means that the *final* ROBDDs will be very similar to a linear chain of nodes, the intermediate steps still require the creation (and disposal) of complex (and costly) ROBDDs. This phenomenon is avoided as much as possible in the hybrid implementation.

(By $\wp_f(Vars)$ we denote the set of all *finite* subsets of *Vars*.)

Definition 8 (Hybrid repr.) *The* hybrid representation *for Pos is*

$$\mathcal{G} \stackrel{\text{def}}{=} \{ \langle G, b \rangle \mid G \in \wp_f(Vars), b \in \mathcal{B}_o, vars(b) \cap G = true(b) = \emptyset \}.$$

The meaning of $\mathcal{G}$'s elements is given by the overloading $[\![\cdot]\!]: \mathcal{G} \to \mathcal{F}$:

$$[\![\langle G, b \rangle]\!] \stackrel{\text{def}}{=} \bigwedge(G) \wedge [\![b]\!],$$

where $\bigwedge\{x_1, \dots, x_n\} \stackrel{\text{def}}{=} x_1 \wedge \cdots \wedge x_n$ and $\bigwedge \emptyset \stackrel{\text{def}}{=} \top$.

Now, we briefly review the operations we need over *Pos* (and thus over $\mathcal{G}$) for the purpose of groundness analysis. The constraint accumulation process requires computing the logical conjunction of two functions, the merge over different computation paths amounts to logical disjunction, whereas projection onto a designated set of variables is handled through existential quantification. Functions of the kind $x \leftrightarrow (y_1, \dots, y_m)$, for $m \geq 0$, accommodate both abstract *mgus* and the combination operation in domains like $\text{Pat}(Pos)$ [9]. Before introducing the $\mathcal{G}$'s

$\mathcal{B}_o$ op	Complexity	Meaning	$\mathcal{G}$ op
$b_1 \barwedge b_2$	$O(\|b_1\|\|b_2\|)$	$[\![b_1]\!] \wedge [\![b_2]\!]$	$g_1 \otimes g_2$
$b_1 \veebar b_2$	$O(\|b_1\|\|b_2\|)$	$[\![b_1]\!] \vee [\![b_2]\!]$	$g_1 \oplus g_2$
$\ddot{\exists}_{\bar{V}} b$	$O(\|b\|^{2^{\|V\|}})$	$\exists_{\bar{V}} [\![b]\!]$	$\exists_{\bar{V}} g$
$\ddot{\bigwedge}(V)$	$O(\|V\|)$	$\bigwedge(V)$	
$x \ddot{\leftrightarrow} V$	$O(\|V\|)$	$x \leftrightarrow \bigwedge(V)$	
$b[1/V]$	$O(\|b\|)$	$[\![b]\!][1/V]$	

Note: $V \subseteq vars(b)$.

Note: $V \neq \emptyset$.

Note: $x \notin V$.

Table 1. Operations defined over $\mathcal{B}_o$ and $\mathcal{G}$.

operations we introduce, by means of Table 1, the needed operations over OBDTs and ROBDDs, their complexity and semantics, as well as the correspondent operations over $\mathcal{G}$. In the sequel we will refer to some operations on OBDTs whose meaning and complexity is specified in the table. The restriction operation $b[1/V]$ (also called *valuation* or *co-factoring*) is used for maintaining the invariant specified in Definition 8. In the definition of the abstract operators used in groundness analysis, the functions of the form $x \leftrightarrow (y_1, \dots, y_m)$ are always *conjuncted* with some other function. For this reason we provide a family of specialized operations $(x, V) \overset{\leftrightarrow}{\otimes} \colon \mathcal{G} \to \mathcal{G}$, indexed over variables and finite sets of variables. The operation $(x, V) \overset{\leftrightarrow}{\otimes}$ builds a representation for $(x \leftrightarrow \bigwedge(V)) \wedge f$, given one for f.

Definition 9 (Operations over $\mathcal{G}$.) *The operation $\otimes \colon \mathcal{G} \times \mathcal{G} \to \mathcal{G}$ is defined, for each $\langle G_1, b_1 \rangle, \langle G_2, b_2 \rangle \in \mathcal{G}$, as follows:*

$$\langle G_1, b_1 \rangle \otimes \langle G_2, b_2 \rangle \overset{\text{def}}{=} \eta\Big(G_1 \cup G_2, b_1 \left[1/(G_2 \setminus G_1) \right] \ddot{\wedge} \, b_2 \left[1/(G_1 \setminus G_2) \right] \Big),$$

where, for each $G \in \wp_f(\mathit{Vars})$ and $b \in \mathcal{B}_o$ such that $G \cap \mathit{vars}(b) = \emptyset$,

$$\eta(G, b) \overset{\text{def}}{=} \begin{cases} \langle G, b \rangle, & \text{if } \mathit{true}(b) = \emptyset; \\ \eta\Big(G \cup \mathit{true}(b), b[1/\mathit{true}(b)] \Big), & \text{otherwise.} \end{cases}$$

The join operation $\oplus \colon \mathcal{G} \times \mathcal{G} \to \mathcal{G}$ is given by

$$\langle G_1, b_1 \rangle \oplus \langle G_2, b_2 \rangle \overset{\text{def}}{=} \Big\langle G_1 \cap G_2, \big(b_1 \ddot{\wedge} \bigwedge(G_1 \setminus G_2) \big) \ddot{\vee} \big(b_2 \ddot{\wedge} \bigwedge(G_2 \setminus G_1) \big) \Big\rangle.$$

For each $\langle G, b \rangle \in \mathcal{G}$, each $V \in \wp_f(\mathit{Vars})$, and $x \in \mathit{Vars}$, the unary operations $\exists_V \colon \mathcal{G} \to \mathcal{G}$ and $(x, V) \overset{\leftrightarrow}{\otimes} \colon \mathcal{G} \to \mathcal{G}$ are given by

$$\exists_V \langle G, b \rangle \overset{\text{def}}{=} \langle G \setminus V, \exists_V b \rangle; \quad \text{and}$$

$$(x, V) \overset{\leftrightarrow}{\otimes} \langle G, b \rangle \overset{\text{def}}{=} \begin{cases} \eta\Big(G \cup V, b[1/(V \setminus G)] \Big), & \text{if } x \in G; \\ \eta\big(G \cup \{x\}, b[1/x] \big), & \text{if } V \subseteq G; \\ \eta\Big(G, b \ddot{\wedge} \big(x \leftrightarrow (V \setminus G) \big) \Big), & \text{if } x \notin G \text{ and } V \not\subseteq G. \end{cases}$$

The following result holds almost by definition.

Theorem 10 *The operations of* Definition 9 *are well-defined. Moreover, for each $g, g_1, g_2 \in \mathcal{G}$, each $V \in \wp_f(\mathit{Vars})$, and $x \in \mathit{Vars}$,*

$$[\![g_1 \otimes g_2]\!] = [\![g_1]\!] \wedge [\![g_2]\!], \qquad [\![g_1 \oplus g_2]\!] = [\![g_1]\!] \vee [\![g_2]\!],$$

$$[\![\exists_V g]\!] = \exists_V [\![g]\!], \qquad [\![(x, V) \overset{\leftrightarrow}{\otimes} g]\!] = (x \leftrightarrow \bigwedge(V)) \wedge [\![g]\!].$$

Notice that $\mathcal{G}$ operations make use of the $\mathcal{B}_o$ (ROBDD) operations only when strictly necessary. When this happens, expensive operations like $\ddot{\wedge}$ and $\ddot{\vee}$ are invoked with operands of the smallest possible size. In particular, we exploit the fact that the restriction operation is relatively cheap. However, we cannot avoid searching for true variables, as the $\otimes$ and $(x, V) \overset{\leftrightarrow}{\otimes}$ operators need that. For this purpose, the procedure implicit in Theorem 7 comes in handy. In programs where many variables are ground the ROBDDs generated will be kept small, and so also the cost of searching will be diminished. As a final remark, observe that in a real implementation the operations which are executed can be further optimized. Without entering into details, the basic analysis step, for what concerns groundness and in a bottom-up framework, generates *macro-operations* of the form $(x_1, V_1) \overset{\leftrightarrow}{\otimes} ((x_2, V_2) \overset{\leftrightarrow}{\otimes} (\cdots ((x_n, V_n) \overset{\leftrightarrow}{\otimes} (g_1 \otimes g_2 \otimes \cdots \otimes g_m)) \cdots))$. These operations can be greatly simplified by first collecting all the true variables in the g_i's in one sweep (a bunch of set unions) and iterating through the $(x_i, V_i) \overset{\leftrightarrow}{\otimes}$ indexes for collecting further true variables. Then the ROBDDs which occur in the macro-operation are restricted using the collected true variables and, at the end of this process, the ROBDD package is invoked over the simplified arguments. Only then we search for further true variables in the resulting ROBDD.

8   Experimental Evaluation

The ideas presented in this paper have been experimentally validated in the context of the development of the CHINA analyzer [2]. CHINA is a data-flow analyzer for $CLP(\mathcal{H}, \mathcal{N})$ languages (i.e. Prolog, $CLP(\mathcal{R})$, clp(FD) and so forth) written in Prolog and C++. It performs bottom-up analysis deriving information on both call and success patterns by means of program transformations and optimized fixpoint computation techniques.

The assessment of the hybrid domain has been done in a quite radical way. In fact, we have compared the standard, pure ROBDD-based implementation of *Pos* against the hybrid domain on the following problem: *deriving, once for each clause's evaluation, a boolean vector indicating which variables are known to be ground and which are not.* This is a very minimal demand for each analysis requiring the knowledge about definitely ground variables *during* the analysis. We have thus performed the analysis of a number of programs on a domain similar to Pat(*Pos*) [9], switching off all the other domains currently supported by CHINA[2]. Pat($\mathfrak{R}$) is a generic structural domain which is parametric with respect to any abstract domain $\mathfrak{R}$. Roughly speaking, Pat($\mathfrak{R}$) associates to each variable the following information:

- a *pattern*, that is to say, the principal functor and subterms which are bound to the variable;
- the "properties" of the variable, which are delegated to the $\mathfrak{R}$ domain (the two implementations of *Pos*, in our case).

As reported in [8], Pat(*Pos*) is a very precise domain for groundness analysis.

The experimental results are reported in Table 2. The table gives, for each program, the analysis times and the number of ROBDD nodes allocated for the standard implementation (STD) and the hybrid one (HYB), respectively. It also shows the ratio STD/HYB for the above mentioned figures (S/H). The computation times have been taken on a 80486DX4 machine with 32 MB of RAM running Linux 1.3.64. The tested programs have become standard for the evaluation of data-flow analyzers. They are a cutting-stock program CS, the generate and test version of a disjunctive scheduling program Disj, a program to put boolean formulas in disjunctive normal form DNF, the Browse program Gabriel taken from

---

[2] Namely, numerical bounds and relations, aliasing, and polymorphic types

	Analysis time (sec)			N. of BDD nodes		
Program	STD	HYB	S/H	STD	HYB	S/H
CS	1.06	0.6	1.77	12387	391	31.7
Disj	1.06	0.6	1.77	72918	176	414.3
DNF	5.17	4.4	1.18	5782	111	52.1
Gabriel	1.13	0.74	1.53	28634	10472	2.73
Kalah	3.92	2.02	1.94	43522	645	67.5
Peep	6.13	5.52	1.11	176402	128332	1.37
PG	0.37	0.25	1.48	3732	86	43.4
Plan	0.59	0.5	1.18	1736	65	26.7

Table 2. Experimental results obtained with the CHINA analyzer.

Gabriel benchmark, an alpha-beta procedure Kalah, the peephole optimizer of SB-Prolog Peep, a program PG written by W. Older to solve a particular mathematical problem, and the famous planning program Plan by D.H.D. Warren.

The results indicate that the hybrid implementation outperforms the standard one in both time and space efficiency. The systematic speed-up obtained was not expected. Indeed, we were prepared to content ourselves with a moderate slowdown which would have been recovered in the reactive combinations. The space figures show that we have achieved significant (and sometimes huge) savings in the number of allocated ROBDD nodes. With the hybrid domain we are thus able to keep the ROBDDs which are created and traversed during the analysis as small as possible. This phenomenon is responsible for the speed-up. It seems that, even for programs characterized by not-so-many ground variables, there are always enough ground variables to make the hybrid implementation competitive. This can be observed, for instance, in the case of the Peep program, which was analyzed with a non-ground, most-general input pattern. The following additional observations are important for a full understanding of Table 2:

1. we are not comparing against a poor standard implementation of *Pos*, as can be seen by comparing the analysis times with those of [8]. The ROBDD package we are using is fine-tuned: it employs separate caches for the main operations (with hit-rates in the range 95%–99% for almost all programs), specialized and optimized versions of the important operations over ROBDDs, as well as aggressive memory allocation strategies. Indeed, we were led to the present work by the apparent impossibility of further optimizing the standard implementation. Moreover, the hybrid implementation has room for improvement, especially for what concerns the handling of bit-vectors.
2. We are not taking into account the cost of garbage-collection for ROBDD nodes. In particular, the sizes of the relevant data-structures were chosen so that the analysis of the tested programs could run to completion without any node deallocation or reallocation.

3. The boolean vectors computed during our test analyses are what is necessary for, say, the quick handling of delayed constraints and goals, and the efficient simplification of aliasing information. However, the experiment does not take into account the inevitable gains which are a consequence of the fast access to ground variables. Furthermore, in a truly reactive combination, the set of ground variables is not needed only at the end of each clause's evaluation (this is the optimistic hypothesis under which we conducted the experimentation), but at each body-atom evaluation for each clause. In this context the hybrid implementation, due to its incrementality, is even more favored with respect to the standard one (which is not incremental at all).

9 Conclusion

We have studied the problem, given an implementation of *Pos* based on ROB-DDs, of determining as efficiently as possible the set of variables which are forced to true in the abstract representation. We have explained why, for the sake of realizing reactive combinations of domains, it is important to detect these variables (which correspond to *ground* ones at the concrete level) as quickly as possible. This problem has not been treated before in the literature [16, 1, 19]. After reviewing the *naïf* approaches, we have presented a simple method of detecting all the true variables in a ROBDD representation at once. We have then proposed a novel hybrid representation for Boolean functions. This representation is designed in a way to take advantage from the observation that most programs (together with their typical queries) have a high percentage of variables which are deemed to be ground at the program points of interest. With the new representation, not only the information about true (ground) variables is always readily available (instead of being scattered all over the ROBDDs), but we are also able to keep the usage of (expensive) ROBDDs at a minimum. This is clearly important for efficiency reasons. In fact, we have presented the experimental results obtained with a prototype implementation of the hybrid domain which outperforms, from any point of view, the standard implementation based on ROBDDs only. Surprisingly enough, we have thus been able to assess the superiority of the hybrid domain even for those cases where fast access to ground variables is not important.

References

1. T. Armstrong, K. Marriott, P. Schachte, and H. Sondergaard. Two classes of boolean functions for dependency analysis. Technical Report 94/211, Dept. Computer Science, Monash University, Melbourne, 1994.
2. R. Bagnara. On the detection of implicit and redundant numeric constraints in CLP programs. In M. Alpuente, R. Barbuti, and I. Ramos, editors, *Proceedings of the "1994 Joint Conference on Declarative Programming (GULP-PRODE '94)"*, pages 312–326, Peñíscola, Spain, September 1994.

3. R. Bagnara. A hierarchy of constraint systems for data-flow analysis of constraint logic-based languages. Technical Report TR-96-10, Dipartimento di Informatica, Università di Pisa, 1996. To appear on a special issue of "Science of Computer Programming".

4. R. Bagnara, R. Giacobazzi, and G. Levi. An application of constraint propagation to data-flow analysis. In *Proceedings of "The Ninth Conference on Artificial Intelligence for Applications"*, pages 270–276, Orlando, Florida, March 1993. IEEE Computer Society Press, Los Alamitos, CA.

5. R. E. Bryant. Graph-based algorithms for boolean function manipulation. *IEEE Transactions on Computers*, C-35(8):677–691, August 1986.

6. R. E. Bryant. Symbolic boolean manipulation with ordered binary-decision diagrams. *ACM Computing Surveys*, 24(3):293–318, September 1992.

7. A. Cortesi, G. Filè, and W. Winsborough. *Prop* revisited: Propositional formula as abstract domain for groundness analysis. In *Proc. Sixth IEEE Symp. on Logic In Computer Science*, pages 322–327. IEEE Computer Society Press, 1991.

8. A. Cortesi, B. Le Charlier, and P. Van Hentenryck. Conceptual and software support for abstract domain design: Generic structural domain and open product. Technical Report CS-93-13, Brown University, Providence, RI, 1993.

9. A. Cortesi, B. Le Charlier, and P. Van Hentenryck. Combinations of abstract domains for logic programming. In *Conference Record of POPL '94: 21st ACM SIGPLAN-SIGACT Symposium on Principles of Programming Languages*, pages 227–239, Portland, Oregon, January 1994.

10. P. Cousot and R. Cousot. Systematic design of program analysis frameworks. In *Proc. Sixth ACM Symp. Principles of Programming Languages*, pages 269–282, 1979.

11. P. Cousot and R. Cousot. Abstract interpretation and applications to logic programs. *Journal of Logic Programming*, 13(2 & 3):103–179, 1992.

12. S. K. Debray. Static Inference of Modes and Data Dependencies in Logic Programs. *ACM Transactions on Programming Languages and Systems (TOPLAS)*, 11(3):418–450, 1989.

13. D. Jacobs and A. Langen. Accurate and efficient approximation of variable aliasing in logic programs. In E. Lusk and R. Overbeek, editors, *Proc. North American Conf. on Logic Programming'89*, pages 154–165. The MIT Press, Cambridge, Mass., 1989.

14. J. Jaffar, S. Michaylov, P. Stuckey, and R. Yap. The CLP($\mathcal{R}$) language and system. *ACM Transactions on Programming Languages and Systems*, 14(3):339–395, 1992.

15. N. D. Jones and H. Søndergaard. A semantics-based framework for the abstract interpretation of Prolog. In S. Abramsky and C. Hankin, editors, *Abstract Interpretation of Declarative Languages*, pages 123–142. Ellis Horwood Ltd, 1987.

16. B. Le Charlier and P. Van Hentenryck. Groundness analysis for Prolog: Implementation and evaluation of the domain prop. In *Proceedings of the ACM SIGPLAN Symposium on Partial Evaluation and Semantics-Based Program Manipulation*, pages 99–110. ACM Press, 1993.

17. C. Mellish. Some global optimizations for a Prolog compiler. *Journal of Logic Programming*, 2:43–66, 1985.

18. V. A. Saraswat. *Concurrent Constraint Programming*. MIT Press Cambridge, Mass., 1993.

19. P. Van Hentenryck, A. Cortesi, and B. Le Charlier. Evaluation of the domain PROP. *Journal of Logic Programming*, 23(3):237–278, June 1995. Extended version of [16].

Dynamic Attribute Grammars
(*Extended Abstract*)

Didier PARIGOT, Gilles ROUSSEL, Martin JOURDAN and Étienne DURIS*

INRIA and Université de Marne-la-Vallée

Abstract. Although Attribute Grammars were introduced long ago, their lack of expressiveness has resulted in limited use outside the domain of static language processing. With the new notion of *Dynamic Attribute Grammars* defined on top of *Grammar Couples*, we show that it is possible to extend this expressiveness and to describe computations on structures that are not just trees, but also on abstractions allowing for infinite structures. The result is a language that is comparable in power to most first-order functional languages, with a distinctive declarative character.

In this paper, we give a formal definition of Dynamic Attribute Grammars and show how to construct efficient visit-sequence-based evaluators for them, using traditional, well-established AG techniques (in our case, using the FNC-2 system).

Keywords: Attribute Grammars, static analysis, implementation, dynamic semantics, applicative programming.

1 Introduction and Related Work

Attribute Grammars were introduced thirty years ago by Knuth [15] and, since then, they have been widely studied [7, 6, 2, 17]. An Attribute Grammar is a declarative specification that describes how attributes (variables) are computed for rules in a particular grammar (i.e., it is syntax-directed). They were originally introduced as a formalism for describing compilation applications and were intended to describe how to decorate a tree representing the program to compile. In this application area, Attribute Grammars were recognized as having these two important qualities:

- they have a natural *structural decomposition* that corresponds to the syntactic structure of the language, and
- they are *declarative* in that the writer only specifies the rules used to compute attribute values, but not the order in which they will be applied.

---

* Gilles Roussel is with Université de Marne-la-Vallée, 2, allée du Promontoire, 93166 Noisy-le-Grand, France; e-mail: `roussel@univ-mlv.fr`. The other authors are with INRIA, Projet OSCAR, Domaine de Voluceau, Rocquencourt, BP 105, 78153 Le Chesnay Cedex, France; e-mail: {Didier.Parigot, Martin.Jourdan, Etienne.Duris}@inria.fr; Web page: `http://www-rocq.inria.fr/oscar/FNC-2/`.

In spite of that, Attribute Grammar specifications are still not as widely used as they could be. We believe that one of the main reasons for this is their lack of expressiveness, which is due to the fact that, because of their historical roots in compiler construction, the notion of (physical) tree was considered as the only way to direct computations. Some works have attempted to respond to this problem by proposing extensions to the classical Attribute Grammar formalism, for instance Circular Attribute Grammars [9], Multi-Attributed Grammars [3], Higher-Order Attribute Grammars [21] or Conditional Attribute Grammars [4]. Our own work [18, 19] has similarities with the latter two (like with HOAGs, the computation tree is not isomorphic to the input tree, and like with CAGs, attribute values can influence the choice of semantic rules to compute) but our approach differs in important respects. First, for us, the notion of *grammar* does *not* necessarily imply the existence of a (physical) *tree* and, in fact, our evaluators can work *without any tree*. Secondly, our implementation technique is a simple derivation of the traditional visit-sequence-based evaluation paradigm and does not require the construction of any additional piece of tree.

Our view of the grammar underlying an Attribute Grammar is similar to the grammar describing all the call trees for a given functional program or all the proof trees for a given logic program: the grammar precisely describes the various possible flows of control. In this context, a production describes an elementary recursion scheme (control flow) [5], whereas the semantic rules describe the computations associated with this scheme (data flow).

It is very important to observe that all the theoretical and practical results on Attribute Grammars are based *only* on the abstraction of the control flow by means of a grammar and not at all on how its instances are obtained at run-time. In particular, this applies to the algorithms for constructing efficient evaluators for various subclasses of Attribute Grammars and the global static analysis methods [10, 2, 17].

In consequence, we present two notions which comply with this view:

- *Grammar Couples* allow to describe recursion schemes independently from any physical structure and/or to exhibit a different combination of the elements of a physical structure. A grammar couple defines an association between a dynamic grammar and a (possibly empty) concrete grammar.
- *Dynamic Attribute Grammars* (DAGs) allow attribute values to influence the flow of control by selecting alternative dynamic productions. We define the new notion of *semantic rules blocks*, decision trees for productions and their semantic rules.

These extensions result in a programming language similar to a first-order language with a functional flavor (because of the single-assignment property) that retains the distinctive declarative character of Attribute Grammars. They have been easily implemented in Olga, the input language to our FNC-2 system [12, 11].

An informal, example-based comparison of Dynamic Attribute Grammars with other programming paradigms appears in [18], together with a discussion of how this leads to fruitful applications regarding analysis and implementation techniques. In this paper, we concentrate instead on the definition and implementation of DAGs. At this point, the semantics of DAGs is given by their functional implementation, as described here; we are working on a more elegant formulation of the semantics, which would be too long to present here anyhow. This paper is a much shortened version of [20], in which the interested reader will find more details, more formalism and all the proofs.

The remainder of this article is divided in two sections. The first one presents successively the classical definition of Attribute Grammars, the two new notions of *Grammar Couple* and *Dynamic Attribute Grammar* and finally the construction of a classical Attribute Grammar which has the same "behavior" as a given DAG (the *Abstract Attribute Grammar*, or AAG, associated with the DAG). The second section demonstrates how to use classical AG-implementation techniques to produce efficient, visit-sequence-based evaluators for DAGs.

2 Dynamic Attribute Grammars

2.1 Recalls on Classical Attribute Grammars

Definition 1 (Context-Free Grammar). A *context-free grammar* is a tuple $G = (N, T, Z, P)$ in which:

- N is a set of non-terminals;
- T is a set of terminals, $N \cap T = \emptyset$;
- Z is the root non-terminal (start symbol), $Z \in N$;
- P is a set of productions, $p : X_0 \rightarrow X_1 \ldots X_n$ with $X_0 \in N$ and $X_i \in (T \cup N)$.

In this paper, we will forget about terminals and parsing problems and consider a grammar as an algebraic definition of a family of trees (or terms or structures).

Definition 2 (Attribute Grammar). An *Attribute Grammar* is a tuple $AG = (G, A, F)$ where:

- $G = (N, T, Z, P)$ is a context-free grammar;
- $A = \bigcup_{X \in N} H(X) \uplus S(X)$ is a set of attributes, with $H(X)$ the *inherited* attributes of $X \in N$ and $S(X)$ the *synthesized* ones;
- $F = \bigcup_{p \in P} F(p)$ is a set of semantic rules, where f_{p,a,X_i} designates the semantic rule defining the attribute occurrence $a(X_i)$ in production $p : X_0 \rightarrow X_1 \ldots X_n$ and $a \in A(X_i)$.

In the previous definitions, there is some ambiguity in the use of symbol X_i. In the CFG definition, they represent non-terminals whereas, in the AG definition, they represent both the non-terminal occurrence (labeled by its position in the production) and the non-terminal (type) itself. However, the position of a name in a production is only relevant for X_0, or to distinguish two non-terminal occurrences and their types. Therefore, we consider a production as a set of distinct names (with a specific one for the left-hand side), each with a type.

Definition 3 (Production). Let V be a universal finite set of *names*. A production $p : X_0 \rightarrow X_1 \dots X_n$ in a CFG is a tuple $((X_0, V_p), type_p)$ in which:

i. $V_p = \{X_1, X_2, \dots, X_n\} \subset V$, with $n = Card(V_p)$, and $X_0 \in V - V_p$;
ii. $type_p : V_p^\oplus \rightarrow N \cup T$, where $V_p^\oplus = \{X_0\} \cup V_p$, is a function which associates to each name a unique type in the set of non-terminals and terminals, such that $type_p(X_0) \in N$.

In the sequel of this paper, we will use the clearest of our two notations for a production—$p : X_0 \rightarrow X_1 \dots X_n$ or $((X_0, V_p), type_p)$—according to the context.
   We now give some notations relative to such a production:

- $LHS(p) = X_0$ and $RHS(p) = V_p$.
- $W_u(p)$, the set of *input* or *used* attribute occurrences in p, and $W_d(p)$, the set of *output* or *defined* attribute occurrences, are defined as usual; $W(p) = W_u(p) \cup W_d(p)$.

We will deal only with well-formed AGs, so $F(p)$ shall contain exactly one semantic rule defining each *output* occurrence. Furthermore, all our AGs will be in normal form.

2.2 Dynamic Attribute Grammars

As said in the introduction, the basis for a Dynamic Attribute Grammar is a grammar which describes the control flow (recursion scheme) of the intended application. This control flow can depend purely on attribute values but also on the shape of some physical tree, which will then be a distinguished parameter to the evaluator. Hence we have to make a difference, but also establish a correspondence, between the grammar which describes the concrete structure and the one which describes the computation scheme (which will "contain" the former, in some sense). This is the motivation for the notion of Grammar Couple.

Definition 4 (Grammar Couple). A *Grammar Couple* $G = (G_d, G_c, Concrete)$ is a pair of context-free grammars $G_d = (N_d, T_d, Z_d, P_d)$ and $G_c = (N_c, T_c, Z_c, P_c)$ and a function $Concrete : P_d \times V \rightarrow (P_c \times V) \cup \{\bot\}$, where:

1. $N_c \subseteq N_d$; $T_d = T_c$; if G_c is not empty[2] then $Z_d = Z_c$.
2. $\forall p_d \in P_d$, we have:
   i. $\forall X \in V_{p_d}^\oplus$, $type_{p_d}(X) \in (N_d - N_c) \Rightarrow Concrete(p_d, X) = \bot$;
   ii. $type_{p_d}(LHS(p_d)) \in (N_d - N_c) \Rightarrow \forall X \in RHS(p_d)$, $type_{p_d}(X) \in (N_d - N_c)$;
   iii. $type_{p_d}(LHS(p_d)) \in N_c \Rightarrow \exists ! \ p_c \in P_c$ such that:
      - $Concrete(p_d, LHS(p_d)) = (p_c, LHS(p_c))$ and $type_{p_d}(LHS(p_d)) = type_{p_c}(LHS(p_c))$;
      - $\forall X \in RHS(p_d)$, $type_{p_d}(X) \in N_c \Rightarrow \exists Y \in V_{p_c}^\oplus$ such that $Concrete(p_d, X) = (p_c, Y)$ and $type_{p_d}(X) = type_{p_c}(Y)$.

---

[2] In completely tree-less applications, such as the factorial function [18], G_c is empty and *Concrete* maps any element to $\bot$.

3. $\forall p, q \in P_d$ such that $type_p(LHS(p)) = type_q(LHS(q))$ and
$Concrete(p, LHS(p)) = Concrete(q, LHS(q))$, we have:
   i. $LHS(p) = LHS(q)$;
   ii. $\forall X \in V_p \cap V_q, type_p(X) = type_q(X)$;
   iii. $\forall X \in V_p \cap V_q, Concrete(p, X) = Concrete(q, X)$.

Given the above constraints, we can unambiguously extend the function $Concrete$ to productions p_d of P_d.

In the previous definition, G_d and G_c respectively represent the *dynamic* and *concrete* grammars, and $Concrete$ gives the concrete production (or name) corresponding to a dynamic one, i.e. a physical tree (or node). When the value of this function is $\perp$ (undefined), it means that the argument is a purely dynamic, or "abstract" object (it corresponds to some pure recursion scheme).

A dynamic production p_d is either purely abstract or associated with a unique corresponding concrete production p_c, which has the same type as LHS. Furthermore, for all non-terminals with a concrete type in the RHS of p_d, there exists in p_c a corresponding non-terminal with the same type. Note that a given physical structure may be referenced more than once in the dynamic production and that the concrete LHS, which by definition is associated with the dynamic LHS, may also be referenced again in the dynamic RHS. *These "special effects" are the essence of DAGs* and allow to express computations that were deemed impossible with classical AGs. The latter effect is illustrated in our **while** example (see below), whereas the former is used in the *double* example of [18].

Condition 3 stems from the constraint that, for two productions with the same LHS type and the same associated $Concrete$[3], the LHS must have the same name and all names common to both productions must have the same type. This implies in particular that, if the corresponding $Concrete$ counterpart of a such common name is not undefined, it is actually the same concrete object.

Our running example in this paper will be to define (an excerpt of) the *dynamic semantics* of a programming language with a DAG describing an interpreter. This application is out of the reach of traditional AGs and is the basis for our translation of denotational semantics into DAGs [16]. Fig. 1 presents the structure of the **while** statement as part of a grammar couple $(G_d, G_c, Concrete)$. **STAT**,**COND** $\in N_d \cup N_c$ respectively represent statements and boolean conditions. **name**:**TYPE** means that **TYPE** is the type of **name** and **name_d=name_c** means that $Concrete(p_d, \text{name\_d}) = (p_c, \text{name\_c})$.[4] $p \in P_c$ is the concrete production which describes that a **while** statement is made of a condition and a body statement. p_r and $p_t \in P_d$ are two dynamic productions which represent the recursive and termination behaviours of a **while** structure.

A semantic rules block is a conditional structure (decision tree) which defines all the dynamic productions that are applicable at a same point (either associated with the same concrete production or the same purely dynamic non-terminal, see the constraints in definition 7 below), their semantic rules and the conditions specifying how to choose between them.

---

[3] with possibly $Concrete = \perp$.

[4] where p_d and p_c are unambiguously defined by the context.

Concrete production $p \in P_c$:

p: `while:STAT -> cond:COND body:STAT`

Dynamic productions p_r and $p_t \in P_d$:

p_r: `w=while:STAT -> cond=cond:COND body=body:STAT loop=while:STAT`

p_t: `w=while:STAT -> cond=cond:COND`

Fig. 1. Part of a grammar couple for the **while** statement

```
( h.env(cond) := h.env(w),                         — common semantic rule R
  ( (s.c(cond)),                                    — boolean expression
    ( w=while:STAT -> cond=cond:COND body=body:STAT loop=while:STAT,
      h.env(body) := h.env(w)                       — true case : ⟨p_r, R'⟩
      h.env(loop) := s.env(body)
      s.env(w) := s.env(loop) ),
    ( w=while:STAT -> cond=cond:COND,               — false case : ⟨p_t, R''⟩
      s.env(w) := h.env(w) ) ) )
```

Fig. 2. The semantic rules block for the **while** statement

Definition 5 (Semantic Rules Block). A semantic rules block b is inductively defined as follows:

$$b = \langle R, \langle e, b, b \rangle \rangle \mid \langle p, R \rangle$$

where R is a possibly empty set of (unconditional) semantic rules, e is a condition (boolean expression over attribute occurrences) and p is a production.

Fig. 2 presents the semantic rules block describing the denotational-like semantics of the **while** statement. Attributes names are prefixed by **h.** for inherited, and **s.** for synthesized. The attribute **env** represents the execution environment (store, etc.) of a statement and **s.c** carries the value of the condition.

In a block, semantic rules are associated with any node of the decision tree whereas the productions appear only at the leaves. The following definition shows how a block is "flattened" into a collection of traditional productions-with-semantic-rules.

Definition 6 ($\mathcal{R}^b$ set). For each block b, $\mathcal{R}^b$ is the set of all semantic rules in b, qualified by the conjunction (path) of conditions that constrain (enable) them and the production to which they are attached:

- $\mathcal{R}^{\langle p, R \rangle} = \{((\varepsilon, p), R)\}$

- $\mathcal{R}^{\langle R, \langle e, b_{true}, b_{false} \rangle \rangle} =$
    let $\mathcal{R}^{b_{true}} = \cup_i((c_i, p_i), R_i),$
         $\mathcal{R}^{b_{false}} = \cup_j((c_j, p_j), R_j)$
    in $\cup_i(((e, true).c_i, p_i), R \cup R_i) \bigcup \cup_j(((e, false).c_j, p_j), R \cup R_j).$

The $\mathcal{R}^b$ set for our **while** example can be derived from Fig. 3 below by forgetting about the DP transformation introduced before definition 9.

For a given semantic rules block b, we define $\mathcal{PR}^b$ as the set of all productions in b: $\mathcal{PR}^b = \{p \mid ((c,p), R) \in \mathcal{R}^b\}$. We say that the pair $((c,p), R)$ is *well-formed* if the semantic rules set R is well-formed for the production p and each condition e in path c refers only to input attribute occurrences of p.

We are now ready to define complete Dynamic Attribute Grammars.

Definition 7 (Dynamic AG). A *Dynamic Attribute Grammar* is a tuple $AG = (G, A, F)$ where:

- $G = (G_d, G_c, Concrete)$ is a grammar couple;
- $A = \bigcup_{X \in N_d} H(X) \uplus S(X)$ is a set of attributes;
- F is a set of semantic rules blocks such that:
  1. $\forall b \in F$, every $((c,p), R) \in \mathcal{R}^b$ is well-formed, as defined above;
  2. $\forall p \in P_d, \exists! \, b \in F$ such that $p \in \mathcal{PR}^b$;
  3. $\forall p, q \in P_d$, with $p \in \mathcal{PR}^{b_i}$ and $q \in \mathcal{PR}^{b_j}$, such that $type_p(LHS(p)) = type_q(LHS(q)) = X$, we have:
     - $X \in (N_d - N_c) \Rightarrow b_i = b_j$;
     - $X \in N_c \Rightarrow (b_i = b_j \Leftrightarrow Concrete(p) = Concrete(q))$.

A Dynamic Attribute Grammar describes a function taking as arguments:

- values for all the inherited attributes of the start symbol (since these are not banned), and
- if the concrete grammar in the grammar couple is not empty, a concrete tree described by this grammar,

and which returns the values of the synthesized attributes of the start symbol. The computation of the attributes is defined in an "obvious" way and is guided at each "dynamic node" by the values of the various conditions and, when relevant, by the production applied at the corresponding concrete node. The formal definition of the semantics of a DAG, based on the notion of consistently attributed dynamic (virtual) trees, is the topic of our present work; in the meantime, it will be defined by its implementation, as described below, and we hope that the sequel of this paper and the examples in [18] will help the reader intuitively grasp the semantics and operation of a DAG.

2.3 Abstract Attribute Grammars

We claimed earlier that Dynamic Attribute Grammars could be implemented using the same techniques as classical AGs. The basic idea is simple [10]:

1. build from the given DAG a classical AG which has the same "behavior" (syntax—i.e., recursion scheme—and dependencies—i.e., data flow);
2. generate the evaluator for this classical AG;
3. transform this evaluator so that it correctly implements the original DAG.

In this section, we show how to construct this equivalent classical AG, which we call the *Abstract Attribute Grammar* (AAG) associated with the DAG.

Let $b = \langle R, \langle e, (p_T, R_T), (p_F, R_F) \rangle \rangle \rangle$ be the simplest form of a (conditional) block. Basically, the productions and semantic rules in the AAG which will reproduce the behavior of this block are, on one hand, p_T associated with the rules in $R \cup R_T$ and, on the other hand, $(p_F, R \cup R_F)$. This is indeed correct from the point of view of the recursion schemes and data flows, and the well-formedness conditions on the DAG will ensure that the resulting AAG will also be well-formed. The definition below formalizes this intuition and adds the very important constraint that no attribute defined by a rule in the groups subject to the condition (R_T and R_F) can be evaluated before the condition.

Definition 8 (Abstract AG). The *Abstract Attribute Grammar* for a given Dynamic Attribute Grammar $DAG = (G = (G_d, G_c, Concrete), A, F)$ is a tuple $AAG = (G_a, A_a, F_a)$ where:

- $G_a = (N_a, T_a, Z_a, P_a)$; $N_a = N_d$; $Z_a = Z_d$; $T_a = T_d$; $A_a = A$;
- $P_a = \{c.p_d : X_0 \rightarrow X_1 \ldots X_{n_{p_d}} \mid \exists b \in F, ((c, p_d), R) \in \mathcal{R}^b$ with $p_d : X_0 \rightarrow X_1 \ldots X_{n_{p_d}} \in P_d\}$;
- $F_a = \cup_{p \in P_a} F_a(p)$ is a set of semantic rules, with $F_a(p) = R$ such that $p = c.p_d$ and $\exists b \in F, ((c, p_d), R) \in \mathcal{F}^b$, with $\mathcal{F}^b$ defined below.

In this definition, $c.p_d$ is just a name for a production in AAG which encodes its origins in DAG: the production p_d and sequence of guards c. For instance, for our **while** example, the two productions in the AAG in Fig. 3 below are the same as p_r and p_t in Fig. 1, up to the production names.

Let DP be the transformation which, to a given semantic rule of the form $f_{p,a,X} : a(X) := exp$ and a condition e seen as an expression over some attribute occurrences, associates the modified semantic rule $DP(f_{p,a,X}, e) : a(X) := dp(exp, e)$, where dp is the polymorphic function defined as $dp(x, y) = x$. The definition of DP extends to set of semantic rules: $DP(R, e) = \{DP(f_{p,a,X}, e) \mid f_{p,a,X} \in R\}$. The purpose of DP is to make sure that a given attribute cannot be evaluated before condition e, without altering its value.

Definition 9 ($\mathcal{F}^b$ set). For each block b, $\mathcal{F}^b$ is the set of all semantic rules in b, qualified *and modified* by the conjunction (path) of conditions that constrain (enable) them and attached to their respective production:

- $\mathcal{F}^{\langle p, R \rangle} = \{((\varepsilon, p), R)\}$

- $\mathcal{F}^{\langle R, \langle e, b_{true}, b_{false} \rangle \rangle} =$
    let $\mathcal{F}^{b_{true}} = \cup_i((c_i, p_i), R_i)$,
    $\quad\mathcal{F}^{b_{false}} = \cup_j((c_j, p_j), R_j)$
    in $\cup_i(((e, true).c_i, p_i), R \cup DP(R_i, e))$
    $\quad\bigcup\cup_j(((e, false).c_j, p_j), R \cup DP(R_j, e))$.

This is nearly the same as the flattened form $\mathcal{R}_b$, except that it makes explicit the "control dependencies" on the conditions. Fig. 3 presents the productions and modified semantic rules in the AAG for the **while** statement.

```
{((((s.c(cond), true),
    w=while:STAT -> cond=cond:COND body=body:STAT loop=while:STAT),
        h.env(cond) := h.env(w)
        h.env(body) := dp(h.env(w),s.c(cond))
        h.env(loop) := dp(s.env(body),s.c(cond))
        s.env(w)    := dp(s.env(loop),s.c(cond))),
 (((s.c(cond), false), w=while:STAT -> cond=cond:COND),
        h.env(cond) := h.env(w)
        s.env(w)    := dp(h.env(w),c(cond))))}
```

Fig. 3. Productions and modified semantic rules in the Abstract AG for the **while** statement

---

It is clear that, given an "abstract" tree that represents the same recursion scheme as some computation described by the DAG, the AAG describes the same computation over this tree: the values of the attributes will be the same and, *a posteriori*, we can check that the conditions will have the same values, too. The other additions to the AAG are pure dependencies which ensure that the evaluation of the conditions and of the attributes alternate in the "right" order. This observation is the basis for the formal definition of the semantics of a DAG, on which we are working.

3 Visit-Sequence-Based Implementation

In this section, we show how to produce evaluators for dynamic AGs based on the visit sequence paradigm [14, 8, 1]. This is our preferred method because: these evaluators reach the best compromise between the time and space efficiency and the generality of the AG class they can implement; this is the paradigm we have implemented in FNC-2 [12] (for the reason just mentioned and for their versatility); and they are the easiest to transform into functions or procedures, which gives a basis for our studies on the relationships between AGs and functional programming [18].

The presentation in this version of the paper is very informal, relying almost entirely on pictures and examples. The formal definitions, the theorems and their proofs appear in [20].

Fig. 4 illustrates the generation process and introduces the various objects it manipulates. It proceeds as follows (the figure numbers refer to the corresponding objects for the **while** example):

1. We construct the abstract AG corresponding to the given dynamic AG and test or make sure that it is *l*-ordered, by exhibiting or constructing appropriate totally-ordered partitions (TOPs) $\{T_X \mid X \in N\}$ of the attributes of each non-terminal. Since not all AGs are *l*-ordered, this may fail for some dynamic AGs. For the **while** example we have $T_{\text{STAT}} = \{\text{h.env}\}\{\text{s.env}\}$ and $T_{\text{COND}} = \{\text{h.env}\}\{\text{s.env, s.c}\}$.

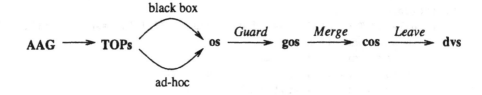

black box

AAG $\longrightarrow$ TOPs $\overbrace{}$ os $\xrightarrow{\text{\textit{Guard}}}$ gos $\xrightarrow{\text{\textit{Merge}}}$ cos $\xrightarrow{\text{\textit{Leave}}}$ dvs

ad-hoc

Fig. 4. The basic idea

$\mathcal{G}uard((s.c(cond), true).p_r, os_{p_r}) =$
    h.env(w), h.env(cond), s.c(cond), $cond_{s.c(cond)}$,
    h.env(body), s.env(body), h.env(loop), s.env(loop), s.env(w)
$\mathcal{G}uard((s.c(cond), false).p_t, os_{p_t}) =$
    h.env(w), h.env(cond), s.c(cond), $cond_{s.c(cond)}$, s.env(w)

Fig. 5. Guarded ordered sequences for the **while** productions

---

2. Using these TOPs, we generate, for each of the productions of the AAG, a separate visit sequence represented by an *ordered sequence os*, i.e. an ordered subset of $W(p)$ such that the total order on *os* respects the partial order $\gamma(p)$ of the augmented dependence graph $D(p)[T_{X_0}, T_{X_1}, \ldots, T_{X_n}]$. *os* is derived from $\gamma(p)$ by topological sort and it is easy to construct the visit sequence from *os*. Note that this step and the previous one are exactly the same as for a traditional AG.

3. Each production in the AAG corresponds to some "guarded production" *c.p* in the dynamic AG. We hence reintroduce in each ordered sequence marks for the evaluation and test of the various conditions (guards) of the dynamic production it corresponds to; for each condition, in the order defined by the path in the decision tree, this occurs as soon as all the attribute occurrences on which it depends are available. This leads to *guarded ordered sequences* (Fig. 5).

4. We then merge all the guarded ordered sequences corresponding to the same block, so as to obtain a single *conditional ordered sequence* structured just like the decision tree of the block (Fig. 6). To make this possible, we have to make sure that these visit sequences are "compatible", i.e. that, for a simple

---

h.env(w), h.env(cond), s.c(cond),
$\langle$ s.c(cond),
    $\langle$ h.env(body), s.env(body), h.env(loop), s.env(loop), s.env(w) $\rangle$,
    $\langle$ s.env(w) $\rangle$ $\rangle$

Fig. 6. Conditional ordered sequence for the **while** block

```
begin 1; eval h.env(cond); visit 1, cond;
⟨ s.c(cond),
    ⟨    eval h.env(body); visit 1, body;
         eval h.env(loop); visit 1, loop;
         eval s.env(w); leave 1 ⟩,
    ⟨    eval s.env(w); leave 1 ⟩ ⟩.
```

Fig. 7. Conditional visit sequence for the **while** block

---

block of the form $\langle R, \langle e, (p_T, R_T), (p_F, R_F) \rangle \rangle$, the parts of the guarded visit sequences for p_T and p_F that appear before the evaluation of the condition e both compute exactly the same collection of attribute occurrences. This point is discussed further below.

5. We transform each conditional ordered sequence into a *conditional visit sequence* by the same process as the traditional transformation of an ordered sequence into a visit sequence (Fig. 7).

6. We cut each conditional visit sequence in "slices" corresponding to the various visits to the LHS node, so as to make each slice a separate *visit function*, and we reintroduce at the beginning of each such function the branching code executed in previous visits.

Because our **while** example is not significant enough to illustrate the last step (there is only one visit), we show in Fig. 8 the (augmented) dependency graphs for two productions of an imaginary abstract AG. These productions depend on a condition over a purely synthesized attribute of a name common to both productions, $s(W)$. If this condition is true, then p_t is applied, otherwise it is p_f. In Fig. 9 we present successively the conditional ordered sequence associated with these productions, the corresponding conditional visit sequence and the dynamic visit sequence.

Let us get back to the notion of *compatibility*, briefly touched upon in step 4 above. Consider a simple block $b = \langle R, \langle e, (p_T, R_T), (p_F, R_F) \rangle \rangle$ and the two guarded ordered sequences $gos_T = \mathcal{G}uard(p_T, os_T) = os'_T.cond_e.os''_T$ and $gos_F = \mathcal{G}uard(p_F, os_F) = os'_F.cond_e.os''_F$ which will be constructed for p_T and p_F. We want to produce a conditional ordered sequence which will: evaluate the attributes "before" the condition; evaluate the condition; according to the value of the latter, continue with one of the sequences or the other. To make this possible, we have to make sure that os'_T and os'_F are *compatible*, i.e. they contain exactly the same set of attribute occurrences. Hence the whole construction relies on the following theorem:

Theorem 10. *Given a block* $b = \langle R, \langle e, (p_1, R_T), (p_2, R_F) \rangle \rangle$ *which induces:*

- $p_T = (e, true).p_1, p_F = (e, false).p_2 \in P_a$,
- os_T *and* os_F *the ordered sequences generated by the topological sort algorithm,*

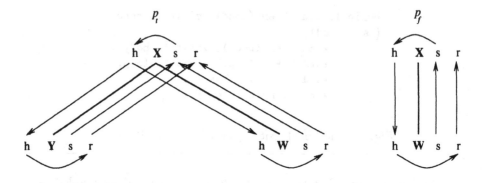

Fig. 8. An example of dependence graph

```
s(W),
⟨ cond,                  — condition over s(W)
    ⟨ s(Y), s(X), h(X), h(Y), h(W), r(Y), r(W), r(X) ⟩,
    ⟨ s(X), h(X), h(W), r(W), r(X) ⟩ ⟩
```

(a) The conditional ordered sequence

```
begin 1; visit 1, W;
⟨ cond,
    ⟨    visit 1, Y; eval s(X); leave 1;
         begin 2; eval h(Y); eval h(W); visit 2, Y;
         visit 2, W; eval r(X); leave 2; ⟩,
    ⟨    eval s(X); leave 1;
         begin 2; eval h(W); visit 2, W; eval r(X); leave 2; ⟩ ⟩
```

(b) The conditional visit sequence

```
begin 1; visit 1, W;
⟨ cond ,
    ⟨ visit 1, Y; eval s(X); ⟩,
    ⟨ eval s(X); ⟩ ⟩
leave 1;
begin 2;
⟨ cond,
    ⟨ eval h(Y); eval h(W); visit 2, Y; visit 2, W; eval r(X); ⟩,
    ⟨ eval h(W); visit 2, W; eval r(X); ⟩ ⟩
leave 2;
```

(c) The dynamic visit sequence

Fig. 9. Example of *Visit* and *Leave* transformations

given $\gamma(p)$ where $p = c.p_d = (e_1, t_1).(e_2, t_2)\ldots(e_n, t_n).p_d$ **do**

$os \leftarrow \epsilon; i \leftarrow 0; S \leftarrow \emptyset;$

repeat

    $i \leftarrow i + 1;$

    if $i = n + 1$ **then** $S \leftarrow W(p)$

    else $S \leftarrow S \cup \mathcal{DD}^+(e_i)$ — *dependency cone of the condition*

    repeat

        compute $\mathcal{E}(os);$ — *the set of attributes ready for evaluation*

        $a(X_i) \leftarrow \mathcal{P}ick(\mathcal{E}(os) \cap S);$

        $os \leftarrow os.a(X_i);$

    until $\mathcal{E}(os) \cap S = \emptyset$

until os is complete.

Fig. 10. <u>Conditional</u> topological sort of $W(p)$

- $gos_T = \mathcal{G}uard(p_T, os_T) = os'_T.cond_e.os''_T$ and $gos_F = \mathcal{G}uard(p_F, os_F) = os'_F.cond_e.os''_F$ the corresponding guarded ordered sequences,

if the choice function used in the topological sort is deterministic, then $os'_T = os'_F$.

In [20], we present two approaches to the construction of ordered sequences and the proof of this compatibility theorem: the first one (*black box*) uses the classical construction of ordered sequences, without any modification, but requires that we start with a slightly more rigid AAG[5] than the one presented earlier; the second one (*ad hoc*) starts with the standard AAG but requires that the construction of ordered sequences (topological sort) is aware of the conditions (see Fig. 10: attributes to evaluate are picked in the "dependency cone" of the successive conditions).

The final form of our evaluators is based on the *visit function* paradigm [21]. An important property of this implementation is that, when we use classical, static storage optimization techniques [13] and, as a last resort, the *binding tree* technique [21], *no* attribute needs to be stored in the tree anymore. It is hence quite appropriate for the implementation of Dynamic AGs, in which the physical tree need not be isomorphic to the computation tree or even exist at all.

The last step before the generation of these visit functions, namely the construction of dynamic visit sequences (Fig. 9), is required to account for the fact that the visit-sequence selection mechanism of Dynamic AGs is richer than that of classical AGs: the latter only depends on the production which is applied at the root of the visited subtree, whereas the former (possibly) uses this information but also the conditions. So, when we cut a conditional visit sequence into "slices" corresponding to the various visits to the LHS, we need to reintroduce

---

[5] The added constraint enforces that no son which is not entirely in the "intersection" of p_T and p_F is visited before the evaluation of condition e. This may lead to the rejection of a few l-ordered, meaningful DAGs.

in each of them the branching code executed in previous visits. This assumes of course that the values of the various conditions computed in one visit are correctly transmitted to subsequent visits as non-temporary local attributes.

This concludes the construction of visit-sequence-based evaluators for Dynamic AGs. Like for traditional AGs, these evaluators are as efficient as possible. When the dynamic AG is evaluable in one pass, the generated visit functions are the same as what one could write by hand in any language with recursive functions; however, when dependencies are more complicated, hand-writing the evaluator is close to impossible, unless one uses some sort of delayed evaluation mechanism—e.g. lazy evaluation of functional programs—, but then our eager evaluators are more efficient. See [18] for a longer discussion of this topic.

4 Conclusion

In this paper we have argued that in the term "Attribute Grammar" the notion of *grammar* does not necessarily imply the existence of an underlying tree, and that the notion of *attribute* does not necessarily mean decoration of a tree. We have presented Dynamic Attribute Grammars, a new, simple extension to the AG formalism which allows the full exploitation of the power of this observation. They are consistent with the general ideas underlying Attribute Grammars, hence we retain the benefits of the results and techniques that are already available in that domain.

Our goal in providing these extensions to the Attribute Grammar formalism is to bring this powerful tool into a larger context of usefulness and applicability. Its declarative and structured programming style and existing static analysis techniques become more general under this extended view and reveal themselves as complementary to other formalisms such as functional programming or inference rule programming [18].

This approach is of practical interest because, as we have shown, the mechanisms necessary to support Dynamic Attribute Grammars were already part of the FNC-2 system, which has proved its usefulness on real applications; this made their implementation easy. It is also promising because it opens the way to the application of good results developed for Attribute Grammars to other programming paradigms.

References

1. Henk Alblas. Attribute evaluation methods. In Alblas and Melichar [2], pages 48–113.
2. Henk Alblas and Bořivoj Melichar, editors. *Attribute Grammars, Applications and Systems*, volume 545 of *Lect. Notes in Comp. Sci.*, Prague, June 1991. Springer-Verlag.
3. Isabelle Attali. *Compilation de programmes TYPOL par attributs sémantiques*. PhD thesis, Université de Nice, April 1989.

4. John Boyland. Conditional attribute grammars. *ACM Transactions on Programming Languages and Systems*, 18(1):73–108, January 1996.
5. Bruno Courcelle and Paul Franchi-Zannettacci. Attribute Grammars and Recursive Program Schemes (i and ii). *Theor. Comp. Sci.*, 17(2 and 3):163–191 and 235–257, 1982.
6. Pierre Deransart and Martin Jourdan, editors. *Attribute Grammars and their Applications (WAGA)*, volume 461 of *Lect. Notes in Comp. Sci.*, Paris, September 1990. Springer-Verlag.
7. Pierre Deransart, Martin Jourdan, and Bernard Lorho. *Attribute Grammars: Definitions, Systems and Bibliography*, volume 323 of *Lect. Notes in Comp. Sci.* Springer-Verlag, August 1988.
8. Joost Engelfriet. Attribute grammars: Attribute evaluation methods. In Bernard Lorho, editor, *Methods and Tools for Compiler Construction*, pages 103–138. Cambridge University Press, 1984.
9. Rodney Farrow. Automatic Generation of Fixed-point-finding Evaluators for Circular, but Well-defined, Attribute Grammars. In *ACM SIGPLAN '86 Symp. on Compiler Construction*, pages 85–98, Palo Alto, CA, June 1986.
10. Martin Jourdan. *Des bienfaits de l'analyse statique sur la mise en œuvre des grammaires attribuées*. Mémoire d'habilitation, Département de Mathématiques et d'Informatique, Université d'Orléans, April 1992.
11. Martin Jourdan and Didier Parigot. *The* FNC-2 *System User's Guide and Reference Manual*. INRIA, Rocquencourt, 1.9 edition, 1993.
12. Martin Jourdan, Didier Parigot, Catherine Julié, Olivier Durin, and Carole Le Bellec. Design, implementation and evaluation of the FNC-2 attribute grammar system. In *ACM SIGPLAN '90 Conf. on Programming Languages Design and Implementation*, pages 209–222. White Plains, NY, June 1990. Published as ACM SIGPLAN Notices, volume 25, number 6.
13. Catherine Julié and Didier Parigot. Space Optimization in the FNC-2 Attribute Grammar System. In Deransart and Jourdan [6], pages 29–45.
14. Uwe Kastens. Ordered attribute grammars. *Acta Informatica*, 13(3):229–256, 1980. See also: Bericht 7/78, Institut für Informatik II, University Karlsruhe (1978).
15. Donald E. Knuth. Semantics of context-free languages. *Math. Systems Theory*, 2(2):127–145, June 1968.
16. Stéphane Leibovitsch. Relations entre la sémantique dénotationnelle et les grammaires attribuées. Rapport de DEA, Université de Paris VII, September 1996.
17. Jukka Paakki. Attribute grammar paradigms — A high-level methodology in language implementation. *ACM Computing Surveys*, 27(2):196–255, June 1995.
18. Didier Parigot, Étienne Duris, Gilles Roussel, and Martin Jourdan. Attribute grammars: a declarative functional language. Rapport de recherche 2662, INRIA, October 1995. ftp://ftp.inria.fr/INRIA/publications/RR/RR-2662.ps.gz.
19. Didier Parigot, Etienne Duris, Gilles Roussel, and Martin Jourdan. Les grammaires attribuées: un langage fonctionnel déclaratif. In *Journées Francophones des Langages Applicatifs 96*, pages 263–279, Val-Morin, Québec, January 1996. Aussi dans les *Actes des journées du GDR Programmation 95*.
20. Didier Parigot, Gilles Roussel, Martin Jourdan, and Étienne Duris. Dynamic attribute grammars. Rapport de recherche 2881, INRIA, May 1996. ftp://ftp.inria.fr/INRIA/publications/RR/RR-2881.ps.gz.
21. S. Doaitse Swierstra and Harald H. Vogt. Higher Order Attribute Grammars. In Alblas and Melichar [2], pages 256–296.

Logic Program Specialisation:
How To Be More Specific

Michael Leuschel* and Danny De Schreye**

K.U. Leuven, Department of Computer Science
Celestijnenlaan 200A, B-3001 Heverlee, Belgium
e-mail: {michael,dannyd}@cs.kuleuven.ac.be

Abstract. Standard partial deduction suffers from several drawbacks when compared to top-down abstract interpretation schemes. Conjunctive partial deduction, an extension of standard partial deduction, remedies one of those, namely the lack of side-ways information passing. But two other problems remain: the lack of success-propagation as well as the lack of inference of global success-information. We illustrate these drawbacks and show how they can be remedied by combining conjunctive partial deduction with an abstract interpretation technique known as more specific program construction. We present a simple, as well as a more refined integration of these methods. Finally we illustrate the practical relevance of this approach for some advanced applications, where it surpasses the precision of current abstract interpretation techniques.

1   Introduction

The heart of any technique for *partial deduction*, or more generally *logic program specialisation*, is a program analysis phase. Given a program P and an (atomic) goal $\leftarrow A$, one aims to analyse the computation-flow of P for all instances $\leftarrow A\theta$ of $\leftarrow A$. Based on the results of this analysis, new program clauses are synthesised.

In partial deduction, such an analysis is based on the construction of finite and usually incomplete[1], SLD(NF)-trees. More specifically, following the foundations for partial deduction developed in [14], one constructs
- a finite set of atoms $S = \{A_1, \ldots, A_n\}$, and
- a finite (possibly incomplete) SLD(NF)-tree τ_i for each $(P \cup \{\leftarrow A_i\})$,

such that:
1) the atom A in the initial goal $\leftarrow A$ is an instance of some A_i in S, and
2) for each goal $\leftarrow B_1, \ldots, B_k$ labelling a leaf of some SLD(NF)-tree τ_l, each B_i is an instance of some A_j in S.

---

* Supported by the Belgian GOA "Non-Standard Applications of Abstract Interpretation"
** Senior Research Associate of the Belgian Fund for Scientific Research
[1] As usual in partial deduction, we assume that the notion of an SLD-tree is generalised [14] to allow it to be incomplete: at any point we may decide not to select any atom and terminate a derivation.

The conditions 1) and 2) ensure that *together* the SLD(NF)-trees $\tau_1, \ldots, \tau_n$ form a *complete description* of all possible computations that can occur for all concrete instances $\leftarrow A\theta$ of the goal of interest. At the same time, the point is to propagate the available input data in $\leftarrow A$ as much as possible through these trees, in order to obtain sufficient accuracy. The outcome of the analysis is precisely the set of SLD(NF)-trees $\{\tau_1, \ldots, \tau_n\}$: a complete, and as precise as possible, description of the computation-flow.

Finally, a code generation phase produces a *resultant clause* for each non-failing branch of each tree, which synthesises the computation in that branch.

In the remainder of this paper we will restrict our attention to *definite* logic programs (possibly with declarative built-ins like \=, is, ...). In that context, the following generic scheme (based on similar ones in e.g. [4, 12]) describes the basic layout of practically all algorithms for computing the sets S and $\{\tau_1, \ldots, \tau_n\}$.

Algorithm 1. (Standard Partial Deduction)
Initialise $i = 0$, $S_i = \{A\}$
repeat
    for each $A_k \in S_i$, compute a finite SLD-tree τ_k for A_k ;
    let $S_i' := S_i \cup \{B_l | B_l$ is an atom in a leaf of some tree τ_k,
          which is not an instance of any $A_r \in S_i\}$;
    let $S_{i+1} := abstract(S_i')$
until $S_{i+1} = S_i$

In this algorithm, *abstract* is a *widening operator*: $abstract(S_i')$ is a set of atoms such that each atom of S_i' is an instance of atom in $abstract(S_i')$. The purpose of the operator is to ensure termination of the analysis.

An analysis following this scheme focusses exclusively on a top-down propagation of call-information. In the separate SLD-trees τ_i, this propagation is performed through repeated unfolding steps. The propagation over different trees is achieved by the fact that for each atom in a leaf of a tree there exists another tree with (a generalisation of) this atom as its root. The decision to create a *set* of different SLD-trees — instead of just creating one single tree, which would include both unfolding steps *and* generalisation steps — is motivated by the fact that these individual trees determine how to generate the new clauses.

The starting point for this paper is that the described analysis scheme suffers from some clear imprecision problems. It has some obvious drawbacks compared to top-down abstract interpretation schemes, such as for instance the one in [1]. These drawbacks are related to two issues: the lack of *success-propagation*, both upwards and side-ways, and the lack of inferring *global* success-information. We discuss these issues in more detail.

1.1 Lack of success-propagation

Consider the following tiny program:

Example 1. $p(X) \leftarrow q(X), r(X)$ $q(a) \leftarrow$ $r(a) \leftarrow$ $r(b) \leftarrow$

For a given query $\leftarrow p(X)$, one possible (although very unoptimal) outcome of the Algorithm 1 is the set $S = \{p(X), q(X), r(X)\}$ and the SLD-trees τ_1, τ_2 and τ_3 presented in Fig. 1.

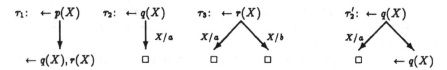

Fig. 1. A possible outcome of Algorithm 1 for Ex. 1 and Ex. 1'

With this result of the analysis, the transformed program would be identical to the original one. Note that in τ_2 we have derived that the only answer for $\leftarrow q(X)$ is X/a. An abstract interpretation algorithm such as the one in [1] would propagate this success- information to the leaf of τ_1, thereby making the call $\leftarrow r(X)$ more specific, namely $\leftarrow r(a)$. This information would then be used in the analysis of $r/1$, allowing to remove the redundant branch. Finally, the success-information, X/a, would be propagated up to the $\leftarrow p(X)$ call, yielding a specialised program:

$$p(a) \leftarrow \qquad q(a) \leftarrow \qquad r(a) \leftarrow$$

which is correct for all instances of the considered query $\leftarrow p(X)$.

Note that this particular example could be solved by the techniques in [4]. There, a limited success-propagation, restricted to only one resolution step, is introduced and referred to as a *more specific resolution step*.

1.2 Lack of inference of global success-information

Assume that we add the clause $q(X) \leftarrow q(X)$ to the program in Ex. 1, yielding Ex. 1'. A possible outcome of Algorithm 1 for the query $\leftarrow p(x)$ now is $S = \{p(X), q(X), r(X)\}$ and τ_1, τ_2', τ_3, where τ_2' is also depicted in Fig. 1.

Again, the resulting program is identical to the input program. In this case, simple bottom-up propagation of successes is insufficient to produce a better result. An additional fix-point computation is needed to detect that X/a is the only answer substitution. Methods as the one in [1] integrate such fix-point computations in the top-down analysis. As a result, the same more specialised program as for Ex. 1 can be obtained.

In addition to pointing out further imprecision problems of the usual analysis scheme, the main contributions of the current paper are to propose a more refined analysis scheme that solves these problems and to illustrate the *applicability* of the new scheme to a *class of applications* in which they are *vital* for successful specialisation. The remainder of the paper is organised as follows. In Sect. 2 we present the intuitions behind the proposed solution and illustrate the extensions on a few simple examples. In Sect. 3 we present more realistic, practical examples and we justify the need for a more refined algorithm. This more refined Algorithm is then presented in Sect. 4 and used to specialise the ground representation in Sect. 5. We conclude with some discussions in Sect. 6.

2 Introducing More Specific Program Specialisation

There are different ways in which one could enhance the analysis to cope with the problems mentioned in the introduction. A solution that seems most promising is to just apply the abstract interpretation scheme of [1] to replace Algorithm 1. Unfortunately, this analysis is based on an AND-OR-tree representation of the computation, instead of an SLD-tree representation. As a result, applying the analysis for partial deduction causes considerable problems for the code-generation phase. It becomes very complicated to extract the specialised clauses from the tree. The alternative of adapting the analysis of [1] in the context of an SLD-tree representation causes considerable complications as well. The analysis very heavily exploits the AND-OR-tree representation to enforce termination.

The solution we propose here is based on the combination of two existing analysis schemes, each underlying a specific specialisation technique: the one of *conjunctive partial deduction* [10, 6] and the one of *more specific programs* [15].[2]

Let us first present an abstract interpretation method based on [15] which calculates more specific versions of programs.

We first introduce the following notations. Given a set of logic formulas P, $Pred(P)$ denotes the set of predicates occuring in P. By $mgu^*(A, B)$ we denote the most general unifier of A and B', where B' is obtained from B by renaming apart wrt A. Next $msg(S)$ denotes the most specific generalisation of the atoms in S. We also define the predicate-wise application msg^* of the msg: $msg^*(S) = \{msg(S^p) \mid p \in Pred(P)\}$, where S^p are all the atoms of S having p as predicate.

In the following we define the well-known non-ground T_P operator along with an abstraction U_P of it.

Definition 2. For a definite logic program P and a set of atoms $\mathcal{A}$ we define:
$T_P(\mathcal{A}) = \{H\theta_1 \ldots \theta_n \mid H \leftarrow B_1, \ldots, B_n \in P \wedge \theta_i = mgu^*(B_i, A_i) \text{ with } A_i \in \mathcal{A}\}$.
We also define $U_P(\mathcal{A}) = msg^*(T_P(\mathcal{A}))$.

One of the abstract interpretation methods of [15] can be seen (see also Sect. 6) as calculating $lfp(U_P) = U_P \uparrow^\infty (\emptyset)$. In [15] more specific versions of clauses and programs are obtained in the following way:

Definition 3. Let $C = H \leftarrow B_1, \ldots, B_n$ be a definite clause and $\mathcal{A}$ a set of atoms. We define $msv_\mathcal{A}(C) = \{C\theta_1 \ldots \theta_n \mid \theta_i = mgu^*(B_i, A_i) \text{ with } A_i \in \mathcal{A}\}$.
The *more specific version* $msv(P)$ of P is then obtained by replacing every clause $C \in P$ by $msv_{lfp(U_P)}(C)$ (note that $msv_{lfp(U_P)}(C)$ contains at most 1 clause).

In the light of the stated problems, an integration of partial deduction with the more specific program transformation seems a quite natural solution. In [15] such an integration was already suggested as a promising future direction. The following example however reveals that, in general, this combination is still too weak to deal with side-ways information propagation.

---

[2] These techniques are rather straightforward to integrate because they use the same abstract domain: a set of concrete atoms (or goals) is represented by the instances of an abstract atom (or goal).

Example 2. (append-last)

```
app_last(L,X) :- append(L,[a],R), last(R,X).
append([],L,L).
append([H|X],Y,[H|Z]) :- append(X,Y,Z).
last([X],X).
last([H|T],X) :- last(T,X).
```

The hope is that the specialisation techniques are sufficiently strong to infer that a query app_last(L,X) produces the answer X=a. Partial deduction on its own is incapable of producing this result. An SLD-tree for the query app_last(L,X) takes the form of τ_1 in Fig. 2. Although the success-branch of the tree produces X=a, there are infinitely many possibilities for L and, without a bottom-up fixed-point computation, X=a cannot be derived for the entire computation. At some point the unfolding needs to terminate, and additional trees for append and last, for instance τ_2 and τ_3 in Fig. 2, need to be constructed.

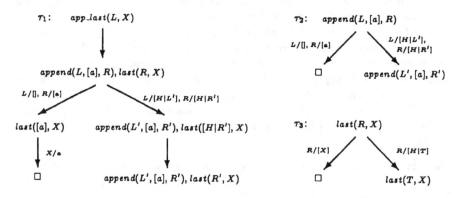

Fig. 2. SLD-trees for Ex. 2

Unfortunately, in this case, even the combination with the more specific program transformation is insufficient to obtain the desired result. We get:

$$T_P(U_P \uparrow 1) = T_P \uparrow 2 = \{ \text{ app_last(a), append([],[a],[a]),}$$
$$\text{append([H],[a],[H,a]), last([X],X), last([H,X],X) }\}$$

after which most specific generalisation yields

$$U_P \uparrow 2 = \{ \text{ app_last(a), append(X,[a],[Y|Z]), last([X|Y], Z) }\}$$

At this stage, all information concerning the last elements of the lists is lost and we reach the fix-point in the next iteration:

$$U_P \uparrow 3 = \{ \text{ app_last(Z), append(X,[a],[Y|Z]), last([X|Y],Z) }\}$$

One could argue that the failure is not due to the more specific programs transformation itself, but to a weakness of the *msg* operator: it's inability to retain information at the end of a data-structure. Note however that, even if we use other abstractions and their corresponding abstract operation proposed in the literature, such as *type-graphs* [8], *regular types* [5] or refined types for compile-time garbage collection of [16], the information still gets lost.

The heart of the problem is that in all these methods the abstract operator is applied to atoms of each predicate symbol *separately*. In this program (and *many, much more relevant others*, as we will discuss later), we are interested in analysing the conjunction append(L,[a],R),last(R,X) with a linking intermediate variable (whose structure is too complex for the particular abstract domain). If we could consider this conjunction as a *basic unit*, and therefore not perform abstraction on the separate atoms, but only on conjunctions of the involved atoms, we would retain a precise side-ways information passing analysis.

In [10] we have developed a minimal extension to partial deduction, called *conjunctive partial deduction*. This technique extends the standard partial deduction approach by:

- considering a set $S = \{C_1, \ldots, C_n\}$ of *conjunctions of atoms* instead of individual atoms, and
- building an SLD-tree τ_i for each $P \cup \{\leftarrow C_i\}$,

such that the query $\leftarrow C$ of interest (which may now be a non-atomic goal) as well as each leaf goal $\leftarrow B_1, \ldots, B_k$ of some SLD-tree τ_i, can be partitioned into conjunctions $C'_1, \ldots, C'_r$, such that each C'_i is an instance of some $C_j \in S$.

The following basic notion is adapted from [14].

Definition 4. (resultant) Let P be a program, $G =\leftarrow Q$ a goal, where Q is a conjunction of atoms, $G_0 = G, G_1, ..., G_n$ a finite derivation for $P \cup \{G\}$, with substitutions $\theta_1, ..., \theta_n$, and let G_n have the form $\leftarrow Q_n$. We say that $Q\theta_1...\theta_n \leftarrow Q_n$ is *the resultant* of the derivation $G_0, G_1, ..., G_n$.

The notion can be generalised to SLD-trees. Given a finite SLD-tree τ for $P \cup \{G\}$, there is a corresponding set of resultants R_τ, including one resultant for each non-failed derivation of τ.

In the partial deduction notion introduced in [14], the SLD-trees are restricted to *atomic* top-level goals. This restriction has been omitted in [10] and therefore resultants of the SLD-trees are not necessarily clauses: their left-hand side may contain a conjunction of atoms. To transform such resultants back into standard clauses, conjunctive partial deduction involves a renaming transformation, from conjunctions to atoms with new predicate symbols, in a postprocessing step. For further details we refer to [10].

Although this extension of standard partial deduction was motivated by totally different concerns than the ones in the current paper (the aim was to achieve a large class of unfold/fold transformations [17] within a simple extension of the partial deduction framework), experiments with conjunctive partial deduction on standard partial deduction examples also showed significant improvements. Only in retrospect we realised that these optimisations were due to considerably improved side-ways information-propagation.

Let us illustrate how conjunctive partial deduction combined with the $msv(.)$ transformation *does* solve Ex. 2. Starting from the goal app_last(X) and using an analysis scheme similar to Algorithm 1, but with the role of atoms replaced by conjunctions of atoms, we can obtain $S = \{$ app_last(X), append(L,[a],R) $\wedge$ last(R,X) $\}$ and the corresponding SLD-trees, which are sub-trees of τ_1 of Fig. 2. Here, "$\wedge$" is used to denote conjunction in those cases where "," is ambiguous.

The main difference with the (standard) partial deduction analysis is that the goal `append(L',[a],R'),last(R',X)` in the leaf of τ_1 is now considered as an undecomposed conjunction. This conjunction is already an instance of an element in S, so that no separate analysis for `append(L',[a],R')` or `last(R',X)` is required. Using a renaming transformation $rename(\text{append}(x,y,z)\wedge\text{last}(z,u))$ = `al(x,y,z,u)` the resulting transformed program is:

```
app_last(L,X) :- al(L,[a],R,X)
al([],[a],[a],a).
al([H|L'],[a],[H | R'], X) :- al(L',[a],R',X).
```

Applying the U_P-operator now produces the sets:
$$U_P \uparrow 1 = \{ \text{al}([],[a],[a],a)\}, \quad U_P \uparrow 2 = \{ \text{al}(X,[a],Y,a), \text{app\_last}(a)\},$$
the latter being a fix-point. Unifying the success-information with the body-atoms in the above program and performing argument filtering produces the desired more specific program:

```
app_last(L,a) :- al(L).
al([]).
al([H|L']) :- al(L').
```

3 Some Motivating Examples

In this section we illustrate the relevance of the introduced techniques by more realistic, practical examples.

3.1 Storing values in an environment

The following piece of code P stores values of variables in an association list and is taken from a meta-interpreter for imperative languages ([9]).

```
store([],Key,Value,[Key/Value]).
store([Key/Value2|T],Key,Value,[Key/Value|T]).
store([K2/V2|T],Key,Value,[K2/V2|BT]) :- Key \= K2,store(T,Key,Value,BT).
lookup(Key,[Key/Value|T],Value).
lookup(Key,[K2/V2|T],Value) :- Key \= K2,lookup(Key,T,Value).
```

During specialisation it may happen that a known (static) value is stored in an unknown environment. When we later retrieve this value from the environment it is often vital to be able to recover this static value. This is very similar to the `append-last` problem of Ex. 2. So again, calculating $msv(P)$, even if we perform a magic-set transformation, does not give us any new information for a query like `store(E,k,2,E1),lookup(E1,k,Val)`. To solve this problem, one needs again to combine abstract interpretation with conjunctive partial deduction (to "deforest" [21] the intermediate environment E_1). The specialised program P' for the query `store(E,k,2,E1),lookup(E1,k,Val)` using e.g. the ECCE ([9]) conjunctive partial deduction system is the following:

```
store_lookup__1([],[k/2],2).
store_lookup__1([k/X1|X2],[key/2|X2],2).
store_lookup__1([X1/X2|X3],[X1/X2|X4],X5) :-
        k \= X1,store_lookup__1(X3,X4,X5).
```

If we now calculate $msv(P')$, we are able to derive that Val must be 2:

```
store_lookup__1([],[k/2],2).
store_lookup__1([k/X1|X2],[k/2|X2],2).
store_lookup__1([X1/X2|X3],[X1/X2,X4/X5|X6],2) :-
        k \= X1,store_lookup__1(X3,[X4/X5|X6],2).
```

Being able to derive this kind of information is of course even more relevant when one can continue specialisation with it. For instance in an interpreter for an imperative language there might be multiple static values which are stored and later on control tests or loops.

3.2 Proving Functionality

The following is a generalisation of the standard definition of functionality (see e.g. [18] or [3]).

Definition 5. We say that a predicate p defined by a program P is *functional wrt the terms* $t_1, \ldots, t_h$ iff for every pair of atoms $A = p(t_1, \ldots, t_h, a_1, \ldots, a_k)$ and $B = p(t_1, \ldots, t_h, b_1, \ldots, b_k)$ we have that:
- $\leftarrow A, B$ has a correct answer θ iff $\leftarrow A, A = B$ has
- $\leftarrow A, B$ finitely fails iff $\leftarrow A, A = B$ finitely fails

In the above definition we allow A, B to be used as atoms as well as terms (as arguments to $= /2$). Also, for simplicity of the presentation we restrict ourselves to correct answers. Therefore it can be easily seen that,[3] if the goal $\leftarrow A', A'$ is a more specific version of $\leftarrow A, B$ then p is functional wrt $t_1, \ldots, t_h$ (because $msv(.)$ preserves computed answers and removing syntactically identical calls preserves the correct answers for definite logic programs).

Functionality is useful for many transformations, and is often vital to get super-linear speedups. For instance it is needed to transform the naive (exponential) Fibonacci program into a linear one (see e.g. [18]). It can also be used to produce more efficient code (see e.g. [3]). Another example arises naturally from the store-lookup code of the previous section. In a lot of cases, specialisation can be greatly improved if functionality of lookup(Key,Env,Val) wrt a given key Key and a given environment Env can be proven (in other words if we lookup the same variable in the same environment we get the same value). For instance this would allow to replace, during specialisation, lookup(Key,Env,V1),lookup(Key,Env,V2),p(V2) by lookup(Key,Env,V1),p(V1).

To prove functionality of lookup(Key,Env,Val) we simply add the following definition:[4] ll(K,E,V1,V2) :- lookup(K,E,V1),lookup(K,E,V2). By specialising

---

[3] The reasoning for computed answers is not so obvious.

[4] This is not strictly necessary but it simplifies spotting functionality.

the query ll(Key,Env,V1,V2) using the ECCE system and then calculating $msv(.)$ for the resulting program, we are able to derive that V1 must be equal to V2:

```
ll(K,E,V,V) :- lookup_lookup__1(K,E,V,V).
lookup_lookup__1(X1,[X1/X2|X3],X2,X2).
lookup_lookup__1(X1,[X2/X3,X4/X5|X6],X7,X7) :-
        X1 \= X2, lookup_lookup__1(X1,[X4/X5|X6],X7,X7).
```

In addition to obtaining a more efficient program the above implies (because conjunctive partial deduction preserves computed answers) that lookup(K,E,V), lookup(K,E,V) is a more specific version of lookup(K,E,V1), lookup(K,E,V2), and we have proven functionality of lookup(Key,Env,Val) wrt Key and Env.

3.3 The Need for a More Refined Integration

So far we have always completely separated the conjunctive partial deduction phase and the bottom-up abstract interpretation phase. The next example, which arose from a practical application described in Sect. 5, shows that this is not always sufficient. Take a look at the following excerpt from a unification algorithm for the ground representation (the full code can be found in [13]), which takes care of extracting variable bindings out of (uncomposed) substitutions.

```
get_binding(V,empty,var(V)).
get_binding(V,sub(V,S),S).
get_binding(V,sub(W,S),var(V)) :- V \= W.
get_binding(V,comp(L,R),S) :- get_binding(V,L,VL), apply(VL,R,S).
apply(var(V),Sub,VS) :- get_binding(V,Sub,VS).
apply(struct(F,A),Sub,struct(F,AA)) :- l_apply(A,Sub,AA).
l_apply([],Sub,[]).
l_apply([H|T],Sub,[AH|AT]) :- apply(H,Sub,AH),l_apply(T,Sub,AT).
```

At first sight this looks very similar to the example of the previous section and one would think that we could easily prove functionality of get_binding(V,S,Bind) wrt a particular variable index V and a particular substitution S. Exactly this kind of information is required for the practical applications in Sect. 5.

Unfortunately this kind of information *cannot* be obtained by fully separated out phases. For simplicity we assume that the variable index V is known to be 1. Taking the approach of the previous section we would add the definition gg(Sub,B1,B2) :- get_binding(1,Sub,B1),get_binding(1,Sub,B2) and apply conjunctive partial deduction and $msv(.)$ to obtain:

```
gg(Sub,B1,B2) :- get_binding_get_binding__1(Sub,B1,B2).
get_binding_get_binding__1(empty,var(1),var(1)).
get_binding_get_binding__1(sub(1,X1),X1,X1).
get_binding_get_binding__1(sub(X1,X2),var(1),var(1)) :- 1 \= X1.
get_binding_get_binding__1(comp(X1,X2),X3,X4) :-
    get_binding_get_binding__1(1,X1,X5,X6),apply(X5,X2,X3),apply(X6,X2,X4).
```

By analysing `apply(I5,I2,I3),apply(I6,I2,I4)` of clause 5 we *cannot* derive that I3 must be equal to I4 because the variables indexes I5 and I6 are different (applying the same substitution on different terms can of course lead to differing results). However, if we re-apply conjunctive partial deduction *before* reaching the fixpoint of U_P, we can solve the above problem. Indeed after one application of U_P we obtain $\mathcal{A} = U_P(\emptyset) = \{$get_binding_get_binding_1(S,B,B)$\}$ and at that point we have that $msv_{\mathcal{A}}(.)$ of clause 5 looks like:

```
get_binding_get_binding__1(comp(I1,I2),I3,I4) :-
    get_binding_get_binding__1(1,I1,V,V),apply(V,I2,I3),apply(V,I2,I4).
```

If we now recursively apply conjunctive partial deduction and $msv(.)$ to `apply(V,I2,I3),apply(V,I2,I4)` and then, again before reaching the fixpoint, to `l_apply(V,I2,I3),l_apply(V,I2,I4)` we can derive functionality of get_binding. The details of this more refined integration are elaborated in the next section.

4 A More Refined Algorithm

We now present an algorithm which interleaves the least fixpoint construction of $msv(.)$ with conjunctive partial deduction unfolding steps. For that we have to adapt the more specific program transformation to work on incomplete SLDNF-trees obtained by conjunctive partial deduction instead of for completely constructed programs.[5]

We first introduce a special conjunction $\perp$ which is an instance of every conjunction, as well as the only instance of itself, and extend the msg such that $msg(S \cup \{\perp\}) = msg(S)$ and $msg(\{\perp\}) = \perp$. We also use the convention that if unification fails it returns a special substitution $fail$. Applying $fail$ to any conjunction Q in turn yields $\perp$. Finally by $\uplus$ we denote the concatenation of tuples (e.g. $\langle a \rangle \uplus \langle b, c \rangle = \langle a, b, c \rangle$).

In the following definition we associate conjunctions with resultants:

Definition 6. (resultant tuple) Let $S = \{Q_1, ..., Q_s\}$ be a set of conjunctions of atoms, and $T = \{\tau_1, ..., \tau_s\}$ a set of finite, non-trivial SLD-trees for $P \cup \{\leftarrow Q_1\}, ..., P \cup \{\leftarrow Q_s\}$, with associated sets of resultants $R_1, ..., R_s$, respectively. Then the tuple of pairs $RS = \langle (Q_1, R_1), ..., (Q_s, R_s) \rangle$ is called a *resultant tuple* for P. An *interpretation* of RS is a tuple $\langle Q'_1, ..., Q'_s \rangle$ of conjunctions such that each Q'_i is an instance of Q_i.

The following defines how interpretations of resultant tuples can be used to create more specific resultants:

Definition 7. (refinement) Let $I = \langle Q'_1, ..., Q'_s \rangle$ be an interpretation of a resultant tuple $RS = \langle (Q_1, R_1), ..., (Q_s, R_s) \rangle$ and $R = H \leftarrow Body$ be a resultant. Let Q be a sub-goal of $Body$ such that Q is an instance of Q_i and such that

---

[5] This has the advantage that we do not actually have to apply a renaming transformation (and we might get more precision because several conjunctions might match).

$mgu^*(Q, Q_i') = \theta$. Then $R\theta$ is called a *refinement of R under RS and I*. R itself and all refinements of $R\theta$ are also called refinements of R under RS and I.

Note that a least refinement does not always exist. Take for instance $R = q \leftarrow p(X, f(T)) \wedge p(T, X)$, $RS = \langle(p(X, Y), R_1)\rangle$ and $I = \langle p(X, X)\rangle$. We can construct an infinite sequence of successive refinements of R under RS and I:
$q \leftarrow p(f(X'), f(T)) \wedge p(T, f(X'))$, $q \leftarrow p(f(X'), f(f(T'))) \wedge p(f(T'), f(X'))$, ...
Hence we denote by $ref_{RS,I}(R)$, a particular refinement of R under RS and I.[6]
A pragmatic approach might be to allow any particular sub-goal to be unified only once with any particular element of I.

Note that in [15], it is not allowed to further refine refinements and therefore only finitely many refinements exist and a least refinement can be obtained by taking the mgu^* of all of them. As we found out through several examples however, (notably the ones of Sect. 3.3 and Sect. 5) this approach turns out to be too restrictive in general. In a lot of cases, applying a first refinement might instantiate R in such a way that a previously inapplicable element of RS can now be used for further instantiation.

We can now extend the U_P operator of Def. 2 to work on interpretations of resultant tuples:

Definition 8. ($U_{P,RS}$) Let $I = \langle Q_1', \ldots, Q_s'\rangle$ be an interpretation of a resultant tuple $RS = \langle(Q_1, R_1), \ldots, (Q_s, R_s)\rangle$. Then $U_{P,RS}$ is defined by $U_{P,RS}(I) = \langle M_1, \ldots, M_s\rangle$, where $M_i = msg(\{H \mid C \in R_i \wedge ref_{RS,I}(C) = H \leftarrow B\})$.

We can now present a generic algorithm which fully integrates the abstract interpretation $msv(.)$ with conjunctive partial deduction. Below, $=_r$ denotes syntactic identity, up to reordering.

We first define an abstraction operation, which is used to ensure termination of the conjunctive partial deduction process (see [6] for some such operations).

Definition 9. (abstraction) A multi-set of conjunctions $\{Q_1, \ldots, Q_k\}$ is an *abstraction* of a conjunction Q iff for some substitutions $\theta_1, \ldots, \theta_k$ we have that $Q =_r Q_1\theta_1 \wedge \ldots \wedge Q_k\theta_k$. An *abstraction operation* is an operation which maps every conjunction to an abstraction of it.

We need the following definition, before presenting the promised algorithm:

Definition 10. (covered) Let $RS = \langle(Q_1, R_1), \ldots, (Q_s, R_s)\rangle$ be a resultant tuple. We say that a conjunction Q is *covered* by RS iff there exists an abstraction $\{Q_1', \ldots, Q_k'\}$ of Q such that each Q_i' is an instance of some Q_j.

Algorithm 11. (Conjunctive Msv)
    Input: a program P, an initial query Q, an unfolding rule *unfold* for P mapping conjunctions to resultants.
    Output: A specialised and more specific program P' for Q.

---

[6] It is probably correct to use $\perp$ if the least refinement does not exist but we have not investigated this.

Initialisation: $i := 0$; $I_0 = \langle \perp \rangle$, $RS_0 = \langle (Q, unfold(Q)) \rangle$
repeat
    for every resultant R in RS_i such that the body B of $ref_{RS_i, I_i}(R)$ is not covered:
        /* perform conjunctive partial deduction: */
        calculate $abstract(B) = B_1 \wedge \ldots \wedge B_q$
        let $\{C_1, \ldots, C_k\}$ be the B_j's which are not instances[7] of conjunctions in RS_i
        $RS_{i+1} = RS_i \uplus \langle (C_1, unfold(C_1)), \ldots (C_k, unfold(C_k)) \rangle$;
        $I_{i+1} = I_i \uplus \underbrace{(\perp \ldots \perp)}_{k}$; $i := i + 1$.

    /* perform one bottom-up propagation step: */
    $I_{i+1} = U_{P,RS_i}(I_i)$; $RS_{i+1} = RS_i$; $i := i + 1$.
    until $I_i = I_{i-1}$
    return a renaming of $\{ref_{RS_i, I_i}(C) \mid (Q, R) \in RS_i \wedge C \in R\}$

Note that the above algorithm ensures coveredness and performs abstraction only when adding new conjunctions, the existing ones are not abstracted (it is trivial to adapt this). This is like in [12] but unlike Algorithm 1.

Algorithm 11 is powerful enough to prove e.g. functionality of get_binding of Sect. 3.3 *and* use it for further specialisation. A detailed execution of the algorithm, proving functionality of multiplication, can be found in [13].

Correctness of Algorithm 11 for preserving Least Herbrand Model as well as computed answers, follows from correctness of conjunctive partial deduction (see [10]) and of the more specific program versions for suitably chosen conjunctions (because [15] only allows one unfolding step, a lot of intermediate conjunctions have to be introduced) and extended for the more powerful refinements of Def 7. Termination, for a suitable abstraction operation (see [6]), follows from termination of conjunctive partial deduction (for the **for** loop) and termination of $msv(.)$ (for the **repeat** loop).

Note that in contrast to conjunctive partial deduction, $msv(.)$ can replace infinite failure by finite failure, and hence Algorithm 11 does not preserve finite failure. However, if the specialised program fails infinitely, then so does the original one (see [15]). The above algorithm can be extended to work for normal logic programs. But, because finite failure is not preserved, neither are the SLDNF computed answers. One may have to look at SLS [19] for a suitable procedural semantics which is preserved.

5 Specialising the Ground Representation

A meta-program is a program which takes another program, the *object* program, as one of its inputs. An important issue in meta-programming is the representation of the object program. One approach is the *ground representation*, which encodes variables at the object level as ground terms. A lot of meta-programming tasks can only be written declaratively using the ground representation. This was e.g. the case for the application in [11], where a simplification procedure

---

[7] Or *variants* to make the algorithm more precise.

for integrity constraints in recursive deductive databases was written as a meta-program. The goal was to obtain a pre-compilation of the integrity checking via partial deduction of the meta-interpreter. However, contrary to what one might expect, partial deduction was then unable to perform interesting specialisation and no pre-compilation could be obtained. This problem was solved in [11] via a new implementation of the ground representation combined with a custom specialisation technique.

The crucial problem in [11] boiled down to a lack of information propagation at the object level. The ground representation entails the use of an explicit unification algorithm at the object level. For the application of [11] we were interested in deriving properties of the result R of calculating unify(A,B,S),apply(H,S,R) where S is a substitution (the *mgu*) and A,B,H are (representations of) partially known atoms. In a concrete example we might have A = status(I,student,Age), B = status(ID,E,A), H = category(ID,E) and we would like to derive that R must be an instance of category(ID',student). However it turns out that, when using an explicit unification algorithm, the substitutions have a much more complex structure than e.g. the intermediate list of Ex. 2. Therefore current abstract interpretation methods, as well as current partial deduction methods alone, fail to derive the desired information.

Fortunately Algorithm 11 provides an elegant and powerful solution to this problem. Some experiments, conducted with a prototype implementation of Algorithm 11 based on the ECCE system [9], are summarised in Table 1. A unification algorithm has been used, which encodes variables as var(VarIndex) and predicates/functors as struct(p,Args). The full code can be found in [13]. All the examples were successfully solved by the prototype and the main ingredient of the success lay with proving functionality of get_binding.

The information propagations of Table 1 could neither be solved by regular approximations ([5]), nor by [15] alone, nor by set-based analysis ([7]) nor even by current implementations of the type graphs of [8]. In summary, Algorithm 11 also provides for a powerful abstract interpretation scheme as well as a full replacement of the custom specialisation technique in [11].[8]

unify(A,B,S),apply(H,S,Res)			
A	B	H	Res
struct(p,[var(1),X])	struct(p,[struct(a,[]),Y])	var(1)	struct(a,[])
struct(p,[X,var(1)])	struct(p,[Y,struct(a,[])])	var(1)	struct(a,[])
struct(p,[X,X])	struct(p,[struct(a,[]),Y])	X	struct(a,[])
struct(F,[var(I)])	X	X	struct(F,[A])
struct(p,[X1,var(1),X2])	struct(p,[Y1,struct(a,[]),Y2])	var(1)	struct(a,[])

Table 1. Specialising the Ground Representation

---

[8] It is sometimes even able to provide better results because it can handle structures with unknown functors or unknown arity with no loss of precision.

6 Discussion and Conclusion

The approach presented in this paper can be seen as a practical realisation of a combined backwards and forwards analysis (see [2]), but using the sophisticated control techniques of (conjunctive) partial deduction to guide the analysis. Of course, in addition to analysis, our approach also constructs a specialised, more efficient program.

The method of [15] is not directly based on the T_P operator, but uses an operator on goal tuples which can handle conjunctions and which is (sometimes) sufficiently precise if deforestation can be obtained by 1-step unfolding without abstraction. For a lot of practical examples this will of course not be the case. Also, apart from a simple pragmatic approach, no way to obtain these conjunctions is provided (this is exactly what conjunctive partial deduction can do).

In Algorithm 11 a conflict between efficiency and precision might arise. But Algorithm 11 can be easily extended to allow different trees for the same conjunction (e.g. use determinate unfolding for efficient code and a more liberal unfolding for a precise analysis).

When using the unification algorithm from [11], instead of the one in [13] Algorithm 11 cannot yet handle all the examples of Table 1. The reason is that the substitutions in [11], in contrast to the ones in [13], are actually *accumulating* parameters, whose deforestation (see [20]) is still an open problem in general.

In conclusion, we have illustrated limitations of both partial deduction and abstract interpretation on their own. We have argued for a tighter integration of these methods and presented a refined algorithm, interleaving a least fixpoint construction with conjunctive partial deduction. The practical relevance of this approach has been illustrated by several examples. Finally, a prototype implementation of the algorithm was able to achieve sophisticated specialisation *and* analysis for meta-interpreters written in the ground representation, outside the reach of current specialisation or abstract interpretation techniques.

Acknowledgments

The authors greatly benefited from stimulating discussions with Jesper Jørgensen and Bern Martens. We also thank Maurice Bruynooghe and anonymous referees for their helpful comments.

References

1. M. Bruynooghe. A practical framework for the abstract interpretation of logic programs. *The Journal of Logic Programming*, 10:91–124, 1991.
2. P. Cousot and R. Cousot. Abstract interpretation and application to logic programs. *The Journal of Logic Programming*, 13(2 & 3):103–179, 1992.
3. S. Debray and D. Warren. Functional computations in logic programs. *ACM Transactions on Programming Languages and Systems*, 11(3):451–481, 1989.
4. J. Gallagher. A system for specialising logic programs. Technical Report TR-91-32, University of Bristol, November 1991.

5. J. Gallagher and D. A. de Waal. Fast and precise regular approximations of logic programs. In P. Van Hentenryck, editor, *Proceedings of the International Conference on Logic Programming*, pages 599–613. The MIT Press, 1994.

6. R. Glück, J. Jørgensen, B. Martens, and M. Sørensen. Controlling conjunctive partial deduction of definite logic programs. *In this Volume*.

7. N. Heintze. Practical aspects of set based analysis. In *Proceedings of the Joint International Conference and Symposium on Logic Programming*, pages 765–779, Washington D.C., 1992. MIT Press.

8. G. Janssens and M. Bruynooghe. Deriving descriptions of possible values of program variables by means of abstract interpretation. *The Journal of Logic Programming*, 13(2 & 3):205–258, 1992.

9. M. Leuschel. The ECCE partial deduction system and the DPPD library of benchmarks. Obtainable via http://www.cs.kuleuven.ac.be/~lpai, 1996.

10. M. Leuschel, D. De Schreye, and A. de Waal. A conceptual embedding of folding into partial deduction: Towards a maximal integration. In *Proceedings of the Joint International Conference and Symposium on Logic Programming*, Bonn, Germany, September 1996. MIT Press. To Appear. Extended version as Technical Report CW 225, Departement Computerwetenschappen, K.U. Leuven. Accessible via http://www.cs.kuleuven.ac.be/~lpai.

11. M. Leuschel and B. Martens. Partial deduction of the ground representation and its application to integrity checking. In J. Lloyd, editor, *Proceedings of the International Logic Programming Symposium*, pages 495–509, Portland, USA, December 1995. MIT Press.

12. M. Leuschel and B. Martens. Global control for partial deduction through characteristic atoms and global trees. In O. Danvy, R. Glück, and P. Thiemann, editors, *Proceedings of the 1996 Dagstuhl Seminar on Partial Evaluation*, LNCS, Schloß Dagstuhl, 1996. To Appear.

13. M. Leuschel and D. Schreye. Logic program specialisation: How to be more specific. Technical Report CW 232, Departement Computerwetenschappen, K.U. Leuven, Belgium, May 1996. Accessible via http://www.cs.kuleuven.ac.be/~lpai.

14. J. W. Lloyd and J. C. Shepherdson. Partial evaluation in logic programming. *The Journal of Logic Programming*, 11:217–242, 1991.

15. K. Marriott, L. Naish, and J.-L. Lassez. Most specific logic programs. *Annals of Mathematics and Artificial Intelligence*, 1:303–338, 1990. Preliminary version in *Proceedings of the Joint International Conference and Symposium on Logic Programming*, pages 909–923, Seattle, 1988. IEEE, MIT Press.

16. A. Mulkers, W. Winsborough, and M. Bruynooghe. Live-structure data-flow analysis for Prolog. *ACM Transactions on Programming Languages and Systems*, 16(2):205–258, 1994.

17. A. Pettorossi and M. Proietti. Transformation of logic programs: Foundations and techniques. *The Journal of Logic Programming*, 19 & 20:261–320, May 1994.

18. M. Proietti and A. Pettorossi. Unfolding-definition-folding, in this order, for avoiding unnecessary variables in logic programs. In J. Małuszyński and M. Wirsing, editors, *Proceedings of PLILP'91*, LNCS 528, Springer Verlag, pages 347–358, 1991.

19. T. C. Przymusinksi. On the declarative and procedural semantics of logic programs. *Journal of Automated Reasoning*, 5(2):167–205, 1989.

20. V. Turchin. Program transformation with metasystem transitions. *Journal of Functional Programming*, 3(3):283–313, 1993.

21. P. Wadler. Deforestation: Transforming programs to eliminate intermediate trees. *Theoretical Computer Science*, 73:231–248, 1990.

Controlling Conjunctive Partial Deduction

Robert Glück[2], Jesper Jørgensen[1], Bern Martens[1], Morten Heine Sørensen[2]

[1] Department of Computer Science, Katholieke Universiteit Leuven,
Celestijnenlaan 200A, B-3001, Heverlee, Belgium. {jesper,bern}@cs.kuleuven.ac.be
[2] Department of Computer Science, University of Copenhagen,
Universitetsparken 1, DK-2100 Copenhagen, Denmark. {glueck,rambo}@diku.dk

Abstract. Partial deduction within Lloyd and Shepherdson's framework transforms different atoms of a goal independently and therefore fails to achieve a number of unfold/fold transformations. A recent framework for *conjunctive partial deduction* allows unfold/fold transformations by specialisation of entire conjunctions, but does not give an actual algorithm for conjunctive partial deduction, and in particular does not address *control* issues (e.g. how to select atoms for unfolding). Focusing on novel challenges specific to local and global control, we describe a generic algorithm for conjunctive partial deduction, refine it into a fully automatic concrete algorithm, and prove termination and correctness.

1 Introduction

Partial deduction, introduced by Komorowski [17] and formalised by Lloyd and Shepherdson [24], takes a program and a query and returns a specialised program tuned towards answering any instance of the query. Partial deduction in Lloyd and Shepherdson's framework cannot achieve certain important optimisations. For example, consider the goal $app(X, Y, T), app(T, Z, R)$ in the program

$$app([\,], Y, Y).$$
$$app([H|X], Y, [H|Z]) \leftarrow app(X, Y, Z).$$

The goal is simple and elegant, but inefficient to execute. Given X, Y, Z and assuming left-to-right execution, $app(X, Y, T)$ constructs from X and Y an intermediate list T which is then traversed to append Z to it. Construction and traversal of intermediate data structures is expensive and redundant. The equivalent goal $da(X, Y, Z, R)$ is more efficient, but its definition is less obvious:

$$da([\,], Y, Z, R) \qquad\quad \leftarrow app(Y, Z, R).$$
$$da([H|X], Y, Z, [H|Rs]) \leftarrow da(X, Y, Z, Rs).$$
$$app([\,], Y, Y).$$
$$app([H|X], Y, [H|Z]) \qquad \leftarrow app(X, Y, Z).$$

Partial deduction in Lloyd and Shepherdson's framework cannot transform the original goal to the more efficient one, because atoms in conjunctive goals are transformed independently, while the example requires merging a conjunction $app(X, Y, T), app(T, Z, R)$ into one new atom $da(X, Y, Z, R)$.

To overcome such limitations, De Schreye, Leuschel and de Waal [19] introduced *conjunctive partial deduction*, an extension of Lloyd and Shepherdson's framework in which entire conjunctions of atoms are specialised, combining the power of unfold-fold transformations with the virtues of partial deduction. However, they did not give a concrete algorithm for conjunctive partial deduction.

This paper aims at a basis for the design of concrete algorithms within this extended framework. We present a generic algorithm for conjunctive partial deduction and refine it into a fully automatic one. Since partial deductions are computed for conjunctions of atoms, rather than for separate atoms, *novel control challenges* specific to conjunctive partial deduction arise. Our solutions to these challenges are the main contribution of the paper.

Section 2 recapitulates the extended framework of [19]. Section 3 gives a generic correct algorithm for conjunctive partial deduction. Section 4 derives a fully automatic, concrete algorithm. Section 5 illustrates the algorithm with examples, which demonstrate that it indeed substantially improves classical partial deduction. Section 6 discusses related work. We assume the reader is familiar with the basic notions of logic programming and partial deduction [22, 24, 10].

This paper is an abridged and somewhat revised version of a technical report [11] where the interested reader may find further comments and examples.

2 Foundations of Conjunctive Partial Deduction

We briefly recall the framework for conjunctive partial deduction by De Schreye, Leuschel and de Waal [19].

We presuppose a given logic language and consider only *definite programs and goals*. A clause has the form $A \leftarrow Q$, where A, A_0, etc. denote atoms and Q, Q_0, etc. conjunctions of atoms. G, G_0, etc. denote goals of the form $\leftarrow Q$, and B, B_0, etc. conjunctions when these appear as bodies of some clauses. $Q \wedge Q'$ denotes the conjunction of Q and Q'; an atom is considered a special case of a conjunction. If Q and Q' are identical modulo variable renaming (and associativity) we write $Q \equiv Q'$. If Q and Q' are identical modulo commutativity (and associativity), we write $Q = Q'$. For a substitution θ and a conjunction Q, $\theta|Q$ is the restriction of θ to the variables in Q. Q' is an instance of Q (Q is more general than Q'), written $Q \preceq Q'$, iff $Q' = Q\theta$ for some θ.

Definition 1. (computed answer, resultant) Let P be a program, $\leftarrow Q_0$ a goal. Let $\leftarrow Q_0, \ldots, \leftarrow Q_n$ be an SLD-derivation of $P \cup \{\leftarrow Q_0\}$, where the sequence of substitutions is $\theta_1, \ldots, \theta_n$. Let $\theta = \theta_1 \circ \ldots \circ \theta_n$. Then the derivation has *computed answer* $\theta|Q_0$ and *resultant* $Q_0\theta \leftarrow Q_n$.

For example, if $Q_{app} \equiv app(X, Y, T) \wedge app(T, Z, R)$ and P_{app} is the program in Section 1, then $P_{app} \cup \{\leftarrow Q_{app}\}$ has SLD-derivation:

$$\leftarrow app(X, Y, T) \wedge app(T, Z, R),$$
$$\leftarrow app(X', Y, T') \wedge app([H|T'], Z, R),$$
$$\leftarrow app(X', Y, T') \wedge app(T', Z, R')$$

with computed answer $\{X \mapsto [H|X'], T \mapsto [H|T'], R \mapsto [H|R']\}$, and resultant
$app([H|X'], Y, [H|T']) \wedge app([H|T'], Z, [H|R']) \leftarrow app(X', Y, T') \wedge app(T', Z, R)$.

Resultants are program clauses if the goal is atomic. In Lloyd and Shepherd-son's framework, this restriction is used to obtain new program clauses from a program and an atomic goal. A *generalised program* is a set of resultants.

Definition 2. (pre-conjunctive partial deduction) Let P be a program, $\mathcal{Q}$ a set of conjunctions. For all $Q \in \mathcal{Q}$, let T_Q be a finite SLD-tree for $P \cup \{\leftarrow Q\}$, and R_Q the associated set of resultants. Let P_Q be the generalised program obtained from P by removing clauses defining predicates that occur in atomic elements of $\mathcal{Q}$ and adding the elements of R_Q, for all $Q \in \mathcal{Q}$. P_Q is a *pre-conjunctive partial deduction* of P wrt $\mathcal{Q}$ (derived from T_Q, $Q \in \mathcal{Q}$).

For instance, for P_{app} and $\mathcal{Q}_{app} = \{app(Y, Z, R), Q_{app}\}$ we have two SLD-trees (selected atoms are underlined):

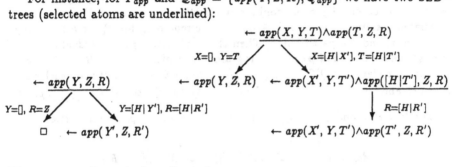

The corresponding set of resultants is:

$app([H|X'], Y, [H|T']) \wedge app([H|T'], Z, [H|R']) \leftarrow app(X', Y, T') \wedge app(T', Z, R')$.
$app([], Y, Y) \wedge app(Y, Z, R) \qquad\qquad\qquad \leftarrow app(Y, Z, R)$.
$app([\ ], Z, Z)$.
$app([H|Y'], Z, [H|R']) \qquad\qquad\qquad\qquad \leftarrow app(Y', Z, R')$.

This is also a pre-conjunctive partial deduction of P_{app} wrt $\mathcal{Q}$. If there were more clauses in P_{app} defining other predicates, these would also have been included.

In order to get from a pre-conjunctive partial deduction to a program, left hand sides must be renamed, so that they become atoms. This is done with *pre-renamings*. Moreover, in the right hand sides one must group atoms together by a *partitioning* into conjunctions that can be *renamed* correspondingly.

Definition 3. (pre-renaming) A *pre-renaming* σ for a pre-conjunctive partial deduction P_Q is a mapping from $\mathcal{Q}$ to atoms such that for all $Q \in \mathcal{Q}$:

1. $vars(\sigma(Q)) \subseteq vars(Q)$.
2. $\sigma(Q)$'s predicate symbol occurs in neither P nor $\sigma(Q')$ for $Q' \in \mathcal{Q} \setminus \{Q\}$.

The simplest pre-renaming for P_Q maps every $Q \in \mathcal{Q}$ to an atom $p(X_1, \ldots, X_n)$, where p is a fresh predicate symbol and $X_1, \ldots, X_n$ are the distinct variables in Q. For example, with $P \equiv P_{app}$ and $\mathcal{Q} \equiv \mathcal{Q}_{app}$ we have as pre-renaming for P_Q:

$\sigma(app(X, Y, T) \wedge app(T, Z, R)) = da(X, Y, T, Z, R)$
$\sigma(app(X, Z, R)) \qquad\qquad\qquad = a(X, Z, R)$

Definition 4. (partitioning) A *partitioning* of a set Q of conjunctions is a map p such that for $Q \in \mathcal{Q}$, $p(Q) = \{Q_1, \ldots, Q_n\}$ and $Q = Q_1 \wedge \ldots \wedge Q_n$.

Definition 5. (renaming) Let σ be a pre-renaming function for P_Q. A *renaming* ρ based on σ is a mapping from conjunctions to atoms such that:

1. if Q is not an instance of an element in $\mathcal{Q}$, then $\rho(Q) = Q$.
2. otherwise, for some θ and $Q' \in \mathcal{Q}$: $Q = Q'\theta$ and $\rho(Q) = \sigma(Q')\theta$.

If there exist elements of $\mathcal{Q}$ with common instances, then there are several renamings associated with the same pre-renaming. Both renaming and partitioning may treat conjunctions that are variants of each other in different ways.

Definition 6. (conjunctive partial deduction) Let P be a program, $\mathcal{Q}$ a set of conjunctions, P_Q a pre-conjunctive partial deduction of P wrt $\mathcal{Q}$ with associated resultant sets R_Q, $Q \in \mathcal{Q}$, σ a pre-renaming for P_Q, ρ a renaming based on σ, and p a partitioning. Then the *conjunctive partial deduction of P (wrt $\mathcal{Q}$, under σ, ρ and p)* is the program P_{Q_ρ} which for each $H \leftarrow B \in R_Q$ contains the clause: $\sigma(Q)\theta \leftarrow \bigwedge_{Q \in p(B)} \rho(Q)$, where θ is a substitution such that $H = Q\theta$, and for each other clause $H \leftarrow B \in P_Q$, the clause: $H \leftarrow \bigwedge_{Q \in p(B)} \rho(Q)$.

For $P = P_{app}$ and $Q = Q_{app}$ we have the conjunctive partial deduction:

$$da([\ ], Y, Y, Z, R) \qquad \leftarrow a(Y, Z, R).$$
$$da([H|X'], Y, [H|T'], Z, [H|R']) \leftarrow da(X', Y, T', Z, R').$$
$$a([\ ], Y, Y).$$
$$a([H|X'], Y, [H|Z']) \qquad \leftarrow a(X', Y, Z').$$

To state the theorem guaranteeing correctness of conjunctive partial deduction, some terminology regarding closedness is required, see [19].

Definition 7. (correct renaming) Let σ be a pre-renaming for P_Q and ρ a renaming based on σ. Then ρ is a *correct* renaming (for P_Q) iff for every clause $H \leftarrow \bigwedge_{Q \in p(B)} \rho(Q)$ in P_{Q_ρ}, every Q in $p(B)$ with $\rho(Q) = \sigma(Q')\theta$ and $V = vars(Q) \backslash vars(\sigma(Q'))$ for some θ and $Q' \in \mathcal{Q}$, $\theta|_V$ is a renaming substitution and the variables in $V\theta$ are distinct from the variables in H, $\rho(Q)$ and $p(B) \backslash \{Q\}$.

Definition 8. (descends from) Given an SLD-tree τ. Let $G =\leftarrow A_1 \wedge \ldots \wedge A_n$ be a goal in τ, A_m the selected atom in G, $A \leftarrow A'_1 \wedge \ldots \wedge A'_k$ a clause of P such that θ is an mgu of A_m and A. Then in $\leftarrow (A_1 \wedge \ldots \wedge A'_1 \wedge \ldots \wedge A'_k \wedge \ldots \wedge A_n)\theta$, for each $i \in \{1, \ldots, k\}$, $A'_i\theta$ descends from A_m, and for each $i \in \{1, \ldots, n\} \backslash \{m\}$, $A_i\theta$ descends from A_i. If A' descends from A, and A'' descends from A', then A'' also descends from A, i.e. the relation is transitive.

Definition 9. (non-trivial) An SLD-tree is *non-trivial* if every atom in every conjunction in a leaf descends from a selected atom. A pre-conjunctive partial deduction P_Q derived from T_Q, $Q \in \mathcal{Q}$, is *non-trivial* if all T_Q are.

Definition 10. (bodies) For a set of resultants R, $R^b = \{B \mid Q \leftarrow B \in R\}$.

Definition 11. (Q-closed wrt p) Let p be a partitioning and Q a set of conjunctions. A conjunction Q is Q-*closed wrt p* iff every element of $p(Q)$ is either an instance of an element of Q or an atom whose predicate symbol is different from those of all atomic elements of Q. A generalised program P is Q-*closed wrt p* iff every element of P^b is Q-closed wrt p.

Definition 12. (p-depends on) Let P be a generalised program, $G = \leftarrow Q$ a goal, and p a partitioning. G *directly p-depends on* a (generalised) clause C in P if some $Q' \in p(Q)$ unifies with the head of C. G *p-depends on* a (generalised) clause C in P if it directly p-depends on C, or it directly p-depends on a (generalised) clause $C' = Q \leftarrow B$ in P and B p-depends on C.

Definition 13. (Q-covered wrt p) Let P be a program, G a goal, p a partitioning, Q a finite set of conjunctions, P_Q a pre-conjunctive partial deduction of P wrt Q, and P^* the set of clauses of P_Q on which G p-depends. $P_Q \cup \{G\}$ is Q-covered wrt p if $P^* \cup \{G\}$ is Q-closed wrt p.

Theorem 14 below now follows from Theorem 3.10 of [19], in a way similar to what is described in Section 4.2 of [24].

Theorem 14. *Let P_{Q_σ} be a conjunctive partial deduction of P wrt Q, under ρ, σ and p. Let ρ be correct for $P_Q \cup \{G\}$ and $P_Q \cup \{G\}$ be Q-covered wrt p, then*

- $P \cup \{G\}$ *has an SLD-refutation with computed answer θ, such that $\theta' = \theta|\rho(G)$, iff $P_{Q_\sigma} \cup \{\rho(G)\}$ has an SLD-refutation with computed answer θ'.*

If in addition P_Q is non-trivial, then

- $P \cup \{G\}$ *has a finitely failed SLD-tree iff $P_{Q_\sigma} \cup \{\rho(G)\}$ has.*

3 A Generic Conjunctive Partial Deduction Algorithm

The framework in Section 2 provides conditions guaranteeing correctness of partial deduction, but does not give an actual algorithm. For this, *control issues* must be addressed, e.g. how to select atoms for unfolding.

We now present a generic algorithm which computes conjunctive partial deductions satisfying the conditions of Theorem 14. The algorithm uses (i) an *unfolding rule* for controlling local unfolding and (ii) an *abstraction operator* for controlling global termination, respectively.

Definition 15. (unfolding rule) An *unfolding rule* U maps a program P and a conjunction Q to the set of resultants derived from a non-trivial SLD-tree for $P \cup \{\leftarrow Q\}$. For a set of conjunctions Q, $U(P, Q) = \cup_{Q \in Q} U(P, Q)$. Occasionally, $U(P, Q)$ will refer to the actual SLD-tree built.

Definition 16. (abstraction operator) An *abstraction operator* A maps any finite set of conjunctions Q to a finite set of conjunctions $A(Q)$ such that

1. if $Q \in A(Q)$, there exists $Q' \in Q$ with $Q' = Q\theta \wedge Q''$ for some Q'' and θ.

2. if $Q \in \mathcal{Q}$, there exist $Q_i \in A(\mathcal{Q})$ and θ_i $(i = 1 \ldots n)$ with $Q = Q_1\theta_1 \wedge \ldots \wedge Q_n\theta_n$.

Note that abstraction of a conjunction can involve splitting and generalising.

The following basic algorithm for conjunctive partial deduction is parameterised by an unfolding rule U and an abstraction operator A.

Algorithm 1

Input: a program P and a goal $\leftarrow Q$
Output: a set of conjunctions $\mathcal{Q}$
Initialisation: $i := 0$; $\mathcal{Q}_0 := \{Q\}$
repeat
    1. $S := U(P, \mathcal{Q}_i)$
    2. $\mathcal{Q}_{i+1} := A(\mathcal{Q}_i \cup S^b)$
    3. $i := i + 1$
until $\mathcal{Q}_i = \mathcal{Q}_{i-1}$ (modulo variable renaming)
output $\mathcal{Q}_i$

When Q is an atom, and abstraction operator A splits every conjunction into atoms, subsequently performing some generalisation on the resulting set, Algorithm 1 is essentially Gallagher's Basic Algorithm [10] restricted to definite programs.

From a program P and a goal $\leftarrow Q$, using some unfolding rule U and abstraction operator A, Algorithm 1 constructs a set of conjunctions $\mathcal{Q}$, which determines a pre-conjunctive partial deduction. From the abstraction, one can determine a partitioning p such that, for goals G to be solved with the specialised program, $P_\mathcal{Q} \cup \{G\}$ is $\mathcal{Q}$-covered wrt p. Then one can determine a correct renaming, and use this to construct a conjunctive partial deduction of P wrt $\mathcal{Q}$, satisfying the conditions for Theorem 14.

To obtain a concrete algorithm it remains to give an unfolding rule and an abstraction operator. These must ensure appropriate specialisation. A too cautious unfolding rule may entail too much abstraction and hence too little specialisation. Too eager unfolding, however, can cause code explosion, slow specialisation and non-termination. The next section addresses these *control problems*.

4 A Concrete Conjunctive Partial Deduction Algorithm

We now refine the above generic algorithm for conjunctive partial deduction into a concrete one. Following [26, 20] for the classical case, we introduce a *tree structure* to record dependencies among conjunctions in the successive $\mathcal{Q}_i$ and choose specific unfolding and abstraction operators. Throughout, we adhere to a conceptual *separation between local and global control* [10, 26, 20].

4.1 Trees for Global Control

Definition 17. (global tree) A *global tree* γ is a labeled tree, where every node N is labeled with a conjunction Q_N. $\mathcal{N}_\gamma$ denotes the set of its labels, and $\mathcal{L}_\gamma \subseteq \mathcal{N}_\gamma$

the set of its leaf labels. For a branch β in γ, $\mathcal{N}_\beta$ denotes the set of conjunctions labeling β's nodes, while $\mathcal{S}_\beta$ is the *sequence* of these labels, in the order they appear in β. For a leaf $L \in \gamma$, β_L denotes the (unique) branch containing L.

As in classical partial deduction, using global trees instead of just sets brings the ability to distinguish between unrelated goals during specialisation and thereby obtain a more specialised program. If two conjunctions in the global tree are on different branches, they are considered unrelated, and an abstraction operator can be defined that takes this into account. This kind of precision seems to be even more crucial here than in the classical context (c.f. Section 5.1).

Algorithm 1 is then refined as follows where each iteration no longer considers all conjunctions in "Q_i", but only those labeling leaves of γ_i (all not yet partially deduced conjunctions in the global tree are indeed leaf labels).

Algorithm 2

Input: a program P and a goal $\leftarrow Q$
Output: a set of conjunctions Q
Initialisation: $i := 0$; $\gamma_0 :=$ the global tree with a single node, labeled Q
repeat
    let γ_{i+1} arise from γ_i as follows:
    for all $L \in \mathcal{L}_{\gamma_i}$:
        for all $B \in (U(P, Q_L))^b$:
            let $\{Q_1, \ldots, Q_n\} := A_{\beta_L}(B) \backslash \mathcal{N}_{\beta_L}$
            and add n children to L with labels $Q_1, \ldots, Q_n$
    $i := i + 1$
until $\gamma_i = \gamma_{i-1}$
output $\mathcal{N}_{\gamma_i}$

The abstraction operators A_β are applied to a single conjunction at a time and, when abstracting the body of a new resultant, they only take the conjunctions in the branch β into account, which the new child nodes are potentially going to extend. Observe that a node N may be added to the global tree in spite of the fact that another node N' with a variant label already appears in it, but not as an ancestor of N. Indeed, both may have different ancestor labels, and if so, then they may be specialised in different ways, although the two label conjunctions are variants.

It remains to fix specific choices for U and A_β, and discuss termination and correctness for the resulting concrete conjunctive partial deduction algorithm.

4.2 Unfolding Rule for Local Control

An unfolding rule U constructs, from a program P and a conjunction Q, the resultants of a non-trivial SLD-tree for $P \cup \{\leftarrow Q\}$. The bodies of the resultants (usually) give rise to new conjunctions that may be added to the global tree γ. So the choice of U for local control determines which new conjunctions will be considered as potential candidates for specialisation at the global level.

Determining U consists in defining how to extend an SLD-tree with new nodes. There exists an extensive literature on this topic in classical partial deduction, see e.g. [2, 4, 25]. We propose a method which is sophisticated enough to usually give good results for the kind of transformations we have in mind.

The following homeomorphic embedding relation $\trianglelefteq$ is adapted from [30, 20]. As usual, $e_1 \prec e_2$ denotes that e_2 is a strict instance of e_1.

Definition 18. (strict homeomorphic embedding) Let X, Y range over variables, f over functors, and p over predicates. Define $\trianglelefteq$ on terms and atoms:

$$X \trianglelefteq Y$$
$$s \trianglelefteq f(t_1, \ldots, t_n) \quad\quad \Leftarrow s \trianglelefteq t_i \text{ for some } i$$
$$f(s_1, \ldots, s_n) \trianglelefteq f(t_1, \ldots, t_n) \Leftarrow s_i \trianglelefteq t_i \text{ for all } i$$
$$p(s_1, \ldots, s_n) \trianglelefteq p(t_1, \ldots, t_n) \Leftarrow s_i \trianglelefteq t_i \text{ for all } i \text{ and } p(t_1, \ldots, t_n) \not\prec p(s_1, \ldots, s_n)$$

Next, we introduce a computation rule, based on $\trianglelefteq$.

Definition 19. (selectable atom) An atom A in a goal at the leaf of an SLD-tree is *selectable* unless it descends from a selected atom A', with $A' \trianglelefteq A$.

Finally, we can present our concrete unfolding rule:

Definition 20. (concrete unfolding rule) Unfold the left-most selectable atom in each goal of the SLD-tree under construction. If no atom is selectable, do not unfold any atom in the goal.

The following theorem is a variant of Kruskal's theorem [18], see also [9].

Theorem 21. *For any infinite sequence $A_0, A_1, \ldots$, for some $0 \leq i < j : A_i \trianglelefteq A_j$.*

The following corollary follows from Definitions 9, 19 and 20, and Theorem 21.

Corollary 22. *Let P be a program, G a goal, and U the unfolding rule in Definition 20. Then $U(P, G)$ is a finite, non-trivial SLD-tree for $P \cup \{G\}$.*

4.3 Abstraction Operator for Global Control

It remains to specify the abstraction operators A_β, deciding which conjunctions are added to the global tree in order to ensure coveredness for bodies of newly derived resultants.

Ensuring coveredness is simple: add to the global tree all (unchanged) bodies of produced resultants as new, "to be partially deduced" conjunctions. However, this strategy leads usually to non-termination, and thus, the need for abstraction arises. For an element B in some $(U(P, Q_L))^\flat$, the abstraction operator A_{β_L} should consider whether adding B to the global level may endanger termination. To this end, A_{β_L} should detect whether B is (in some sense) bigger than another label already occurring in S_{β_L}, since adding B might then lead to some systematic growing behaviour resulting in non-termination.

According to Definition 16, abstraction allows two operations: conjunctions can be split and generalised. There are many ways this can be done and the concrete way will (usually) directly rely on the relation detecting growing behaviour. In this paper, we use homeomorphic embedding for *both* purposes.

Since we aim to remove shared, but unnecessary variables from conjunctions, there is no point in keeping atoms together that do not share variables. We will therefore always break up conjunctions into *maximal connected subparts* and abstraction will only consider these. In other words, resultant bodies will be automatically split into such connected chunks and it will be the latter that are considered by the abstraction operator proper.

Global termination then follows in a way similar to the local one.

Definition 23. (maximal connected subconjunctions) Given conjunction $Q \equiv A_1 \wedge \ldots \wedge A_n$, the collection $\mathrm{mcs}(Q) = \{Q_1, \ldots, Q_m\}$ of *maximal connected subconjunctions* is defined by:

1. $Q = Q_1 \wedge \ldots \wedge Q_m$
2. If a variable occurs in both A_i and A_j where $i < j$, then A_i occurs before A_j in the same Q_k.

Definition 24. (ordered instance, generalisation) A conjunction Q' is an *(ordered) instance* of another conjunction Q, $Q \leq Q'$, iff $Q' \equiv Q\theta$. Given two conjunctions Q and Q'. An *(ordered) generalisation* of Q and Q' is a conjunction Q'' such that $Q'' \leq Q$ and $Q'' \leq Q'$. A *most specific (ordered) generalisation* of Q and Q' is an ordered generalisation Q'' such that Q'' is an ordered instance of every ordered generalisation of Q and Q'.

For two conjunctions $Q \equiv A_1 \wedge \ldots \wedge A_n$ and $Q' \equiv A'_1 \wedge \ldots \wedge A'_n$ where A_i and A'_i have the same predicate symbols for all i, a most specific generalisation $\lfloor Q, Q' \rfloor$ exists, which is unique modulo variable renaming.

We now extend the definition of homeomorphic embedding to conjunctions.

Definition 25. (homeomorphic embedding) Define $\trianglelefteq$ by:

$$Q \equiv A_1 \wedge \ldots \wedge A_n \trianglelefteq Q' \equiv Q_1 \wedge A'_1 \wedge \ldots \wedge Q_n \wedge A'_n \wedge Q_{n+1} \Leftarrow A_i \trianglelefteq A'_i \text{ for all } i \text{ and } Q' \not\prec Q$$

Note that occurrences of the same variable in different atoms may be considered different. The proofs of the following two propositions are similar to the proofs of Propositions 3.23 and 3.24 in the extended version of [20].

Proposition 26. *If $Q_3 \leq Q_2$, then $Q_1 \trianglelefteq Q_3 \Rightarrow Q_1 \trianglelefteq Q_2$.*

So, a generalisation of a given conjunction will only embed conjunctions already embedded by the given one.

Proposition 27. *Suppose $Q_2 \leq Q_1$. Then $Q_1 \trianglelefteq Q_2$ iff $Q_1 \equiv Q_2$.*

To complete the definition of abstraction, it remains to decide how to split a maximal connected subconjunction Q' deriving from some $B \in (U(P, Q_L))^b$, when it indeed embeds a goal Q on the branch β considered.

Assume that $Q \equiv A_1 \wedge \ldots \wedge A_n$ is embedded in Q'. An obvious way is to split Q' into $A'_1 \wedge \ldots \wedge A'_n$ and R, where A'_i embeds A_i, and R contains the remaining atoms of Q'. This may not suffice since R can still embed a goal in S_{β_L}. Thus, in order to obtain a set of conjunctions not embedding any label in S_{β_L}, we *recursively repeat splitting and generalisation* on R.

There can be several conjunctions in S_{β_L} embedded in Q', and Q' can embed conjunctions in various ways. We cut the Gordian knot by abstracting wrt the node closest to leaf L. Next, we split in a way that is the *best match* wrt to connecting variables. Consider two conjunctions $Q \equiv p(X, Y) \wedge q(Y, Z)$ and $Q' \equiv p(X, T) \wedge p(T, Y) \wedge q(Y, Z)$. Q' embeds Q and, to rectify this, we can either split Q' into $p(X, T) \wedge q(Y, Z)$ and $p(T, Y)$, or into $p(X, T)$ and $p(T, Y) \wedge q(Y, Z)$. Of these, the second way is the best match because it maintains the sharing of Y. A straightforward method for approximating best matches is the following.

Definition 28. (best matching conjunction) Given conjunctions $Q, Q_1, ..., Q_n$ all containing the same number of atoms and such that Q_i embeds Q for all i's. A best matching conjunction Q_j is one for which $\lfloor Q_j, Q \rfloor$ is equal to a minimally general element[3][4] in the set $\{\lfloor Q_i, Q \rfloor | 1 \le i \le n\}$.

Definition 29. (splitting) Given conjunctions $Q \equiv A_1 \wedge ... \wedge A_n$ and Q'' such that $Q \trianglelefteq Q''$. Let Q' be the lexicographically leftmost subsequence[5] consisting of n atoms in Q'' such that $Q \trianglelefteq Q'$ and Q' is a best match among all subsequences Q^* consisting of n atoms in Q'' such that $Q \trianglelefteq Q^*$. Then $split_Q(Q'')$ is the pair (Q', R) where R is the conjunction containing the remaining atoms of Q'' in the same order as they appear in Q''.

We now make the abstraction operators A_β fully concrete in Algorithm 2.

Algorithm 3 For a global tree branch β, $S_\beta = [B_0, ..., B_n]$, define A_β by:

Input: a conjunction Q
Output: a set $\{Q_1, ..., Q_n\}$ with $Q = Q_1\theta_1 \wedge ... \wedge Q_n\theta_n$ and $\forall i, j : B_i \trianglelefteq Q_j \Rightarrow B_i \equiv Q_j$.
Initialisation: Let $Q = \emptyset$ and $\mathcal{M} = mcs(Q)$;
repeat
    1. Let $M \in \mathcal{M}$, $\mathcal{M} := \mathcal{M} \setminus \{M\}$;
    2. If there exists a largest i such that $B_i \trianglelefteq M$ and $B_i \not\equiv M$, then
        (a) $(M_1, M_2) := split_{B_i}(M)$;
        (b) $W := \lfloor M_1, B_i \rfloor$;
        (c) $Q := Q \cup mcs(W)$;
        (d) $\mathcal{M} := \mathcal{M} \cup mcs(M_2)$.
    3. Else $Q := Q \cup \{M\}$;
until $\mathcal{M} = \emptyset$;
output Q;

---

[3] An element Q of a set $\mathcal{Q}$ is minimally general iff there does not exist another element Q' in $\mathcal{Q}$ such that Q' is an (strict) instance of Q.
[4] Among the minimally general elements, one can select as follows. Consider graphs representing conjunctions where nodes represent occurrences of variables and there is an edge between two nodes iff they refer to occurrences of the same variable. A best match is then a Q_j with a maximal number of edges in the graph for $\lfloor Q_j, Q \rfloor$.
[5] By the *lexicographically leftmost subsequence* of atoms in a conjunction we mean the one with the smallest tuple of position indexes, ordered lexicographically.

Note that A_β is indeed an abstraction operator in the sense of Definition 16, abstracting a singleton $\{Q\}$. It is this property which ensures the existence of a partitioning (and a renaming) such that the output of Algorithm 2 leads to a conjunctive partial deduction satisfying the conditions of Theorem 14. The issue of finding a good renaming is briefly addressed in [19]. For lack of space, we cannot provide further details here. We do prove *termination* of Algorithm 2.

Proposition 30. *Algorithm 3 terminates. A conjunction $Q \in \mathcal{Q}$ either does not embed any $B_i \in \mathcal{L}_\beta$, or it is a variant of some such B_j.*

Proof. Upon every iteration, a conjunction is either removed from $\mathcal{M}$, or is replaced by finitely many strictly smaller conjunctions. Termination follows.
For the second part of the proposition, a conjunction Q is added to $\mathcal{Q}$ if either there is a $B_i \equiv Q$, or $Q \equiv \mathrm{mcs}(\lfloor M_1, B_i \rfloor)$ where $B_i \trianglelefteq M_1$ and for no $i < j$, $B_j \trianglelefteq M_1$. Since $B_k \trianglelefteq B_i$ for no $k < i$, Proposition 26 implies that $B_l \trianglelefteq Q$ for no $l \neq i$. Finally, Proposition 27 ensures that if $B_i \trianglelefteq Q$, then they are variants. $\square$

So, abstraction according to Algorithm 3 is well defined: its use ensures that no label in a branch of the global tree embeds an earlier label. The following theorem then is, again, a variant of Kruskal's Theorem.

Theorem 31. *Algorithm 2 terminates if U is a terminating unfolding operator and the A_β's are defined as in Algorithm 3.*

4.4 Refinements of the Algorithm

There are several ways in which the above algorithm can be refined further. Space does not allows a detailed discussion here, so we shall mention only two traditional techniques. Both techniques must be tuned to ensure non-triviality of the SLD-trees obtained by 'gluing' together the resulting smaller trees.

The simplest technique is as follows: If a conjunction Q' at a leaf in an SLD-tree is a variant (instance) of a conjunction $Q \in \mathcal{N}(\gamma_i)$, then unfolding stops at that leaf. We call this refinement the *variant (instance) check rule*. Note that applying this rule may lead to different specialisation of Q', since unfolding Q may have led to an SLD-tree, different from the subtree that can be built from Q', and its leaves may have been abstracted in another way than those in the latter (sub)tree would.

Another technique applies variant (instance) checking in a post-processing phase. At the end of specialisation, it inspects the SLD-trees connected to the conjunctions in $\mathcal{N}(\gamma)$, and removes from them all subtrees rooted in nodes whose goal body is a variant (instance) of a conjunction in $\mathcal{N}(\gamma)$. This optimisation can lead to less specialisation for essentially the same reasons as the one above. We call the second technique the *post variant (instance) check rule*.

5 Examples

In this section, we present examples illustrating optimisations that can be achieved by conjunctive partial deduction. We will, unless explicitly stated otherwise, use

Algorithm 2 with the concrete strategy formulated in Section 4, as well as the *variant check rule* and the *post variant check rule* described in Subsection 4.4. Further examples can be found in [11] and [19].

5.1 Double Append

Initially, the global tree contains a single node labeled $app(X, Y, T)$, $app(T, Z, R)$. Unfolding produces the SLD-tree shown below.

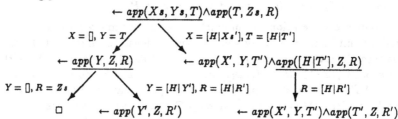

Note that the tree is indeed non-trivial. The fresh conjunctions to be considered are $app(Y', Z, R')$ and $app(X', Y, T')$, $app(T', Z, R')$. The abstraction operator returns both unchanged. The second one, however, is a variant of the initial one, and therefore is not incorporated in the global tree. Since we use the post variant check rule from Subsection 4.4, we remove (safely) the subtree below $app(Y, Z, R)$ in the SLD-tree in Subsection 4.2. The SLD-tree of $app(Y', Z, R')$ will be identical to the removed subtree (except for variable renaming). Then no more goals need to be considered, and the algorithm will terminate. From the result, one can construct the following conjunctive partial deduction; for details on renaming, see [19].

$$
\begin{aligned}
da([\,], Y, Y, Z, R) &\leftarrow a(Y, Z, R). \\
da([H|X'], Y, [H|T'], Z, [H|R']) &\leftarrow da(X', Y, T', Z, R'). \\
a([\,], Y, Y). & \\
a([H|X'], Y, [H|Z']) &\leftarrow a(X', Y, Z').
\end{aligned}
$$

This is almost the desired program except for the redundant third argument of *da*. As shown in [21], such redundant arguments can easily be removed by using a better renaming function, yielding the program shown in Section 1.

This example also illustrates a point mentioned in Section 4.1: It is even more crucial to use global trees for conjunctive partial deduction than in a classical context. If we run an algorithm based on sets of conjunctions, then $app(X', Y, T')$, $app(T', Z, R')$ embeds $app(Y, Z, R)$ and abstraction splits the conjunction $app(X', Y, T')$, $app(T', Z, R')$ into two separate atoms. Consequently, no optimisation is obtained.

5.2 Rotate-Prune

Consider the rotate-prune program, adopted from [28]:

$$
\begin{aligned}
rotate(leaf(N), leaf(N)). & \\
rotate(tree(L, N, R), tree(L', N, R')) &\leftarrow rotate(L, L'), rotate(R, R'). \\
rotate(tree(L, N, R), tree(R', N, L')) &\leftarrow rotate(L, L'), rotate(R, R').
\end{aligned}
$$

$prune(leaf(N), leaf(N))$.
$prune(tree(L, 0, R), leaf(0))$.
$prune(tree(L, s(N), R), tree(L', s(N), R')) \leftarrow prune(L, L'), prune(R, R')$.

The goal $rotate(T1, T2)$ is true if the tree $T2$ arises by interchanging the left and right subtree in zero or more nodes of $T1$, and $prune(T1, T2)$ is true if $T2$ arises be replacing each subtree of $T1$ with label 0 by a leaf labeled 0. Given $T1$, the goal $rotate(T1, U), prune(U, T2)$ first rotates and then prunes $T1$ by means of an intermediate variable U.

The goal $rp(T1, T2)$ arising by the technique in Section 4, avoids the intermediate data structure and so is more efficient. This is equivalent to what unfold/fold transformations can do [28].

$rp(l(N), l(N))$.
$rp(t(L, 0, R), l(0)) \qquad\qquad \leftarrow r(L), r(R)$.
$rp(t(L, s(N), R), t(L', s(N), R')) \leftarrow rp(L, L'), rp(R, R')$.
$rp(t(L, s(N), R), t(R', s(N), L')) \leftarrow rp(L, L'), rp(R, R')$.
$r(l(N))$.
$r(t(L, N, R)) \qquad\qquad\qquad \leftarrow r(L), r(R)$.

6 Related Work

Burstall and Darlington introduced unfold/fold transformations in functional programming [5]; *deforestation* [34] and *tupling* [6] are two automatic instances of the technique. Similar transformations have been introduced in logic programming [31, 27] for removing redundant variables from logic programs [28].

The relationship between partial deduction and unfold/fold transformation has already been discussed [3, 29, 27] but with an emphasis on how specialisation of logic programs can be understood in an unfold/fold setting. Pettorossi and Proietti [27] describe a technique for classical partial deduction based on unfold/fold rules. Their technique relies on a simple folding strategy involving no generalisation, so termination is not guaranteed. Similar approaches are described in [28, 29]; in [29] generalisation is present in the notion of "minimal foldable upper portion" of an unfolding tree.

Turchin's supercompiler [32, 14] can also do deforestation. Supercompilation performs *driving* (normal-order unfolding and unification-based information propagation) and *generalisation* (a form of abstraction) [33, 30]. Tree structures are used to record the history of configurations [12]. The connection between driving and classical partial deduction was established in [13].

Recently, a transformation scheme has been proposed for functional-logic languages based on an automatic unfolding algorithm that builds narrowing trees [1]. A generic algorithm is provided that does not depend on the eager or lazy nature of the narrowing to be defined. Effects similar to driving and partial deduction can be achieved due to the unification-based mechanism of narrowing.

Finally, in classical partial deduction [24, 10, 8], the goals at the leaves of the SLD-trees are always cut up into atoms before being specialised further. Therefore, any information obtained by subsequently further specialising one atom in such a goal can never be used when specialising the other atoms in that same goal. Consequently, conjunctive partial deduction can have a major impact on the quality of specialisation even in cases where the objective is not elimination of unnecessary variables, but just specialisation of programs with respect to some known input. The experiments reported in [16] confirm this conjecture. In particular, determinate unfolding often leads to little or no specialisation with classical partial deduction, but performs much better with conjunctive partial deduction.

Acknowledgements. Special thanks to Danny De Schreye, André de Waal, Michael Leuschel, Torben Mogensen and Maurizio Proietti for discussions on this work. Michael Leuschel provided valuable feedback on an earlier version of this paper.

Robert Glück, Bern Martens, and Morten Heine Sørensen were partially supported by the DART project funded by the Danish Natural Sciences Research Council. Bern Martens is a postdoctoral fellow of the K.U. Leuven Research Council. Jesper Jørgensen was supported partly by the HCM Network "Logic Program Synthesis and Transformation" and the Belgian GOA "Non-Standard Applications of Abstract Interpretation".

References

1. M. Alpuente, M. Falaschi, G. Vidal. Narrowing-driven partial evaluation of functional logic programs. *ESOP'96*. LNCS 1058, 45–61, Springer-Verlag, 1996.
2. R. Bol. Loop checking in partial deduction. *Journal of Logic Programming*, 16(1&2):25–46, 1993.
3. A. Bossi, N. Cocco, S. Dulli. A method for specializing logic programs. *ACM Transactions on Programming Languages and Systems*, 12(2):253–302, 1990.
4. M. Bruynooghe, D. De Schreye, B. Martens. A general criterion for avoiding infinite unfolding during partial deduction. *New Generation Computing*, 11(1):47–79, 1992.
5. R.M. Burstall, J. Darlington. A transformation system for developing recursive programs. *Journal of the ACM*, 24(1):44–67, 1977.
6. W.-N. Chin. Towards an automated tupling strategy. In *Symposium on Partial Evaluation and Semantics-Based Program Manipulation*. 119–132. ACM Press, 1993.
7. O. Danvy, R. Glück, P. Thiemann (eds.). *Partial Evaluation*, LNCS 1110, Springer-Verlag, 1996.
8. D. De Schreye, M. Leuschel, B. Martens. Program specialisation for logic programs. Tutorial presented at [23].
9. N. Dershowitz, J.-P. Jouannaud. Rewrite systems. In J. van Leeuwen (ed.), *Handbook of Theoretical Computer Science*, 244–320, Elsevier, 1992.
10. J. Gallagher. Tutorial on specialisation of logic programs. In *Symposium on Partial Evaluation and Semantics-Based Program Manipulation*, 88–98. ACM Press, 1993.
11. R. Glück, J. Jørgensen, B. Martens, and M. Sørensen. Controlling conjunctive partial deduction of definite logic programs. Technical Report CW 226, Departement Computerwetenschappen, K.U. Leuven, Belgium, February 1996.

12. R. Glück, A.V. Klimov. Occam's razor in metacomputation: The notion of a perfect process tree. In P. Cousot, et al. (eds.), *Static Analysis*. LNCS 724, 112–123, Springer-Verlag, 1993.

13. R. Glück, M.H. Sørensen. Partial deduction and driving are equivalent. In M. Hermenegildo and J. Penjam (eds.), *Programming Language Implementation and Logic Programming*. LNCS 844, 165–181, Springer-Verlag, 1994.

14. R. Glück, M.H. Sørensen. A roadmap to metacomputation by supercompilation. In [7].

15. N.D. Jones, C.K. Gomard, P. Sestoft. *Partial Evaluation and Automatic Program Generation*. Prentice Hall, 1993.

16. J. Jørgensen, M. Leuschel, B. Martens. Conjunctive partial deduction in practice. Logic Program Synthesis and Transformation 1996. To appear.

17. J. Komorowski. Partial evaluation as a means for inferencing data structures in an applicative language: A theory and implementation in the case of Prolog. In *Symposium on Principles of Programming Languages*, 255–167. ACM Press, 1982.

18. J.B. Kruskal. Well-quasi-ordering, the tree theorem, and Vazsonyi's conjecture. *Transactions of the American Mathematical Society*, 95:210–225, 1960.

19. M. Leuschel, D. De Schreye, A. de Waal. A conceptual embedding of folding into partial deduction: Towards a maximal integration, JICSLP'96, 1996. To appear.

20. M. Leuschel, B. Martens. Global control for partial deduction through characteristic atoms and global trees. In [7].

21. M. Leuschel, M.H. Sørensen. Redundant argument filtering of logic programs, 1996. Logic Program Synthesis and Transformation 1996. To appear.

22. J.W. Lloyd. *Foundations of Logic Programming*. Springer-Verlag, 1987.

23. J.W. Lloyd (ed.). *Logic Programming: Proceedings of the 1995 International Symposium*. MIT Press, 1995.

24. J.W. Lloyd, J.C. Shepherdson. Partial evaluation in logic programming. *Journal of Logic Programming*, 11(3-4):217–242, 1991.

25. B. Martens, D. De Schreye. Automatic finite unfolding using well-founded measures. *Journal of Logic Programming*, 1996. 28(2):89–146, 1996.

26. B. Martens, J. Gallagher. Ensuring global termination of partial deduction while allowing flexible polyvariance. In L. Sterling (ed.), *International Conference on Logic Programming*. 597–611, MIT Press, 1995.

27. A. Pettorossi, M. Proietti. Transformation of logic programs: Foundations and techniques. *Journal of Logic Programming*, 19 & 20:261–320, 1994.

28. M. Proietti, A. Pettorossi. Unfolding – definition – folding, in this order for avoiding unnecessary variables in logic programs. In *Programming Language Implementation and Logic Programming*. LNCS 528, 347–358, Springer-Verlag, 1991.

29. M. Proietti, A. Pettorossi. The loop absorption and the generalization strategies for the development of logic programs and partial deduction. *Journal of Logic Programming*, 16:123–161, 1993.

30. M.H. Sørensen, R. Glück. An algorithm of generalization in positive supercompilation. In [23], 465–479.

31. H. Tamaki, T. Sato. Unfold/fold transformation of logic programs. In S-Å. Tärnlund (ed.), *International Conference on Logic Programming*. 127–138, 1984.

32. V.F. Turchin. The concept of a supercompiler. *ACM Transactions on Programming Languages and Systems*, 8(3):292–325, 1986.

33. V.F. Turchin. The algorithm of generalization in the supercompiler. In D. Bjørner, A.P. Ershov, N.D. Jones (eds.), *Partial Evaluation and Mixed Computation*. 531–549. North-Holland, 1988.

34. P. Wadler. Deforestation: Transforming programs to eliminate intermediate trees. *Theoretical Computer Science*, 73:231–248, 1990.

Unfold/Fold Transformations of Concurrent Processes [1]

Nicoletta De Francesco and Antonella Santone

Dipartimento di Ingegneria dell'Informazione
Università di Pisa, Italy

Abstract. Program transformation is a technique for obtaining, starting from a program P, a semantically equivalent one, which is "better"
than P with respect to a particular goal. Traditionally, the main goal
of program transformation was obtaining more efficient programs, but,
in general, this technique can be used to produce programs written in a
syntactic form satisfying some properties. Program transformation techniques have been extensively studied in the framework of functional and
logic languages, where they were applied mainly to obtain more efficient
and readable programs. All these works are based on the Unfold/Fold
program transformation method developed by Burstall and Darlington
in the context of their recursive equational language. The use of Un-
fold/Fold based transformations for concurrent languages is a relevant
issue that has not yet received an adequate attention. In fact the existing
proposals of transformations of concurrent programs are not based on a
general Unfold/Fold transformation theory. The aim of this paper is to
define such a theory for the concurrent calculus CCS and to prove it
correct.

1 Introduction and Overview

Program transformation is a technique for obtaining, starting from a program
P, a semantically equivalent one, which is "better" than P with respect to a
particular goal. Traditionally, the main goal of program transformation was obtaining more efficient programs, but, in general, this technique can be used to
produce programs written in a syntactic form satisfying some properties.

Program transformation techniques have been extensively studied in the
framework of functional and logic languages [5, 9, 19, 24, 25, 26], where they
were applied mainly to obtain more efficient and readable programs. All these
works are based on the Unfold/Fold program transformation method developed
by Burstall and Darlington [5] in the context of their recursive equational language. The method is based on a set of rules manipulating a set of mutually
recursive definitions. It consists in building a sequence of equivalent programs,
each obtained by the preceding ones by means of the application of a rule. The
rules are based on *Unfolding* and *Folding*, i.e., expansion and contraction of
sub-expressions of a program, using the definitions of the preceding programs.

---

[1] This work has been partially funded by Progetto Coordinato CNR ANATRA.

The use of Unfold/Fold based transformations for concurrent languages is a relevant issue that has not yet received an adequate attention. In fact the existing proposals of transformations of concurrent programs (see, for example, [20, 29]) are not based on a general Unfold/Fold transformation theory. The aim of this paper is to define such a theory for the concurrent calculus CCS [22] and to prove it correct. A CCS program is a set of mutually recursive definitions that can be manipulated by syntactic transformations to obtain a semantically equivalent program in which a particular property is syntactically evident.

In this paper we define a set of transformation rules for CCS. These are a specialization of classical program transformation rules, such as Folding and Unfolding. It is well known [27] that, while Unfolding preserves program equivalence, its inverse, i.e. Folding, when used without restriction, can cause loss of information. The study of conditions to ensure folding safeness is a major topic in program transformation. In the functional and logic programming areas many proposals have been made of safe folding rules: the first one was that of Tamaki and Sato [27], in which the set of definitions is partitioned into "old" and "new" ones, and unrestricted folding is allowed only for old definitions, while it is constrained when applied to the new ones. Subsequent proposals (see, for example, [15, 23]), were devoted to find weaker conditions for the application of folding, still maintaining its safeness. In this paper we introduce an elegant safe folding rule for CCS, based on a well-known process algebra notion, i.e. *Guardedness*. Besides being very simple, this rule is very general and powerful and, differently from most proposals for logic programs, the condition it imposes do not depend on the transformation history, but is checkable only by inspecting the program to be folded.

In the paper the transformation rules are proved correct with respect to the CCS semantics. The detailed proof we show is built differently from the proof of analogous theorems for logic programs (see [25, 27]), since it uses bisimulation techniques.

Finally, we show two examples of application of Unfold/Fold transformations of CCS. First we use our rules to transform, if possible, a full CCS program into an equivalent program whose semantics is a finite transition system. This is achieved by trying to obtain a program in which the "growing" operators, such as parallel composition and restriction, do not occur. If the transformation succeeds, it becomes feasible to use the existing verification environments [1, 4, 7, 8, 13, 14], which are based on an internal finite state representation of the program. Moreover, the transformation process can be seen as a way to prove finiteness of CCS programs. As a second example, we show how it is possible to prove the equivalence between two BPP programs by transforming one into the other, where BPP [6] is a subset of CCS for which equivalence is decidable. Thus, our transformational approach can be seen as unifying in a common framework a set of different techniques of program analysis.

This paper is the first attempt, to our knowledge, of formally defining and proving correct a general Unfold/Fold program transformation methodology for a concurrent calculus. The results we have achieved suggest that this area of research is very promising.

Section 2 recalls some notions related to CCS and program transformation methodology. Section 3 defines our methodology, while Section 4 shows some applications. Section 5 compares the work with existing ones, concludes and illustrates future work.

2 Preliminaries

2.1 CCS

We assume that the reader is familiar with the basic concepts of process algebras and CCS. We summarize the most relevant definitions below, and we refer to [22] for more details. The CCS syntax we consider is the following:

$$p ::= \mu.p \mid nil \mid p + p \mid p|p \mid p\backslash A \mid x \mid p[f]$$

Terms generated by p ($Terms$) are called *process terms* (called also *processes* or *terms*); x ranges over a set $\{x, y, \ldots\}$ of constants ($Const$). A constant is defined by a constant definition $x \stackrel{\text{def}}{=} p_x$, ($p_x$ is called the *body* of x).

As usual, there is a set of visible actions $Vis = \{a, \overline{a}, b, \overline{b}, \ldots\}$ over which α ranges, while μ, ν range over $Act = Vis \cup \{\tau\}$, where τ denotes the so-called *internal action*. We denote by $\overline{\alpha}$ the action complement: if $\alpha = a$, then $\overline{\alpha} = \overline{a}$, while if $\alpha = \overline{a}$, then $\overline{\alpha} = a$. By nil we denote the empty process.

The operators to build process terms are prefixing ($\mu.p$), summation ($p + p$), parallel composition ($p|p$), restriction ($p\backslash A$) and relabelling ($p[f]$), where $A \subseteq Vis$ and $f : Vis \rightarrow Vis$ such that $f(\overline{\alpha}) = \overline{f(\alpha)}$. We also extend f to Act by decreeing that $f(\tau) = \tau$ and we assume that Vis is finite. The precedence of the operators is given by the following list, in increasing order: $+$, $|$, $.$, $\backslash A$, $[f]$ (parentheses will be avoided wherever possible).

A CCS program is a pair $\langle \mathcal{D}, p \rangle$, where $p \in Terms$ and $\mathcal{D}$ is a finite set of constant definitions. Given a term p, a sub-term of p is *weakly guarded* (or simply *guarded*) *in* p if it occurs in a term q such that $\mu.q$ is a sub-term of p. We say that a CCS program $\langle \mathcal{D}, p \rangle$ is *standard* if: i) there is only one definition for each constant; ii) p and each constant body are *closed*, i.e. contain only constants defined in $\mathcal{D}$; and iii) each constant occurrence is weakly guarded in each constant body.

The operational semantics of a CCS term p with a set $\mathcal{D}$ of constant definitions is given by a set of inference rules defining a relation $\rightarrow_{\mathcal{D}} \subseteq Terms \times Act \times Terms$. The relation is the least relation satisfying the rules. If $(p, \mu, q) \in \rightarrow_{\mathcal{D}}$, we write $p \stackrel{\mu}{\rightarrow}_{\mathcal{D}} q$. The SOS rules [22] are recalled in figure 1.

A *labelled transition system* (or simply *transition system*) TS is a quadruple $(S, T, \rightarrow, s_0)$, where S is a set of states, T is a set of transition labels, $s_0 \in S$ is the initial state, and $\rightarrow \subseteq S \times T \times S$. If $(s, \mu, s') \in \rightarrow$, we write $s \stackrel{\mu}{\rightarrow} s'$. Given a program $P = \langle \mathcal{D}, p \rangle$, the *operational semantics* of P is the transition system $SOS(P) = (Terms, Act, \rightarrow_{\mathcal{D}}, p)$, where $\rightarrow_{\mathcal{D}}$ is the relation defined by SOS.

$$\textbf{Act } \frac{}{\mu.p \xrightarrow{\mu}_{D} p} \qquad \textbf{Sum}_1 \frac{p \xrightarrow{\mu}_{D} p'}{p+q \xrightarrow{\mu}_{D} p'} \qquad \textbf{Sum}_2 \frac{q \xrightarrow{\mu}_{D} q'}{p+q \xrightarrow{\mu}_{D} q'}$$

$$\textbf{Com}_1 \frac{p \xrightarrow{\mu}_{D} p'}{p|q \xrightarrow{\mu}_{D} p'|q} \qquad \textbf{Com}_2 \frac{q \xrightarrow{\mu}_{D} q'}{p|q \xrightarrow{\mu}_{D} p|q'} \qquad \textbf{Com}_3 \frac{p \xrightarrow{\alpha}_{D} p' \quad q \xrightarrow{\overline{\alpha}}_{D} q'}{p|q \xrightarrow{\tau}_{D} p'|q'}$$

$$\textbf{Res } \frac{p \xrightarrow{\mu}_{D} p'}{p \backslash A \xrightarrow{\mu}_{D} p' \backslash A} \; \mu, \overline{\mu} \notin A \quad \textbf{Rel } \frac{p \xrightarrow{\mu}_{D} p'}{p[f] \xrightarrow{f(\mu)}_{D} p'[f]} \qquad \textbf{Con } \frac{p_x \xrightarrow{\mu}_{D} p'}{x \xrightarrow{\mu}_{D} p'} \; (x \stackrel{\text{def}}{=} p_x \in D)$$

Figure 1: Operational Semantics of CCS

A finite computation of a CCS term p with D is a sequence $\mu_1 \mu_2 \cdots \mu_n$ of labels such that $p_0 \xrightarrow{\mu_1}_{D} \cdots \xrightarrow{\mu_n}_{D} p_n$ with $p = p_0$. A term q such that there is a computation $p \xrightarrow{\mu_1}_{D} \cdots \xrightarrow{\mu_n}_{D} q$ is a *derivative* of p with D. If $n = 1$, q is an *immediate derivative* of p.

Let $TS_1 = (S_1, T_1, \rightarrow_{D_1}, s_{0_1})$ and $TS_2 = (S_2, T_2, \rightarrow_{D_2}, s_{0_2})$ be transition systems and let $s_1 \in S_1$ and $s_2 \in S_2$. s_1 and s_2 are *strongly equivalent* (or simply *equivalent*) $(s_1 \cong s_2)$ if there exists a *strong bisimulation* that relates s_1 and s_2.
$\mathcal{B} \subseteq S_1 \times S_2$ is a strong bisimulation if $\forall (r, s) \in \mathcal{B}$ (where $\mu \in T_1 \cup T_2$)

- $r \xrightarrow{\mu}_{D_1} r'$ implies $\exists s' : s \xrightarrow{\mu}_{D_2} s'$ and $(r', s') \in \mathcal{B}$;
- $s \xrightarrow{\mu}_{D_2} s'$ implies $\exists r' : r \xrightarrow{\mu}_{D_1} r'$ and $(r', s') \in \mathcal{B}$.

TS_1 and TS_2 are said to be *equivalent* $(TS_1 \cong TS_2)$ if a strong bisimulation exists relating s_{0_1} and s_{0_2}. Given two CCS programs $P = \langle D, p \rangle$ and $Q = \langle D', q \rangle$, we say that P is *equivalent* to Q $(P \cong Q)$ if $SOS(P) \cong SOS(Q)$.

In [22] a set of laws is defined, which axiomatize strong equivalence, for example $p \backslash A \backslash A \cong p \backslash A$. An important law is the *Expansion Law*: for each $q = (p_1 \mid \cdots \mid p_n) \backslash A$, with $n \geq 1$, it holds

$$q \cong \sum \left\{ \mu.(p_1 \mid \cdots \mid p_i' \mid \cdots \mid p_n) \backslash A : p_i \xrightarrow{\mu} p_i', \; \mu \notin (A \cup \overline{A}) \right\}$$
$$+ \sum \left\{ \tau.(p_1 \mid \cdots \mid p_i' \mid \cdots \mid p_j' \mid \cdots \mid p_n) \backslash A : p_i \xrightarrow{\alpha} p_i', \; p_j \xrightarrow{\overline{\alpha}} p_j', \; i < j \right\}$$

It holds that, if each constant occurrence is guarded in q, then the summation is finite.

2.2 Program Transformation

The Unfold/Fold transformation approach was introduced in [5] to manage functional programs and then used for logic programs [25, 26]. This approach is based on the construction, by means of a *strategy*, of a sequence $\{P_k\}$ of programs each obtained by the preceding ones using of a transformation rule. The rules are based on *unfolding* and *folding*, i.e. expansion and contraction of a subexpression of P_k using the definitions of P_k or of a preceding program. Other rules are used, as, for example, *definition elimination* and *introduction*. Each program in the sequence is related with the preceding ones by a particular semantic notion. In general, the methodologies may differ in the rules they adopt and/or in the strategy they follow, and each methodology is proved correct with respect to a particular semantics of the language.

3 The Transformation Rules

In this section we present the transformation rules of our methodology. They allow us to build a sequence $\{P_k\}$, $k \geq 0$, of CCS programs each one obtained by the preceding ones by the application of a rule. All the programs of the sequence $\{P_k\}$ are strongly equivalent.

We use the following definition. Given the terms q and r, the pair $[q/r]$ denotes *substitution*. If r is a sub-term of a term p, the application of a substitution to p, denoted as $p[q/r]$, results in the term obtained from p by substituting q for r in p.

The first rule is *Unfolding* and substitute a constant name x with the body of the definition of x belonging to a preceding or to the same program.

Unfolding. Let $P_k = \langle \mathcal{D}, p \rangle$ be a program and let $D \in \mathcal{D}$ be the constant definition $x \stackrel{\text{def}}{=} p_x$ such that the constant y occurs in p_x. Suppose that the definition D' : $y \stackrel{\text{def}}{=} q$ belongs to a program P_j, with $0 \leq j \leq k$. If we *unfold* D using D' in P_j, we obtain the program $P_{k+1} = \langle (\mathcal{D} - \{D\}) \cup \{x \stackrel{\text{def}}{=} p_x[q/y]\}, p \rangle$.

For example, suppose that $P_0 = \langle \{x \stackrel{\text{def}}{=} c.y \mid a.nil, \ y \stackrel{\text{def}}{=} b.y\}, \ x \rangle$. After an unfolding step we obtain the program $P_1 = \langle \{x \stackrel{\text{def}}{=} c.b.y \mid a.nil, \ y \stackrel{\text{def}}{=} b.y\}, \ x \rangle$.

It is well known that the Unfolding rule is safe, in the sense that it produces semantically equivalent programs. Its inverse, the *Folding* rule, is harmful in general. In the Folding rule we substitute a term p with a constant name x such that there is a definition $x \stackrel{\text{def}}{=} p$ in a preceding or in the same program. But it is well known [24, 25, 27] that unrestricted folding may cause loss of information, as in the case of the program $\langle \{x \stackrel{\text{def}}{=} a.nil\}, x \rangle$ which can be folded, obtaining $\langle \{x \stackrel{\text{def}}{=} x\}, x \rangle$. However, information can be lost also in non trivial cases: consider the program $P_0 = \langle \{x \stackrel{\text{def}}{=} a.nil, \ y \stackrel{\text{def}}{=} a.nil\}, \ x \rangle$; after a folding step we obtain the program $P_1 = \langle \{x \stackrel{\text{def}}{=} a.nil, \ y \stackrel{\text{def}}{=} x\}, \ x \rangle$. If now we re-apply folding using the definition of y in P_0, we obtain the program $P_2 = \langle \{x \stackrel{\text{def}}{=} y, \ y \stackrel{\text{def}}{=} x\}, \ x \rangle$ such that $P_2 \not\cong P_0$. A safe solution is to allow folding of a program P_k using only the definitions of P_k and not those of the preceding programs (provided we do not use self-folding). But in this way most of the power of the approach is lost. For these reasons, in the functional and logic programming areas many proposals were made of weaker conditions for the application of folding, still maintaining its safeness. In [27] the set of definitions is partitioned into "old" and "new" ones, allowing folding only for old definitions and imposing restrictions on the new ones: essentially, a new definition can be folded only if it has been unfolded at least once. Other proposals can be found in [3, 15, 18, 23].

For CCS we propose the following safe folding rule, which simply allows folding only for weakly guarded sub-terms.

Guarded-Folding. Let $P_k = \langle \mathcal{D}, p \rangle$ be a program and let $D \in \mathcal{D}$ be the constant definition $x \stackrel{\text{def}}{=} p_x$ such that q is a weakly guarded sub-term of p_x. Suppose that $D' : y \stackrel{\text{def}}{=} q$ is a definition belonging to a program P_j, with $0 \leq j \leq k$. If we *fold* D using D' in P_j, we obtain the program $P_{k+1} = \langle (\mathcal{D} - \{D\}) \cup \{x \stackrel{\text{def}}{=} p_x[y/q]\}, p \rangle$.

Intuitively, using Guarded-Folding we do not lose any information since the "first" events of each constant body remain unaltered and this has the same effect achieved when the definition to be folded has been already unfolded, which is the condition described in [27]. Note that the condition on folding does not depend on the transformation history, as most of the existing conditions do, but is checkable by inspecting only the program to be folded.

The *Definition Introduction* rule adds a new constant definition:

Definition Introduction. Let be $P_k = \langle \mathcal{D}, p \rangle$. If there is no definition for the constant x in $P_0, \ldots, P_k$ and q is a term in which all the occurring constants are defined in $\mathcal{D}$ and are weakly guarded, we can *introduce* the definition of x, obtaining the program $P_{k+1} = \langle \mathcal{D} \cup \{x \stackrel{\text{def}}{=} q\}, p \rangle$.

We now define a set containing the constants possibly reachable from a term p during the computations starting from p.

Definition 1 (Reachable constants: $\mathcal{R}_{\mathcal{D}}(p)$). Given a term p and a set $\mathcal{D}$ of constant definitions, we define the set $\mathcal{R}_{\mathcal{D}}(p) \subseteq Const$ of constants reachable from a term p as $\mathcal{R}_{\mathcal{D}}(p) = \rho_n(p)$, where n is the number of the constant definitions in $\mathcal{D}$ and, $\forall i \geq 0$ $\rho_i : Terms \rightarrow 2^{Const}$ is defined as follows:

$$\rho_i(nil) = \emptyset$$
$$\rho_i(\mu.p) = \rho_i(p)$$
$$\rho_i(p + q) = \rho_i(p) \cup \rho_i(q)$$
$$\rho_i(p \mid q) = \rho_i(p) \cup \rho_i(q)$$
$$\rho_i(p \backslash A) = \rho_i(p)$$
$$\rho_i(p[f]) = \rho_i(p)$$
$$\rho_i(y) = \begin{cases} \emptyset & \text{if } i = 0 \\ \rho_{i-1}(p_y) \cup \{y\} & \text{if } i \geq 1 \text{ and } y \stackrel{\text{def}}{=} p_y \in \mathcal{D} \end{cases}$$

For example, if $\mathcal{D} = \{x \stackrel{\text{def}}{=} c.b.y, y \stackrel{\text{def}}{=} b.y, z \stackrel{\text{def}}{=} a.nil\}$, then $\mathcal{R}_\mathcal{D}(a.x|b.nil) = \{x, y\}$.

The following lemma holds:

Lemma 2. *Given a term p and a set $\mathcal{D}$ of constant definitions, for each constant y occurring in a derivative of p with $\mathcal{D}$, $y \in \mathcal{R}_\mathcal{D}(p)$.*

Proof. First note that, by definition,

1. for each $i \leq j, i \geq 0$, $\rho_i(p) \subseteq \rho_j(p)$;
2. $y \in \rho_i(x)$ and $x \in \rho_1(p)$ implies $y \in \rho_{i+1}(p)$.

Consider y occurring in a derivative of p. If y occurs in p, then $y \in \rho_1(p)$ and, by (1), $y \in \rho_n(p) = \mathcal{R}_\mathcal{D}(p)$. Otherwise, the set of constants $C = \{x_1, \ldots, x_k\}, k \geq 1$, exists, with $x_i \neq x_j$ and $x_i \neq y$, for each $1 \leq i, j \leq k$, such that $y \in \rho_1(p_{x_k})$, $x_1 \in \rho_1(p)$ and, if $k > 1$, $x_j \in \rho_1(p_{x_{j-1}})$ for $j \in \{2, \ldots, k\}$. By point (2) above, we have that $y \in \rho_{k+1}(p)$. Since $k < n$ ($y \notin C$), then $y \in \rho_n(p) = \mathcal{R}_\mathcal{D}(p)$. $\square$

Note that $\mathcal{R}_\mathcal{D}(p)$ is a super set of the set of constants that actually occur in the derivatives of p: this means that it may occur that a constant in $\mathcal{R}_\mathcal{D}(p)$ is not reached in any computation starting from p. However, it is not decidable whether a constant can be actually reached from p.

The *Definition Elimination* rule deletes a definition, provided that the corresponding constant is not reachable from p:

Definition Elimination. Let $P_k = \langle \mathcal{D}, p \rangle$ be a program and let $D \in \mathcal{D}$ be the constant definition $x \stackrel{\text{def}}{=} p_x$. If $x \notin \mathcal{R}_\mathcal{D}(p)$, we *eliminate* the definition of x, obtaining the program $P_{k+1} = \langle \mathcal{D} - \{D\}, p \rangle$.

The following lemma holds:

Lemma 3. *If P_{k+1} is obtained from P_k by means of an application of the Definition Elimination rule, then, $P_k \cong P_{k+1}$.*

Proof. The proof follows from lemma 2.

The following rule allows us to perform simple equivalence preserving rewritings of terms occurring in the constant bodies.

Simplification. Let be $P_k = \langle \mathcal{D}, p \rangle$, $D \in \mathcal{D}$ the constant definition $x \stackrel{\text{def}}{=} p_x$ and q a sub-term of p_x. If for each $\mathcal{D}'$, $\langle \mathcal{D}', q \rangle \cong \langle \mathcal{D}', q' \rangle$, we *simplify* D in P_k, obtaining the program $P_{k+1} = \langle (\mathcal{D} - \{D\}) \cup \{x \stackrel{\text{def}}{=} p_x[q'/q]\}, p \rangle$.

Lemma 4. *If P_{k+1} is obtained from P_k by means of an application of the Simplification rule, then $P_k \cong P_{k+1}$.*

Proof. By defining a suitable bisimulation.

Note that the property expressed in the rule ensures that the rule itself can be applied independently from the constant definitions of a program. The rule allows us to use the properties of the CCS operators to simplify the terms. For example, we can rewrite $p\backslash A\backslash B$ as $p\backslash A \cup B$ or $(p+q)\backslash A$ as $p\backslash A + q\backslash A$. A particular case is the application of the Expansion law when the partners of the parallel composition are weakly guarded.

Note that all our transformation rules are applied to the constant definitions of a program $\langle \mathcal{D}, p \rangle$ and not to the term p. We do not lose generality, since we can consider, instead of a program $\langle \mathcal{D}, p \rangle$, the equivalent program $\langle \mathcal{D} \cup \{x \stackrel{\text{def}}{=} p\}, x \rangle$, where x is different from all constants occurring in $\mathcal{D}$.

3.1 Correctness of the transformation system

In this section we prove that, by using the rules defined in the preceding section, we obtain a sequence of equivalent programs. The proof is built differently from the proof of analogous theorems for logic programs [18, 25, 27], since it uses bisimulation techniques.

The following lemma states that all programs of a transformation sequence, starting from a standard program, are standard.

Lemma 5. *Let be given a transformation sequence* $\{P_k\}$ *such that* P_0 *is standard; then each* p_i *in* $\{P_k\}$ *is standard.*

Proof. By definition of the transformation rules.

From now we assume transformation sequences such that P_0 is standard. Let be given a transformation sequence $\{P_k\}$. We denote as $\mathcal{D}_i$ the constant definitions of program P_i belonging to the sequence and with p_x^i the body of constant x in $\mathcal{D}_i$. Moreover, we use $\stackrel{\mu}{\to}_i$ instead of $\stackrel{\mu}{\to}_{\mathcal{D}_i}$.

We will use the following definitions. A θ-*substitution* is a substitution $[x/p_x^i]$ or $[p_x^i/x]$, for each x and each i such that x is defined in P_i and $P_i \in \{P_k\}$. A θ-*substitution sequence* σ is a, possibly empty, finite sequence of θ-substitutions. With $|\sigma|$ we denote the length of σ. The *inverse* of a θ-substitution $[p_x^i/x]$ is $[x/p_x^i]$ and the *inverse* of $[x/p_x^i]$ is $[p_x^i/x]$. Moreover, concatenation between sequences is represented by juxtaposition and λ denotes the empty sequence.

The following lemma states that i) the bodies of a same constant in different programs of a transformation sequence can be transformed into each other by a θ-substitution sequence; and ii) the same holds for the immediate derivatives of the constants.

Lemma 6. *Let be given* P_j *and* P_k *belonging to a transformation sequence* $\{P_k\}$ *obtained with Unfolding, Guarded Folding and Definition Introduction. For each* $x \in \mathcal{D}_j \cap \mathcal{D}_k$, *the following holds:*

1. *a θ-substitution sequence $\sigma_x^{j,k}$ exists such that $p_x^j \sigma_x^{j,k} = p_x^k$;*
2. *$x \xrightarrow{\mu}_j p$ implies $x \xrightarrow{\mu}_k p\sigma_x^{j,k}$.*

Proof. (1) Let be $j \leq k$. If S is the sequence of transformation steps leading from P_j to P_k, let S' be the sub-sequence of S containing Foldings and Unfoldings modifying the body of x, i.e. transforming p_x^j into p_x^k. We have that $\sigma_x^{j,k}$ is the sequence of the θ-substitutions made by S' and $\sigma_x^{k,j}$ is the inverse of the sequence containing the inverse of the θ-substitutions made by S'.

(2) $\sigma_x^{j,k}$ substitutes only weakly guarded sub-terms of p_x^j, since Folding is guarded and, by lemma 5, constant occurrences are guarded in each constant body. $\square$

For example, given the following transformation sequence:

$P_0 : \langle \{x \overset{\text{def}}{=} a.b.x, \ y \overset{\text{def}}{=} b.x\}, \ y\rangle$

$P_1 : \langle \{x \overset{\text{def}}{=} a.b.a.b.x, \ y \overset{\text{def}}{=} b.x\}, \ y\rangle$

$P_2 : \langle \{x \overset{\text{def}}{=} a.b.a.y, \ y \overset{\text{def}}{=} b.x\}, \ y\rangle$

We have: $\sigma_x^{0,2} = [a.b.x/x][y/b.x]$, and $\sigma_x^{2,0} = [b.x/y][x/a.b.x]$

The following lemma is the nucleus of our proof. It shows that a bisimulation exists between any two programs of a transformation sequence. The bisimulation contains pairs composed of a process p and the process obtained by applying any substitution sequence to p.

Lemma 7. *Let be given P_j and P_k belonging to a transformation sequence $\{P_k\}$ obtained with Unfolding, Guarded Folding and Definition Introduction starting from the initial program $\langle \mathcal{D}, s\rangle$. Then, for each j, k, $P_j \cong P_k$.*

Proof. We define the following set of pairs:

$$S = \{(p, p\sigma)|\sigma \text{ is a } \theta\text{-substitution sequence }\}$$

We are going to show that S is a strong bisimulation relating the states of $SOS(P_j)$ with those of $SOS(P_k)$. More precisely, if p is a state of $SOS(P_j)$ and $p\sigma$ is a a state of $SOS(P_k)$, then i) $p \xrightarrow{\mu}_j q$ implies that a θ-substitution sequence $\overline{\sigma}$ exists such that $p\sigma \xrightarrow{\mu}_k q\overline{\sigma}$; and ii) $p\sigma \xrightarrow{\mu}_k q$ implies that a θ-substitution sequence $\overline{\sigma}$ exists such that $p \xrightarrow{\mu}_j q'$ and $q = q'\overline{\sigma}$.

The proof is made by induction on the length of σ.

– *Base.* $|\sigma| = 0$.

1. $p \xrightarrow{\alpha}_j q$. If no constant is derived for executing α, then $\overline{\sigma} = \lambda$. Otherwise, let x be the constant executing α. First note that $x \in \mathcal{D}_k$: in fact p is a state of $SOS(P_k)$ and all programs in the transformation sequence are closed, by lemma 5. Let $\sigma_x^{j,k}$ be the θ-substitution sequence as defined by lemma 6, point (1). By lemma 6, point (2), if $x \xrightarrow{\alpha}_j u$, then $x \xrightarrow{\alpha}_k u\sigma_x^{j,k}$. Thus we have $\overline{\sigma} = \sigma_x^{j,k}$.

The case of $p \xrightarrow{\tau}_j q$ can be proved in a similar way.

2. $p \xrightarrow{\alpha}_k q$. The proof is similar to that of case 1): either $\overline{\sigma} = \lambda$ or $\overline{\sigma} = \sigma_x^{k,j}$.

- Induction step. $|\sigma| = n > 0$.

   1. $p \xrightarrow{\alpha}_j q$. Suppose that $\sigma = \sigma'\theta$ with $|\sigma'| = n - 1$ and $\theta = [r/t]$ is the last θ-substitution of α. By inductive step, we have that $\overline{\sigma}'$ exists such that $p\sigma' \xrightarrow{\alpha}_k q\overline{\sigma}'$. If t is not used by $p\sigma'$ for executing α (the minimum sub-term of $p\sigma'$ producing α is not a sub-term of t), then $p\sigma'\theta \xrightarrow{\alpha}_k q\overline{\sigma}'\theta$. Otherwise, consider the two possible kinds of θ.

      a. $\theta = [x/p_x^i]$, i.e. α is executed by the sub-term p_x^i of $p\sigma'$, i.e. $p\sigma' \xrightarrow{\alpha}_k p\sigma'[u/p_x^i]$ and $p_x^i \xrightarrow{\alpha}_k u$. We have $p_x^i \xrightarrow{\alpha}_i u$, since the constant occurrences are guarded in each constant body (lemma 5). Thus $x \xrightarrow{\alpha}_i u$ and, by lemma 6, point (2), we have $x \xrightarrow{\alpha}_k u\sigma_x^{i,k}$. Thus we have $\overline{\sigma} = \overline{\sigma}'\sigma_x^{i,k}$.

      b. $\theta = [p_x^i/x]$. Similar to the previous point with $\overline{\sigma} = \overline{\sigma}'\sigma_x^{k,i}$.

      The case of $p \xrightarrow{\tau}_j q$ can be proved in a similar way.

   2. $p\sigma \xrightarrow{\mu}_k q$. Similar to the previous case.

The initial state, i.e. s, is always the same for all programs of the transformation sequence, since the rules modify only the definitions. Thus (s, s) belongs to $\mathcal{S}$ ($\sigma = \lambda$) and thus $SOS(P_j) \cong SOS(P_k)$. □

We are now ready to state the main theorem:

Theorem 8. *Let be given a sequence $\{P_k\}$, $k \geq 0$, of CCS programs each one obtained from the preceding ones by means of the application of one of all the transformation rules. Suppose that no rule different from Definition Elimination is applied after a Definition Elimination. Then, for each j, k, $P_j \cong P_k$.*

Proof. The proof for the prefix of $\{P_k\}$ starting at P_0 and ending at the application of the first Elimination can be done using lemma 7 and lemma 4, while for the rest of the sequence it follows from lemma 3. □

4 Examples of application

We first apply the transformation rules for simplifying the syntactic structure of CCS programs. In particular, given a program P, the aim of the transformation process is to obtain a program, say Q, semantically equivalent to P, in which the operators of restriction, relabelling and parallel composition are removed. If we succeed, we have that $SOS(Q)$ is finite [22], while $SOS(P)$ may be not finite. This transformation is meaningful, since most of the existing verification environments [1, 7, 13, 14] for CCS-like languages are based on an internal finite state representation of the processes, allowing the verification of logical properties and the application of efficient algorithms to decide whether two processes are bisimilar [2, 16, 17]. Consider the program:

$$P_0 : \langle\ x \stackrel{\text{def}}{=} a.b.x\backslash\{c\} + c.x,$$
$$y \stackrel{\text{def}}{=} \overline{b}.y,$$
$$z \stackrel{\text{def}}{=} d.(x \mid y)\backslash\{b\},\ z\rangle$$

Note that $SOS(P_0)$ is infinite.

We *unfold* the definition of the constant z using the definitions of x and y in P_0:

$P_2 : \langle\, x \stackrel{\text{def}}{=} a.b.x\backslash\{c\} + c.x,$
$\quad\quad y \stackrel{\text{def}}{=} \overline{b}.y,$
$\quad\quad z \stackrel{\text{def}}{=} d.(a.b.x\backslash\{c\} + c.x \mid \overline{b}.y)\backslash\{b\},\ z\rangle$

We apply the Simplification rule (Expansion law) to the constant definition z:

$P_3 : \langle\, x \stackrel{\text{def}}{=} a.b.x\backslash\{c\} + c.x,$
$\quad\quad y \stackrel{\text{def}}{=} \overline{b}.y,$
$\quad\quad z \stackrel{\text{def}}{=} d.(a.\tau.(x\backslash\{c\} \mid y)\backslash\{b\} + c.(x \mid \overline{b}.y)\backslash\{b\}),\ z\rangle$

We *introduce* two constant definitions, u and w, and we *fold* the definition of z using the newly introduced definitions:

$P_7 : \langle\, x \stackrel{\text{def}}{=} a.b.x\backslash\{c\} + c.x,$
$\quad\quad y \stackrel{\text{def}}{=} \overline{b}.y,$
$\quad\quad z \stackrel{\text{def}}{=} d.(a.u + w),$
$\quad\quad u \stackrel{\text{def}}{=} \tau.(x\backslash\{c\} \mid y)\backslash\{b\},$
$\quad\quad w \stackrel{\text{def}}{=} c.(x \mid \overline{b}.y)\backslash\{b\},\ z\rangle$

We *unfold* the definitions of the constants u and w using the definitions of x and y in P_0:

$P_{10} : \langle\, x \stackrel{\text{def}}{=} a.b.x\backslash\{c\} + c.x,$
$\quad\quad y \stackrel{\text{def}}{=} \overline{b}.y,$
$\quad\quad z \stackrel{\text{def}}{=} d.(a.u + w),$
$\quad\quad u \stackrel{\text{def}}{=} \tau.((a.b.x\backslash\{c\} + c.x)\backslash\{c\} \mid \overline{b}.y)\backslash\{b\},$
$\quad\quad w \stackrel{\text{def}}{=} c.(a.b.x\backslash\{c\} + c.x \mid \overline{b}.y)\backslash\{b\},\ z\rangle$

We apply, to the constant definitions u and w, the Simplification rule: Expansion law and the following strong equivalence laws [22]:

$$(p+q)\backslash A \cong p\backslash A + q\backslash A,\ p+nil \cong p,\ p\backslash A\backslash A \cong p\backslash A,\ (\mu.p)\backslash A \cong \begin{cases} \mu.p\backslash A & \text{if } \mu, \overline{\mu} \notin A \\ nil & \text{otherwise} \end{cases}$$

$P_{11} : \langle\, x \stackrel{\text{def}}{=} a.b.x\backslash\{c\} + c.x,$
$\quad\quad y \stackrel{\text{def}}{=} \overline{b}.y,$
$\quad\quad z \stackrel{\text{def}}{=} d.(a.u + w),$
$\quad\quad u \stackrel{\text{def}}{=} \tau.a.\tau.(x\backslash\{c\} \mid y)\backslash\{b\},$
$\quad\quad w \stackrel{\text{def}}{=} c.(a.\tau.(x\backslash\{c\} \mid y)\backslash\{b\} + c.(x \mid \overline{b}.y)\backslash\{b\}),\ z\rangle$

We *fold* the definitions of the constants u and w using their definitions in P_7:

$P_{14} : \langle\ x \stackrel{\text{def}}{=} a.b.x\backslash\{c\} + c.x,$

$\quad\quad y \stackrel{\text{def}}{=} \bar{b}.y,$

$\quad\quad z \stackrel{\text{def}}{=} d.(a.u + w),$

$\quad\quad u \stackrel{\text{def}}{=} \tau.a.u,$

$\quad\quad w \stackrel{\text{def}}{=} c.(a.u + w),\ z \rangle$

We *eliminate* the definition of the constants x and y, since they are not reachable from z, obtaining the final program, in which parallel composition, restriction and relabelling do not occur:

$P_{16} : \langle\ z \stackrel{\text{def}}{=} d.(a.u + w),$

$\quad\quad u \stackrel{\text{def}}{=} \tau.a.u,$

$\quad\quad w \stackrel{\text{def}}{=} c.(a.u + w),\ z \rangle$

In [11] we have defined a *strategy*, i.e an algorithm specifying the order of application of the rules, which is proved to be more powerful than many existing methods for building finite representations of CCS programs [10, 21, 28] (not based on program transformation). The strategy cannot be used as a decision procedure for the finiteness of CCS programs, since this problem is undecidable.

4.1 Proving bisimulation equivalence

As second example of application of our transformation methodology, we show how it is possible to prove the equivalence between two CCS programs by transforming one into the other. Let us consider the subset of CCS, denoted as BPP [6], not including restriction and relabelling and not allowing communication. It is well-known that for BPP bisimulation equivalence is decidable: in [6] a method to prove equivalence is shown, using tableaux, which are a kind of proof tree. Consider the following two BPP programs P_0 and Q (the example is in [6]):

$P_0 : \langle\ x_1 \stackrel{\text{def}}{=} a.(x_1|x_4),$

$\quad\quad x_4 \stackrel{\text{def}}{=} b.nil,\ x_1 \rangle$

$Q : \langle\ x_2 \stackrel{\text{def}}{=} a.x_3,$

$\quad\quad x_3 \stackrel{\text{def}}{=} a.(x_3|x_4) + b.x_2,$

$\quad\quad x_4 \stackrel{\text{def}}{=} b.nil,\ x_2 \rangle$

We *introduce* a constant definition y_1 and we *fold* the definition of x_1 of P_0 using the newly introduced definition:

$P_2 : \langle\ x_1 \stackrel{\text{def}}{=} a.y_1,$

$\quad\quad y_1 \stackrel{\text{def}}{=} x_1|x_4,$

$\quad\quad x_4 \stackrel{\text{def}}{=} b.nil,\ x_1 \rangle$

We *unfold* the definition of the constant y_1 using the definitions of x_1 and x_4 in P_2:

$$P_4 : \langle\ x_1 \stackrel{def}{=} a.y_1,$$
$$y_1 \stackrel{def}{=} a.y_1|b.nil,$$
$$x_4 \stackrel{def}{=} b.nil,\ x_1 \rangle$$

We apply the Simplification rule, using the Expansion law and the law $p|nil \cong p$ [22], to the constant definition y_1, obtaining:

$$P_5 : \langle\ x_1 \stackrel{def}{=} a.y_1,$$
$$y_1 \stackrel{def}{=} a.(y_1|b.nil) + b.a.y_1,$$
$$x_4 \stackrel{def}{=} b.nil,\ x_1 \rangle$$

We *fold* the definition of the constant y_1 using the definitions of x_1 and x_4 in P_5:

$$P_7 : \langle\ x_1 \stackrel{def}{=} a.y_1,$$
$$y_1 \stackrel{def}{=} a.(y_1|x_4) + b.x_1,$$
$$x_4 \stackrel{def}{=} b.nil,\ x_1 \rangle$$

which is equal (isomorphic) to Q.

We are going to investigate the possibility of defining a *strategy* able to decide whether a BPP program is transformable into another one.

5 Conclusions

We have presented a transformation methodology for CCS, that can be used to transform CCS programs into equivalent ones with a particular structure. An interesting aspect of the approach is that it unifies in a common framework a set of different techniques of program analysis: different applications are based on the same rules, applied according to different strategies. For example, we have shown two applications of the methodology: obtaining finite state representations of processes and deciding bisimulation equivalence.

We remark the novelty of the Guarded Folding rule, which uses the well-known notion of guardedness and is a very general and simple safe folding rule for CCS. Moreover, the applicability of the rule depends only on a property of the program to be folded and not of the entire transformation sequence, as occurs for almost all known folding rules for functional and logic programming. We are actually defining *strategies*, i.e. algorithms defining an order of application of the rules, with different transformation goals [12].

In [20] program transformation rules are defined for the LOTOS concurrent specification language, with the aim of supporting program design. This approach differs from our methodology, since we are mainly based on Unfolding and Folding, while this is not the case of [20], where the transformations essentially consist in manipulations of terms by means of rewriting rules.

In [29] transformation rules are defined, belonging to an environment for the specification of PSF programs, using, among others, some kind of unfolding and folding. However, the notion of transformation sequence is not formalized and no attention is paid to the correctness of folding. In fact, a very restrictive version of folding seems to be used, allowing using only the definitions occurring in the program to be folded.

As future work, it is interesting to study the feasibility of defining transformation rules and strategies which are correct with respect to other semantics for concurrency, for example, weak bisimulation equivalence instead of strong one.

Moreover, transformation rules and strategies can be defined to check properties of programs, for example deadlock freeness. In these cases, the programs of the transformation sequence may be not equivalent to each other, since it only needs to keep the property verified.

Acknowledgment. We are grateful to Roberto Barbuti for useful comments and suggestions.

References

1. T. Bolognesi, M. Caneve. *A tool for the analysis of Lotos specifications.* In K. Turner (ed.) Formal description techniques, pp. 201-216. Amsterdam: North-Holland 1989.

2. T. Bolognesi, S. Smolka. *Fundamental results for the verification of observational equivalence: a survey.* In Proc. IFIP WG 6.1 7th Conference on Protocol Specification, Testing and Verification. Amsterdam: North-Holland 1987.

3. A. Bossi and N. Cosso. *Basic Transformation operations which preserve Computer Answer Substitutions of Logic Programs.* Bulletin of the EATCS, n.54, October 1994, pp.207-223.

4. A. Bouali, S. Gnesi, S. Larosa. *The integration Project for the JACK Environment.* Bulletin of the EATCS, n.54, October 1994, pp.207-223.

5. R.M. Burstall, J. Darlington. *A Transformation System for Developing Recursive Programs.* J. ACM 24(1): pp. 44-67 (1977).

6. S. Christensen, Y. Hirshfeld and F. Moller. *Bisimulation is Decidable for all Basic Parallel Processes.* In Proceedings of CONCUR'93, number 715 in Lecture Notes in Computer Science, pp. 143-157. Springer-Verlag, 1993.

7. R. Cleaveland, J. Parrow, B. Steffen. *The concurrency workbench: operating instructions.* Tech. Notes Sussex University, 1988.

8. R. Cleaveland, J. Parrow, B. Steffen. *Model Checking and Abstraction. The Concurrency Workbench.* Proceedings of Automatic Verification Methods for Finite State Systems. Lecture Notes in Computer Science 407, Springer-Verlag, 1990, pp. 24-37.

9. S.K. Debray. *Unfold/Fold Transformations and Loop Optimization of Logic Programs.* In Proceedings of SIGPLAN '88, Conference on Programming Language Design and Implementation. Atlanta, Georgia, SIGPLAN Not. 23(7): pp. 297-307 (1988).

10. N. De Francesco, P. Inverardi. *Proving Finiteness of CCS Processes by Non-standard Semantics.* Acta informatica, vol.31, n.1, 1994, pp. 55-80.

11. N. De Francesco, A. Santone. *A Program Transformations Methodology for CCS.* In Proceedings of the Fifth Italian Conference of Theoretical Computer Science, Ravello, Italy, November 1995.

12. N. De Francesco, A. Santone. *Transforming Concurrent Processes.* Internal Report IR-2/94, Dipartimento di Ingegneria dell'Informazione, Univ. of Pisa.

13. R. De Simone, D. Vergamini. *Aboard AUTO.* INRIA Technical Report 111, 1989.

14. J. Fernandez.: Aldebaran. *Un system de verification par reduction de processus communicantes.* Ph.D. Thesis, Université de Grenoble, 1988.

15. P.A. Gardner and J.C. Shepherdson. *Unfold/Fold Transformations of Logic Programs.* in Computational Proofs: Essays in honour of G. Robinson (1991).

16. J.F. Groote, F.W. Vaandrager. *An efficient algorithm for branching bisimulation and stuttering equivalence.* In M. S. Paterson (ed.) Automata, languages and programming. Proceedings (Lect. Notes Comput. Sci., vol 443, pp. 626-638) Berlin, Heildelberg, New York: Springer 1990.

17. P.C. Kanellakis, S.A. Smolka. *CCS Expressions, finite state processes and three problems of equivalence.* Inf. Comput. 86 (1990).

18. T. Kawamura and T. Kanamori. *Preservation of stronger equivalence in unfold/fold logic program transformation.* In Theoretical Computer Science, vol. 75, pp.139-156 (1990).

19. L. Kott. *About Transformation System.* A Theoretical Study, 3ème Colloque International sur la Programmation, Dunod, Paris, 1978, pp. 232-247.

20. *Catalogue of LOTOS Correctness Preserving Transformations.* ESPIT Project, Final Deliverable, April 1992.

21. E. Madelaine, D. Vergamini. *Finiteness conditions and structural construction of automata for all process algebras.* In Proceedings, 2nd Workshop on Computer-Aided Verification. DIMACS Technical report 90-31, June 1990.

22. R. Milner. *Communication and Concurrency.* Prentice-Hall, 1989.

23. A. Pettorossi, M. Proietti. *The Loop Absorption and The Generalization Strategies for the Development of Logic Programs and Partial Deduction.* Journal of Logic Programming 1993, 16, pp. 123-161.

24. A. Pettorossi, M. Proietti. *Rules and Strategies for Program Transformation.* In State-of-the-Art. Report on Formal Program Development, Rio de Janeiro, Brazil. Lecture Notes in Computer Science 755, Springer, New York, 1993, pp. 263-304.

25. A. Pettorossi, M. Proietti. *Transformation of Logic Programs: Foundations and Techniques.* In J. Logic Programming 1994, 19,20: pp.261-320.

26. A. Takeuchi. *Affinity between Meta Interpreters and Partial Evaluation.* In H.J. Kugler (ed.), Proceedings of Information Processing '86. North-Holland, Amsterdam, 1986, pp. 279-282.

27. H. Tamaki, T. Sato. *Unfold/Fold Transformation of Logic Programs.* In:S.-Å. Tärnlund (ed.), Proceedings of the 2nd International Conference on Logic Programming, Uppsala, Sweden, 1984, pp.127-138.

28. D. Taubner. *Finite representations of CCS and TCSP programs by automata and Petri nets.* Lecture Notes in Computer Science, vol. 369. Berlin, Heidelberg, New York: Springer 1989.

29. G. Veltink. *The PSF toolkit.* Computer Networks and ISDN Systems, North Holland, 25, pp. 875-898 (1993).

Semantics-Based Compiling:
A Case Study in Type-Directed Partial Evaluation

Olivier Danvy and René Vestergaard

BRICS *
Computer Science Department
Aarhus University **

Abstract. We illustrate a simple and effective solution to semantics-based compiling. Our solution is based on "type-directed partial evaluation", and

- our compiler generator is expressed in a few lines, and is efficient;
- its input is a well-typed, purely functional definitional interpreter in the style of denotational semantics;
- the output of the generated compiler is effectively three-address code, in the fashion and efficiency of the Dragon Book;
- the generated compiler processes several hundred lines of source code per second.

The source language considered in this case study is imperative, block-structured, higher-order, call-by-value, allows subtyping, and obeys stack discipline. It is bigger than what is usually reported in the literature on semantics-based compiling and partial evaluation.

Our compiling technique uses the first Futamura projection, *i.e.*, we compile programs by specializing a definitional interpreter with respect to the program. Specialization is carried out using type-directed partial evaluation, which is a mild version of partial evaluation akin to λ-calculus normalization.

Our definitional interpreter follows the format of denotational semantics, with a clear separation between semantic algebras, and valuation functions. It is thus a completely straightforward stack-based interpreter in direct style, which requires no clever staging technique (currying, continuations, binding-time improvements, *etc.*), and does not rely on any other framework (attribute grammars, annotations, *etc.*) than the typed λ-calculus. In particular, it uses no other program analysis than traditional type inference.

The overall simplicity and effectiveness of the approach has encouraged us to write this paper, to illustrate this genuine solution to denotational semantics-directed compilation, in the spirit of Scott and Strachey. Our conclusion is that λ-calculus normalization suffices for compiling by specializing an interpreter.

* Basic Research in Computer Science,
  Centre of the Danish National Research Foundation.
** Ny Munkegade, Building 540, DK-8000 Aarhus C, Denmark.
  E-mail: {danvy, jrvest}@brics.dk

1 Introduction

1.1 Denotational semantics and semantics-implementation systems

Twenty years ago, when denotational semantics was developed [23, 37], there were high hopes for it to be used to specify most, if not all programming languages. When Mosses developed his Semantics Implementation System [25], it was with the explicit goal of generating compilers from denotational specifications.

Time passed, and these hopes did not materialize as concretely as was wished. Other semantic frameworks are used today, and other associated semantics-implementation systems as well. Two explanations could be that (1) domains proved to be an interesting area of research *per se*, and they are studied today quite independently of programming-language design and specification; and (2) the λ-notation of denotational semantics was deemed untamable — indeed writing a denotational specification can be compared to writing a program in a module-less, lazy functional language without automatic type-checker.

As for semantics-implementation systems, there have been many [1, 13, 16, 22, 25, 28, 29, 31, 34, 35, 38, 39, 40], and they were all quite complicated. (Note: this list of references is by no means exhaustive. It is merely meant to be indicative.)

1.2 Partial evaluation

For a while, partial evaluation has held some promise for compiling and compiler generation, through the Futamura projections [17, 18]. The first Futamura projection states that specializing a definitional interpreter with respect to a source program "compiles" the source program from the defined language to the defining language [32]. This idea has been applied to a variety of interpreters and programming-language paradigms, as reported in the literature [7, 17].

One of the biggest and most successful applications is Jørgensen's BAWL, which produces code that is competitive with commercially available systems, given a good Scheme implementation [19]. The problem with partial evaluation, however, is the same as for most semantics-implementation system: it requires an expert to use it successfully.

1.3 Type-directed partial evaluation

Recently, the first author has developed an alternative approach to partial evaluation which is better adapted to specializing interpreters and strikingly simpler [8]. The approach is type-directed and amounts to normalizing a closed, well-typed program, given its type (see Figure 1). The approach has been illustrated on a toy programming language, by transliterating a denotational specification into a definitional interpreter, making this term closed by abstracting all the (run-time) semantics operators, applying it to the source program, and normalizing the result.

Type-directed partial evaluation thus merely requires the user to write a purely functional, well-typed definitional interpreter, to close it by abstracting its semantic operators, and to provide its type. The type is obtained for free, using ML or Haskell. No annotations or binding-time improvements are needed.

The point of the experiment with a toy programming language [8] is that it can be carried out at all. The point of this paper is to show that the approach scales up to a non-trivial language.

$$t \in \text{Type} ::= b \mid t_1 \times t_2 \mid t_1 \to t_2$$

$$\text{reify} = \lambda t.\lambda v.\downarrow^t v$$
$$\downarrow^b v = v$$
$$\downarrow^{t_1 \times t_2} v = \underline{\text{pair}}(\downarrow^{t_1} \overline{\text{fst}} \, v, \downarrow^{t_2} \overline{\text{snd}} \, v)$$
$$\downarrow^{t_1 \to t_2} v = \underline{\lambda} x_1.\downarrow^{t_2} (v \, \overline{@} \, (\uparrow_{t_1} x_1))$$
$$\text{where } x_1 \text{ is fresh.}$$

$$\text{reflect} = \lambda t.\lambda e.\uparrow_t e$$
$$\uparrow_b e = e$$
$$\uparrow_{t_1 \times t_2} e = \overline{\text{pair}}(\uparrow_{t_1} \underline{\text{fst}} \, e, \uparrow_{t_2} \underline{\text{snd}} \, e)$$
$$\uparrow_{t_1 \to t_2} e = \overline{\lambda} v_1.\uparrow_{t_2} (e \, \underline{@} \, (\downarrow^{t_1} v_1))$$

$$\text{residualize} = \text{statically-reduce} \circ \text{reify}$$

The down arrow is read *reify*: it maps a static value and its type into a two-level λ-term [27] that statically reduces to the dynamic counterpart of this static value. Conversely, the up arrow is read *reflect*: it maps a dynamic expression into a two-level λ-term representing the static counterpart of this dynamic expression.

In residualize, reify (resp. reflect) is applied to types occurring positively (resp. negatively) in the source type.

N.B. In practice, residual let expressions need to be inserted to maintain the order of execution, *à la* Similix [5]. This feature makes it possible to specialize direct-style programs with the same advantages one gets when specializing continuation-passing programs, and is described elsewhere [9].

Fig. 1. Type-directed partial evaluation (a.k.a. residualization)

1.4 Disclaimer

We are not suggesting that well-typed, compositional and purely definitional interpreters written in the fashion of denotational semantics are the way to go always. This method of definition faces the same problems as denotational semantics. For example, it cannot scale up easily to truly large languages, which has motivated *e.g.*, the development of Action Semantics [26].

Our point is that given such a definitional interpreter, type-directed partial evaluation provides a remarkably simple and effective solution to semantics-based compiling.

1.5 This paper

We consider an imperative language with block structure, higher-order and mutually recursive procedures, call-by-value, and that allows subtyping. We write a direct-style definitional interpreter that is stack-based, reflecting the traditional call/return strategy of Algol 60 [30], but is otherwise completely straightforward.[3]

---

[3] Being stack-based is of course not a requirement. An unstructured store would also need to be threaded throughout, but its implementation would require a garbage collector [23].

We specialize it and obtain three-address code that is comparable to what can be expected from a compiler implemented *e.g.*, according to the Dragon Book [1].

This experiment is significant for the following reasons:

Semantics-implementation systems: Our source language is realistic. Our compiler generator is extremely simple (it is displayed in Figure 1). Our language specification is naturally in direct style and requires no staging transformations [20]. Our compiler is efficient (several hundred lines per second). Our target code is reasonable.

We are not aware of other semantics-implementation systems that yield similar target code with a similar efficiency. In any case, our primary goal is not efficiency. Our point here is that the problem of semantics-based compiling can be stated in such a way that a solution exists that is extremely simple and yields reasonable results.

Partial evaluation: Similar results can be obtained using traditional partial evaluation, but not as simply and not as efficiently.

An online partial evaluator incurs a significant interpretive overhead. An offline partial evaluator necessitates a binding-time analysis, and then either incurs interpretive overhead by direct specialization, or requires its user to generate a generating extension. Furthermore, an offline partial evaluator usually requires binding-time improvements, which are an art in themselves [17, Chapter 12].

It is our experience that in a way, partial evaluators today are too powerful: our present experiment shows that λ-calculus normalization is enough for compiling by interpreter specialization.

1.6 Overview

Section 2 presents the essence of semantics-based compiling by type-directed partial evaluation. Section 3 briefly outlines our source programming language. Based on this description, it is simple to transcribe its denotational specification into a definitional interpreter [32]. We describe one such interpreter in Section 4, and display the outline of it in Figure 6. It is well-typed. Given its type and a source program such as the one in Figure 3, we can residualize the application of the interpreter to the source program and obtain a residual program such as the one in Figure 4. Each residual program is a specialized version of the definitional interpreter and appears as three-address code. We use the syntax of Scheme to represent this three-address code, but it is trivial to map it into assembly code.

2   The essence of semantics-based compiling by type-directed partial evaluation

Our point here is that to compile programs by interpreter specialization, λ-calculus normalization is enough.

Interpreter specialization: the first Futamura projection states that specializing an interpreter with respect to a program (*i.e.*, performing all the interpreter operations that only depend on the program, but not on its input) amounts to compiling this program into the defining language of the interpreter [17]. Along with the second and third Futamura projections, this property has been instrumental to the renaissance of partial evaluation in the 80's [18].

Normalization is enough: the technique of type-directed partial evaluation is otherwise used to normalize simply typed programs extracted from proofs. There, it is referred to as "normalization by evaluation" [3, 4]. Type-directed partial evaluation slightly differs in that to make it fit call-by-value, we insert let expressions naming residual expressions to avoid code and computation duplication.

Throughout, we consider Schmidt-style denotational specifications [34], *i.e.*, specifications with a clear separation between semantic algebras, and valuation functions. We normalize the result of applying the main valuation function to a program, given the type of its denotation. The result is a combination of semantic-algebra operations, sequentialized with let expressions, and thus corresponding to three-address code [1].

Let us illustrate this point with one extremely simple example. We consider a microscopic imperative language and its definitional interpreter (Figure 2). Applying this interpreter to a source program yields a functional value. Normalizing it yields a textual representation of the dynamic semantics of the source program, *i.e.*, its compiled version: a sequence of semantic-algebra operations.

2.1 Syntax

The following BNF specifies our microscopic imperative language. A program consists of a sequence of zeros and ones terminated by a stop.

$$p \in \text{Program} ::= c$$
$$c \in \text{Command} ::= \text{stop} \mid i \text{ ; } c$$
$$i \in \text{Instruction} ::= \text{zero} \mid \text{one}$$

2.2 Semantic algebra

The valuation functions uses a semantic algebra consisting of a store and two store-transforming operations f and g.

2.3 Valuation functions

We respectively interpret zero and one with f and g.

$$C : \text{Command} \rightarrow \text{Store} \rightarrow \text{Store} \qquad \mathcal{I} : \text{Instruction} \rightarrow \text{Store} \rightarrow \text{Store}$$
$$C[\![\text{stop}]\!] = \lambda\sigma.\sigma \qquad\qquad\qquad \mathcal{I}[\![\text{zero}]\!] = f$$
$$C[\![i \text{ ; } c]\!] = \lambda\sigma.C[\![c]\!](\mathcal{I}[\![i]\!]\sigma) \qquad \mathcal{I}[\![\text{one}]\!] = g$$

2.4 Compiling by normalization

Figure 2 displays a direct-style definitional interpreter, expressed in Scheme. This interpreter is curried: when applied to a source program, it returns a higher-order procedure expecting f and g and returning a store transformer. We have parameterized it with f and g merely for convenience (precisely: to make it a closed term, *i.e.*, a term without free variables that can be characterized with its type).

```
(define-record (Stop))
(define-record (Sequence i c))
(define-record (Zero))
(define-record (One))

(define meaning
  (lambda (c)
    (lambda (f g)
      (letrec ([meaning-command
                (lambda (c)
                  (case-record c
                   [(Stop) (lambda (s) s)]
                   [(Sequence i c) (lambda (s)
                                     ((meaning-command c)
                                      ((meaning-instruction i) s)))]))]
               [meaning-instruction
                (lambda (i)
                  (case-record i
                   [(Zero) f]
                   [(One) g]))])
        (meaning-command c)))))

(define-base-type sto "s")
(define-compound-type one (sto -!> sto) "f" alias)
(define-compound-type two (sto -!> sto) "g" alias)
(define-compound-type denotation-type ((one two) => sto -!> sto))
```

Fig. 2. Microscopic definitional interpreter

The figure also shows the definition of the abstract syntax as records, and the definition of the types of the store, of f, and g. The function type of f and g is annotated with "!" to indicate that they operate on a single-threaded value, and thus that their application should be named with a let expression [9].

Let p denote the source program "zero; one; zero; one; stop". In the following Scheme session, we residualize the application of the definitional interpreter with respect to the type of the denotation. The result is the text of the corresponding normal form, $i.e.$, of the dynamic semantics of p.

```
> (load "tdpe.scm")
> (load "mic-def-int.scm")
> (residualize (meaning p) 'denotation-type)
(lambda (f g)
  (lambda (s0)
    (let* ([s1 (f s0)]
           [s2 (g s1)]
           [s3 (f s2)])
      (g s3))))
```

This residual Scheme program is the specialized version of the interpreter of Figure

2 with respect to the source program p. It performs the run-time actions of p, sequentially. The interpretive overhead is gone.

2.5 Assessment

This microscopic example is significant for at least three reasons.

This is semantics-based compilation: we have compiled a program based on the semantics of a programming language.

This is partial evaluation: we have specialized a definitional interpreter with respect to a source program.

This is normalization: all we have used is a λ-calculus normalizer.

Furthermore, the target language of the normalizer (a flat sequence of let expressions) has the same structure as three-address code as described in the Dragon book [1]. Translating residual programs into assembly language therefore does not amount to writing a compiler for the λ-calculus, but more simply to writing the back-end of a standard compiler. The method is thus not a step sideways, but an actual step forward in the process of compiling a source program. In essence, it makes it possible to derive the front-end of a compiler from a definitional interpreter.

Methodologically, our type-directed partial evaluator is simpler than a traditional semantics-implementation system or a standard partial evaluator for three more reasons:

1. Normalization is simpler than partial evaluation.
2. Type-directed partial evaluation does not require one to re-implement the λ-calculus: it relies on an existing implementation (presently Scheme, but ML or Haskell would do just as well).
3. There is no need to massage (a.k.a. stage [20]) the definitional interpreter to derive [the front-end of] the compiler. It is enough to follow the format of denotational semantics: semantic algebras, and valuation functions.

We come back to these issues in Section 6.

The example language of this section is deliberately microscopic, but it captures the essence of our case study. Examples of semantics-based compiling by type-directed partial evaluation have been published for Paulson's Tiny language [8, 9], which is an imperative while-language traditional in the semantics community [16]. In this paper, we explore semantics-based compiling with a more substantial programming language, in an effort to explore the applicability of type-directed partial evaluation.

3 A block-structured procedural language with subtyping

The following programming language is deliberately reminiscent of Reynolds's idealized Algol [33], although it uses call-by-value. We briefly present it here. A full description is available in a companion technical report [10] and in the second author's MS thesis (forthcoming).

3.1 Abstract Syntax

The language is imperative: its basic syntactic units are commands. It is block-structured: any command can have local declarations. It is procedural: commands can be abstracted and parameterized. It is higher-order: procedures can be passed as arguments (though not returned, to enable stack discipline for activation records) to other procedures. Finally it is typed and supports subtyping in that an integer value can be assigned to a real variable, a procedure expecting a real can be passed instead of a procedure expecting an integer, *etc.*

$$
\begin{array}{lll}
p, \langle pgm \rangle & \in Pgm & \text{—domain of programs} \\
c, \langle cmd \rangle & \in Cmd & \text{—domain of commands} \\
e, \langle exp \rangle & \in Exp & \text{—domain of expressions} \\
i, \langle ide \rangle & \in Ide & \text{—domain of identifiers} \\
d, \langle decl \rangle & \in Decl & \text{—domain of declarations} \\
t, \langle type \rangle & \in Type & \text{—domain of types} \\
o, \langle btype \rangle & \in BType & \text{—domain of base types}
\end{array}
$$

$$
\begin{array}{ll}
\langle pgm \rangle ::= & \langle cmd \rangle \\
\langle decl \rangle ::= & \textbf{Var } \langle ide \rangle : \langle btype \rangle = \langle exp \rangle \\
& | \ \textbf{Proc } \langle ide \rangle \ ((\langle ide \rangle{:}\langle type \rangle, \ldots, \langle ide \rangle{:}\langle type \rangle)) = \langle cmd \rangle \\
\langle cmd \rangle ::= & \textbf{skip} \ | \ \textbf{write } \langle exp \rangle \ | \ \textbf{read } \langle ide \rangle \ | \ \langle cmd \rangle \ ; \langle cmd \rangle \\
& | \ \langle ide \rangle := \langle exp \rangle \ | \ \textbf{if } \langle exp \rangle \ \textbf{then } \langle cmd \rangle \ \textbf{else } \langle cmd \rangle \\
& | \ \textbf{while } \langle exp \rangle \ \textbf{do } \langle cmd \rangle \ | \ \textbf{call } \langle ide \rangle \ ((\langle exp \rangle, \ldots, \langle exp \rangle)) \\
& | \ \textbf{block } ((\langle decl \rangle, \ldots, \langle decl \rangle)) \ \textbf{in } \langle cmd \rangle \\
\langle exp \rangle ::= & \langle lit \rangle \ | \ \langle ide \rangle \ | \ \langle exp \rangle \ \langle op \rangle \ \langle exp \rangle \\
\langle lit \rangle ::= & \langle bool \rangle \ | \ \langle int \rangle \ | \ \langle real \rangle \\
\langle op \rangle ::= & + \ | \ \times \ | \ - \ | \ < \ | \ = \ | \ \textbf{and} \ | \ \textbf{or} \\
\langle btype \rangle ::= & \textbf{Bool} \ | \ \textbf{Int} \ | \ \textbf{Real} \\
\langle type \rangle ::= & \langle btype \rangle \ | \ \textbf{Proc } ((\langle type \rangle, \ldots, \langle type \rangle))
\end{array}
$$

3.2 Semantics

The language is block structured, procedural, and higher-order. Since it is also typed, we define the corresponding domain of values inductively, following its typing structure. Our implementation is stack-based, and so we want to pass parameters on top of the stack. We thus define the denotation of procedures as a store transformer, whose elements are functions accepting a stack whose top frame contains parameters of an appropriate type. We furthermore index the denotation of a procedure with its free variables.

The store can hold untagged booleans, integers, reals, and procedures. It is accessed with typed operators. We define expressible values (the result of evaluating an expression) to be type-annotated storable values. A denotable value (held in the environment) is a reference to the stack, paired with the type of the corresponding stored value.

The stack holds a sequence of activation records which are statically (for the environment) and dynamically (for the continuation) linked via base pointers, as is traditional in Algol-like languages [1, 30]. An activation record is pushed at each procedure call, and popped at each procedure return. A block (of bindings) is pushed whenever we enter the scope of a declaration, and popped upon exit of this scope. Each block extends the current activation record. Procedures are call-by-value: they are passed the (storable) values of their arguments on the stack [1, 30]. The global store pairs a push-down stack and i/o channels. It is addressed through type-indexed operators.

The language is statically typed: any type mismatch yields an error. In addition, subtyping is allowed: any context expecting a value of type t ($i.e.$, assignments and parameter passing) accepts an expressible value whose type is a subtype of t. Our coercions at higher type simulate intermediate procedures that coerce their arguments as required by their types [33]. Along the same lines, the type-directed partial evaluator of Figure 1 is simply a coercion from static to dynamic [8].

We want the language to obey a stack discipline. Stack discipline can only be broken when values may outlive the scope of their free variables. This can only occur when an identifier i of higher type is updated with the value of an identifier j which was declared in the scope of i. We thus specify that at higher type, i must be local to j.

4 A definitional interpreter and its specialization

We have transcribed the denotational specification of Section 3 into a definitional interpreter which is compositional and purely functional [32, 36]. We make the interpreter a closed term by abstracting all its free variables at the outset ($i.e.$, the semantic operators fix, test, $etc.$). Figure 6 displays the skeleton of the interpreter.

As in Section 2, we can then residualize the application of the definitional interpreter to any source program, with respect to the codomain of the definitional interpreter, $i.e.$, with respect to the type of the meaning of a source program. The result is a textual representation of the dynamic semantics of the source program, $i.e.$, of its step-by-step execution without interpretive overhead.

Figure 3 displays such a source program. Figures 4 and 5 display the resulting target program, unedited (except for the comments).

---

block Var x : Int $=$ 100
    Proc $print$ (y : Real) $=$ write y
    Proc p (q : Proc(Int), y : Int) $=$ call q ($x + y$)
in call p ($print$, 4)

Fig. 3. Sample source program

```
(lambda (fix test int-to-real conj disj eq-bool read-int read-real
         read-bool write-int write-real write-bool add-int mul-int
         sub-int less-int eq-int add-real mul-real sub-real less-real
         eq-real push-int push-real push-bool push-proc push-func
         push-al push-base-pointer pop-block update-base-pointer
         pop-frame lookup-int lookup-real lookup-bool lookup-proc
         lookup-func update-int update-real update-bool update-proc
         update-func current-al lookup-al update-al) ...
```

Fig. 4. Sample target program (specialized version of Fig. 6 with respect to Fig. 3)

```
...
(lambda (s)
  (let* ([s   (push-int 100 s)]   ;;; decl. of x
         [a0  (current-al s)]
         [s   (push-proc
                 (lambda (s)        ;;; decl. of print (code pointer)
                   (let ([r1 (lookup-real 0 0 s)])
                     (write-real s r1)))
                 s)]
         [s   (push-al a0 s)]      ;;; decl. of print (access link)
         [a2  (current-al s)]
         [s   (push-proc
                 (lambda (s)    ;;; decl. of p (code pointer)
                   (let* ([p3 (lookup-proc 0 0 s)]
                          [a4 (lookup-al 0 1 s)]
                          [i5 (lookup-int 1 0 s)]
                          [i6 (lookup-int 0 2 s)]
                          [i7 (add-int i5 i6)]
                          [s  (push-al a4 s)]
                          [s  (push-base-pointer s)]
                          [s  (push-int i7 s)]
                          [s  (update-base-pointer s 1)]
                          [s  (p3 s)])
                     (pop-frame s)))
                 s)]
         [s   (push-al a2 s)] ;;; decl. of p (access link)
         [p8  (lookup-proc 0 3 s)]
         [a9  (lookup-al 0 4 s)]
         [p10 (lookup-proc 0 1 s)]
         [a11 (lookup-al 0 2 s)]
         [s   (push-al a9 s)]
         [s   (push-base-pointer s)]
         [s   (push-proc
                 (lambda (s)   ;;; coercion of print (code pointer)
                   (let* ([i12 (lookup-int 0 0 s)]
                          [a13 (current-al s)]
                          [s   (push-al a13 s)]
                          [s   (push-base-pointer s)]
                          [s   (push-real (int-to-real i12) s)]
                          [s   (update-base-pointer s 1)]
                          [s   (p10 s)])
                     (pop-frame s)))
                 s)
         [s   (push-al a11 s)] ;;; coercion of print (access link)
         [s   (push-int 4 s)]
         [s   (update-base-pointer s 3)]
         [s   (p8 s)]              ;;; actual call to p
         [s   (pop-frame s)])
    (pop-block s 5)))))
```

Fig. 5. Fig. 4 (continued and ended)

```
(define meaning
  (lambda (p)
    (lambda (fix test ...)
      (lambda (s)
        (letrec ([meaning-program (lambda (p s) ...)]
                 [meaning-command
                   (lambda (c r s)
                     (case-record c
                       ...
                       [(Assign i1 e)
                        (case-record e
                          [(Ide i2)
                           (let ([(Pair x1 t1) ((cdr r) i1)]
                                 [(Pair x2 t2) ((cdr r) i2)])
                             (if (or (is-local? x1 x2)
                                     (and (is-base-type? t1)
                                          (is-base-type? t2)))
                                 (update t1 x1
                                         (coerce t2 t1 (lookup t2 x2 s))
                                         s)
                                 (wrong "not stackable")))]
                          [else
                           (let ([(Pair x1 t1) ((cdr r) i1)]
                                 [(ExpVal t2 v2)
                                  (meaning-expression e r s)])
                             (update t1 x1 (coerce t2 t1 v2) s))])]
                       ...))]
                 [meaning-expression (lambda (e r s) ...)]
                 [meaning-operator (lambda (op v1 v2) ...)]
                 [meaning-declarations (lambda (ds r s) ...)]
                 [meaning-declaration (lambda (d r s) ...)])
          (meaning-program p s))))))
```

Fig. 6. Skeleton of the medium definitional interpreter

The source program of Figure 3 illustrates block structure, non-local variables, higher-order procedures, and subtyping. The body of Procedure p refers to the two parameters of p and also to the global integer-typed variable x. Procedure p expects an integer-expecting procedure and an integer. It is passed the real-expecting procedure *print*, which is legal in the present subtyping discipline. Procedure *print* needs to be coerced into an integer-expecting procedure, which is then passed to Procedure p.

The residual program of Figure 4 is a specialized version of the definitional interpreter of Figure 6 with respect to the source program of Figure 3. It is a flat Scheme program threading the store throughout and reflecting the step-by-step execution of the source program. The static semantics of the source program, *i.e.*, all the interpretive steps that only depend on the text of the source program, has been processed at partial-evaluation time: all the location offsets are solved and all primitive operations are properly typed. The coercion, in particular, has been residualized as a call to an intermediate procedure coercing its integer argument to a real and calling Procedure *print*.

The target language of this partial evaluator is reminiscent of continuation-passing style without continuations, otherwise known as *nqCPS*, *A-normal forms* [11], or *monadic normal forms* [15], *i.e.*, for all practical purposes, three-address code, as in the Dragon book [1]. It can be indifferently considered as a Scheme program or be translated into assembly language.

5 Assessment

5.1 The definitional interpreter

Our definitional interpreter has roughly the same size as the denotational specification of Section 3: 530 lines of Scheme code and less than 16 Kb. This however also includes the treatment of functions, which we have elided here.

The semantic operations occupy 120 lines of Scheme code and about 3.5 Kb.

5.2 Compiler generation

Generating a compiler out of an interpreter, using type-directed partial evaluation, amounts to specializing the type-directed partial evaluator with respect to the type of the interpreter (applied to a source program) [8, Section 2.4]. The improvement obtained by eliminating the type interpretive overhead is negligible in practice.

5.3 Compiling efficiency

We have constructed a number of source programs of varying size (up to 18,000 lines), and have observed that on the average, compiling takes place at about 400 lines per second on a SPARC station 20 with two 75 Mhz processors running Solaris 2.4, using R. Kent Dybvig's Chez Scheme Version 4.1u. On a smaller machine, a SPARC Station ELC with one 33 Mhz processor running SunOS 4.1.1, about 100 lines are compiled per second, again using Chez Scheme.

5.4 Efficiency of the compiled code

The compiled code is of standard, Dragon-book quality [1]. It accounts for the dynamic interpretation steps of the source program. As this paper is going to press, we do not have actual figures yet about the efficiency of assembly code (only of intermediate code).

5.5 Interpreted vs. compiled code

Compiled intermediate code runs four times faster than interpreted code, on the average, in Scheme. This is consistent with traditional results in partial evaluation [7, 17].

6 Related work

6.1 Semantics-implementation systems

Our use of type-directed partial evaluation to specialize a definitional interpreter very precisely matches the goal of Mosses's Semantics Implementation System [25], as witnessed by the following recent quote [26]:

"SIS [...] took denotational descriptions as input. It transformed a denotational description into a λ-expression which, when applied to the abstract syntax of a program, reduced to a λ-expression that represented the semantics of the program in the form of an input-output function. This expression could be regarded as the 'object code' of the program for the λ-reduction machine that SIS provided. By applying this code to some input, and reducing again, one could get the output of the program according to the semantics."

When SIS was developed, functional languages and their programming environment did not exist. Today's definitional interpreters can be (1) type-checked automatically and (2) interactively tested. Correspondingly, today's λ-reduction machines are simply Scheme, ML, or Haskell systems. Alternatively, though, we can translate our target three-address code directly into assembly language.

SIS was the first semantics-implementation system, but as mentioned in Section 1, it was followed by a considerable number of other systems. All of these systems are non-trivial. Some of them are definitely on the sophisticated side. None of them are so simple that they can, in a type-directed fashion and in a few lines, as in Figure 1,

1. take a well-typed, runnable, unannotated definitional interpreter in direct style, as in Figure 6, together with a source program, as in Figure 3; and
2. produce a textual representation of its dynamic semantics, as in Figure 4.

6.2 Compiler derivation

Deriving compilers from interpreters is a well-documented exercise by now [12, 24, 40]. These derivations are significantly more involved than the present work, and require significant more handcraft and ingenuity. For example, the source interpreter usually has to be expressed in continuation-passing style.

6.3 Partial evaluation

The renaissance of partial evaluation we see in the 90s originates in Jones's Mix project [18], which aimed at compiling by interpreter specialization and at generating compilers by self-application. This seminal work has paved the way for further work on partial evaluation, namely with offline strategies and binding-time improvements [7, 17]. Let us simply mention two such works.

Definitional interpreter for an imperative language: In the proceedings of POPL'91 [6], Consel and Danvy report the successful compilation and compiler generation for an imperative language that is much simpler than the present one (procedureless and stackless). The quality of the residual code is comparable, but a full-fledged partial evaluator is used, including source annotations, and so are several non-trivial binding-time improvements, most notably continuations.

Definitional interpreter for a lazy language: In the proceedings of POPL'92 [19], Jørgensen reports the successful compilation and compiler generation for a lazy language of a commercial scale. The target language is the high-level programming language Scheme. The quality of the result is competitive with contemporary implementations, given an efficient Scheme implementation. Again, a full-fledged partial evaluator is used, including source annotations, and so is a veritable arsenal of binding-time improvements, including continuations.

This work: In our work, we use λ-calculus normalization, no annotations, no binding-time analysis, no binding-time improvements, and no continuations. Our results are of Dragon-book quality.

7 Conclusion

We hope to have shown that type-directed partial evaluation of a definitional interpreter does scale up to a realistic example with non-trivial programming features. We would also like to point out that our work offers evidence that Scott and Strachey were right, each in their own way, when they developed Denotational Semantics: Strachey in that the λ-calculus provides a proper medium for encoding at least traditional programming languages, as illustrated by Landin [21]; and Scott for organizing this encoding with types and domain theory. The resulting format of denotational semantics proves ideal to apply a six-lines λ-calculus normalizer (using a higher-order functional language) and obtain the front-end of a semantics-based compiler towards three-address code — a strikingly concise and elegant solution to the old problem of semantics-based compiling.

8 Limitations

Modern programming languages (such as ML) have more type structure than Algol-like languages, in that whereas the type of the denotation of an Algol program is always the same, the type of the denotation of an ML program depends on the type of this program. Such languages are beyond the reach of the current state-of-the-art of type-directed partial evaluation, which is simply typed. Higher type systems are necessary — a topic for future work.

Acknowledgements

Grateful thanks to John Hatcliff, Nevin Heintze, Julia L. Lawall, Peter Lee, Karoline Malmkjær, Peter D. Mosses, and Peter O'Hearn for discussions and comments; and to the referees, for their lucid reviews.

References

1. Alfred V. Aho, Ravi Sethi, and Jeffrey D. Ullman. *Compilers: Principles, Techniques and Tools.* Addison-Wesley, 1986.
2. France E. Allen, editor. *Proceedings of the 1982 Symposium on Compiler Construction*, SIGPLAN Notices, Vol. 17, No 6, Boston, Massachusetts, June 1982. ACM Press.
3. Thorsten Altenkirch, Martin Hofmann, and Thomas Streicher. Categorical reconstruction of a reduction-free normalization proof. In David H. Pitt and David E. Rydeheard, editors, *Category Theory and Computer Science*, number 953 in Lecture Notes in Computer Science, pages 182–199, 1995.

4. Ulrich Berger and Helmut Schwichtenberg. An inverse of the evaluation functional for typed λ-calculus. In *Proceedings of the Sixth Annual IEEE Symposium on Logic in Computer Science*, pages 203–211, Amsterdam, The Netherlands, July 1991. IEEE Computer Society Press.

5. Anders Bondorf and Olivier Danvy. Automatic autoprojection of recursive equations with global variables and abstract data types. *Science of Computer Programming*, 16:151–195, 1991.

6. Charles Consel and Olivier Danvy. Static and dynamic semantics processing. In Robert (Corky) Cartwright, editor, *Proceedings of the Eighteenth Annual ACM Symposium on Principles of Programming Languages*, pages 14–24, Orlando, Florida, January 1991. ACM Press.

7. Charles Consel and Olivier Danvy. Tutorial notes on partial evaluation. In Susan L. Graham, editor, *Proceedings of the Twentieth Annual ACM Symposium on Principles of Programming Languages*, pages 493–501, Charleston, South Carolina, January 1993. ACM Press.

8. Olivier Danvy. Type-directed partial evaluation. In Guy L. Steele Jr., editor, *Proceedings of the Twenty-Third Annual ACM Symposium on Principles of Programming Languages*, pages 242–257, St. Petersburg Beach, Florida, January 1996. ACM Press.

9. Olivier Danvy. Pragmatics of type-directed partial evaluation. In Olivier Danvy, Robert Glück, and Peter Thiemann, editors, *Partial Evaluation*, number 1110 in Lecture Notes in Computer Science, Dagstuhl, Germany, February 1996. To appear.

10. Olivier Danvy and René Vestergaard. Semantics-based compiling: A case study in type-directed partial evaluation. Technical report BRICS-RS-96-13, Computer Science Department, Aarhus University, Aarhus, Denmark, May 1996.

11. Cormac Flanagan, Amr Sabry, Bruce F. Duba, and Matthias Felleisen. The essence of compiling with continuations. In David W. Wall, editor, *Proceedings of the ACM SIGPLAN'93 Conference on Prg. Lng. Design and Implementation*, SIGPLAN Notices, Vol. 28, No 6, pages 237–247, Albuquerque, New Mexico, June 1993. ACM Press.

12. Daniel P. Friedman, Mitchell Wand, and Christopher T. Haynes. *Essentials of Programming Languages*. The MIT Press and McGraw-Hill, 1991.

13. Harald Ganzinger, Robert Giegerich, Ulrich Mönke, and Reinhard Wilhem. A truly generative semantics-directed compiler generator. In Allen [2], pages 172–184.

14. Susan L. Graham, editor. *Proceedings of the 1984 Symposium on Compiler Construction*, SIGPLAN Notices, Vol. 19, No 6, Montréal, Canada, June 1984. ACM Press.

15. John Hatcliff and Olivier Danvy. A generic account of continuation-passing styles. In Hans-J. Boehm, editor, *Proceedings of the Twenty-First Annual ACM Symposium on Principles of Prg. Lng.*, pages 458–471, Portland, Oregon, January 1994. ACM Press.

16. Neil D. Jones, editor. *Semantics-Directed Compiler Generation*, number 94 in Lecture Notes in Computer Science, Aarhus, Denmark, 1980.

17. Neil D. Jones, Carsten K. Gomard, and Peter Sestoft. *Partial Evaluation and Automatic Program Generation*. Prentice Hall International Series in Computer Science. Prentice-Hall, 1993.

18. Neil D. Jones, Peter Sestoft, and Harald Søndergaard. MIX: A self-applicable partial evaluator for experiments in compiler generation. *LISP and Symbolic Computation*, 2(1):9–50, 1989.

19. Jesper Jørgensen. Generating a compiler for a lazy language by partial evaluation. In Andrew W. Appel, editor, *Proceedings of the Nineteenth Annual ACM Symposium on Principles of Programming Languages*, pages 258–268, Albuquerque, New Mexico, January 1992. ACM Press.

20. Ulrik Jørring and William L. Scherlis. Compilers and staging transformations. In Mark Scott Johnson and Ravi Sethi, editors, *Proceedings of the Thirteenth Annual*

ACM Symposium on Principles of Programming Languages, pages 86-96, St. Petersburg, Florida, January 1986.

21. Peter J. Landin. A correspondence between Algol 60 and Church's lambda notation. *Communications of the ACM*, 8:89-101 and 158-165, 1965.

22. Peter Lee. *Realistic Compiler Generation*. MIT Press, 1989.

23. Robert E. Milne and Christopher Strachey. *A Theory of Programming Language Semantics*. Chapman and Hall, London, and John Wiley, New York, 1976.

24. Lockwood Morris. The next 700 formal language descriptions. In Carolyn L. Talcott, editor, *Special issue on continuations (Part I)*, LISP and Symbolic Computation, Vol. 6, Nos. 3/4, pages 249-258. Kluwer Academic Publishers, December 1993.

25. Peter D. Mosses. SIS — semantics implementation system, reference manual and user guide. Technical Report MD-30, DAIMI, Computer Science Department, Aarhus University, Aarhus, Denmark, 1979.

26. Peter D. Mosses. Theory and practice of Action Semantics. In *Proceedings of the 1996 Symposium on Mathematical Foundations of Computer Science*, Lecture Notes in Computer Science, 1996. To appear.

27. Flemming Nielson and Hanne Riis Nielson. *Two-Level Functional Languages*, volume 34 of *Cambridge Tracts in Theoretical Computer Science*. Cambridge University Press, 1992.

28. Larry Paulson. Compiler generation from denotational semantics. In Bernard Lorho, editor, *Methods and Tools for Compiler Construction*, pages 219-250. Cambridge University Press, 1984.

29. Uwe Pleban. Compiler prototyping using formal semantics. In Graham [14], pages 94-105.

30. B. Randell and L. J. Russell. *Algol 60 Implementation*. Academic Press, New York, 1964.

31. Martin R. Raskovsky. Denotational semantics as a specification of code generators. In Allen [2], pages 230-244.

32. John C. Reynolds. Definitional interpreters for higher-order programming languages. In *Proceedings of 25th ACM National Conference*, pages 717-740, Boston, Massachusetts, 1972.

33. John C. Reynolds. The essence of Algol. In van Vliet, editor, *International Symposium on Algorithmic Languages*, pages 345-372, Amsterdam, The Netherlands, 1982. North-Holland.

34. David A. Schmidt. *Denotational Semantics: A Methodology for Language Development*. Allyn and Bacon, Inc., 1986.

35. Ravi Sethi. Control flow aspects of semantics-directed compiling. In Allen [2], pages 245-260.

36. Joseph Stoy. Some mathematical aspects of functional programming. In John Darlington, Peter Henderson, and David A. Turner, editors, *Functional Programming and its Applications*. Cambridge University Press, 1982.

37. Joseph E. Stoy. *Denotational Semantics: The Scott-Strachey Approach to Programming Language Theory*. MIT Press, 1977.

38. Mitchell Wand. Deriving target code as a representation of continuation semantics. *ACM Transactions on Programming Languages and Systems*, 4(3):496-517, 1982.

39. Mitchell Wand. A semantic prototyping system. In Graham [14], pages 213-221.

40. Mitchell Wand. From interpreter to compiler: a representational derivation. In Harald Ganzinger and Neil D. Jones, editors, *Programs as Data Objects*, number 217 in Lecture Notes in Computer Science, pages 306-324, Copenhagen, Denmark, October 1985.

Implementing Memoization for Partial Evaluation

Peter Thiemann

Wilhelm-Schickard-Institut, Universität Tübingen, Sand 13, D-72076 Tübingen, Germany, E-mail: thiemann@informatik.uni-tuebingen.de

Abstract. Memoization is a key ingredient in every partial evaluator. It enables folding by caching previously specialized functions. It is essential to make polyvariant specialization terminate. Its implementation is reasonably straightforward in a standard specializer that represents functions by closures. With the advent of handwritten program-generator generators (PGGs), implementing memoization gets harder, because PGGs use efficient standard representations of data at specialization time.

We present several implementations of memoization for PGGs that are able to deal with all features of current partial evaluators, specifically partially static data and functions. The first implementation is based on message passing. It is simple, portable, and efficient, but only suitable for untyped higher-order languages such as Scheme. The second implementation is geared towards typed language such as SML. Whereas the first two implementations are completely portable, our third implementation exploits introspective features that may not be available in all implementations.

Finally, we demonstrate that PGGs can solve the termination problem for partial evaluation. Our new incremental memoization algorithm performs incremental specialization and guarantees that specialization terminates whenever standard evaluation does.

Keywords: partial evaluation, automatic program transformation, incremental specialization, termination of partial evaluation, reflection.

Partial evaluation is a powerful program-specialization technique based on constant propagation. Given the *static* (known) parameters of a source program, partial evaluation constructs a *residual program*—a specialized version of the program, which on application to the remaining *dynamic* parameters produces the same result as the original program applied to all parameters. *Offline* partial evaluation [10,18] consists of two phases, binding-time analysis (BTA) and static reduction. BTA transforms a program and the binding times (static/dynamic) of the parameters into an annotated program. Subsequently, the specializer applies the program to the static input, reducing static expressions and rebuilding dynamic ones.

Specialization and Memoization Specialization is *polyvariant*: Each function in the source program may result in an arbitrary number of specialized versions in the residual program. The specializer must maintain a *specialization cache* to produce a finite residual program. The cache is a mapping from static parts of argument lists to residual function names. It works as follows:

Suppose the specializer calls function f on arguments $\bar{a}$. First, the specializer *extracts the static skeleton $\bar{s}$ and the dynamic parts $\bar{d}$* (predetermined by the BTA) from $\bar{a}$. Then, the specializer checks whether $f_{\bar{s}}$ is present in the cache. If that is not the case, the specializer enters $f_{\bar{s}}$ into the cache, *creates a cloned version $\bar{c}$ of $\bar{a}$*, all dynamic parts replaced by fresh variables, and specializes f's body with respect to $\bar{c}$. In any case, the specializer generates a residual function call $f_{\bar{s}}(\bar{d})$.

Specialization Points Not every function call needs to be memoized. However, memoizing too many function calls leads to poor residual programs, whereas memoizing too few calls leads to nonterminating specialization. Nontermination is a problem, because specialization is more eager than standard evaluation. It processes both branches of dynamic conditionals and also the bodies of dynamic abstractions. This may introduce loops not present under standard evaluation. The most effective way to break these loops is to introduce new *sp-functions* for dynamic conditionals and abstractions [5,7]. With this setup the specializer only memoizes calls to sp-functions and unfolds all others.

Partially Static Data Partially static data [27, 28] consists of a static skeleton and dynamic parts. For example, a (static) pair can have a static component and a dynamic one; the length of a list may be known statically, but the elements of the list may be dynamic; or a static function may have free variables with dynamic components. Partially static data increases the power of a partial evaluator considerably. It is a standard feature of current partial evaluators (e.g., [6,9]).

Program-Generator Generators In the standard approach to partial evaluation, there is a specializer **spec**, a source program p, and some input data divided into a static part inp_s and a dynamic part inp_d. The specification for **spec** is the *mix equation* [18,19]:

$$[\![p']\!]\ \text{inp}_d = [\![p]\!]\ \text{inp}_s\ \text{inp}_d \qquad \text{where} \qquad p' = [\![\text{spec}]\!]\ p\ \text{inp}_s \qquad (1)$$

Double self-application of the specializer constructs a program-generator generator **cogen** [11,37]. This **cogen** is a generator of program generators. Consider again the program p with inputs inp_s and inp_d. Applying **cogen** to p yields a program p-gen with some interesting properties:

$$\begin{aligned}
\text{p-gen} &= [\![\text{cogen}]\!]\ p \\
p' &= [\![\text{p-gen}]\!]\ \text{inp}_s \\
\text{result} &= [\![p']\!]\ \text{inp}_d = [\![p]\!]\ \text{inp}_s\ \text{inp}_d
\end{aligned} \qquad (2)$$

p-gen is a program generator specific to p. It accepts the static input of p and produces a specialized residual program p'. For this reason p-gen is called a *generating extension* of p. The interest in cogens and generating extensions is not just theoretical: Specialization with generating extensions is usually four to ten times faster than direct specialization [5, 27] [18, Chapter 4.10].

Hand-written Program-Generator Generators Holst and Launchbury [21] have discovered that cogen can be written by hand. We call such a hand-written program-generator generator **PGG**. PGGs solve the infamous encoding problem which hindered the development of efficient self-applicable specializers for typed languages; a PGG can be written in a different language, as long as it can parse and unparse programs; a PGG is not constrained by the limited capabilities of a specializer. The same is true for the generating extensions produced. They can freely exploit all features of their implementation language, not just those that are amenable to specialization. A final point in favor of PGGs is the simplification of correctness proofs. By now, there are several PGGs for functional languages: SML [3], Scheme [12], the lambda calculus [8, 23, 36].

1 Overview of This Work

The goal of PGGs in using the underlying language implementation to perform static computations conflicts with the necessity to provide an (intensional) equality for functions. Therefore, PGGs for functional languages [3, 12] have so far lacked a memoization mechanism for functional values. Section 2 describes a simple and efficient implementation of memoization for arbitrary partially static data, including functions. It is based on message passing and applies to dynamically typed higher-order programming languages (e.g., Scheme [17]). Unfortunately, this implementation cannot be used in a PGG for an ML-style typed language, because it is not well-typed. Therefore, Section 3 develops a memoization algorithm for typed higher-order languages. The key problem here is the development of a well-typed representation for closures.

Section 4 introduces an approach to memoization that exploits introspective features. The specializer reuses the closure representation of the underlying language implementation to perform memoization.

Section 5 shows that PGGs (in Scheme) are well suited to incremental specialization. An incremental specializer constructs the residual program on demand. It specializes a function only if the execution of the residual program actually calls its specialized version. Combined with a slight modification of the insertion of sp-functions, we can guarantee that specialization terminates for some input if and only if standard evaluation does so the same input.

Some knowledge of Scheme [17], ML [25], and partial evaluation [18] is a prerequisite to this paper.

```
(define (static-constructor ctor closed-value vvs bts)
  (let ((ctor-vvs (cons ctor vvs)))
    (lambda (what)
      (case what
        ((value)   (apply closed-value vvs))
        ((static)  (project-static ctor-vvs bts))
        ((dynamic) (project-dynamic ctor-vvs bts))
        ((clone)   (static-constructor
                    ctor
                    closed-value
                    (cdr (clone-dynamic ctor-vvs bts))
                    bts))
        (else      (error "bad argument ~a" what))))))
```

Fig. 1. Encoding for Partially Static Constructors

2 Memoization by Message Passing

For a dynamically typed language we can implement memoization for partially
static data using a simple, portable, and efficient encoding as functions.

Recall that the specializer must perform four operations on every data object:

1. obtain its value (so that static computation can proceed),
2. extract its static parts (for caching),
3. extract its dynamic parts (to build lists of residual arguments and formal
   parameters), and
4. clone its dynamic parts by replacing them with fresh variables.

We represent all partially static data (be it functions or constructed data) in a
generating extension by functions. The function static-constructor in Fig. 1
implements this representation (in Scheme). It factorizes the fixed static parts
of a partially static value from its changing dynamic parts. Cloning changes the
dynamic parts by replacing them with fresh variables. The fixed part ctor is the
name of the constructor (or the unique label of the lambda) which is used for
memoization. closed-value is the constructor function. For a partially static
function f it is an abstraction which accepts the values of f's free variables
and delivers the function as its result. The arguments of the constructor live
separately in the list vvs which contains the arguments of the constructor (the
values of the free variables in case of a function). With this separation there is
no restriction regarding the "real" representation of partially static structures.
They can be represented by vectors, functions, and so on. vvs is the argument
list for the constructor. Finally, bts contains the binding times of the elements
of vvs.

As an example, we demonstrate in Fig. 2 the encoding of (lambda (x) y)
with unique label c142, once with free static variable y = 5 (left column) and
then once with y a free dynamic variable (right column).

The projection functions, *project-static*, *project-dynamic*, and *clone-dynamic*,
are well-known [18, Ch.10.2]. They extract the static part or the dynamic part

```
> (define consty                          > (define consty
>   (static-constructor                   >   (static-constructor
>    'c142                                 >    'c142
>    (lambda (y) (lambda (x) y))           >    (lambda (y) (lambda (x) y))
>    (list y) '(STATIC))                   >    (list 'y) '(DYNAMIC)))
> ; apply the function                    >
> ((consty 'value) 'arg-for-x)            > ((consty 'value) 'arg-for-x)
5                                         'y
> ; get the static skeleton               >
> (consty 'static)                        > (consty 'static)
'(c142 5)                                 '(c142)
> ; get the dynamic parts                 >
> (consty 'dynamic)                       > (consty 'dynamic)
'()                                       '((y))
> ; clone the value                       >
> (define cloned (consty 'clone))         > (define cloned (consty 'clone))
> ; same static skeleton                  >
> (cloned 'static)                        > (cloned 'static)
'(c142 5)                                 '(c142)
                                          > (cloned 'dynamic)
```

Fig. 2. A Partially Static Function   `'((clone-3))`

```
(define (project-static value bts)
  (let ((ctor (car value)) (values (cdr value)))
    (cons ctor
          (let loop ((values values) (bts bts))
            (if (null? values)
                '()
                (let ((skeleton (loop (cdr values) (cdr bts))))
                  (if (static? (car bts))
                      (let ((static-value (car values)))
                        (if (procedure? static-value)
                            (append (static-value 'STATIC) skeleton)
                            (cons static-value skeleton)))
                      skeleton)))))))
```

Fig. 3. Implementation of *project-static*

from a partially static value, or they replace the dynamic parts of a value by fresh variables. What is new in our setting is that they may encounter static data encoded as a function in which case they must pass the respective message to it as outlined above. To convey the idea, we show the implementations of *project-static* in Fig. 3. We omit the other functions, as they pose no new problems.

3 Typed Memoization

Unfortunately the message-passing approach shown in Sec. 2 does not work in an ML-style typed language. The type of the abstraction (lambda (what) ...) in *static-constructor* (Fig. 1) depends on the value of what. This is not surprising as the function implements method dispatch in the representation of static constructors. The abstraction (lambda (what) ...) has no ML type, because the result of the 'value message is a function and the result of the 'static message is a list.

Hence, we have to perform some variant of closure conversion [30]. It is, however, well-known that closure conversion is not straightforward in a typed setting [26]. The untyped appraoch closure conversion introduces a datatype AllClosures which has a constructor for each abstraction in the program. The constructor takes the values of the abstraction's free variables. We replace abstractions with the appropriate closure of type AllClosures and each function application with a case dispatch on the closure. However, in a typed setting a type conflict arises unless all functions have the same type.

For concreteness we consider a monomorphic subset of Standard ML [25]. We concentrate on a monomorphic language because of typing problems with the specialization cache. This issue is usually side-stepped by monomorphic expansion.

Applying Closure Analysis When we assume the availability of the explicitly typed source program (after type reconstruction) and the results of a closure analysis (see e.g., [14, 33, 35]), we can solve the typing problem. Suppose each program point is marked with a unique label $\ell \in$ Labels. An (equational) flow analysis partitions Labels into disjoint *flow classes* $L_1 \cup \ldots \cup L_n$ such that values of expressions with label $\ell \in L_i$ are never mixed up with values of expressions with labels in L_j, for $i \neq j$. Moreover, unless the source program has a type error, all expressions in the same flow class have the same type.

We further assume that the membership in a flow class is made explicit in the types. That is, the type $\tau \to_i \tau'$ is the type of a function in flow class L_i. We represent such a function as a pair of type $(FC_i \to \tau \to \tau') \times FC_i$. That is, we abstract the free variables from the original functions and package them in some data type FC_i.

The data type FC_i has constructors FV_ℓ for each $fn_\ell\ x\ =>\ E$ where $\ell \in L_i$ (in this section, we adopt ML syntax for expressions and types). The arguments of the constructor FV_ℓ are the free variables of $fn_\ell\ x\ =>\ E$ and their annotated types are $\tau_{\ell 1}, \ldots, \tau_{\ell m_\ell}$.

We replace

$$\overline{fn_\ell\ x\ =>\ E}^c = (fn\ (FV_\ell(x_1, \ldots, x_{m_\ell}))\ =>\ fn\ x\ =>\ \overline{E}^c, FV_\ell(x_1, \ldots, x_{m_\ell}))$$

where $x_1 \ldots x_n = FV(E)$ and we replace each application $(E_1\ E_2)$ in which E_1 has type $\tau \to_i \tau'$ with

$$\overline{(E_1\ E_2)}^c = let\ (cv, fvs)\ =\ \overline{E_1}^c\ in\ ((cv\ fvs)\ \overline{E_2}^c)\ end.$$

This program transformation induces a type transformation as follows.

$$\overline{\tau_1 \to_i \tau_2}^c = (FC_i \to \overline{\tau}^c \to \overline{\tau'}^c) \times FC_i$$
$$\overline{(\tau_1, \ldots, \tau_n)\chi}^c = (\overline{\tau_1}^c, \ldots, \overline{\tau_n}^c)\chi$$

Here χ stands for an arbitrary type constructor different from $\to$. As the type transformation also applies to free variables of functions, we obtain the definition of FC_i:

datatype FC_i = ... | FV_ℓ of $(\overline{\tau_{\ell 1}}^c * \ldots * \overline{\tau_{\ell m_\ell}}^c)$ | ...

The program transformation can be performed on a per-flow-class basis. The resulting program is well-typed, since all program points in L_i simultaneously change their type from $\tau \to_i \tau'$ to $(FC_i \to \overline{\tau}^c \to \overline{\tau'}^c) \times FC_i$. The transformed application is also well-typed: As $(E_1\ E_2)$ is well-typed, E_2 must have type τ and $(E_1\ E_2)$ must has type τ'. In the transformed expression, cv has type $FC_i \to \overline{\tau}^c \to \overline{\tau'}^c$ and fvs has type FC_i. Therefore, $(cv\ fvs)$ has type $\overline{\tau}^c \to \overline{\tau'}^c$ and can be applied to $\overline{E_2}^c$ of type $\overline{\tau}^c$ to yield a result of type $\overline{\tau'}^c$.

The Static Skeleton To encode static skeletons we introduce a type FCS_i for each flow class L_i with one constructor FVS_ℓ for each function in flow class i with an argument for each free variable of the function.

datatype FCS_i = ... | FVS_ℓ of $(\overline{\tau_{\ell 1}}^s * \ldots * \overline{\tau_{\ell m_\ell}}^s)$ | ...

The function $\overline{\tau}^s$ works on *binding-time annotated types* (as output by a BTA) where each type constructor is annotated with a binding time S or D (static or dynamic). It constructs the type of the static skeleton for a value of type τ. We use υ to denote an annotated type with its top level annotation stripped off.

$$\overline{\upsilon^D}^s = \text{unit}$$
$$\overline{\tau_1 \to_i^S \tau_2}^s = FCS_i$$
$$\overline{(\tau_1, \ldots, \tau_n)\chi^S}^s = (\overline{\tau_1}^s, \ldots, \overline{\tau_n}^s)\chi$$

In other words: dynamic values are mapped to the unit type, static functions are mapped to the type of the static skeleton of their free variables, other static data is mapped to itself with the subcomponents mapped recursively.

In the typed case, each memoized function has its own specialization cache [3]. Otherwise, the cache may not be well-typed, for its type depends on the static part of the arguments. We use type and flow information to construct the implementation of each dynamic call. Consider a call $f^D(E_1, \ldots, E_n)$ and assume that E_i has type τ_i. The static skeleton is a tuple $(s_1, \ldots, s_n)$ of type $\overline{\tau_1}^s \times \ldots \times \overline{\tau_n}^s$ with the components determined by $s_i = get\_static(E_i, \tau_i)$.

$$get\_static(E, \tau) = \begin{cases} () & \tau = \upsilon^D \\ E & \tau = B^S \\ project\_static_\ell(E) & \tau = \tau' \to_\ell^S \tau'' \end{cases}$$

That is, we return () for dynamic values, the value itself for static values of base type $B \in \{\texttt{unit}, \texttt{int}, \ldots\}$, and the static projection of the value for static functional values.

Using *get_static*, the definition of *project_static* is straightforward.

$$project\_static_\ell(cv, fvs) = case\ fvs\ of$$
$$\ldots \mid FV_\ell(x_1, \ldots, x_{m_\ell}) \Rightarrow FVS_\ell(\ldots, get\_static(x_k, \tau_{\ell k}), \ldots) \mid \ldots$$

The PGG precomputes the function *get_static* as it is not ML-typable in a generating extension. However, the resulting *project_static$_\ell$* functions are typable, once the occurrences of *get_static* are expanded. Their type is

$$project\_static_i : (FC_i \to \overline{\tau}^c \to \overline{\tau'^c}) \times FC_i \to FCS_i$$

where i ranges over all flow classes. The result type FCS_i of *project_static$_i$* is an equality type as all function types in the argument have been recursively replaced by their corresponding closure types. Hence, the generating extensions can use these values as keys in the specialization cache.

For each functional flow class L_i we specify a function *project_dynamic$_i$* : $FC_i \to$ Code *list*.

$$project\_dynamic_i(cv, fvs) = case\ fvs\ of$$
$$\ldots \mid FV_k(x_1, \ldots, x_{m_k}) \Rightarrow get\_dynamic(x_1, \tau_1)get\_dynamic(x_2, \tau_2) \ldots [\ ] \mid \ldots$$

Here, we assume the macro definition

$$get\_dynamic(w, \tau)l = \begin{cases} w :: l & \tau = v^D \\ l & \tau = B^S \\ project\_dynamic_i(w)@l & \tau = \tau' \to_i^S \tau'' \end{cases}$$

where $w :: l$ denotes construction of a list with head w and tail l, and @ denotes list concatenation. And finally, the specification of cloning.

$$get\_clone(w, \tau) = \begin{cases} gen\,Variable() & \tau = v^D \\ w & \tau = B^S \\ clone\_dynamic_\ell(w) & \tau = \tau' \to_\ell^S \tau'' \end{cases}$$

$$clone\text{-}dynamic_i : FC_i \to FC_i$$
$$clone\_dynamic_\ell(cv, fvs) = case\ fvs\ of$$
$$\ldots \mid FV_k(x_1, \ldots, x_{m_k}) \Rightarrow (cv, FV_k(\ldots, get\_clone(x_i, \tau_i), \ldots)) \mid \ldots$$

Failure of the Obvious The extra types FCS_i for the static skeletons appear artificial. After all, a separate type for the static skeleton is not necessary in the untyped case. Thus, let us consider using a parameterized type FC_i, both for the value and for the static skeleton. This datatype has one parameter for each free variable of each lambda in the flow class L_i.

To see what happens, consider the following example ML program:

```
fun loop (n, g) = if n=0 then g else loop (n-1, fn y => g y)
fun f n = loop (n, fn z => z)
```

As both abstractions can appear as the parameter g of loop it is clear that they belong to the same flow class. Therefore, we define a datatype

```
datatype 'a FC = FV1 of unit | FV2 of 'a
```

encoding the free variables of the abstractions. The result after transformation:

```
val fnx = (fn (FV1 ()) => fn z => z, FV1 ())
fun fny g = (fn (FV2 g) => fn z => let val (cv, fvs) = g in cv fvs z end,
             FV2 g)

fun loop_m (n, g) = if n=0 then g else loop_m (n-1, fny g)
fun f_m n = loop_m (n, fnx)
```

Unfortunately, the transformed program does not type-check anymore. The functions fnx and fny have the following types:

```
val fnx : ('a FC -> 'b -> 'b) * 'c FC
val fny : 'a -> ((('b -> 'c -> 'd) * 'b) FC -> 'c -> 'd) * 'a FC
```

Function fny embeds the type of its first parameter in the type of its result. We have constructed loop_m in such a way that fnx as well as fny fnx and fny (fny fnx) (and so on recursively) can occur as parameters of fny. Therefore the type checker complains about a circular type:

```
Error: pattern and expression in val rec dec don't agree (circularity)
  pattern:     (((('Z -> 'Y -> 'X) * 'Z) FC -> 'Y -> 'X) * 'W FC)
  expression: 'W
  in declaration:
    loop_m = ...
```

For this reason we have to use two different data types, one to encode functional values and another for the static skeleton.

4   Memoization Using Introspection

Our function static-constructor constructs an explicit closure for a function although the underlying implementation represents the function as a closure anyway. If an implementation provides introspective operations to access the underlying representation we can avoid that overhead. Most implementations provide the necessary operations for debugging purposes or for use by the compiler:

- obtain the values of the free variables of a function,
- obtain the code part of a function, and
- construct a function from its code part and the values of its free variables.

However, the specializer must be able to reconstruct the binding times of the free variables. Therefore, each variable must be bound to a pair consisting of the variable's value and its binding time. We have no other hope of reconstructing the binding time, as the sequence of variables in the closure provided by the system is not predictable.

To be more specific, suppose the system provides the following functions:

- **reify-closure**, which accepts a procedure and returns a closure, and
- **reflect-closure**, which accepts a closure and returns a procedure.

In this context a closure is a record type providing the following operations:

- **(make-closure label vals)** creates a new closure with label **label**, which must be obtained from another closure using **closure->label**, and list of free variables **vals**,
- **(closure->label closure)** returns a unique label identifying the function represented by **closure**, for example the address of the function's code, and
- **(closure->vals closure)** returns the list of the values of the free variables of the function represented by the closure.

Next, we need operations to encode bindings:

- **(make-binding value btime)** pairs a value and a binding time,
- **(binding->value binding)** returns the value component, and
- **(binding->btime binding)** returns the binding time.

To support other partially static data structures, we suppose the following encoding of constructed data.

- **(make-constructor ctor args bts)** creates a data structure with constructor **ctor**, arguments **args**, and binding times **bts**,
- **(constructor->ctor cval)** returns the constructor of a constructed value,
- **(constructor->args cval)** returns the arguments of the constructor of a constructed value,
- **(constructor->bts cval)** returns the binding times of the arguments of the constructor of a constructed value, and
- **(constructor? obj)** returns **#f** unless the argument is a constructed data structure.

In order to make it work, we have to change *project-static* etc. In Fig. 3, we replace the body of the (let ((static-value (car values))) ...) with

```
(cond ((procedure? static-value)
       (append (project-static-proc static-value) skeleton))
      ((constructor? static-value)
       (append (project-static-ctor static-value) skeleton))
      (else
       (cons static-value skeleton)))
```

and define the procedures project-static-proc and project-static-ctor:

```
(define (project-static-proc proc)
  (let ((closure (reify-closure proc)))
    (let ((freevals (closure->vals closure)))
      (project-static (cons (closure->label closure)
                            (map binding->value freevals))
                      (map binding->btime freevals)))))
```

```
(define (project-static-ctor cval)
  (project-static (cons (constructor->ctor cval)
                        (constructor->args cval))
                  (constructor->bts cval)))
```

The possibility to exploit reflective features is a unique feature of PGGs. A cogen generated by self-application cannot utilize such a feature, as it is derived from a specializer which has its own implementation of environments.

The current version 0.44 of Scheme 48 [20] has exactly the features that we need. Specifically, the procedures

- `make-closure` accepts a template (which contains a unique identification, literals, and code) and an environment (a vector) to build a closure,
- `closure-template` extracts the template from a closure,
- `template-id` extracts the unique identification from a template, and
- `closure-env` extracts the environment from a closure.

This is all we need to get things to work.

5 Incremental Memoization

In Scheme with `eval` [29], generating extensions can perform incremental specialization just by changing the memoization code. The idea is that the specializer only processes code when there is a demand to run it. No time is spent specializing code which is never run. This is analogous to the difference between call-by-value and call-by-need: With call-by-value all arguments of functions are evaluated once, whereas with call-by-need arguments of functions are evaluated at most once. Therefore incremental specialization *terminates more often* than standard specialization.

The fine thing is that we do not have to change anything in our PGG except the treatment of dynamic function calls. Fig. 4 shows the new definition.

When we start the generating extension it performs a call to the goal function (see Fig. 4), which defines a top-level procedure which accepts the dynamic parameters and returns the text of a call to this procedure.

The procedure constructed by the initial call behaves as follows. When it is called with actual dynamic parameters, it first goes away to create the text of the specialized function, using the static parameters remembered from the initial call. Next, it overwrites its own definition with the definition of the specialized function and calls the specialized function just constructed with the dynamic parameters.

When the recursive specialization process reaches a memoized function call, the same mechanism as for the initial call comes into play. Thus, the specialized program is constructed interleaved with its own execution. The specialization of a procedure starts upon the first call to its specialized variant.

The code uses the top-level variable `*dummy-definition-buffer*` to construct a top-level function definition from the compiled abstraction generate. We first assign the function to `*dummy-definition-buffer*` and then bind that value to a new name.

```
(define (memo-call fn bts args)
  (let*
      ((full-pp    (cons fn args))
       (static-pp (project-static full-pp bts))
       (dynamics  (project-dynamic full-pp bts))
       (actuals   (apply append dynamics))
       (found
        (or (assoc static-pp *spec-cache*)
            (let* ((new-name    (gensym fn))
                   (cloned-pp   (clone-dynamic full-pp bts))
                   (new-formals (apply append
                                       (project-dynamic cloned-pp bts)))
                   (new-entry   (spec-cache! (cons static-pp new-name)))
                   (generate
                    (lambda actuals
                      (let* ((new-def
                               '(DEFINE (,new-name ,@new-formals)
                                  ,(apply
                                    (eval fn (interaction-environment))
                                    (cdr cloned-pp))))
                             (dummy (add-to-residual-program! new-def))
                             (dummy
                               (eval new-def (interaction-environment))))
                        (apply (eval new-name (interaction-environment))
                               actuals)))))
              (set! *dummy-definition-buffer* generate)
              (eval '(DEFINE ,new-name *DUMMY-DEFINITION-BUFFER*)
                    (interaction-environment))
              (cons static-pp new-name))))
       (res-name  (cdr found)))
    ;; generate call to fn with actual arguments
    '(,res-name ,@actuals)))
(define *dummy-definition-buffer*)
```

Fig. 4. Implementation of Memoized Function Calls for Incremental Specialization

Termination With a little change in the introduction of sp-functions incremental specialization terminates whenever standard evaluation does. We can get the correct behavior by moving the sp-functions to the *branches* of dynamic conditionals and to the *bodies* of dynamic abstractions. This way, we only specialize those branches and bodies that are actually used in the execution of the specialized program.

6 Related Work

Self-applicable partial evaluators [6, 9] also employ dual representations of functions to generate efficient program-generator generators (cogens) and generating extensions. This theme reappears in our closure representations which separates the function part from the environment part in the representation of functions.

Minamide, Morrisett, and Harper [26] propose existential types to type the environment part of closures. This is appropriate in their intermediate code setting, which supports existential types. Standard ML does not support them, though [25]. Moreover, existential types would not solve the memoization problem as the dynamic call must be able to *compare* two closures. If the closure representation is abstract, such a comparison is impossible.

The termination of partial evaluation is usually addressed by means of program analysis. Holst [15] and Glenstrup and Jones [13] have defined enhanced BTA algorithms to ensure termination. Andersen and Holst [1] have defined a termination analysis for higher-order specialization. Our current approach is orthogonal as it builds on incremental specialization.

Intricate call graph analyses have been developed to find a set of memoized calls which is as small as possible but still ensures terminating specialization [19, 31, 32]. Our algorithm to insert sp-functions is a variation of Bondorf and Danvy's algorithm [5, 7] which works satisfactory in practice.

The idea of specializing data types to avoid type problems has been used before, for example by Steele [34].

7 Conclusions

We have presented four contributions to the implementation of memoization for partial evaluation. We have developed implementations of memoization for partially static functions, for untyped and for typed languages. Furthermore, language implementations that supply introspective features support an implementation of memoization which reuses the internal representation of functions. Finally, we have developed a framework for doing incremental specialization with generating extensions. With a slight variation of the standard insertion of sp-functions, incremental specialization solves all termination problems associated with partial evaluation.

The latter two features can only be achieved in the PGG framework: The introspective implementation exploits the representation of functions by the implementation and incremental specialization relies on inerleaving the actual execution with the specialization.

Furthermore, all of these techniques work with multiple levels of binding times [12]. The untyped techniques are all implemented in our PGG [36].

References

1. Peter Holst Andersen and Carsten Kehler Holst. Termination analysis for offline partial evaluation of a higher order functional language. In Radhia Cousot, editor, *Proc. International Static Analysis Symposium, SAS'96*, Aachen, Germany, September 1996. Springer-Verlag. LNCS.

2. Lars Birkedal and Morten Welinder. Partial evaluation of Standard ML. Rapport 93/22, DIKU, University of Copenhagen, 1993.

3. Lars Birkedal and Morten Welinder. Hand-writing program generator generators. In Manuel V. Hermenegildo and Jaan Penjam, editors, *Programming Languages, Implementations, Logics, and Programs (PLILP '94)*, volume 844 of *Lecture Notes in Computer Science*, pages 198–214, Madrid, Spain, September 1994. Springer-Verlag.

4. Dines Bjørner, Andrei P. Ershov, and Neil D. Jones, editors. *Partial Evaluation and Mixed Computation*, Amsterdam, 1988. North-Holland.

5. Anders Bondorf. Automatic autoprojection of higher order recursive equations. *Science of Programming*, 17:3–34, 1991.

6. Anders Bondorf. *Similix 5.0 Manual*. DIKU, University of Copenhagen, May 1993.

7. Anders Bondorf and Olivier Danvy. Automatic autoprojection of recursive equations with global variables and abstract data types. *Science of Programming*, 16(2):151–195, 1991.

8. Anders Bondorf and Dirk Dussart. Improving CPS-based partial evaluation: Writing cogen by hand. In Peter Sestoft and Harald Søndergaard, editors, *Proc. ACM SIGPLAN Workshop on Partial Evaluation and Semantics-Based Program Manipulation PEPM '94*, pages 1–10, Orlando, Fla., June 1994. ACM.

9. Charles Consel. A tour of Schism. In David Schmidt, editor, *Proc. ACM SIGPLAN Symposium on Partial Evaluation and Semantics-Based Program Manipulation PEPM '93*, pages 134–154, Copenhagen, Denmark, June 1993. ACM Press.

10. Charles Consel and Olivier Danvy. Tutorial notes on partial evaluation. In *Proc. 20th Annual ACM Symposium on Principles of Programming Languages*, pages 493–501, Charleston, South Carolina, January 1993. ACM Press.

11. Yoshihiko Futamura. Partial evaluation of computation process — an approach to a compiler-compiler. *Systems, Computers, Controls*, 2(5):45–50, 1971.

12. Robert Glück and Jesper Jørgensen. Efficient multi-level generating extensions for program specialization. In Doaitse Swierstra and Manuel Hermenegildo, editors, *Programming Languages, Implementations, Logics, and Programs (PLILP '95)*, volume 982 of *Lecture Notes in Computer Science*, Utrecht, The Netherlands, September 1995. Springer-Verlag.

13. Arne John Glenstrup and Neil D. Jones. Bta algorithms to ensure termination of offline partial evaluation. In *PSI-96: Andrei Ershov Second International Memorial Conference, Perspectives of System Informatics*, Novosibirsk, Russia, June 1996.

14. Fritz Henglein. Efficient type inference for higher-order binding-time analysis. In Hughes [16], pages 448–472. LNCS 523.

15. Carsten Kehler Holst. Finiteness analysis. In Hughes [16], pages 473–495. LNCS 523.

16. John Hughes, editor. *Functional Programming Languages and Computer Architecture*, Cambridge, MA, 1991. Springer-Verlag. LNCS 523.

17. Institute of Electrical and Electronic Engineers, Inc. IEEE standard for the Scheme programming language. IEEE Std 1178-1990, New York, NY, 1991.

18. Neil D. Jones, Carsten K. Gomard, and Peter Sestoft. *Partial Evaluation and Automatic Program Generation*. Prentice Hall, 1993.

19. Neil D. Jones, Peter Sestoft, and Harald Søndergaard. An experiment in partial evaluation: The generation of a compiler generator. In J.-P. Jouannaud, editor, *Rewriting Techniques and Applications*, pages 124–140, Dijon, France, 1985. Springer-Verlag. LNCS 202.

20. Richard A. Kelsey and Jonathan Rees. A tractable Scheme implementation. *Lisp and Symbolic Computation*, 7(4):315–335, 1994.
21. John Launchbury and Carsten Kehler Holst. Handwriting cogen to avoid problems with static typing. In *Draft Proceedings, Fourth Annual Glasgow Workshop on Functional Programming*, pages 210–218, Skye, Scotland, 1991. Glasgow University.
22. Julia Lawall and Olivier Danvy. Continuation-based partial evaluation. In LFP 1994 [24], pages 227–238.
23. Julia Lawall and Olivier Danvy. Continuation-based partial evaluation. Extended version of [22] from ftp://ftp.daimi.aau.dk/pub/danvy/Papers/, January 1995.
24. *Proc. 1994 ACM Conference on Lisp and Functional Programming*, Orlando, Florida, USA, June 1994. ACM Press.
25. Robin Milner, Mads Tofte, and Robert Harper. *The Definition of Standard ML*. MIT Press, 1990.
26. Yasuhiko Minamide, Greg Morrisett, and Robert Harper. Typed closure conversion. In *Proc. 23rd Annual ACM Symposium on Principles of Programming Languages*, pages 271–283, St. Petersburg, Fla., January 1996. ACM Press.
27. Torben Æ. Mogensen. Partially static structures in a self-applicable partial evaluator. In Bjørner et al. [4], pages 325–347.
28. Torben Æ. Mogensen. Separating binding times in language specifications. In *Proc. Functional Programming Languages and Computer Architecture 1989*, pages 14–25, London, GB, 1989.
29. Jonathan Rees. The Scheme of things: The June 1992 meeting. *Lisp Pointers*, V(4), October 1992.
30. John C. Reynolds. Definitional interpreters for higher-order programming. In *ACM Annual Conference*, pages 717–740, July 1972.
31. Peter Sestoft. The structure of a self-applicable partial evaluator. In Harald Ganzinger and Neil D. Jones, editors, *Programs as Data Objects*, pages 236–256, Copenhagen, Denmark, October 1985. Springer-Verlag. LNCS 217.
32. Peter Sestoft. Automatic call unfolding in a partial evaluator. In Bjørner et al. [4], pages 485–506.
33. Olin Shivers. *Control-Flow Analysis of Higher-Order Languages*. PhD thesis, School of Computer Science, Carnegie Mellon University, Pittsburgh, PA 15213, May 1991. Also technical report CMU-CS-91-145.
34. Guy L. Steele Jr. Building interpreters by composing monads. In *Proc. 21st Annual ACM Symposium on Principles of Programming Languages*, pages 472–492, Portland, OG, January 1994. ACM Press.
35. Dan Stefanescu and Yuli Zhou. An equational framework for the flow analysis of higher-order functional programs. In LFP 1994 [24], pages 318–327.
36. Peter Thiemann. Cogen in six lines. In R. Kent Dybvig, editor, *Proc. International Conference on Functional Programming 1996*, pages 180–189, Philadelphia, PA, May 1996. ACM Press, New York.
37. Valentin F. Turchin. The use of metasystem transition in theorem proving and program optimization. In *International Conference on Automata, Languages, and Programming. Seventh ICALP*, volume 85 of *Lecture Notes in Computer Science*, pages 645–657, Noordwijkerhout, The Netherlands, 1980. Springer-Verlag.

Higher Order Deforestation

G.W.Hamilton

Department of Computer Science
University of Keele
Keele
Staffordshire UK ST5 5BG
e-mail: *geoff@cs.keele.ac.uk*

Abstract. Intermediate data structures are widely used in functional programs. Programs which use these intermediate structures are usually a lot easier to understand, but they result in loss of efficiency at run-time. In order to reduce these run-time costs, a transformation algorithm called *deforestation* was proposed by Wadler which could eliminate intermediate structures. However, this transformation algorithm was formulated only for first order functional programs. In this paper, it is shown how the original deforestation algorithm can be extended to deal with higher order functional programs. A *treeless form* of higher order expression is defined which creates no intermediate structures. Higher order treeless form is an easily recognised form of expression, and any function definition can easily be generalised so that it is in this form. It is shown that the higher order deforestation algorithm will terminate if all function definitions are in this form. This algorithm is then compared with related work.

1 Introduction

The use of intermediate structures, lazy evaluation and higher order functions in functional programming facilitates a more elegant and readable style of programming (see [8]), but it often results in inefficient programs. One solution to this problem is to transform these programs to more efficient equivalent programs. A transformation algorithm called *deforestation* was proposed in [17] which can eliminate intermediate structures from first order functional programs. This algorithm was extended to allow a restricted higher order facility by treating higher order functions as macros. This mechanism does not cover all uses of higher order functions.

In this paper, it is shown how the deforestation algorithm can be extended to handle higher order expressions directly, thus covering all uses of higher order functions. This paper provides two major contributions. Firstly, a *treeless form* of higher order expression is defined which is easy to recognise and for which the higher order deforestation algorithm is guaranteed to terminate. Secondly, it is shown how this algorithm compares with other methods for removing intermediate structures from higher order programs. It is found that some commonly used higher order functions are not in treeless form, so some intermediate structures cannot be removed from programs using these functions.

The remainder of this paper is organised as follows. In Section 2, the higher order language on which the described transformations are to be performed is introduced. In Section 3, higher order treeless form is defined, and it is shown how function definitions can be generalised so that they are in this form. In Section 4, the higher order deforestation algorithm is described. In Section 5, the higher order deforestation theorem is stated and proved correct. In Section 6, it is shown how this algorithm compares with other methods for removing intermediate structures from higher order programs, and Section 7 concludes.

2   Language

The language for which the described transformations are to be performed is a simple higher order functional language as given in Fig. 1.

$$
\begin{array}{lll}
prog ::= & e_0 & \\
& \textbf{where} & \\
& f_1 = e_1 & \text{program} \\
& \quad\vdots & \\
& f_n = e_n & \\
& & \\
e \quad ::= v & & \text{variable} \\
\mid c\ \{e\} & & \text{constructor application} \\
\mid f & & \text{function variable} \\
\mid \lambda v.e & & \text{lambda expression} \\
\mid \textbf{case}\ e'\ \textbf{of}\ <p:e> & & \text{case expression} \\
\mid e\ e' & & \text{function application} \\
& & \\
p \quad ::= c\ \{v\} & & \text{pattern}
\end{array}
$$

Fig. 1. Language Grammar

The notation $\{e\}$ represents a series of zero or more constructs of the form given by e and the notation $<p:e>$ represents a series of one or more constructs of the form given by $p:e$.

Programs in the language consist of an expression to evaluate and a set of function definitions. It is assumed that the language is typed using the Milner polymorphic typing system [11, 4], so all functions must have a finite number of arguments. It is also assumed that the compiler for the language implements the full laziness technique described in [7]. Nested function definitions are not allowed in the language. Programs involving nested definitions can be transformed into this restricted form of program using a technique called *lambda lifting* [9].

For the purposes of this paper, constants (e.g. numbers) and basic functions $(+,*,>,square,$ etc.) can be considered to be variables. Each constructor has a fixed arity (for example, Nil has arity 0, and $Cons$ has arity 2) and each constructor application must be saturated.

Within **case** expressions of the form **case** e' **of** $< p : e >$, e' is called the *selector*, and $< p : e >$ are called the *branches*. The patterns in **case** expressions may not be nested. Methods to transform **case** expressions with nested patterns to ones without nested patterns are described in [1] and [16].

An example program in the language is shown in Fig. 2.

$$fold\ (+)\ 0\ (map\ square\ (until\ (>\ n)\ (repeat\ (+\ 1)\ 1)))$$
where
$$
\begin{aligned}
fold\ \ &=\lambda f.\lambda a.\lambda xs.\,\textbf{case}\ xs\ \textbf{of}\\
&\qquad\qquad Nil\qquad\quad : a\\
&\qquad\qquad Cons\ x\ xs : f\ x\ (fold\ f\ a\ xs)\\[6pt]
map\ \ &=\lambda f.\lambda xs.\,\textbf{case}\ xs\ \textbf{of}\\
&\qquad\qquad Nil\qquad\quad : Nil\\
&\qquad\qquad Cons\ x\ xs : Cons\ (f\ x)\ (map\ f\ xs)\\[6pt]
until\ \ &=\lambda p.\lambda xs.\,\textbf{case}\ xs\ \textbf{of}\\
&\qquad\qquad Nil\qquad\quad : Nil\\
&\qquad\qquad Cons\ x\ xs : \textbf{case}\ (p\ x)\ \textbf{of}\\
&\qquad\qquad\qquad\qquad\qquad True\ \ : Nil\\
&\qquad\qquad\qquad\qquad\qquad False : Cons\ x\ (until\ p\ xs)\\[6pt]
repeat\ &=\lambda f.\lambda x.Cons\ x\ (repeat\ f\ (f\ x))
\end{aligned}
$$

Fig. 2. Example Program

This program calculates the sum of the squares of the numbers from 1 to n. The function *repeat* is used to create a list of integers starting with 1, with each subsequent number increasing by 1. The function *until* is used to select the first n of these. The function *map* is used to square each of these numbers, and the function *fold* is used to add these together.

As in [17], an expression other than a **case** expression is defined to be *linear* with respect to a variable if the number of occurrences of the variable within the expression is not more than one. A **case** expression is defined to be linear with respect to a variable if the total number of occurrences of the variable within the selector and any branch of the expression is not more than one. For example, the function *fold* given in Fig. 2 is linear with respect to the variable a, but it is not linear with respect to the variable f.

3 Higher Order Treeless Form

In this section, a higher order treeless form of expression is defined which is similar to the first order blazed treeless form defined in [17]. In the first order blazed treeless form defined in [17], expressions are *blazed*[1] according to whether or not they can be eliminated by the deforestation algorithm. Expressions blazed $\oplus$ can be eliminated, but expressions blazed $\ominus$ cannot. This blazing was performed according to the type of the expressions; expressions of structured type are blazed $\oplus$ and expressions of basic type are blazed $\ominus$.

In higher order treeless form, expressions are blazed as follows. Function arguments and **case** selectors which are not variables are blazed $\ominus$; these are intermediate structures which will be transformed separately and will not be removed by the higher order deforestation algorithm. No other expressions are blazed; these are equivalent to expressions which are blazed $\oplus$ in [17][2].

In higher order treeless form, variables can also be blazed at their binding occurrence[3]. All non-linear variables are blazed in this way. Expressions cannot be substituted for blazed variables, and will be transformed separately by the higher order deforestation algorithm. This ensures that expressions which are expensive to compute will not be duplicated. For example, consider a function call *square e* where *square* is a non-linear function defined as $\lambda x.x * x$. If e is an expression which is expensive to compute, then the unfolded expression $e * e$ will be less efficient than the original expression *square e*. This situation is avoided by blazing the bound variable x to give the function definition $\lambda x^{\ominus}.x * x$. The function argument will be transformed separately in any applications, and will not cause any duplication of work[4].

Higher order treeless form is defined as follows.

Definition 1 (Higher Order Treeless Form). *An expression is in higher order treeless form if all function arguments and* **case** *selectors which are not variables are blazed, and all non-linear variables are blazed at their binding occurrence.*

□

Expressions in higher order treeless form must therefore satisfy the grammar given in Fig. 3 where, in addition, each non-linear variable is blazed at its binding occurrence and each function contained within the expression has a higher order treeless definition.

---

[1] In forestry, blazing is the operation of marking a tree by making a cut in its bark.

[2] For the remainder of this paper if an expression is said to be blazed, it is assumed that it is annotated with $\ominus$, as $\ominus$ is the only blazing annotation which is used.

[3] This is the occurrence of a variable as the bound variable in a lambda abstraction, or within the pattern of a **case** expression.

[4] This relies upon the fact that the language is implemented using the full laziness technique described in [7], since it would be possible that the function argument is a partially applied function into which an expression has been substituted and the expression would be re-evaluated each time the function is fully applied.

$$
\begin{aligned}
te \ ::= \ &v \\
&| \ c \ \{te\} \\
&| \ f \\
&| \ \lambda v.te \\
&| \ \textbf{case} \ te' \ \textbf{of} \ < p : te > \\
&| \ te \ te'
\end{aligned}
$$

$$
\begin{aligned}
te' \ ::= \ &v \\
&| \ te^{\ominus}
\end{aligned}
$$

Fig. 3. Higher Order Treeless Form

Unfortunately, a lot of useful higher order functions are not in higher order treeless form. For example, none of the function definitions given in Fig. 2 are in this form. However, function definitions can be generalised so that they are in higher order treeless form as follows. Within higher order treeless expressions, function arguments and **case** selectors which are not variables must be blazed. All function arguments and **case** selectors which are not variables are therefore blazed. Non-linear variables within higher order treeless expressions must be blazed at their binding occurrence. All non-linear variables are therefore blazed in this way. The generalisation of the program in Fig. 2 is shown in Fig. 4.

$$
\begin{aligned}
&fold \ (+) \ 0 \ (map \ square \ (until \ (> \ n) \ (repeat \ (+ \ 1) \ 1))) \\
&\textbf{where} \\
&fold \quad = \lambda f^{\ominus}.\lambda a.\lambda xs. \ \textbf{case} \ xs \ \textbf{of} \\
&\qquad\qquad\qquad\quad Nil \qquad\qquad : a \\
&\qquad\qquad\qquad\quad Cons \ x \ xs : f \ x \ (fold \ f \ a \ xs)^{\ominus} \\
\\
&map \quad = \lambda f^{\ominus}.\lambda xs. \ \textbf{case} \ xs \ \textbf{of} \\
&\qquad\qquad\qquad\quad Nil \qquad\quad : Nil \\
&\qquad\qquad\qquad\quad Cons \ x \ xs : Cons \ (f \ x) \ (map \ f \ xs) \\
\\
&until \quad = \lambda p^{\ominus}.\lambda xs. \ \textbf{case} \ xs \ \textbf{of} \\
&\qquad\qquad\qquad\quad Nil \qquad\qquad : Nil \\
&\qquad\qquad\qquad\quad Cons \ x^{\ominus} \ xs : \textbf{case} \ (p \ x)^{\ominus} \ \textbf{of} \\
&\qquad\qquad\qquad\qquad\qquad\qquad\quad True \ \ : Nil \\
&\qquad\qquad\qquad\qquad\qquad\qquad\quad False : Cons \ x \ (until \ p \ xs) \\
\\
&repeat = \lambda f^{\ominus}.\lambda x^{\ominus}.Cons \ x \ (repeat \ f \ (f \ x)^{\ominus})
\end{aligned}
$$

Fig. 4. Example Program Generalised

$$\mathcal{T}[\![e^{\Theta}]\!] \qquad\qquad = (\mathcal{T}[\![e]\!])^{\Theta} \qquad\qquad\qquad\qquad\qquad (1)$$

$$\mathcal{T}[\![v\,\{e\}]\!] \qquad\qquad = v\,\{(\mathcal{T}[\![e]\!])^{\Theta}\} \qquad\qquad\qquad\qquad (2)$$

$$\mathcal{T}[\![c\,\{e\}]\!] \qquad\qquad = c\,\{\mathcal{T}[\![e]\!]\} \qquad\qquad\qquad\qquad\quad (3)$$

$$\mathcal{T}[\![f\,\{e'\}]\!] \qquad\qquad = \mathcal{T}[\![e\,\{e'\}]\!] \qquad\qquad\qquad\qquad\quad (4)$$
$$\text{where } f \text{ is defined by } f = e$$

$$\mathcal{T}[\![\lambda v.e]\!] \qquad\qquad = \lambda v.\mathcal{T}[\![e]\!] \qquad\qquad\qquad\qquad\quad (5)$$

$$\mathcal{T}[\![(\lambda v.e')\,e^{\Theta}\,\{e''\}]\!] = (\lambda v.\mathcal{T}[\![e'\,\{e''\}]\!])\,(\mathcal{T}[\![e]\!])^{\Theta} \qquad (6a)$$

$$\mathcal{T}[\![(\lambda v^{\Theta}.e')\,e\,\{e''\}]\!] = (\lambda v^{\Theta}.\mathcal{T}[\![e'\,\{e''\}]\!])\,(\mathcal{T}[\![e]\!])^{\Theta} \qquad (6b)$$

$$\mathcal{T}[\![(\lambda v.e')\,e\,\{e''\}]\!] \ = \mathcal{T}[\![e'[e/v]\,\{e''\}]\!] \qquad\qquad (6c)$$

$$\mathcal{T}[\![(\textbf{case } e^{\Theta} \textbf{ of } <p':e'>)\,\{e''\}]\!] \qquad\qquad\qquad\qquad (7)$$
$$= \textbf{case } (\mathcal{T}[\![e]\!])^{\Theta} \textbf{ of } <p':\mathcal{T}[\![e'\,\{e''\}]\!]>$$

$$\mathcal{T}[\![(\textbf{case } (v\,\{e\}) \textbf{ of } <p':e'>)\,\{e''\}]\!] \qquad\qquad\qquad (8)$$
$$= \textbf{case } (\mathcal{T}[\![v\,\{e\}]\!])^{\Theta} \textbf{ of } <p':\mathcal{T}[\![e'\,\{e''\}]\!]>$$

$$\mathcal{T}[\![(\textbf{case } (c\,\{e\}) \textbf{ of } <p':e'>)\,\{e''\}]\!] \qquad\qquad\qquad (9)$$
$$= \mathcal{T}[\![(\lambda\{v\}.e'_i\,\{e''\})\,\{e\}]\!]$$
$$\text{where } p'_i : e'_i \in <p':e'> \text{ and } p'_i = c\,\{v\}$$

$$\mathcal{T}[\![(\textbf{case } (f\,\{e'\}) \textbf{ of } <p'':e''>)\,\{e'''\}]\!] \qquad\qquad\quad (10)$$
$$= \mathcal{T}[\![(\textbf{case } (e\,\{e'\}) \textbf{ of } <p'':e''>)\,\{e'''\}]\!]$$
$$\text{where } f \text{ is defined by } f = e$$

$$\mathcal{T}[\![(\textbf{case } ((\lambda v.e')\,e^{\Theta}\,\{e''\}) \textbf{ of } <p''':e'''>)\,\{e''''\}]\!] \qquad (11a)$$
$$= (\lambda v.\mathcal{T}[\![(\textbf{case } (e'\,\{e''\}) \textbf{ of } <p''':e'''>)\,\{e''''\}]\!])\,(\mathcal{T}[\![e]\!])^{\Theta}$$

$$\mathcal{T}[\![(\textbf{case } ((\lambda v^{\Theta}.e')\,e\,\{e''\}) \textbf{ of } <p''':e'''>)\,\{e''''\}]\!] \qquad (11b)$$
$$= (\lambda v^{\Theta}.\mathcal{T}[\![(\textbf{case } (e'\,\{e''\}) \textbf{ of } <p''':e'''>)\,\{e''''\}]\!])\,(\mathcal{T}[\![e]\!])^{\Theta}$$

$$\mathcal{T}[\![(\textbf{case } ((\lambda v.e')\,e\,\{e''\}) \textbf{ of } <p''':e'''>)\,\{e''''\}]\!] \qquad (11c)$$
$$= \mathcal{T}[\![(\textbf{case } (e'[e/v]\,\{e''\}) \textbf{ of } <p''':e'''>)\,\{e''''\}]\!]$$

$$\mathcal{T}[\![(\textbf{case } ((\textbf{case } e \textbf{ of } <p':e'>)\,\{e''\}) \textbf{ of } <p''':e'''>)\,\{e''''\}]\!] \qquad (12)$$
$$= \mathcal{T}[\![(\textbf{case } e \textbf{ of } <p':\textbf{case } (e'\,\{e''\}) \textbf{ of } <p''':e'''>>)\,\{e''''\}]\!]$$

Fig. 5. Transformation Rules for Higher Order Deforestation

4 The Higher Order Deforestation Algorithm

The higher order deforestation algorithm is a set of transformation rules which attempt to convert a given expression into a higher order treeless equivalent. The transformation rules for the given language are shown in Fig. 5.

These rules cover all possible kinds of expression (blazed, variable, constructor, function, lambda and **case**). In rules (1), (2) and (3), the transformation rules are applied recursively to the sub-expressions of the expression being transformed. In rule (4), the function variable in an application is replaced with its body. In rule (5), the transformation rules are applied recursively to the body of a lambda expression. In rule (6), the argument in a lambda application is substituted for the lambda variable (provided neither of these are blazed) within the lambda body.

All six possibilities for the selector of a **case** expression are considered in rules (7) - (12). In rules (7) and (8), the transformation rules are applied recursively to the sub-expressions of the expression being transformed. In rule (9), when the selector is a constructor application, pattern matching is applied and the **case** expression is replaced by the appropriate branch. This is where intermediate structures are actually removed by deforestation by avoiding the need for the intermediate constructor application. In rules (10) and (11), when the selector is a function application or lambda application, the application is transformed in the same manner as for rules (4) and (6). In rule (12), when the selector is another **case** expression, the outer **case** expression is distributed across the branches of the inner one.

Rules (6) - (9) and (11) - (12) are valid only if there is no name clash between the free and bound variables of the expression being transformed. It is always possible to rename the bound variables of the expression so that this condition applies.

As is the case for the first order deforestation algorithm described in [17], the higher order algorithm as given will not necessarily terminate. Termination is achieved only through the introduction of appropriate new function definitions. Any infinite sequence of transformation steps in a well-typed program must involve the unfolding of a function call. A new function definition is therefore introduced before the application of rules (4) and (10). The right hand sides of these function definitions are the expressions which were about to be transformed. When an expression is encountered later in the transformation which matches the right hand side of one of these function definitions (modulo renaming of variables), it is replaced by an appropriate call of the corresponding function.

Transformation rules (4) and (10) which were previously of the form $\mathcal{T}[\![e]\!] = \mathcal{T}[\![e']\!]$ must therefore be changed as shown in Fig. 6 to make this more explicit. These rules are similar to the rules for first order deforestation given in [3]. The additional parameter ϕ contains the set of expressions which have been encountered before during the transformation and the associated function name which was introduced. This additional parameter must also be passed to all other transformation rules.

$$\mathcal{T}[\![e]\!] \, \phi = f \, v_1 \dots v_n, \text{ if } (f' \; = \; \lambda v_1' \dots v_n'.e'') \in \phi \text{ and } e \; = \; e''[v_1/v_1', \dots, v_n/v_n']$$

$$= f v_1 \dots v_n, \text{ otherwise}$$
where
$$f \; = \; \lambda v_1 \dots v_n.(\mathcal{T}[\![e']\!] \, \phi')$$
$$\phi' = \phi \cup \{f \; = \; \lambda v_1 \dots v_n.e\}$$
$v_1 \dots v_n$ are the free variables in e

Fig. 6. Extended Transformation Rules for Higher Order Deforestation

The result of transforming the program in Fig. 4 is shown in Fig. 7. It can be seen that all the intermediate lists in the program have been eliminated.

$$g \, 1 \, n$$
where
$$g = \lambda m.\lambda n. \, \text{case } (m \; > \; n)^\Theta \text{ of}$$
$$\qquad\qquad True \; : 0$$
$$\qquad\qquad False : ((square \; m)) \; + \; (g \; (m \; + \; 1)^\Theta \; n)^\Theta$$

Fig. 7. Result of Applying Higher Order Deforestation Algorithm

Another example of applying the higher order deforestation algorithm is shown in Fig. 8 and Fig. 9. The program in Fig. 8 can be used to determine whether a complex number k, represented by a pair, is a member of the Mandelbrot set. This is the case if the iterative formula $z := z^2 + k$ converges with an initial value of $(0,0)$ for z. It is impossible to find all the points for which the iteration converges, but it is possible to find an approximation to the Mandelbrot set. The sequence of iterations will diverge if the size of the complex number exceeds 2. Any point for which the iteration has not diverged after a fixed number of iterations can be assumed to lie within the set. The function *next* is used to calculate the value of the next iteration of the formula from the previous one. The function *repeat* is used to produce an infinite list of the values given by the iterations of the formula. The function *until* is used to take the values in this list until it is found that they will diverge. The function *morethan* determines whether more than n iterations are required before it can be determined that the sequence diverges. If this is the case, then the point k is assumed to be in the Mandelbrot set. It is assumed that the functions +, *square* and *size* are defined on complex numbers and are built-in functions of the language. The result of transforming this program is shown in Fig. 9. Again, it can be seen that all the intermediate lists in the program have been eliminated.

$morethan\ n\ (until\ (diverges)\ (repeat\ (next\ k)\ (0,0)))$
where
$morethan = \lambda n.\lambda xs.\ \textbf{case}\ n\ \textbf{of}$
$\qquad\qquad\qquad\quad Zero\quad : True$
$\qquad\qquad\qquad\quad Succ\ n : \textbf{case}\ xs\ \textbf{of}$
$\qquad\qquad\qquad\qquad\qquad\qquad Nil\qquad\ : False$
$\qquad\qquad\qquad\qquad\qquad\qquad Cons\ x\ xs : morethan\ n\ xs$

$until\qquad = \lambda p.\lambda xs.\ \textbf{case}\ xs\ \textbf{of}$
$\qquad\qquad\qquad\quad Nil\qquad : Nil$
$\qquad\qquad\qquad\quad Cons\ x\ xs : \textbf{case}\ (p\ x)^{\ominus}\ \textbf{of}$
$\qquad\qquad\qquad\qquad\qquad\qquad True\ : Nil$
$\qquad\qquad\qquad\qquad\qquad\qquad False : Cons\ x\ (until\ p\ xs)$

$diverges\ = \lambda z.(size\ z)^{\ominus}\ >\ 2$

$repeat\quad = \lambda f.\lambda x.Cons\ x\ (repeat\ f\ (f\ x)^{\ominus})$

$next\qquad = \lambda k.\lambda z.k\ +\ (square\ z)^{\ominus}$

Fig. 8. Another example Program

$f\ n\ k\ (0,0)$
where
$f = \lambda n.\lambda k.\lambda z.\ \textbf{case}\ n\ \textbf{of}$
$\qquad\qquad\qquad Zero\quad : True$
$\qquad\qquad\qquad Succ\ n : \textbf{case}\ ((size\ z)^{\ominus}\ >\ 2)^{\ominus}\ \textbf{of}$
$\qquad\qquad\qquad\qquad\qquad\quad True\ : False$
$\qquad\qquad\qquad\qquad\qquad\quad False : f\ n\ k\ (k\ +\ (square\ z)^{\ominus})^{\ominus}$

Fig. 9. Result of Applying Higher Order Deforestation Algorithm

5   The Higher Order Deforestation Theorem

As one of the main contributions of this paper is to define a treeless form of
function definition for which the deforestation algorithm terminates, details of
a termination proof are given here. In order to be able to prove that the higher
order deforestation algorithm always terminates, it is sufficient to show that
there are bounds on the depth and width of the terms encountered during transformation. If these are bounded, then there will be a finite number of terms
encountered (modulo renaming of variables), and a renaming of a previous term
must eventually be encountered. The algorithm will therefore be guaranteed to
terminate.

In order to prove that there is a bound on the depth of terms encountered during transformation, it is shown that all terms which are encountered must satisfy a particular grammatical form. It is then shown that there is a bound on the depth of the terms described by this grammar. First of all, it must be defined what is meant by the depth of the terms encountered during transformation.

Definition 2 (Depth of Terms). *The depth of terms encountered by the higher order deforestation algorithm is defined as shown in Fig. 10.*

□

$$
\begin{aligned}
&\mathcal{D}[\![v]\!] && = 1 \\
&\mathcal{D}[\![c\ \{e\}]\!] && = 1 + max(\{\mathcal{D}[\![e]\!]\}) \\
&\mathcal{D}[\![f]\!] && = 1 \\
&\mathcal{D}[\![\lambda v.e]\!] && = 1 + \mathcal{D}[\![e]\!] \\
&\mathcal{D}[\![\text{case } e \text{ of } <p : e'[\{e''/v\}]>]\!] = max(<\mathcal{D}[\![e']\!]>) + max(\mathcal{D}[\![e]\!], \{\mathcal{D}[\![e'']\!]\}) \\
&\mathcal{D}[\![e[\{e'/v\}]\ e'']\!] && = \mathcal{D}[\![e]\!] + max(\{\mathcal{D}[\![e']\!]\}, \mathcal{D}[\![e'']\!])
\end{aligned}
$$

Fig. 10. Depth of Terms Encountered by the Higher Order Deforestation Algorithm

In this definition, the substitution of terms for variables is made explicit. The terms are therefore considered to be in the form of a graph.

Definition 3 (Grammar of Terms). *The grammar of terms encountered by the higher order deforestation algorithm is given by $de_d(x, y)$, as defined in Fig. 11, where d is the maximum depth of the right hand sides of all the function definitions accessible from the term.*

□

In the definition of the grammar of terms $de_d(x, y)$, x corresponds to the depth of the term before the substitution of values for its free variables and y corresponds to the *order* of the term (as described in [17], where a term of order zero has no terms substituted for its free variables, and a term of order $o + 1$ has terms of order o substituted for its free variables).

Lemma 4 (On Grammar of Terms). *All terms encountered by the higher order deforestation algorithm are described by the grammar $de_d(d, n)$, where d is the maximum depth of all function definitions accessible from within the original term being transformed, and n is the depth of the original term being transformed.*

□

$$
\begin{array}{lll}
de_d(x,y) ::= v & \text{if } x \geq 0 \text{ and } y \geq 0 \\
\quad | \; c \; \{de_d(x-1,y)\} & \text{if } x > 0 \text{ and } y \geq 0 \\
\quad | \; f & \text{if } x \geq 0 \text{ and } y \geq 0 \\
\quad | \; \lambda v. de_d(x-1,y) & \text{if } x > 0 \text{ and } y \geq 0 \\
\quad | \; \mathbf{case} \; de_d'(x-1,y) \; \mathbf{of} \; < p : de_d(x,0)[\{de_d(d,y-1)/v\}] > & \\
\quad\quad\quad\quad\quad\quad\quad\quad\quad\quad\quad\quad\quad\quad\quad\quad\quad\quad\quad\quad\quad & \text{if } x > 0 \text{ and } y \geq 0 \\
\quad | \; (de_d(x,0)[\{de_s(d,y-1)/v\}]) \; de_d'(x-1,y) & \text{if } x > 0 \text{ and } y \geq 0 \\
\quad | \; de_d(x,0)[< de_d(d,y-1)/v >] & \text{if } x \geq 0 \text{ and } y > 0 \\
\\
de_d'(x,y) ::= v & \text{if } x \geq 0 \text{ and } y \geq 0 \\
\quad | \; de_d(d,y-1) & \text{if } x \geq 0 \text{ and } y > 0 \\
\quad | \; de_d(x,y)^\ominus & \text{if } x \geq 0 \text{ and } y \geq 0 \\
\end{array}
$$

Fig. 11. Grammar of Terms Encountered by the Higher Order Deforestation Algorithm

Proof. It is shown for each transformation rule that if the original term to be transformed satisfies the given grammar, then any terms which need to be further transformed will also satisfy this grammar. □

Lemma 5 (On Depth of Terms). *The depth of all terms described by the grammar $de_d(d,n)$ is bounded by $d \times (n+1)$.*

□

Proof. It is shown that the depth of each possible term in the grammar $de_d(x,y)$ is bounded by $x + (d \times y)$ by induction on the variables x and y. □

Lemma 6 (On Width of Terms). *There is a bound on the width of all terms encountered by the higher order deforestation algorithm.*

□

Proof. It is shown that each transformation rule preserves the well-typedness of the original program. Infinitely wide terms cannot therefore occur as they would be ill-typed. □

The deforestation theorem given in [17] can now be extended to the higher order deforestation theorem as follows.

Theorem 7 (Higher Order Deforestation Theorem). *Every expression in which each non-linear variable is blazed at its binding occurrence, and which contains only occurrences of functions with higher order treeless definitions can be transformed to an equivalent higher order treeless expression without loss of efficiency.*

□

Proof. The proof of termination of the higher order deforestation algorithm follows immediately from Lemmata 4, 5 and 6. A proof of the correctness of the algorithm can be found in [13], and is not considered here. □

6   Comparison With Related Work

A substantial amount of work has been performed on extending deforestation for first order functional programs [3, 6, 15, 14]. Not so much work has been done on trying to extend it for higher order functional programs.

The first order deforestation algorithm described in [17] was extended to allow a restricted higher order facility by treating higher order functions as macros. These macros can have higher order arguments, but are not allowed to be recursive. This lack of recursion guarantees that all higher order macro calls can be expanded out to an equivalent first order expression at compile-time. Although these macros are not allowed to be recursive, they can still use a form of local recursion by introducing **where** expressions in which only first order functions are allowed to be recursive. Macros can be defined only when function-type arguments are passed unchanged in each recursive call of a function. In these cases, the use of macros can serve to make functions linear in their function-type arguments, thus allowing transformations to be performed which can not be performed by the higher order deforestation algorithm. For example, all the function definitions given in Fig. 2 can be made linear in their function-type arguments through the use of macros. These arguments would be blazed by the higher order deforestation algorithm and transformed separately in all applications. If these arguments create or destroy structures, the structures would not be removed by the higher order deforestation algorithm. For example, consider the following expression:

$$map \ (map \ square) \ xss$$

During the transformation of this expression, the function $(map \ square)$ will be blazed, so the lists of squares created by applications of this function will not be removed.

There are many higher order functions which cannot be defined using macros. For example, consider the functions *altmap* and *listmap* shown in Fig. 12.

$altmap \ = \lambda f.\lambda g.\lambda xs. \textbf{case} \ xs \ \textbf{of}$
$\qquad\qquad\qquad Nil \qquad : Nil$
$\qquad\qquad\qquad Cons \ x \ xs : Cons \ (f \ x) \ (altmap \ g \ f \ xs)$

$listmap = \lambda fs.\lambda xs. \textbf{case} \ fs \ \textbf{of}$
$\qquad\qquad\qquad Nil \qquad : Nil$
$\qquad\qquad\qquad Cons \ f \ fs : \textbf{case} \ xs \ \textbf{of}$
$\qquad\qquad\qquad\qquad\qquad Nil \qquad : Nil$
$\qquad\qquad\qquad\qquad\qquad Cons \ x \ xs : Cons \ (f \ x) \ (listmap \ fs \ xs)$

Fig. 12. Example Functions Which Cannot Be Defined Using Macros

The function *altmap* cannot be defined using macros because the first two arguments f and g are swapped in the recursive call of the function. The function *listmap* cannot be defined using macros because it is not possible to define a list of functions using macros. In the work described here, the deforestation algorithm has been reformulated so that it applies to all higher order functions directly. As a result, it is possible to transform expressions involving the functions shown in Fig. 12. Perhaps more importantly, there is a loss of *transparency* when macros are used, as it is harder for the programmer to see where intermediate structures will be eliminated. With the higher order deforestation algorithm described in this paper it is much easier for the programmer to see where this will occur.

An extension of deforestation to handle higher order functions is described in [3]. This extension involves transforming programs to remove higher order features. Not all higher order features can be removed by this transformation, but it produces a specialised form of higher order program. This specialised form of program can then be transformed to remove intermediate structures using an extension of the deforestation algorithm. Other higher order features may re-appear as a result of this deforestation, so they need to be removed again before the deforestation can continue. This problem could be avoided if the deforestation algorithm were reformulated to apply to all higher order functions directly, as is done in this paper. No separate transformation would then be required to remove the higher order features from a program. The algorithm used in [3] can successfully transform some functions with non-linear function-type arguments, although this may result in a loss of laziness. This algorithm is therefore applicable to a wider range of expressions than the algorithm described in this paper. However, the programs resulting from the transformation in [3] can be much larger than the input. Also, the algorithm is very complicated and it is very difficult for the programmer to see where intermediate structures will be eliminated.

A transformation for removing higher order features from programs by partial evaluation is described in [2]. This transformation is applicable only to a subset of higher order programs in which all higher order expressions are *variable-only* or *constant*. Variable-only higher order expressions are functions in which the function-type arguments are all variables in each recursive call to the function. This is a similar restriction to that made in this paper, and also in [3], but is less restrictive than the form of expression which can be defined using a macro. Constant higher order expressions are the primitive functions of the language. There is no restriction that arguments are linear in this work, so a loss of efficiency may occur. If there were such a restriction, the transformation would be applicable to a similar range of expressions which can be transformed by the algorithm described in this paper, but again there would be a lack of transparency for the programmer.

A reformulation of the deforestation algorithm which can be applied to higher order functional programs is described in [10]. The transformation rules are given as three mutually recursive functions, and are therefore not as intuitive as the rules given in this paper. More importantly, no higher order treeless form is defined for the algorithm in [10], so there is no guarantee that the algorithm will terminate. Also, there is no guarantee that the expression resulting from the transformation will be more efficient than the original expression.

Another reformulation of the deforestation algorithm which can be applied to all higher functional programs is described in [12]. The transformation rules are presented in a more straightforward manner than in [10] by identifying the next redex within the expression being transformed. However, no treeless form is defined in this paper either, so there is no guarantee that the algorithm will terminate or that the result will be more efficient. A similar reformulation is also given in [13]. Termination of this algorithm is guaranteed by stopping the transformation after a given number of steps, but no treeless form is defined to allow a general method for ensuring the termination of the algorithm.

A different technique for achieving much the same effect as deforestation is described in [5]. This technique involves defining functions which consume lists in terms of the function *foldr*, and functions which produce lists in terms of the function *build*. When calls of the functions *foldr* and *build* appear next to each other, they can be coalesced to avoid the production of an intermediate list. This technique can remove some intermediate lists which are not removed by the higher order deforestation algorithm, but it applies only to functions defined on lists which can be written efficiently in terms of *foldr* and *build*, and requires that calls of these functions appear next to each other. It is therefore applicable to a different set of expressions than the algorithm described in this paper.

7 Conclusion

In this paper, it has been shown how the deforestation algorithm given in [17] can be extended to handle higher order functional programs. A higher order treeless form, which creates no intermediate structures, was defined. Higher order treeless form is an easily recognised form of expression, and any function definition can easily be generalised so that it is in this form. It was shown that the higher order deforestation algorithm will terminate if all function definitions are in this form. This algorithm was compared with other methods for removing intermediate structures from higher order programs.

A prototype implementation of the higher order deforestation algorithm has been completed, and was used to transform the example programs in this paper. The inclusion of such an implementation in a functional language compiler would allow a more thorough evaluation of the worth of higher order deforestation. However, the initial findings have been that some intermediate structures cannot be eliminated from expressions containing some commonly used higher order functions such as *map* and *fold* which are non-linear in their function-type arguments. These functions are a problem because the deforestation algorithm uses a call-by-name evaluation strategy, but the language on which it operates uses a call-by-need evaluation strategy. If the deforestation algorithm could be re-formulated in terms of a call-by-need evaluation strategy then this problem could be overcome. Research is continuing in this area.

References

1. L. Augustsson. Compiling Pattern Matching. In *Functional Programming Languages and Computer Architecture*, volume 201 of *Lecture Notes in Computer Science*, pages 368–381. Springer-Verlag, 1985.
2. F. Bellegarde. A Transformation System Combining Partial Evaluation with Term Rewriting. Technical Report CS/E 94-010, Dept. of Computer Science, Oregon Graduate Institute, 1994.
3. Wei-Ngan Chin. *Automatic Methods for Program Transformation*. PhD thesis, Imperial College, University of London, July 1990.
4. L. Damas and R. Milner. Principal Type Schemes for Functional Programs. In *Proceedings of the Ninth ACM Symposium on Principles of Programming Languages*, pages 207–212, 1982.
5. A. Gill. *Cheap Deforestation for Non-Strict Functional Languages*. PhD thesis, Glasgow University, September 1995.
6. G.W. Hamilton. *Compile-Time Optimisation of Store Usage in Lazy Functional Programs*. PhD thesis, University of Stirling, October 1993.
7. R.J.M. Hughes. Supercombinators: A New Implementation Method for Applicative Languages. In *Proceedings of the ACM Conference on LISP and Functional Programming*, pages 1–10, 1982.
8. R.J.M. Hughes. Why Functional Programming Matters. *The Computer Journal*, 32(2):98–107, April 1989.
9. T. Johnsson. Lambda Lifting: Transforming Programs to Recursive Equations. In *Proceedings of the Workshop on Implementation of Functional Languages*, pages 165–180, February 1985.
10. S. Marlow and P. Wadler. Deforestation for Higher-Order Functions. In *Proceedings of the Fifth Annual Glasgow Workshop on Functional Programming*, pages 154–165, July 1992.
11. R. Milner. A Theory of Type Polymorphism in Programming. *Journal of Computer and System Science*, 17:348–375, 1978.
12. K. Nielsen and M. H. Sørensen. Deforestation, Partial Evaluation, and Evaluation Orders. Unpublished, 1995.
13. D. Sands. Proving the Correctness of Recursion-Based Automatic Program Transformations. In *Sixth International Conference on Theory and Practice of Software Development (TAPSOFT)*, volume 915 of *Lecture Notes in Computer Science*, pages 681–695. Springer-Verlag, 1995.
14. H. Seidl. Integer Constraints to Stop Deforestation. In *Proceedings of the European Symposium on Programming*, 1996.
15. M. H. Sørensen. A Grammar-Based Data-Flow Analysis to Stop Deforestation. In *Lecture Notes in Computer Science*, volume 787, pages 335–351, 1994.
16. P. Wadler. Efficient Compilation of Pattern Matching. In S.L. Peyton Jones, editor, *The Implementation of Functional Programming Languages*, pages 78–103. Prentice Hall, 1987.
17. P. Wadler. Deforestation: Transforming Programs to Eliminate Trees. *Theoretical Computer Science*, 73:231–248, 1990.

Scheduling Expression DAGs for Minimal Register Need

Christoph W. Keßler

Universität Trier, FB 4 – Informatik
D-54286 Trier, Germany
email: kessler@psi.uni-trier.de

Abstract. Generating schedules for expression DAGs that use a minimal number of registers is a classical NP–complete optimization problem. Up to now an exact solution could only be computed for small DAGs (with up to 20 nodes), using a trivial $O(n!)$ enumeration algorithm. We present a new algorithm with worst–case complexity $O(n2^{2n})$ and very good average behaviour. Applying a dynamic programming scheme and reordering techniques, it is able to defer the combinatorial explosion and to generate an *optimal* schedule not only for small DAGs but also for medium–sized ones with up to 50 nodes, a class that contains nearly all DAGs encountered in typical application programs. Experiments with randomly generated DAGs and large DAGs from real application programs confirm that the new algorithm generates optimal schedules quite fast. We extend our algorithm to cope with delay slots and multiple functional units, two common features of modern superscalar processors.

1 Introduction

Register allocation and instruction scheduling are the most important optimization problems in the code generation phase of a compiler.

Global register allocation by coloring a register interference graph [8, 7] is still the state of the art and has been refined by several heuristic techniques [2, 6, 9]. Spill code is automatically generated until the register need of the code does not exceed the number of physical registers. The graph coloring approach works on a given fixed schedule of the instructions. This typically results in a suboptimal usage of registers and increased register need: In earlier work [18] we have shown that for large randomly generated basic blocks the register need could be reduced by approximately 30 percent on the average by suitably reordering the instructions within a range permitted by the data dependences among them.

Using fewer registers is essential if the target machine has not enough registers to evaluate an expression without storing intermediate results in the main memory (*spilling*). This is especially important for vector processors which usually have a small number of vector registers (e.g., the CRAY vector computers have 8 vector register of 64 × 64 bit) or a register file that can be partitioned into a number of vector registers of a certain length (e.g., the vector acceleration units of the CM5 have register files of length 128 × 32 bit that can be partitioned into 1, 2, 4 or 8 vector registers, see [29]). A vector operation is evaluated by splitting it into appropriate stripes and computing the stripes one after another. If the register file is partitioned into a small number of vector registers, each of them can hold more elements and the vector operations can be split into fewer stripes. This saves startup times and results in a faster computation. On the other hand, if such a small number of vector registers has to be enforced by holding some intermediate results not in vector registers but in the main memory, the overall execution time increases again due to the additional memory references. Exploiting this trade–off, an optimal number of vector registers can be found [20]. — Using fewer registers also pays off if less registers are to be saved and restored at procedure calls.

Basic blocks are typically rather small, with up to 20 instructions. Nevertheless, scientific programs often contain also larger basic blocks, due to e.g. complex arithmetic expressions and array indexing. Larger basic blocks can also be produced by compiler techniques such as loop unrolling [10] and trace scheduling [12]. Therefore, it is important to derive register allocation techniques that cope with rather large basic blocks [15].

First, we consider the problem of reordering the instructions of a basic block whose dependence graph is a DAG, in order to just minimize the register need. For the simplest case where instructions are not delayed (i.e., take unit time to complete and do not overlap) and partial recomputations are not admitted, this is a classical NP–complete problem [27]. Some heuristic methods (e.g., [19, 21]) have been proposed. Only if the DAG is a tree, the labeling algorithm of Sethi and Ullman [28] yields an optimal solution; its run time is linear in the number of instructions; spilling of registers is not considered. [1] proposes a dynamic programming algorithm which computes an optimal schedule for *trees* in linear time that uses a given, fixed number of registers and contains spill code where required.

Modern microprocessors have sophisticated hardware features like pipelining and multiple functional units that exhibit further challenges for scheduling. Currently, register allocation is generally subordinated to scheduling because both optimization goals often conflict with each other. Typically there are enough registers available such that remarkable speedup can be obtained from scheduling improvements rather than from better register usage.

In the presence of delayed instructions or multiple functional units, the register requirements are either completely ignored for scheduling (e.g., [3]), or the DAG is assumed to be a tree [4, 26, 31], or heuristic techniques are applied [4, 5, 14, 16, 25]. In the presence of a loop, the quality of instruction scheduling may be improved by suitably overlapping subsequent iterations: Software pipelining (e.g., [11, 23, 24]) transforms a loop such that independent instructions from several consecutive iterations may be executed concurrently. Most approaches focus on instruction scheduling and ignore register requirements; nevertheless, this technique tends to increase operand lifetimes, and thus, the register need.

[5] shows that separating register allocation and instruction scheduling produces inefficient code. But even for basic blocks, we are currently not aware of any method that integrates register allocation and scheduling whose dependence graph is a DAG, that is guaranteed to find an *optimal* solution for register allocation or both register need and completion time. In fact, nothing better than $O(n!)$ [21] was known up to now, making the problem intractable for basic blocks of more than 15–20 instructions.

In this paper we present a new algorithm based on dynamic programming that reduces the worst–case bound to $O(n2^{2n})$. Tests for large basic blocks from real scientific programs and for suites of randomly generated basic blocks have shown that the algorithm makes the problem generally solvable for the first time also for medium–sized basic blocks with up to 40–50 instructions, a class that contains nearly all basic blocks encountered in real programs.

The time complexity can be further reduced because we can exploit massive parallelism present in the algorithm.

We further show how the method can be adapted to scheduling for delayed instructions and multiple functional units.

2 DAG schedules

We assume that we are generating code for a RISC–style single processor machine with general–purpose registers numbered consecutively (1, 2, 3, ...) and a countable sequence of memory locations. The arithmetic machine operations are three–address instructions (unary and binary arithmetic operations on registers. For the first part of this paper, we assume that each instruction takes one unit of time to execute, i.e. the result of an instruction can be used by the next instruction in the next time slot. The extension of our work for delay slots is discussed in section 7.

Each input program can be partitioned into a number of basic blocks. On the machine instruction level, a *basic block* is a sequence of three–address-instructions that can only be entered via the first instruction and only be left via the last one. The data dependencies in a basic block can be described by a *directed acyclic graph (DAG)*. The leaves of the DAG are the variables occurring as operands in the basic block; the inner nodes represent intermediate results. An example is given in Fig. 1.

Let $G = (V, E)$ be such a DAG with n nodes.

Definition 1. A *schedule* S of a DAG G is a bijective mapping of the nodes in V to the set of time slots $\{1, ..., n\}$ such that for all inner nodes $v \in V$ with children $v_1, ..., v_k$ holds $S(v) > S(v_i)$, $i = 1, ..., k$, i.e. v is computed only after all its children $v_1, ..., v_k$ have been computed.

This implies that a schedule is *complete*, i.e. all nodes are scheduled at some time slot between 1 and n, and the schedule contains *no recomputations*, i.e., each node of the DAG is scheduled only once. Moreover, the schedule is *consistent* because the precedence constraints are preserved. Thus, a schedule is just a topological order of G.

Definition 2. A mapping *reg*: $V \to \{1, 2, ...\}$ is called a (consistent) *register allocation* for S, if for all nodes $u, v, w \in V$ the following holds: If u is a child of w, and $S(u) < S(v) < S(w)$, i.e. v is scheduled by S between u and w, then $reg(w) \neq reg(u) \neq reg(v)$.

Definition 3. Let R_S denote the set of register allocations for a schedule S. Then,

$$m(S) = \min_{reg \in R_S} \left\{ \max_v \ reg(v) \right\}$$

is called the *register need* of the schedule S. A schedule S for a DAG G is called *optimal* if for all possible schedules S' of G holds $m(S') \geq m(S)$.

Computing an optimal register allocation for a given schedule is straightforward. The technique of usage counts was first proposed in [13]: Let *new_reg*() be a function which returns an unoccupied register and marks it 'occupied'. Let *free_reg*(r) be a function that marks register r 'unoccupied' again. *new_reg*() is called each time a node is scheduled. *free_reg*($reg(u)$) is called immediately after[1] the last parent of node u has been scheduled. To determine this event, we keep a usage counter for each node u which counts the number of u's parent nodes already scheduled. Obviously, a register allocation for a given schedule can be computed with run time linear in the number of DAG edges, which is at most twice the number of instructions. — If one desires to keep register usage as *unequal* as possible (in order to obtain good candidates for a posteriori spilling of registers), sorting the unoccupied registers requires an additional factor of $O(\log n)$, as proposed in [21].

In general, there will exist several optimal schedules for a given DAG. The problem of computing an optimal schedule for a DAG is NP–complete [27].

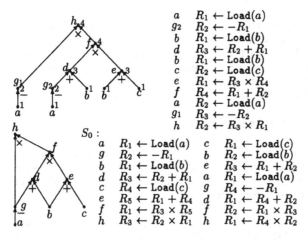

$$
\begin{array}{ll}
a & R_1 \leftarrow \text{Load}(a) \\
g_2 & R_2 \leftarrow -R_1 \\
b & R_1 \leftarrow \text{Load}(b) \\
d & R_3 \leftarrow R_2 + R_1 \\
b & R_1 \leftarrow \text{Load}(b) \\
c & R_2 \leftarrow \text{Load}(c) \\
e & R_1 \leftarrow R_3 \times R_4 \\
f & R_4 \leftarrow R_1 + R_2 \\
a & R_2 \leftarrow \text{Load}(a) \\
g_1 & R_3 \leftarrow -R_2 \\
h & R_2 \leftarrow R_3 \times R_1
\end{array}
$$

S_0 :

$$
\begin{array}{llll}
a & R_1 \leftarrow \text{Load}(a) & c & R_1 \leftarrow \text{Load}(c) \\
g & R_2 \leftarrow -R_1 & b & R_2 \leftarrow \text{Load}(b) \\
b & R_1 \leftarrow \text{Load}(b) & e & R_3 \leftarrow R_1 + R_2 \\
d & R_3 \leftarrow R_2 + R_1 & a & R_1 \leftarrow \text{Load}(a) \\
c & R_4 \leftarrow \text{Load}(c) & g & R_4 \leftarrow -R_1 \\
e & R_5 \leftarrow R_1 + R_4 & d & R_1 \leftarrow R_4 + R_2 \\
f & R_1 \leftarrow R_3 \times R_5 & f & R_2 \leftarrow R_1 \times R_3 \\
h & R_3 \leftarrow R_2 \times R_1 & h & R_1 \leftarrow R_4 \times R_2
\end{array}
$$

Fig. 1. Example: Suppose the expression tree for $(-a) \times ((-a+b) \times (b+c))$ has been scheduled using the Labeling algorithm of *Sethi/Ullman* with minimal register need 4. — Common subexpression elimination results in a DAG G, reducing the number of instructions to be executed. If G is scheduled according to S_0, now 5 registers are required. The better schedule on the right obtained by reordering the instructions needs only 4 registers, which is optimal.

Let N_G denote the number of different schedules S for a DAG G with n nodes. N_G obviously depends on the structure of the DAG. Clearly N_G is less than $n!$, the number of permutations of the instructions. Our hope is that this is a very coarse upper bound and that N_G is not too high for small and medium–sized DAGs. Then we could just generate *all* N_G possible schedules for a given DAG G and select an optimal one among them.

Let us begin with a naive approach using an algorithm for topological sorting to generate these schedules. Topological sorting performs n steps. Each step selects one of the nodes, say v, with indegree zero, schedules it, and deletes all edges from v to its parents. Note that some of v's parents may get indegree 0, thus they become selectable in the following step.

We use an array $S[1:n]$ of nodes of G to store the current (partial) schedule S. Let z_0 be the set of all leaves of G, i.e. the nodes with initial indegree zero, and let $INDEG_0$ be an array containing the initial indegree of every node. The call $nce(z_0, INDEG_0, 1)$ of the following recursive <u>algorithm *nce*</u> yields all possible schedules of G.

---

[1] On most target architectures, the target register of an instruction may also be identical to one of the source registers (i.e., $reg(w) = reg(u)$ may be possible in Def. 2). Then, the register of u can be freed immediately *before* issuing the last parent of u. In the context of (strip–mined) vector instructions, however, the architecture may require registers to be mutually different.

```
function nce(z, INDEG, pos)
  if pos = n + 1  // S[1:n] is a complete schedule of G //
  then print S; compute register allocation for S and print it;
  else for all v ∈ z do  // expand for next node v of current S: //
           let P be the set of all parent nodes of v in G
           for all w ∈ P do INDEG'[w] ← INDEG[w] - 1 od;
           for all u ∉ P do INDEG'[u] ← INDEG[u] od;
           let P' be the subset of those nodes of P which have indegree 0;
           z' ← z - {v} ∪ P';
           S[pos] ← v;
           nce(z', INDEG', pos + 1);  od fi
```

It is easy to see that the algorithm has a recursive nesting depth of n. For each recursive call, a copy of the current set z and of the current array $INDEG$ must be generated, so the required space is $O(n^2)$. The iterations of the **for all** loop over z could be executed in parallel. If this loop is executed in sequential, copying can be avoided; thus space $O(n)$ will suffice. The run time of nce depends on the structure of the given DAG G and of the number of possibilities for the choice of the next node for S, i.e. the cardinality of z in each step of the algorithm.

The total run time of nce is proportional to the total number of generated schedules. Thus, the run time is bounded by $O(n! \cdot n)$, because for each call we either update the $INDEG$ array or print a schedule.[2] The *real* number of schedules generated will be considerably smaller than the worst case bound $n!$ because only a small fraction of the permutations are valid schedules. Nevertheless, algorithm nce is impractical for DAGs with more than 15 nodes; our prototype implementation of nce already needs several days for DAGs of size around 20.

How can we reduce this complexity? One approach, following those in [19] and [21], restricts the set of schedules considered to *contiguous schedules*:

Definition 4. A schedule S of a DAG $G = (V, E)$ is called *contiguous*, if for each node $v \in V$ with children v_1 and v_2 the following is true: if w is a predecessor of v_2 but not of v_1, and $S(v_1) < S(v_2)$, then $S(v_1) < S(w)$.

A contiguous schedule has thus the property that for each binary node v, all nodes of the complete subDAG of one of v's children are scheduled first, before any node belonging to the remaining subDAG rooted at v is scheduled. — While general schedules can be generated by variants of topological–sort, contiguous schedules are generated by variants of *depth–first search*.

Restriction to contiguous schedules degrades the worst-case complexity from $O(n!)$ to $O(2^n)$. While this is still exponential, for most practical cases the run time appears to be much smaller after clever pruning of the search space [21]. However, the heuristic may not find an optimal schedule because it might be non-contiguous. There are DAGs for which a general schedule exists that uses fewer registers than every contiguous schedule (see [21]). — Moreover, if delayed instructions or multiple functional units are to be considered (see sections 7 and 8), contiguous schedules tend to be inferior to noncontiguous ones, because at contiguous schedules it is much more typical that a parent node is scheduled directly after its child, which may cause a structural hazard.

---

[2] We can easily eliminate a factor of n if we use the fact that the root r of the DAG must always be the last node in a schedule, i.e. $S(r) = n$, terminating the recursion at nesting level $n - 1$.

3 The new algorithm

How can the exhaustive search performed by *nce* be improved? *nce* builds a decision tree, called the *selection tree*, $T = (Z', H')$. The set Z' of nodes, called the *selection nodes*, contains all the *instances* z' of the zero–indegree sets of DAG nodes that occur as the first parameter z in a call to *nce* during the execution of the algorithm. A directed edge $h = (z'_1, z'_2) \in H'$, called *selection edge*, connects two selection nodes $z'_1, z'_2 \in Z'$ iff there is a step in *nce* that directly generates z'_2 from z'_1 by selecting a DAG node from z'_1 and scheduling it. Clearly, the selection tree has one root that corresponds to the initial set z_0 of zero–indegree DAG nodes.

All leaves of the selection tree are instances of the empty set of DAG nodes. The number of selection edges leaving a selection node $z \in Z'$ is equal to the cardinality of z.

Let *scheduled*(z) denote the set of DAG nodes that have already been scheduled when function *nce* is called with first parameter z. In particular, all DAG predecessors of the DAG nodes in z belong to *scheduled*(z), see Fig. 2. We have observed that in such a selection tree, there occur generally several different instances $z' \in Z'$ of the same set z. We will modify the algorithm *nce* in such a way that these multiple occurrences of z are eliminated. Thus, the computation of the modified algorithm will result in a *selection DAG* rather than a selection tree. Let us first introduce some notation.

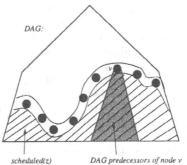

Fig. 2. A snapshot of a DAG being processed by algorithm *nce*.

Definition 5. A *selection DAG* $D = (Z, H)$ is a directed acyclic graph. The set Z of selection nodes contains all *different* sets z generated by *nce*. An edge $h \in H$ connects two selection nodes $z_1, z_2 \in Z$ iff there is a step in *nce* that directly generates z_2 from z_1.

Note that a selection DAG has a single root, namely z_0, and a single sink, the empty set $\emptyset$.

Example: Fig. 3 shows an example DAG G and the selection DAG computed for it.

Each selection edge (z_1, z_2) is annotated with the DAG node v that is selected when going from z_1 to z_2. Consider a path $\pi = (z_0, z_1, z_2, ..., z_{n-1}, z_n)$ in the selection DAG D. The *inscription* $I(\pi) = v_1 v_2 ... v_n$ of the path π is the concatenation of all DAG node names v_j annotated with the selection edges (z_{j-1}, z_j), $j = 1, ..., n$.

For each $z \in Z$, we define by $G_z = (scheduled(z), E \cap (scheduled(z) \times scheduled(z)))$ the subgraph of G induced by *scheduled*(z). Note that $G = G_\emptyset$.

Lemma 6. *Each path π in the selection DAG $D = (Z, H)$ from the root to a node $z \in Z$ corresponds one-to-one to a schedule of scheduled(z).*

Proof. by induction on the length of π. Initially, the path inscription is empty, z is the root, namely z_0, and *scheduled*$(z) = \emptyset$. Let z be an inner node of D. z has

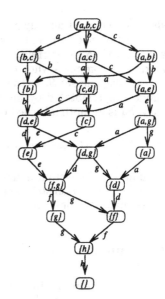

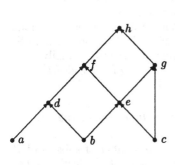

Fig. 3. An example DAG and its selection DAG

some direct predecessor y in D. y scheduled a DAG node $v \in y$, changing the set of zero–indegree nodes from y to z. We have thus $scheduled(z) - scheduled(y) = \{v\}$. We apply the induction hypothesis to y and concatenate each schedule for $scheduled(y)$ with the scheduling of v, resulting in a schedule for $scheduled(z)$.

This means that subpaths corresponding to different partial schedules of the same subsets of nodes end up in the same selection node, e.g. the paths inscripted a, b, c and b, c, a in Fig. 3 both end up in selection node $\{d, e\}$. If we read the edge annotations along any path from the root to the sink of the selection DAG, we obtain a valid schedule of G.

Corollary 7. *All paths π in the selection DAG $D = (Z, H)$ from the root to a node $z \in Z$ have equal length $L(z)$.*

Corollary 8. *D is leveled, i.e. the nodes z of D can be arranged in n levels $L_1, ..., L_n$ such that edges in D connect only nodes in neighbored levels L_i, L_{i+1}, $i = 1, ..., n - 1$.*

Proof. Set $i = L(z)$ in corollary 7.

We further define:
Σ_z as the set of all schedules for G_z;
S_z as one of the schedules in Σ_z with minimal register need, and
$m_z = m(S_z)$ as this minimal register need. Note that $m_\emptyset$ is then the register need of an optimal schedule for G.
    The definition of Σ_z and the selection of S_z from Σ_z is well–defined due to Lemma 6.
    The new algorithm ncc constructs the selection DAG instead of the selection tree. At any creation of a new zero–indegree set z, it inspects whether the same DAG node set has already been created before. Because D is leveled (corollary

8), it needs only to inspect already generated selection nodes in the current level L. If such a selection node z does not yet exist, a new selection node z is created and S_z is initialized to the current schedule S. Otherwise, if the selection node z already exists, it computes whether the current schedule S or the schedule S_z uses fewer registers, and set S_z to the better schedule of these two. Finally, each selection node z is annotated by an optimal schedule S_z of *scheduled*(z), and consequently, $S_\emptyset$ is an optimal schedule for the DAG G.

Theorem 9. *The worst–case time complexity of algorithm ncc is* $O(n2^{2n})$.

Proof. The number of selection nodes is bound by the number of subsets of V which is 2^n. In each selection step we have to inspect one level of selection nodes which has less than 2^n nodes. Each comparison of two z sets costs at most $O(n)$.

4   Improvement

We improve the algorithm *ncc* by the following modification: Instead of entering all selection nodes of the same level into the same set L_i, we subdivide L_i into sets L_i^0, L_i^1, ..., L_i^K where K is some upper bound of the minimal number of registers required for G.[3] Now we store in L_i^k exactly those selection nodes z of L_i that have register need $m_z = k$. Now, we no longer have to look up all L_i^k, $k = 1, ..., K$ when looking for equality of z sets because of data dependencies:

Lemma 10. *The predecessors of a selection node in L_{i+1}^k are located in either L_i^{k-1} or L_i^k.*

Proof. Appending a DAG node v to an existing schedule S with register need $m(S)$ giving a new schedule S' yields $m(S) \leq m(S') \leq m(S) + 1$ since we could be required to allocate a new register for v that was previously unused, and a composed schedule S' can never take less registers than any of its sub-schedules.

This leads to the data dependencies in the selection graph illustrated in Fig. 4.

We use this theorem to free storage for levels as soon as they are not required any more.

The data dependencies impose a partial order of the selection steps. Hence, we can change our algorithm's order of constructing selection nodes as long as there is no conflict with these data dependencies. For instance, we can change the priority of the time slot axis over the register need axis, which corresponds, roughly speaking, just to a loop interchange. The resulting algorithm *ncv* can finish computing selection nodes as soon as the (first) selection node is entered into level L_n, because it represents a valid schedule with minimal register need — just what we want! Thus, expensive computation of later unused, inefficient partial schedules is deferred as far as possible — if we are lucky, to a point that needs not be considered any more because a solution has been found meanwhile.

---

[3] K could be a priori determined by using contiguous schedule techniques or by just choosing a random schedule of G. If storage is not too scarce, we can conservatively choose $K = n$.

5 Parallelization

There are several possibilities to exploit parallelism in *ncv*:

- exploiting the structure of the data dependencies among the lists L_i^k (see Fig. 4): all lists L_i^{j-i}, $i = 1, 2, ...$ (the lists on the jth "wavefront" diagonal) can be computed concurrently in step j, for $j = 1, ..., n + K$.
- further subdivision of a list L_i^k into sublists of roughly equal size and expanding the selection nodes in these sublists concurrently. Note that this requires a parallel list data structure that guarantees that the same selection node is not erroneously inserted twice at the same time.
- parallelization of the lookup routine (according to previous item).
- parallelization of the expansion step itself.

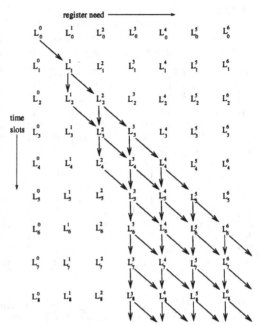

Fig. 4. Data dependencies among the sets L_i^k of selection nodes

Particularly, the second and third item promise the exploitation of massive parallelism.

We are currently implementing the parallel version of *ncv* on a massively parallel shared memory multiprocessor, the SB-PRAM [17], using the parallel programming language Fork95 [22].

6 Experimental Results

We have implemented *nce*, *ncc* and *ncv*, and have applied them to hundreds of randomly generated test DAGs and to larger DAGs taken from real application programs. Some of the experimental results are shown in Tables 1 and 2. All measurements were taken on a SUN SPARC-20.

The random DAGs are generated by initializing a predefined number of nodes and by selecting a certain number of them as leaf nodes. Then, the children of inner nodes are selected randomly. We observed:

- *nce* is not practical for DAGs with more than 20 nodes and often takes inacceptable time for DAGs with 15 to 20 nodes.
- *ncc* reduces the number of different contiguous schedules considerably. It is, roughly spoken, practical for DAGs with up to 40 nodes, sometimes also for larger DAGs, very depending on the DAG's structure. A timeout feature, controlled e.g. by a compiler option, should be provided for practical use that switches to a heuristic method if the deadline is exceeded..

- *ncc* is particularly suitable for "slim" DAGs because the zero–indegree sets z always remain small.
- *ncv* defers the combinatorial explosion to a later point of time but, of course, cannot always avoid it for larger and more complex DAGs. For some DAGs in the range of 41...50 nodes and for nearly all DAGs with more than 50 nodes *ncv* runs out of space and time.

n	T_{ncv}	$m_\emptyset$	n	T_{ncv}	$m_\emptyset$	n	T_{ncv}	$m_\emptyset$
24	0.8 sec	8	36	32.4 sec	10	42	23.4 sec	10
26	1.5 sec	7	37	3:00.8 sec	9	42	46.9 sec	11
26	0.8 sec	7	38	56.1 sec	10	43	43:30.6 sec	9
27	0.1 sec	8	38	2:38.8 sec	9	43	23:51.7 sec	9
28	1.4 sec	8	38	28.8 sec	9	44	3:44.6 sec	11
30	4.6 sec	8	38	7.0 sec	10	44	5:20.7 sec	12
31	22.5 sec	7	38	3:35.8 sec	9	44	18.9 sec	11
31	48.6 sec	7	39	10:01.7 sec	10	44	10:30.9 sec	10
32	17.5 sec	8	39	34.4 sec	9	45	58:01.7 sec	10
32	1:14.9 sec	8	39	43.1 sec	10	46	36:46.0 sec	12
33	4.6 sec	10	39	3:39.6 sec	9	46	55:59.8 sec	10
34	25.3 sec	7	39	1:44.8 sec	10	47	22:30.0 sec	11
34	54.3 sec	9	41	14:28.1 sec	9	49	1:09:37.2 sec	10
35	34.4 sec	10	41	1:48.6 sec	11	50	32:58,1 sec	12
36	14.9 sec	10	41	1:09.3 sec	10	51	19:01.2 sec	13

Table 1. *ncv* applied to some random DAGs. For all these DAGs, *nce* failed because of running out of space and time.

Source	DAG	n	T_{ncv}	$m_\emptyset$
LL 14	second loop	19	0.12 sec	4
LL 20	inner loop	23	0.48 sec	6
MDG	calc. cos, sin	26	0.44 sec	7
SPEC77	spher. flow	27	0.93 sec	7
SPEC77	mult. FFT	49	23:26.0 sec	7

Table 2. *ncv* applied to some DAGs taken from real programs (LL = Livermore Loop Kernels; MDG = molecular dynamics, and SPEC77 = atmospheric flow simulation; the last two are taken from the Perfect Club Benchmark Suite). *nce* failed for all DAGs because of running out of space and time.

7 Filling delay slots

Up to now, we assumed that there are no delay slots to be filled since the result of an operation was available at the beginning of the next machine cycle. However, modern processors often have operations with one or more delay slots. These delay slots may be filled by subsequent operations that do not use the result of the delayed operation. If there are no such operations available, a NOP instruction has to be inserted to fill the delay slot. We will show how our technique can be easily extended to cope with delay slots.

For each DAG node v, let *delay*(v) denote the number of delay slots required by the operation performed at v. For a given schedule S, we compute a mapping T of the DAG nodes to the set $\{1, 2, ...\}$ of physical time slots as follows:

function *time* (**schedule** S of a **DAG** G with n nodes)
Initially we set $t = 1$. Then,
for the DAG nodes u_i in the order induced by S, i.e., $u_1 = S^{-1}(1)$, $u_2 = S^{-1}(2)$, ...
do if u_i has a left child l **then** $t = \max(t, T(l) + delay(l) + 1$ **fi**
  if u_i has a right child r **then** $t = \max(t, T(r) + delay(r) + 1$ **fi**
  $T(u_i) = t$; $t = t + 1$; **od**
return $\max_i(T(u_i) + delay(u_i))$;

The algorithm returns the time which is required to execute the basic block reordered according to schedule S.

We are faced with the problem that we now get a second optimization goal: minimizing $time(S)$, i.e. the number of NOPs, in addition to minimizing the number $m(S)$ of registers. Comparing two schedules S_1 and S_2 becomes more difficult. Clearly, if $time(S_1) < time(S_2)$ and $m(S_1) \leq m(S_2)$ or if $time(S_1) \leq time(S_2)$ and $m(S_1) < m(S_2)$ we prefer S_1 over S_2. In the context of our previous algorithm, this means that S_1 would be kept in the lists of schedules, and S_2 would be thrown away. But what happens if S_1 and S_2 have both equal register need and equal number of NOPs, or, even worse, if $time(S_1) > time(S_2)$ but $m(S_1) < m(S_2)$ (or vice versa)? The only safe method is to keep both S_1 and S_2 in the lists for later expansion. This clearly increases the computational work.

But we apply the same trick as above to defer computationally expensive expansions to a later point in time. In addition to the previous partition of the selection nodes into lists L_i^k (cf. Fig. 4), we add a third dimension to the space of lists of execution nodes z, namely execution time $time(S_z)$. Specifically, a list $L_i^{k,d}$ contains the selection nodes z with $|scheduled(z)| = i$ and $m_z = k$ and $time(S_z) = d$. The structure of data dependencies among the $L_i^{k,d}$ results from

Lemma 11. *Let $maxdelay = \max_v delay(v)$. The predecessors of a selection node in $L_{i+1}^{k,d}$ are located in $L_i^{k-1,D}$ or $L_i^{k,D}$, with D ranging from $d - maxdelay$ to d.*

Proof. Evidence regarding k was already given in Lemma 10. Appending a DAG node v to an existing schedule S with execution time $time(S)$, giving a new schedule S', yields $time(S) \leq time(S') \leq time(S) + maxdelay$ since v can be placed safely $maxdelay$ time slots after the last time slot occupied by S.

Another difficulty arises. For the previous algorithm, ncv, all optimal schedules, with respect to register need, were equivalent also when later used as subschedules in subsequent stages of the selection DAG. Thus, ncv needed to keep only one optimal schedule for each $z \in L_i^k$. But, as we outlined above, this is now no longer true because we have now more than one optimization direction. Thus, ncv may keep a "wrong" optimal schedule and may throw away the "right" ones.

This is illustrated in the following example (cf. Fig. 3): When selection node $\{d, e\}$ has been completed, ncv keeps only one optimal schedule for $scheduled(\{d, e\}) = \{a, b, c\}$, e.g. (b, c, a). The optimal solution found by ncv may follow a path through $\{d, e\}$. But if the final schedule should still require only 4 registers, ncv *must* continue with node d. But the schedule (b, c, a, d) enforces a NOP after issuing a if the DAG leaves have one delay slot (delayed Load). Thus the final schedule computed may be suboptimal w.r.t. execution time because the decision to keep only (b, c, a) at $\{d, e\}$ was made too early.

To repair this deficiency, we must keep *all* optimal schedules for the $L_i^{k,d}$ rather than only one. Clearly, this increases optimization time (and space) considerably, since all optimal schedules for $scheduled(z)$ have to be taken into consideration now when expanding selection node z.

As we have two different optimization goals (number of registers and number of NOPs) we have to consider trade-offs between them. We can select one of them as primary goal of optimization and the other one as a secondary goal, which determines the order of stepping through the search space $\{L_i^{k,d}\}_{i,k,d}$. Or we formulate a mixed criterion (e.g., a weighted sum of k and d) that results in the algorithm traversing the search space in a wavefront manner. It is up to the user to formulate his favorite optimization goal.

We implemented algorithm ncn, the modification of ncv for delay slots, for the processor of the SB-PRAM [17] that has a delayed Load with one delay slot; all other operations perform in one cycle. We decided to minimize execution time as a primary goal and register need as a secondary goal. It is very easy now to backtrack the algorithm if one is willing to trade more NOPs for decreased register space. The results for several DAGs at different delay configurations are given in Tab. 3. It appears that the program runs quickly out of space for $n > 25$ in the case of delayed Loads of 1 delay slot, and for $n > 20$ if more delay slots are assumed. This is due to the unavoidable (but perhaps optimizable) replication of schedules described above. Clearly, our test implementation of ncn still wastes a lot of space. Further research has to be done here. In any case ncn appears to be feasible at least for small DAGs.

DAG	n	delay slots for Loads	avg. delay slots for compute	T_{ncn}	min. reg. need	#nops at min. reg. need	reg. need at min. #nops	min. #nops
LL 14	19	1	0	2.2 sec	4	4	5	0
		2	0.5	15.2 sec	4	11	6	1
LL 20	23	1	0	18.5 sec	6	0	6	0
random	17	1	0	0.7 sec	5	1	6	0
random	19	1	0	6.4 sec	5	2	6	0
random	19	1	0	14.8 sec	5	4	6	0
random	20	1	0	30.3 sec	6	2	7	0
random	21	1	0	11.8 sec	8	0	8	0
random	25	1	0	10.4 sec	7	0	7	0
random	15	2	0.5	0.1 sec	5	3	6	1
random	16	2	0.5	4.1 sec	5	3	6	1
random	16	2	0.5	1.1 sec	6	1	7	0
random	17	2	0.5	10.2 sec	5	7	6	1
random	19	2	0.5	62.5 sec	5	9	8	0
random	21	2	0.5	5.5 sec	6	2	7	0
random	22	2	0.5	45.3 sec	6	5	7	0

Table 3. Real and random DAGs, submitted to ncn with two target machine constellations: (1) delayed Load with one delay slot, and (2) delayed Load with 2 delay slots and delayed Compute with 0 or 1 delay slots (randomly chosen with probability 0.5). Columns 6 and 7 show register need and number of NOPs if register need is minimized; columns 8 and 9 show the results if the number of NOPs is minimized. For DAGs of more than 25 resp. 22 nodes our ncn implementation ran out of space. Interesting tradeoffs between register need and execution time occur mainly for small DAGs.

In general, optimization seems to be the faster, the more limitations and dependencies there are. Thus it is a straightforward idea to extend our method for processors with multiple functional units.

8 Multiple functional units

In the presence of multiple functional units it becomes possible to exploit fine grained parallelism. Consider a schedule S and two DAG nodes u, v such that v is scheduled directly after u. If u is not a DAG predecessor of v, u and v could be executed in parallel, provided that both are ready to be issued and functional units are available for the operations to be performed at u and v.

In contrast to VLIW machines, today's superscalar microprocessors do not rely on compilers to schedule operations to functional units. Scheduling is done on-line in hardware by a dispatcher unit. The dispatcher is able to issue several subsequent instructions from the instruction stream in the same clock cycle as long as there are (1) enough functional units available to execute them, and (2) there are no structural hazards such as control dependencies or data dependencies that would prohibit parallel execution These dependences are determined on-line by the dispatcher. If a subsequent instruction v is control or data dependent on a previous one, u, that has just been issued in this cycle, or if all suitable functional units are busy, the later instruction has to be delayed.

We see that this on–line scheduling performed by the dispatcher is indeed bounded by the rather small lookahead. Thus, it is a reasonable idea to reorder the instruction stream at compile time to facilitate the dispatcher's job. In order to optimize the schedule in this context, we need exact knowledge of the hardware features such as number, type, and speed of functional units, and the dispatcher's functionality which is then just simulated during optimization, as we already did for the pipeline behaviour in the previous section.

We can extend algorithm ncn for this case. The result is an optimal schedule S with issuing–time slots T and a mapping F of the DAG nodes to the functional units, such that the overall time required by S is minimized. T and F are computed as side–effects of the modified function $time$ which just imitates the dispatcher's functionality.

9 Related Work

Vegdahl [30] applies a similar idea to instruction scheduling only. He first constructs the entire selection DAG, which is not leveled there, and then applies a shortest path algorithm. In contrast, we compute also partial costs and thus construct only those nodes of the selection DAG which may belong to an optimal path (schedule). His method directly generalizes to Software Pipelining. However, register requirements are not considered at all.

10 Conclusion

We have presented a new algorithm ncv that computes a schedule of a given expression DAG which uses a minimal number of registers. ncv makes it possible, for the first time, to solve this classical optimization problem also for medium-sized DAGs. Based upon the experimental results we conclude that ncv is feasible for usage in optimizing compiler passes; regarding DAGs of medium size, a timeout should be specified, depending on program size and the importance of this particular DAG for the overall execution time of the program. If ncv reaches this deadline without the solution being completed, we should switch to contiguous schedules, as proposed in [21]. For DAGs with more than 50 nodes, we should immediately restrict ourselves to contiguous schedules since it is not very probable that the solution can be completed before the deadline. But nearly all the DAGs occurring in real application programs are of small or medium size and can thus be processed by ncv.

We have proposed several ideas how to exploit massive parallelism in *ncv*.

We have shown how to adapt the algorithm to scheduling in the presence of delayed instructions and multiple functional units. First results for *ncn* show that an optimal solution for any optimization direction can be computed in a reasonable amount of time for small DAGs with up to 20–25 nodes.

Note also that for test compilations, any legal schedule is sufficient, which can be determined in linear time. The optimization algorithms presented here need only be run in the final, optimizing compilation of an application program. Moreover, they need only be applied to the most time–critical parts of a program, e.g. the bodies of innermost loops.

Future research will address techniques, other than trace scheduling [12], that extend these optimizations beyond basic block boundaries. It may also be interesting to combine these algorithms with software pipelining techniques in the presence of loops, maybe in a way similar to [30].

Acknowledgements The author thanks Anton M. Ertl, Dr. Arno Formella, and Prof. Dr. Helmut Seidl for valuable comments on an earlier version of this paper.

References

1. A.V. Aho and S.C. Johnson. Optimal Code Generation for Expression Trees. *Journal of the ACM*, 23(3):488–501, July 1976.
2. D. Bernstein, M.C. Golumbic, Y. Mansour, R.Y. Pinter, D.Q. Goldin, H. Krawczyk, and I. Nahshon. Spill code minimization techniques for optimizing compilers. In *Proc. ACM SIGPLAN Programming Language Design and Implementation*, pages 258–263, 1989.
3. D. Bernstein and I. Gertner. Scheduling expressions on a pipelined processor with a maximal delay on one cycle. *ACM Trans. on Progr. Lang. and Systems*, 11(1):57–67, Jan. 1989.
4. D. Bernstein, J.M. Jaffe, and M. Rodeh. Scheduling arithmetic and load operations in parallel with no spilling. *SIAM J. Comput.*, 18:1098–1127, 1989.
5. D.G. Bradlee, S.J. Eggers, and R.R. Henry. Integrating Register Allocation and Instruction Scheduling for RISCs. In *Proc. 4th Int. Conf. on Architectural Support for Programming Languages and Operating Systems*, pages 122–131, Apr. 1991.
6. Preston Briggs, Keith Cooper, Ken Kennedy, and Linda Torczon. Coloring heuristics for register allocation. In *Proc. ACM SIGPLAN Programming Language Design and Implementation*, 1989.
7. G.J. Chaitin. Register allocation & spilling via graph coloring. *ACM SIGPLAN Notices*, 17(6):201–207, 1982.
8. G.J. Chaitin, M.A. Auslander, A.K. Chandra, J. Cocke, M.E. Hopkins, and P.W. Markstein. Register allocation via coloring. *Computer Languages*, 6:47–57, 1981.
9. Fred C. Chow and John L. Hennessy. Register allocation by priority-based coloring. *ACM SIGPLAN Notices*, 19(6):222–232, 1984.
10. J.J. Dongarra and A.R. Jinds. Unrolling Loops in Fortran. *Software – Practice and Experience*, 9(3):219–226, 1979.
11. C. Eisenbeis, S. Lelait, and B. Marmol. The meeting graph: a new model for loop cyclic register allocation. In *Proc. 5th Workshop on Compilers for Parallel Computers*, pages 503–516. Dept. of Computer Architecture, University of Malaga, Spain. Report No. UMA-DAC-95/09, June 28–30 1995.
12. Joseph A. Fisher. Trace scheduling: A technique for global microcode compaction. *IEEE Transactions on Computers*, C-30(7):478–490, July 1981.

13. R.A. Freiburghouse. Register allocation via usage counts. *Comm. ACM*, 17(11), 1974.

14. P.B. Gibbons and S.S. Muchnick. Efficient instruction scheduling for a pipelined architecture. In *Proc. SIGPLAN Symp. on Compiler Construction*, pages 11–16, July 1986.

15. J.R. Goodman and W. Hsu. Code scheduling and register allocation in large basic blocks. In *Proc. Int. Conf. on Supercomputing*, pages 442–452, July 1988.

16. John Hennessy and Thomas Gross. Postpass Code Optimization of Pipeline Constraints. *ACM Transactions on Programming Languages and Systems*, 5(3):422–448, July 1983.

17. Jörg Keller, Wolfgang J. Paul, and Dieter Scheerer. Realization of PRAMs: Processor Design. In *Proc. WDAG94, 8th Int. Workshop on Distributed Algorithms*, *Springer Lecture Notes in Computer Science vol. 857*, pages 17–27, 1994.

18. C.W. Keßler. Code–Optimierung quasiskalarer vektorieller Grundblöcke. Diploma thesis, University of Saarbrücken (Germany), 1990.

19. C.W. Keßler, W.J. Paul, and T. Rauber. A Randomized Heuristic Approach to Register Allocation. In *Proc. 3rd Symp. on Programming Language Implementation and Logic Programming*, pages 195–206. Springer LNCS vol. 528, Aug. 1991.

20. C.W. Keßler, W.J. Paul, and T. Rauber. Scheduling Vector Straight Line Code on Vector Processors. In R. Giegerich and S.L. Graham, editors, *Code Generation – Concepts, Tools, Techniques*, pages 77–91. Springer Worksh. in Computing Series, 1992.

21. C.W. Keßler and T. Rauber. Generating optimal contiguous evaluations for expression DAGs. *Computer Languages*, 21(2):113–127, 1996.

22. C.W. Keßler and H. Seidl. Integrating Synchronous and Asynchronous Paradigms: The Fork95 Parallel Programming Language. In W. Giloi, S. Jähnichen, and B. Shriver, editors, *Proc. 2nd Int. Conf. on Massively Parallel Programming Models*, pages 134–141. Los Alamitos: IEEE Computer Society Press, Oct. 1995. See also: Technical Report 95-05, FB IV Informatik, Universität Trier, http://www.informatik.uni-trier.de/ ~kessler/fork95.html.

23. Monica Lam. Software pipelining: An effective scheduling technique for VLIW machines. In *Proc. SIGPLAN Symp. on Compiler Construction*, pages 318–328, July 1988.

24. J. Llosa, M. Valero, and E. Ayguade. Bidirectional scheduling to minimize register requirements. In *Proc. 5th Workshop on Compilers for Parallel Computers*, pages 534–554. Dept. of Computer Architecture, University of Malaga, Spain. Report No. UMA-DAC-95/09, June 28–30 1995.

25. Rajeev Motwani, Krishna V. Palem, Vivek Sarkar, and Salem Reyen. Combining Register Allocation and Instruction Scheduling (Technical Summary). Technical Report TR 698, Courant Institute of Mathematical Sciences, New York, July 1995.

26. Todd A. Proebsting and Charles N. Fischer. Linear–time, optimal code scheduling for delayed–load architectures. In *Proc. ACM SIGPLAN Programming Language Design and Implementation*, pages 256–267, June 1991.

27. R. Sethi. Complete register allocation problems. *SIAM J. Comput.*, 4:226–248, 1975.

28. R. Sethi and J.D. Ullman. The generation of optimal code for arithmetic expressions. *Journal of the ACM*, 17:715–728, 1970.

29. Thinking Machines Corp. Connection Machine Model CM-5. Technical Summary. TMC, Cambridge, MA, Nov. 1992.

30. Steven R. Vegdahl. A Dynamic-Programming Technique for Compacting Loops. In *Proc. 25th Annual IEEE/ACM Int. Symp. on Microarchitecture*, pages 180–188. Los Alamitos: IEEE Computer Society Press, 1992.

31. R. Venugopal and Y.N. Srikant. Scheduling expression trees with reusable registers on delayed-load architectures. *Computer Languages*, 21(1):49–65, 1995.

Beyond Depth-First: Improving Tabled Logic Programs through Alternative Scheduling Strategies

Juliana Freire   Terrance Swift   David S. Warren

Department of Computer Science
State University of New York at Stony Brook
Stony Brook, NY 11794-4400
{juliana,tswift,warren}@cs.sunysb.edu

Abstract. Tabled evaluations ensure termination of logic programs with finite models by keeping track of which subgoals have been called. Given several variant subgoals in an evaluation, only the first one encountered will use program clause resolution; the rest uses answer resolution. This use of answer resolution prevents infinite looping which happens in SLD. Given the asynchronicity of answer generation and answer return, tabling systems face an important scheduling choice not present in traditional top-down evaluation: How does the order of returning answers to consuming subgoals affect program efficiency?

This paper investigates alternate scheduling strategies for tabling in a WAM implementation, the SLG-WAM. The original SLG-WAM had a simple mechanism of scheduling answers to be returned to callers which was expensive in terms of trailing and choice point creation. We propose here a more sophisticated scheduling strategy, Batched Scheduling, which reduces the overheads of these operations and provides dramatic space reduction as well as speedups for many programs. We also propose a second strategy, Local Scheduling, which has applications to non-monotonic reasoning and when combined with answer subsumption can improve the performance of some programs by arbitrary amounts.

1   Introduction

Tabling extends the power of logic programming since it allows the computation of recursive queries at the speed of Prolog. This property has led to the use of tabling for new areas of logic programming — not only for deductive database style applications, but other fixpoint-style problems, such as program analysis. Ensuring that these new applications run efficiently in terms of time and space may require the use of different *scheduling strategies*. The possibility of different useful strategies derives from an intrinsic asynchrony in tabling systems between the generation of answers and their return to a given consuming tabled subgoal. Depending on how and when the return of answers is scheduled, different strategies can be formulated. Furthermore, these different strategies can benefit the serious research and industrial applications which are beginning to emerge.

To take a well-known instance, in order to efficiently evaluate queries to disk-resident data, a tabling system should provide set-at-a-time processing analogous to the semi-naive evaluation of a magic-transformed [2] program, so that communication and I/O costs are minimized. To address this, a separate paper defined a breadth-first set-at-a-time strategy for the SLG-WAM [15] of XSB[1] and proved it *iteration equivalent* to the semi-naive evaluation of a magic transformed program [8]. Unlike XSB's original tuple-at-a-time engine, the engine based on the breadth-first strategy showed very good performance for disk accesses.

Of course tabled evaluations must also be efficient in terms of time and space for in-memory queries. [16] showed that, compared to Prolog, tabled evaluation incurred a minimal execution time overhead under several different criteria of measurement. However, memory is also a critical resource for computations, and stack space for consuming tabled subgoals can be reclaimed only when it can be ensured that all answers have been returned to them. Since the choice of scheduling strategy can influence when this condition happens, it can affect the amount of space needed for a computation.

Finally, a number of tabling applications require more than the simple recursion needed for Horn programs. Resolving a call to a negative literal requires completely evaluating the subgoal contained in the literal, along with all other dependent subgoals. In a similar manner, waiting until part of an evaluation has been completely evaluated can also benefit programs that use *answer subsumption* (e.g. [12]), in which only the most general answers need to be maintained and returned to consuming subgoals. When answer subsumption is seen as taking place over arbitrary lattices (rather than just the lattice of terms), it captures aspects of tabled evaluations for program analyses (see e.g. [4, 10]), for deductive database queries that use aggregates [17], and for answers involving constraints [9].

This paper motivates and describes two new types of scheduling for tabled logic programs:

- We describe Batched Scheduling which is highly efficient for in-memory programs that do not require answer subsumption.
- We describe Local Scheduling, which provides an elegant strategy to evaluate both fixed-order stratified programs, and programs which use answer subsumption.
- We provide detailed results of experiments comparing these two strategies with XSB's original Single Stack Scheduling (described in [16]). They show that:
    - Batched Scheduling can provide an order of magnitude space reduction over the original strategy, as well as reliably provide a significant reduction in time.
    - Local Scheduling can provide large speedups for programs that require answer subsumption, while incurring a relatively small constant cost for programs that do not.

2 Scheduling SLG Evaluations

Review of SLG Terminology

Full details of the concepts and terminology presented in this section can be found in [3]. In an SLG evaluation predicates can be either tabled or non-tabled,

---

[1] XSB is freely available at http://www.cs.sunysb.edu/~sbprolog.

in which case SLD resolution is used. Evaluations in tabling systems are usually modeled by a forest of resolution trees containing a tree for every tabled subgoal present in an evaluation. SLG trees have nodes of the form:

$$answer\_template : status : goal\_list$$

(see, e.g. Figures 1 and 3). The *answer_template* is used to maintain variable bindings made to the tabled subgoal during the course of resolution, and the *goal_list* contains unresolved goals. For definite programs, which are the main focus of this paper, *status* is one of the set: *generator*, *active* (or, synonymously, *consuming*), *interior*, *answer*, and *disposed*. The roots of SLG trees are created when new tabled subgoals are selected. These roots have status *generator*, and are also called *generator nodes*. Program clause resolution is used to produce the children of generator nodes; in SLG, this resolution occurs through the SUBGOAL CALL operation. The node calling a tabled subgoal is denoted as a *consuming* or *active* node and its children will be produced by answer clause resolution (through the ANSWER RETURN operation). An answer corresponds to a leaf node of a tree whose *goal_list* is empty. Conceptually, the NEW ANSWER operation can be seen as adding these answers to a table where they are associated with the subgoals that are the roots of their trees. *Interior* nodes represent nodes whose selected literals are *non-tabled* and for which SLD resolution (i.e., program clause resolution in all cases) is used.

Subgoals that occur in trees that have been *completely evaluated* are marked as *disposed*. Sets of subgoals are *completely evaluated* when all possible answers have been derived for them. This concept of *complete evaluation* of a subgoal is necessary for negation and is useful for the early reclamation of stack space in our implementation. When a subgoal is found to be completely evaluated, its non-answer nodes are marked as disposed through the COMPLETION operation.

Any finite SLG evaluation can be seen as a sequence of forests or *SLG systems*. As applicable operations are performed, the evaluation proceeds moving from system to system. Given a particular SLG system, a subgoal S_1 *depends on* a subgoal S_2 iff neither S_1 nor S_2 are completed, and there is a node in the tree for S_1 whose selected literal is S_2. This dependency relation gives rise to a *Subgoal Dependency Graph* (SDG) for each SLG system. Since the dependency relation is non-symmetric, the SDG is a directed graph and can be partitioned into strongly connected components, or SCCs. Note that the dependency graph may be labeled with different types of dependencies: positive or negative dependencies in normal programs, or aggregate dependencies in deductive database programs. Given the usual dependency labelings for normal programs, these SDGs can be related to the dynamic stratification of [13] in the sense that a program is dynamically stratified if there is a dynamic computation rule which avoids labeled SDGs that have cycles through negation. We thus refer to the unlabeled SDG as a *pre-stratification* of a system.

Single Stack Scheduling

The scheduling of resolution in Prolog [1] is conceptually simple. The engine performs forward execution for as long as it possibly can. If it cannot — because of failure of resolution, or because all solutions to the initial query are desired

— it checks a scheduling stack (the choice point stack) to determine a *failure continuation* to execute.

The SLG-WAM differs from the WAM in that, in addition to resolving program clauses, it also resolves answers against active nodes. A natural way to extend the WAM paradigm to return answers to an active node is to distinguish between the acts of returning old answers to new active nodes — answers that were already in the table when the active node was created — and returning new answers to old active nodes. The first case is simple: When a new active node is created, a choice point is set up to backtrack through answers in the table much as if they were unit clauses. To handle the second case, whenever a new answer is derived for which there are existing active nodes, an answer return choice point is placed on the choice point stack. This choice point will manage the resolution of the new answer with each of the active nodes. Forward execution is then continued until failure, at which time the top of the choice point stack is then used for scheduling. The choice point stack thus serves as a scheduling stack for both returning answers and resolving program clauses. Accordingly, we call this scheduling strategy Single Stack Scheduling. The operational semantics of this scheduling strategy was described in detail in [14] and forms the basis of XSB's SLG-WAM as described in [15]. The following example demonstrates how this strategy works.

Example 1. Consider the following double-recursive transitive closure

```
:- table p/2.
a(1,2). a(1,3). a(2,3).
p(X,Y) :- p(X,Z), p(Z,Y).
p(X,Y) :- a(X,Y).
```

and the query ?- p(1,Y). The forest of SLG trees for this program at the end of the evaluation is shown in Fig. 1, and Fig. 2 shows snapshots of the choice point stack at different points of the evaluation.

Let us examine the actions of Single Stack Scheduling in detail. When the top-level query is called, it is inserted into the table (since p/2 is a tabled subgoal) and a generator choice point is created, which corresponds to the root of the new SLG tree in node 1. Program clause resolution is then used to create node 2. Since the selected literal in node 2 is a variant of a tabled subgoal, a new active choice point frame (corresponding to the consuming node 2) is laid down to serve as an environment through which to return answers, and the stacks are frozen (see Fig. 2(a)), so that backtracking will not *overwrite* any frames below that point. In addition, if there were any answers in the table, the RetryActive instruction would backtrack through them and return each to the active node. Since there are no answers in the table for p(1,Y), the second clause for p/2 is tried. As the selected literal is not a tabled predicate, SLD resolution is applied and a Prolog choice point is laid down for a/2. The evaluation then gives rise to an answer, p(1,2) (in node 4). Since there are no variants of p(1,2) associated with p(1,Y), the answer is inserted into the table, and an answer return choice point is laid down (Fig. 2(a)).

When the engine backtracks into the answer return choice point for p(1,2) (see Fig. 2(b)), the AnswerReturn instruction freezes the stacks and returns the

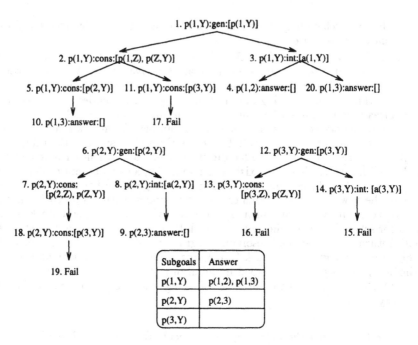

Fig. 1. *SLG evaluation under Single Stack Scheduling*

answer to all active nodes[2]. In this case, the answer will be returned to node 2, which in turn will trigger a call to p(2,Y). The evaluation of p(2,Y) (see node 6) is similar to that of node 1: It is inserted into the table and a **generator choice point** is laid down for it. It will eventually generate an answer (p(2,3) in node 9), which is inserted into the table for p(2,Y). In addition, an **answer return choice point** is laid down and the bindings for the answer are propagated to node 5, which will then derive the answer p(1,3). When p(1,3) is returned to node 2, it prompts a call to p(3,Y).

A **generator** and a **new active choice point** are laid down for p(3,Y). But this subgoal fails, and can be completed. Upon completion, the choice points for p(3,Y) can be reclaimed — as Fig. 2(c) shows. At this point, the engine backtracks into the **answer return choice point** p(2,3), and this answer is returned to the consuming node 7. Node 7 then calls p(3,Y), which is completed and has no answers, and thus the engine fails. The subgoal p(2,Y) is now completely evaluated, and space for it can be reclaimed in the stacks (see Fig. 2(d)).

The evaluation then returns to the choice point for a/2 (node 3), and the next clause is tried. The answer p(1,3) is generated (node 20), but since a variant of this answer is already in the table (from node 10), the engine simply fails. Finally, when the engine backtracks to the generator node for p(1,Y) (node 1) and there are no other choices to be tried, the last subgoal in the system can be completed.

---

[2] As an optimization, in the SLG-WAM after an **answer return choice point** returns the answer to the last active node, it removes itself from the backtracking chain — this is represented in Fig. 2 by dotted frames.

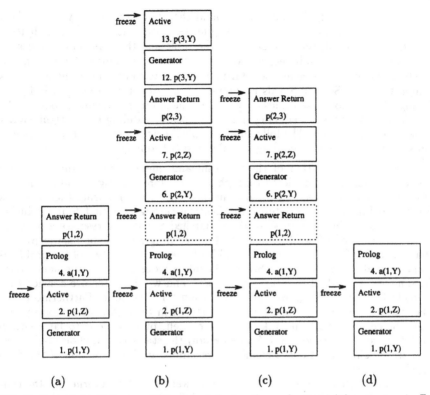

Fig. 2. *Snapshots of the completion stack during the evaluation of the program in Example 1 under Single Stack Scheduling*

While single-stack scheduling is simple to conceptualize, it contains several drawbacks. First, the integration of the action of returning answers into the mechanism of the choice point stack makes Single Stack Scheduling not easily adaptable to a parallel engine [6]. Another problem is memory usage: In order to perform answer clause resolution at different points in the SLG forest, the stacks have to be frozen so that the environment can be correctly reconstructed at the different points. This need to freeze stacks may lead to inefficient space usage by the SLG-WAM, as some frames might get trapped (e.g., the Prolog choice point in Fig. 2(b)). Finally, the addition of new choice points and the need to move around in the SLG forest to return answers means that trailed variables must be continually set and reset to switch binding environments, causing further inefficiencies.

3 Batched Scheduling

Batched Scheduling can be seen as an attempt to address the problems with Single Stack Scheduling mentioned above. Indeed, versions 1.5 and higher of XSB use this new strategy as a default. As its name implies, Batched Scheduling minimizes the need to freeze and move around the search tree simply by *batching* the return of answers. That is, if the engine generates answers while evaluating a particular subgoal, they are added to the table and the subgoal continues its normal evaluation until it resolves all available program clauses. Only then will it return the answers it generated during the evaluation to consuming nodes. As demonstrated in Section 5, this new strategy makes better use of space: By reducing the need to freeze branches it reduces the number of trapped nodes in the search tree. Along with reducing space, Batched Scheduling shows significantly better execution times. The following example illustrates some of the differences between Single Stack Scheduling and Batched Scheduling.

Example 2. The execution of the program and query from Example 1 under Batched Scheduling is depicted through the SLG forest in Fig. 3 and a sequence of choice point stacks in Fig. 4. As can be seen from comparing the forests in Fig. 1 and Fig. 3, the procedures are identical through the first four resolution steps, but differ in the fifth step. Here, Batched Scheduling resolves a program clause against node 3 while Single Stack Scheduling returns the answer p(1,2) that was derived in step 4 to node 2. This difference reflects two of the problems mentioned above. First, Single Stack Scheduling requires an environment switch from node 3 to node 2 to return the answer, and will later require a swich *back* to node 3 to finish program clause expansion for that node. Furthermore, the unexpanded program clause for node 3 is stored in the engine as a choice point. This choice point not only takes up space itself, but the need to later switch back to it requires freezing (at AnswerReturn) the stack at that choice point (see Fig. 2(b)). This frozen space cannot be reclaimed until completion of the SCC in which it lies.

A similar difference occurs when the answer p(2,3) is returned to the consuming node 6. In the choice point stack of Fig. 2(c), the return of this answer requires the placement of an explicit choice point and a freeze. In Fig. 4 both of these overheads are avoided.

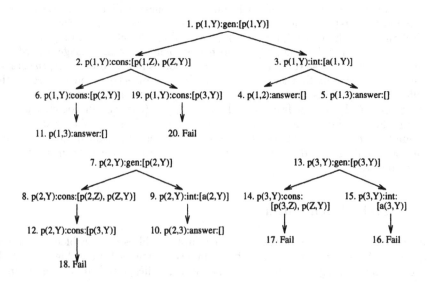

Fig. 3. *SLG evaluation under Batched Scheduling*

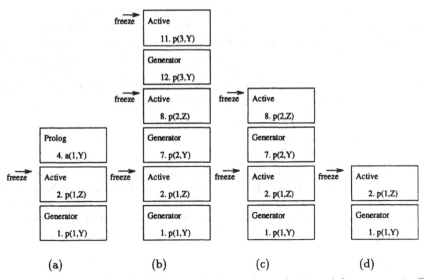

Fig. 4. *Snapshots of the completion stack during the evaluation of the program in Example 1 under Batched Scheduling*

Rather than creating explicit **answer return choice points**, as in Single Stack Scheduling, Batched Scheduling controls answer return through a designated node in each SCC called a *leader*[3]. When the **generator choice point** has exhausted all program clause resolution, rather than disposing of the choice point, as in Prolog, the failure continuation instruction for the choice point becomes a CheckComplete instruction. If the **generator choice point** corresponds to a subgoal that is a leader of an SCC, the action of this instruction is to cycle through the subgoals in the SCC to return unresolved answers to every consuming node whose selected literal is in the SCC. Batched Scheduling is related to fixpoint style algorithms of deductive databases. The engine iteratively backtracks to the CheckComplete instruction for the leader of an SCC. This leader then switches environments to a consuming node, *Cons*, that has a non-empty delta set of answers. (If there is no such *Cons*, the fixpoint for the SCC has been reached and the subgoals in the SCC can be completed). Each new answer for *Cons* is resolved through backtracking as with unit clauses (as in the RetryActive instruction of Single Stack Scheduling). Furthermore, the engine resolves answers against *Cons* as long as there are any answers to resolve, and may resolve answers in the same iteration they are added. This latter step gives good performance for in memory queries, but makes the Batched Scheduling algorithm differ from traditional goal-oriented formulations of semi-naive fixpoint[4] such as Magic evaluation [2].

Batched Scheduling bears some resemblance to other two independently developed approaches: the ET* algorithm from [5] and the AMAI from [10]. How-

---

[3] In the SLG-WAM each subgoal is labeled with a unique depth-first number (DFN) reflecting its location in the stack, which maintains the exact order in which subgoals are called. The leader of an SCC is the subgoal in that SCC with the lowest DFN (i.e., the subgoal in the SCC that was first called).

[4] Details of these differences can be found in [7].

ever, in [5], Fan and Dietrich do not consider strongly connected components in the fixpoint check, and their strategy is *fair* for answers, what might cause inefficiencies. In [10], Janssens et al. describe an abstract machine specialized for abstract interpretation and use a similar scheduling strategy for their fixpoint iterations. Even though they take SCCs into account, these are detected statically, whereas in our engine in order to evaluate general logic programs (with negation), SCCs have to be determined at run time.

4 Local Scheduling

In Local Scheduling the engine evaluates a single SCC at a time. In other words, answers are returned outside of an SCC (that is, to consuming nodes in trees whose root subgoal is not in the SCC) only after that SCC is completely evaluated. The action of Local Scheduling can easily be seen through the following example of stratified evaluation.

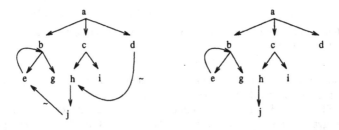

(a) Negative dependencies　　　　(b) No negative dependencies

Fig. 5. *Subgoal dependency graphs for program* P *of Example 3 under different search strategies*

Example 3. Let *P* be the modularly stratified program
:- table a/0,b/0,c/0,d/0,e/0,g/0,h/0,i/0,j/0.

```
a:-b,c,d.       b:-e.          c:-h.
                b:-g.          c:-i.

d:- ~h.         e:-b,s.        g.

h:-j.           j:- ~e.        i.
```

for which the query ?- a is to be evaluated. If evaluated under either Single Stack Scheduling or Batched Scheduling, an SDG will be produced with cascading negative dependencies as shown in Fig. 5(a). Even though there is no cycle through negation, detecting this property can complicate the evaluation of stratified programs. However if Local Scheduling is used, a *simpler* SDG is created, as depicted in Fig. 5(b). To attain this latter SDG, each independent SCC is completely evaluated before returning any answers to subgoals outside the SCC — making the search depth-first with respect to SCCs. In Local Scheduling, the SCCs {b, e} and {g} are completely evaluated before b returns any answers to

a. Thus, **e** is completely evaluated when ~**e** is called and negative dependencies are not created. Both the negative link from j to **e**, and that from d to h are avoided, since both **e** and h are completed by the time they are called negatively.

Local Scheduling can improve the performance of programs that benefit from answer subsumption in the following manner. Answer subsumption can be performed as a variation of the SLG NEW ANSWER operation. While adding an answer, the engine may check whether that answer is more general than those currently in the table. If it is more general, this new answer is added and the subsumed answers are removed. Given that Local Scheduling evaluates each SCC completely before returning any answers out of it, we are guaranteed that only the most general answers will be returned out of that SCC. This process is presented in detail in Example 4.

anc(mary,bob).
anc(john,bob).
anc(louis,mary).
anc(eve,john).
anc(eve,mary).
anc(joan,louis).
anc(carl,eve).
anc(carl,louis).

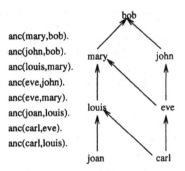

Fig. 6. *Ancestor relation for Example 4*

Example 4. Consider the following variation of the same generation program which finds the smallest distance between two people in the same generation

```
sgi(X,Y)(I) :-
        ancestor(X,Z),
        subsumes(min)(sgi(Z,Z1),I1),
        ancestor(Y,Z1),
        I is I1+1.
sgi(X,X)(0).
:- subsumes(min)(sgi(joan,carl),I).
```

where **subsumes(min)/2** is a tabled predicate that performs answer subsumption by deleting all non-minimal answers every time it adds an answer to the table. Given the facts in Fig. 6, there are a number of ways this query can be evaluated. It is well-known that for shortest-path like problems, a breadth-first search can behave asymptotically better than depth-first. Nevertheless, in this example a breadth-first search is still not *optimal*.

In the above query we are trying to find how close **joan** and **carl** are. Note that they have three common ancestors (**louis**, **mary** and **bob**), and thus they are cousins of 1st, 2nd and 3rd degree. If evaluated under breadth-first (the behavior of Batched Scheduling for this example), all possible subpaths between **joan** and **carl** are considered, and if at some point during the evaluation a subpath is found whose length is less than those so far derived, it is immediately propagated even though it may not be minimal. For instance, Batched Scheduling first finds the distance between two immediate ancestors of **joan** and **carl** to be 2, and concludes the distance between **joan** and **carl** themselves is 3. Then evaluation continues and a new distance between the immediate ancestors if found to be 1, a new answer (I=2) is generated for the top-level query. Finally, the minimal distance between **joan** and **carl** is found to be 1 and the *correct* answer is returned.

If Local Scheduling is used instead, only minimal subpaths are propagated, and the engine is able to prune a number of superfluous choices.

5 Experimental Results

Due to space limitations details on the implementations of the strategies have been omited[5]. In this section we compare both execution time and memory usage of SLG-WAM engines based on the different scheduling strategies described in the paper. XSB v. 1.4 uses Single Stack Scheduling, XSB v. 1.5 uses Batched Scheduling and XSB Local uses Local Scheduling. For execution time, we considered not only the running time, but also the dynamic count of SLG-WAM instructions and operations. Benches were run on a SPARC2 with 64MB RAM under SUNOS.

Transitive Closure	reach(X,Y) :- arc(X,Y).
	reach(X,Y) :- reach(X,Z), arc(Z,Y).
Shortest-Path	sp(X,Y)(D) :- arc(X,Y,D).
	sp(X,Y)(D) :- subsumes(min)(sp(X,Z),D1), arc(Z,Y,D2), D is D1+D2.
Same Generation	sgi(X,Y)(D) :- arc(X,Y).
	sgi(X,Y)(D) :- arc(X,Z), subsumes(min)(sgi(Z,Z1),D1), arc(Y,Z1), D is D1+1.

Table 1. *Bench programs*

The bench programs consisted of variations of transitive closure, same-generation and shortest-path on various graphs (the programs are described in Table 1). We experimented with graphs that have well defined structures, such as linear chains and complete binary trees, as well as less regular graphs, based on Knuth's *Words*[6].

5.1 Performance of Batched Scheduling

Let us first examine the differences between Single Stack Scheduling and Batched Scheduling for left-recursive transitive closure on a linear chain containing 1024 nodes, with the query **reach(1,X)**. Under Single Stack Scheduling, first all facts are used (by backtracking through the facts for **arc/2** in the first clause) and when the active node is laid down for the subgoal in the second clause, each

---

[5] Implementation details are given in the expanded version of this paper available at http://www.cs.sunysb.edu/~sbprolog.

[6] The nodes of this graph are the 5757 more common 5-letter English words; there is an arc between two words if they differ in a single character [11].

answer in the table is consumed. If a new answer is derived in this process, computation is suspended and the new answer is immediately returned, by freezing the stacks and pushing an answer return choice point onto the choice point stack. Under Batched Scheduling strategy, all answers in the table are returned before any newly derived answer is considered.

We profiled the SLG-WAM instructions and the main difference between XSB v. 1.4 and XSB v. 1.5 for this example lies in the fact that since answer return choice points are no longer used, AnswerReturns are replaced by Retry-Actives. Since RetryActive requires fewer (about 30% less) machine instructions than AnswerReturn, the tradeoff is beneficial. Also, since Batched Scheduling requires less stack freezing, it utilizes memory better. Fig. 7(a) gives the total stack space usage (local, global, choice point, trail, and completion stack) for the three strategies for the same left-recursive transitive closure and query on chains of varying lengths. Note that whereas memory consumption grows linearly with the number of facts for XSB v. 1.4, the space remains constant for XSB v. 1.5 (and also for Local) at 2.7 Kbytes.

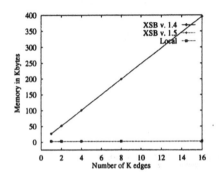 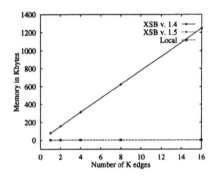

(a) Linear chains of varying length

(b) Complete binary trees of varying height

Fig. 7. *Total memory usage for left-recursive transitive closure*

The SLG-WAM instruction count for left-recursive transitive closure on complete binary trees of varying height are similar to those for chains. However, the batching of answer resolution reduces the need for the engine to move around in the SLG forest and thus Batched Scheduling also save trails and untrails. As a result, memory savings are even bigger than for chains, as Fig. 7(b) shows (note that for the two new strategies the space remains constant at 2.88Kbytes).

The times for the different engines to compute the transitive closure on trees and chains is given in Fig. 8. The speedup of XSB v. 1.5 over XSB v. 1.4 for these examples varies between 11 and 16%.

Single Stack Scheduling as its name implies, uses a stack-based scheduling for answers, and so when executing transitive closure over, say a binary tree, traverses the tree in a depth-first manner. Because Batched Scheduling effectively uses a queue for returning answers, when executing (left-recursive) transitive closure it will traverse the same tree in a breadth-first manner. Accordingly, optimization problems such as shortest-path that can (1) be formulated through left-recursive transitive closure, and (2) benefit from a breadth-first search, can

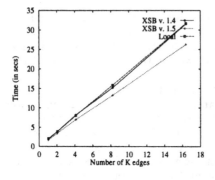
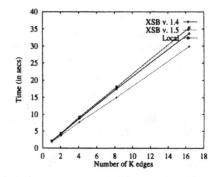

(a) Linear chains of varying length

(b) Complete binary trees of varying height

Fig. 8. *Times for left-recursive transitive closure*

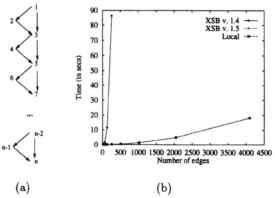

(a)   (b)

Fig. 9. *(b) Shows the time in secs. for XSB v. 1.4, XSB v. 1.5 and Local to find the shortest-path between the endpoints (1 and n) of a graph of the form depicted in (a)*

be run more efficiently under Batched Scheduling[7].

To demonstrate this, we compared the running times for the different engines using the shortest-path program in Table 1. First we considered the artificial graph shown in Fig. 9(a). If a depth-first search is used to compute the shortest-path between nodes 1 and n in this graph, it will run in exponential time. However the shortest path can be computed in polynomial time if the graph is searched in a breadth-first manner. Fig. 9(b) shows the times XSB v. 1.4, XSB v. 1.5 and Local take to compute sp(1,n)(Dist) for different values of n. In addition to running slower, XSB v. 1.4 ran out of memory on graphs with more than 512 nodes. We also considered more realistic graphs, variations of Knuth's Words, and the speedups are substantial as Fig. 10 shows.

---

[7] It is worth pointing out that only the underlying data structures are searched in a breadth-first manner. The depth-first nature of program clause resolution in the WAM is maintained through all strategies discussed in this paper.

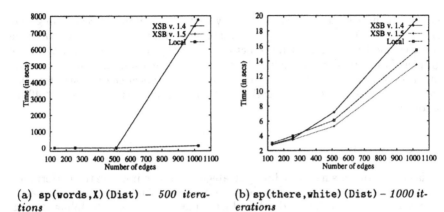

(a) `sp(words,X)(Dist)` – *500 itera-tions*

(b) `sp(there,white)(Dist)` – *1000 it-erations*

Fig. 10. *Timings for shortest-path on Words*

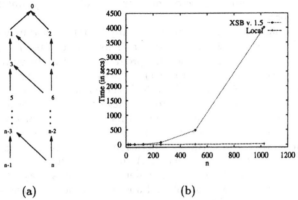

(a)   (b)

Fig. 11. *(b) shows the execution time for the query* `subsumes(min)(sgi(n-1,n),I)` *on graphs of the form depicted in (a) for varying* n

5.2   Performance of Local Scheduling

Since the return of answers out of an SCC has to be delayed until the SCC is completely evaluated, the implementation of Local Scheduling incurs the cost of explicitly returning an answer to the generator node, rather than sharing the bindings as in Batched Scheduling and Single Stack Scheduling. This results in the duplication of the number of **RetryActive** instructions and in a higher number of environment switches.

As for memory consumption, Local Scheduling has the same constant behavior as Batched Scheduling for transitive closure on trees and chains, as evidenced in Fig. 7 (notice that the lines for Local and XSB v. 1.5 overlap). In Fig. 8 we can see that Local adds a roughly constant 15% overhead to XSB v. 1.5, and the execution times for the Local engine are comparable to XSB v. 1.4. Local also has approximately the same performance as XSB v. 1.5 for shortest-path on variations of the Words graph and on the artificial graph of Fig. 9(a) (see Fig. 9(b) and Fig. 10).

We have stated that for programs that can benefit from answer subsumption

Local Scheduling can perform arbitrarily better than Batched Scheduling. The graph in Fig. 11(b) substantiates this statement. This experiment measured the times to find the shortest distance between the two *deepest* nodes (n-1 and n) on graphs of the form depicted in Fig. 11(a) for varying n, using the same-generation program of Example 4. Note that the times for the Local engine vary from 0.06 to 15.7 seconds, whereas for XSB v. 1.5, they range between 0.09 and 4007.8 seconds.

6 Conclusion

This paper proposes new scheduling strategies that can improve the performance — memory usage and execution time – of tabled evaluations. Due to its performance improvement, Batched Scheduling is now the default scheduling strategy for XSB. The gains from this strategy are twofold: by eliminating the answer return choice point and the freezing of stacks done at AnswerReturn, memory usage is greatly reduced; and because of the reduction of trailings/untrailings, the execution time decreases.

Local Scheduling can perform asymptotically better than Batched Scheduling when combined with answer subsumption. This can be of use in many different areas such as aggregate selection and program analysis. In addition, Local Scheduling may have an important role to play in evaluating programs under the well-founded semantics [18]. Currently in XSB the engine may have to construct part of the SDG to check for loops through negation. Since Local Scheduling maintains exact SCCs, it does not require this step as was demonstrated by Example 3. Furthermore, when negative literals actually are involved in a loop through negation, SLG uses a DELAY operation to attempt to break the loop. This use of DELAY may create an answer A that is *conditional* on the truth of some unevaluated literal. However, other derivation paths may create an *unconditional* answer for A (for example, all answers considered in this paper are unconditional). Clearly conditional answers are not needed for A if there is a corresponding unconditional answer, and the use of DELAY gives rise to a form of answer subsumption, leading to another advantage of locality. As the well-founded semantics becomes used by practical programs, the advantages of Local Scheduling may become increasingly necessary for their efficient evaluation.

Acknowledgements: This work was supported in part by CAPES-Brazil, and NSF grants CDA-9303181 and CCR-9404921.

References

1. H. Aït-Kaci. *WAM: A Tutorial Reconstruction.* MIT Press, 1991.
2. C. Beeri and R. Ramakrishnan. On the Power of Magic. *Journal of Logic Programming*, 10(3):255–299, 1991.
3. W. Chen and D.S. Warren. Tabled Evaluation with Delaying for General Logic Programs. *JACM*, 43(1):20–74, January 1996.
4. S. Dawson, C.R. Ramakrishnan, and D.S. Warren. Practical Program Analysis Using General Purpose Logic Programming Systems — A Case Study. In *Proceedings of the ACM Conference on Programming Language Design and Implementation (PLDI)*, pages 117–125. ACM, 1996.

5. C. Fan and S. Dietrich. Extension Table Built-ins for Prolo. *Software–Practice and Experience*, 22(7):573–597, July 1992.

6. J. Freire, R. Hu, T. Swift, and D.S. Warren. Exploiting Parallelism in Tabled Evaluations. In *7th International Symposium, PLILP 95 - LNCS Vol. 982*. Springer-Verlag, 1995.

7. J. Freire, T. Swift, and D.S. Warren. Batched answers: An alternative strategy for tabled evaluations. Technical Report 96/2, Department of Computer Science, State University of New York at Stony Brook, 1996.

8. J. Freire, T. Swift, and D.S. Warren. Taking I/O seriously: Resolution reconsidered for disk. Technical Report 96/4, Department of Computer Science, State University of New York at Stony Brook, 1996.

9. J. Jaffar and J.-L. Lassez. Constraint logic programming. In *Proceedings of the 14th Annual ACM Symposium on Principles of Programming Languages (POPL)*, pages 111–119, 1987.

10. G. Janssens, M. Bruynooghe, and V. Dumortier. A Blueprint for an Abstract Machine for Abstract Interpretation of (Constraint) Logic Programs. In *Proceedings of the International Symposium on Logic Programming (ILPS)*, 1995.

11. D. E. Knuth. *The Stanford GraphBase: A Platform for Combinatorial Computing*. Addison Wesley, 1993.

12. G. Köstler, W. Kiessling, H. Thöne, and U. Güntzer. Fixpoint iteration with subsumption in deductive databases. *Journal of Intelligent Information Systems (JIIS)*, 4(2):123–148, March 1995.

13. T.C. Przymusinski. Every logic program has a natural stratification and an iterated least fixed point model. In *Proceedings of the ACM Symposium on Principle of Database Systems (PODS)*, pages 11–21, 1989.

14. T. Swift. *Efficient Evaluation of Normal Logic Programs*. PhD thesis, Department of Computer Science, State University of New York at Stony Brook, 1994.

15. T. Swift and D. S. Warren. An Abstract Machine for SLG Resolution: Definite Programs. In *Proceedings of the International Symposium on Logic Programming (ILPS)*, pages 633–654, 1994.

16. T. Swift and D. S. Warren. Analysis of sequential SLG evaluation. In *Proceedings of the International Symposium on Logic Programming (ILPS)*, pages 219–238, 1994.

17. A. van Gelder. Foundations of Aggregation in Deductive Databases. In *Proceedings of the International Conference on Deductive and Object-Oriented Databases (DOOD)*, pages 13–34, 1993.

18. A. van Gelder, K.A. Ross, and J.S. Schlipf. Unfounded sets and well-founded semantics for general logic programs. *JACM*, 38(3):620–650, 1991.

Program Sharing: A New Implementation Approach for Prolog

Xining Li

Department of Computer Science
Lakehead University
Thunder Bay, Canada
E-mail: xli@flash.lakeheadu.ca

Abstract. *Structure Sharing* (SS) and *Structure Copying* (SC) are two commonly used term representation methods in various Prolog systems. SS was used in earlier Prolog implementations while SC has been accepted as the *de facto* standard in modern Prolog implementations. Most abstract machines dedicated to Prolog, such as the Warren Abstract Machine(WAM) and the Vienna Abstract Machine(VAM), adopt SC as the fundamental component to implement efficient unification. However, practical comparison of SS and SC shown that programs can be written which make any one method almost arbitrarily worse than the other. In this paper, I propose a new Prolog implementation approach - *Program Sharing* (PS). The major contribution of this work is that PS has the advantages of both SC (representing terms of different types to fit in the size of a machine word) and SS (low overhead in constructing a dynamic structure instance), and the concept of program sharing could be used to realize all special-case instruction-driven unification. This method has been adopted in the design of a new Prolog abstract machine - the LAM$^{\frac{1}{2}}$. I have implemented an experimental LAM$^{\frac{1}{2}}$-emulator in C. Benchmarks show that this new approach is at least as efficient as the WAM-based systems in general while exhibits much better performance to those tasks involving large, complex data structures.

1 Introduction

On an abstract level, two very different methods - Structure Sharing (SS) and Structure Copying (SC), are used to implement term unification in various Prolog systems. SS was first introduced by Boyer and Moore [1] and used in earlier Prolog implementations, such as DEC-10 Prolog [2] and MProlog [3]. The first report of SC implementation came from Bruynooghe [4] and has been accepted as the *de facto* standard in modern Prolog implementations. The abstract machines dedicated to Prolog, such as the WAM [5][6] and the VAM [7], adopt SC as the fundamental component to implement efficient unification. Most of the high performance Prolog systems, such as Aquarius, BIM, Quintus, SICStus and wamcc, are based on the WAM or some WAM-like abstract machine with improved efficiency [8][9][10].

"Although the WAM is a distillation of a long line of experience in Prolog implementation, it is by no means the only possible point to consider in the design space. For example, whereas the WAM adopts *structure copying* to represent Prolog terms, the *structure sharing* representation used in the Marseille and DEC-10 implementation still has much to recommend it"[11].

In this paper, I will briefly compare SS and SC, revisit the principle of SS, and propose a new term representation method - *Program Sharing*. The idea of PS is originated from SS. The significant differences, however, are that PS only needs one pointer to represent a dynamic instance of a structure, and the shared resources are no longer structure skeletons but executable code. The major contribution of this work is that PS has the advantages of both SC (representing terms of different types to fit in the size of a machine word) and SS (low overhead in constructing a dynamic structure instance), and the concept of program sharing could be used to realize all special-case instruction-driven unification.

A new Prolog abstract machine - $LAM^{\frac{1}{2}}$ - will be briefly discussed in section 4. An experimental C-emulator of the $LAM^{\frac{1}{2}}$ has been implemented. I will present the empirical results of the emulator on a small set of hand-translated benchmarks (the translator of Prolog to $LAM^{\frac{1}{2}}$ instructions is in progress). Two existing Prolog systems, SICStus 2.1 (emulated) and BIN-Prolog 3.30, have been compared under the same environment. Performance evaluation shows that the $LAM^{\frac{1}{2}}$ emulator is at least as efficient as the WAM-based systems in general while exhibits much better performance to those tasks involving large, complex data structures.

2 A Brief Review of SC and SS

In a SC system, terms of different types are represented to fit in the size of a machine word/register. Non-structure terms can be handled quite efficiently in most cases. Their unification operations could be simplified into matches and assignments. When a variable comes to stand for a structure, however, a concrete *instance* of the structure must be created in the heap, which includes copying the ground description of the structure and allocating a heap cell for every argument in the structure. Copying a complex structure is a time consuming operation. Furthermore, SC method conceals the knowledge about structures. As soon as a structure has been copied into the heap, the information about its arity and argument types becomes indirectly accessible. Only the instance pointer can be carried around in the future unification. The efficient special term treatments are no longer applicable to a structure instance and its arguments. Therefore, when two terms to be unified are both structure instances, a general unification procedure will be invoked to carry out the stack-based full unification. This procedure forces each pair of terms to go through a sequence of unavoidable operations: push, pop, dereferencing, tag-checking and unification.

On the other hand, a SS system takes advantage of the fact that different instances of the same term could share a single prototype and differ only in their variable bindings. Therefore, the cost of constructing a new structure instance is quite low: it only needs an environment allocation plus a *molecule* assignment. Why has this scheme been abandoned in the latter Prolog implementations? A

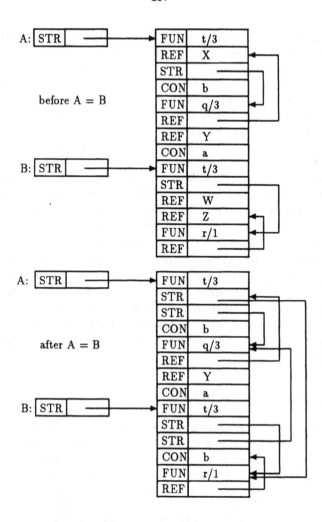

Fig. 1. Term Representations of Structure-Copying

major reason is that a molecule, which is used to represent a dynamic instance of a structure, consists of two components: a pointer to the skeleton of the structure together with a pointer to the global stack frame which contains the variable instances of the structure. There are three commonly used methods for handling molecules: to embed these two components in a single machine word, to allocate two machine words to each variable catering to the contingency that it might be bound to a structure instance, or to allocate a single machine word to each variable which either refers to a non-structure binding or points to a two-cell molecule created on the heap. The problems involved with these methods are that the first scheme makes it impossible to cope with large address space

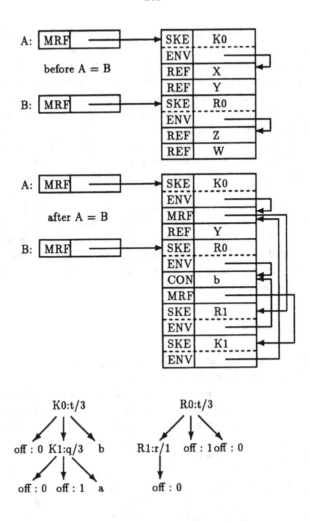

Fig. 2. Term representations of Structure-Sharing

on 32-bit machines, the second method wastes half of the local/global space on non-structure bindings, while the third increases the usage of the global space.

Consider the following Prolog example:

```
?- p(A), q(B), A = B.
p(t(X, q(X, Y, a), b)).
q(t(r(Z), W, Z)).
```

The execution of the query will create two structure instances referenced by A and B respectively and then unify A and B. Fig. 1 and Fig. 2 illustrate term representations of SC and SS, before and after A = B. The third molecule handling scheme, implemented in MProlog, is used in SS representation. A molecule is represented in two successive machine words delimited by a dotted line. When a molecule becomes the binding of a variable, it is created on the heap and its pointer with a tag MRF (molecule reference) is assigned to the variable. In addition, Fig. 2 also shows the structure skeletons in directed graphs, where *off : i* indicates the offset of the *i*th variable in its environment. For this example, SC needs 14 global cells while SS requires 12 global cells to carry out the query.

SC and SS have been thoroughly investigated in [12] [13]. It is faster to create terms in a SS system while it is faster to access (unify) terms in a SC system. Comparison between them shown that programs can be written which make any one method almost arbitrarily worse than the other. As Mellish remarked:"the comparison between structure sharing and its alternative is not a simple one, and no quick answer can be given as to which approach is best. It is interesting, however, that a significant factor in the decision is the relationship between the word size and address size of the machine on which the system is implemented. Unfortunately, neither of the systems discussed is optimal in its use of the local and global stacks. It remains to be seen whether mixed approach can be devised that have the advantages of both."[12]

3 From SS to PS

The idea of SS is to separate static information of a structure from its dynamic instances. Consequently, the static information, *i.e.*, the structure skeleton, could be shared by all instances of the structure, if only care is taken to let them have different variables. I adopt the same idea in my proposal - Program Sharing. The significant differences, however, are that PS only needs one pointer to represent a dynamic instance of a structure, and the shared static information is no longer structure skeletons but executable code.

With PS, nested structures are flattened and then be translated into a set of code segments. Each flattened structure has a unique entry to its code segment. Like SC, PS represents terms of different types to fit the size of a machine word. On the other hand, comparing with SS method, the problem of using two-cell molecules is because we do need a structure skeleton pointer (structure code entry in PS), and an environment pointer. Where is the environment indicator in my scheme? I use a so called *structure code stub* mechanism to solve the two-pointer problem. When a procedure is invocated, an integral heap frame is allocated to hold global variables as well as the structure code entries occurred in the matched clause. I call the heap cell holding a structure code entry as the structure code stub, or just the *stub* in our latter discussion. A binding to a structure instance is in fact bound to its stub address. This stub will serve on two purposes: the stub address is the environment base for executing the structure code, and the stub content gives the entry to the structure code. For example, if a variable binding is a pointer to a stub, then by accessing the stub we have the entry to the code segment which defines the necessary instructions for the structure unification, and by the pointer itself we get the environment base which will be consulted during unification to access global variables and

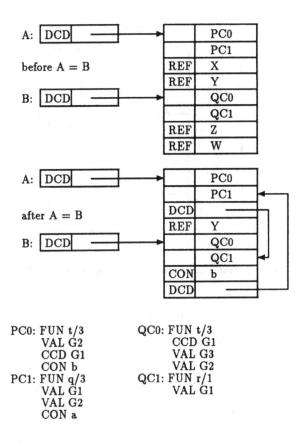

PC0: FUN t/3	**QC0:** FUN t/3
VAL G2	CCD G1
CCD G1	VAL G3
CON b	VAL G2
PC1: FUN q/3	**QC1:** FUN r/1
VAL G1	VAL G1
VAL G2	
CON a	

Fig. 3. Term representations of Program-Sharing

stubs occurred in the structure.

With this setup, Fig. 3 gives the term representation of PS for the example in previous section. When procedure p/1 is called by goal p(A), four heap cells are allocated as an integral heap frame to hold global variables and stubs occurred in p/1, where the first two cells are initialized by stubs (PC0 and PC1) and the next two cells are unbound variables (X and Y). The execution of p/1 will assign a dynamic instruction - stub address of PC0 with opcode DCD - to variable A. The similar behavior happens for the call of q(B). The unification of A and B thus involves four basic pair-wise operations: a functor matching and three assignments. For this example, PS requires only 8 heap cells to carry out the query, while SC and SS need 14 and 12 heap cells respectively.

In SS, variable indices are calculated against a common frame base. If a variable is allocated at the ith cell of the frame, then $\mathit{off} : i$ will be used in all structure/substructure skeletons. For example, $\mathit{off} : 0$ refers to the same variable X in both skeletons of K0 and K1. On the other hand, PS introduces a scope

Global frame

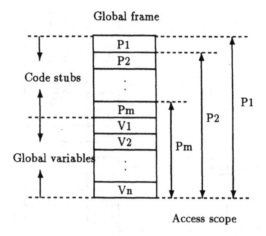

Fig. 4. Frame Allocation and Access Scope of PS

rule to compute the offsets of variables/stubs occurred in each code segment. Suppose that there are m structure code stubs and n global variables occurred in a clause, Fig. 4 shows the heap frame allocated upon the invocation of the clause and illustrates the access scopes of different code segments, where the first m heap cells are stubs which are initialized by code entries of P1 to Pm, and the next n heap cells are global variables. Let G_i represent the ith frame cell against a stub address, then G_{m+1} refers to V1 in code P1 whereas G_1 refers to the same variable in code Pm. Thus, each structure code segment uses the scoped index calculation to decide the offsets of its arguments. The code segments in Fig. 3 have revealed such a fact, for example, G_2 denotes variable X in PC0 whereas G_1 represents the same variable in PC1.

Considering the memory utilization, it is certain that both PS and SS consume less local space than SC, this has been discussed by [12]. As regards global space utilization, PS is clearly better than SS, because it uses one-cell stubs to replace two-cell molecules. Here, I briefly compare the global space consumption of PS and SC.

For a given Prolog program, the number of structure instances to be created in execution is somehow independent of term representation methods. However, different term representation methods require a variable amount of global space for constructing an individual instance. In general, to construct a structure instance T of the form $f(T_1, T_2, ..., T_m)$, the global cells required by PS and SC are shown in Table 1.

	ground(T)	non-ground(T)	$T == [X|L]$
SC	$m+1$	$m+1$	2
PS	0	$\leq m+1$	3

Table 1: Global cells required in constructing a structure instance

In Table 1, non-ground($\mathcal{T}$) indicates that $\mathcal{T}$ contains variables. It is possible that some of T_i's are ground terms and some are repeated variables, thus the global cells required by PS is less than or equal to $m+1$. We use $m+1$ to indicate the number of global cells, however, the 1 in SC represents the cell allocated to the functor of $\mathcal{T}$ whereas in PS it represents the cell assigned to the stub of $\mathcal{T}$. The worst case of PS is to construct a list structure of the form [X|L]. Three cells are required where one cell for its stub and two cells for X and L. On the other hand, SC needs only 2 global cells to represent such a special structure (a list is handled as a structure without functor). From this analysis, I conclude that PS will take no more than 1.5 times of global space as much as SC in the worst case whereas SC will lose by arbitrary amounts in its worst case.

As evidenced by our discussion, to create structure instances in execution, SC turns static information to dynamic; SS maintains static information but involves great overhead for handling molecules; whereas PS takes the advantages of both SC and SS, *i.e.*, it makes static information directly executable instructions and spends much less overhead for handling dynamics. PS is very promising in both time and space utilization, especially for those tasks involving large, complex data structures.

4 LAM$^{\frac{1}{2}}$

Program sharing scheme not only bridges the gap between SS and SC, but also provides a novel basis for designing new Prolog abstract machine. In this section, I will briefly discuss the principle of the LAM$^{\frac{1}{2}}$ (a detailed report on this subject is in progress). We start by outlining the significant differences between the WAM, the VAM and the LAM$^{\frac{1}{2}}$:

- The WAM embeds unification instructions within control sequences and adopts a single engine for both control and unification. On the other hand, the LAM$^{\frac{1}{2}}$ separates control and unification code and cooperates two engines: an one-program-counter (1P) control engine and a two-program-counter (2P) unification engine (this is what the $\frac{1}{2}$ stands for).
- The WAM specifies a set of tags to distinguish terms of different types while the LAM$^{\frac{1}{2}}$ treats terms as executable instructions during unification. In addition, the WAM defines a set of special instructions for handling lists while the LAM$^{\frac{1}{2}}$ treats lists as normal structures.
- The WAM uses a set of general purpose registers as an interface and a two-stage operation (*put-get*) to pass arguments through the interface from a caller to a callee. The LAM$^{\frac{1}{2}}$ eliminates the parameter passing bottleneck by unifying caller and callee's arguments in one step.
- Although the LAM$^{\frac{1}{2}}$ looks like the VAM$_{2P}$ in the sense that they both use the merged caller-callee unification, yet there are two essential differences. First, the VAM$_{2P}$ is basically a SC-based machine, although it eliminates superfluous data on the heap for unifying ground structures. As same as the

WAM, the VAM_{2P} treats terms as tagged data. On the contrary, the $LAM^{\frac{1}{2}}$ is a PS-based machine which shares code instead of copying structures. The $LAM^{\frac{1}{2}}$ sees terms as executable instructions. Secondly, the VAM_{2P} defines separate sets of instructions for head and goal arguments. To enable fast decoding of a pair of instructions, the sum of a goal instruction and a head instruction must be unique. On the other hand, the $LAM^{\frac{1}{2}}$ specifies a set of neutral unification instructions. During execution, an entry to a delayed structure code can be carried by any variable and later be invoked at any place - no matter this variable occurs in a head or a goal. As the matter of fact, Krall and Neumerkel have already noticed this problem: "Another improvement in the VAM_{2P} spirit under investigation is to delay parts of the head unification unless they are needed. In this way, VAM will be more similar to a structure sharing interpreter in cases where structure sharing is more efficient than structure copying"[7].

- In the WAM, the global stack (heap) is used as the container of structure instances. New term instances being constructed are incrementally piled on the top of what already exist in the heap. The heap cells are accessed either by indirect addressing or through a specific register which always contains the next available address on the heap. In the $LAM^{\frac{1}{2}}$, a global frame is an integral memory block which contains global variables and stubs extracted from a clause declaration. It is allocated in the same way as the local stack which reflects chronological order of procedure calls. As a result, the base-plus-index addressing method is used to access local and global variables (stubs).

- The WAM creates structure instances on the fly. If execution is bouncing (backtracking and forwarding) around goals of a clause, structures in those goals might be frequently constructed and destroyed. On the other hand, the $LAM^{\frac{1}{2}}$ initializes all stubs of a clause at the entry of the clause invocation. As long as the clause is active, those stubs can be safely accessed no matter how goals of the clause are executed.

- Two WAM instructions, get_value and unify_value, require the availability of full unification. The $LAM^{\frac{1}{2}}$ implements all special-case instruction-driven unification.

To achieve the best performance, the $LAM^{\frac{1}{2}}$ assumes that a mode declaration is attached to each predicate definition. The mode information can be obtained by user-declaration or through global analysis during compilation. Some modern Prolog implementations also consult this information to generate optimized code. The $LAM^{\frac{1}{2}}$ defines three modes, (+:in, $\wedge$:out, ?:in/out), to indicate the input-argument properties of a procedure. During code generation, we are only interested to the modes of corresponding structure arguments declared in the head of a clause.

A structure argument is a selector if it is ground or its input mode is +. For a non-ground structure argument, the input mode guarantees that it, as well as its nested substructures, can not be instantiated to any variable under any circumstances. The execution of a selector code might consult the current local and global environments, but never change the environment registers.

A structure argument is a pure constructor if its input mode is $\wedge$, *i.e.*, it will always be bound to a variable. This mode will help to generate optimized code such that some global variables occurred inside the structure need not be initialized. As a pure constructor will be bound to an arbitrary variable during execution, a stub is allocated in the global environment to represent its dynamic instance.

A structure argument is a dual if its input mode is ?, that is, it may be used as a selector or a constructor. A dual structure is processed as a constructor except that all global variables occurred inside the structure must be initialized if they don't have a first occurrence.

Although the LAM$^{\frac{1}{2}}$ adopts an 1P-engine for control and a 2P-engine for unification, this can not be seen in code generation. Code segment of a clause is generated with respect to the clause definition. It is also worth to note that the purpose of mode declaration is to improve performance, and deriving mode information through global analysis has become a practical tool for Prolog.

To facilitate the code generation, a Prolog program is first transformed to the LAM$^{\frac{1}{2}}$ assembly code and then be mapped to the LAM$^{\frac{1}{2}}$ abstract machine code. Let R denote a register variable, G a global variable, L a local variable, C a constant, N an integer, E a code entry, and V a R/L/G variable. Table 2 and 3 give the unification instructions (in assembly form) and a subset of control instructions respectively.

The LAM$^{\frac{1}{2}}$ control instructions similar to the WAM's counterpart, which include stack allocation, initialization, execution control, nondeterministic control, and environment manipulation. Unification instructions, however, are defined and implemented in a totally different style. Now, I lay my emphasis on the aspect of unification. From the LAM$^{\frac{1}{2}}$ point of view, there is virtually no data in a pure Prolog program. All terms are coded into LAM$^{\frac{1}{2}}$ unification instructions. Unification is purely pair-wise instruction driven. Objects stored in the execution environment (local stack and global stack) are no longer data objects but either directly executable LAM$^{\frac{1}{2}}$ instructions or code segment entries. These objects will be interpreted as tagged data only in arithmetic operations or some builtin predicates.

Operator	Operand	Meaning
VAR	V	an uninitialized variable or a void variable if V is absent
VAL	V	a variable's value
SCD	E	a selector
CCD	G	a constructor
FUN	C	a functor
CON	C	a constant
INT	N	an integer
NIL		a nil structure

Table 2: Unification Instructions

Operator	OD1	OD2	OD3	Meaning
ALH	N1	N2		allocate a global frame N1: # of initialized global cells N2: # of uninitialized global cells
ALB	N1	N2	N3	allocate both global and local frames N1, N2 as above N3: # of local cells
UNI	E			invoke unification engine E: callee's head unification entry
STB	G	E		initialize a constructor stub G: a stub offset E: the constructor code entry
ENV	N			environment set-up N: # of local cells allocated
CAL	V	E1	E2	call a procedure V: a variable for switching the call or direct call if V is absent E1: caller's goal unification entry E2: callee's control or jump-table entry
LAC	V	E1	E2	last call. V, E1, E2 as above
LOP	V	E1	E2	last chain call. V, E1, E2 as above
PCD				proceed execution
TRY	E			try me else E
RTY	E			retry me else E
TST				trust me

Table 3: Control Instructions

To illustrate the LAM$^{\frac{1}{2}}$ code generation, let us consider a deterministic *append* procedure. Its LAM$^{\frac{1}{2}}$ assembly code is shown in Fig. 5 where an instruction with a trailing star indicates the last instruction of a unification code segment, and an assembly directive .TBL defines a branching table with entries corresponding to variable, nil, constant and structure respectively.

```
:- append(_, ∧, +).
append(L, L, []).
append(L1, [X|L2], [X|L3],):- append(L1, L2, L3).
```

```
ap/3:         .TBL  fail    ap/3.1    fail    ap/3.2
ap/3.1:       UNI   ap/3.1.u.0
              PCD
ap/3.2:       ALH   0       3
              STB   G0      ap/3.2.u.3
              UNI   ap/3.2.u.0
              LOP   R1      ap/3.2.u.1    ap/3

ap/3.1.u.0:   VAR   R0
              VAL   R0
              NIL*
ap/3.2.u.0:   VAR   R0
              CCD   G0
              SCD*  ap/3.2.u.2
ap/3.2.u.1:   VAL   R0
              VAR   G2
              VAL*  R1
ap/3.2.u.2:   VAR   G1
              VAR*  R1
ap/3.2.u.3:   VAL   G1
              VAL*  G2
```

Fig. 5. Append/3 LAM$^{\frac{1}{2}}$ code

Mapping names and instructions in the source assembly code to addresses of run-time objects and abstract machine-level instructions is done by the LAM$^{\frac{1}{2}}$ assembler. Unification instructions have the same coding format: a single (32-bit) machine word consisting of a 4-bit op-code, a 1-bit Last-instruction flag, and a 27-bit operand. Table 4 shows the mapping from assembly instructions to machine-level instructions. Three machine-level instructions, uv, dc and bv, do not have a direct mapping with the assembly code. They are dynamic unification instructions. Instruction uv indicates a unbound variable if its operand is a self-referential pointer, bv is used for avoiding unnecessary trailing/detrailing operations, while dc is used to form a dynamic constructor instruction. The difference between dc and cc is that the former's operand is the absolute address of a stub and the latter's operand is the offset of a stub to the current environment. Four static machine-level instructions, namely, nl, cn, in, and sc, can transform to dynamic instructions. A dynamic instruction is one which can become the binding of a variable. Dereferencing operation terminates when a dynamic instruction is reached. Instructions cc and fn are not dynamic instructions, because a cc binding will always be replaced by its dynamic form dc, while a fn binding violates the law of the first-order logic.

Op-code	Symbol	Operand	Meaning	Mapping
0000	uv	address	a dynamic variable*	
0001	cc	offset	a static constructor	CCD G
0010	gv	offset	a global variable	VAR G
0011	gu	offset	a global value	VAL G
0100	lv	offset	a local variable	VAR L
0101	lu	offset	a local value	VAL L
0110	rv	address	a register variable	VAR R
0111	ru	address	a register value	VAL R
1000	dv	null	a void variable	VAR
1001	nl	null	a nil structure	NIL
1010	cn	address	a constant	CON C
1011	dc	address	a dynamic constructor*	
1100	bv	address	a bridge variable*	
1101	fn	address	a functor	FUN C
1110	in	integer	an integer	INT N
1111	sc	address	a selector	SCD E

Table 4: Abstract Machine Unification Instructions

Like a common processor, the 2P unification engine has the cycle of *fetching*, *decoding* and *executing*, except that it fetches two instructions simultaneously. The decoding phase branches each op-code pair to its corresponding operation. The way of creating this correspondence is to employ a matrix mapping table. An op-code pair will serve as indices to the matrix in order to select a location which contains the operation entry. Table 5 shows the decoding matrix, where the first row enumerates the callee-side op-codes, the first column gives the caller-side op-codes, and an entry in the matrix indicates the operation to be performed. In the matrix, a n_n combination indicates that no operation is required, and a x_x represents an illegal operation. Most of operations are symmetric, such as v_i and i_v, and each of them deals with a special case of unification. For example, the v_i operation simply assigns the head-side instruction to the goal-side variable, and the i_v operation does the reverse assignment. The L-flag is very important in determining the termination of unification. However, space does not permit a detailed discussion of these operations and the usage of the L-flag.

G/H	uv	cc	gv	gu	lv	lu	rv	ru	dv	nl	cn	dc	bv	fn	in	sc
uv	u_u	u_c	u_g	x_x	x_x	x_x	x_x	x_x	x_x	u_i	u_i	u_i	v_b	x_x	u_i	u_i
cc	c_u	t_t	c_v	i_a	c_v	i_a	c_v	i_e	n_n	x_x	x_x	t_t	c_v	x_x	x_x	t_t
gv	g_u	v_c	v_v	i_a	v_v	i_a	v_r	i_e	v_o	v_i	v_i	v_i	v_b	x_x	v_i	v_i
gu	x_x	a_i	a_v	a_a	a_v	a_a	a_r	a_e	n_n	a_i	a_i	x_x	x_x	x_x	a_i	a_i
lv	x_x	v_c	l_g	v_a	v_v	v_a	v_r	i_e	v_o	v_i	v_i	v_i	l_b	x_x	v_i	v_i
lu	x_x	a_i	a_i	a_a	a_v	a_a	a_r	a_e	n_n	a_i	a_i	x_x	x_x	x_x	a_i	a_i
rv	x_x	x_x	x_x	x_x	x_x	x_x	x_x	x_x	x_x	x_x	x_x	x_x	x_x	x_x	x_x	x_x
ru	x_x	e_i	e_i	e_a	e_i	e_a	a_v	e_e	n_n	e_i	e_i	x_x	x_x	x_x	e_i	e_i
dv	x_x	n_n	o_v	n_n	o_v	n_n	o_v	n_n	n_n	n_n	n_n	x_x	x_x	x_x	n_n	n_n
nl	i_u	x_x	i_v	i_a	i_v	i_a	i_v	i_e	n_n	n_n	x_x	x_x	i_v	x_x	x_x	x_x
cn	i_u	x_x	i_v	i_a	i_v	i_a	i_v	i_e	n_n	x_x	i_i	x_x	i_v	x_x	x_x	x_x
dc	i_u	t_t	i_v	x_x	i_v	x_x	i_v	x_x	x_x	x_x	x_x	t_t	i_v	x_x	x_x	t_t
bv	b_v	v_c	b_v	x_x	b_l	x_x	x_x	x_x	x_x	v_i	v_i	v_i	v_b	x_x	v_i	v_i
fn	x_x	x_x	x_x	x_x	x_x	x_x	x_x	x_x	x_x	x_x	x_x	x_x	x_x	i_i	x_x	x_x
in	i_u	x_x	i_v	i_a	i_v	i_a	i_v	i_e	n_n	x_x	x_x	x_x	i_v	x_x	i_i	x_x
sc	i_u	t_t	i_v	i_a	i_v	i_a	i_v	i_e	n_n	x_x	x_x	t_t	i_v	x_x	x_x	t_t

Table 5: Decoding Matrix

I have implemented a $LAM^{\frac{1}{2}}$ C-emulator which copes with a small set of builtin predicates and without stack overflow checking. The $LAM^{\frac{1}{2}}$ emulator is compiled using gcc 2.7.2 with the -O option. It uses the features offered by the GNU C to declare global register variables and to transfer control through indirect jump instead of case switch. Timings of a small set of hand-translated benchmarks are in millisecond measured on a SUN SPARC IPC with 8 megabytes of memory. Table 6 gives the $LAM^{\frac{1}{2}}$ benchmark statistics which include the number of logic inferences (procedure calls), control instructions and unification instruction-pairs executed, average number of instructions per logic inference, maximum global and local space (words) consumed, execution time and KLIPS. Table 7 compares the performances of the $LAM^{\frac{1}{2}}$ emulator, SICStus 2.1 (emulated) and BIN-Prolog 3.30.

It should be pointed out that my experimental results only give a rough performance evaluation. First, the $LAM^{\frac{1}{2}}$ emulator is not a complete system. It does not perform stack-overflow checking. Adding this function could influence the empirical results. However, an idea proposed by [10] suggests to use UNIX memory manager to raise an exception signal in case of stack overflow, and therefore eliminates costly software tests. Secondly, benchmarks are small and hand-translated with optimizations based on annotated mode. This is unfair towards the compared systems because mode information helps to generate better code. Despite these factors, the performance evaluation suggests that the

$LAM^{\frac{1}{2}}$ emulator is as efficient as the WAM-based systems in general while exhibits much better performance to those tasks involving large, complex data structures, as evidenced by the *zebra* (Zebra Puzzle by Claude Sammut) and the *puzzle* (Music Man Puzzle by Paul Tarau) benchmarks. Interesting readers might want to compare these two benchmarks with the performances of some well-known Prolog compilers, they will find that the $LAM^{\frac{1}{2}}$ C-emulated results are even competitive with the execution times of the native code.

	nrev30	qsort50	tak(18,10,6)	queen8	serialise	mu	puzzle	zebra
Logic Inferences	496	373	8889	1680	227	605	4693	15708
C-instructions	1550	2331	75556	12219	1530	4036	25709	80828
U-Instr-pairs	2475	2069	35556	9252	2706	6055	48542	247403
Instr-per-LI	8.11	11.8	12.5	12.8	18.7	16.7	15.8	20.1
Max global	1365	816	0	89	364	84	258	35
Max local	215	59	201	147	549	119	502	168
Execution time(ms)	3.67	3.85	121	19.3	4.43	11.36	80.0	332
KLIPS	135	97	73	87	51	53	58	47

Table 6: $LAM^{\frac{1}{2}}$ Benchmark Statistics

	nrev30	qsort50	tak(18,10,6)	queen8	serialise	mu	puzzle	zebra
LAM	3.67	3.85	121	19.3	4.43	11.36	80	332
SIC	4.00	7.00	241	35.2	5.68	9.80	140	551
BIN	5.50	8.00	250	37.0	7.50	12.16	140	700

Table 7: Performance Comparison

Although there is a suggestion that it is unreliable to use LIPS as the performance unit, I believe that the LIPS does somehow reflect the performance of a Prolog system for real Prolog programs. Some Prolog systems have remarkable peak performances. For deterministic or arithmetic programs, these systems could achieve over 1 MLIPS. However, for backtracking and unification intensive programs, their performances degenerate to several tens KLIPS. The reason of this, I believe, is not only because different procedures carry out different amounts of work, but also (mainly) because these systems adpot SC as their term representation method which is not an ideal model for handling large, complicated data structures. On the other hand, the difference of the LIPS measurements under the $LAM^{\frac{1}{2}}$ emulator is much smaller.

5 Conclusion

In this paper, I have briefly compared two commonly used term representation methods in implementing Prolog, and proposed a new approach - Program Sharing. The major contribution of this research is that PS has the advantages of both SC (representing data object in a single machine word) and SS (low overhead in constructing a dynamic structure instance). PS could be viewed as a superior alternative to SC and SS in implementing high performance logic programming systems.

Based on PS, a Prolog abstract machine - the $LAM^{\frac{1}{2}}$ has been designed. From the $LAM^{\frac{1}{2}}$ point of view, there is virtually no data in a pure Prolog program.

All terms are compiled into and handled as executable instructions. Unification is purely pair-wise instruction driven. Objects stored in execution environment are no longer tagged data but either directly executable unification instructions or code segment entries. Performance evaluation shows that this new approach is very promising in both time and space utilization, especially for those tasks involving large, complex data structures.

Study on the $\text{LAM}^{\frac{1}{2}}$ is now being concentrated on the refinement of the instruction set, completing the emulator to cope with full Prolog, and the design of a $\text{LAM}^{\frac{1}{2}}$-based compiler. In addition, the $\text{LAM}^{\frac{1}{2}}$ offers a great potential in the design of a simple but efficient logic machine in hardware. This will be another subject of my future work.

Finally, I would like to express my appreciation to the Natural Science and Engineering Council of Canada for supporting this research. The anonymous referees helped to improve this paper. Special thanks to Dr. Bart Demoen for providing benchmark statistics with SICStus.

References

1. R. S. Boyer and J. S. Moore. The Sharing of Structure in Theorem Proving Programs. *Machine Intelligence 7 (B. Meltzer and D. Miche, eds.)*, Edinburgh University Press, 1972, pp. 101-116.

2. D. H. D. Warren. Logic Programming and Compiler Writing. *Technique Report: DAI 44, University of Edinburgh*, 1977.

3. Z. Farkas, P. Koves and P. Szeredi. MProlog: An Implementation Overview. *Implementations of Logic Programming Systems, Kluwer Academic Publishers*, 1994, pp. 103-117.

4. M. Bruynooghe. An Interpreter for Predicate Programs: Part 1. *Technique Report CW 16*, Katholieke Universiteit Leuven, 1976.

5. D. H. D. Warren. An Abstract Prolog Instruction Set. *Technical Note 209*, SIR International, 1983.

6. H. Ait-Kaci. Warren's Abstract Machine: a Tutorial Reconstruction. *MIT Press*, 1991.

7. A. Krall and U. Neumerkel. The Vienna Abstract Machine. In *PLILP'90, LNCS. Springer*, 1990.

8. P. Van Roy and A. M. Despain. High-Performance Logic Programming with the Aquarius Prolog Compiler. *IEEE Computer*, Vol. 25, No. 1, 1992, pp. 54-68.

9. E. Tick and G. Succi. Implementations of Logic Programming Systems. *Kluwer Academic Publishers*, 1994.

10. P. Codognet and D. Diaz. wamcc: Compiling Prolog to C. *PLILP'95, The MIT Press*, 1995.

11. D. H. D. Warren. Foreword in *Warren's Abstract Machine: a Tutorial Reconstruction. MIT Press*, 1991, pp. xiii-xiv.

12. C. S. Mellish. An Alternative to Structure Sharing in the Implementation of a Prolog Interpreter. *Logic Programming, Academic Press*, 1982.

13. M. Bruynooghe. The Memory Management of Prolog Implementations. *Logic Programming, Academic Press*, 1982.

Systematic Extraction and Implementation of Divide-and-Conquer Parallelism

Sergei Gorlatch

University of Passau, D–94030 Passau, Germany

Abstract. Homomorphisms are functions that match the divide-and-conquer paradigm and thus can be computed in parallel. Two problems are studied for homomorphisms on lists: (1) parallelism *extraction*: finding a homomorphic representation of a given function; (2) parallelism *implementation*: deriving an efficient parallel program that computes the function. A systematic approach to parallelism extraction proceeds by generalization of two sequential representations based on traditional *cons* lists and dual *snoc* lists. For some non-homomorphic functions, e.g., the maximum segment sum problem, our method provides an embedding into a homomorphism. The implementation is addressed by introducing a subclass of distributable homomorphisms and deriving for them a parallel program schema, which is time optimal on the hypercube architecture. The derivation is based on equational reasoning in the Bird-Meertens formalism, which guarantees the correctness of the parallel target program. The approach is illustrated with function *scan* (parallel prefix), for which the combination of our two systematic methods yields the "folklore" hypercube algorithm, usually presented *ad hoc* in the literature.

1 Motivation and Notation

The problem of programming parallel machines can be managed if put on a solid formal basis, which allows to address both correctness and performance issues during the design process, rather than as an afterthought. This paper deals with divide-and-conquer parallelism by studying functions called homomorphisms.

Definition 1. A function h defined on lists is a *homomorphism* iff there exists a binary associative operation $\circledast$ such that, for all lists x and y:

$$h(x \mathbin{+\!\!+} y) = h(x) \circledast h(y) \tag{1}$$

where $+\!\!+$ is the list concatenation.

Intuitively this means that the value of h on the concatenated list depends in a particular way, using the *combine operation* $\circledast$, on the values of h applied to the pieces of the list. The computations of $h(x)$ and $h(y)$ are independent and can be carried out in parallel, so (1) can be viewed as expressing the well-known divide-and-conquer paradigm. Examples of homomorphisms are simple functions, such as summing up the elements of a list of numbers, and also more complicated and important functions like *scan* (prefix sums) [5].

In the Bird-Meertens formalism (BMF) [4, 26], functions including homomorphisms are defined on arbitrary composite types (trees, arrays, etc.), and equational reasoning is used for deriving programs by transformation [29]. The use of higher-order functions has been popular in the data-parallel setting [18].

We restrict ourselves to non-empty lists and use the following notation (for brevity, definitions are informal):

$[\alpha]$ the type of lists whose elements are of type α;

$+\!\!\!+$ list concatenation;

$\circ$ backward functional composition;

$map\,f$ *map* of an unary function f, i.e. $map\,f\,[x_1,\ldots,x_n] = [fx_1,\ldots,fx_n]$;

$red\,(\odot)$ *reduce* with a binary associative operation $\odot : \alpha \to \alpha \to \alpha$,
       $red\,(\odot)\,[x_1,\ldots,x_n] = x_1 \odot x_2 \odot \ldots \odot x_n$;

$<\,>$ Backus' FP *construction*: $<f_1,\ldots,f_n>x = (f_1\,x,\ldots,f_n\,x)$;

$zip\,(\odot)$ combines elements of two lists of equal length with operation $\odot$,
       $zip\,(\odot)\,([x_1,\ldots,x_n],[y_1,\ldots,y_n]) = [(x_1 \odot y_1),\ldots,(x_n \odot y_n)]$.

Theorem 2 (Bird [4]). *Function h is a homomorphism iff it can be factored into the composition:*

$$h = red\,(\circledast) \circ (map\,f) \tag{2}$$

We write $hom\,(f,\circledast)$ for the unique homomorphism with combine operation $\circledast$, such that $h\,([a]) = f\,(a)$, for all a. The theorem provides a standard parallelization pattern for all homomorphisms as a composition of two *stages* [13]. Whereas the first stage in (2), *map*, is totally parallel, the reduction can be computed in parallel on a tree-like structure, with $\circledast$ applied in the nodes.

There are two main problems with homomorphisms:

• *Parallelism extraction.* It would be desirable to be able to extract the homomorphic parallelism of a given function h, i.e., to find the corresponding combine operation $\circledast$ satisfying property (1). For functions like *length* this construction is simple, but already for the *scan* function it requires a formal correctness proof [23] or intuition [15]. For non-homomorphic functions, the problem is how to "massage" them into a homomorphism [7].

• *Parallelism implementation.* The reduction stage of (2) may be inefficient: e.g., for functions which yield lists, its direct implementation has linear time complexity because of communication, and this cannot be improved by increasing the number of processor [27].

We propose systematic approaches to both problems and present them as follows. In Section 2, we consider two sequential functional representations, based on *cons* and *snoc* lists, and show that their generalization as terms can be used for extracting a homomorphic representation. Section 3 extends this method to non-homomorphic functions and illustrates it for a well-known problem, maximum segment sum. In Section 4, we consider homomorphisms whose direct parallel implementation suffers from high communication costs and introduce a subclass, called DH (distributable homomorphisms), for which these costs can be cut down. A common parallel implementation schema for DH is derived and mapped onto a hypercube in Section 5. We illustrate with the *scan* function: its homomorphic representation is extracted in Section 2; then, in Section 6, it is systematically adjusted to the DH-format and implemented on the hypercube, yielding the "folklore" algorithm, which is usually presented in an *ad hoc* manner [25]. We compare to the related work in Section 7 and then conclude.

2 Extracting Homomorphisms

We restrict ourselves to finite non-empty lists. Whereas homomorphic representations use list concatenation, traditional functional programming is based on the constructors *cons* and *snoc*. We use $\cdot:$ for *cons*, which attaches an element at the front of the list, and $:\cdot$ for *snoc*, which attaches the element at the list's end.

Definition 3. List function h is called *leftwards* (*lw*) iff there exists a binary operation $\oplus$, such that $h\,(a \cdot: y) = a \oplus h(y)$ for all elements a and lists y. Dually, function h is *rightwards* (*rw*) iff, for some $\otimes$, $h\,(x :\cdot b) = h(x) \otimes b$.

Since $\oplus$ and $\otimes$ may be complicated, many functions are either *lw* or *rw* or both. Following fact was proved by Meertens and presented systematically by Gibbons [9, 11].

Theorem 4. *Function h is a homomorphism iff it is leftwards and rightwards.*

Unfortunately, as pointed out in [11], the theorem does not provide a way to construct the homomorphic representation of a function from its *lw* and *rw* terms. We try to rectify this by introducing a new definition.

Definition 5. Function h is called *left-homomorphic* (*lh*) iff there exists (possibly non-associative) combine operation $\oplus$, such that $h\,(a \cdot: y) = h\,([a]) \oplus h\,(y)$. The dual definition of *right-homomorphic* (*rh*) function is obvious.

Every *lh* (*rh*) function is also *lw* (*rw*), but, e.g., function g is *lw* but not *lh*:

$$g\,[a] = |a|$$
$$g\,(a \cdot: y) = \text{if}\ \ a \le g\,(y)\ \ \text{then}\ \ |a + g\,(y)|\ \ \text{else}\ \ |a - g\,(y)|$$

Theorem 6. *If function h is a homomorphism with combine operation $\circledast$, i.e., $h = \mathrm{hom}\,(f, \circledast)$, then h is both lh and rh with the same combine operation. If function h is lh or rh, and the combine operation is associative, then h is a homomorphism with this combine operation.*

Proof: see [12], where we prove a slightly stronger proposition.

The following example (courtesy of J. Gibbons) shows why the test for associativity in the second part of the theorem is necessary. The identity function *id* on lists can be defined as both *lh* and *rh* with combine operation: $u \circledast v = [head\,u] \mathbin{+\!\!+} init\,v \mathbin{+\!\!+} tail\,u \mathbin{+\!\!+} [last\,v]$, but it is clearly not a homomorphism with this operation.

Theorem 6 suggests a possible way to find a homomorphic representation: construct a *cons* definition of the function in the *lh* format (or, dually, find an *rh* representation on *snoc* lists) and prove that the combine operation is associative. Sometimes this simple method works, as the following example of function *length*, computing the length of a list, demonstrates.

Example 1. Since $length([a]) = 1$, we have $f = one$, where $one(x) = 1$. The *cons*-definition: $length(a : y) = 1 + length(y) = length([a]) + length(y)$. Thus *length* is *lh*. From Theorem 6 and associativity of $+$: $length = hom(one, +)$.

Our next example demonstrates that the method with *lh/rh* representations does not always go that smoothly.

Example 2. A more complicated example is function *scan* which, for an associative operation $\odot$ and a list, returns the list of the "running totals" with $\odot$, e.g.: $scan(\odot)([a, b, c, d]) = [a, a \odot b, a \odot b \odot c, a \odot b \odot c \odot d]$.

The sequential *cons* definition of *scan* is as follows:

$$scan(\odot)(a : y) = a : (map(a \odot)(scan(\odot)y)) \tag{3}$$

Here, so-called sectioning is exploited in that we fix one argument of $\odot$ and obtain the unary function $(a \odot)$, which can be *mapped*.

Representation (3) does not match the *lh* format because a is used where only $scan[a]$ is allowed. Since $scan[a] = [a]$, there are different possibilities to express a via $scan[a]$, e.g., $a = fst(scan[a])$ or $a = last(scan[a])$, or we could use $((scan[a]) +\!\!+)$ for $(a :)$. Thus we obtain six possible terms for $\circledast$; however, none of these terms defines an associative operation!

Let us try to use rightwards-homomorphy in the *snoc* definition:

$$scan(\odot)(x : b) = (scan(\odot)x) : (last(scan(\odot)x) \odot b) \tag{4}$$

Alas, we run into a similar problem as for *cons* lists: both obvious substitutions for b, namely $fst(scan[b])$ and $last(scan[b])$, lead to a non-associative operation, and thus we are still not able to express the *scan*-function as a homomorphism.

We proceed with general considerations and then get back to the example. According to Definition 1, there is a term TH over $h(x)$ and $h(y)$ that defines an associative operation: $TH : h(x) \circledast h(y)$. For term T, let $T.\{u \mapsto c\}$ denotes the result of substituting c for variable u in T. The following two terms, built from TH by substitutions: $TL = TH.\{x \mapsto [a]\}$ and $TR = TH.\{y \mapsto [b]\}$, are obviously in the *lh* and *rh* format (see Definition 5), correspondingly.

Terms TL and TR are semantically equivalent to all *cons* and *snoc* representations of function h, correspondingly. In Example 2, we have unsuccessfully tried to pick a *cons* term TC or a *snoc* term TS and to transform them into the desired format using various equalities of the theory of lists. In the following, $T_1 \overset{E}{=} T_2$ means that terms T_1 and T_2 are semantically equivalent in equational theory E.

Relations between the terms introduced so far are illustrated in the following diagram by solid lines:

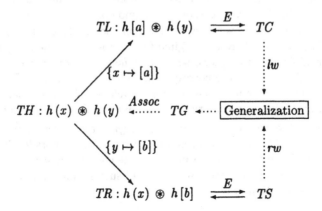

Our ultimate goal is to find term TH from given TC and TS, e.g., for *scan* function, TC and TS are the right-hand sides of (3) and (4), correspondingly. We use so-called *generalization* or *anti-unification* of terms [16].

Definition 7. *Generalization* in equational theory E of terms T_1 and T_2 w.r.t. substitutions σ_1 and σ_2 is term $TG = Gen_E\{T_1 \mid \sigma_1, T_2 \mid \sigma_2\}$, which satisfies $TG.\{\sigma_1\} \stackrel{E}{=} T_1$ and $TG.\{\sigma_2\} \stackrel{E}{=} T_2$.

Theorem 8. *If an lw term TC and an rw term TS, both for function h, are generalized to the term $Gen_E\{TC \mid \{x \mapsto [a]\}, TS \mid \{y \mapsto [b]\}\}$, which defines an associative operation ⊛, then h is a homomorphism with ⊛ as combine operation.*

We call the generalization in Theorem 8 the *CS-Generalization* (CS for "Cons + Snoc") in the theory of lists E. The envisaged CS method of finding the combine operation can be understood from the above diagram by moving along the dotted arrows. Two terms provided by the user, TC for a *cons* and TS for a *snoc* representation of function h, are first checked to be in the *lw/rw* format, correspondingly. If so, they are CS-generalized to term TG, and then associativity of the operation defined by TG is checked.

For function *scan*, representation (3) is obviously *lw* and (4) is *rw*. Their CS-generalization yields term

$$TG = scan(\odot)\,x \mathbin{+\mkern-10mu+} (\,map\ (last(scan(\odot)\,x)\odot)\ (scan(\odot)\,y)\,)$$

The operation ⊛ defined by TG is associative:

$$u \circledast v = u \mathbin{+\mkern-10mu+} map\,(last(u)\odot)\,v \tag{5}$$

Therefore, *scan* is a homomorphism: $scan(\odot) = hom([.], \circledast)$, with ⊛ from (5).

Designing a CS-generalization procedure and investigating its properties is our present topic of research, which is beyond the scope of this paper.

The next section shows that the CS approach is even more useful in case of non-homomorphic functions.

3 Almost-Homomorphisms

Many practical non-homomorphic functions are so-called *almost-homomorphism*: they are convertible to a composition of a homomorphism and some adjusting function. Cole [7] reports several case studies on constructing a homomorphism as a tuple of functions, where the original function is one of the components. [1]

The main difficulty is to guess, which *auxiliary functions* must be included in a tuple and then to find the corresponding combine operation. Usually, this requires a lot of ingenuity from the program developer. We show that the "cons + snoc" approach allows to construct tuple-homomorphisms systematically.

Example 3. We consider the *maximum segment sum* (*mss*) problem – a *programming pearl* [3], which has been studied by many authors [4, 7, 26, 28].

Given a list of integers, function *mss* finds the contiguous segment of the list whose members have the largest sum among all such segments and returns this sum, e.g., in the notation of [7]:

$$mss\,[\,2, -4, 2, -1, 6, -3\,] = 7$$

where the result is contributed by the segment $[2, -1, 6]$. The empty segment is defined to have sum 0, so the result is always non-negative.

Let us first express function *mss* over *cons* lists. For some element a and list y, it may well be the case that $mss\,(a \,:\, y) = (mss\,[a]) \uparrow (mss\,y)$, where $\uparrow$ returns the larger of its two integer arguments. But we must not overlook the possibility that the true segment of interest includes both a and some (initial) segment of y. Therefore, we have to introduce an auxiliary function *mis* which yields the sum of the *maximum initial segment*. We add the definition of *mis* and obtain the following closed definition of the tuple function $< mss, mis >$ on *cons* lists:

$$mss\,(a \,:\, y) = mss\,[a] \uparrow mss\,y \uparrow (a + mis\,y)$$
$$mis\,(a \,:\, y) = mis\,[a] \uparrow (a + mis\,y)$$

Our approach requires to define *mss* on *snoc* lists. This leads to another auxiliary function, *mcs*, yielding the sum of the *maximum concluding segment*:

$$mss\,(x \,:\, b) = mss\,x \uparrow (mcs\,x + b) \uparrow mss\,[b]$$
$$mcs\,(x \,:\, b) = (mcs\,x + b) \uparrow mcs\,[b]$$

The introduction of tuples requires the following natural extension of the CS method: (1) the notion of homomorphism is straightforwardly extended for tuples; (2) generalization works for representations of the *union tuple* which in the *mss*-example is: $< mss, mis > \cup < mss, mcs > \, = \, < mss, mis, mcs >$.

Trying to find a *cons*-definition for *mcs* and a *snoc*-definition for *mis*, we see that, e.g., the concluding segment of $(a \,:\, y)$ may be the whole list, so we need to know its sum, which no (combination) of the three functions can yield. We have to introduce one more auxiliary function *ts* (for *total sum*).

---

[1] Actually, every function can be made "homomorphic" by tupling with the identity function, however, this trivial case is clearly of no interest for parallelization.

The constructed quadruple $< mss, mis, mcs, ts >$ has following *cons* and *snoc* representations which are obviously *lw* and *rw*, correspondingly:

$$
\begin{array}{l|l}
mss\,(a : y) = mss\,[a]\uparrow(a + mis\,y)\uparrow mss\,y & mss\,(x : b) = mss\,x\uparrow(mcs\,x + b)\uparrow mss\,[b] \\
mis\,(a : y) = mis\,[a]\uparrow(a + mis\,y) & mis\,(x : b) = mis\,x\uparrow(ts\,x + b) \\
mcs\,(a : y) = mcs\,y\uparrow(a + ts\,y) & mcs\,(x : b) = mcs\,[b]\uparrow(mcs\,x + ts\,[b]) \\
ts\,(a : y) = ts\,[a] + ts\,y & ts\,(x : b) = ts\,x + ts\,[b]
\end{array}
$$

After applying the CS-generalization procedure pair-wise (see [12] for details) we obtain the following combine operation:

$$
\begin{aligned}
(mss\,x, mis\,x, mcs\,x, ts\,x) \circledast (mss\,y, mis\,y, mcs\,y, ts\,y) = \\
(\,mss\,x \uparrow (mcs\,x + mis\,y) \uparrow mss\,y\,,\ mis\,x \uparrow (ts\,x + mis\,y)\,, \\
mcs\,y \uparrow (mcs\,x + ts\,y)\,,\ (ts\,x + ts\,y)\,)
\end{aligned}
$$

Since $\circledast$ is associative, our tuple is the homomorphism: $< mss, mis, mcs, ts >=$ $hom\,(f, \circledast)$, where f determines the result of the tuple on singleton list:

$$
f\,(a) = < mss, mis, mcs, ts > [a] = (a\uparrow 0,\ a\uparrow 0,\ a\uparrow 0,\ a)
$$

The target function *mss* is therefore computable as follows:

$$
mss = fst \circ red\,(\circledast) \circ (map\,f)
$$

If both function f and operation $\circledast$ require constant time, the total time complexity of this homomorphic algorithm is $O(\log n)$. The processor number can be reduced to $O(n/\log n)$ by simulating lower levels of the tree sequentially, based on Brent's theorem [25]. Therefore, the algorithm is both time and cost optimal.

In [12], we apply our "*cons + snoc* with generalization" method also to the parsing problem for so-called input-driven languages [8].

4 Concatenating and Distributable Homomorphisms

In this section, we address the second problem of the paper, finding an efficient parallel implementation for a given homomorphism.

The well-known difficulty arises when the output of a list homomorphism is a list again. In this case, the combine term has $+\!\!+$ as its top function: $com\text{-}op\,(u, v) = f\,(u, v) +\!\!+ g\,(u, v)$; we call such homomorphisms *concatenating*. The reduce stage starts from the singleton lists after the map stage and arrives at a "long" result list at the root of the tree. The communication of lists of growing length induces linear execution time, independently of the number of processors [27].

From (5) follows that *scan* is a concatenating homomorphism. However, there exist parallel logarithmic algorithms for *scan* with good performance on parallel machines [25]: rather than producing a monolithic output list, they distribute it between processors. Our goal is to derive such algorithms systematically.

From now on, we restrict ourselves to *powerlists* [21] of length 2^k, $k = 0, 1, \ldots$ with *balanced* concatenation and reduction: $x +\!\!+ y$ and $red\,(\odot)\,(x +\!\!+ y)$ are defined iff $length\,x = length\,y = 2^k$.

Definition 9. Distributable combine operation, $\oplus\!\!\otimes$, on lists x and y of equal length:

$$x \,\oplus\!\!\otimes\, y \;=\; zip\,(\oplus)\,(x, y) \;+\!\!\!+\; zip\,(\otimes)\,(x, y) \tag{6}$$

where $\oplus$ and $\otimes$ are arbitrary binary associative operations on elements.

Definition 10. *Distributable homomorphism* (DH), denoted $(\oplus\updownarrow\otimes)$ for associative operations $\oplus$ and $\otimes$, is the unique homomorphism: $\oplus\updownarrow\otimes \;=\; hom([.], \oplus\!\!\otimes)$ with $\oplus\!\!\otimes$ defined by (6).

Figure 1 illustrates, how DH is computed on a concatenation of two lists; dashed arrows denote replication of the partial results.

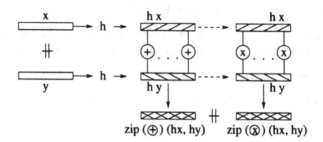

Fig. 1. Distributable homomorphism: an illustration

As a simple example, let us consider the function *sumd*: for a list of numbers $x \;=\; [x_1, x_2, \ldots, x_n]$, it yields: $sumd\ x \;=\; [sum\,x, sum\,x, \ldots, sum\,x]$, where $sum\ x \;=\; x_1 + x_2 + \cdots + x_n$ yields the sum of the list elements. It is easy to express *sumd* in the component-wise format (6):

$$sumd\,(x \,+\!\!\!+\, y) = zip\,(+)\,(sumd\,x, sumd\,y) \;+\!\!\!+\; zip\,(+)\,(sumd\,x, sumd\,y)$$

Hence, $sumd \;=\; +\!\updownarrow\!+$. Generally, we will use the function called "distributed reduction", defined as $redd\,(\odot)\,x \;=\; [red\,(\odot)\,x, red\,(\odot)\,x, \ldots, red\,(\odot)\,x]$:

$$redd\,(\odot) \;=\; \odot\!\updownarrow\!\odot \tag{7}$$

This function is implemented as **AllReduce** primitive in the MPI standard [30].

5 Towards an Efficient Parallel Implementation

Our ultimate goal is to find a provably correct and efficient parallel implementation for all DH functions. In this section, we first design an architecture-independent implementation schema and then map it onto hypercube topology. For that, we introduce some auxiliary functions on powerlists.

Our first two functions do simple rearrangements:

$$att : nat \rightarrow \alpha \rightarrow (nat, \alpha) \qquad glue : \alpha \rightarrow (nat, \alpha) \rightarrow (nat, \alpha, \alpha)$$
$$att\ i\ x \;=\; (i, x) \qquad\qquad glue\ a\ (i, b) \;=\; (i, a, b)$$

Function *permute* interchanges pair-wise elements which have a given distance between their positions in the list, (the distance is the first argument of *permute*). The function attaches to each element a flag which is equal to 0, if the element has changed its position to the left and 1, otherwise:

$permute : nat \rightarrow [\alpha] \rightarrow [(nat, \alpha)]$
$permute\ k\ (x +\!\!\!+ y) = permute\ k\ x +\!\!\!+ permute\ k\ y ,$ if $(k < length(x))$
$permute\ k\ (x +\!\!\!+ y) = map\,(att\,0)\ y +\!\!\!+ map\,(att\,1)\ x ,$ if $(k = length(x))$

Function *triples* composes a list and the result of its permutation together:

$triples : nat \rightarrow [\alpha] \rightarrow [(nat, \alpha, \alpha)]$
$triples\ k\ x = zip\,(glue)\,(x,\ permute\ k\ x)$

Function *apply* performs one of two binary operations ($\oplus$ or $\otimes$) on the elements of a list of triples, depending on the value of the flag:

$apply : ((\alpha \rightarrow \alpha \rightarrow \alpha), (\alpha \rightarrow \alpha \rightarrow \alpha)) \rightarrow (nat, \alpha, \alpha) \rightarrow \alpha$
$apply\ (\oplus, \otimes)\,(i,\ a,\ b) = if\ (i = 0)\ then\ (a \oplus b)\ else\ (b \otimes a)$

Figure 2 illustrates how function *permute* and the next introduced function, *step*, work on a 4-element list.

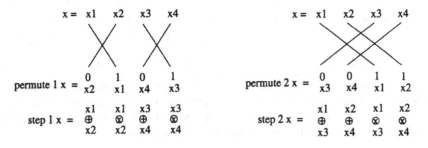

Fig. 2. Functions *permute* and *step*: an illustration

$step : nat \rightarrow ((\alpha \rightarrow \alpha \rightarrow \alpha), (\alpha \rightarrow \alpha \rightarrow \alpha)) \rightarrow [\alpha] \rightarrow [\alpha]$
$step\ k\ (\oplus, \otimes) = map\,(apply\,(\oplus, \otimes)) \circ (triples\ k)$

The following function, *iter*, does a sequence of *step* applications:

$iter : nat \rightarrow nat \rightarrow ((\alpha \rightarrow \alpha \rightarrow \alpha), (\alpha \rightarrow \alpha \rightarrow \alpha)) \rightarrow [\alpha] \rightarrow [\alpha]$
$iter\ k\ j\ (\oplus, \otimes) = id ,$ if $(k = j)$
$iter\ k\ j\ (\oplus, \otimes) = (iter\,(2 * k)\ j\ (\oplus, \otimes)) \circ (step\ k\ (\oplus, \otimes)) ,$ if $(k < j)$

The definition of *iter* is *tail-recursive*, with an obvious iterative implementation, rather than the usual *cascading recursion* in a homomorphism. The following theorem establishes the equivalence of these two forms.

Theorem 11. *For arbitrary associative $\oplus$ and $\otimes$ and lists of length 2^k:*

$$\oplus \updownarrow \otimes = iter\ 1\ k\ (\oplus, \otimes) \tag{8}$$

Proof: by induction on k.

The theorem provides a common iterative computation schema for all DH functions. The next step is to map this architecture-independent solution onto a particular processor topology. As an example, let us consider the hypercube.

Our lists of length $n = 2^k$ are stored in a k-dimensional hypercube with n nodes. The standard encoding is used: the position i, $0 \leq i < n$, of a list is stored in the node i, whose index is the k-bit binary representation of i.

The access function on hypercube:

$$hyp : [\alpha] \rightarrow nat \rightarrow \alpha$$

yields, for list x and index i, the ith element of x.

Each processor of the hypercube can communicate directly with its k neighbours, whose indices differ in one bit position; this position determines the dimension, in which the communication takes place. In each dimension, $n/2$ pairs of processors can communicate simultaneously, without dilation or congestion. For processor i, its partner in the dimension $d = 1, 2, \ldots, k$ is computed as $p(i, d) = xor(i, 2^{d-1})$, where xor is "bit-wise exclusive OR".

Definition 12. Function $swap$ expresses a pattern of the hypercube behaviour:

$$swap : nat \rightarrow ((\alpha \rightarrow \alpha \rightarrow \alpha), (\alpha \rightarrow \alpha \rightarrow \alpha)) \rightarrow [\alpha] \rightarrow [\alpha]$$

$$hyp \ (swap \ d \ (\oplus, \otimes) \ x) \ i \ = \ (hyp \ x \ i) \ \oplus \ (hyp \ x \ (p(i, d))) \ , \quad \text{if } i < p(i, d)$$
$$(hyp \ x \ (p(i, d))) \ \otimes \ (hyp \ x \ i) \ , \quad \text{otherwise}$$

$$\text{where } length(x) = 2^k \ , \ p(i, d) = xor(i, 2^{d-1}), \ 1 \leq d \leq k, \ 0 \leq i < 2^k.$$

From the definition follows that to compute the result of $swap$ in processor i, this processor must access the element in position $p(i, d)$, i.e., communicate with its neighbour in dimension d. Thus, $swap$ consists of pair-wise, two-directional communication in one dimension, followed by computation.

The following proposition establishes the correspondence between one step of the iterative solution (8) and one application of $swap$.

Theorem 13. *For lists of length 2^k and $1 \leq d \leq k$, holds:*

$$step \ (2^{d-1}) \ (\oplus, \otimes) \ = \ swap \ d \ (\oplus, \otimes) \tag{9}$$

Introducing the notation:

$$swap^k \ (\oplus, \otimes) \ = \ (swap \ k \ (\oplus, \otimes)) \ \circ \ \cdots \ \circ \ (swap \ 2 \ (\oplus, \otimes)) \ \circ \ (swap \ 1 \ (\oplus, \otimes))$$

we obtain from Theorem 11 and Theorem 13 the following:

Corollary 14 (Common Hypercube Implementation). *Every DH can be computed on the 2^k-node hypercube by a sequence of swaps, with the dimensions counting from 1 to k:*

$$\oplus \updownarrow \otimes \ = \ swap^k \ (\oplus, \otimes) \tag{10}$$

Schema (10) expresses a standard way of programming hypercubes; its implementation as the target SPMD program with explicit message passing can be generated easily.

6 Implementation of Scan

In this section, we derive a parallel program that computes the *scan*-function. Let us first check whether the *scan* function is DH. Its combine operator:

$$scan\,(\odot)\,(x + \!\!\!+ y) \;=\; S_1 \circledast S_2 \;=\; S_1 + \!\!\!+ \; map\,((last\,S_1)\,\odot)\;S_2, \qquad (11)$$
$$\text{where } S_1 \,=\, scan\,(\odot)\,x, \; S_2 \,=\, scan\,(\odot)\,y.$$

Our task is to express the right-hand side of (11) in the component-wise format (6), with both sides of $+\!\!\!+$ in the *zip*-form. The part on the left of $+\!\!\!+$: $S_1 = zip\,(\pi_1)\,(S_1, S_2)$, where π_1 yields the first element of a pair.

The obvious way to express the part on the right of $+\!\!\!+$ component-wise is to "replicate" the element $last\,(S_1)$. Since $last\,(scan\,(\odot)\,x) = red\,(\odot)\,x$, the replication yields $(redd\,(\odot)\,x)$. This allows us to reformulate $\circledast$ component-wise:

$$S_1 \circledast S_2 \;=\; zip\,(\pi_1)\,(S_1, S_2) + \!\!\!+ \; zip\,(\odot)\,(R_1, S_2) \qquad (12)$$

where the introduced function, *redd*, is used: $R_1 = redd\,(\odot)\,x$.

Like for almost-homomorphisms above, we "tuple" both functions together: $< scan\,(\odot),\, redd\,(\odot) >$. To fit the DH format, we massage this tuple into a new function, *scred*, which yields a list of pairs instead of pair of lists:

$$scred\,(\odot) \;=\; zip\,(\diamond) \,\circ\, < scan\,(\odot),\, redd\,(\odot) > \qquad (13)$$

where $a \diamond b = (a, b)$, for elements a and b.

Since *redd* itself matches the DH format (7) with the combine operator:

$$R_1 \ominus R_2 \;=\; zip\,(\odot)\,(R_1, R_2) + \!\!\!+ \; zip\,(\odot)\,(R_1, R_2) \qquad (14)$$

no additional auxiliary functions are necessary.

Function *scred* can be expressed as follows:

$$scred\,(\odot) \;=\; (\oplus \updownarrow \otimes) \,\circ\, map\,(pair), \qquad (15)$$

where function *pair* transforms an element into a pair; operations $\oplus$ and $\otimes$ work on pairs of elements $s_i \in S_i$, $r_i \in R_i$ and are directly read off from (12), (14):

$$pair\,a = (a, a)$$
$$(s_1, r_1) \oplus (s_2, r_2) = (s_1,\, r_1 \odot r_2) \qquad (16)$$
$$(s_1, r_1) \otimes (s_2, r_2) = (r_1 \odot s_2,\, r_1 \odot r_2)$$

From (13)-(15) follows the expression of *scan*, adjusted to the DH format:

$$scan\,(\odot) \;=\; (map\,\pi_1) \,\circ\, (\oplus \updownarrow \otimes) \,\circ\, (map\,pair) \qquad (17)$$

where *pair*, $\oplus$, $\otimes$ are defined by (16).

Thus, we have adjusted the *scan* function to the DH format. The tuple structure, its initialization by function *pair*, and the computations expressed by $\oplus$ and $\otimes$ in (16), are all the results of the systematic adjustment process.

We can now directly rewrite (17) by using the implementation schema (10) and thus obtain the hypercube program for *scan*:

$$scan(\odot) = (map\ \pi_1) \circ swap^k(\oplus, \otimes) \circ (map\ pair) \tag{18}$$

with *pair*, $\oplus$ and $\otimes$ from (16).

This is the well-known "folklore" implementation [25]. In Figure 3, it is illustrated for the 2-dimensional hypercube which is computing $scan(+)$ [1, 2, 3, 4].

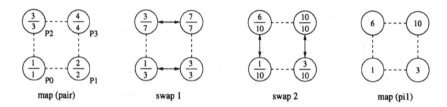

map (pair)   swap 1   swap 2   map (pi1)

Fig. 3. Computing *scan* on a hypercube

Implementation (18) consists of three stages: pairing, repeating swaps and projecting. For a list of length $n = 2^k$, we need n processors. Both the pairing and the projection stage require constant time. The central stage is the sequential loop with k swaps; in each swap, pairs of elements are communicated and computations are performed on pairs as well, so every swap requires constant time. Hence, the time is $O(k) = O(\log n)$, our implementation is *time optimal*.

The cost (time-processor product [25]) is $O(n \log n)$, whereas the cost of the sequential computation is $O(n)$, so the implementation is *not cost optimal*. To improve it, we must use fewer processors, with each processor working with a segment of the input list. Formal derivation of a time and cost optimal algorithm for this practical situation exploits BMF-transformations which involve data distributions; this is the subject of another paper [14].

7   Related Work

Our approach to parallelism extraction can be compared with [15] since we consider the same examples. On simple examples like *length*, we actually do the same. For *scan*, rather involved calculations and intuition are required in [15] to obtain ⊛; here the advantages of the systematic CS-approach are evident. For almost-homomorphisms, the method of [15] is not suitable at all. In [2], the existence of leftwards and rightwards algorithms is used as an evidence that a homomorphic algorithm exists; unlike our approach, the authors do not provide a method to derive it.

Our solution for the maximum segment sum problem is similar to those provided earlier by Smith [28] and Cole [7]. Our contribution is the systematic CS-method which, first, provides a uniform way of introducing the necessary auxiliary functions and, second, exploits a rigorous generalization procedure for deriving the resultant combine operation on tuples.

Parallelization of the *scan* function has a rich history, starting from the seminal work by Ladner and Fisher [20]. Meanwhile, parallel algorithms for *scan* are a part of folklore [25], and are usually presented in an *ad hoc* manner.

There are few exceptions, to which we compare our approach. Mou [6, 22] specifies the *scan* algorithm within an algebraic model of divide-and-conquer and suggests an optimization, which is similar to ours; the tuple structure arises by a non-formal argument and the result is not proved formally. A tree algorithm has been verified formally by O'Donnell [23], and later derived formally by J. Gibbons [10]. Kornerup [17] arrives formally at the algorithm by Ladner and Fisher in the recursive powerlist notation. Our approach differs in that our target implementation (1) is a result of the systematic, provably correct adjustment and specialization process and (2) is obtained in an iterative form, where all stages of computations and communication can be seen explicitly.

The construction of function *iter* is a special case of the compound list operations by Kumar and Skillicorn [19], which we use here for a different purpose. Our restriction to lists of length 2^k has also much in common with the powerlists by Misra [21]. Unlike him, we get rid of the explicit recursion in the target program by introducing iterative constructs. However, our approach is more restrictive, since we do not consider the list interleaving constructor ⋈ used by Misra.

An approach similar to ours in deriving an architecture-independent solution and mapping it onto particular topologies has been taken by Achatz and Schulte [1]. We consider a more special class DH, which allows us to exploit additional transformations. Our approach can be extended to an arbitrary number of processors [14], unlike the SIMD model used in [1].

The general implementation schema for DH functions on the hypercube resembles the common structure of *ascending* algorithms studied in the seminal paper by Preparata and Vuillemin [24]. We view this analogy is a promising sign for research towards building a taxonomy of functions with respect to their efficient parallel implementations.

8 Conclusion and Future Work

We propose an approach to exploiting divide-and-conquer parallelism in functions on lists, which consists of two steps: first, parallelism extraction by finding a homomorphic representation of the given function, second, parallelism implementation by adjusting the function to the DH format and using the common parallel implementation schema.

We claim that our approach is more systematic than the methods presented previously, for the following reasons:

- At the *parallelism extraction* step, the user provides two sequential definitions of a given function in a closed leftwards and rightward form. According to Theorem 4, a difficulty in finding an *lw* or *rw* form indicates that the function might be non-homomorphic. The requirement of closeness, as we see in the *mss* example, "guides" the introduction of the necessary auxiliary functions. The rest of the job is done by the generalization procedure.

- At the *parallelism implementation* step, the function must be cast in the DH format, which again serves as a guide for the user. After that, the implementation schema is customized correspondingly.

Methodologically, an important feature of the parallelism extraction step is that it is based on sequential thinking: the developer is required to provide two sequential functional programs, which are then transformed by the generalization procedure. Considerations involving data and control dependences, which are usual in parallelization techniques, are completely avoided.

The contribution to the implementation methodology is in the definition of the DH class of functions on lists and the formal derivation of a common efficient parallel implementation schema for all functions of the class. The derivation is based on the semantically sound transformation rules of the BMF, which guarantees its correctness. The performance of the common target implementations is easily predictable and conforms with the known estimates.

Our future work includes designing a standard generalization procedure for the CS method and also extending a class of functions for which efficient parallel implementation schemata for various architectures can be built systematically.

9 Acknowledgments

I am grateful to Murray Cole, Alfons Geser, Jeremy Gibbons, Christian Lengauer, Lambert Meertens and Christoph Wedler for discussing different parts of the manuscript. The anonymous referees helped a lot to make it a better paper.

The author was partially supported by the DAAD cooperation programs ARC and PROCOPE, and by the Project INTAS-93-1702.

References

1. K. Achatz and W. Schulte. Architecture independent massive parallelization of divide-and-conquer algorithms. In B. Moeller, editor, *Mathematics of Program Construction*, Lecture Notes in Computer Science 947, pages 97–127, 1995.
2. D. Barnard, J. Schmeiser, and D. Skillicorn. Deriving associative operators for language recognition. *Bulletin of EATCS*, 43:131–139, 1991.
3. J. Bentley. Programming pearls. *Communications of the ACM*, 27:865–871, 1984.
4. R. S. Bird. Lectures on constructive functional programming. In M. Broy, editor, *Constructive Methods in Computing Science*, NATO ASO Series F: Computer and Systems Sciences. Vol. 55, pages 151–216. Springer Verlag, 1988.
5. G. Blelloch. Scans as primitive parallel operations. *IEEE Trans. on Computers*, 38(11):1526–1538, November 1989.
6. B. Carpentieri and G. Mou. Compile-time transformations and optimizations of parallel divide-and-conquer algorithms. *ACM SIGPLAN Notices*, 20(10):19–28, 1991.
7. M. Cole. Parallel programming with list homomorphisms. *Parallel Processing Letters*, 5(2):191–204, 1994.
8. A. Gibbons and W. Rytter. *Efficient Parallel Algorithms*. Cambridge Univ. Press, 1988.

9. J. Gibbons. The third homomorphism theorem. *J. Fun. Programming*. To appear.

10. J. Gibbons. Upwards and downwards accumulations on trees. In R. Bird, C. Morgan, and J. Woodcock, editors, *Mathematics of Program Construction*, Lecture Notes in Computer Science 669, pages 122–138, 1992.

11. J. Gibbons. The third homomorphism theorem. Technical report, Univ. of Auckland, 1994.

12. S. Gorlatch. Constructing list homomorphisms. Technical Report MIP-9512, Universität Passau, 1995.

13. S. Gorlatch. Stages and transformations in parallel programming. In M. Kara et al., editors, *Abstract Machine Models for Parallel and Distributed Computing*, pages 147–162. IOS Press, 1996.

14. S. Gorlatch. Systematic optimal parallelization of scan and other list homomorphisms. In *Proceedings of the Euro-Par'96*. LNCS, to appear, 1996.

15. Z. Grant-Duff and P. Harrison. Parallelism via homomorphisms. *Parallel Processing Letters*. To appear.

16. B. Heinz. Lemma discovery by anti-unification of regular sorts. Technical Report 94-21, TU Berlin, May 1994.

17. J. Kornerup. Mapping a functional notation for parallel programs onto hypercubes. *Information Processing Letters*, 53:153–158, 1995.

18. H. Kuchen, R. Plasmeijer, and H. Stolze. Distributed implementation of a data-parallel functional language. In *PARLE'94, LNCS 817*, pages 464–477, 1994.

19. K. Kumar and D. Skillicorn. Data parallel geometric operations on lists. *Parallel Computing*, 21(3):447–459, 1995.

20. R. Ladner and M. Fischer. Parallel prefix computation. *J. ACM*, 27:831–838, 1980.

21. J. Misra. Powerlist: a structure for parallel recursion. *ACM TOPLAS*, 16(6):1737–1767, 1994.

22. Z. G. Mou. Divacon: A parallel language for scientific computing based on divide and conquer. In *Proc. 3rd Symposium on the Frontiers of Massively Parallel Computation*, pages 451–461, October 1990.

23. J. O'Donnell. A correctness proof of parallel scan. *Parallel Processing Letters*, 4(3):329–338, 1994.

24. F. Preparata and J. Vuillemin. The cube-connected cycles: A versatile network for parallel computation. *Communications of the ACM*, 24(5):300–309, 1981.

25. M. J. Quinn. *Parallel Computing*. McGraw-Hill, Inc., 1994.

26. D. Skillicorn. *Foundations of Parallel Programming*. Cambridge Univ. Press, 1994.

27. D. Skillicorn and W. Cai. A cost calculus for parallel functional programming. *Journal of Parallel and Distributed Computing*, 28:65–83, 1995.

28. D. Smith. Applications of a strategy for designing divide-and-conquer algorithms. *Science of Computer Programming*, (8):213–229, 1987.

29. D. Swierstra and O. de Moor. Virtual data structures. In B. Moeller, H. Partsch, and S. Schuman, editors, *Formal Program Development*, Lecture Notes in Computer Science 755, pages 355–371.

30. D. Walker. The design of a standard message passing interface for distributed memory concurrent computers. *Parallel Computing*, 20:657–673, 1994.

Functional Skeletons Generate Process Topologies in Eden

Luis A. Galán   Cristóbal Pareja   Ricardo Peña*

Departamento de Informática y Automática
Universidad Complutense de Madrid
e-mail: {lagalan,cpareja,ricardo}@dia.ucm.es
Fax: (34-1) 394 4607

Abstract. We present a collection of skeletons that are appropriate to instantiate process systems in the functional-concurrent language Eden [BLOM96]. Eden is a functional language providing facilities for the explicit definition and instantiation of processes. Skeletons in this language are just higher order functions having process definitions as parameters. We introduce skeletons for both transformational (i.e. deterministic) and reactive (usually non deterministic) process topologies and illustrate their use by applying them to several examples. Some comparisons to the skeletons literature are also established.

Keywords: Functional programming, concurrent programming, parallel programming, skeletons, higher order functions.

1   Introduction

Functional languages are often said to be amenable for implicit parallelism but, in order to get enough profit from it, decisions have to be taken to see whether to evaluate an expression in parallel is worthwhile or not. Several solutions have been proposed, ranging between two extremes: one of them is to leave the responsibility of deciding when and how to evaluate in parallel to the programmer. This is usually expressed by means of annotations within the functional program [Hud86, Kel89, PvE93]. Another is to leave such decisions to the compiler [Bra93].

Functional skeletons [Col89, DFH+93, Ski93] constitute a compromise between these two extremes: on one hand, a skeleton is a parameterized algorithmic scheme which can be instantiated with particular functions as actual parameters, thus becoming a program. On the other hand, it expresses a concrete process structure that can be recognized as such by the compiler, so that its parallelism can be appropriately exploited.

Higher order functions are the natural way to express skeletons in a functional language [KPS94, Kes95]. It has also been observed that a restricted set of skeletons —just as it happens with higher order functions— are usually enough to express most computation patterns. So, skeletons are receiving much attention in the last few years as a means of exploiting parallelism in functional programs.

---

* Supported by the Spanish Ministry of Education and Science in the context of the German-Spanish Acción Integrada no. 142-B.

M. Cole [Col89] proposed —in an imperative framework— the skeleton principle, and suggested a first collection of them, and how to predict the resulting program efficiency.

Two early attempts of describing process topologies in a functional framework are *Para-Functional Programming* [Hud86] and the language Caliban [Kel89]. In both cases annotations are used by the programmer to indicate that an expression should be evaluated in parallel. In the Hudak approach, even the processor responsible for that evaluation is given in the annotation. Normally, a concrete underlying architecture is assumed. Only static, or at least bounded, process networks can be coped with.

In the language P^3L [DMO$^+$92, BDO$^+$93], a brief collection of predefined skeletons and a set of tools mapping them to concrete architectures are proposed. Also here, the network size must be known before processes start running.

In J. Darlington and his collaborators' work [DFH$^+$93], the emphasis is put on how to transform programs to fit them into known skeletons. They are proposing a kind of *program derivation* method in which programs are transformed into more efficient parallel versions, having in mind a concrete machine architecture. In a later work [DGTY95], they show how to combine skeletons in different ways to produce complex parallel topologies.

Other interesting work has been devoted to actual implementations of skeletons, either by including these implementations as predefined ones in the compiler [Bra93], or by using lower level annotations to spawn processes or/and to place them in particular processors [Kes95].

The approach to parallelism followed by Eden is explained in [BLOM96, BLOMP96] where a comparison to other concurrent declarative languages is also given. Eden is aimed not only to the parallel execution of functional programs but also to the definition of general reactive systems, so non-determinism is also allowed. Section 2 introduces its main characteristics.

In Eden, skeletons are not related to concrete architectures. The target machine for Eden programs is assumed to be a distributed and fully interconnected one, i.e. it can communicate any couple of processors with a similar delay and simultaneously handle many communications. The mapping and balancing problems (i.e. where a new process should be created) are assumed to be efficiently managed by the underlying run-time environment. So, skeletons are seen as an abstract way of defining process topologies and they will be used both for creating static and dynamic process networks.

Frequently, process topologies consist of many instances of a few process schemes. Also, topologies use to remain the same, while component processes can be freely interchanged with others having a similar communication structure. It is a good habit in functional languages to express this redundancy by making an extensive use of higher order functions. This is the approach followed in this paper: skeletons are higher order functions having as parameters what we call *process abstractions*. A process abstraction is just a parameterized process scheme that can be instantiated in different ways. Skeletons receive process abstractions, together with some size/shape parameters, and dynamically instantiate process topologies of varying size. In Eden, skeletons are programmer-defined functions and so, they are not limited to be a fixed collection.

In what follows, we distinguish two kinds of skeletons: *transformational* ones and *reactive* ones. Transformational skeletons are devoted to deterministic programs, i.e. those (normally terminating) programs calculating a result from a set of arguments. Reactive skeletons abstract reactive systems, i.e. those (normally non-terminating and non-deterministic) programs maintaining some interaction with its environment, and not necessarily yielding a final result. This is a novel aspect of this paper. Reactive process topologies are not usually considered in the skeleton literature.

The plan of the paper is as follows: after this section, we briefly introduce Eden, explaining the syntax and the meaning of the constructions used in this paper. In Section 3, we present a collection of transformational skeletons and illustrate their use with simple examples. In Section 4, reactive skeletons are presented and they are illustrated with typical examples of concurrent systems. The last section draws a brief conclusion.

2 A bird's-eye view of Eden

Eden is a functional language providing constructions for the explicit definition of processes and for establishing communication between them. It is suitable both for parallel and for concurrent programming, including in the later reactive systems, and is tailored for execution in distributed memory architectures. A thorough description of the language and of its operational semantics can be found in [BLOM96] and [BLOM95]. In [BLOMP96], a collection of sophisticated examples programmed in Eden is presented.

Eden extends the lazy functional language Haskell [HPJW92] by new syntactic constructs for explicitly defining and instantiating processes. These processes exchange values via communication channels modelled essentially by lazy lists. They are asynchronous, unidirectional, and one-to-one. Communication is implicit, i.e. no special primitives are provided to send or to receive messages. This is achieved by simply connecting an output channel of a process to an input channel of another process. Messages are automatically buffered, so sending a value through a channel never blocks the sending process, while awaiting a value from a channel may block the receiving process. In principle, direct communication is only possible between a parent process and his children processes. But, whenever a parent process simply transmits the values generated by a child to an input channel of another child, it will be "bypassed", and channels will be automatically installed between the corresponding producer and consumer processes. This feature is called *automatic bypassing*.

These constructions are enough to express (deterministic) parallelization of sequential functional programs. In addition, Eden incorporates special concepts for the efficient treatment of general reactive systems:

Dynamic creation of reply channels: This feature simplifies the generation of complex communication topologies and increases the flexibility of the language: at run time, a process may dynamically create new input channels and transmit their "names" to remote processes through previously existing channels. A process receiving these names may either transmit them to another process, or use them to send replies to the originator process.

Predefined nondeterministic processes: In order to model nondeterministic many-to-one and one-to-many communication in process systems, Eden provides predefined nondeterministic MERGE and SPLIT processes. Eden has a two level semantics: the user-defined process level and the system process level. User-defined processes are seen as deterministic mappings from input channels to output channels. Nondeterminism is handled only at the system level.

In what follows, we introduce the Eden syntax for the constructions used in this paper, namely the ones for process definition, process instantiation, and nondeterministic processes. Dynamic reply channels are not covered here.

2.1 Process abstractions and process instantiations

Process abstractions specify process behaviour, while process instantiations specify actual creation of processes. The later is done by supplying suitable input values to some process abstraction. A process abstraction maps input values $in_1, \ldots, in_m$ to output values $exp_1, \ldots, exp_n$. It is specified by using the following syntax:

$$absName \; par_1 \ldots par_k \quad = \textbf{process} \quad (in_1, \ldots, in_m) \; \text{->} \; (exp_1, \ldots, exp_n)$$
$$\textbf{where} \quad equation_1$$
$$\ldots$$
$$equation_r$$

The keywords **process** and **where** and the symbol -> are concrete syntax for a new construction. The visibility rules of this construction allow us to use identifiers $in_1, \ldots, in_n$ corresponding to the input *channels*, in the equations following the **where** keyword. When $exp_1, \ldots, exp_n$ are simple enough, the equations and the **where** keyword can be omitted.

A process abstraction is a parameterized process scheme, where par_1, ..., par_k are parameters of any type. The result of the whole construction is a value of the predefined type **Process a b**. The body of a process abstraction consists of a list of expressions $exp_1, \ldots, exp_n$ defining the output channels. The optional **where** part can be used to introduce local variables and some auxiliary functions referenced in the above mentioned expressions.

A process abstraction can be seen as a special kind of λ-abstraction having the following type:

$$absName :: \tau_1 \; \text{->} \; \ldots \; \text{->} \; \tau_k \; \text{->} \; \textbf{Process} \; (\tau_1', \ldots, \tau_m') \; (\bar{\tau}_1, \ldots, \bar{\tau}_n)$$

where $\tau_1, \ldots, \tau_k$ denote the types of the parameters and $\tau_1', \ldots, \tau_m'$ and $\bar{\tau}_1, \ldots, \bar{\tau}_n$ are respectively the input and output channel types. A process may have as input (respectively, output) a single channel, a tuple of channels (as in the display above), a list of channels, or any other type expression. Additionally, when a channel is a list (i.e. of type [a]), the implementation will transmit its contents element by element as in stream based languages. In order to correctly infer types, some conventions apply:

- If the inferred type for a (respectively, for b) in **Process a b** is a tuple, each component of it will be considered a separate channel by the implementation.

- If a channel has type [a], it will be treated as a stream by the implementation.
- Once a channel "type" has been inferred, none of its type subexpressions are allowed to be channels.

Sometimes, these default rules are not convenient for the programmer. In order to overrule them, *type annotations* can be introduced. The annotation <a> expresses that a is a channel. For instance, the annotation [<a>] means "list of channels". Otherwise, a single stream channel would be inferred. Similarly, the annotation <(a,b)> means a single channel transmitting a tuple of values. Otherwise, a tuple of channels would be assumed. Of course, no nested channel annotations are allowed. In what follows, we will explicitly provide types for all processes. Should the type not contain annotations, it will correspond to the type inferred by the compiler.

Process creation takes place when a process abstraction with no unbound parameters is applied to a tuple of inport expressions. This is called *process instantiation* and defines the tuple of outports of the newly created process:

$$absName\ e_1 \ldots e_k\ \#\ (input\_exp_1, \ldots, input\_exp_m)$$

where # is a predefined infix operator (#) :: Process a b -> a -> b denoting process aplication. It associates to the right and has binding precedence 0. Often, process instantiations occur in equations of the form:

$$(out_1, \ldots, out_n) = absName\ e_1 \ldots e_k\ \#\ (input\_exp_1, \ldots, input\_exp_m)$$

While in lazy functional programs there is always demand for the evaluation of the topmost expression driving the computation, in Eden there is always demand for the evaluation of the process outports. If a process has several outports, it is divided into several *concurrent threads*, one for each outport definition. If outports are assembled in a tuple and defined by a single expression, there will be a unique thread for their evaluation. This leads to a natural distinction of two levels of concurrency: processes and threads within processes.

Also, in order to increase parallelism, the following evaluation convention applies: all process instantiations contained in the current top level environment are eagerly evaluated, regardless of whether its output values are demanded or not. This convention may in some cases create speculative parallelism if care is not taken of, but it is very useful in many circumstances.

2.2 Communication and synchronization

Communication channels transmit completely evaluated values of arbitrary type. Stream channels correspond essentially to lazy lists and, accordingly, they are fully compatible with the corresponding list types. Streams are lazy with respect to the (:) constructor, but eager with respect to the head of the list, in correspondence with the decision of communicating completely evaluated expressions.

Communication between processes only takes place via communication channels. They are asynchronous and connect normally one sender to one receiver process. Multicasting can be easily achieved by simply connecting the output channel of one process to input channels of several other processes. The semantics of this construction is message duplication. Each channel provides a transmission buffer into which fully evaluated objects are transferred by the sender process. As soon as a value of the corresponding type has been transmitted in full, the channel is closed and the communication port is abolished. Stream channels are closed when the [] constructor is transmitted. Information transfer via communication channels is done automatically. No explicit send or receive commands are needed by the programmer who simply specifies *what* has to be output.

If a concurrent thread within a process needs some value from an inport whose channel buffer is empty, this thread will be suspended until the corresponding sender process writes some value into the channel buffer. However, the evaluation of outports is independent of the consumption of the produced values.

The input and output ports specified in the process abstraction are established on process creation, but additional ones can be introduced later during the process "life" when either child processes are instantiated or dynamic reply channels are used. How is this reflected in the process interface? To answer this question we distinguish two different points of view: from the denotational one, where processes are seen as functions mapping input parameters into output ones, the process interface does never change. This coincides with the (process abstraction) users view. But from the operational point of view process interfaces in fact change because, when children processes are created, new connections with parent processes are established. However, this interface can be seen as an "internal" one, only known to the process abstraction implementer . Therefore, Eden supports modular design by making explicit the external interface in the process header, but hiding the internal one inside the implementation.

2.3 Nondeterministic Processes

Nondeterminism is introduced in Eden by special predefined process abstractions. They encapsulate nondeterminism and thus do not destroy referential transparency within user-defined processes. Furthermore, the introduction of separate processes to model nondeterministic behaviour improves modularity and simplifies the incremental analysis of process systems.

The MERGE process abstraction creates a nondeterministic process *fairly* merging a list of stream channels and producing a single stream channel of the same type. We also introduce an analogous process abstraction SPLIT nondeterministically distributing the contents of its single input stream into a set of output streams:

```
MERGE :: Process [<[a]>] [a]
SPLIT :: Process [a] [<[a]>]
```

A typical application of the MERGE process is the modelling of many-to-one communications. For instance, in a client-server system several clients may send requests to a single server. This situation can be modelled by using a MERGE process merging the requests in a fair way into a single input channel going to the server, so without fixing a deterministic order in which process requests will arrive. Our fair merge easily generalizes to a *priorized* merge which would have a list with the priorities associated to the input channels as a parameter.

3 Transformational skeletons

Here, we review some skeletons proposed in the literature and express them as Eden process networks. We apply them to some examples and comment on how Eden features may extract the parallelism implicit in these topologies. Frequently, to appropriately exploit this parallelism several skeletons must be combined, or/and some pre/post-processing is needed in order to adapt the input data to the skeleton or to extract the final results.

3.1 Pipelines

A pipeline is just a list of processes composed in such a way that the output channel of every process is connected to the input channel of the next one in the pipe. Parallelism is achieved if these channels transmit *streams* of data. Pipes in Eden can be easily described by a `foldr` application to a binary composition of processes:

```
(>>):: Process a b -> Process b c -> Process a c
p >> q = process left -> q # p # left
pipe:: [Process [a] [a]] -> Process [a] [a]
pipe = foldr (>>) pipeId where pipeId = process left -> left
```

Sometimes, it is useful to provide for a bi-directional data flow. This can be done by a simple modification of the above definition:

```
(<<>>):: Process (a,b) (a,b) -> Process (a,b) (a,b) -> Process (a,b) (a,b)
p1 <<>> p2 = process (iright,ileft) -> (oright,oleft)
             where (midr,oleft) = p1 # (iright,midl)
                   (oright,midl) = p2 # (midr,ileft)
pipeB:: [Process ([a],[b]) ([a],[b])] -> Process ([a],[b]) ([a],[b])
pipeB = foldr (<<>>) pipeBId
        where pipeBId = process (iright,ileft) -> (iright,ileft)
```

The binary operators themselves can be useful to define pipes in which processes have different types. For instance, if we have p1::Process [a] [b], p2::Process [b] [c] and p3::Process [c] [d], we can define:

```
mypipe :: Process [a] [d]
mypipe = p1 >> p2 >> p3
```

Example 1. Hamming numbers. A previous Eden solution to this problem can be found in [BLOM96]. A list of different prime numbers is given and the pipeline returns the list of all natural numbers having (some of) these primes as the only prime factors. The pipe has as many processes as the initial list, each one devoted to a prime factor:

```
hamming :: [Int] -> [Int]
hamming primes =  pipe (map mergeWithPows primes) # [1]
mergeWithPows p = process left -> right
                  where right = 1 : merge (tail left) (map (*p) right)
```

pipe (map mergeWithPows [2, 3, 5])

Fig. 1. One-directional pipeline for the Hamming numbers problem

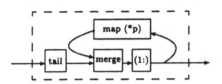

Fig. 2. A pipeline component

The `merge` function is just the standard one merging two ordered lists. The resulting pipeline and a detail of the component processes can be respectively seen in Figure 1 and in Figure 2.

In some circumstances, it is appropriate to have pipelines in which all the component processes are identical. Its definition is just a particular case of the previously defined pipes:

```
repeatN :: Int -> a -> [a]
repeatN n x = take n (repeat x)
pipeN :: Int -> Process [a] [a] -> Process [a] [a]
pipeN n p = pipe (repeatN n p)
pipeBN :: Int -> Process ([a],[b]) ([a],[b]) -> Process ([a],[b]) ([a],[b])
pipeBN n p = pipeB (repeatN n p)
```

Finally, it could also be useful to have pipes in which the number of components is dynamically decided depending on the input data. We propose the following generic definition for them:

```
dynPipe :: ([a] -> Bool) -> Process [a] [a] -> Process [a] [a]
dynPipe q p = process xs -> if q xs then xs else dynPipe q p # p # xs
```

3.2 Grids

A grid is a two-dimensional structure in which component processes are connected to four neighbours. We convene that input channels come in from left and top sides of each component, and output channels go out from right and bottom sides of it. A natural way of defining such a topology is by using arrays. The following function receives a list of m process abstractions lists, each one of length n, and instantiate them in a grid fashion. Please note that type annotations are mandatory here:

```
gridMN :: [[Process (a,b) (a,b)]] -> Process ([<a>],[<b>]) ([<a>],[<b>])
gridMN pss = process (lefts,tops) -> (rights,bots) where
  grid = array ((0,0),(m-1,n-1))
    ([[((0,0),pss!!0!!0 # (lefts!!0,tops!!0))] ++
      [((0,j),pss!!0!!j # (fst (grid!(0,j-1)),tops!!j)) | j<-[1..n-1]] ++
      [((i,0),pss!!i!!0 # (lefts!!(i),snd (grid!(i-1,0)))) | i<-[1..m-1]] ++
      [((i,j),pss!!i!!j # (fst (grid!(i,j-1)),snd (grid!(i-1,j)))) |
                i<-[1..m-1], j<-[1..n-1]])
  m = length pss
```

```
n = length (head pss)
rights = [fst (grid!(i,n-1)) | i <- [0..m-1]]
bots   = [snd (grid!(m-1,i)) | i <- [0..n-1]]
```

Here, the auxiliary array grid :: Array (Int,Int) (a,b) is used to provide channel connections between all the processes.

An alternative way of defining the same topology is by making an extensive use of higher order functions as we did with pipelines. Now, we define binary operators to add a component to a row and to add a row to a grid. Note again the use of type annotations:

```
(>:) :: Process (a,b) (a,b) -> Process (a,[<b>]) (a,[<b>])
                           -> Process (a,[<b>]) (a,[<b>])
p >: ps = process (left,tops) -> (right,bots)
        where (x:xs)     = tops
              (mid,y)    = p  # (left,x)
              (right,ys) = ps # (mid,xs)
              bots       = y:ys
(>>:) :: Process (a,[<b>]) (a,[<b>]) -> Process ([<a>],[<b>])
                                     -> ([<a>],[<b>])
ps >>: pss = process (lefts,tops) -> (rights,bots)
           where (l:ls)    = lefts
                 (r,mids)  = ps  # (l,tops)
                 (rs,bots) = pss # (ls,mids)
                 rights    = r:rs
```

We need identity processes to start with when constructing each row or the complete grid:

```
idRow :: Process (a,[<b>]) (a,[<b>])
idRow = process (left,[]) -> (left,[])
idGrid :: Process ([<a>],[<b>]) ([<a>],[<b>])
idGrid = process ([],xs) -> ([],xs)
```

Then, the grid definition is just a repeated application of the foldr higher order function:

```
gridMN :: [[Process (a,b) (a,b)]] -> Process ([<a>],[<b>]) ([<a>],[<b>])
gridMN pss = foldr (>>:) idGrid rows
           where rows = [foldr (>:) idRow ps | ps <- pss]
```

Example 2. Matrix multiplication. To multiply a $m \times n$ matrix by an $n \times l$ one, we will instantiate a $m \times n$ grid in which each processing element will contain the corresponding value of the first matrix. Consecutive length-n columns of the second matrix will be feed through the n top channels of the grid. The resulting m rows of the product matrix will go out from the m right channels of the grid.

```
multElem :: Num a => a -> Process ([a],[a]) ([a],[a])
multElem x = process (ileft, itop) -> (zipWith f itop ileft, itop)
           where f y z = x*y + z
matMult :: Num a => [[a]] -> [[a]] -> [[a]]
matMult ass bss = result
              where (result,_) = gridMN pss # (zeroesRows,bss)
                    zeroesRows = repeatN (length ass) (repeat 0)
                    pss = map (map multElem) ass
```

In Figure 3 we show the following multiplication example, in which the first matrix is $\begin{pmatrix} 3 & 2 \\ 5 & 7 \end{pmatrix}$ and the second one is $\begin{pmatrix} 8 & 2 & 5 & \dots \\ 7 & 3 & 4 & \dots \end{pmatrix}$. Thanks to the default Eden feature of providing a concurrent thread to compute each output channel of a process, the vertical data flow proceeds in parallel with the horizontal computation of scalar products.

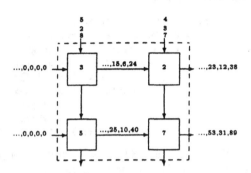

Fig. 3. Matrix multiplication as an application of the grid topology

3.3 Farms

This skeleton applies the same process abstraction to a set of independent input channels. It corresponds to the higher order function map:

```
farm :: Process a b -> Process [<a>] [<b>]
farm p = process xs -> f xs
         where f []       = []
               f (x:xx) = (p # x) : f xx
```

The function f repeatedly instantiates copies of process p. It could also have been done by replacing the recursive invocation f xx by a recursive invocation such as farm p # xx but, in this case, we would have instantiated a number of not very useful processes. We present an application of farm in the next section, where farm is used in the context of another well known skeleton.

3.4 Divide and conquer

This skeleton instantiates a dynamic tree of processes, each one receiving an input channel from his parent process and returning an output channel to it. The farm skeleton is used to generate the set of children processes of a given process. Its description in Eden is as follows:

```
divCon :: (a -> Bool) -> (a -> b) -> (a -> [a]) -> (a -> [b] -> b)
          -> Process a b
divCon trivial solve split combine = process x -> y where
  y = if trivial x then solve x
      else combine x (farm (divCon trivial solve split combine) # split x)
```

Note here that, whenever y is demanded and the boolean expresion trivial x has been evaluated to False, the farm instatiation becomes top-level (demanded by combine). Then, process creation takes place eagerly.

One of the several applications of this skeleton is R. Bird's homomorphisms over lists (denoted $\oplus/ \circ f*$). It corresponds to the particular case in which the combine function ignores x: $a \oplus b =$ combine _ [a, b].

Example 3. Quicksort:

```
quickSort :: Ord a => Process [a] [a]
quickSort = divCon trivial id splitHd combine
            where trivial l    = length l <= 1
                  splitHd (x:l) = splitAux x l
                  splitAux x [] = [[],[]]
                  splitAux x (y:l) | y<=x = [y:u,v]
                                   | y>x  = [u,y:v]
                                  where [u,v] = splitAux x l
                  combine (x:_) [l1, l2] = l1 ++ [x] ++ l2
```

We remark that Eden's eager creation of processes and eager evaluation of output channels increase the parallelism of this solution: the downwards data flow proceeds as soon as each node process receives the first element of its input list. So, splitting the original list is done in parallel by an increasing number of processes. The upwards "pipeline" is also done in parallel due to eager evaluation of output channels.

4   Reactive skeletons

In this section, we show how to instantiate in Eden some process topologies which are common in reactive systems. Sometimes, reactive systems constitute "closed" process graphs in the sense that each output channel of every process is connected to some input channel of another process. From the functional point of view, a skeleton instantiating such a process net would produce no value as a result. These skeletons will then present the following aspect:

$$skel :: \tau_1 \rightarrow \ldots \rightarrow \tau_n \rightarrow \text{Process } () \; ()$$
$$skel \; p_1 \ldots p_n = \text{process } () \rightarrow ()$$
$$\text{where } decls$$

They will be instantiated in the usual way $skel \; p_1 \ldots p_n \; \# \; ()$ and, due to the eager process creation convention, all process instantiations appearing in the **where** clause will be immediately done.

4.1   Client-server

In this topology, several *client* processes ask a single *server* process for some service. We include a MERGE process to model the non determinism in the arrival of requests to the server, and a *distributor* process in order to split the output from the server into a list of channels, each one dedicated to one client. The resulting topology is shown in figure 4, where a client-server skeleton is

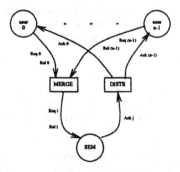

Fig. 4. A client-server skeleton

instantiated with a semaphore. The distributor process is deterministic and can be made generic provided a "distribution" function f::a -> Int is given:

```
type Client a b = Process [a] [b]
type Server a b = Process [a] [b]

distr :: (b -> Int) -> Process [b] [<[b]>]
distr f = process input -> cycle input
        where  cycle (m:ms) = insert m (f m) (cycle ms)
               insert x 0 (ys:yss) = (x:ys):yss
               insert x (k+1) (ys:yss) = ys:(insert x k yss)

clientServer :: [Client b a] -> Server a b -> (b -> Int) -> Process () ()
clientServer cs serv f = process () -> () where
                             outClients = zipWith (#) cs outDist
                             inServer   = MERGE # outClients
                             outServer  = serv # inServer
                             outDist    = distr f # outServer
```

Example 4. We show a simple FIFO semaphore to achieve mutual exclusion between the critical regions of a set of users. The program is self explanatory. We
assume that emptyQ, empty, add, first and del are the typical queue operations.

```
data Signal = Req Int | Ack Int | Rel Int

distFun (Ack i) = i

user :: Int -> Client Signal Signal
user i    = process input -> thinking input
            where thinking xs          = Req i : hungry xs
                  hungry (Ack i : xs) = eating xs
                  eating xs            = Rel i : thinking xs

semaphore :: Server Signal Signal
semaphore = process input -> cycle True emptyQ input where
 cycle True  q (Req i : ss) = Ack i : cycle False q ss
 cycle False q (Req i : ss) = cycle False (add q i) ss
 cycle False q (Rel i : ss) = if empty q then cycle True q ss
                              else Ack (first q) : cycle False (del q) ss

semMutex = clientServer (map user [0..n-1]) semaphore distFun
```

4.2 Ring

A ring topology having a single channel connecting every two neighbours in the
ring can be easily defined in terms of the pipe function presented in Section 3.1.
We also define bi-directional rings by using the pipeB function defined in the
same section:

```
ring :: [Process a a] -> Process () ()
ring (p:ps) = process () -> () where link = p # next
                                     next = pipe ps # link
ringB :: [Process (a,b) (a,b)] -> Process () ()
ringB (p:ps) = process () -> () where (in2,out2) = p # (in1,out1)
                                      (in1,out1) = pipeB ps # (in2,out2)
```

Example 5. A typical example of two-ways ring is a token-passing ring, i.e. a mutual exclusion system where a ring-shaped set of processes share a **token**. A process must hold the token in order to enter the critical region. If it does not hold it, it asks its right neighbour for it. Requests for the token travel counterclockwise through the ring, while token acknowledgements travel clockwise, as it is shown in Figure 5. The token is released whenever there is a request for it and it is not currently being used by the (only) process holding it. We present only the external view of this ring:

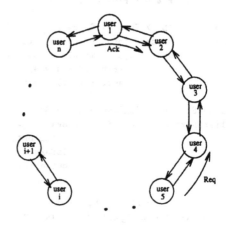

Fig. 5. A ring skeleton instantiation

```
data Req      = Req
data Ack      = Ack
type RingProc = Process ([Ack],[Req]) ([Ack],[Req])
mutexRing     = ringB ps
```

4.3 Graph

A connected graph of processes is the most general topology we can define. We present in this section a skeleton receiving as parameters the graph description and a list of *node* processes. Then, it instantiates a node process for each vertex of the graph, and connects the nodes according to the graph edges. For each edge joining vertices A and B, it provides a channel going from $node_A$ to $node_B$, and another one in the opposite direction. The graph description is just an array of adjacency lists, and nodes in the node list are given in correspondence with the array indices, i.e. the first node in the list is the node we wish to instantiate for vertex zero, and so on. Undirected edges are represented in the graph description by two directed edges (i.e. if vertex u is adjacent to vertex v, then u is in the adjacency list of v and v is in the adjacency list of u). We adopt the convention that, if v is the vertex in position p_v in u's adjacency list, and u is vertex in position p_u in v's adjacency list, then the p_v-th output channel of u is connected to the p_u-th input channel of v:

```
type Graph    = Array Int [Int]
type Node a   = Process [<a>] [<a>]
net           :: Graph -> [Node a] -> Process () ()
net g nodes   = process () -> () where
   outchans  = [node # inchans i|(node,i) <- zip nodes [0..]]
   inchans i = [outchans!!k!!p|k <- g!i,(j,p) <- zip (g!k) [0..],j==i]
```

Example 6. We show an application of the graph topology to the generalized dining philosopher problem presented by Chandy and Misra in [CM84]. A detailed description of the Eden solution to this problem can be found in [BLOMP96]. There, we only instantiated a ring of five nodes. Every node contained four processes: a philosopher, a secretary, a MERGE and a distributor process. We are assuming here that the nodes corresponding to each graph vertex have already been defined and our problem now is to instantiate the complete graph of nodes. Let us call node0, node1, node2, node3, node4 and node5 to the Node processes corresponding to the graph vertices of Figure 6. Then, the instantiation of the process graph would be as follows:

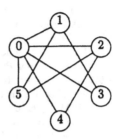

Fig. 6. A concrete graph topology

```
philGraph = array (0,5) [(0,[1,2,3,4,5]),(1,[0,3,5]),(2,[0,4,5]),
                         (3,[0,1]),(4,[0,2]),(5,[0,1,2])]
philNet   = net philGraph [node0, node1, node2, node3, node4, node5]
```

5   Conclusions

We have presented two skeleton families that are appropriate to instantiate both transformational parallel algorithms and reactive concurrent systems. They have been expressed as higher order functions written in the functional-concurrent language Eden. Having a skeletons catalogue very much simplifies concurrent programming in Eden because the programmer can concentrate on writing process abstractions, and this essentially amounts to defining functions. So, writing concurrent programs in this framework presents a difficulty rather similar to that of writing ordinary functional programs.

Eden's special characteristics, in particular eager evaluation of output channels, eager process creation and the possibility of providing a concurrent thread for each output channel, seem to extract a high degree of parallelism from the presented skeletons.

Present work is devoted to the denotational semantics of Eden (at present we have only defined an operational one) and to develop formal techniques to analyze safety and liveness properties in Eden programs.

Acknoledgements

We want to thank Rita Loogen, Herbert Kuchen, Yolanda Ortega, Manuel Núñez, Pedro Palao and the anonymous referees for their comments on a previous version of this paper.

References

[BDO+93]   B. Bacci, M. Danelutto, S. Orlando, S. Pelagatti, and M. Vanneschi. P^3L: a Structured High-level Parallel Language, and its Structured Support. Technical Report HPL-PSC-93-55, Pisa Science Center. Hewlett-Packard Laboratories., May 1993.

[BLOM95] S. Breitinger, R. Loogen, and Y. Ortega-Mallén. Eden: Language definition and operational semantics. Technical Report, Philipps-Universität Marburg, Germany, 1995.

[BLOM96] S. Breitinger, R. Loogen, and Y. Ortega-Mallén. Towards a declarative language for concurrent and parallel programming. In *Glasgow Workshop on Functional Programming 1995*. Springer-Verlag, 1996.

[BLOMP96] S. Breitinger, R. Loogen, Y. Ortega-Mallén, and R. Peña. Eden, the Paradise of Functional-Concurrent Programming. Technical Report DIA-UCM-20/96, Universidad Complutense de Madrid, Spain. Also available as http://www.mathematik.uni-marburg.de/~loogen/paper/paradise.ps. A short version of it can be found in EUROPAR'96, LNCS Springer-Verlag (to appear), 1996.

[Bra93] T. A. Bratvold. A Skeleton-Based Parallelising Compiler for ML. In *Proceedings of the fifth International Workshop on the Implementation of Functional Languages*, pages 23–33, September 1993.

[CM84] K. M. Chandy and J. Misra. The drinking philosophers problem. *ACM Transactions on Programming Languages and Systems*, 6:632–646, 1984.

[Col89] M. Cole. *Algorithmic Skeletons: Structured Management of Parallel Computation*. Research monographs in parallel and distributed computing. Pitman, 1989.

[DFH+93] J. Darlington, A. J. Field, P. J. Harrison, P. H. J. Kelly, D. W. N. Sharp, and Q. Wu. Parallel Programming using Skeleton Functions. In *PARLE'93: Parallel Architectures and Languages Europe*. Springer-Verlag, Jun. 1993.

[DGTY95] J. Darlington, Y. Guo, H. W. To, and J. Yang. Parallel Skeletons For Structured Composition. In *Proceedings of the 15th ACM Sigplan Symposium on Principles and Practice of Parallel Programming*, 1995.

[DMO+92] M. Danelutto, R. Di Meglio, S. Orlando, S. Pelagatti, and M. Vanneschi. A methodology for the development and the support of massively parallel programs. *Future Generation Computer Systems. North-Holland*, 8(1–3), July 1992.

[HPJW92] P. Hudak, S. Peyton-Jones, and P. Wadler. Report on the Functional Programming Language Haskell. version 1.2. *ACM SIGPLAN Notices*, 27(5), May 1992.

[Hud86] P. Hudak. Para-Functional Programming. *IEEE Computer*, 19(8):60–69, August 1986.

[Kel89] P. Kelly. *Functional Programming for Loosely-Coupled Multiprocessors*. Pitman, 1989.

[Kes95] M. Kesseler. Constructing skeletons in Clean: The bare bones. In A. P. Wim Bohm and John T. Feo, editors, *High Performance Functional Computing*, pages 182–192, April 1995.

[KPS94] H. Kuchen, R. Plasmeijer, and H. Stoltze. Distributed Implementation of a Data Parallel Functional Language. In *Parallel Architectures & Languages Europe, PARLE'94. LNCS 817*, pages 464–477. Springer-Verlag, 1994.

[PvE93] R. Plasmeijer and M. van Eekelen. *Functional Programming and Parallel Graph Rewriting*. Addison-Wesley, 1993.

[Ski93] D.B. Skillicorn. The Bird-Meertens Formalism as a parallel model. In J.S. Kowalik and L. Grandinetti, editors, *Software for Parallel Computation*, volume 106 of *NATO ASI Series F*, pages 120–133. Springer-Verlag, 1993.

ProFun - A Language for Executable Specifications[*]

Thomas Gehrke, Michaela Huhn

Institut für Informatik
Universität Hildesheim, D-31113 Hildesheim, Germany
Phone: (+49)(5121) 883-743, Fax: 883-768
{gehrke,huhn}@informatik.uni-hildesheim.de

Abstract. We present a new programming language *ProFun* which is aimed for the specification and prototype implementation of reactive systems. *ProFun* combines the paradigms of concurrent and functional programming. A formal operational semantics is developed as a basis for verification techniques. We have implemented a *ProFun*-compiler which uses $C++$ as its target language.

Keywords: Executable Specifications, Language Design, Integration of Concurrent and Functional Programming, Formal Reasoning.

1 Introduction

Reactive and distributed systems are of increasing importance in theory and practice of computer science. Various languages for the specification and implementation of reactive systems have been developed to integrate two major aspects of reactive systems: the description of the structure and dynamic behaviour of a system *and* the handling of data.

Process algebras [Mil89, Hoa85] are commonly used to specify the reactions of a system on external events from its environment by means of communication and internal actions and a set of operators to describe more complex behaviour like choice, sequential and parallel composition. Process algebras provide a powerful theory on behavioural preorders and equivalences developed during the last decade. Behavioural equivalences like *bisimulation* [Mil89] allow for formal reasoning on correctness issues of distributed systems and are the basis for several tools for automated verification of such systems. Usually, process algebras focus on the structure and dynamic behaviour of the system and neglect the data.

Functional programming languages [Bac78, FH88] offer the capability to specify data on a very abstract level. Features like referential transparency, abstract data types, higher-order functions and exception handling improve program development and support rapid-prototyping. On the other hand the formal embedding of functional programs in a non-declarative environment (e.g. input/output handling) is rather difficult [Mog91].

[*] This work was partially supported by the HCM Network "EXPRESS" (Expressiveness of Languages for Concurrency).

We present a new language *ProFun* ("Processes with Functions") which is designed for specification and prototype implementation of reactive systems. *ProFun* integrates the paradigms of process algebras with synchronous communication and strict functional programming languages and shall support formal reasoning on specifications.

We agree with [BLOM] that concurrent programming is more than just parallelising existing sequential programs: the concurrency paradigm raises needs of structuring concepts in the language to specify the distribution of the system. In difference to approaches which aim to parallelise functional programs, in *ProFun* the specification of the system structure and behaviour is separated from the data handling within a process. Therefore, *ProFun* consists of two sublanguages. The first one is based on process algebras, the second is a functional programming language for the data handling within a process. In opposite to concurrent functional languages like *CML* [Rep93] and *Facile* [Tho93] the two sublanguages are integrated *asymmetrically*. Functional expressions may be part of the behavioural operators, (e.g. a value v may be sent on a channel c, denoted by $c!v$) but not vice versa, i.e. process terms are not part of the functional sublanguage. The two sublanguages can be understood as two layers: local data transformations of the subsystems are described on the first layer. This layer is embedded in a second one that deals with the hierarchical structure of systems and the interaction between the components. The data part can only influence the dynamic behaviour of the system via the interface provided by the operators of the process algebraic sublanguage.

Our main argument in favour of the strict separation of the data part from the behavioural part of the language is the possibility to adopt *existing* verification techniques well established for one part of the language: proof methods for abstract data types can be used to verify the data handling of a system whereas process algebraic techniques can be applied to prove the behavioural part correct. The rest of the paper is organised as follows: in sections 2 and 3 we introduce the syntax and the operational semantics of *ProFun*. A specification of the Bakery protocol is discussed in section 4. Section 5 briefly describes the implementation. Related work is considered in section 6.

2 The Language

ProFun consists of two sublanguages which are integrated asymmetrically. The data sublanguage (or "computation sublanguage") is a strict and purely functional language similar to core *Standard ML* [HMM86]. It provides abstract data types, exception handling, higher-order functions and pattern matching. As the properties of strict functional languages are well understood we concentrate in the following on the behavioural sublanguage (or "coordination sublanguage") and its integration with the data language. A complete presentation of the data language can be found in [Geh96]. The syntax of *ProFun* is given in fig. 1.

In the behavioural sublanguage the hierarchical system structure is represented by processes which are described by *process schemes*. A process scheme describes a set of similar process instances which differ by their local data. It consists of

```
program    ::=  process { process }
process    ::=  PROCESS ident ( paramlist ) [ EXITTYPE type ] ;
                [ DATA DECLARATIONS datadec { datadec } ]
                [ PROCESS DECLARATIONS process { process } ]
                BEHAVIOUR procterm
                ENDPROCESS ident ;
paramlist  ::=  [ type ident { , type ident } ]
procterm   ::=  nothing
                | stop
                | expr ! expr
                | expr ? ident
                | exit expr
                | eval ident = expr
                | if expr then procterm else procterm end
                | choose ( procterm { , procterm } )
                | test ident = expr success procterm failure handler end
                | procterm ; procterm
                | spawn ident ( arglist )
                | receive ident from parterm
                | restart ( arglist )
arglist    ::=  [ expr { , expr }]
parterm    ::=  |ident| ( ident ( arglist ) { , ident ( arglist ) } )
handler    ::=  [ ( expr → procterm ) | { ( expr → procterm ) | }]
                ( default → procterm )
datadec    ::=  ident = expr ;
                | exception ident [ of type ] ;
                | sumtype ident = ident of type {| ident of type } ;
                | prodtype ident = ident of type { , ident of type } ;
expr       ::=  op_un expr | expr op_bin expr
                | if expr then expr else expr
                | local ident = expr; {ident = expr;} in expr
                | function type ( expr { expr } → expr )
                              { | ( expr { expr } → expr ) }
                | raise expr
                | try expr handle
                        ( expr → expr )
                        { | ( expr → expr ) }
                | const | expr expr | ( expr )
type       ::=  int | bool | string | unit | typevar | ident |
                type list | type channel | type → type | ( type )
op_un      ::=  not | −
op_bin     ::=  + | − | * | / | mod | and | or |
                < | <= | > | >= | = | #
const      ::=  number | ident | boolconst | stringconst | listconst
                prodconst | void | expr.ident | new_channel ( type )
listconst  ::=  nil | cons | [ ] | [ expr {, expr } ]
prodconst  ::=  ident { ident = expr { , ident = expr } }
```

Fig. 1. Syntax of *ProFun*.

three main parts: data declarations, process declarations and a process term. In the data declarations part the local data of the process are declared by use of the operations of the data sublanguage. The process declarations part contains declarations of local process schemes. The third section contains a process term which determines the behaviour of the process instances. *ProFun* provides synchronous bidirectional communication via typed channels. Channels are implemented as values of a specific data type and can be created dynamically.

Now we briefly describe the operations of the behavioural sublanguage (see nonterminal *procterm* in figure 1). *nothing* is the void action with no effect to be used as a fill-in if the syntax demands the occurrence of an action and no effects are aspired by the programmer. *stop* denotes the inactive process (corresponding to 0 in CCS [Mil89]). The actions *!* and *?* represent send- and receive-operations on channels. *eval* computes the value of its expression and binds it to the implicitly declared identifier. *exit* terminates the execution of a process instance and determines its return value. *if, choose* and *test* are choice operators. The internal choice operator *if* selects one of its two alternatives via the result of a boolean expression. A *choose* offers different alternatives (process terms), each beginning with a communication action offered to the environment of the process. If an environmental process contains the counterpart of one of the communications offered, the corresponding process term is selected and executed whereas all other alternatives are dropped. The third choice operator *test* is used for exception handling on the process layer. If the corresponding expression is evaluated to a regular value, the process term after *success* is selected. If the result is an (via *raise*) activated exception, the corresponding process term is determined by *pattern matching*. If no match is possible, the *default* alternative is executed.

ProFun provides two operators for creating new process instances. Using *spawn* a new instance of the addressed process scheme is created, which is executed concurrently to the spawning instance. It is possible to parametrise the new process instance by arguments. The operator *receive* is used to compute a value by parallelising its computation. The computation is split into different parts, each executed by its own process instance. The process containing the *receive*-operator is blocked until all instances are terminated. After termination a *combine* function (similar to combine functions in *Esterel* [BG88]) is applied to the return values of the instances to compute the resulting value of the operator. The last operator *restart* is used for tail recursion in processes. *restart* restarts the current process instance without terminating the old one and creating a new one. Therefore, tail recursion can be handled more efficiently.

Scoping is closely related to the hierarchical structure of processes. The identifiers declared in the data section of a process scheme are visible in the local process schemes and in the scheme's process term. Identifiers can be declared in the process term implicitly (e.g. *value* in figure 2). The scope of an implicitly declared identifier extends to the end of the actual process term (e.g. the alternative of a choice operator).

In figure 2 an example in *ProFun* is given. The process scheme *FIFO_Memory* specifies a memory cell storing a queue of numbers. This queue is bound to the

```
PROCESS FIFO_Memory (int list queue);
DATA DECLARATIONS
  append = function int list->int list->int list
                (nil l          -> l)
              | ((cons h t) l -> cons h (append t l));
  empty = function int list->bool
                (nil          -> true)
              | ((cons h t) -> false);
BEHAVIOUR
  if empty queue then
    put? value; restart(append queue [value])
  else
    choose (
      put? value; restart(append queue [value]),
      get! head queue; restart(tail queue)
    )
  end
ENDPROCESS FIFO_Memory;
```

Fig. 2. Example: FIFO memory process scheme.

parameter *queue* and is represented by an integer list. The environment can send numbers via the channel *put*, which are appended to the queue, and asks for the current head of the queue via the channel *get* (we assume that both channels are declared in the environment). In the data section of the process scheme two functions are declared, namely *append* and *empty*. Both functions use pattern matching to determine the computation to be performed. The process term consists of an internal choice operator *if*. If the queue is empty, it is only possible to send a value via *put* to the cell. Otherwise the external choice operator *choose* offers communication on both channels to the environment. When receiving a value on the *put* channel, the process is restarted with a new queue, the concatenation of the old queue and a one-element list with the value received. After sending the head of the queue the process is restarted with the remainder of the old queue. A *FIFO_Memory* with the empty list as the initial parameter is created via *spawn FIFO_Memory(nil)*.

3 Sketch of the Operational Semantics

Now we sketch the *integrated operational semantics* of *ProFun*. The formal semantics is defined for well-formed and well-typed syntactic terms and consists of two parts, one for each sublanguage. Because of the asymmetric integration of the data language into the behavioural language the semantics for the latter makes use of the semantics of the former as a "black box". Thus we will use the structural approaches known for functional languages and process algebras, resp., for the definition of the semantics. A different approach can be found in semantics for *Concurrent ML* [FH95] where the semantics of the behaviour and the data are not defined separately, e.g. the semantics of the functional *let*-expression is defined using parallelism. Another approach is presented in [Pie93] where data are considered as abbreviations of more complex process terms which are expanded to give them a semantics. Thus in [Pie93] one formalism is sufficient to define the formal semantics of the whole language but with the drawback of a rather unintuitive semantics of the data part in terms of process derivations.

The data sublanguage is defined by using three reduction relations [Loo90], which model the elementary reduction steps ($\rightarrow$), reduction in context ($\Rightarrow$), and the control flow caused by activated exceptions ($\rightarrow_{exn}$). Reduction states are represented by tuples (exp, env) where exp is an expression and env an environment binding the free variables in exp to values. Environments are treated dynamically as stacks. Whenever a scope-defining construct is reached during execution, a new set for the identifiers defined in that scope is added to the environment. After leaving the current scope the corresponding set is removed. We denote the set of all environments by ENV.

The reduction semantics of a tuple (exp, env) is the normal form v to which the expression is reduced: $red[(exp, env)] = v$. We illustrate the reduction relations by presenting the rules for function application.

$$\frac{(E_1, env) \Rightarrow (E_1', env)}{(E_1\ E_2, env) \Rightarrow (E_1'\ E_2, env)} \tag{1}$$

$$\frac{(E_2, env) \Rightarrow (E_2', env)}{(v\ E_2, env) \Rightarrow (v\ E_2', env)} \tag{2}$$

$$(f\ v_1 \dots v_n, env) \rightarrow (E_i\sigma, env) \tag{3}$$

$$(f\ v_1 \dots v_{i-1}\ (raise\ x)\ E_{i+1} \dots E_n, env) \rightarrow_{exn} (raise\ x, env) \tag{4}$$

Because of the eager evaluation semantics the function expression and the argument expressions have to be evaluated before the rule (3) is applicable. Therefore, in rules (1) and (2) the reduction of the expressions of the function application is defined. In rule (1) the expression representing the function is evaluated, in rule (2) the arguments of the function application are reduced. Afterwards the function application is performed as an elementary reduction step by rule (3). Via pattern matching a suitable rule from the function declaration is selected (indicated by the index i) and the formal parameters of the i-th rule are substituted by the substitution σ. Rule (4) is used to handle the occurrence of an activated *exception* during the evaluation of the argument expressions. In this case the evaluation of the remaining expressions is disabled and the result of the expression is the activated exception.

The semantics of the behavioural sublanguage is given by two labelled transition systems (LTS). Following [NN93], the first LTS describes the local effects of the actions and operations and the second models the global system behaviour.

The asymmetrical integration of both formalisms can be seen at rule (5). If an operation of the behavioural sublanguage needs the evaluation of expressions, the evaluation is done by the reduction rules of the data sublanguage. After reduction the resulting value can be used by the operator.

Let T_Σ be the set of all process terms, $P \in T_\Sigma$ a process term and env an environment. Then $Z = (P, env)$ is a state of the local transition system. Let $\mathcal{Z} = \{Z \mid Z = (P, env), P \in T_\Sigma, env \in \text{ENV}\}$ be the set of the local states. $\mathcal{L}$ denotes the set of labels, which contains at least the labels $\tau, c(x), \overline{c(x)}$ and $\phi(.)$. τ represents internal behaviour, $c(x)$ denotes a read action, $\overline{c(x)}$ a write action (c is a channel name) and ϕ signals the creation of a new process instance.

To model the behaviour of a process term $P \in T_\Sigma$ a labelled transition system $< \mathcal{L}, \mathcal{Z}, \rightsquigarrow, (P, \mathcal{I}) >$ is used. $(P, \mathcal{I})$ is the initial state of the modelled process where $\mathcal{I}$ denotes the initial environment containing the formal parameters of the process and their values (environments are represented by lists of sets where each set contains the identifiers and the corresponding values of a single scope). The transition relation $\rightsquigarrow$ is defined as usually by inference rules. For example, the following rules define the local effects of the communication actions.

$$\frac{red[(E, env)] = v}{(c!E, env) \overset{\tau}{\rightsquigarrow} (c!v, env)} \tag{5}$$

$$\frac{\exists\, s \in \text{CTYP} : v \in \text{VALUE}^s \land c \in \text{CHAN}^s}{(c!v, env) \overset{\overline{c(v)}}{\rightsquigarrow} (nothing, env)} \tag{6}$$

$$(c?x, env) \overset{c(v)}{\rightsquigarrow} (nothing, include(x, v, env)) \tag{7}$$

Before the send action in rule (6) can be applied, its parameter has to be evaluated. This is described in rule (5): if the expression for the send action's parameter can be reduced to v, the process containing the send action can do so by a transition labelled τ which indicates local behaviour. CTYP denotes the ground type expressions without type variables, VALUE^s the values of type s and CHAN^s the channels of type s. In rule (7) the local behaviour of the receive action is described. After receiving a value v, the value is bound to the identifier x and included in the current scope of the environment.

The LTS for the description of the global system behaviour uses *process pools* as states. A process pool is a partial function $PP : PID \rightarrow \mathcal{Z}$ which maps process identifiers to the local states of the associated process instances. Whenever a new process instance is created, a unique process identifier (PID) is generated to identify this instance. The initial process pool of a program execution contains one instance for each global process scheme. The transitions of the LTS are labelled by sets of process identifiers representing the instances which participate in the respective transition.

As an example of an inference rule for the global LTS we consider again the rule for communication:

$$\frac{(B_1, env_1) \overset{\overline{c(v)}}{\rightsquigarrow} (B_1', env_1'), (B_2, env_2) \overset{c(v)}{\rightsquigarrow} (B_2', env_2')}{PP[p_1 \mapsto (B_1, env_1)][p_2 \mapsto (B_2, env_2)] \overset{\{p_1, p_2\}}{\Longrightarrow} PP[p_1 \mapsto (B_1', env_1')][p_2 \mapsto (B_2', env_2')]} \tag{8}$$

If two processes execute corresponding communication actions, the global transition system models the communication as a combined transition which is labelled with a set containing the process numbers of the participating processes. The notation $PP[p_i \rightarrow Z_i]$ is taken from [NN93] to describe the current local state Z_i of process instance p_i in the process pool PP.

$$\frac{\forall i \in \{1, ..., n\} : red[(E_i, env)] = v_i}{(spawn\ P(E_1, ..., E_n), env) \overset{\tau}{\rightsquigarrow} (spawn\ P(v_1, ..., v_n), env)} \tag{9}$$

$$\frac{p = newpid()}{(spawn\ P(v_1, ..., v_n), env) \overset{\phi(P(v_1,...,v_n),p)}{\rightsquigarrow} (nothing, env)} \tag{10}$$

$$\frac{(B_1, env) \overset{\phi(P(v_1,...,v_n),p')}{\rightsquigarrow} (B_1', env)}{PP[p \mapsto (B_1, env)] \overset{\{p,p'\}}{\Longrightarrow} PP[p \mapsto (B_1', env)][p' \mapsto \Theta(P, [v_1, ..., v_n])]} \tag{11}$$

As a second example we consider the creation of a process instance. The rules (9) and (10) describe the local behaviour of a process performing a *spawn*. In rule (9) the arguments of the new instance are computed. In rule (10) a new unique process identifier is generated to identify the new instance. The *spawn* expression is reduced to *nothing*. The corresponding transition is labelled with the event ϕ which denotes the creation of a process instance. The name of the process scheme, the parameters and the process identifier are attached as parameters. Rule (11) describes to global effects of process creation. The process pool is updated by adding the initial state of the new instance. The initial state is the result of the function Θ, which initialises the parameters $[v_1, ..., v_n]$ in the local environment of p' and generates a prefix of *eval* actions that evaluate the local data of p'.

4 Example: The Bakery Protocol

In this section we give a *ProFun*-specification of the so-called Bakery protocol [GK94]. The Bakery protocol is a simple protocol used in busy shops (in particular bakeries) to serve customers. Whenever a customer enters the shop she picks a sequence number *next* (in the range of $[0 \ldots n-1]$) that will be shown at the service point when it is her turn to be served.

In *ProFun* (see figure 4) the protocol is modelled as follows: The channels *enter* and *leave* connect the protocol to its environment. They are defined on the system level whereas the other parts are internal for the Bakery protocol. According to the modulo number n a bunch of *Buffer*-processes are started. Each *Buffer* synchronises via its own *get*- and *put*-channel with the *Enter*- and *Server*-process and provides a place for one customer who is waiting for service. *Enter* has access to a list of the *get*-channels to the *Buffers* and controls by its local identifier *next* which *Buffer* will be used for the next incoming customer. The *Server* receives its next job via the *put*-channel from the *Buffer* in turn. The sequencing of the customers is achieved by the selection of the channels associated with the

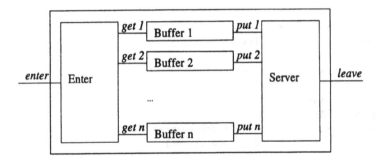

Fig. 3. Bakery protocol with n places

next Buffer. Thus the situation where a customer with an incorrect sequencing number arrives at the *Server* is excluded automatically.

In opposite to the situation in the bakery where the sequence number to be served is broadcast among the customers in the shop, we had to introduce a unique pair of channels for each buffer because *ProFun* does not allow broadcast or multi-party-synchronisation.[2] In that *ProFun* agrees with the synchronisation mechanisms as defined in LOTOS [ISO87] and μCRL [GP91]. But in difference to these specification languages synchronisation on the data value is also prevented in *ProFun*. In LOTOS and μCRL a communication action like

```
get? Job_with_Num{num=next,client}                                    (*)
```

can be specified. It indicates that the *Server* wants to participate in a communication but only if the first value *num* offered by the sending *Buffer* equals the *Server*'s value *next*. Such a synchronisation on data values allows to simulate broadcast. This is not possible in *ProFun* where the mechanism that ensures the synchronisation on a data value has to be made explicit already in the specification of the processes. One may argue that *ProFun* enforces a lower abstraction level for the specification of distributed systems that is too close to implementation. But this also can be seen as an advantage: The complete synchronisation structure of a system has to be made explicit in its *ProFun*-specification and is strictly separated from the data handling. Thus an implementation of a *ProFun*-specification in a more efficient programming environment will coincide in more aspects with the behaviour of the *ProFun*-specification. In particular, scheduling problems like livelocks, deadlocks, or unbounded delay become obvious already in the *ProFun*-specification. In our example, a naive low level implementation of the synchronisation on a data value like (*) may contain an unbounded or even infinite sequence of *show* and *test* actions caused by an impertinent customer who permanently offers her job to the *Server* and is rejected because it is not her turn. We argue that a formal verification of properties of *ProFun*-specifications is more expressive w.r.t. the actual behaviour of a real implementation of the system.

---

[2] Thus a solution with a single pair of *get* and *put* channels common to all buffers would require an additional synchronisation procedure to determine the customer owning the correct sequence number (that equals the *next*-value of the *Server*).

```
enter = new_channel(Job);
leave = new_channel(Result);
nth = function int -> 'a list -> 'a
          (0 (cons h t) -> h)
        | (n (cons h t) -> nth (n-1) t);

PROCESS BakeryProtocol(int n);
DATA DECLARATIONS
prodtype Ch_List_Pair = first of Job channel list,
                        snd of Job channel list;

work = function Job -> Result (...)   % service offered to the customers %

PROCESS DECLARATIONS

PROCESS Initialize(int n, Job channel list get_list, Job channel list put_list)
EXITTYPE Ch_List_Pair;
BEHAVIOUR
    if n=0 then exit Ch_List_Pair{first=get_list,snd=put_list}
    else eval get_ch=new_channel(Job); eval put_ch=new_channel(Job);
         spawn Buffer(get_ch,put_ch);
         restart (n-1, cons get_ch get_list, cons put_ch put_list)
    end
ENDPROCESS Initialize;

PROCESS Enter(int next, Job channel list get_list);
BEHAVIOUR
    enter? job; (nth next get_list)! job;
    restart((next+1) mod n, get_list)
ENDPROCESS Enter;

PROCESS Buffer(Job channel get, Job channel put);
BEHAVIOUR
  get? job; put! job;
  restart(get,put)
ENDPROCESS Buffer;

PROCESS Server(int next, Job channel list put_list);
BEHAVIOUR
  (nth next put_list)? client; leave! work(client);
  restart((next+1) mod n,put_list)
ENDPROCESS Server;

BEHAVIOUR
    receive ch_list_p from Initialize(n,nil,nil);
    spawn Enter(0,ch_list_p.first); spawn Server(0,ch_list_p.snd)
ENDPROCESS BakeryProtocol;
```

Fig. 4. *ProFun* specification of the Bakery protocol

In particular, we hope that the interface strictly encapsulating the data of the processes will allow the adoption of verification tools with minor modifications. As an example we considered in [GH96] a correctness property of the Bakery protocol which is supposed to work as a FIFO-Buffer with $(n + 1)$ places.

5 Implementation

Another main topic when developing a new language is its practical expressiveness. Hence we developed a compiler prototype that allows to compile a subset of the language into $C++$ code [Str92]. Not implemented yet are the exception handling (including the *test*-operator) and the support for product and sum types. The compiler has already been used for the specification and simulation of some distributed algorithms and a medium size case study on a distributed bank system.

The compiler was designed as a tool for rapid-prototyping. It allows to compile *ProFun* specifications into executable code which simulates distribution by the multi-threading capabilities of the Solaris operating system [Sun94].

$C++$ was chosen as the target language for several reasons:

- the language in the release of Solaris includes a library which provides multi-threading,
- the object oriented facilities ease the realisation of the data types of *ProFun*: the data types are implemented as a class hierarchy where the root class contains the common methods for data handling,
- and $C++$ is a widely used language which is supported by tools and additional libraries.

As implementation language for the compiler itself *Standard ML* in the release of New Jersey [Bel93] was chosen. Compiling a program can be understood as a transformational operation which can be naturally expressed in functional languages. By the tools *lexgen* and *sml-yacc* a support for the implementation of the analysis phases of the compiler is given.

The source code of the compiler embraces 130 lines for the definition file of the scanner, 330 lines for the parser and 2700 lines for the semantical analysis and code generation. The runtime library consists of 1000 lines of $C++$ code.

A *ProFun* source program is translated to $C++$ code which is compiled to an executable file for Solaris. Due to the possibility of executing process instances in parallel, the program is mapped to a task containing several threads which represent the program's process instances. Every thread consists of a $C++$ function which contains the generated code for the associated process scheme.

Channels are implemented as instances of a channel class using templates to realise polymorphism. The class contains methods which perform synchronisation and value transfer between communicating processes.The function *new_channel* creates channels dynamically. In order to guarantee weak fair executions of the program, two FIFO-queues are associated with each channel. If a process wants to communicate via a channel, it sends a read or a write request to the channel that is stored in the corresponding queue. If both queues contain at least one request, the first processes of the queues are chosen as communication partners. The expressions of the data sublanguage are evaluated by an abstract machine PVM which is similar to the machine presented in [Ler90]. The machine consists of two stacks and four registers. The first stack is used for reduction of operators and function application, the second for the management of variables. The content of the registers determine the states of the stacks. Instead of interpreting byte code, the statements of the PVM are coded as $C++$-functions in the runtime library. The execution of a statement is performed via a call to the corresponding function. Therefore, the PVM contains no program counter and control flow is managed by the real machine.

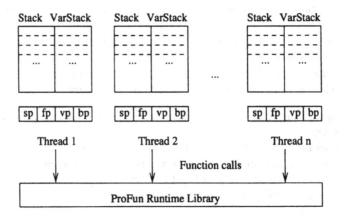

Fig. 5. Instances of the virtual machine.

Each created process instance needs its own copy of the virtual machine to evaluate its local data operations without interfering with other process instances. Therefore, when a new instance of a process is created, it achieves a new instance of the virtual machine (see figure 5). The functions of the data sublanguage are mapped to $C++$-functions which are parametrised with the stacks and the registers of the corresponding instance of the virtual machine.

The lack of the ability to declare local functions in $C++$ increased the complexity of managing global identifiers. Local processes are allowed to access the identifiers defined in the surrounding processes, which enables the sharing of data between process instances. Due to the declarative usage of data this access is limited to read access. Therefore, at the creation of a local process a corresponding data structure is generated containing the values of the global identifiers. This data structure is passed as an argument to the thread that realises the process.

Another problem arose from the implementation of the external choice operator *choose*. On the one hand the alternatives of this operator have to behave like processes for communication issues. On the other hand these alternatives have to be considered as process terms, not real processes (e.g. a *restart* in one alternative must restart the whole process, not only the alternative). In the implementation this problem is solved as follows: the communication action at the beginning of each alternative is realised as a process. The rest of the alternatives are coded into the function which implements the process with the *choose*-operator. If one of the communication actions is chosen, the processes containing the communication actions of the other alternatives are terminated. The selected process signals its success to the process with the *choose* which performs the remaining actions of the chosen alternative.

6 Related Work and Conclusions

We strongly believe that an asymmetric integration of an functional languages in a coordination language reduces the complexity of the dynamic structure of systems and eases the verification of systems described in *ProFun*. Examples for a symmetric integration are *Facile* or *CML* where a functional language (in both cases ML) is enriched by non-declarative concepts like synchronisation and spawning. This gives the programmer the freedom to mix up imperative and declarative programming styles arbitrarily. Both languages provide operators to transform a process term into a functional expression (which may be communicated via channels and modified by functions) and vice versa. Thus the specified system can be reconfigured dynamically. The dynamic reconfiguration of a system (called "mobility") is also a major concern in the π-calculus [3] [MPW92, Pie93].

But the additional expressivity also makes the formal reasoning on correctness issues of the specified systems more complicate. For these languages static analysis (e.g. type inference) necessarily gives weaker results. Moreover, new verification techniques have to be investigated [FHJ95, AD96] for such a generalised framework. We aim to adopt and combine *existing* verification techniques that are already well established for process algebras [Mil89, Bae90] and functional programming [Cle87] respectively. To achieve this goal it appears more promising to provide a restricted interface between both paradigms as it is done in *ProFun*. The functional concurrent language *Erlang* differs in various aspects from *ProFun*. *Erlang* is type-less and communication is based on asynchronous message passing. The addressee of a message is a process identifier, thus conceptual a unique port is associated with each process to receive messages which is a major difference to the channel-based synchronisations in process algebras. Additionally primitives to deal with real time are incorporated in *Erlang*.

An similar asymmetric integration of the data sublanguage into a process algebra can be found in the specification languages LOTOS [BB87], standardised in [ISO87], and μCRL [GP91]. Both languages combine process algebras with abstract data types (ADT). ADTs are well-suited for formal verification, but - compared to functional languages - implementations of ADT languages are

---

[3] In contrary to the other languages a functional expression in the π-calculus abbreviates more complex process terms that simulate the evaluation of the expression.

unsatisfactory inefficient. Thus the execution of prototypes generated from a specification is restricted to rather small examples. Secondary, ADTs lack a built-in exception handling mechanism. Therefore an ADT is usually extended by specific values for the different kinds of exceptions possible. But this technique leads to an increased expense in handling the extended ADT in specification and it does not include the control flow management provided by built-in exception handling[4]. In our opinion the specification of data types in a functional language makes a good compromise between applicability and a strict formal reasoning on specifications. A first larger case study was presented on a workshop on "Concurrency in Information Systems" in Braunschweig in January and proved the applicability of the new language.

Some practical work has to be done on the compiler. The implementation of the remaining elements of *ProFun* will be finished soon. Next we plan to develop a code generator which generates code for the *Java*-machine. This will increase the portability of *ProFun*. Moreover, because of the integrated garbage collector of the machine, we will achieve memory management for free. Another topic for future work is the implementation of libraries providing commonly used data structures and process architectures.

Acknowledgements

We are grateful to U. Goltz, P. Niebert, A. Rensink, H. Wehrheim, A. Stümpel and T. Firley for fruitful discussions and comments. In particular, we benefited from their experience on the integration of a data sublanguage into a process algebra.

References

[AD96] Robert Amadio and Mads Dam. Towards a modal theory of types for the π-calculus. R96:03, SICS, 1996.

[Bac78] J. Backus. Can programming be liberated from the von Neumann style? A functional style and its algebra of programs. *Communications of the ACM*, 21:613–641, 1978.

[Bae90] J.C.M. Baeten, editor. *Applications of Process Algebra*. Cambridge University Press, 1990.

[BB87] Tommaso Bolognesi and Ed Brinksma. Introduction to the ISO specification language LOTOS. *Computer Networks and ISDN System*, 14:25–59, 1987.

[Bel93] Bell Laboratories,AT&T. *Standard ML of New Jersey – User's Guide (Version 0.93)*, Feb 1993.

[BG88] G. Berry and G. Gonthier. The Esterel Synchronous Programming Language: Design, Semantics, Implementation. Technical report, ENSMP and INRIA, 1988.

[BLOM] K. Bohlmann, R. Loogen, and Y. Ortega-Mallén. Specification of Concurrent Process Systems in a Functional Setting. Technical report, Universität Marburg.

---

[4] For these (and other) reasons in the aspired new LOTOS standard E-LOTOS the integration of a functional language for data handling is proposed [Pec94].

[Cle87] D. Clement. The Natural Dynamic Semantics of Mini-Standard ML. In E. Hartmut, R. Kowalski, and G. Levi, editors, *TAPSOFT'87*, volume 250 of *LNCS*, pages 67–81. Springer, 1987.

[FH88] A.J. Field and P.G. Harrison. *Functional Programming*. Addison Wesley, 1988.

[FH95] W. Ferreira and M. Hennessy. Towards a Semantic Theory of CML. Technical report, University of Sussex, 1995.

[FHJ95] W. Ferreira, M. Hennessy, and A. Jeffrey. A Theory of Weak Bisimulation for Core CML. Technical Report 05/95, University of Sussex, 1995.

[Geh96] Thomas Gehrke. Eine Programmiersprache für verteilte Systeme mit funktionalem Datenanteil. Master's thesis, Universität Hildesheim, 1996.

[GH96] Thomas Gehrke and Michaela Huhn. *ProFun* – a Language for Executable Specifications. Technical Report HIB 17/96, Universität Hildesheim, 1996.

[GK94] J.F. Groote and H. Korver. A correctness proof of the bakery protocol in μCRL. In A. Ponse et al., editor, *Algebra of Communicating Processes*, Workshops in Computing, pages 63–86. Springer, 1994.

[GP91] J.F. Groote and A. Ponse. Proof theory for μCRL: a language for processes with data. Technical Report CS-R9138, CWI, 1991.

[HMM86] R. Harper, D. MacQueen, and R. Milner. Standard ML. Technical Report ECS-LFCS-86-2, Dep. of Computer Science, University of Edinburgh, 1986.

[Hoa85] C.A.R. Hoare. *Communicating Sequential Processes*. Prentice Hall, 1985.

[ISO87] ISO – OSI. LOTOS – A Formal Description Technique Based on the Temporal Ordering of Observational Behaviour. DIS 8807, 1987.

[Ler90] Xavier Leroy. The ZINC Experiment: An economical implementation of the ML language. Technical Report 117, Institut National de Recherche en Informatique et Automatique (INRIA), 1990.

[Loo90] Rita Loogen. *Parallele Implementierung funktionaler Programmiersprachen*. Springer, 1990.

[Mil89] Robin Milner. *Communication and Concurrency*. Prentice Hall, 1989.

[Mog91] Eugenio Moggi. Notions of computation and monads. *Information and Computation*, 93:55 – 92, 1991.

[MPW92] R. Milner, J. Parrow, and D. Walker. A calculus of mobile processes. *Information and Computation*, 100:1–40, 41–77, 1992. parts I and II.

[NN93] Flemming Nielson and Hanne Riis Nielson. From CML to Process Algebras. In *Proceedings of CONCUR '93*, volume 715 of *LNCS*. Springer, 1993.

[Pec94] Charles Pecheur. A Proposal for Data Types for E-LOTOS. Technical report, University of Liège, 1994.

[Pie93] Benjamin C. Pierce. Programming in the Pi-Calculus - An Experiment in Programming Language Design. Technical report, Department of Computer Science, University of Edinburgh, 1993.

[Rep93] J.H. Reppy. CML: A Higher-order Concurrent Language. Technical report, Cornell University, 1993.

[Str92] B. Stroustrup. *The C++ programming language*. Addison–Wesley, 1992.

[Sun94] Sun Microsystems GmbH. *Multithreaded Programming Guide*, 1994.

[Tho93] B. Thomsen et al. Facile Antigua Release Programming Guide. Technical Report ECRC-93-20, ECRC GmbH, München, 1993.

From Term Rewriting to Generalised Interaction Nets

Maribel Fernández
LIENS (CNRS URA 1327)
École Normale Supérieure
45 Rue d'Ulm, 75005 Paris, France
maribel@dmi.ens.fr

Ian Mackie
LIX (CNRS URA 1439)
École Polytechnique
91128 Palaiseau Cedex, France
mackie@lix.polytechnique.fr

Abstract. In this paper we present a system of interaction that generalises Lafont's interaction nets by allowing computation in several nets in parallel and communication through a state. This framework allows us to represent large classes of term rewriting systems, genuine parallel functions, non-determinism, communication, sharing, and hence can be used to code features from Standard ML and Concurrent ML.

1 Introduction

Term rewriting systems can be regarded as a multi-paradigm specification language, or as an abstract model of computation (abstract in the sense that they specify actions but not control; they are free from strategies). Lafont's interaction nets are a graphical framework based on net rewriting which is much closer to a real model of computation in that all the operations are made explicit, including discarding and copying of data. Moreover, interaction nets can be regarded as a distributed model of computation since all reductions are local.

In a previous paper [2] we began a programme of research which aims to bridge the gap between these two separate formalisms: we presented a series of translations from interaction nets to various classes of term rewriting systems, and studied various properties that are preserved under the translations. The aim of the present paper is to complete the study of the correspondence between interaction nets and term rewriting systems, by showing translations of term rewriting systems into interaction nets. This is a first step towards the development of an interaction-net based implementation of term rewriting languages.

Due to the intrinsic limitations of interaction nets (they only capture confluent and sequential computations) not all term rewriting systems can be encoded. However, for the class of *match-sequential orthogonal constructor systems* [17] we give a general encoding into interaction nets. We then look at more general classes of term rewriting systems, and investigate what we need to add to interaction nets to allow a full encoding.

We identify several features that we would like to capture that are not included in the interaction net framework. Since interaction nets only capture sequential and deterministic computations, the main additions that we consider concern non-determinism and parallel functions, such as "parallel-or" defined by: por tt $x \to$ tt, por x tt $\to$ tt, por ff ff $\to$ ff. In addition, we would like to code notions such as communication, so that we can send and receive data between disjoint nets which is required to code languages such as CML [16], and state so that we can code references, as in ML [15].

In this paper we propose a new system of interaction that captures the above, but retains the spirit of Lafont's interaction nets. The generalisation we propose consists of allowing computation in *several interaction nets in parallel*, which can communicate through a *state*. In particular, we still consider a graphical framework and binary interactions, but we permit interactions through the state (a kind of "indirect interaction"), which allows the encoding of all the above notions in a clean and uniform way. As particular cases, we show how to encode the whole class of orthogonal (i.e. left-linear and non-overlapping) constructor systems, which is used in most programming languages based on term rewriting, and also overlapping systems such as the system defining the parallel-or function.

Other models of computation derived from interaction nets with different purposes have been proposed by Laneve [11], who introduced *interaction systems* as combinatory reduction systems that correspond to interaction nets without the linearity condition (but still sequential), and Honda [5] who defined a calculus of concurrent processes in which the connecting edges are not necessarily binary (Lafont's interaction nets can be seen as a particular case, although the framework of concurrent processes is quite different from the graphical framework of interaction nets). In contrast, the generalised interaction nets we propose can represent parallel computations while retaining the essence of Lafont's interaction nets. We define a set of combinators that can be used to manipulate (interact through) the state, thus making possible the encoding of references and communication. By restricted use of these combinators we obtain Lafont's interaction nets as a particular case, and also parallel nets without side effects which inherit all the properties of interaction nets.

Interaction nets have been successfully used for the implementation of various λ-calculi [12]. We study interaction nets from the term rewriting point of view with the hope of making these implementation ideas applicable also to term rewriting systems and to languages that combine term rewriting and λ-calculus. We hope that generalised interaction nets will also allow us to code more general classes of rewrite systems, such as combinatory reduction systems.

The rest of this paper is structured as follows. In the next section we recall the basic concepts used in the rest of the paper. In Section 3 we give the first set of translations from term rewriting systems to interaction nets. In Section 4 we investigate the structures that we need to code general term rewriting systems; in particular this leads to interaction nets with state. In Section 5 we look at several case studies to show how to code additional features into our nets. Finally, in Section 6 we conclude our ideas and suggest further directions.

2 Background

We refer the reader to [1, 8] for a detailed account of rewrite systems, and to [10] for interaction nets; here we briefly recall the basic definitions.

Term rewriting systems. A *signature* $\mathcal{F}$ is a finite set of *function symbols* together with their (fixed) arity. $\mathcal{X}$ denotes a denumerable set of *variables*, and $T(\mathcal{F}, \mathcal{X})$ denotes the set of *terms* built up from $\mathcal{F}$ and $\mathcal{X}$. The *subterm* of t at position p is denoted by $t|_p$ and the result of replacing $t|_p$ with u at position p in t is denoted by $t[u]_p$. This notation is also used to indicate that u is a subterm of t. A term is *linear* if each variable occurs at most once.

A *term rewriting system* is a set of rewrite rules $R = \{l_i \to r_i\}_i$, where $l_i \notin \mathcal{X}$ and $Var(r_i) \subseteq Var(l_i)$. A term t rewrites to a term u at position p with the rule $l \to r$ and the substitution σ, written $t \xrightarrow[l \to r]{p} u$, or simply $t \to u$, if $t|_p = l\sigma$ and $u = t[r\sigma]_p$. We denote by $\to^+$ (resp. $\to^*$) the transitive (resp. transitive and reflexive) closure of the rewrite relation $\to$. R is *left-linear* if all left-hand sides of rules in R are linear; *non-overlapping* if there are no critical pairs; *orthogonal* if it is left-linear and non-overlapping.

Interaction nets. An interaction net (Σ, IR) is specified by a set Σ of symbols (*agents*), each with an arity (degree) $n \in \mathbf{N}$ ($n \geq 1$) which is the number of edges attached to it, and a set IR of *interaction rules*. A *net* on Σ is an undirected graph with nodes labeled by symbols in Σ. The points of contact of edges with nodes are called *ports*. Each agent has a distinguished port labeled with an arrow, called the *principal port*, where interaction can take place. All the other ports are called *auxiliary ports*. Interaction rules are activated when two agents are connected on their principal port. There is at most one rule for each pair of agents. The following diagram shows the general form of an interaction rule, where N is a any net. Note that the interface is preserved.

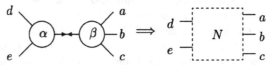

As examples, we show the rules of two ubiquitous agents, namely the *erase* (ϵ), which deletes everything it interacts with, and the *duplicator* (δ), which copies everything. These are represented by the following diagrams, where α is any node.

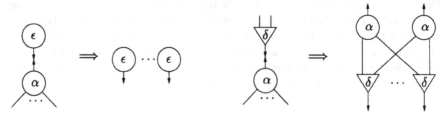

We say that a net is in *normal form* when no interactions are possible. By construction, the net rewriting process is *confluent*. Moreover, since the local interface is preserved during interaction there is scope for a truly parallel implementation.

3 From Term Rewriting Systems to Interaction Nets

Interaction nets provide an alternative view of rewriting that is easier to work with (since it is graphical), and easier to implement (since they are more explicit with respect to copying/discarding of data, and the reduction process is local). But term rewriting is a very rich field, with well established theories and results such as type systems, termination proof techniques, etc. The study of the relationships between these two formalisms allows results to be transferred from one framework to the other. In [2] we showed the following mappings from classes of interaction nets to rewrite systems:

Class of Interaction Nets	Class of Rewrite Systems
Discrete Semi-simple Nets	First-order Term Rewriting Systems (linear and non-overlapping)
Non-Dependent Semi-simple Nets	First-order Term Rewriting Systems (left-linear and non-overlapping)
Dependent Semi-simple Nets	Combinatory Reduction Systems (left-linear and non-overlapping)

In this section we continue the study of the above correspondence by showing how to translate in the opposite direction. We focus on *orthogonal term rewriting systems*.

It is not possible to encode an arbitrary system of this class into interaction nets. The first problem is that there is no uniform translation for rules that express relations between *constructors*, like: $Pred(Succ(x)) \rightarrow x$, $Succ(Pred(x)) \rightarrow x$, since agents can only interact on their principal ports. However, if we consider the class of term rewriting systems that is used in most functional programming languages, constructor systems, then this problem does not arise. A *constructor system* is a term rewriting system with the property that the signature can be partitioned into a set C of constructors and a set D of defined functions, and every left-hand side $f(t_1, \ldots, t_n)$ of a rule satisfies $f \in D$ and $t_1, \ldots, t_n \in T(C, X)$. A constructor system is then specified by a triple (D, C, R), where R is the set of rewrite rules of the system.

It is still not possible to encode an arbitrary function definition of this class as an interaction net: the limitation of binary interactions does not allow us to encode non-sequential functions like the well-known BP function of Berry and Plotkin. Note that this is an orthogonal constructor system, but it is not sequential. Interaction nets can only code function definitions where patterns can be examined in some sequential order. This property is called *match-sequentiality*, and is decidable for orthogonal constructor systems [17].

In the rest of this section we show that orthogonal match-sequential constructor systems can be encoded as interaction nets, by showing a translation from this class of rewrite systems to (non-dependent) interaction nets. We then show that the left-linearity condition can be dropped if we consider a call-by-value strategy of evaluation for the term rewrite system.

Translating Match-sequential Orthogonal Constructor Systems. Constructor systems contain rules of the form $f(l_1,\ldots,l_n) \to t$ where $l_1,\ldots,l_n \in T(\mathcal{C}, \mathcal{X})$ and are called the *patterns* of the rewrite rule. In a match-sequential rewrite system, given a function f of arity n, there is a sequence $(i_1,\ldots,i_k)$, $0 \le k \le n$, of *indexes* of patterns such that pattern-matching can be safely done in the order indicated by the sequence. The case of an empty sequence of indexes ($k = 0$) corresponds to a function defined by a rule of the form $f(\vec{x}) \to t$ (we use vectors to denote sequences, which can be empty).

By adding new function symbols to the signature, we can assume without loss of generality that all the patterns have depth less than or equal to 1. Moreover, because the system is match-sequential, we can transform each function definition so that each function has at most one index (see [7] for a detailed description of these transformations). Hence, in the following we will consider constructor systems with left-linear rules of the form $f(\vec{x}, c(\vec{z}), \vec{y}) \to t$, where $c \in \mathcal{C}$, $\vec{x}, \vec{y}, \vec{z} \in \mathcal{X}$, and the position of $c(\vec{z})$ corresponds to the index i of f. We will translate a constructor system over the signature $(\mathcal{D}, \mathcal{C})$ into an interaction net system with agents:

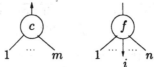

for each $c \in \mathcal{C}$ of arity m, and $f \in \mathcal{D}$ of arity n with index i. In addition, for each $f \in \mathcal{D}$ of arity n with an empty sequence of indexes (this implies that no pattern-matching is needed for f) we consider the agents:

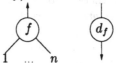

The dummy agent d_f is needed to code the rules for f as binary interactions, as we see below. Note that in this case the output port of f is the principal port, as in the case of constructors.

We now define (by induction) a translation function Θ that takes a term t in the signature $(\mathcal{D}, \mathcal{C})$ and produces a net with the above set of agents.

1. If $t \in \mathcal{X}$ then $\Theta(t)$ is just an edge.
2. If $t = c(t_1,\ldots,t_n)$ and $c \in \mathcal{C}$, $\Theta(t)$ is the net given in Fig. 1(a).
3. If $t = f(t_1,\ldots,t_n)$ and $f \in \mathcal{D}$ with index i, $\Theta(t)$ is the net in Fig. 1(b).
4. If $t = f(t_1,\ldots,t_n)$ and $f \in \mathcal{D}$ with an empty list of indexes, then t will be translated using the dummy function d_f. $\Theta(t)$ is the net in Fig. 1(c).

If t is a linear term we are done, otherwise we define $\Theta'(t)$ as the net obtained from $\Theta(t)$ by connecting the edges corresponding to occurrences of non-linear variables in t to δ nodes (duplicators).

To complete the encoding of a constructor system into an interaction net, we show the translation of the set of rewrite rules. We distinguish two cases. A rule of the form $f(\vec{x}, c(\vec{z}), \vec{y}) \to t$ defining an n-ary function f with index i, is translated as the interaction rule given in Fig. 1(d), where $\Theta'(t)$ is obtained from

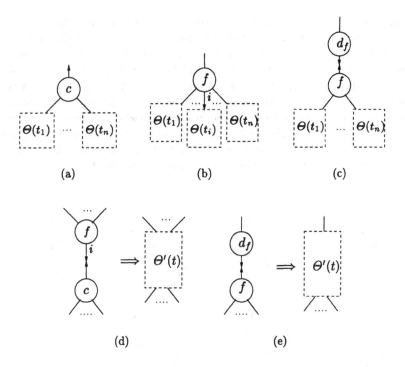

Fig. 1.

the net $\Theta(t)$ by connecting the edges that correspond to non-linear variables in t to δ nodes (duplicating), and adding ϵ nodes (erasing) for the variables of the left-hand side that do not appear in t. If $l \to r$ is right-linear and $Var(l) = Var(r)$ then $\Theta'(r) = \Theta(r)$. A rule of the form $f(\vec{x}) \to t$ will be coded as a binary interaction using d_f, as shown in Fig. 1(e), where $\Theta'(t)$ is defined as above.

Correctness of the translation. We only give a brief sketch of the proof. It consists of two parts. First we show that a sequence of shared-rewrite steps (see [9] for details on shared-rewriting) $s \to^+ t$ using rules in R can be simulated by a sequence of interactions from $\Theta'(s)$ using the translation of R. Then we use a result of Kennaway *et al.* [6] that shows that in the case of orthogonal systems, shared-rewriting can simulate standard rewriting. This completes the proof.

Non-linearity and Overlappings. We address first the problem of encoding match-sequential non-overlapping constructor systems *with non-linear left-hand sides.* Let us consider a simple example: $f(c(x), x) \to t$. This rule can be applied only to terms of the form $f(c(t_1), t_2)$ where t_1 and t_2 are equal. The translation function defined previously is not correct for non-left-linear rules: in order to mimic term reduction, we have to code the function that tests syntactical equality of terms as an interaction net. We can represent such a function by an agent *eq* with 3 ports, corresponding to the two arguments and the result, and we will arbitrarily choose the left argument to be the principal port. Since *eq* can only interact with constructors, this forces a *call-by-value strategy* on our encoding.

To simplify the presentation we consider only rewriting on ground terms (terms without variables), and assume that normal forms are constructor terms. The encoding of terms is done in exactly the same way as before. For the rules we just give an example. Figure 2 shows the translation of the system containing the rule $f(c(x), x) \to t$ in a signature f, c, a, b where $a, b, c \in C$, a is nullary, b is binary, and c is unary. The generalisation is straightforward.

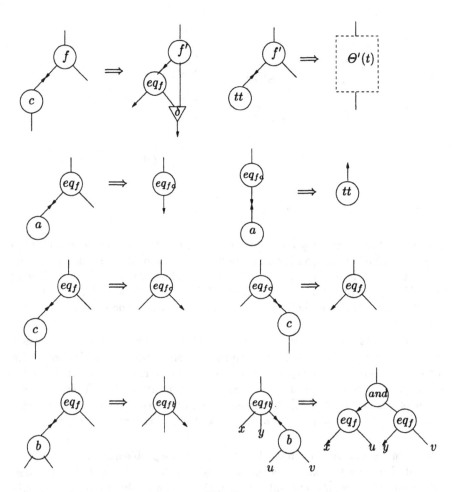

Fig. 2.

The problem of overlapping patterns is more delicate. Rules like $f(c(x)) \to a$

and $f(c(x)) \rightarrow b$ are perfectly acceptable, although the system is not confluent. Interaction nets are confluent by definition; only one interaction rule can
be defined for each pair of agents, preventing the encoding of rules like the ones
above. Of course, an overlapping system may be confluent, an interesting example being the class of *weakly-orthogonal* rewrite systems: left-linear systems
that have only trivial critical pairs of the form (t,t). The translation function
defined before can be directly applied to weakly-orthogonal constructor systems
that are match-sequential: in this case the only possible overlappings are at the
root position, between a left-hand side l and another left-hand side instance of
l (note that the assumption of match-sequentiality is crucial here); then it is
sufficient to translate only the most general rules that create a critical pair.

4 Generalised Interaction Nets

Thus far the most general class of term rewriting system that we have been able
to code completely in interaction nets is the class of match-sequential, orthogonal
constructor systems. Here we generalise the interaction net framework so that all
orthogonal constructor systems, and also overlapping systems can be encoded.

We add the notion of a *state* to the interaction net framework. That is to
say that we consider the interaction system together with a state that we can
allocate, update and read values. In particular, we see generalised interaction
nets as parallel interaction nets that communicate via the state.

The main reason for this choice is that having a notion of state allows us
to have *interaction by indirection*. We maintain the binary interaction (with a
reference node) but can have multiple pointers to a single net via the state (this
is crucial for capturing sharing of values). By keeping the restriction to binary
interactions, our generalised interaction nets inherit the properties of interaction
nets (asynchrony, locality, confluence) when restricted to computations in one
net. The interactions between different nets are restricted to interactions through
the state.

To explain how this works we define several interaction rules that are examples of basic combinators for state manipulation. These operations are identified
using the same nomenclature as for references in ML [15]. In Fig. 3 we introduce
the nodes that we are going to use, and give the corresponding interaction rules
for each operation in Fig. 4. These are all explained as follows.

Fig. 3. Nodes

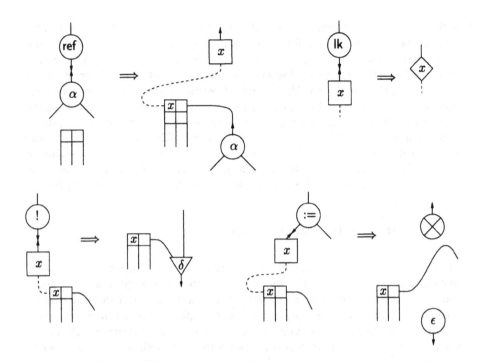

Fig. 4. Interaction rules with state

Allocation of a new cell (ref N). This operation creates a new memory location, say x, and assigns to it an initial net N. The interaction produces a new node which we draw as a square holding the memory location. We draw a dashed line to show that this node is "pointing to" the state.

Read (dereferencing $!x$). This operation reads out a copy of the net in memory location x. Note that we use the interaction net machinery to copy the contents using the δ node.

Look (lk). This behaves in a similar way to read, except the net in the location is *not* copied. An indirection node, drawn as a diamond containing a pointer to the memory location, then allows interactions through the state. Of course only a limited kind of interaction can be done, which we specify below. Remark that there is no principal port for this indirection node; it is there solely to delimit the dashed line from the edges of the interaction net.

Update (assignment $x := N$). This operation assigns the new net N to the memory location x and deletes the old net in memory (using the ϵ node). Remark that the correctness of some systems may require that we evaluate the net N to normal form before making the assignment and deleting the old net. This would mean that we only allow values in the state.

Unit (⊗) used to code the result of assignment.

We emphasise that we still maintain the restriction of binary interaction rules, but allow many pointers to the same memory cell (indicated by a dashed line). We now have the possibility to define interaction rules that operate through the state, via the indirection node. We adopt a notational convention for the latter to simplify the diagrams, as shown in Fig. 5(a). Rather than writing an interaction via the state we write the interaction rule with a dashed line and the name of the location. Figure 5(b) shows the interaction rules that we allow.

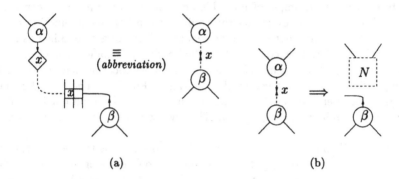

(a)   (b)

Fig. 5.

It is important to note that in this kind of rule we preserve the interface of the node α interacting through the state, hence we are not able to change the contents of the memory; just pattern match. This is the feature that allows us to get extra sharing in this framework.

We end this section with a few remarks about our nets. We have extended the framework of interaction nets to allow computation in several nets in parallel. These parallel interaction nets can communicate through the state, which requires that we have a global entity. Hence our interaction system does not preserve locality of interaction nets. However, this is only the case for the specific memory operations. One of the main reasons for introducing state was to break the confluence property of interaction nets, to allow non-deterministic computation. There is a simple condition on our interaction system that ensures that confluence is maintained, and that is that there is only one assignment to each memory location. A simple way to avoid side-effects would be to restrict to only using the ref and lk operations on the state.

There is a natural extension of Lafont's type system [10] for our generalised interaction nets, where we use ref types of ML. It is then possible to check that all rewrite rules preserve types.

We remark that we have only presented some examples of combinators for state manipulation. For many applications one might need additional, or modified, rules; for example, to code reference counting, mutual exclusion, etc. Also it may be necessary to impose some order of evaluation on the rules to ensure the desired behaviour, in particular for assignment. In the examples that follow, we omit these details. Of course, for interaction nets that do not use the state, we preserve all the properties of Lafont's interaction nets. Note also that garbage collection forces evaluation of discarded computations that may contain assignments.

4.1 Translation of non-match-sequential systems

We begin with an example of how this new interaction framework can code a richer class of systems by giving the coding of the parallel-or function defined above. Let us assume that the two arguments of the **por** are compiled as nets P and Q which are connected to nodes called arg. A **por** node is then introduced which takes only one argument, which is a memory location, say x. The initial configuration of nodes is given by the diagram in Fig. 6(a). The node $\perp$ is introduced to represent an undefined value in the state, and should not be confused with a non-terminating computation. The rewrite rules for the nodes introduced are given in Fig. 6(b).

The net N that we have omitted to draw corresponds to the following program which is easily represented as an interaction net using pattern matching through the state: if $!x =$ tt then tt else (if $!x = \perp$ then for else ff). The intuition is that if either argument returns tt then this value will be assigned to the state, where the **por** node can interact with it. If either argument returns ff, then we look at the value already in the state. If the value is tt then we do nothing, if the value is $\perp$ then we place a **for** node ("false-or") indicating that we have to wait for the other argument. If there is already **for** in the state then the final value will be false so we can assign this value to the state where the **por** function can interact. Note that there is no rule for the interaction **por-for** hence the system will *deadlock* in the case of **por** ff $\Omega =$ **por** Ω ff (here Ω is a non-terminating computation). This example provides the essential ideas that can be used to code non-sequential rewrite systems into nets. We next present in more detail the translation of orthogonal non-match-sequential constructor systems.

Given a constructor system R over the signature $(\mathcal{D}, \mathcal{C})$, we consider in turn the rules defining each $f \in \mathcal{D}$. Without loss of generality we assume f to be defined by rules of the form $f(\vec{C}[\vec{x}]) \to t$, where the patterns C_i are either a variable or a constructor. We code the rules for an n-ary f using an agent arg_i $(1 \leq i \leq n)$ for each argument, which will put in a memory location, say x, the result of evaluating that argument. The memory location x will contain n-tuples of constructor symbols and $\perp$ (initially all $\perp$, and getting more constructors as the arg agents add them). We use new agents to represent the n-tuples; in other words, x contains nets of the form:

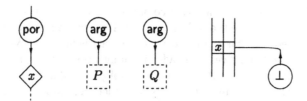

(a) Initial configuration

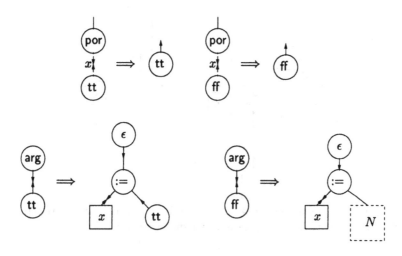

(b) Rewrite rules

Fig. 6. Parallel-or

where each x_i is either $\perp$ or a constructor c_j, and the number of auxiliary ports is equal to the sum of the arities of the constructors appearing in the n-tuple.

We use an agent f to represent the function f, which will interact through the state with the n-tuples placed by the **arg** agents. There will be a set of interaction rules for each rule defining f in R (with a right-hand side that corresponds to the translation $\Theta'(t)$ of the right-hand side t of the rule, as in Section 3). Note that the encoding of parallel-or is an optimised version of this method of translation, where we take profit of the symmetry of the patterns to use only one **arg** agent, and only one value for ("false-or") to represent the pairs $\perp$ff and ff$\perp$.

5 Case Studies

In this section we show how to encode a series of computational features into our interaction system, some of which go beyond term rewriting systems.

Standard ML References. The basic combinators introduced were given using the notation of ML, hence the coding is direct. However, a call-by-value strategy on the nets is required for the correct (sequential) behaviour. We give a small example, which we hope gives some additional intuitions about how our interaction system works. Consider the program: let val y = ref 3 in $(y := S(!y); !y)$ end. y is a binder, hence we compile the body of the let and bind all occurrences of y to the net representing ref 3. If we perform the interaction of the ref 3, giving a memory location x, and the duplication of the references, we get the following:

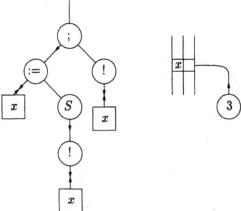

To complete this example, we give the rewrite rules for the additional nodes, which are the sequential composition and successor function:

We leave it as an exercise to the reader to use these rules to reduce this term to its normal form, which gives the result 4 as expected.

Communication. A notion of send and receive, both synchronous and asynchronous, on a channel can be coded using assignment. It is also possible to code process forking, which would involve the creation of a new net that would communicate on a channel (a memory location).

Sharing. One of the greatest achievements of interaction nets is the ability to code optimal reduction in the λ-calculus; see [3] for example. However, there is no way of sharing *values* which have to be copied due to the linearity condition of interaction rules. This arises since two pointers to a value (coded with a δ node) forces copying, even if the rule was just "inspecting" the value. This can be overcome in the new framework, by pattern matching through the state.

Non-determinism can be coded as a simple variant of the technique used for parallel-or. A simple example is given by the following rewrite system: amb $x\,y \rightarrow$

x, amb x y → y. The initial configuration is the same as for parallel-or (replace por by amb). The rewrite rules for the agents are given by:

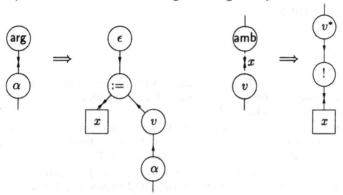

The arg node interacts with any agent and assigns the net connected to that agent to the memory location x, together with a new node v (for "value") to indicate that there is a value in the state. amb simply reads out the value. The node v^* is introduced which interacts with the v node and annihilate each other. Therefore, as soon as a value has been assigned to the location x, the amb agent will read out the result which will be the last value assigned to that location.

6   Conclusions

We have completed the study of the correspondences between interaction nets and first-order term rewriting systems, that we initiated in [2]. We have shown how to encode some restricted classes of constructor systems into interaction nets. To extend this to richer classes of term rewriting systems we were led to extend the paradigm of interaction to include a notion of state, which was shown to allow the coding of general constructor term rewriting systems. In addition, the new interaction system is sufficiently general to code a number of other features, such as references, communication and sharing.

We are currently developing implementations of term rewriting systems based on parallel nets. Most implementations of term rewriting use graph rewriting (see e.g. [6]), a related formalism which also allows sharing of computation. Graph rewriting is more flexible than interaction nets in that left-hand sides are not restricted. However, interaction nets have the advantage of being easier to implement (possibly distributed) since the rewrite rules are local and asynchronous.

Some directions for further investigation are the encoding of: higher-order rewrite systems like combinatory reduction systems (the reverse direction, i.e. coding interaction nets as combinatory reduction systems was studied in [2]), ML (including exceptions and I/O), threads in CML, process calculi (such as the π-calculus [13], and an understanding of π-nets [14]), equational rewriting, and narrowing (for the encoding of logic programming).

This would provide a common basis where we can study models and implementations of systems, for example the combination of λ-calculus with term rewriting systems.

Acknowledgement. The work of Ian Mackie was funded by EC project No. ERB4001GT940674: The Geometry of Interaction and the Implementation of Programming Languages.

References

1. N. Dershowitz and J.-P. Jouannaud. Rewrite Systems. In J. van Leeuwen, editor, *Handbook of Theoretical Computer Science: Formal Methods and Semantics*, volume B. North-Holland, 1989.

2. M. Fernández and I. Mackie. Interaction nets and term rewriting systems (extended abstract). In H. Kirchner, editor, *Trees in Algebra and Programming – CAAP'96*, number 1059 in LNCS, Springer-Verlag, 1996.

3. G. Gonthier, M. Abadi, and J.-J. Lévy. The geometry of optimal lambda reduction. In *Proc. ACM Symposium Principles of Programming Languages*, 1992.

4. C. Hankin, I. Mackie, and R. Nagarajan, editors. *Theory and Formal Methods of Computing 94: Proceedings of the Second Imperial College Workshop*. Imperial College Press, 1995.

5. K. Honda and N. Yoshida. Combinatory representation of mobile processes. In *Proc. 21st ACM Symposium on Principles of Programming Languages*, 1994.

6. J. R. Kennaway, J. W. Klop, M. R. Sleep, and F. J. de Vries. On the adequacy of graph rewriting for simulating term rewriting. *ACM TOPLAS*, 16(3):493–523, 1994.

7. J. Kennaway. Implementing term rewrite languages in DACTL. *Theoretical Computer Science*, 72:225–249, 1990.

8. J.-W. Klop. Term Rewriting Systems. In S. Abramsky, D. Gabbay, and T. Maibaum, editors, *Handbook of Logic in Computer Science*, volume 2. Oxford University Press, 1992.

9. M. Kurihara and A. Ohuchi. Non-copying term rewriting and modularity of termination. Hokkaido University.

10. Y. Lafont. Interaction nets. In *Proc. 17th ACM Symposium on Principles of Programming Languages*, 1990.

11. C. Laneve. *Optimality and Concurrency in Interaction Systems*. PhD thesis, Università degli Studi di Pisa, 1993.

12. I. Mackie. A λ-evaluator based on interaction nets. In Hankin et al. [4].

13. R. Milner. The polyadic π-calculus: A tutorial. Technical Report 91-180, LFCS, Department of Computer Science, University of Edinburgh, 1991.

14. R. Milner. Action calculi II: π-nets with boxes and replication. Technical report, LFCS, Department of Computer Science, University of Edinburgh, 1993.

15. R. Milner, M. Tofte, and R. Harper. *The Definition of Standard ML*. MIT Press, 1990.

16. J. Reppy. CML: A higher-order concurrent language. *ACM SIGPLAN Notices*, 26(6):294–305, 1991.

17. S. Thatte. A refinement of strong sequentiality for term rewriting systems with constructors. *Information and Computation*, 72:46–65, 1987.

Type Isomorphisms for Module Signatures

María-Virginia Aponte[1] and Roberto Di Cosmo[2]

[1] CNAM Conservatoire National des Arts et Métiers - 292, rue St. Martin - 75003 Paris France
E-mail:aponte@cnam.fr
[2] DMI-LIENS (CNRS URA 1347) Ecole Normale Supérieure - 45, Rue d'Ulm - 75230 Paris CEDEX 05 - France
E-mail:dicosmo@dmi.ens.fr

Abstract. This work focuses on software reuse for languages equipped with a module system. To retrieve modules from a library, it is quite reasonable to use module signatures as a search key, up to a suitable notion of signature isomorphism.

We study a formal notion of isomorphism for module signatures, which naturally extends the notion of isomorphism for types in functional languages. Isomorphisms between module types surprisingly have non-trivial interactions with the theory of isomorphisms of the base language to which the module system is added. We investigate the power of this notion in equating module signatures, and we study its decidability. This work does not impose any limitative assumption on the module system as we handle type declarations in signatures, type sharing and higher order modules.

KEYWORDS: typing and structuring systems, programming environments, module systems, ML, retrieval of functions in function libraries.

1 Introduction

Powerful module systems such as SML's [11, 5, 12] or Ada's [13] are essential tools for code reuse. Reuse requires a method to find modules. We suggest to use signatures as search keys, up to type isomorphism, a notion which have been proven relevant as a basis for advanced library search tools in functional libraries [16], and additionally for proposing extensions to the ML type inference mechanism [2].

An isomorphism is one way to identify types t and w for which any object of type t can be coerced into an object of type w and conversely, without losing information. That is, t and w contain the same information, organized in a different way. There is a well-known example: the types $(t \times w) \to r$ and $t \to (w \to r)$ are equivalent.

A highly illustrating example of Rittri's shows how the same function can happen to have very different-looking types, depending on some unpredictable coding choices on the programmer's side (see table 1).

Language	Name	Type
ML of Edinburgh LCF	itlist	$\forall X.\forall Y.(X \to Y \to Y) \to List(X) \to Y \to Y$
CAML	list_it	"
Haskell	foldl	$\forall X.\forall Y.(X \to Y \to X) \to X \to List(Y) \to X$
SML of New Jersey	fold	$\forall X.\forall Y.(X \times Y \to Y) \to List(X) \to Y \to Y$
The Edinburgh SML Library	fold_left	$\forall X.\forall Y.(X \times Y \to Y) \to Y \to List(X) \to Y$

Table 1. Different typings for the same functionality

Nevertheless, these different types turn out to be *isomorphic* types, which was the basis for Rittri's idea [15]: when looking for a function with a given type, a search tool must retrieve all the functions with isomorphic types, and not just those with syntactically equal types. For this, we need a decidable theory of type isomorphisms.

The study of type isomorphism for the typed λ-calculus, both explicit (system F) and implicit (Core-ML) has already been solved [3], leading to complete and decidable axiomatizations of isomorphisms and to efficient library search tools based on types. Exemples of application are library search systems for functions in typed functional languages (like LML, Haskell and CamlLight). The CamlLight system [17], for example, comes equipped with such a tool, `camlsearch`; here are some typical examples of its use:

```
> camlsearch -s -e "string*int*int -> string" /usr/local/lib/caml-light/
sub_string : string -> int -> int -> string

> camlsearch -s -e "'a*('a->'b->'a)*'b list ->'a" /usr/local/lib/caml-light/
it_list : ('a -> 'b -> 'a) -> 'a -> 'b list -> 'a
list_it : ('b -> 'a -> 'a) -> 'b list -> 'a -> 'a
```

It is now clear that in the future, libraries will not be a flat set of functions, but rather a set of well-organized *modules*, each coming with its set of defined types and functions. In this framework, the necessity to retrieve programs (or modules) in an independent way from the unpredictable structuring and coding choices of the programmer, is an even greater challenge. We show below an example of two functors that we intuitively want to identify.

```
module UnifyCurry :
        functor (t:TERMS)
        functor (s:SUBSTITUTION with s.termtype = t.termtype):
        sig ... unify: t.termtype -> t.termtype -> s.substtype end

module UnifyUnCurry :
    functor (sig module t:TERMS
                module s:SUBSTITUTION with s.termtype = t.termtype end):
          sig ... findunifier: t.termtype * t.termtype -> s.substtype end
```

Table 2. Different typings and structuring for the same functionalities

The goal of the present work is to tackle this challenge, studying in a precise way how to combine SML-like modules and isomorphisms of types. We develop a notion of equivalence of module types (also called signatures in SML) that parallels the equivalence of types induced by type isomorphisms. This equivalence notion can be applied to the retrieval of software components in libraries of modules.

The key idea is to export the analogy between simple types with products and module types [1] to derive from each of the type isomorphisms for core-ML a similar module type equivalence. These equivalences capture structural modifications of modules that are significantly more complex than a simple reordering of components. We strive to give a *general* solution, handling explicitly type declarations in signatures, type sharing specifications and higher-order modules. We have chosen to work with Leroy's proposal for module systems [6], which is now implemented in the Objective Caml language (available as [10]), to be quite easier to work with than the original SML module system.

Let us finally mention that all the work done here can be immediately applied to module systems like ADA's packages and *generics*.

The remainder of this paper is organized as follows. In the next section we briefly recall the essential features of Leroy's module system. In section 3, we informally define the equivalence between module signatures, which is formalized in section 4. In section 5, we discuss the decidability of our notion of equivalence. Finally, we present conclusions and directions for future research.

2 The module system

Our signature language is a subset of the manifest module language developed by X. Leroy [6, 9]. This language is sintactically similar to SML modules [12, 7]. The module language described has two base constructs: basic modules (structures), and functions from modules to modules (functors). Signatures are the types of modules (structure signatures or functor signatures). Structure signatures are sequences of type specifications. Functor signatures are actually dependent types: the type of a functor body may refer to a type identifier $x.t$ coming from the functor argument x. The single keyword module introduces both structure and functor specifications. In the grammar of figure 1, v ranges over value identifiers, t over type identifiers and x over module names.

Module types:
$$S ::= \texttt{sig } D \texttt{ end} \qquad \text{structure type}$$
$$| \texttt{ functor } (x : S)S \quad \text{functor dependent type}$$

Structure signature body:
$$D ::= \epsilon \mid C; D$$

Signature components:
$$C ::= \texttt{val } v_e : \tau \qquad \text{value specification}$$
$$| \texttt{ type } t_e \qquad \text{abstract type specification}$$
$$| \texttt{ type } t_e = \tau \qquad \text{manifest type specification}$$
$$| \texttt{ module } x_e : S \qquad \text{module specification}$$

Type expressions:
$$\tau ::= t \qquad \text{type identifier}$$
$$| \ p.t \qquad \text{type path}$$
$$| \ \tau \to \tau \qquad \text{function type}$$
$$| \ \tau \star \tau \qquad \text{product type}$$

Structure paths:
$$p ::= x \mid p.x$$

Extended identifiers:
$$id_e ::= id \mid p.id$$

Fig. 1. The signature language

The structure path $m.x$ denotes the module component x of structure m. The path $p.x$ refers to the component x from an arbitrarily nested structure given by path p. Identifiers in structure paths must correspond to structure identifiers.

Type paths $(p.t)$ and value paths $(p.v)$ provide access to type and value identifiers from nested structures. Two occurrences of the path $p.t$ always correspond to the same type. On the other hand, manifest types can be equivalent even when coming from different type paths: they only have to be specified with (provably) equivalent type annotations.

We extend identifiers to paths: v_e, t_e and x_e are extended identifiers for values, types and modules. Extended identifiers cannot appear in a programmer defined signature. They are used during equivalence checking to rename identifiers bound in flattened signatures. We justify their use, and show examples, later in section 3.2. The syntactic class id_e introduces extended identifiers for the class id ranging on value, types and module identifiers.

Modules à la SML can be seen as a set of modular constructs (the module language) built on top of a statically-typed language (the base language). To keep this paper simple, we restrict the set of type constructors of the base language to products and functions.

3 Defining module isomorphism

Isomorphism between two types can be formalized using *converters*, that is, functions to coerce any object of one type into an object of the other type, as long as there is no loss of information:

Definition 1 (Isomorphic types) *Two types A and B are isomorphic iff there exist conversion* functions $f : B \to A$ *and* $f' : A \to B$ *such that*

$$\forall M : A, \quad f(f' \, M) = M : A \, and \, \forall N : B, \quad f'(f \, N) = N : B.$$

Analogously, we give a semantic definition of signature isomorphism, as follows:

Definition 2 (Isomorphic module signatures) *Two module signatures S and S' are isomorphic iff there exist conversion* functors $f : S \to S'$ *and* $f' : S' \to S$ *such that*

$$\forall s' : S', \quad f(f' \, s') = s' : S' \, and \, \forall s : S, \quad f'(f \, s) = s : S.$$

Characterizing isomorphisms of signatures is more complex than for simple types: we have to deal not with one language but two, the base language and the module language. In the remainder of this section, we take as starting point the results for isomorphism on the base types [2] and try to apply it to modules.

3.1 A first naive approximation

A simple analogy can be made between the SML module language and a typed functional language: structures correspond to basic values, functors to functions and signatures to types. Moreover, as structures are sequences of component declarations including other modules, they can be seen as named products of modules, values and types [1].

Thus, it is tempting to adapt the known isomorphism rules to module types built with named products and arrows, and then compare signatures componentwise using the already known results on isomorphism for base types [3]. Here is an example of two signatures that can be shown isomorphic in this way:

```
sig                               sig
  val filter:                       val filter:
    ('a->bool)->'a list->'a list        ('a list)*('a->bool)->'a list
  val list_it:                      val list_it:
    ('a->'b->'a)->'a->'b list->'a       ('a*'b -> 'b)->'a list->'b->'b
end                               end
```

Unfortunately, this simple technique only discovers few isomorphisms: essentially those on signatures having identical skeletons, including the same number and names of components (modulo some limited permutations) and without type declarations.

3.2 Equivalence via signature transformations

Our approach of equivalence relies on a simple idea already used for base language types: we consider that two signatures are equivalent if they can be transformed (preserving equivalence) into componentwise isomorphic signatures.

It is easy to associate to each one of these transformations a corresponding pair of conversion functors establishing an isomorphism. In this section we discuss informally the transformations and equivalences over signatures we aim to capture in a formal framework.

Names of components Few programmers choose exactly the same identifiers for module components with identical semantics. During equivalence verification we consider possible mismatch of names between components with isomorphic types.

Interaction between base and module types Structures in the module language can be seen as named products of simple types. When we do not impose the same names on type-isomorphic components, we can freely mix products from the module language (i.e, sequences of components) and products from the base language. The signatures below are semantically equivalent:

```
sig  val a: int*bool  end
sig  val a1: int; val a2: bool  end
```

A similar equivalence arises for type declarations. These two equivalences lead to the following transformations: we decompose value specifications, and manifest type specifications, that are annotated by a product type, into as many value or type specifications as there are components in the product type.

Structural equivalence Structures declare components (values, types, or modules), which can be organized in many different ways. We consider two kinds of equivalences between structurally different signatures. First, components with isomorphic types can be declared in different orders; second, they can be declared at different levels of sub-structure nesting. Thus, during equivalence checking we flatten all inner structures in signatures before comparing them componentwise.

Nevertheless, flattening of structure signatures must be performed carefully in order to preserve type dependencies over type identifiers bound within them. In the signature below, the type of b depends on the type t bound in the substructure x.

```
sig
  module x : sig type t = int; val a: t end
  type t = bool; val b: x.t
end
```

To flatten the inner module x, a natural solution is to lift all its declarations:

```
sig type t = int;  val a: t;  type t = bool; val b: x.t  end
```

However, the path x.t in the type of b does not correspond any more to a bound type in this signature. To be correct, this transformation must also rename all references outside x of names bound within x. Yet this renaming can produce name clashes, and even change typing. Consider below the result of renaming the type name x.t into t: the type of b changes from int into bool. This simplistic transformation is erroneous:

```
sig type t = int; val a: t; type t = bool; val b: t  end
```

To avoid this problem, we extend the syntax of identifiers to paths, and while lifting declarations from x, we rename every occurrence (even bounding ones) of any component u bound within x into the path x.u. The signature above is transformed into:

```
sig  type x.t = int; val x.a: x.t;  type t = bool; val b: x.t end
```

Notice that this renaming remains local to x: the specification type t = int is modified into type x.t = int, and thus, any reference to t outside x remains (correct and) unchanged.

Curried functors In the base type language the following equivalence holds: $s_1 \rightarrow s_2 \rightarrow s \equiv s_1 \times s_2 \rightarrow s$. Analogously, we consider that functor signatures are equivalent if their (curried) arguments put together (as in products) are componentwise isomorphic. For instance, consider the functors f and g below:

```
module f :  functor(x: S1) functor(y: S2) S
module g :  functor(x: S3) S
```

We consider that they are equivalent if transforming functor f into

```
module f ' : functor (z: sig module x:S1; module y: S2 end) S
```

ends up in a functor f' such that its argument z has a signature componentwise isomorphic to S. This amounts to perform a transformation on curried functors analogous to that used for simple types: put in products all arguments of a functor. In module types, this corresponds to using a single argument having a substructure for each one of the functor arguments. Combined with flattening, this transformation can be used to check equivalence in presence of curried functors.

Equivalence of sharing specifications Type sharing specifications are used in functor signatures to express compatibility between type components of different arguments. Each functor below specifies sharing on two types t and w within theirs arguments.

```
signature S1 = sig type t=int end; signature S2 = sig type w=int end
module f : functor(x: S1) functor (y: sig type w = x.t end) S
module g : functor(y: S2) functor (x: sig type t = y.w end) S
```

We consider two functors equivalent if, when they specify sharing, the sharing specified is exactly the same on types equivalent across the functors. In this example, beacause x.t and y.w in f and y.w and x.t in g are all specified as int, they can be considered as equivalent across functors. Moreover, both functors specify exactly the same sharing, namely, the equivalence of the type components x.t and y.w.

Sharing is specified using manifest type specifications, and manifest type specifications induce an equivalence relation on type identifiers and congruences on type expressions. Thus, sharing specifications do not need a particular transformation during equivalence checking: they are simply taken in account as manifest type specifications in signatures. Thus, the two functor above can be proved equivalent after transforming them using the usual rules on functor equivalence (in particular those on curried funtors).

4 An axiomatization of signature isomorphism

We formalize the ideas presented above, by presenting a set of equivalence rules for *checking* signature isomorphism. The main goal of these rules is to say whether a set of equivalences E between two signatures S_1 and S_2 can be used to establish an isomorphism between them. This will be written:

$$E \vdash S1 \equiv S2$$

Module signatures can contain specifications for type components that can be referred to later on in the signature, and this type information may be necessary to determine equivalences for the remainder of the signature. Thus, our equivalence rules check whether two signatures are isomorphic *both* with respect to an *equivalence type context* E, which records equalities on type identifiers declared in the two signatures checked for isomorphisms, *and* with respect to two local contexts L and R, containing each the type equivalence information local to the left or right signature. Our rule system uses the following equivalence judgements:

$$E, L, R \vdash S \equiv S' \text{ signature iso} \qquad E \vdash \tau \text{ iso}_{base} \sigma \text{ base type iso}$$
$$E, L, R \vdash \tau \text{ iso } \tau' \quad \text{cross base type iso} \quad A \vdash \tau \approx \tau' \qquad \text{local base type equiv}$$

We classify these judgements into two kinds: those stating equivalence between types of two different signatures (either between type components, or between whole signatures), and those stating equivalence between (base language) types local to one of the compared signatures. We call the former *cross equivalences* and the latter *local equivalences*. Equivalence contexts are distinguished in a similar way: the equivalence context E is a cross context, while L (for left) and R (for right) are local contexts. The context A above stands for any of these local contexts.

Both cross and local equivalences are necessary to determine isomorphism between signatures, as shown in the example below:

```
signature S = sig  type t = int;  val a: t * t  end
signature S' = sig  type w = int;  val p : int * w  end
```

In order to prove S equivalent to S', we must show a cross equivalence between the type identifiers t and w, and between the types t * t and int * w. The former is immediate, but for the latter we need to use type information local to each signature, namely, that t is specified as int in S, and w as int in S'. Thus, to show equivalence of components a: t*t and p: int*w, the cross context E contains {type t = w}, and the local contexts are L = (type t = int) and R = (type w = int).

In the following rules, we need an auxiliary normalisation function norm associating to each signature S a signature S' (its normal form), as detailed in figure 7. Finally, we will write $E \vdash S1 \equiv S2$ for $E, \emptyset, \emptyset \vdash S1 \equiv S2$.

4.1 The isomorphism rules

We give a formal axiomatic presentation of our rules for *checking* signature isomorphism. For this, we assume given a cross context E, containing already the appropriate cross equations to check the equivalence. We then use the various transformations discussed above to test equivalence with respect to E. Due to the symmetry of equivalence judgments, we will often present only the rule for the left case, with a name ending with a -L suffix. We will also often talk generically about a rule, with no suffix, when meaning both the right and the left rule.

The rules in figure 2 compare componentwise two signatures, reordering and renaming components. Rule (Comp-fun) compares functor components. An analogous rule for structure components is subsumed by the rule (Flatten), that also captures flattening as presented in section 3.2.

Rules in figure 3 deal with interactions between base-language product types and products implicit in sequences of signature components. Whenever we can use base-language isomorphisms to show that a component has a product type, we split it in two components. The rules in figure 4 show how the isomorphisms for the base language can be lifted to isomorphisms of the types that appear in the module signatures (these types can indeed contain path expressions, that are not part of the base language).

Rules in figure 5 account for the equivalence relation on types induced by manifest type specifications local to each compared signature [6].

Notation 3 (Fully substituted form) *The rules in figure 5 can be seen as a function $\phi(A, \tau) = \tau'$, that given a type τ and an environment A, performs all possible substitution of identifiers from A in τ.*

Rules in figure 6 deal with functor equivalences. These rules use normalization, which is only needed to flatten functor arguments before checking equivalence of bodies. Rule (Functor-decompose) compares two functors by comparing argument signatures and result signatures. In this rule, E contains the cross type equations (for type identifiers coming from both functor arguments) needed to verify equivalence on functor bodies. Here, normalization of arguments guarantees, first, that the correct type paths are held in E; and second, that type declarations in arguments are flattened. These are necessary steps to apply rule (Eq-type-path) on functor arguments when used as hypothesis to derive equivalences of bodies. Rules (Functor-uncurry) deal with curried functors as explained in section 3.2.

Semantic soundness We can now show that all our equivalence rules are semantically sound.

Proposition 4 Semantic soundness. *Assume that S, S' are module signatures such that $E \vdash S \equiv S'$. Then, there exist conversion functors $f : S \to S'$ and $f' : S' \to S$ such that:*

$$\forall s' : S', \quad f(f' \, s') = s' \text{ and } \forall s : S, \quad f'(f \, s) = s.$$

Proof. To each of the equivalence rules one can associate a pair of conversion functors, as hinted in the informal discussion. Then one can build the conversion functors associated to a full proof by composing the simpler ones associated to each equivalence used in the derivation.

5 Deciding module isomorphism

From the definition in the previous section it is not really evident that, given a cross context E, the property $E \vdash S_1 \equiv S_2$ is decidable, as not all the rules transform a decision problem into a smaller one: notably, the Mix rules replace one component with *two* other ones, while splitting products.

Indeed, decidability depends in an essential way on the properties of isomorphisms of the base language. Consider the rule Mixtype-L: to prove $E, L, R \vdash S_1; \text{type } t = \tau; S \equiv S'$ one has first to establish $E, L; \text{type } t = t_1 * t_2, R \vdash S_1; \text{type } t_1 = \tau_1; \text{type } t_2 = \tau_2; S \equiv S'$ where $L \vdash \tau \approx \tau_1 * \tau_2$, i.e. $L \vdash \phi(L, \tau) \text{ isobase } \tau_1 * \tau_2$.

This rule reminds us, like all the Comp rules, that if isomorphism in the base language is not decidable, neither can be isomorphism at the module level.

But it also tells us that if we do not have enough information on τ_1 and τ_2, we are in the presence of a potential cause of nontermination: if the equivalence classes of the base language isomorphism are infinite (this is the case for second order isomorphisms, which are nevertheless decidable, as shown in [4]), or if either one of τ_1 or τ_2 is not strictly *smaller*, according to an appropriate measure, than τ (and this is the case in the presence of recursive types), then there may be an infinite number of derivations with the same root and the brute-force search for a legal derivation may not terminate. This fact highlights once more the tight relationship that exists between isomorphisms at the base language level, and isomorphisms of modules. If the base language isomorphisms are decidable in a sophisticated way that can cope with potentially infinite equivalence classes of isomorphic types, then the module isomorphisms will probably also be decidable, but by means of a specialized algorithm, which is not simply built on top of the existing decision procedure for the base language.

Nevertheless, here are some general necessary conditions for decidability.

Proposition 5 Decidability w.r.t. E. *Assume the following conditions:*

- *the equivalence classes of the base language isomorphism are finite (or pseudo-finite, i.e., finite up to alpha renaming of bound type variables as in ML and F), and*

- *there is a well founded measure m such that if $\tau \equiv \tau_1 * \tau_2$, then $m(\tau) > m(\tau_i)$, $i = 1, 2$.*

Then, signature isomorphism w.r.t. a given E is decidable.

Proof. (sketch) It is enough to show that the brute-force construction of all proof derivations, given E, terminates.

The first condition ensures that at any step only a finite number of subproblems is generated (the trick for handling pseudo-finiteness is to consider only isomorphic types with the same bound variables in the Mix rule, and only renaming of bound variables to already existing bound variables in the Comp rules). The second condition ensures that only a finite number of Mix rules can be used in a derivation (as each application of the rule decreases the overall measure of all types on which Mix can be applied). This is sufficient, as all other rules strictly decrease the size of the subproblems.

Remark. The conditions for termination are not as restrictive as they might seem: for example all theories of isomorphisms found in [3] satisfy them.

Now that we know how to *check* whether a given set of cross equivalences E is enough to derive the equivalence of the two signatures, what about *finding* all such E's?

Proposition 6 Decidability. *If signature isomorphism w.r.t. E is decidable, then so is the problem of finding all E such that $E \vdash S_1 \equiv S_2$*

Proof. The equations in E that are relevant for signature equivalence are only those involving the possible paths in the two given signatures. Hence we can use decidability of signature isomorphism checking w.r.t. a given E to build an algorithm for isomorphism checking: just try all the relevant E's.

It is possible to give a more refined algorithm to find all possible valid E for a given specific base language.

6 Conclusions and future work

We have presented a notion of module isomorphism that parallels the semantic notion of type isomorphism. This notion is at the same time conceptually simpler and technically richer than previous proposals (for example [18]).

We showed that, when dealing with module interconvertibility, one can no longer separate the module language from the base language, as long as the base language has types such as products or records, and that this fact can have important consequences on the decidability of the module isomorphisms: this is quite reasonable, and nevertheless essentially new.

We also showed how, using Leroy's formalism, sharing and higher order modules can fit nicely and naturally in our framework: the system presented here does not have the usual restrictions to first order modules, and does not sweep sharing (one of the most important features in this kind of modules) under the carpet. Nevertheless, like Leroy's calculus [6], our system does not account for the full transparency problem of higher-order functors. A solution would be to adapt our equivalence system to Leroy's applicative functors semantics [8], but this is still under investigation. Proceeding from here, we can now address some further problems, both on the practical and theoretical side:

Module matching up to isomorphism There are two orthogonal problems when reusing code from a library: one is the different representations of the same functionality (captured by our notion of isomorphism); the other is how to combine several pieces from the library to build the functionality that we need. While our work focuses on the first problem, there has been work dealing with the second: [14], for example, studies a language with higher-order parametric module signatures, and shows how to translate a library of higher order modules into a logic program. The execution of this program generates all possible compositions of modules that result in a module containing at least all components specified in the query. This approach, based on an extension of signature matching does not account for the problem of equivalence of representations, which is central to our work, nor for type sharing in signatures. Nevertheless, it would be interesting to combine the two approaches: this would require an axiomatization of subsumption up to isomorphism.

Semantic soundness and completeness An important feature of previous work on isomorphisms of types is the existence of a soundness and completeness proof for the isomorphism inference system (see [3] for a survey): this guarantees that only relevant information is retrieved, and that nothing is missed during a search. While semantic soundness for our set of rules can be shown easily using the conversion functors associated to each inference rule, semantic completeness is a much more difficult task: even for the base language types for the systems presented in [3], the proof relies on a very complex analysis of a special class of typed λ-terms. The most promising approach seems to try to exploit the analogy between module types and base language types to recover the completeness result for modules from completeness on base language type isomorphisms.

Acknowledgements

The authors would like to thank Mathias Felleisen and Xavier Leroy for pleasurable discussions and careful reading of the paper.

References

1. María Virginia Aponte. Extending records typing to type parametric modules with sharing. In *20th symposium on Principles of Programming Languages*, 1993.
2. Roberto Di Cosmo. Type isomorphisms in a type assignment framework. In *19th Ann. ACM Symp. on Principles of Programming Languages (POPL)*, pages 200–210. ACM, 1992.
3. Roberto Di Cosmo. *Isomorphisms of types: from λ-calculus to information retrieval and language design*. Birkhauser, 1995. ISBN-0-8176-3763-X.
4. Roberto Di Cosmo. Second order isomorphic types. A proof theoretic study on second order λ-calculus with surjective pairing and terminal object. *Information and Computation*, pages 176–201, June 1995.

5. Robert Harper, Robin Milner, and Mads Tofte. A type discipline for program modules. In *Theory and Practice of Programming Languages*, volume 250 of *Lecture Notes in Computer Science*. Springer Verlag, 1987.

6. Xavier Leroy. Manifest types, modules, and separate compilation. In *21st symposium on Principles of Programming Languages*, pages 109–122. ACM Press, January 1994.

7. Xavier Leroy. A syntactic approach to type generativity and sharing (extended abstract). In *Record of the 1994 ACM-SIGPLAN Workshop on ML and its Applications*, pages 1–12. INRIA, June 1994.

8. Xavier Leroy. Applicative functors and fully transparent higher-order modules. In *22nd symposium on Principles of Programming Languages*. ACM Press, January 1995.

9. Xavier Leroy. The Caml Special Light system. Technical report, INRIA, Roquencourt, Le Chesnay Cedex 78153, France, 1995. Available as `ftp://ftp.inria.fr/lang/caml-light/csl*`.

10. Xavier Leroy. The Objective Caml reference manual. Technical report, INRIA, Roquencourt, Le Chesnay Cedex 78153, France, 1996. Available as `ftp://ftp.inria.fr/lang/caml-light/ocaml*`.

11. David MacQueen. Modules for standard ML. In *ACM Symposium on Lisp and Functional Programming*, 1984.

12. Robin Milner, Mads Tofte, and Robert Harper. *The Definition of Standard ML*. The MIT Press, 1990.

13. Departement of Defense DoD. *Ada reference manual*. 1983.

14. Patrick Parot. Automatisation d'une bibliothèque de modules. In *Journées Francophones des Langages Applicatifs*, pages 75–98, 1995.

15. Mikael Rittri. *Searching program libraries by type and proving compiler correctness by bisimulation*. PhD thesis, University of Göteborg, Göteborg, Sweden, 1990.

16. Mikael Rittri. Using types as search keys in function libraries. *Journal of Functional Programming*, 1(1):71–89, 1991.

17. Pierre Weis and Xavier Leroy. *Le langage Caml*. InterÉditions, 1993.

18. Amy Moormann Zaremsky and Jeannette M. Wing. Signature matching: a key to reuse. In *SIGSOFT*, December 1993. Also available as CMU-CS-93-151, May 1993.

(Paren)

$$\frac{E, L, R \vdash D \;\equiv\; D'}{E, L, R \vdash \mathbf{sig}\; D \;\mathbf{end} \;\equiv\; \mathbf{sig}\; D' \;\mathbf{end}}$$

(Comp-value)

$$\frac{E, L, R \vdash \tau \;\mathbf{iso}\; \tau' \quad E, L, R \vdash D_1; D_2 \;\equiv\; D_1'; D_2'}{E, L, R \vdash D_1; \mathbf{val}\; a : \tau; D_2 \;\equiv\; D_1'; \mathbf{val}\; b : \tau'; D_2'}$$

(Comp-type)

$$\frac{E, L, R \vdash \tau \;\mathbf{iso}\; \tau' \quad E \supseteq \{\mathbf{type}\; t = r\} \\ E, L; \mathbf{type}\; t = \tau, R; \mathbf{type}\; r = \tau' \vdash D_1; D_2 \;\equiv\; D_1'; D_2'}{E, L, R \vdash D_1; \mathbf{type}\; t = \tau; D_2 \;\equiv\; D_1'; \mathbf{type}\; r = \tau'; D_2'}$$

(Comp-abs-type)

$$\frac{E, L, R \vdash D_1; D_2 \;\equiv\; D_1'; D_2' \quad E \supseteq \{\mathbf{type}\; t = r\}}{E, L, R \vdash D_1; \mathbf{type}\; t; D_2 \;\equiv\; D_1'; \mathbf{type}\; r; D_2'}$$

(Comp-fun)

$$\frac{E, L, R \vdash F \;\equiv\; F' \quad F, F' \;\text{functor signatures} \\ E, L, R \vdash D_1; D_2 \;\equiv\; D_1'; D_2'}{E, L, R \vdash D_1; \mathbf{module}\; f : F; D_2 \;\equiv\; D_1'; \mathbf{module}\; f' : F'; D_2'}$$

(Flatten-L)

$$\frac{E, L, R \vdash D_1; D\{n \leftarrow x.n \mid n \in BV(D)\}; D_2 \;\equiv\; S}{E, L, R \vdash D_1; \mathbf{module}\; x : \mathbf{sig}\; D \;\mathbf{end}; D_2 \;\equiv\; S}$$

Fig. 2. Structure compatibility rules

(Mixvalue-L)

$$\frac{E, L, R \vdash D_1; \mathbf{val}\; a_1 : \tau_1; \mathbf{val}\; a_2 : \tau_2; D_2 \;\equiv\; S \quad L \vdash \tau \approx \tau_1 * \tau_2}{E, L, R \vdash D_1; \mathbf{val}\; a : \tau; D_2 \;\equiv\; S}$$

(Mixtype-L)

$$\frac{E, L; \mathbf{type}\; t = t_1 * t_2, R \vdash D_1; \mathbf{type}\; t_1 = \tau_1; \mathbf{type}\; t_2 = \tau_2; D_2 \;\equiv\; S \\ L \vdash \tau \approx \tau_1 * \tau_2}{E, L, R \vdash D_1; \mathbf{type}\; t = \tau; D_2 \;\equiv\; S}$$

Fig. 3. Mix products rules

(Iso-E)
$$E \cup \{\text{type } t = w\} \vdash t \text{ iso}_{base} \, w$$

(Iso-ELR)
$$\frac{L \vdash \tau \approx \tau' \quad R \vdash \sigma \approx \sigma' \quad E \vdash \tau' \text{ iso}_{base} \, \sigma'}{E, L, R \vdash \tau \text{ iso } \sigma}$$

Fig. 4. Base language isomorphisms

(Eq-type)
$$A; \text{type } t = \tau \vdash t \approx \tau$$

(Eq-type-path)
$$A; \text{module } p : \text{sig } D_1; \text{type } t = \tau; D_2 \text{ end} \vdash p.t \approx \tau\{x \leftarrow p.x \mid x \in BV(p)\}$$

(Subst)
$$\frac{A \vdash \tau \approx \tau' \quad A \vdash C[\tau'] \approx \sigma}{A \vdash C[\tau] \approx \sigma}$$

Fig. 5. Type equivalence rules

(Functor-decompose)
$$\begin{array}{c} N_1 = \text{norm}(S_1) \quad N_2 = \text{norm}(S_2) \\ E, L, R \vdash \text{module } x : N_1 \quad \equiv \quad \text{module } y : N_2 \\ E, L; \text{module } x : N_1, R; \text{module } y : N_2 \vdash S'_1 \quad \equiv \quad S'_2 \\ \hline E, L, R \vdash \text{functor}(x : S_1)S'_1 \quad \equiv \quad \text{functor}(y : S_2)S'_2 \end{array}$$

(Functor-uncurry-L)
$$\begin{array}{c} E, L, R \vdash \text{functor}(z : \text{sig module } x : S_1; \text{module } y : S_2 \text{ end}) \\ S_3\{x.n \leftarrow z.x.n \mid n \in BV(x)\}\{y.n \leftarrow z.y.n \mid n \in BV(y)\} \quad \equiv S \\ \hline E, L, R \vdash \text{functor}(x : S_1)\text{functor}(y : S_2)S_3 \quad \equiv \quad S \end{array}$$

Fig. 6. Functor equivalence rules

A   The normalization rules

We present here the definition of the norm function that associates to a module signature its *normal form* (essentially flattening signatures using (Flatten)).

$$\text{norm}(\textbf{val } a : \tau; D) \longrightarrow \textbf{val } a : \tau; \text{norm}(D)$$
$$\text{norm}(\textbf{type } t; D) \longrightarrow \textbf{type } t; \text{norm}(D)$$
$$\text{norm}(\textbf{type } t = \tau; D) \longrightarrow \textbf{type } t = \tau; \text{norm}(D)$$
$$\text{norm}(\textbf{module } x : \textbf{sig } D \textbf{ end}; D') \longrightarrow \text{norm}(D\{n \leftarrow x.n \mid n \in BV(D)\}; D')$$
$$\text{norm}(\textbf{module } f : F; D) \longrightarrow \textbf{module } f : F; \text{norm}(D)$$
$$\text{if } F \text{ is a functor signature}$$

Fig. 7. The rewriting rules for normalization

Decidability of Logic Program Semantics
and Applications to Testing

Salvatore Ruggieri

Dipartimento di Informatica, Università di Pisa
Corso Italia 40, 56125 Pisa, Italy
e-mail: ruggieri@di.unipi.it

Abstract. We consider the decidability problem of logic program semantics, focusing in particular on the least Herbrand model, the least term model and the S-semantics. A declarative characterization is given for a large class of programs whose semantics are decidable sets. In addition, we show how decidability is strongly related to (black box) testing. In our terminology, the testing problem consists of checking whether or not the formal semantics of a program includes a given *finite* set of atoms. We show that the testing problem for a program is decidable iff its formal semantics is a decidable set.
Interestingly, the decision procedure used to check whether an atom belongs to the S-semantics of a program has a natural implementation in the logic programming paradigm itself, in the form of a Prolog meta-program. Consequently, this provides us with a basic tool for testing. Theory and tools are refined to consider the use of non-standard predicates, such as arithmetic built-in's and the meta-predicate demo.

1 Introduction

Many declarative semantics have been proposed in the logic programming literature, with different aims and objectives. In particular, we concentrate on the declarative extensions of the least Herbrand model semantics (or M-semantics) known as the least term model semantics of Clark [8] (or C-semantics of Falaschi et al. [10]), and the S-semantics of Bossi et al. [5]. They have been proposed as the most promising candidates for a declarative interpretation for logic and pure Prolog programs. Each semantics associates a set of atoms to each program.

In [2], the relationships between the three semantics are studied, with several results on their relative information ordering. In this paper, we consider the problem of deciding whether $M(P)$, $C(P)$ or $S(P)$ are decidable sets. We identify a large class of programs P, called *bounded* programs, such that $M(P)$, $C(P)$ and $S(P)$ are decidable sets, by providing a procedure for deciding whether an atom A belongs to the semantics of P. Interestingly, the decision procedure has an intuitive implementation in the logic programming paradigm itself, in the form of a Prolog meta-program. In particular, the well-studied class of *acceptable* logic programs, introduced in [4], is a sub-class of bounded programs. They coincide with the class of programs such that the LD-tree of every ground query is finite. As Apt and Pedreschi claim, most of the practical Prolog programs belong to this class. In addition to termination, acceptable programs have several interesting properties, including independence from the underlying first order language, modularity, and an efficient *declarative debugging* approach. We show that bounded programs are operationally characterized as the class of programs such that for every ground query Q the number of *LD-refutations* starting with Q is finite.

Our study is directly related to testing. Software testing is an important stage in program development. It covers more than one third of the development time, and requires a high degree of specialization of the developers. Although testing cannot show the absence of errors, but only the presence, it is still a necessary stage, even when a formal proof of correctness is provided. The testing techniques can be divided into "black box" - or *declarative* - and "white box" - or *procedural* - techniques. White box testing occurs when test data are chosen with reference to the structure of the program to demonstrate that the internal behavior is satisfactory. Black box testing occurs when test data are chosen using the requirement documents (*validation* testing), or the formal specification (*verification* testing), or a previous version of the program (*regression* testing), and pays no regard to the internal behavior of the program, and in particular to the underlying control mechanisms.

In our terminology the testing problem consists of checking whether or not the formal semantics of a program includes a given *finite* set of atoms. This set represents a collection of test data provided by the requirement documents, the formal specification or a previous version of the program. The testing problem is undecidable in the general case of logic programs, since they have the full power of Turing machines. We relate semantics decidability and testing by showing that the testing problem for a program P and a semantics $\mathcal{F}$ is decidable iff $\mathcal{F}(P)$ is a decidable set. Therefore, our procedure for semantics decidability can be used as a simple automatic tool for testing bounded logic programs.

From the definition of testing, it is clear that we concentrate on black box testing. The declarative nature of logic programming separates the concerns of correctness and efficiency. At least in principle, to realize this potential advantage, we must be able to reason on programs (development, correctness proof, termination, testing, debugging, etc.) on the only basis of their declarative semantics. For this reason, it seems more appropriate in this setting to reason on black box testing, rather than white box testing, by abstracting away from the underlying operational model. Unfortunately, the use of non-standard predicates (arithmetic built-in's, non-declarative control, etc.), mainly due to efficiency reasons, spoils the declarative reading of logic programming. Therefore, we must carefully consider the possibility of reasoning on those predicates by appropriately extending the declarative semantics. In this paper, we extend the $\mathcal{S}$-semantics and the meta-program implementing the decision procedure in order to reason on programs with arithmetic.

Although an extensive literature on testing of imperative programming languages exists, in logic programming there is no formal basis or tool for testing. The only papers on the topic we are aware of are [11] and [6], where two testing methodologies are presented, which are founded on a description of the test space in terms of context-free grammars, constraint systems, and algebraic specifications. However, it is worth mentioning that there are several proposals concerning declarative *debugging* and *diagnosis* [9, 13] of logic programs. Therefore, it seems appropriate at this stage to have a proposal for a formal approach to testing, to be later integrated with other techniques. This paper represents a first step towards that objective.

Preliminaries We use in this paper the standard notation of Apt [1], when not specified otherwise. A (first order) language L is a pair $\langle \Sigma_L , \Pi_L \rangle$ of non–empty sets: the set of function symbols Σ_L, and the set of predicate symbols Π_L. Every symbol in a language is assigned a non–negative arity. Given two languages $L = \langle \Sigma_L , \Pi_L \rangle$ and $M = \langle \Sigma_M , \Pi_M \rangle$, we say that M *extends* L iff $\Sigma_M \supseteq \Sigma_L$ and $\Pi_M \supseteq \Pi_L$.
We use U_L to denote the set of ground terms on L, $Atom_L$ the set of atoms on L, B_L the Herbrand base on L. B_P the Herbrand base on L_P, and U_P is the set of ground terms on L_P. We denote with L the underlying language a program is defined on. Usually, one considers $L = L_P$. LD-resolution is SLD-resolution together with the (Prolog) left-most selection rule.
An atom is called *pure* if it is of the form $p(x_1,\ldots,x_n)$ where $x_1,\ldots,x_n$ are different variables. The size $size(t)$ of a ground term t is the number of function symbols occurring in it. Finally, we denote by N the set of natural numbers.

2   Relating semantics decidability to testing

In this section, we establish some fundamental relations between logic program semantics decidability and declarative testing. We restrict to consider a semantics as a function from programs to sets of atoms. Then, for a semantics $\mathcal{F}$ and a program P, $\mathcal{F}(P)$ is a set of atoms.
In the literature, several declarative semantics have been considered as alternatives to the standard least Herbrand model $\mathcal{M}(P)$. We mainly focus on two of them, namely the $\mathcal{C}$-semantics of Falaschi et al. [10] (also known as the least term model of Clark [8]) and the $\mathcal{S}$-semantics of Bossi et al. [5]. After that, the testing problem is introduced and proved undecidable for the class of logic programs with respect to each of the mentioned semantics.

Definition 1. For a logic program P we define

$$\mathcal{M}(P) = \{ A \in B_L \mid P \models A \}$$
$$\mathcal{C}(P) = \{ A \in Atom_L \mid P \models A \}$$
$$\mathcal{S}(P) = \{ A \in Atom_L \mid A \text{ is a computed instance of a pure atom } \}. \quad \square$$

It is out of the scope of this paper to discuss properties and relations among those semantics. We only report from [5] a result that clarifies the relevance of the $\mathcal{S}$-semantics. With $mgi(Q, \mathcal{Q})$ we denote the set of computed instances of Q and every finite subset of $\mathcal{Q}$. The following theorem states that it is possible to reconstruct the set of computed instances of P and Q starting from $\mathcal{S}(P)$.

Theorem 2. *The set of computed instances of a program P and a query Q coincides with $mgi(Q, \mathcal{S}(P))$.* □

We now define the testing problem for logic programs. Consider two finite sets: one of atoms which should belong to the formal semantics of the program, and the other of atoms which should not belong. In practice, these sets are provided by an analysis of the requirement documents (*validation* testing), of the formal specification (*verification* testing) or of a previous version of the program (*regression* testing.) Testing a program on this pair of sets of atoms means checking that the formal semantics of the program includes every atom in the first set and no atom in the second one.

Definition 3. A logic program P is tested w.r.t. a semantic $\mathcal{F}$ on a couple of finite sets of atoms (I, S) iff

$$I \ \subseteq \ \mathcal{F}(P) \ \subseteq \ Atom_L \setminus S$$ □

An atom A such that $A \in I$ and $A \notin \mathcal{F}(P)$ is called an *incompleteness symptom*. If $A \in \mathcal{F}(P)$ and $A \notin Atom_L \setminus S$, then A is called an *incorrectness symptom*. The *testing problem* consists of deciding whether a program P is tested w.r.t. $\mathcal{F}$ on a given couple (I, S). In this paper, we are concerned with a formal theory and some practical tools to make the testing problem decidable. A further stage in the program development process, called *diagnosis problem*, consists of determining the program components which are sources of incompleteness or incorrectness symptoms. The next simple result clarifies the relation between the testing problem and the semantics decidability issue.

Theorem 4. *For a program P and a semantics $\mathcal{F}$, the following statements are equivalent*

(i)   the testing problem is decidable,
(ii)   the testing problem is semi-decidable,
(iii) $\mathcal{F}(P)$ is a decidable set.

Proof. *(i → ii)* is obvious. Let us prove *(ii → iii)*. Suppose the testing problem is semi-decidable, and consider, for an atom A, the sets $I = \{ A \}$ and $S = \emptyset$. Then it is semi-decidable whether $I \subseteq \mathcal{F}(P)$, i.e. $A \in \mathcal{F}(P)$. Symmetrically, by considering $I = \emptyset$ and $S = \{ A \}$, it is semi-decidable whether $A \notin \mathcal{F}(P)$. As a result, $\mathcal{F}(P)$ is a decidable set. To prove *(iii → i)*, we recall that the complement of a decidable set is decidable as well. Then as I and S are supposed finite, it is decidable whether $I \subseteq \mathcal{F}(P)$ and $S \subseteq Atom_L \setminus \mathcal{F}(P)$, i.e. $I \subseteq \mathcal{F}(P) \subseteq Atom_L \setminus S$. □

As a consequence, the testing problem is undecidable for the class of logic programs w.r.t. all the introduced semantics.

Corollary 5. *The testing problem is undecidable for the class of logic programs w.r.t. the least Herbrand model semantics, the C-semantics, and the S-semantics.*

Proof. In general, for a logic program P the set $\mathcal{M}(P)$ is undecidable, as the class of logic programs is Turing equivalent (for a formal proof see [1].) Since $\mathcal{C}(P) \cap B_L = \mathcal{M}(P)$, if $\mathcal{C}(P)$ were decidable then $\mathcal{M}(P)$ would be decidable as well. Finally, if $\mathcal{S}(P)$ were decidable then $\mathcal{C}(P)$ would be decidable as well. This because an atom is in $\mathcal{C}(P)$ iff any of its anti-instances (that are finite, modulo renaming) is in $\mathcal{S}(P)$. □

The aim of the following section is to identify a suitable large class of logic programs for which the introduced declarative semantics are decidable, and *a fortiori* the testing problem is decidable.

3 Bounded programs

First, we define level mappings and ground instances of logic programs. They are the basic tools our framework is based on.

Definition 6. Given a program P

- a *level mapping* is a function $|\ | : B_L \to N$ of ground atoms to natural numbers. $|\ |$ is recursive if it is total and computable. $|A|$ is called the level of A.
- $ground_L(P)$ denotes the set of ground instances of clauses from P w.r.t. the language L. □

We introduce the class of *bounded* programs, defined as follows. We require that the level of the head of a ground instance of a clause is greater than the level of every atom in the body if the body is true in a model of the program.

Definition 7. A program P is *bounded by* $|\ | : B_L \to N$ *and a Herbrand interpretation* I iff I is a model of P, and for every $A \leftarrow B_1, \ldots, B_n$ in $ground_L(P)$

$$I \models B_1, \ldots, B_n \quad implies \quad |A| > |B_i| \quad for\ i \in [1, n]$$

P is *bounded* if it is bounded by some $|\ |$ and I. □

The class of bounded logic programs is large enough to include most of the programs of practical use. In particular, it includes the class of acceptable logic program, introduced by Apt and Pedreschi [4]. Acceptable programs have a number of properties well-suited for a good programming practice, including termination, modularity, independence from the language, and an efficient *declarative debugging* approach proposed by Comini et al. [9].

Intuitively, the definition of acceptability requires that for every clause, the level of the head of any of its ground instances is greater than the level of each atom in the body which might be selected further in a LD-derivation.

Definition 8. A program P is *acceptable by* $|\ | : B_L \to N$ *and a Herbrand interpretation* I iff I is a model of P, and for every $A \leftarrow B_1, \ldots, B_n$ in $ground_L(P)$:

$$for\ i \in [1, n] \quad I \models B_1, \ldots, B_{i-1} \quad implies \quad |A| > |B_i|$$

P is *acceptable* if it is acceptable by some $|\ |$ and I. □

Consider, as an example, the program SAT for propositional satisfiability:

satisfiable(Formula) ← *There is a true instance of Formula*

```
satisfiable(true).
satisfiable(X ∧ Y) ← satisfiable(X), satisfiable(Y).
satisfiable(not X) ← invalid(X).

invalid(false).
invalid(X ∧ Y) ← invalid(X).
invalid(X ∧ Y) ← invalid(Y).
invalid(not X) ← satisfiable(X).
```

SAT is acceptable by $|\ |$ and B_L, where

$$|\text{satisfiable}(t)| = |\text{invalid}(t)| = size(t)$$

We point out that the model and the level mapping would have been correctly inferred by any of the existing tools for the analysis of termination, such as those based on abstract interpretation [7] or constraint solving [18].

We sum up the termination property of acceptable programs we are interested in by means of the following Lemma reported from [14].

Lemma 9. *A logic program is acceptable iff the LD-tree of every ground query (written in any language) is finite.* □

Therefore, a Prolog interpreter universally terminates for an acceptable program and a ground query. However, the Theorem does not hold for non-ground queries. For instance, the LD-tree of SAT and the query satisfiability(X ∧ Y) is infinite. Therefore, a Prolog interpreter is not a complete decision procedure w.r.t. $\mathcal{C}$ or $\mathcal{S}$-semantics, even though it is so w.r.t. $\mathcal{M}$-semantics.

Bounded logic program are characterized by a similar operational property: they coincide with the class of programs with finitely many refutations starting with a ground query. Therefore, they *strictly* include the class of acceptable programs. The proof of the following theorem is reported in Appendix A.

Theorem 10. *A program is bounded iff for every ground query Q (written in any language), the number of LD-refutations starting with Q is finite.* □

It is worth noting that no restriction is assumed on the first order language in which the ground query is written. Differently from acceptable programs, a Prolog interpreter is not guaranteed to terminate for bounded programs and ground queries, even though other selection strategies may be complete. Consider the following *generate & test* program CHECK.

```
check  ← forall(N),q(s(N)).

forall(0).
forall(s(N))  ← forall(N), p(s(N)).

p(s(0)).
q(s(s(0))).
```

CHECK is bounded by | | and { q(s(s(0))), p(s(0)), forall(0), check, forall(s(0)) }, where

$$|\text{check}| = 2$$
$$|\text{forall}(s^k(0))| = k$$
$$|\text{p}(s^k(0))| = |\text{q}(s^k(0))| = 0$$

Declaratively, check is a logical consequence of CHECK iff there exists n such that $p(k)$ holds for $k \in [1, n]$ and $q(n + 1)$ holds. However, the LD-tree for the query check is infinite. As a consequence of Lemma 9, CHECK is not acceptable. We point out that, by the strong completeness of SLD-resolution, the notion of *boundedness* is independent from a specific selection-rule, because the characterization of bounded programs given in Theorem 10 can be re-stated in terms of any selection rule. Therefore, our theory abstracts away from the underlying operational model. In other words, we can apply the results of the further sections to any bounded logic program, independently from the operational model, i.e. from the specific selection rule and search strategy (such as Prolog's, Gödel's, etc.)

An immediate consequence of the proof of Theorem 10 is that the length of a refutation for P and a ground atom A is bounded. Denoting with n_P the maximum number of atoms (> 1) occurring in the body of a clause of P, an upper bound is $l(|A|)$ where

$$l(k) = \frac{n_P^{k+1} - 1}{n_P - 1}$$

As a consequence, an upper bound for the length of a refutation for a ground query $Q = A_1, \ldots, A_n$ is $l(Q) = \Sigma_{i=1}^n l(|A_i|)$. This observation suggests a decision procedure for $A \in \mathcal{M}(P)$ consisting of finding out a LD-refutation for A among the LD-derivations with length lower or equal than $l(|A|)$. The procedure is effective if | | is a recursive level mapping.

Theorem 11. *For a program P bounded by a recursive level mapping, $\mathcal{M}(P)$ is a decidable set.* □

One can show that acceptable programs are a strict subclass of programs bounded by recursive level mappings[1]. However, the decision procedures for the two classes

---

[1] In particular, in [4] it is shown that if P is acceptable then it is acceptable by $\mathcal{M}(P)$ and | |, where $|A|$ is the number of nodes of a LD-tree for P and A. As a consequence, P is bounded by $\mathcal{M}(P)$ and | |, with | | recursive level mapping.

are quite different, in the sense that for acceptable programs it is not needed to know the level mapping whereas that information is needed for bounded programs. For this reason, we will maintain the distinction between the two classes in the following Section.

3.1 Decidability results

Theorem 10 and Lemma 9 allow us to achieve further results. In the next two lemmata, we show that it is decidable whether a query is a correct or computed instance of another query, when considering acceptable programs or programs bounded by a recursive level mapping.

Lemma 12. *Let P be an acceptable program or a program bounded by a recursive level mapping, and Q, Q' two queries. Then it is decidable whether Q' is a correct instance of Q and P.*

Proof. Q' is a correct instance of Q and P iff Q' is a logical consequence of P and an instance of Q. Since it is decidable whether a query is an instance of another, we only have to show that it is decidable whether Q' is a logical consequence of P. By the well-known *Theorem on Constants* (see e.g. Shoenfield [16]) Q' is a logical consequence of P iff $Q'\theta$ is a logical consequence of P, where θ is a substitution mapping all of the variables of Q' into distinct new constants - not occurring in P or Q'. By Correctness and Strong Completeness of SLD–resolution, $Q'\theta$ is a logical consequence of P iff there is a LD-refutation for it. By Theorem 10 or Lemma 9 we have that it is decidable whether $Q'\theta$ - and then Q' - is a logical consequence of P. □

The proof reduces the problem to a decision procedure for a ground query which is provided by Lemma 9 for acceptable programs and Theorem 10 for bounded programs. The decidability in the case of computed instances is stated in the next lemma.

Lemma 13. *Let P be an acceptable program or a program bounded by a recursive level mapping, and Q, Q' two queries. Then it is decidable whether Q' is a computed instance of Q and P.* □

Proof. We provide a decision for establishing whether Q' is a computed instance of Q and P. Let θ be a substitution mapping all of the variables of Q' into distinct new constants - not occurring in P or Q'.
The query $Q'\theta$ is ground and therefore, by Theorem 10 or Lemma 9, there is a finite (modulo renaming) set $\{\xi_1, ..., \xi_m\}$, $m \geq 0$, of LD-refutations for it and P. Moreover we can compute $\xi_1, ..., \xi_m$ since the LD-tree of P is finite if P is acceptable and since the length of each ξ_i is bounded by $l(Q'\theta)$ if P is bounded. For each ξ_i, consider the prefix ξ_i' of the LD-derivation for Q using the same sequence of clauses of ξ_i until possible, i.e. until an empty query or a non-unifiable left-most atom is reached. Let $Q_1', ..., Q_n'$ be the computed answers of the successful ξ_i''s (in general $n \in [0, m]$.) Let us show the following fact

$$Q' \text{ computed inst. of } Q \text{ and } P \text{ iff } Q' \text{ renaming of } Q_i' \text{ for some } i \in [1, n] \quad (1)$$

The *if* part is trivial. To prove the *only–if* part, we notice that if Q' is a computed instance of Q and P with a LD-refutation ξ, then Q' is a computed instance of Q' and P with a LD-refutation ξ', which uses the same sequence of clauses of ξ. The conclusion then follows from the observation that $\xi'\theta$ (the refutation obtained by replacing in ξ' every variable x of Q' by $x\theta$) is a LD-refutation for $Q'\theta$ which uses the same sequence of clauses of ξ'.

We point out that the Q'_i's are computable since we can compute $\xi_1,\ldots,\xi_m$. Finally, as it is decidable whether two queries are variants, it follows from (1) that it is decidable whether Q' is a computed instance of Q and P. $\quad\square$

As an example, it is decidable whether `satisfiable(not(X ∧ false))` is a computed instance of `SAT` and Q =`satisfiable(not(X ∧ Y))`. Notice, however, that the plain Prolog execution of `SAT` and Q does not allow to solve that question by an exhaustive enumeration of the computed instances of Q, since there are infinitely many of them. In addition, if we remove the unit clause of `invalid`, the Prolog execution of the resulting program `SAT1` and `invalid(X)` runs into an infinite computation. In this case, the plain Prolog execution is not sufficient to test `SAT1` on `invalid(false)`, which reveals to be an incompleteness symptom. The same reasoning applies to `CHECK` and the query `check`. From the last results, we conclude that all the semantics here considered are decidable.

Theorem 14. *For a program P acceptable or bounded by a recursive level mapping, $\mathcal{M}(P), \mathcal{C}(P)$ and $\mathcal{S}(P)$ are decidable sets.* $\quad\square$

Theorem 14 and Theorem 4 allow us to conclude that the testing problem is decidable for bounded and acceptable programs.

Corollary 15. *The testing problem is decidable for the class of acceptable programs and programs bounded by a recursive level mapping w.r.t. the least Herbrand model, the C-semantics, and the S-semantics.* $\quad\square$

The importance of this result is mainly due to the relevance of the classes under consideration. It is worth mentioning that most of the programs reported in any basic book of programming, such as [17], belong to these classes. Even though it is undecidable whether a program is acceptable, there are several studies and (semi-automatic) tools for inferring acceptability of a program (and many of them can be easily adapted to infer boundedness.) For instance, by means of abstract interpretation [7] or constraint solving [18] techniques (recursive) level mapping can be automatically inferred and passed to our decision procedure. Summing up, the following steps should be followed in the testing process of logic programs:

1. *Choice a test data set,*
2. *Infer a model and a (recursive) level mapping, such that the program is bounded by the model and the level mapping,*
3. *Call the decision procedure on the test data,*

4. *Call a declarative debugger on detected incorrectness/incompleteness symptoms.*

Step *(1)* is always critical in every testing methodology, and it is based on a deep analysis of the requirement documents or of the formal specifications. Steps *(2)* is not fully automatizable, even though, as discussed, there are some existing tools that can effectively help to solve the problem. Step *(3)* consists of a trivial call to our decision procedure. Finally, in step *(4)* a debugger is called on the detected symptoms and possibly on the proof trees constructed in *(3)*.

4 Prolog implementation of the decision procedure

The proof of Theorem 12 suggests a testing procedure for the S-semantics[2] employing mechanisms from the logic programming paradigm itself, such as unification and LD-derivations. Therefore, it is natural to try to develop an implementation in Prolog.

First, consider the case of acceptable programs. Given two queries Q', Q, in the proof of Theorem 12 the variables of Q' are consistently replaced with new distinct constants. Then a Prolog interpreter for P and the resulting query is called, building up a *finite* LD-tree. Actually, we need a slight modification of the underlying Prolog interpreter, such that when a refutation is found, the computed instance Q'' (if it exists) of P and Q is computed using the same sequence of clauses of that refutation. Finally, if Q'' is a variant of Q' then we can state that Q' is a computed instance of Q. If no variant of Q' is found in this way, then Q' is not a computed instance of Q.

We translate this reasoning in a decision procedure in the form of a Prolog meta-program. We assume a set of facts { new_const(i, a_i) }, where a_i are fresh distinct constants, for $1 \leq i \leq M$. M is an upper bound for the number of variables of a test query. The predicate constants($N1$, Ls, $N2$) replaces the $N2 - N1$ variables appearing in Ls with $a_{N1}, \ldots a_{N2-1}$, implementing the replacement of variables with new constants. In addition, we design a variant of the Vanilla meta-interpreter which behaves as expected when a LD-refutation is found. In order to trace back the sequence of clauses used in a derivation, we assume that a distinct identifier k is associated with each clause C_k from P.

Definition 16. For a logic program P, we denote with TEST(M, P) the program below together with the set of facts { new_const(i, a_i) } where $1 \leq i \leq M$ and the a_i's are fresh distinct constants.

```
test_s(Q1, Q) :-
    constants(1, Q1, _),
    demo(Q1, Q),
    constants(1, Q, _),
    Q = Q1.
```

---

[2] The procedures for M and C semantics are a simplification of that for S-semantics.

```
constants(N, [], N).

constants(N, [X|L], N2) :-
   var(X),
   new_const(N, X),
   N1 is N + 1,
   constants(N1, L, N2).

constants(N, [X|L], N1) :-
   nonvar(X),
   X =.. [F|L1],
   constants(N, L1, N1),
   constants(N1, L, N2).

demo([], []).

demo([A|As], [B|Bs]) :-
   clause(A, Ls, Id),
   demo(Ls, L1s),
   demo(As, Bs),
   clause(B, L1s, Id).
```

clause$(A, [B_1, \ldots, B_n], k)$.   *for every* $C_k = A : -B_1, \ldots, B_n \in P$ □

Given a query $Q = Q_1, \ldots, Q_n$ we write $[Q]$ as a shorthand for $[Q_1, \ldots, Q_n]$. The next Theorem states the termination of the meta-program.

Theorem 17. *Let* P *be an acceptable program, and* Q', Q *two queries. Then every LD-derivation for* TEST(M, P) *and* test_s($[Q']$, $[Q]$) *is finite.*   □

It is worth mentioning that the proof mainly shows that the meta-program defined by **demo** and **clause** is acceptable, when the object program is acceptable, and then uses the well-known termination properties of acceptable programs. For an overview of a general criterion for lifting properties from the object program up to a meta-interpreter, we refer the reader to [15].

In addition, the following theorem states the correctness of TEST. *(i)* is an immediate consequence of Theorem 12. *(ii)* is implied by *(i)* and Theorem 17.

Theorem 18. *Let* P *be an acceptable program, and* Q', Q *two variable disjoint queries, each of which with at most* M *variables. Then*

(i) Q' *is a computed instance for* P *and* Q *iff there exists a Prolog computed instance for* TEST(M, P) *and* test_s($[Q']$, $[Q]$)*;*

(ii) Q' *is not a computed instance for* P *and* Q *iff there exists a Prolog finitely failed tree for* TEST(M, P) *and* test_s($[Q']$, $[Q]$)*.*   □

With an analogous reasoning, we present a correct and complete decision procedure for programs bounded by recursive level mappings. We define TEST-B(M, P) as TEST(M, P) but with the following modifications to test_s and demo:

```
test_s(Q1, Q, N) :-
    constants(1, Q1, _),
    demo(Q1, Q, N),
    constants(1, Q, _),
    Q = Q1.

demo([], [], _).

demo([A|As], [B|Bs], N) :-
    N > 0,
    clause(A, Ls, Id),
    N1 is N - 1,
    demo(Ls, L1s, N1),
    demo(As, Bs, N),
    clause(B, L1s, Id).
```

Intuitively, a call to demo([Q'], [Q], N) involves an attempt to construct a proof tree for Q' whose depth is at most N. For a program P bounded by a recursive level mapping $| \ |$, Theorems 17 and 18 can be extended to TEST-B(M, P) and test_s([Q'], [Q], N), where N is an upper bound for the depth of a proof tree of an atom in Q'. As shown in the proof of Theorem 10, an upper bound is $max_{i=1..n}|A_i| + 1$, where $A_1, \ldots, A_n$ is any ground instance of Q'.

5 Programming with arithmetic built-in's

Several built-in's have been added to pure Prolog in order to overcome efficiency problems. Unfortunately, most of them have no declarative interpretation within first order logic. In this section, we consider an extension of S-semantics and our approach to include the treatment of arithmetic built-in's ([17]). In particular, we deal with <, pointing out that the same reasonings apply to <=, =:=, is, >, >= as well.

A program with arithmetic is a logic program in which the predicate < can appear only in the body of a clause. According to [17], we stipulate that a LD-derivation for a program with arithmetic and a query ends in an error if an atom n < m is selected and n, m are not ground arithmetic expressions (in short, gae's.) If n, m are gae's then we stipulate that the LD-derivation fails if $value(n)$, i.e. the natural number denoted by n, is equal or greater than $value(m)$, i.e. the natural number denoted by m. If the value of n is lower than that of m, the resolvent is the rest of the goal. This is the procedural semantics of < in Prolog. It is worth noting that the resulting LD-trees are still finitely branching. Next definition extends S-semantics to programs with arithmetic.

Definition 19. The S_{ar}-semantics of a program with arithmetic P is the set

$$S_{ar}(P) = \cup_{i \geq 0} S(P \cup M_<^i)$$

where $\{M_<^i\}_{i \geq 0}$ is a chain of finite sets such that

$$\cup_{i \geq 0} M_<^i = \{ n<m \mid n, m \text{ gae's} \wedge value(n) < value(m) \}.$$ $\square$

We point out that $\mathcal{S}_{ar}(P)$ is well-defined since it does not depend on the particular chain chosen. However, at this stage Theorem 2, which fully justifies the interests in $\mathcal{S}$-semantics, cannot be immediately extended. For instance, for the program P

```
p ← 0 < X.
```

it is clear that $\mathbf{p} \in \mathcal{S}_{ar}(P)$, even though the only LD-derivation for P and $\mathbf{p}$ ends in an error. Excluding the case of "wrong" computations, we can extend Theorem 2 as follows (we recall the existence of several approaches [3] to (statically) prove absence from arithmetic errors.)

Theorem 20. *Assume that no LD-derivation for a program with arithmetic P and a query Q ends in an error. Then the set of computed instances of P and Q w.r.t. the left-most selection rule, coincides with $mgi(Q, \mathcal{S}_{ar}(P))$.*

Proof. By definition 19 and the definition of mgi, if $Q' \in mgi(Q, \mathcal{S}_{ar}(P))$ then there exists i such that $Q' \in mgi(Q, \mathcal{S}(P \cup M_<^i))$. Noting that $P \cup M_<^i$ is a logic program, by Theorem 2 and Strong completeness of SLD-resolution there exists a LD-derivation ξ for $P \cup M_<^i$ and Q with computed instance Q'. Since no LD-derivation ends in an error, we have that ξ is a LD-derivation for the program with arithmetic P. Conversely, a LD-derivation for Q and the program with arithmetic P with computed instance Q' is also a LD-derivation for Q and the logic program $P \cup M_<^i$, for some i. Therefore, by Theorem 2, $Q' \in mgi(Q, \mathcal{S}(P \cup M_<^i))$ and then $Q' \in mgi(Q, \mathcal{S}_{ar}(P))$. □

This theorem gives us a method to extend Theorems 17 and 18 to programs with arithmetic, under the additional hypothesis that no LD-derivation for P and Q ends in an error. Let us suppose that the atom $n < m$ is selected in a LD-derivation for P and Q'. The proof of Theorem 20 shows that LD-resolution for programs with arithmetic behaves like LD-resolution where the selected clauses is $n < m$. Therefore, we simply add to $\mathbf{TEST}(M, P)$ the following meta-level interpretation of $<$. Again, we refer the reader to [15] for a general method able to show that the LD-derivation of the meta-program does not end in an error when this property holds for the object-program.

```
demo([ X < Y |As], [ X < Y |Bs]) :-
    X < Y,
    demo(As, Bs).
```

6 Discussion

Semantics Several other semantics have been proposed in the literature. We can easily extend our results to include the following two.

Definition 21. We write $B \leq A$ for two atoms A, B if A is an instance of B. We write $B < A$ when $B \leq A$ and A, B are not variants.

$$\mathcal{MC}(P) = \{ A \in Atom_L \mid P \models A \text{ and } P \not\models B \text{ for any } B < A \}$$
$$\mathcal{FF}(P) = \{ A \in B_L \mid \text{there exists a f.f. SLD-tree for } P \text{ and } A \} \qquad \square$$

The set $\mathcal{MC}(P)$ of the more general correct instances coincides with that of computed instances $\mathcal{S}(P)$ when considering *subsumption free* programs (see [2]), namely, those with no computed instances A, B such that $A < B$. $\mathcal{FF}(P)$ is the well-known finite failure set of P.

It is straightforward to show that the testing problem is decidable for an acceptable program or a program bounded by a recursive level mapping w.r.t. $\mathcal{MC}$. $\mathcal{MC}(P)$ is a decidable set by Lemma 12 and the observation that there are finitely many atoms (modulo renaming) which are more general of a given atom. If P is acceptable then $\mathcal{FF}(P)$ is a decidable set by Lemma 9. However, with our results we cannot conclude that $\mathcal{FF}(P)$ is a decidable set in the case of programs bounded by a recursive level mapping.

Extensions As we pointed out in the introduction, the use of non-standard predicates has to be balanced with the possibility of extending in a natural and intuitive way the declarative semantics. In this paper we extended the $\mathcal{S}$-semantics in order to formalize and justify a testing procedure for programs with arithmetic. Further research is needed towards a declarative description of other non-standard predicates. For instance, the meta-predicate demo can be easily included in the meta-program by adding the clause

```
demo([ demo(A)| As], [ demo(B) |Bs]) :-
    demo([A], [B]),
    demo(As, Bs).
```

Consider a program P containing meta-calls to demo, and suppose that it is acceptable by a level mapping $||$ such that $|demo(A)| > |A|$. Then termination and correctness of the resulting reflective meta-interpreter $TEST(M, P)$ are formally justified respectively by a variant of Theorem 17 and [12, Theorem 2.23].

7 Conclusions

In this paper, we investigated the decidability issue of several declarative semantics of logic programs, and related it to testing. For a large class of logic programs, we proved that the testing problem is decidable by providing a decision procedure in the form of a Prolog meta-program. We are confident that our approach can be successfully integrated with other frameworks for which (semi-)automatic tools exist already. We believe that this is a promising research area, where further work is needed in order to produce an effective tool, which covers the treatment of non-standard predicates according to some (declarative) extension of the considered semantics.

Acknowledgements I am grateful to M. Gabbrielli, D. Pedreschi and the anonymous referees for many helpful comments.

References

1. K.R. Apt. Logic programming. In J. van Leeuwen, editor, *Handbook of Theoretical Computer Science*, volume B, pages 493–574. Elsevier, 1990.

2. K.R. Apt, M. Gabbrielli, and D. Pedreschi. A Closer Look at Declarative Interpretations. Technical Report CS-R9470, Centre for Mathematics and Computer Science, Amsterdam, 1994. To appear in *Journal of Logic Programming*.

3. K.R. Apt and E. Marchiori. Reasoning about Prolog programs: from modes through types to assertions. *Formal Aspects of Computing*, 6A:743–764, 1994.

4. K.R. Apt and D. Pedreschi. Studies in Pure Prolog: Termination. In J. W. Lloyd, editor, *Symposium on Computational Logic*. Springer-Verlag, Berlin, 1990.

5. A. Bossi, M. Gabbrielli, G. Levi, and M. Martelli. The S-semantics Approach: Theory and Applications. *Journal of Logic Programming*, 19,20:149–197, 1994.

6. L. Bougè, N. Choquet, L. Fribourg, and M. Gaudel. Test sets generation from algebraic specifications using logic programming. *Journal of System and Software*, 6(4), 1986.

7. M. Bruynooghe. A Practical Framework for the Abstract Interpretation of Logic Programs. *New Generation Computing*, 10(2):91–124, 1991.

8. K.L. Clark. Predicate logic as a computational formalism. Technical Report DOC 79/59, Imperial College, Dept. of Computing, 1979.

9. M. Comini, G. Levi, and G. Vitiello. Efficient detection of incompleteness errors in the abstract debugging of logic programs. In *AADEBUG'95*, 1995.

10. M. Falaschi, G. Levi, M. Martelli, and C. Palamidessi. A Model-Theoretic Reconstruction of the Operational Semantics of Logic Programs. *Information and Computation*, 102(1):86–113, 1993.

11. M. Gorlick, C.F. Kesselman, D. Marotta, and D. Stott Parker. MOCKINGBIRD: A Logical Methodology for Testing. *Journal of Logic Programming*, 8(1,2), 1990.

12. G. Levi and D. Ramundo. A Formalization of Metaprogramming for Real. In D.S. Warren, editor, *Proceedings Tenth International Conference on Logic Programming*, pages 354–373. The MIT Press, 1993.

13. L. Naish. Declarative Diagnosis of Missing Answers. *New Generation Computing*, 10:255–285, 1991.

14. D. Pedreschi and S. Ruggieri. Termination is language-independent. In M. Alpuente et. al., editor, *Proc. of the GULP-PRODE'94 Joint Conference on Declarative Programming*. Univ. Politecnica de Valencia, 1994.

15. D. Pedreschi and S. Ruggieri. Verification of Metainterpreters. Technical Report TR-96-23, Dipartimento di Informatica, Università di Pisa, 1996. Accepted for publication in *Journal of Logic and Computation*.

16. J. Shoenfield. *Mathematical logic*. Addison Wesdley, Reading, 1967.

17. L. Sterling and E. Shapiro. *The Art of Prolog*. The MIT Press, 1986.

18. J.D. Ulmann and A. van Gelder. Efficient tests for top-down termination of logical rules. *Journal of the ACM*, 35(2):345–373, 1988.

A Proofs

First, we show that the class of bounded logic programs is closed w.r.t. the underlying language L, i.e. a program is bounded w.r.t. a language iff it is bounded w.r.t. every language. This fact is directly implied by the following lemma.

Lemma 22. *A program is bounded w.r.t. L iff it is bounded w.r.t. L_P.*

Proof. The only-if part is straightforward. It is sufficient to consider the restrictions of the level mapping and the model to the language L_P. Conversely, consider $|\ | : B_P \to N$ and $I \subseteq B_P$, such that I is a model of P and for every $A \leftarrow B_1, \ldots, B_n$ in $ground_{L_P}(P)$ $I \models B_1, \ldots, B_n$ implies $|A| > |B_i|$ for $i \in [1, n]$. Let $H : B_L \to B_L$ be a function such that $H(A)$ is obtained by replacing every maximal subterm in A whose principal function symbol f is not in L_P with a ground term $t_f \in U_P$. We show that P is bounded w.r.t. L by considering $|\ |' : B_L \to N$ and $I' \subseteq B_L$ such that for $A \in B_{\langle \Sigma_L, \Pi_P \rangle}$

$$|A|' = |H(A)| \qquad A \in I' \Leftrightarrow H(A) \in I$$

Consider $A \leftarrow B_1, \ldots, B_n$ in $ground_L(P)$ and $I' \models B_1, \ldots, B_n$. We point out that $H(A) \leftarrow H(B_1), \ldots, H(B_n)$ is in $ground_{L_P}(P)$, and that by definition of I', $I \models H(B_1), \ldots, H(B_n)$. Since I is a model of P, we conclude $I \models H(A)$ and then $I' \models A$, i.e. I' is a model of P. Since P is bounded w.r.t. L_P, $|H(A)| > |H(B_i)|$ for $i \in [1, n]$. By definition of $|\ |'$ this implies $|A|' > |B_i|'$ for $i \in [1, n]$. Therefore, we conclude that P is bounded w.r.t. L under the hypothesis that it is bounded w.r.t. L_P. $\square$

We assume the reader familiar with proof trees (see [8].) We recall only that for a ground atom A, $A \in \mathcal{M}(P)$ iff there exists a ground proof tree for A and P.

Theorem 10
Proof. By Lemma 22 it is sufficient to prove the thesis for a fixed language L.

If) We show that the program is bounded by $\mathcal{M}(P)$ and a level mapping $|\ |$ such that $|A|$ is the maximum depth of a proof tree for A. $|\ |$ is well-defined since the number of nodes in a proof tree is bounded by the length of some LD-refutation, hence finite. By König's Lemma the depth of the proof tree is finite. Let $A \leftarrow B_1, \ldots, B_n$ be a ground instance of a clause C from P, and suppose that the body is true in the least Herbrand model. Then there exists at least one proof tree for each B_i. As a consequence, given a proof tree T_i for B_i, for any $i \in [1, n]$, we can construct a proof tree for A, with T_i as a sub-tree. Therefore, $|A| > |B_i|$ for $i \in [1, n]$.

Only if) We point out that if there are infinitely many LD-refutations for P and a ground query Q then their lengths are unbounded. This implies that the depths of the proof trees for a ground atom A appearing in Q are unbounded. On the contrary, we will show that for every ground atom A, $|A| + 1$ is an upper bound for the depth of a proof tree for A. We point out that the depth of a ground proof tree is not lower than that of a proof tree. This is immediate since any ground instance of a proof tree is a ground proof tree. Therefore, to show that $|A| + 1$ is an upper bound for the depth of a proof tree for A it is sufficient to prove that $|A| + 1$ is an upper bound for the depth of a ground proof tree for A. The proof of this fact is on induction on $|A|$.
If $|A| = 0$ then the depth of a proof tree is at most 1. Otherwise there is $A \leftarrow B_1, \ldots, B_n$ in $ground_L(P)$ such that there exist ground proof trees for each B_i. Since I is a model of P, we would have that $I \models B_1, \ldots, B_n$ and then $|A| > |B_i|$ for $i \in [1, n]$. This is impossible since $|A| = 0$.
Suppose now $|A| = n + 1$ and let ξ be a ground proof tree for A. If the depth of ξ is 1 then the conclusion follows. Otherwise there is $A \leftarrow B_1, \ldots, B_n \in ground(P)$ such that the B_i's are the sons of A and there exist ground proof trees for each B_i. Therefore, $I \models B_1, \ldots, B_n$ and then $|A| > |B_i|$ for $i \in [1, n]$. We can then apply the induction hypothesis on the B_i's and conclude that the depth of the proof trees for the B_i's are lower or equal than $|B_i| + 1$. Consequently, the depth of the proof tree for A is bounded by $max\{|B_i| + 2\}$ which is lower or equal than $|A| + 1$. $\square$

PIDGETS
Unifying Pictures and Widgets in a Constraint-Based Framework for Concurrent Functional GUI Programming

Enno Scholz

Department of Computer Science, Freie Universität Berlin
Takustr. 9, 14195 Berlin, Germany
scholz@inf.fu-berlin.de

Abstract. A framework for programming graphical user interfaces (GUIs) in a functional programming language, called PIDGETS, is presented. From the point of view of graphical user interfaces, the contribution of PIDGETS is to unify two concepts traditionally kept separate in GUI programming, namely, static *pictures* and dynamic, input-sensitive *widgets*. From the point of view of functional programming, the contribution of PIDGETS is to introduce a monad suitable for encapsulating objects whose values evolve over time, for arranging these objects in directed acyclic graphs, and for maintaining functional constraints between their values using a lazy evaluation scheme.

1. Introduction

Recently, the subject of using pure functional languages to program graphical user interfaces (GUIs) has received much attention. A number of systems for functional GUI programming have emerged, e.g., FUDGETS [Carlsson, Hallgren 93], GADGETS [Noble, Runciman 93], BRIX [Serrarens 95], HAGGIS [Finne, Peyton Jones 95], OPALWIN [Grieskamp et al. 96]. They demonstrate that, in principle, it is feasible to build functional GUIs without incurring undue performance penalties. This paper presents another functional GUI system called PIDGETS.

From a GUI point of view, the contribution of PIDGETS is to unify two concepts traditionally kept separate in GUI programming, namely, *pictures* and *widgets*. Widgets are the basic building blocks from which GUIs are composed, such as checkbuttons, menus, and scroll bars. They are able to detect and react to user events but the shapes they can take are limited, in particular, they must usually be rectangular. Pictures are graphical objects within widgets which can be of arbitrary shape, but they cannot handle user events.

At the core of PIDGETS, there is a collection of abstract data types which serve as a high-level interface to the services provided by the Display PostScript client library for the X Window system [Adobe 93]. These data types enable arbitrary device-independent PostScript pictures to be put together and manipulated using pure functions. Moreover, PostScript pictures can be displayed in windows and equipped with monadic imperative handlers which are invoked whenever a user event occurs while the mouse pointer's hot spot is over the area colored by the picture. Since these handlers may in turn change the picture's onscreen appearance, arbitrary widgets may be constructed as composite pictures. Correspondingly, widgets are amenable to arbitrary PostScript transformations such as coloring, rotation, scaling, overlaying, and clipping while staying fully functional. Moreover, PIDGETS allows pictures to be nested to form not only trees, but directed acyclic graphs: one picture may appear on the screen multiple times, in multiple windows and with different transformations applied to it, such that events occurring to one instance are indistinguishable from events occurring to another instance and such that, when the picture changes its appearance, the changes become visible in all places it appears on the screen.

From the point of view of functional programming, the contribution of PIDGETS is to introduce a monad suitable for representing objects whose values evolve over time. Such objects may be arranged as nodes in a directed acyclic graph whose edges are functional dependencies maintained by the system using a lazy recalculation scheme. PIDGETS pictures are a special case of such evolving objects whose current value can be thought of as the picture's current appearance.

The PIDGETS framework has been implemented as an extension to Mark Jones's Gofer interpreter [Jones 94]. Over time, its C++ runtime system has evolved into a full-fledged GUI framework for C++ which is described in [Scholz, Bokowski 96].

The paper is organized as follows: The following section introduces the constraint-maintenance monad used in PIDGETS. Section 3 gives an overview of the abstract data types used to represent PostScript graphics objects. Section 4 shows how constraints and graphics interact. Section 5 demonstrates the use of concurrency in PIDGETS. Section 6 gives the details of input handling and hit detection. Section 7 discusses the virtues and shortcomings of the Gofer-based implementation of PIDGETS. Sections 8 and 9 review related work and draw conclusions.

2. Constraints

This section presents the constraint-maintenance monad introduced by PIDGETS.

Primitives

Like most Haskell systems, Gofer has a facility for creating and accessing mutable variables as defined in [Launchbury, Peyton Jones 94]. The PIDGETS interface to mutable variables is given below.

```
type Var a

new_Var    ::  a → IO (Var a)
read_Var   ::  Var a → IO a
write_Var  ::  Var a → a → IO ()
```

new_Var a creates a new mutable variable with an initial value *a*; *read_Var v* reads *v*'s value; *write_Var v a'* destructively updates *v*'s value with *a'*.

This is the interface of type constructor *Expr* that is built into PIDGETS:

type **Expr** *a*		
read_Expr	::	*Expr a → IO a*
var	::	*Var a → Expr a*
result_Expr	::	*a → Expr a*
map_Expr	::	*(a → b) → Expr a → Expr b*
join_Expr	::	*Expr (Expr a) → Expr a*

A term of type *Expr a* denotes an object, called an *expression*, whose *current value* evolves over time. In this paper, the term "expression" is used exclusively to mean "a term of type *Expr a*". The current value of an expression can be queried using the imperative *read_Expr*. However, imperatively querying the current value of an expression is a relatively rare activity in PIDGETS programming; mostly, expressions are composed using pure functions. Function *var v* returns an expression whose current value, at any time, is the current value of variable *v*. *result_Expr* turns a value of type *a* into an expression whose current value is *a* throughout its lifetime. *map_Expr f ea* returns an expression *eb* whose current value is, at any given time, the result of applying *f* to the current value of *ea*. Operationally, a change in the current value of *ea* will entail a change in the current value of *eb*. *join_Expr eea* returns an expression *ea* whose current value is, at any given time, the current value of the current value of *eea*. Operationally, both a change in the current value of *eea* and a change in the current value of the current value of *eea* will entail a change in the current value of *ea*.

In Gofer, *Expr* can be declared to be an instance of type class *Monad* in the following way:

```
instance Functor Expr where   map    =  map_Expr
instance Monad  Expr where   result =  result_Expr
                             join   =  join_Expr
```

This enables monad comprehension syntax defined in [Wadler 90] to be used. For instance, *[a + b | a ← ea, b ← eb]* denotes the expression whose current value, at any time, is the sum of the current values of *ea* and *eb*.

Example

The following example illustrates that, in PIDGETS, expressions are subject to *lazy evaluation*:

```
do v1 ← new_Var "Hi "; v2 ← new_Var "world!\n"
    let e = [ s1++s2 | s1 ← var v1,
                       s2 ← var v2] -- read_Expr e would return "Hi world\n"
    write_Var v1 "Hello "           -- read_Expr e would return "Hello world\n"
    write_Var v2 "Pidgets!\n"       -- read_Expr e would return "Hello Pidgets\n"
    ... etc. ...
```

For instance, if *read_Expr e* is only called at the end of the above program fragment, the concatenation of the current values of *v1* and *v2* has only been calculated once, and not thrice as would be the case if constraints were maintained using *eager evaluation*. For longer strings, the difference may be significant.

Abstractions

In the following, it will be convenient to use the standard arithmetic functions with expressions:

instance Num a ⇒ Num (Expr a) where ea + ea' = [a + a' | a ← ea, a' ← ea']
ea - ea' = [a - a' | a ← ea, a' ← ea']
... etc. ...

3. Graphics

As mentioned above, PIDGETS uses the PostScript graphics model [Adobe 90] for describing graphics, and its implementation is based on the Display PostScript client library for the X window system [Adobe 93]. PIDGETS separates the PostScript imaging model from the PostScript language and from the Display PostScript client library for X Windows. The functional programmer is provided with the full power of (device-independent) Display PostScript while enjoying all the capabilities of a modern functional programming language and without having to deal with issues related to the PostScript language and the X Window system.

Primitives

In this subsection, the following data types will be defined: *Pictures* are device-independent PostScript page descriptions. Pictures may be displayed in *windows*. Roughly, pictures are composed from *paths*, and paths are composed from *subpaths*. To describe the positions of graphical elements in the PostScript coordinate system, *vectors* and *rectangles* are introduced.

Note that of all the primitive functions provided by PIDGETS to create and manipulate pictures, paths, etc., only those required by the paper's example programs are presented in this section; moreover, a few primitives are presented in a slightly simplified form. For a comprehensive treatment, refer to [Scholz 96].

Vectors and Rectangles

Vectors are used to specify points, distances, and scales in the PostScript coordinate system where one unit equals 1/72 inch. Rectangles are useful for specifying bounding boxes.

type **Vector** =	*(Expr Float, Expr Float)*	
type **Rectangle** =	*(Vector, Vector)*	

A vector is given by two floating point expressions denoting its x and y components. A rectangle is given by the vectors pointing to its lower left and upper right corners.

Subpaths

A subpath represents a sequence of connected, infinitely thin *segments*. Each segment is either a straight line, a circular arc, or a Bezier curve. A subpath implicitly has a *current point*.

```
type SubPath
startAt  ::  Vector → SubPath
lineTo   ::  SubPath → Vector → SubPath
connect  ::  SubPath → SubPath → SubPath
```

startAt (x, y) creates an empty subpath with a given current point *(x, y)*. *subpath* `lineTo` *(x, y)* creates a new subpath which has the same shape as *subpath* except that the new subpath's current point is *(x, y)* and that the new subpath contains one segment more than *subpath*, namely, a line segment from *subpath*'s current point to *(x, y)*. *subpath1* `connect` *subpath2* appends *subpath2* to *subpath1* by translating *subpath2* such that its starting point coincides with *subpath1*'s current point. The new current point is the translated current point of *subpath2*.

Paths

A path can be created (for instance) by *closing* a subpath or by outlining a string. A path has no current point.

```
type Path
closed ::  SubPath → Path
string ::  Expr String → Expr String → Path
```

closed subpath closes *subpath* by adding a line segment from its current point to its starting point, forgetting the current point. *string fontName s* constructs a path which represents the outline of a string *chars* in font *fontName* with size 100 point, positioning the string's origin in point *(0,0)*.

Pictures

In PIDGETS, pictures are the principal means for representing on-screen graphics.

```
type Picture
fill     ::  Path → Picture
stroke   ::  Expr Float → Path → Picture
overlay  ::  Picture → Picture → Picture
```

fill path fills the area enclosed by *path* with black ink; *stroke lineWidth path* draws along *path* with black ink in a given line width *lineWidth*. *overlay over under* puts *over* on top of *under* such that colored parts of *over* obscure colored parts of *under*.

Colors

Using *color*, pictures may be colored in one of the color systems supported by PostScript.

type **Color**		
rgb	::	*Expr Float → Expr Float → Expr Float → Color*
color	::	*Color → Picture → Picture*

For instance, *rgb* creates a color in the RGB color system. Note that *color* changes
the color of every colored point in its argument picture to the new color.

Shapes

Pictures, paths, and subpaths are all instances of type class *Shape*, i.e., they are
amenable to affine transformations, their bounding box may be queried, and they
may be tested for emptiness.

class **Shape** a where	**translate**	::	*Vector → a → a*
	scale	::	*Vector → a → a*
	rotate	::	*Expr Float → a → a*
	boundingBox	::	*a → Rectangle*
	isEmpty	::	*a → Expr Bool*

Windows

Pictures can be displayed in *windows*.

type **Window**		
new_Window	::	*String → String → Int → Int → Int → Int → IO Window*
write_Window	::	*Window → Picture → IO ()*
diagonal_Window	::	*Window → Vector*

Given the name of an X display, a window title, and the desired window coordinates,
new_Window opens a window which initially displays the empty picture. The picture
displayed in a window can be set using *write_Window*. The vector describing a
window's current diagonal can be queried using the pure function *diagonal_Window*.

Abstraction

star n creates a path outlining an *n*-pronged star with fixed-size prongs.

```
star :: Int → Path
star n =   let prong = startAt (expr 0.0, expr 0.0)
                       `lineTo` (expr 5.0, expr 10.0)
                       `lineTo` (expr 10.0, expr 0.0)
           in  closed (foldr1 connect [ rotate (expr ((-i * 360.0) / fromInteger n))
                                        prong
                                      | i ← [1.0 .. fromInteger n]])
```

Example

myStar overlays a filled and a stroked version of *star 9* and colors, scales, and
translates the resulting picture. The result of displaying *myStar* in a window is given
in Fig. 1.

myStar :: Picture
myStar = *translate (expr 100.0, expr 100.0)*
(scale (expr 4.0, expr 2.0)
(overlay (stroke(expr 4.0)
(star 9))
(color (rgb (expr 1.0) (expr 0.0) (expr 0.0))
(fill (star 9)))))

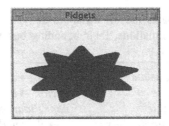

Fig. 1: Screen dump of *myStar*

Abstractions

The arithmetic operations on vectors are defined componentwise:

instance Num Vector where (x,y) + (x',y') = *(x+x', y+y')*
(x,y) - (x',y') = *(x-x', y-y')*
... etc. ...

The following functions return a rectangle's corners, center, and its diagonal vector.

lowerLeft, lowerRight, diagonal, center, upperLeft, upperRight ::

Rectangle → Vector

diagonal (ll, ur) = *ur - ll*
center (ll, ur) = *(ll + ur) / (expr 2.0, expr 2.0)*
... etc. ...

Note how these definitions use vector arithmetics.

beside translates *picture2* to align its lower left corner with *picture1*'s lower right corner.

beside :: Picture → Picture → Picture
beside picture1 picture2 = *overlay pict1*
(translate (lowerRight (boundingBox picture1)
- lowerLeft (boundingBox picture2))
picture2)

hbox arranges a list of pictures in a horizontal row.

hbox :: [Picture] → Picture
hbox = foldr1 beside

fitWithin scales and translates a shape such that its bounding box coincides with a given rectangle.

fitWithin :: Shape a ⇒ Rectangle → a → a
fitWithin rect shape =
    translate (lowerLeft rect)
        (scale (diagonal rect / diagonal (boundingBox shape))
            (translate (- lowerLeft (boundingBox shape))
            shape))

4. Combining Constraints and Graphics

Primitives

In PIDGETS, graphical objects, i.e., pictures, paths, subpaths, and colors, are just distinguished kinds of expressions:

> *type **Picture** = Expr PictureVal*
> *... etc. ...*

For instance, the type of the current value of a picture is *PictureVal*. However, there are no operations whatsoever defined on type *PictureVal*; it is just there to make the abstractions defined on expressions available on pictures. It is helpful to think of the current value of a graphical object as being its current appearance. For instance, the appearance of *string fontName s* is not fixed but rather, its appearance is constrained to be, at any time, the result of outlining the current value of string expression *s* in the font specified by the current value of string expression *fontName*.

Here the lazy evaluation mechanism of the *Expr* monad significantly improves performance: since recalculating an object's appearance involves expensive calls to the Display PostScript interpreter, it is important only to recalculate a picture's appearance when the system finds the time to update the contents of the window it is displayed in, and not every time the picture changes.

Example

Using *beside* and *fitWithin*, we can define the first version of the PIDGETS hello world program:

helloWorld1 =
    do font_Var ← new_Var"Helvetica-Bold"
       window ← new_Window "" "Pidgets" 0 0 300 300
       write_Window window (fitWithin ((expr 0.0, expr 0.0),
                           diagonal_Window window)
                           (beside (fill (string (var font_Var)
                                   (expr "Hello ... ")))
                           (fill (string (var font_Var)
                                 (expr "... world!")))))
      sleep 10
      write_Var font_Var "Courier-Bold"

It opens a window and shows the strings *"Hello ..."* and *"... world!"*. At any time (i.e., initially, after the application has changed the string's font, and whenever the user resizes the window) the system maintains the following graphical constraint: The bounding boxes of the strings are exactly aligned, they are displayed in the same font, and their combined bounding box exactly fills the window (see Fig. 2).

Fig. 2: Screen dumps of *helloWorld1*

5. Concurrency

In GUI programming, concurrency is widely held to be helpful for structuring programs that produce graphical output autonomously. Consequently, PIDGETS provides a set of concurrency primitives based on synchronous message passing; their design rationale and semantics are described at length in [Scholz 95].

Primitives

fork t creates causes expression *t* to be evaluated in a new thread executing concurrently with the thread executing *fork*. A thread executing *sleep n* is delayed for at least *n* seconds.

```
fork    ::  IO () → IO ()
sleep   ::  Int → IO ()
```

Abstractions

The imperative *new_moving* creates a shape whose appearance is constrained to be the appearance of *shape*, moving by the distance specified by the current values of vector (*xDelta_Expr, yDelta_Expr*) each second.

```
new_moving :: Shape shape ⇒ Vector → shape → IO shape
new_moving (xDelta_Expr, yDelta_Expr) shape =
    do positionVar ← new_Var (0.0, 0.0)
       let loop = do (xCurr, yCurr) ← read_Var positionVar
                     xDelta ← read_Expr xDelta_Expr
                     yDelta ← read_Expr yDelta_Expr
                     write_Var positionVar (xCurr+xDelta, yCurr + yDelta)
                     sleep 1
                     loop
           fork loop
           result (translate (map fst (var positionVar), map snd (var positionVar))
                       shape)
```

6. Handling input

Primitives

In PIDGETS, user events occurring while the mouse pointer's hot spot is over a picture may be intercepted by associating the picture with a handler, turning it into a a so-called *pidget* (i.e. a picture ga*dget*).

data Event	= *Move*	*Float Float*
	| *ButtonPress*	*Float Float Int*
	| *ButtonRelease*	*Float Float Int*
	... *etc.* ...	
pidget	:: *(Event → IO ()) → Picture → Picture*	
grabMouse	:: *IO ()*	
releaseMouse	:: *IO ()*	
dispatch	:: *Picture → Event → IO ()*	

pidget handler picture returns a picture *picture'* whose appearance is identical to that of *picture*. While *picture'* is displayed in a window, any time a user event *event* occurs while the mouse pointer's hot spot is over a pixel colored by *picture'*, and *picture'* is the outermost pidget term in the picture displayed by the window, *handler event* is executed. The events *ButtonPress x y n* or *ButtonRelease x y n* indicate that the *n*-th mouse button has been pressed or released at position (x, y) in the pidget's coordinate system; the event *Move x y* indicate's that the mouse pointer has moved to position (x, y).

It is important to realize that the x and y coordinates of the mouse pointer are reported *in the coordinate system of the pidget*. For instance, assume that a top-level window displays the picture *picture1 = translate (expr 20.0, expr 10.0) (pidget handler picture2)*. Then, if the mouse pointer moves to the point with the window-relative coordinates *(x, y)*, and if *(x, y)* is within the area colored by *picture1*, *handler (Move (x – 20) (y – 10))* is executed.

Moreover, a handler can grab the mouse using *grabMouse*, which causes all future user events to be dispatched directly to the handler (without any handlers of other, possibly enclosing pidgets getting a chance to interfere), until the mouse is released again with *releaseMouse*. The window-relative coordinates of grabbed events are transformed with the same transformation as the one that was used to transform the event in reaction to which the handler effected the mouse grab. Moreover, an event can be dispatched to an arbitrary picture using *dispatch*. Note that invoking *grabMouse*, *releaseMouse*, or *dispatch* outside of a handler is a run-time error.

Abstraction

The imperative *new_draggable* illustrates the use of pidgets. The appearance of the pidget returned by *new_draggable picture* is constrained to be the appearance of *picture*, translated to a position – initially (0,0) – that the user can choose by dragging with the mouse. The pidget's handler controls a mutable variable containing information about the current translation of picture, whether the mouse button is currently down, and – in case it is – at which position the mouse button was pressed. Whenever the user presses a mouse button over the translated picture, the pidget's handler is invoked: subsequent mouse motions cause the picture to be translated correspondingly. When the user releases the mouse button, the pidget becomes idle again and subsequent mouse motions are dispatched to *picture*.

```
new_draggable :: Picture → IO Picture
new_draggable picture =
    do state_Var ← new_Var (False, 0.0, 0.0, undefined, undefined)
        let positionVector = ([ xCurrent | (_, xCurrent, _, _, _)← var state_Var ],
                              [ yCurrent | (_, _, yCurrent, _, _)← var state_Var ])
            resultPicture = translate positionVector picture
            handler event =
                do (buttonIsDown, xCurrent, yCurrent, xOffset, yOffset)
                                                    ← read_Var state_Var
                    case event of
                    ButtonPress x y 1 →
                        do write_Var state_Var (True, xCurrent, yCurrent,
                                                    xCurrent - x, yCurrent - y)
                            grabMouse
                    Move x y | buttonIsDown →
                            write_Var state_Var (buttonIsDown, x+xOffset,
                                                    y+yOffset, xOffset, yOffset)
                    ButtonRelease _ _ 1 →
                        do write_Var state_Var (False, xCurrent, yCurrent,
                                                    undefined, undefined)
                            releaseMouse
                    other →
                            dispatch resultPicture other
        result (pidget handler resultPicture)
```

Example

Using *new_moving* and *new_draggable*, we can refine the hello world application.

```
helloWorld2 =
    do worldInMotion ← new_moving (expr 2.4, expr 2.4)
                                    (fill (string (expr "Helvetica-Bold")
                                            (expr "... world!")))
        draggableWorldInMotion ← new_draggable worldInMotion
        window ← new_Window "" "Pidgets" 0 0 300 300
        write_Window window
                    (fitWithin ((expr 0.0, expr 0.0), diagonal_Window window)
                            (overlay (fill (string (expr "Helvetica-Bold")
                                            (expr "Hello ... ")))
                                draggableWorldInMotion))
```

Initially, the toplevel window displays the string *"Hello ..."* on top of the string *"... world!"*, scaled such that their combined bounding box exactly fits the window. However, the string *"... world!"* starts to slowly move to the right and up, away from the *"Hello ..."* string. It would move out of the area visible in the window were it not for the existence of the enclosing *fitWithin*, which ensures that, at any time, the combined bounding box of the two strings exactly coincides with the toplevel window's real estate. Additionally, the string *"...world"* is draggable, allowing the user to drag it to the left and down, even past *"Hello ..."*.

Fig. 3: Screen dumps of *helloWorld2*

In *helloWorld2*, it is worthwhile to contemplate the interplay of the functional and the imperative program parts: Only where objects with mutable state are created or changed, imperative programming using the IO monad is required. Whenever relationships between groups of objects are specified, pure functional programming is employed. Moreover, *helloWorld2* demonstrates that the functional and imperative combinators developed so far are indeed completely general, in that they can be composed in arbitrary ways.

7. Related Work

Many of the ideas found in PIDGETS can be traced back to existing work on GUI programming in imperative languages, in particular, to FRESCO [Linton, Price 93], AMULET [McDaniel, Myers 95] and the NEXTSTEP operating system [NEXT Inc. 92]. Moreover, the design of PIDGETS has been influenced by the study of the functional GUI framework HAGGIS [Finne 96]. Thus it is worthwhile to compare PIDGETS to each of these systems.

FRESCO

The idea of unifying the representation of graphics, GUI objects, transformations, and layout in the notion of *glyphs* was presented in [Calder, Linton 90] and implemented in the frameworks INTERVIEWS [Linton et al. 89] and FRESCO. PIDGETS maps glyphs to PostScript pictures such that – in the terminology of FRESCO – every *composite glyph* is identified with a PostScript transformation, every *leaf glyph* is identified with a PostScript path description, and every *viewer* is identified with a pidget. However, in FRESCO, the responsibility for invalidating and repainting the screen in the face of updates, for maintaining constraints, and for supplying hit detection algorithms is placed with the programmer.

NeXTSTEP

In the NEXTSTEP operating system, two languages exist side by side: PostScript is used to describe all graphics, Objective C is used as the application programming language. On the level of Objective C, the programmer accesses the graphical capabilities of the operating system by means of a number of classes called the *Application Kit*. Since the Display PostScript interpreter's interface to NEXTSTEP is almost identical to its interface to the X Window system, applications having to extend the Application Kit face many of the problems described in [Scholz, Bokowski 96].

AMULET

AMULET takes a very high-level approach, relieving the programmer of tasks like redrawing and notifying the systems when a redraw is necessary; every picture element is automatically a GUI element, with full hit detection supported by the system. Like PIDGETS, it is based on a machinery for constraint maintenance. However, the graphical objects supplied by AMULET are restricted to a few basic shapes, for instance, rectangles, arcs, and polygons. Moreover, the transformations supported on graphical objects are significantly less expressive than those supported by PIDGETS, for instance, no graphical objects may currently be rotated or clipped to non-rectangular shapes, and non-atomic graphical objects cannot be scaled. AMULET allows arbitrary graphical objects to be enhanced with behavior by associating with them one out of a set of five built-in *interactors*; in contrast, PIDGETS allows arbitrary behaviors to be associated with pictures.

HAGGIS

In HAGGIS, pictures are represented by an algebraic data type, allowing them to be decomposed with pattern-matching. HAGGIS does not seem to provide any direct means of performing hit or collision detection on pictures, testing them for emptiness, or calculating a picture's bounding box. Nevertheless, the HAGGIS picture data type supports high-level concepts such as *structured translation* enabling picture combinators similar to the ones presented in this paper to be expressed. The most obvious difference between the two systems seems to be that HAGGIS maintains the traditional distinction between static pictures and dynamic widgets (represented by types *Picture* and *DisplayHandle*, respectively) which PIDGETS strives to eliminate; in particular, picture combinators may not be applied to widgets.

8. Implementation

Because PIDGETS is implemented as an extension to the Gofer interpreter, it inherits Gofer's fast compilation speed and pleasant interactive environment along with its – compared to the large Haskell compilers – moderate execution speed. However, due to substantial optimizations in the C++ runtime system, the performance of PIDGETS appears to be quite good in practice, for instance, the *new_moving* and *new_draggable* abstractions of Sections 5 and 6 are able to move objects around the screen rather quickly and smoothly (thanks to double-buffering). Unfortunately, PIDGETS does not inherit Gofer's portability: the whole of Gofer's source code has been ported to C++ and the PIDGETS runtime system depends on C++ templates and the presence of the Display PostScript extension in the X server.

The current implementation has a few shortcomings, to be remedied shortly: Only one open window is supported, Gofer's garbage collector and the C++ storage deallocation have not been matched properly yet, and some advanced features of Display PostScript, such as querying font information, are not available yet.

9. Conclusion

We have given an overview of the PIDGETS framework for GUI programming. The two main characteristics of PIDGETS are its high-level interface to the services of the Display PostScript System and its constraint maintenance monad. Their integration enabled us to eliminate the traditional distinction between pictures and widgets. We have shown how a number of abstractions capturing common interactive graphics metaphors like draggability, autonomous motion, and layout combinators could be constructed on top of the PIDGETS primitives in a very concise way. Moreover, we argue that the introduction of the constraint-maintenance monad helped to significantly reduce the amount of imperative programming required in the construction of these abstractions.

Acknowledgements

I thank Peter Achten, Magnus Carlsson, Manuel Chakravarty, Sigbjørn Finne, Wolfgang Grieskamp, Paul Hudak, Peter Löhr, Rob Noble, Simon Peyton Jones, Colin Taylor, David N. Turner, Philip Wadler, and the anonymous referees for their comments on different versions of the PIDGETS system. Moreover, I thank my colleague Boris Bokowski for innumerable fruitful discussions on the design of PIDGETS, and for being a constant source of moral support.

References

[Adobe 90] Adobe Inc.: *PostScript Language Reference Manual, Second Edition*, Addison-Wesley 1990

[Adobe 93] Adobe Inc.: *Programming the Display PostScript System with X*, Addison-Wesley 1993

[Calder, Linton 90] P. Calder, M. Linton: *Glyphs: Flyweight Objects for User Interfaces*, Proceedings of the ACM Symposium on User Interface Software and Technology, Snowbird, Utah, 1990

[Carlsson, Hallgren 93] M. Carlsson, T. Hallgren: *FUDGETS - A Graphical User Interface in a Lazy Functional Language*, Conference on Functional Programming Languages and Computer Architectures, 1993

[Finne, Peyton Jones 95] S. Finne, S.L. Peyton Jones: *Composing HAGGIS*, 5th Eurographics Workshop on Programming Paradigms in Computer Graphics, Maastricht, 1995

[Finne 96] S. Finne: *The Haggis Manual*, edition 0.02, Glasgow University, 1996

[Grieskamp et al. 96] W. Grieskamp, T. Frauenstein, P.Pepper, M. Südholt: *Functional Programming of Communicating Agents and its Application to Graphical User Interfaces*, 2nd International Conference on Perspectives in System Informatics, Novosibirsk, 1996

[Hudak et al. 92] P. Hudak, S. Peyton Jones, P. Wadler (editors): *Report on the Programming Language Haskell: Version 1.1*, ACM SIGPLAN Notices, 27 (5), May 1992

[Jones 94] M. Jones: *Gofer 2.21/2.28/2.30 Release Notes*, available by anonymous ftp from *ftp.cs.yale.edu*, 1994

[Launchbury, Peyton Jones 94] J. Launchbury, S.L. Peyton Jones: *Lazy Functional State Threads*, Conference on Programming Language Design and Implementation, Orlando, FL, June 1994

[Linton et al. 89] M. Linton, J. Vlissides, P. Calder: *Composing User Interfaces with InterViews*, IEEE Computer 22, 2, pp. 8-22, 1989

[Linton, Price 93] M. Linton, C. Price: *Building Distributed User Interfaces with Fresco*, Proceedings of the 7th X Technical Conference, Boston, Massachussets, pp. 77-87, 1993

[McDaniel, Myers 95] R. McDaniel, B. Myers: *Amulet's Dynamic and Flexible Prototype-Instance Object and Constraint System in C++*, Technical Report CMU-HCII-95-104, Carnegie-Mellon University, July 1995

[NeXT Inc. 92] NeXT Inc.: *NeXTSTEP General Reference Volume1*, Addison Wesley, 1992

[Noble, Runciman 95] R. Noble, C. Runciman: *GADGETS: Lazy Functional Components for Graphical User Interfaces*, PLILP 1995

[Scholz 95] E. Scholz: *Four Concurrency Primitives for Haskell*, Haskell Workshop Proceedings, Yale University Research Report YALEU/DCS/RR-1075, 1995

[Scholz 96] E. Scholz: *Pidgets Programmer's Manual* (in preparation), 1996

[Scholz, Bokowski 96] E. Scholz, B. Bokowski: *Pidgets++ – A C++ Framework Unifying PostScript Pictures, Graphical User Interface Objects, and Lazy One-Way Constraints*, TOOLS 20 USA, Santa Barbara, CA, July 1996

[Serrarens 95] P. Serrarens: *BriX, A Deterministic Concurrent Functional X Windows System*, Technical Report, Bristol University, 1995

[Wadler 92] P. Wadler: *The Essence of Functional Programming*, 16th ACM SIGPLAN-SIGACT Symposium on Principles of Programming Languages, 1992

Generalized β–Reduction and Explicit Substitutions [*]

Fairouz Kamareddine and Alejandro Ríos

Department of Computing Science, 17 Lilybank Gardens, University of Glasgow, Glasgow G12 8QQ, Scotland, fax: +44 41 330 4913, email: fairouz@dcs.gla.ac.uk and rios@dcs.gla.ac.uk

Abstract. Extending the λ-calculus with either explicit substitution or generalised reduction has been the subject of extensive research recently which still has many open problems. Due to this reason, the properties of a calculus combining both generalised reduction and explicit substitutions have never been studied. This paper presents such a calculus λsg and shows that it is a desirable extension of the λ-calculus. In particular, we show that λsg preserves strong normalisation, is sound and it simulates classical β-reduction. Furthermore, we study the simply typed λ-calculus extended with both generalised reduction and explicit substitution and show that well-typed terms are strongly normalising and that other properties such as subtyping and subject reduction hold.

1 Introduction

1.1 The λ-calculus with generalised reduction

In $((\lambda_x.\lambda_y.N)P)Q$, the function starting with λ_x and the argument P result in the redex $(\lambda_x.\lambda_y.N)P$ which when contracted will turn the function starting with λ_y and Q into a redex. This fact has been exploited by many researchers and reduction has been extended so that the future redex based on the matching λ_y and Q is given the same priority as the other redex. Attempts at generalising reduction can be summarized by three axioms:

(θ) $((\lambda_x.N)P)Q \rightarrow (\lambda_x.NQ)P,$ (γ) $(\lambda_x.\lambda_y.N)P \rightarrow \lambda_y.(\lambda_x.N)P,$
(γ_C) $((\lambda_x.\lambda_y.N)P)Q \rightarrow (\lambda_y.(\lambda_x.N)P)Q.$

These rules attempt to make more redexes visible. γ_C e.g., makes sure that λ_y and Q form a redex even before the redex based on λ_x and P is contracted. By compatibility, γ implies γ_C. Moreover, $((\lambda_x.\lambda_y.N)P)Q \rightarrow_\theta (\lambda_x.(\lambda_y.N)Q)P$ and hence both θ and γ_C put λ adjacently next to its matching argument. θ moves the argument next to its matching λ whereas γ_C moves the λ next to its matching argument. θ can be equally applied to explicitly and implicitly typed systems. The transfer of γ or γ_C to explicitly typed systems is not straightforward however, since in these systems, the type of y may be affected by the reducible pair λ_x, P. E.g., it is fine to write $((\lambda_{x:*}.\lambda_{y:x}.y)z)u \rightarrow_\theta (\lambda_{x:*}.(\lambda_{y:x}.y)u)z$ but not

---

[*] This work was carried out under EPSRC grant GR/K25014.

to write $((\lambda_{x:*}.\lambda_{y:x}.y)z)u \to_{\gamma_C} (\lambda_{y:x}.(\lambda_{x:*}.y)z)u$. Hence, we study θ-like rules in this paper. Now, we discuss where generalised reduction has been used (cf. [24]).

[32] introduces the notion of a *premier redex* which is similar to the redex based on λ_y and Q above (which we call *generalised redex*). [33] uses θ and γ (and calls the combination σ) to show that the perpetual reduction strategy finds the longest reduction path when the term is Strongly Normalising (SN). [37] also introduces reductions similar to those of [33]. Furthermore, [22] uses θ (and other reductions) to show that typability in ML is equivalent to acyclic semi-unification. [35] uses a reduction which has some common themes with θ. [30] and [11] use θ whereas [25] uses γ to reduce the problem of β-strong normalisation to the problem of weak normalisation (WN) for related reductions. [23] uses θ and γ to reduce typability in the rank-2 restriction of the 2nd order λ-calculus to the problem of acyclic semi-unification. [27, 38, 36, 26] use related reductions to reduce SN to WN and [21] uses similar notions in SN proofs. [2] uses θ (called "let-C") as a part of an analysis of how to implement sharing in a real language interpreter in a way that directly corresponds to a formal calculus. [16] uses a more extended version of θ where Q and N are not only separated by the redex $(\lambda_x.N)P$ but by many redexes (ordinary and generalised). [16] shows that generalised reduction makes more redexes visible allowing flexibility in reducing a term. [6] shows that with generalised reduction one may indeed avoid size explosion without the cost of a longer reduction path and that λ-calculus can be elegantly extended with definitions which result in shorter type derivations. Generalised reduction is strongly normalising (cf. [6]) for all systems of the cube (cf. [3]) and preserves strong normalisation of classical reduction (cf. [13]).

1.2 The λ-calculus with explicit substitution

Functional programming and in particular partial evaluation may benefit from explicit substitution. For example, given $xx[x := y]$, we may not be interested in having yy as the result of $xx[x := y]$ but rather only $yx[x := y]$. In other words, we only substitute one occurrence of x by y and continue the substitution later. This issue of being able to follow substitution and decide how much to do and how much to postpone, has become a major one in functional language implementation (cf. [31]). Another wish is to execute substitutions only when necessary. For this purpose one may decide to postpone substitutions as long as possible ("lazy evaluations"). This can yield profits, since substitution is an inefficient, maybe even exploding, process by the many repetitions it causes. This is the ground for the so-called graph reduction (cf. [31]). Most theorem provers (Nuprl [7], Coq [12]) use explicit substitutions in their implementation in order to replace locally (rather than globally) some abbreviated term. This avoids explosion when it is necessary that a variable be replaced by a huge term only in specific places so that a certain theorem can be proved.

Most literature on the λ-calculus considers substitution as an implicit operation: the computations to perform substitution are usually described with operators which do not belong to the language of the λ-calculus. The last fifteen years have seen an interest in formalising substitution explicitly; various calculi including new operators to denote substitution have been proposed. Amongst these calculi we mention $C\lambda\xi\phi$ (cf. [10]); the calculi of categorical combinators (cf. [8]); $\lambda\sigma$, $\lambda\sigma_{\uparrow}$, $\lambda\sigma_{SP}$ (cf. [1, 9, 34]) referred to as the $\lambda\sigma$-family; $\lambda\upsilon$ (cf. [4]), a descendant of the $\lambda\sigma$-family; $\varphi\sigma BLT$ (cf. [15]), $\lambda\mathbf{exp}$ (cf. [5]), λs (cf. [17]), λs_e (cf. [19]) and $\lambda\zeta$ (cf. [29]). All these calculi (except $\lambda\mathbf{exp}$) are described in a de Bruijn setting where natural numbers play the role of the classical variables.

In [17], we extended the λ-calculus with explicit substitutions by turning de Bruijn's meta-operators into object-operators offering a style of explicit substitution that differs from that of $\lambda\sigma$. The resulting calculus λs remains as close as possible to the λ-calculus from an intuitive point of view. The main interest in introducing the λs-calculus (cf. [17]) was to provide a calculus of explicit substitutions which would both preserve strong normalisation and have a confluent extension on open terms (cf. [19]). There are calculi of explicit substitutions which are confluent on open terms: the $\lambda\sigma_{\uparrow}$-calculus (cf. [9]), but the non-preservation of strong normalisation for $\lambda\sigma_{\uparrow}$, for the rest of the $\lambda\sigma$-family and for the categorical combinators, has been proved (cf. [28]). There are also calculi which satisfy the preservation property: the $\lambda\upsilon$-calculus (cf. [4]), but this calculus is not confluent on open terms. Recently, the $\lambda\zeta$-calculus (cf. [29]) has been proposed as a calculus which preserves strong normalisation and is itself confluent on open terms. It works with two new applications that allow the passage of substitutions within classical applications only if these applications have a head variable. This is done to cut the branch of the critical pair which is responsible for the non-confluence of $\lambda\upsilon$ on open terms. Unfortunately, $\lambda\zeta$ is not able to simulate one step β-reduction as shown in [29], it simulates only a "big step" β-reduction. This lack of the simulation property is an uncommon feature among calculi of explicit substitutions. On the other hand, λs has been extended to λs_e which is confluent on open terms (cf. [19]) and simulates one step β-reduction but the preservation of strong normalisation is still an open problem.

1.3 Combining generalised reduction and explicit substitution

All the research mentioned above is a living proof for the importance and usefulness of generalised reduction and explicit substitutions. Moreover, a system where reduction is generalised and substitution is explicit, gives a more flexible way of evaluating programs thanks to the advantages of step-wise substitution and the ability of reducing more redexes.

Before such a combination can be used as a powerful basis for programming, we need to check that this combination is sound and safe exactly like we checked that each of explicit substitutions and generalised reductions are sound and safe. This paper shows that extending the λ-calculus with both concepts results in theories that are confluent, preserve termination, and simulate β-reduction.

Generalised reduction $g\beta$, has never been introduced in a de Bruijn setting. Explicit substitution, has almost always been presented in a de Bruijn setting. For this reason, we combine $g\beta$-reduction and explicit substitution in a de Bruijn setting giving the first calculus of generalised reduction à la de Bruijn. As we need to describe generalised redexes in an elegant way, we use a notation suitable for this purpose *the item notation* (cf. [14]).

In Section 2 we introduce the calculus of generalised reduction, the λg-calculus, in item notation with de Bruijn indices and prove its confluence.

In Section 3 we extend the λs-calculus with $\rightarrow_{g\beta}$ into the λsg-calculus. We show that λsg is sound with respect to λg, simulates $g\beta$ and is confluent.

In Section 4 we prove that the λsg-calculus preserves λs-strong normalisation and conclude that a is λ-SN $\Leftrightarrow$ a is λs-SN $\Leftrightarrow$ a is λg-SN $\Leftrightarrow$ a is λsg-SN.

In Section 5 the simply typed versions of the λs- and λsg-calculi are presented and subject reduction, subtyping, and SN of well typed terms are proved.

This article is an abridged version of [20], where more detailed proofs are given.

2 The λg-calculus

We assume familiarity with de Bruijn notation. Since generalised β-reduction is easily described in item notation, we adopt the item syntax (cf. [16, 14] for the advantages of item notation) and write $a\,b$ as $(b\,\delta)a$ and $\lambda.a$ as $(\lambda)a$.

Definition 1 *The* set of terms Λ, *is defined as follows:* $\Lambda ::= \mathbf{N} | (\Lambda\,\delta)\Lambda | (\lambda)\Lambda$
We let $a, b, \ldots$ range over Λ and $m, n, \ldots$ over $\mathbf{N}$ (positive natural numbers). $a = b$ means that a and b are syntactically identical. We write $a \lhd b$ when a is a subterm of b. We assume the usual definition of compatibility.

$(\lambda x\lambda y.zxy)(\lambda x.yx) \rightarrow_\beta \lambda u.z(\lambda x.yx)u$ translates to $(\lambda\lambda 521)(\lambda 31) \rightarrow_\beta \lambda 4(\lambda 41)1$. Note that we did not simply replace 2 in $\lambda 521$ by $\lambda 31$. Instead, we decreased 5 as one λ disappeared, and incremented the free variables of $\lambda 31$ as they occur within the scope of one more λ. For incrementing the free variables we need updating functions U_k^i, where k tests for free variables and $i - 1$ is the value by which a variable, if free, must be incremented:

Definition 2 $U_k^i : \Lambda \rightarrow \Lambda$ *for $k \geq 0$ and $i \geq 1$ are defined inductively:*

$$U_k^i((a\,\delta)b) = (U_k^i(a)\,\delta)U_k^i(b)$$
$$U_k^i((\lambda)a) = (\lambda)(U_{k+1}^i(a))$$
$$U_k^i(n) = \begin{cases} n+i-1 & \text{if } n > k \\ n & \text{if } n \leq k \end{cases}$$

Now we define meta-substitution. The last equality substitutes the intended variable (when $n = j$) by the updated term. If n is not the intended variable, it is decreased by 1 if it is free (case $n > j$) as one λ has disappeared and if it is bound (case $n < j$) it remains unaltered.

Definition 3 *The* meta-substitutions at level j, *for $j \geq 1$, of a term $b \in \Lambda$ in a term $a \in \Lambda$, denoted $a\{\!\{j \leftarrow b\}\!\}$, is defined inductively on a as follows:*

$$((a_1\delta)a_2)\{\!\{j \leftarrow b\}\!\} = ((a_1\{\!\{j \leftarrow b\}\!\})\delta)(a_2\{\!\{j \leftarrow b\}\!\})$$
$$((\lambda)c)\{\!\{j \leftarrow b\}\!\} = (\lambda)(c\{\!\{j+1 \leftarrow b\}\!\})$$
$$n\{\!\{j \leftarrow b\}\!\} = \begin{cases} n-1 & \text{if } n > j \\ U_0^j(b) & \text{if } n = j \\ n & \text{if } n < j \end{cases}$$

The following gives the properties of meta-substitution and updating (cf. [17]):

Lemma 1 *Let* a, b, $c \in \Lambda$. *We have:*
1. *for* $k < n < k+i$: $U_k^{i-1}(a) = U_k^i(a)\{\!\{n \leftarrow b\}\!\}$.
2. *for* $l \leq k < l+j$: $U_k^i(U_l^j(a)) = U_l^{j+i-1}(a)$.
3. *for* $k+i \leq n$: $U_k^i(a)\{\!\{n \leftarrow b\}\!\} = U_k^i(a\{\!\{n-i+1 \leftarrow b\}\!\})$.
4. *for* $i \leq n$: $a\{\!\{i \leftarrow b\}\!\}\{\!\{n \leftarrow c\}\!\} = a\{\!\{n+1 \leftarrow c\}\!\}\{\!\{i \leftarrow b\{\!\{n-i+1 \leftarrow c\}\!\}\}\!\}$.
5. *for* $l+j \leq k+1$: $U_k^i(U_l^j(a)) = U_l^j(U_{k+1-j}^i(a))$.
6. *for* $n \leq k+1$: $U_k^i(a\{\!\{n \leftarrow b\}\!\}) = U_{k+1}^i(a)\{\!\{n \leftarrow U_{k-n+1}^i(b)\}\!\}$.

In order to introduce generalised β-reduction we need some defintions (cf. [14]).

Definition 4 Items, segments *and* well-balanced segments (w.b.) *are defined respectively by:* $\mathcal{I} ::= (\Lambda\delta) \mid (\lambda) \quad \mathcal{S} ::= \phi \mid \mathcal{I}\mathcal{S} \quad \mathcal{W} ::= \phi \mid (\Lambda\delta)\mathcal{W}(\lambda) \mid \mathcal{W}\mathcal{W}$ *where ϕ is the empty segment. Hence, a segment is a sequence of items.* $(a\,\delta)$ *and* (λ) *are called δ- and λ-item respectively. We let* I, J, ... *range over* $\mathcal{I}$; S, S', ... *over* $\mathcal{S}$ *and* W, U, ... *over* $\mathcal{W}$. *For a segment* S, $\lg S$, *is given by:* $\lg \phi = 0$, $\lg(I\,S) = 1 + \lg S$. *The number of main λ-items in* S, $N(S)$, *is given by:* $N(\phi) = 0$, $N((a\,\delta)S) = N(S)$ *and* $N((\lambda)S) = 1 + N(S)$.

Definition 5 λ-calculus *is the reduction system* $(\Lambda, \rightarrow_\beta)$, *where* $\rightarrow_\beta$ *is the least compatible reduction on* Λ *generated by the β-rule:* $(a\delta)(\lambda)b \rightarrow a\{\!\{1 \leftarrow b\}\!\}$.

Definition 6 Generalised β, $\rightarrow_{g\beta}$, *is the least compatible reduction on* Λ *generated by the $g\beta$-rule:* $(a\delta)W(\lambda)b \rightarrow W(b\{\!\{1 \leftarrow U_0^{N(W)+1}(a)\}\!\})$ *where W is w.b. The λg-calculus is the reduction system* $(\Lambda, \rightarrow_{g\beta})$.

Remark 1 *The β-rule is an instance of the $g\beta$-rule.*

Proof: Take $W = \phi$ and check $U_0^1(a) = a$. $\qquad\square$

Now, let us briefly explain the relation between $\rightarrow_{g\beta}$ and $\rightarrow_\theta$, $\rightarrow_\gamma$, $\rightarrow_{\gamma C}$ given in the introduction. As $\rightarrow_\gamma$ implies $\rightarrow_{\gamma C}$, we ignore the latter. It would be helpful if we write $\rightarrow_\theta$ and $\rightarrow_\gamma$ in item notation:

$$(Q\delta)(P\delta)(\lambda_x)N \rightarrow_\theta (P\delta)(\lambda_x)(Q\delta)N \qquad (P\delta)(\lambda_x)(\lambda_y)N \rightarrow_\gamma (\lambda_y)(P\delta)(\lambda_x)N$$

Note how in $\rightarrow_\theta$, the start of a redex $(P\delta)(\lambda_x)$ is moved (or reshuffled) giving $(Q\delta)$ the chance to find its matching (λ) in N. In $\rightarrow_\gamma$ the same happens but now it is (λ_y) which is given the chance to look for its matching $(-\delta)$. Only once reshuffling has taken place, can the newly found redex be contracted. $\rightarrow_{g\beta}$ on the other hand avoids reshuffling and contracts the redex as soon as it sees the matching of δ and λ.

We define segments' updating and meta-substitution and prove some properties.

Definition 7 *Let* $S \in \mathcal{S}$, a, $b \in \Lambda$, $k \geq 0$ *and* $n, i \geq 1$.
We define $U_k^i(S)$ *and* $S\{\!\{n \leftarrow a\}\!\}$ *by:*

$$U_k^i(\phi) = \phi \qquad\qquad \phi\{\!\{n \leftarrow a\}\!\} = \phi$$
$$U_k^i((b\,\delta)S) = (U_k^i(b)\,\delta)U_k^i(S) \qquad ((b\,\delta)S)\{\!\{n \leftarrow a\}\!\} = (b\{\!\{n \leftarrow a\}\!\}\,\delta)(S\{\!\{n \leftarrow a\}\!\})$$
$$U_k^i((\lambda)S) = (\lambda)(U_{k+1}^i(S)) \qquad ((\lambda)S)\{\!\{n \leftarrow a\}\!\} = (\lambda)(S\{\!\{n+1 \leftarrow a\}\!\})$$

Lemma 2 *Let S, T be segments and $a, b \in \Lambda$. The following hold:*

1. $U_k^i(ST) = U_k^i(S)U_{k+N(S)}^i(T)$ *and* $U_k^i(S\,a) = U_k^i(S)U_{k+N(S)}^i(a)$
2. $\lg(S) = \lg(U_k^i(S))$, $N(S) = N(U_k^i(S))$ *and if S w.b. then $U_k^i(S)$ w.b.*
3. $(S\xi)\{\!\{n \leftarrow a\}\!\} = S\{\!\{n \leftarrow a\}\!\}\,\xi\{\!\{n + N(S) \leftarrow a\}\!\}$ *for ξ a segment or a term*
4. *If $r \in \{\lg, N\}$ then $r(S) = r(S\{\!\{n \leftarrow a\}\!\})$. If S w.b. then $S\{\!\{n \leftarrow a\}\!\}$ w.b.*

Proof: All by induction on S. For 2. and 4. use 1. and 3. respectively. $\square$

Lemma 3 *Let $a, b \in \Lambda$. If $a \twoheadrightarrow_{g\beta} b$ then $a =_\beta b$.*

Proof: First prove by induction on a that $a \to_{g\beta} b$ implies $a =_\beta b$. To show the case $(c\delta)W(\lambda)d \to_{g\beta} W(d\{\!\{1 \leftarrow U_0^{N(W)+1}(c)\}\!\})$ use induction on $\lg W$. $\square$

Theorem 1 (Confluence of λg) *The λg-calculus is confluent.*

Proof: Use Lemma 3 and Remark 1 (cf. [16]). $\square$

Next, we ensure the good passage of $g\beta$-reduction through $\{\!\{\leftarrow\}\!\}$ and U_k^i:

Lemma 4 *Let $a, b, c, d \in \Lambda$. The following hold:*

1. *If $c \to_{g\beta} d$ then $U_k^i(c) \to_{g\beta} U_k^i(d)$.*
2. *If $c \to_{g\beta} d$ then $a\{\!\{n \leftarrow c\}\!\} \twoheadrightarrow_{g\beta} a\{\!\{n \leftarrow d\}\!\}$.*
3. *If $a \to_{g\beta} b$ then $a\{\!\{n \leftarrow c\}\!\} \twoheadrightarrow_{g\beta} b\{\!\{n \leftarrow c\}\!\}$.*

Proof: 1. By induction on c. 2. and 3. By induction on a. $\square$

3 The λs- and λsg-calculi

The idea is to handle explicitly the meta-operators of definitions 2 and 3. Hence, the syntax of the λs-calculus is obtained by adding two families of operators:

1. Explicit substitution operators $\{\sigma^j\}_{j \geq 1}$ where $(b\,\sigma^j)a$ stands for a where all free occurrences of the variable representing j are to be substituted by b.

2. Updating operators $\{\varphi_k^i\}_{k \geq 0 \ i \geq 1}$ needed for working with de Bruijn indices.

Definition 8 *The* set of terms, *noted* Λs, *of the λs-calculus is given as follows:*

$$\Lambda s ::= \mathbb{N} \mid (\Lambda s\, \delta)\Lambda s \mid (\lambda)\Lambda s \mid (\Lambda s\, \sigma^j)\Lambda s \mid (\varphi_k^i)\Lambda s \quad \text{where} \quad j, i \geq 1, \quad k \geq 0.$$

We let a, b, c range over Λs. A term $(a\, \sigma^j)b$ is called a closure. *Furthermore, a term containing neither σ's nor φ's is called a* pure term. *Λ denotes the set of pure terms. $\delta\lambda$-segments are those whose main items are either δ- or λ-items, i.e. $\mathcal{DL} ::= \phi \mid (\Lambda s\, \delta)\mathcal{DL} \mid (\lambda)\mathcal{DL}$. Compatibility is extended by adding: $(a\, \sigma^j)c \to (b\, \sigma^j)c$, $(c\, \sigma^j)a \to (c\, \sigma^j)b$ and $(\varphi_k^i)a \to (\varphi_k^i)b$ whenever $a \to b$.*

Definition 9 Items, segments *and* well-balanced segments *for Λs are defined as follows:* $\mathcal{I}s ::= (\Lambda s\, \delta) \mid (\lambda) \mid (\Lambda s\, \sigma^j) \mid (\varphi_k^i) \qquad \mathcal{S}s ::= \phi \mid \mathcal{I}s\,\mathcal{S}s$

$$\mathcal{W}s ::= \phi \mid (\Lambda s\, \delta)\mathcal{W}s(\lambda) \mid \mathcal{W}s\,\mathcal{W}s$$

We let I, J, ... range over $\mathcal{I}s$; S, S', ... over $\mathcal{S}s$ and W, U, ... over $\mathcal{W}s$. We call $(a\, \sigma^j)$ and (φ_k^i), σ- and φ-item respectively. $\lg(S)$ is trivially extended to $S \in \mathcal{S}s$ and $N(S)$ is extended by: $N((a\, \sigma^j)S) = N(S)$ and $N((\varphi_k^i)S) = N(S)$.

As the λs-calculus updates and substitutes explicitly, we include a set of rules which are the equations in definitions 2 and 3 oriented from left to right.

Definition 10 *The λs-calculus is the reduction system $(\Lambda s, \rightarrow_{\lambda s})$, where $\rightarrow_{\lambda s}$ is the least compatible reduction on Λs generated by the following rules:*

σ-generation	$(b\,\delta)(\lambda)a \longrightarrow (b\,\sigma^1)a$
σ-λ-transition	$(b\,\sigma^j)(\lambda)a \longrightarrow (\lambda)(b\,\sigma^{j+1})a$
σ-app-transition	$(b\,\sigma^j)(a_1\delta)a_2 \longrightarrow ((b\,\sigma^j)a_1\delta)\,(b\,\sigma^j)a_2$
σ-destruction	$(b\,\sigma^j)\mathbf{n} \longrightarrow \begin{cases} \mathbf{n}-1 \text{ if } n > j \\ (\varphi_0^j)b \text{ if } n = j \\ \mathbf{n} \quad \text{ if } n < j \end{cases}$
φ-λ-transition	$(\varphi_k^i)(\lambda)a \longrightarrow (\lambda)(\varphi_{k+1}^i)a$
φ-app-transition	$(\varphi_k^i)(a_1\delta)a_2 \longrightarrow ((\varphi_k^i)a_1\delta)(\varphi_k^i)a_2$
φ-destruction	$(\varphi_k^i)\mathbf{n} \longrightarrow \begin{cases} \mathbf{n}+i-1 \text{ if } n > k \\ \mathbf{n} \qquad \text{ if } n \leq k \end{cases}$

We use λs to denote this set of rules. The calculus of substitutions *associated with the λs-calculus is the reduction system generated by the set of rules $s = \lambda s - \{\sigma\text{-generation}\}$ and we call it the s-calculus.*
The λsg-calculus is the calculus whose set of rules is $\lambda sg = \lambda s + \{g\sigma\text{-generation}\}$:

$$g\sigma\text{-generation} \qquad (b\,\delta)W(\lambda)a \longrightarrow W((\varphi_0^{N(W)+1})b\,\sigma^1)a \qquad W \text{ w.b}, W \neq \phi$$

Note that in the λsg-calculus we do not merge σ-generation and $g\sigma$-generation in a new $g\sigma$-generation which admits $W = \phi$ because in that case we would obtain, when $W = \phi$, the rule $(b\delta)(\lambda)a \rightarrow ((\varphi_0^1 b)\sigma^1)a$, and this is not a generalisation of the original σ-generation of the λs-calculus.

σ-generation starts β-reduction by generating a substitution operator (σ^1). σ-app and σ-λ allow this operator to travel throughout the term until its arrival to the variables. If a variable should be affected by the substitution, σ-destruction (case $j = n$) carries out the substitution by the updated term, thus introducing the updating operators. Finally the φ-rules compute the updating. We state now the following theorem of the λs-calculus (cf. [19]).

Theorem 2 *The s-calculus is strongly normalising and confluent on Λs, hence s-normal forms are unique. The set of s-normal forms is exactly Λ. If $s(a)$ denotes the s-normal form of a, then for $a, b \in \Lambda s$: $s((a\,\delta)b) = (s(a)\,\delta)s(b)$, $s((\lambda)a) = (\lambda)(s(a))$, $s((\varphi_k^i)a) = U_k^i(s(a))$ and $s((b\,\sigma^j)a) = s(a)\{\!\{j \leftarrow s(b)\}\!\}$.*

Lemma 5 *Let $a, b \in \Lambda s$, if $a \rightarrow_{(g)\sigma-gen} b$ then $s(a) \rightarrow\!\!\!\rightarrow_{(g)\beta} s(b)$.*

Proof: Induction on a using Lemma 4 and Theorem. 2. For the case with g, note that if W is w.b then $s(W\,a) = s(W)s(a)$, where the s-nf of a $\delta\lambda$-segment is given by: $s(\phi) = \phi$, $s((a\,\delta)S) = (s(a)\,\delta)s(S)$ and $s((\lambda)S) = (\lambda)s(S)$. $\square$

Corollary 1 *Let $a, b \in \Lambda s$, if $a \twoheadrightarrow_{\lambda sg} b$ then $s(a) \twoheadrightarrow_{g\beta} s(b)$.*

Corollary 2 (Soundness) *Let $a, b \in \Lambda$, if $a \twoheadrightarrow_{\lambda sg} b$ then $a \twoheadrightarrow_{g\beta} b$.*

Hence, the λsg-calculus is correct w.r.t. the λg-calculus, i.e. λsg-derivations of pure terms ending with pure terms can also be derived in the λg-calculus.

Moreover, the λsg-calculus is powerful enough to simulate $g\beta$-reduction.

Lemma 6 (Simulation of $\rightarrow_{g\beta}$) *Let $a, b \in \Lambda$, if $a \rightarrow_{g\beta} b$ then $a \twoheadrightarrow_{\lambda sg} b$.*

Proof: Induction on a using Lemma 4. $\qquad\qquad\qquad\qquad\qquad\qquad\qquad$ $\square$

Theorem 3 (Confluence of λsg) *The λsg-calculus is confluent on Λs.*

Proof: Use the interpretation method (cf. [9]), Corollary 1, confluence of the λg-calculus and Lemma 6. $\qquad\qquad\qquad\qquad\qquad\qquad\qquad\qquad\qquad$ $\square$

4 The λsg-calculus preserves λs-SN

The technique used here to prove preservation of strong normalisation (PSN) is the same used in [4] to prove PSN for λv and in [17] to prove PSN for λs.

Notation 1 *We write $a \in \lambda$-SN resp. $a \in \lambda r$-SN when a is strongly normalising in the λ-calculus resp. in the λr-calculus for $r \in \{g, sg, s\}$. We write $a \underset{p}{\rightarrow} b$ to denote that p is the occurrence of the redex which is contracted. Therefore $a \underset{\epsilon}{\rightarrow} b$ means that the reduction takes place at the root. If no specification is made the reduction must be understood as a λsg-reduction. We denote by $\prec$ the prefix order between occurrences of a term. Hence if p, q are occurrences of the term a such that $p \prec q$, and we write a_p (resp. a_q) for the subterm of a at occurrence p (resp. q), then a_q is a subterm of a_p. E.g., if $a = 2\sigma^3((\lambda 1)4)$, we have $a_1 = 2$, $a_2 = (\lambda 1)4$, $a_{21} = \lambda 1$, $a_{211} = 1$, $a_{22} = 4$. Since $2 \prec 21$, a_{21} is a subterm of a_2.*

The following three lemmas assert that all the σ's in the last term of a derivation beginning with a λ-term must have been created at some previous step by a (generalised) σ-generation and trace the history of these closures. The first lemma deals with one-step derivation where the redex is at the root; the second generalises the first; the third treats arbitrary derivations.

Lemma 7 *If $a \rightarrow C[(e\,\sigma^i)d]$ then one of the following must hold:*
1. *$a = (e\,\delta)(\lambda)d$, $C = \square$ and $i = 1$.*
2. *$a = (e'\,\delta)W(\lambda)d$, $W \neq \phi$, $C = W\square$, $e = (\varphi_0^{N(W)+1})e'$ and $i = 1$.*
3. *$a = C'[(e\,\sigma^j)d']$ for some context C', some term d' and some natural j.*

Proof: Since the reduction is at the root, check for every rule $a \rightarrow a'$ in λsg that if $(e\,\sigma^i)d$ occurs in a' then either 1. or 2. or 3. follows. $\qquad\qquad$ $\square$

Lemma 8 *If $a \rightarrow C[(e\,\sigma^i)d]$ then one of the following must hold:*
1. *$a = C[(e\,\delta)(\lambda)d]$ and $i = 1$.*
2. *$a = C'[(e'\,\delta)W(\lambda)d]$, $C = C'[W\square]$, $e = (\varphi_0^{N(W)+1})e'$ and $i = 1$.*
3. *$a = C'[(e'\,\sigma^i)d']$ where $e' = e$ or $e' \rightarrow e$.*

Proof: Induction on a, using lemma 7 for the reductions at the root. $\square$

Lemma 9 *If $a_1 \to \ldots \to a_{n+1} = C[(e\,\sigma^i)d]$, there exist $e', d' \in \Lambda s$ with $e' \twoheadrightarrow e$ and, either $a_1 = C'[(e'\,\sigma^j)d']$ or for some $k \leq n$ and W w.b., $a_k = C'[(e'\,\delta)W(\lambda)d']$ and $a_{k+1} = C'[W((\varphi_0^{N(W)+1})e'\,\sigma^1)d']$ or, if $W = \phi$, $a_{k+1} = C'[(e'\,\sigma^1)d']$.*

Proof: Induction on n and use the previous lemma. $\square$

We define now internal and external reductions. An internal reduction takes place at the left of a σ^i operator. An external reduction is a non-internal one. Our definition is inductive rather than starting from the notion of internal and external position as in [4].

Definition 11 *The reduction $\xrightarrow{\text{int}}_{\lambda sg}$ is defined by the following rules:*

$$\frac{a \to_{\lambda sg} b}{(a\,\sigma^i)c \xrightarrow{\text{int}}_{\lambda sg} (b\,\sigma^i)c} \qquad \frac{a \xrightarrow{\text{int}}_{\lambda sg} b}{(a\,\delta)c \xrightarrow{\text{int}}_{\lambda sg} (b\,\delta)c} \qquad \frac{a \xrightarrow{\text{int}}_{\lambda sg} b}{(c\,\delta)a \xrightarrow{\text{int}}_{\lambda sg} (c\,\delta)b}$$

$$\frac{a \xrightarrow{\text{int}}_{\lambda sg} b}{(\lambda)a \xrightarrow{\text{int}}_{\lambda sg} (\lambda)b} \qquad \frac{a \xrightarrow{\text{int}}_{\lambda sg} b}{(c\,\sigma^i)a \xrightarrow{\text{int}}_{\lambda sg} (c\,\sigma^i)b} \qquad \frac{a \xrightarrow{\text{int}}_{\lambda sg} b}{(\varphi_k^i)a \xrightarrow{\text{int}}_{\lambda sg} (\varphi_k^i)b}$$

Definition 12 *The reduction $\xrightarrow{\text{ext}}_s$ is defined by induction. The axioms are the rules of the s-calculus and the inference rules are the following:*

$$\frac{a \xrightarrow{\text{ext}}_s b}{(a\,\delta)c \xrightarrow{\text{ext}}_s (b\,\delta)c} \qquad \frac{a \xrightarrow{\text{ext}}_s b}{(c\,\delta)a \xrightarrow{\text{ext}}_s (c\,\delta)b} \qquad \frac{a \xrightarrow{\text{ext}}_s b}{(\lambda)a \xrightarrow{\text{ext}}_s (\lambda)b}$$

$$\frac{a \xrightarrow{\text{ext}}_s b}{(c\,\sigma^i)a \xrightarrow{\text{ext}}_s (c\,\sigma^i)b} \qquad \frac{a \xrightarrow{\text{ext}}_s b}{(\varphi_k^i)a \xrightarrow{\text{ext}}_s (\varphi_k^i)b}$$

An external (generalised) σ-generation is defined by the rule $(g)\sigma$-generation and the five inference rules above where $\xrightarrow{\text{ext}}_s$ is replaced by $\xrightarrow{\text{ext}}_{(g)\sigma-gen}$.

Remark 2 *By inspection of the inference rules, $a \xrightarrow{\text{int}}_{\lambda sg} \text{n}$ is impossible and:*
- *If $a \xrightarrow{\text{int}}_{\lambda sg} (\lambda)b$ then $a = (\lambda)c$ and $c \xrightarrow{\text{int}}_{\lambda sg} b$.*
- *If $a \xrightarrow{\text{int}}_{\lambda sg} (c\,\delta)b$ then $a = (e\,\delta)d$ and $((d \xrightarrow{\text{int}}_{\lambda sg} b$ and $e = c)$ or $(e \xrightarrow{\text{int}}_{\lambda sg} c$ and $d = b))$.*

Note that $\dfrac{a \xrightarrow{\text{ext}}_s b}{(a\,\sigma^i)c \xrightarrow{\text{ext}}_s (b\,\sigma^i)c}$ and $\dfrac{a \xrightarrow{\text{ext}}_{(g)\sigma-gen} b}{(a\,\sigma^i)c \xrightarrow{\text{ext}}_{(g)\sigma-gen} (b\,\sigma^i)c}$ are excluded from the definitions of external s-reduction and external (generalised) σ-generation, respectively. Thus external reductions will not occur at the left of a σ^i operator and we write $\xrightarrow{+}_\beta$ instead of $\twoheadrightarrow_\beta$ in the following (compare with Lemma 5):

Proposition 1 *Let $a, b \in \Lambda s$, if $a \xrightarrow{\text{ext}}_{(g)\sigma-gen} b$ then $s(a) \xrightarrow{+}_{(g)\beta} s(b)$.*

Proof: Induction on a (as in Lemma 5). Note that when $a = c\,\sigma^i d$, the reduction cannot take place within d because it is external, and this is the only case that forced us to consider the reflexive-transitive closure because of lemma 4.2. □

The following is needed in Lemma 11 and hence in the Preservation Theorem.

Lemma 10 (Commutation Lemma) *Let $a, b \in \Lambda s$ such that $s(a) \in \lambda$-SN and $s(a) = s(b)$. If $a \xrightarrow{\text{int}}_{\lambda sg} \cdot \xrightarrow{\text{ext}}_s b$ then $a \xrightarrow{\text{ext}}_s{}^+ \cdot \xrightarrow{\text{int}}_{\lambda sg} b$.*

Proof: By a careful induction on a analysing the positions of the redexes. The proof is exactly the same as that of the Commutation Lemma in [17] □

Lemma 11 *Let $a \in \lambda g$-$SN \cap \Lambda$ and $a \to_{\lambda sg} b_1 \to_{\lambda sg} \cdots \to_{\lambda sg} b_n \to_{\lambda sg} \cdots$, an infinite derivation. There exists N such that for every $i \geq N$, the reductions $b_i \to_{\lambda sg} b_{i+1}$ are internal.*

Proof: Analogous to the proof of the corresponding lemma in [17]. □

In order to prove the Preservation Theorem we need two definitions.

Definition 13 *An infinite λsg-derivation $a_1 \to \cdots \to a_n \to \cdots$ is* minimal *if for every step $a_i \xrightarrow{p} a_{i+1}$, any derivation starting with $a_i \xrightarrow{q} a'_{i+1}$, if $p \prec q$, is finite.*

The idea of a minimal derivation is that if one rewrites at least one of its steps within a subterm of the actual redex, then an infinite derivation is impossible.

Definition 14 *The syntax of skeletons and the skeleton of a term are as follows:*
$$\text{Skeletons} \quad K ::= \mathbf{N} \mid (K\,\delta)K \mid (\lambda)K \mid ([.]\,\sigma^j)K \mid (\varphi_k^i)K$$

$$Sk(\mathbf{n}) = \mathbf{n} \quad Sk((a\,\delta)b) = (Sk(a)\,\delta)Sk(b) \quad Sk((b\,\sigma^i)a) = ([.]\,\sigma^i)Sk(a)$$
$$Sk((\lambda)a) = (\lambda)Sk(a) \qquad Sk((\varphi_k^i)a) = (\varphi_k^i)Sk(a)$$

Remark 3 *Let $a, b \in \Lambda s$. If $a \xrightarrow{\text{int}}_{\lambda sg} b$ then $Sk(a) = Sk(b)$.*

Theorem 4 (Preservation of λs-SN) *For every $a \in \Lambda$, if a is strongly normalising in the λs-calculus then a is strongly normalising in the λsg-calculus.*

Proof: Assume $a \in \lambda s$-SN, $a \notin \lambda sg$-SN and take a minimal infinite λsg-derivation $\mathcal{D} : a \to a_1 \to \cdots \to a_n \to \cdots$. Lemma 11 gives N such that for $i \geq N$, $a_i \to a_{i+1}$ is internal. By Remark 3, $Sk(a_i) = Sk(a_{i+1})$ for $i \geq N$. As there are only a finite number of closures in $Sk(a_N)$ and as the reductions within these closures are independent, an infinite subderivation $\mathcal{D}'$ of $\mathcal{D}$ must take place within the same and unique closure in $Sk(a_N)$ and $\mathcal{D}'$ is also minimal. Let C be the context such that $a_N = C[(d\,\sigma^i)c]$ and $(d\,\sigma^i)c$ is the closure where $\mathcal{D}'$ takes place:
$$\mathcal{D}' : a_N = C[(d\,\sigma^i)c] \xrightarrow{\text{int}}_{\lambda sg} C[(d_1\,\sigma^i)c] \xrightarrow{\text{int}}_{\lambda sg} \cdots \xrightarrow{\text{int}}_{\lambda sg} C[(d_n\,\sigma^i)c] \xrightarrow{\text{int}}_{\lambda sg} \cdots$$
Since a is a pure term, Lemma 9 ensures the existence of $I \leq N$ such that either
$$a_I = C'[(d'\,\delta)(\lambda)c'] \to a_{I+1} = C'[(d'\sigma^1)c'] \text{ and } d' \twoheadrightarrow d \text{ or}$$
$$a_I = C'[(d'\,\delta)W(\lambda)c'] \to a_{I+1} = C'[W((\varphi_0^{N(W)+1})d'\sigma^1)c'] \text{ and } d' \twoheadrightarrow d.$$
Let us consider in the first and second cases respectively, the infinite derivations:

$\mathcal{D}''$: $a \twoheadrightarrow a_I \twoheadrightarrow C'[(d\delta)(\lambda)c'] \to C'[(d_1\delta)(\lambda)c'] \to \cdots \to C'[(d_n\delta)(\lambda)c'] \cdots$

$\mathcal{D}'''$: $a \twoheadrightarrow a_I \twoheadrightarrow C'[(d\delta)W(\lambda)c'] \to C'[(d_1\delta)W(\lambda)c'] \to \cdots \to C'[(d_n\delta)W(\lambda)c'] \cdots$

In $\mathcal{D}''$ and $\mathcal{D}'''$, the redex in a_I is within d' which is a proper subterm of $(d'\,\delta)(\lambda)c'$ (of $(d'\,\delta)W(\lambda)c'$ in the second case), whereas in $\mathcal{D}$ the redex in a_I is $(d'\,\delta)(\lambda)c'$ (in the second case $(d'\,\delta)W(\lambda)c'$) and this contradicts the minimality of $\mathcal{D}$. □

Corollary 3 *For every* $a \in \Lambda$*, the following equivalences hold:*
$a \in \lambda g\text{-}SN$ *iff* $a \in \lambda sg\text{-}SN$ *iff* $a \in \lambda\text{-}SN$ *iff* $a \in \lambda s\text{-}SN$

Proof: By Remark 1 and Theorem 4, $a \in \lambda s\text{-}SN$ iff $a \in \lambda sg\text{-}SN$. Due to [13], $a \in \lambda\text{-}SN$ iff $a \in \lambda g\text{-}SN$. Due to [17], $a \in \lambda\text{-}SN$ iff $a \in \lambda s\text{-}SN$. □

5 The typed λs- and λsg-calculi

We prove λsg-SN of well typed terms using the technique developped in [18] to prove λs-SN and suggested to us by P.-A. Melliès as a successful technique to prove λv-SN (personal communication). We recall the syntax and typing rules for the simply typed λ-calculus in de Bruijn notation. The types are generated from a set of basic types T with the binary type operator $\to$. Environments are lists of types. Typed terms differ from the untyped ones only in the abstractions which are now marked with the type of the abstracted variable.

Definition 15 *The syntax for the simply typed λ-terms is given as follows:*

Types	$T ::= T \mid T \to T$
Environments	$\mathcal{E} ::= nil \mid T, \mathcal{E}$
Terms	$\Lambda_t ::= \mathbf{n} \mid (\Lambda_t\,\delta)\Lambda_t \mid (T\,\lambda)\Lambda_t$

We let A, B, ... range over T; E, E_1, ... over $\mathcal{E}$ and a, b, ... over Λ_t.
The typing rules are given by the typing system **L1** *as follows:*

$$(\mathbf{L1} - var) \quad A, E \vdash 1 : A \qquad\qquad (\mathbf{L1} - \lambda) \quad \frac{A, E \vdash b : B}{E \vdash (A\,\lambda)b : A \to B}$$

$$(\mathbf{L1} - varn) \; \frac{E \vdash \mathbf{n} : B}{A, E \vdash \mathbf{n}+1 : B} \qquad (\mathbf{L1} - app) \; \frac{E \vdash b : A \to B \quad E \vdash a : A}{E \vdash (a\,\delta)b : B}$$

If E is the environment $E_1, E_2, \ldots, E_n$, we shall use the notation $E_{\geq i}$ for the environment $E_i, E_{i+1}, \ldots, E_n$, analogously $E_{\leq i}$ stands for $E_1, \ldots, E_i$, etc.

Definition 16 *The syntax for the* simply typed λs-terms *is given as follows:*

$$\Lambda s_t \; ::= \; \mathbf{N} \mid (\Lambda s_t\,\delta)\Lambda s_t \mid (T\,\lambda)\Lambda s_t \mid (\Lambda s_t\,\sigma^i)\Lambda s_t \mid (\varphi_k^i)\Lambda s_t \quad i \geq 1,\ k \geq 0.$$

Types and environments are as above. The typing rules of the system **Ls1** *are: The rules* **Ls1-var**, **Ls1-varn**, **Ls1-λ** *and* **Ls1-app** *are exactly the same as* **L1-var**, **L1-varn**, **L1-λ** *and* **L1-app**, *respectively. The new rules are:*

$$(\mathbf{Ls1} - \sigma) \; \frac{E_{\geq i} \vdash b : B \quad E_{<i}, B, E_{\geq i} \vdash a : A}{E \vdash (b\,\sigma^i)a : A} \qquad (\mathbf{Ls1} - \varphi) \; \frac{E_{\leq k}, E_{\geq k+i} \vdash a : A}{E \vdash (\varphi_k^i)a : A}$$

The simply typed λs- and λsg-calculi are defined by the same rules of the untyped versions, except that abstractions in the typed versions are marked with types.

Definition 17 $a \in \Lambda s_t$ *is a well typed term* if for some environment E and type A, $E \vdash_{\mathbf{Ls1}} a : A$. We note Λs_{wt} the set of well typed terms.

The aim of this section is to prove that every well typed λs-term a is λsg-SN (and hence λs-SN). To do so, we show $\Lambda s_{wt} \subseteq \Xi \subseteq \lambda sg$-SN, where
$$\Xi = \{a \in \Lambda s_t : \text{for every subterm } b \text{ of } a, \ s(b) \in \lambda g\text{-}SN\}.$$
To prove $\Lambda s_{wt} \subseteq \Xi$ (Proposition 2) we need to establish some useful results such as subject reduction, soundness of typing and typing of subterms:

Lemma 12 Let S be a segment, A, B types and a, b, $c \in \Lambda s_t$. We have:
1. $E \vdash S((\varphi_0^i)a\,\delta)(c\,\delta)(B\,\lambda)b : A$ iff $E \vdash S(c\,\delta)(B\,\lambda)((\varphi_0^{i+1})a\,\delta)b : A$
2. $E \vdash S((\varphi_0^i)(\varphi_0^j)a\,\delta)b : A$ iff $E \vdash S((\varphi_0^{i+j-1})a\,\delta)b : A$
3. $E \vdash S(a\,\delta)(B\,\lambda)b : A$ iff $E \vdash S(a\,\sigma^1)b : A$

Proof: All by induction on S. $\qquad\qquad\square$

Lemma 13 (Shuffle Lemma) Let S be an arbitrary segment, W a w.b. segment and a, $b \in \Lambda s_t$, then $E \vdash S(a\,\delta)W\,b : A$ iff $E \vdash SW((\varphi_0^{N(W)+1})a\,\delta)\,b : A$.

Proof: By induction on W using Lemma 12. If $W = \phi$, it is immediate since $E' \vdash d : D$ iff $E' \vdash (\varphi_0^1)d : D$. Let us assume $W = (c\,\delta)U(B\,\lambda)V$, with U, V w.b..
$E \vdash S(a\,\delta)(c\,\delta)U(B\,\lambda)V\,b : A$ iff (IH)
$E \vdash S(a\,\delta)U((\varphi_0^{N(U)+1})c\,\delta)(B\,\lambda)V\,b : A$ iff (IH)
$E \vdash SU((\varphi_0^{N(U)+1})a\,\delta)((\varphi_0^{N(U)+1})c\,\delta)(B\,\lambda)V\,b : A$ iff (Lemma 12.1)
$E \vdash SU((\varphi_0^{N(U)+1})c\,\delta)(B\,\lambda)((\varphi_0^{N(U)+2})a\,\delta)V\,b : A$ iff (IH, twice)
$E \vdash S(c\,\delta)U(B\,\lambda)V((\varphi_0^{N(V)+1})(\varphi_0^{N(U)+2})a\,\delta)b : A$ iff (Lemma 12.2)
$E \vdash S(c\,\delta)U(B\,\lambda)V((\varphi_0^{N(V)+N(U)+2})a\,\delta)b : A$ $\qquad\square$

Lemma 14 (Subject reduction) If $E \vdash_{\mathbf{Ls1}} a:A$, $a \rightarrow_{\lambda sg} b$ then $E \vdash_{\mathbf{Ls1}} b:A$.

Proof: Induction on a. If the reduction is not at the root, use IH. Else, show for every rule $a \rightarrow b$ that $E \vdash_{\mathbf{Ls1}} a : A$ implies $E \vdash_{\mathbf{Ls1}} b : A$. Case σ-gen, use Lemma 12.3. Case $g\sigma$-gen: If $E \vdash (a\,\delta)W(B\,\lambda)b : A$ then, by Lemma 13, we have $E \vdash W((\varphi_0^{N(W)+1})a\,\delta)(B\,\lambda)b : A$ and, by Lemma 12.3, we conclude $E \vdash W((\varphi_0^{N(W)+1})a\,\sigma^1)b : A$. $\qquad\square$

Corollary 4 Let $E \vdash_{\mathbf{Ls1}} a : A$, if $a \rightarrow_{\lambda sg} b$ then $E \vdash_{\mathbf{Ls1}} b : A$.

Lemma 15 (Typing of subterms) If $a \in \Lambda s_{wt}$ and $b \lhd a$ then $b \in \Lambda s_{wt}$.

Proof: By induction on a. If b is not an immediate subterm of a, use IH. Else, the last rule used to type a has a premise in which b is typed. $\qquad\square$

Lemma 16 (Soundness of typing) If $a \in \Lambda_t$, $E \vdash_{\mathbf{Ls1}} a : A$ then $E \vdash_{\mathbf{L1}} a : A$.

Proof: Easy induction on a. $\qquad\square$

Proposition 2 $\Lambda s_{wt} \subseteq \Xi$.

Proof: Let $a \in \Lambda s_{wt}$ and b a subterm of a. By Lemma 15, $b \in \Lambda s_{wt}$ and by Corollary 4, $s(b) \in \Lambda s_{wt}$. Since $s(b) \in \Lambda$ (Thm. 2), Lemma 16 gives $s(b)$ is **L1**-typable. But classical typable λ-terms are strongly normalising in the λ-calculus. Hence, $s(b) \in \lambda$-SN and, by Corollary 3, $s(b) \in \lambda g$-SN. Therefore $a \in \Xi$. $\quad\square$

We prove now $\Xi \subseteq \lambda sg$-SN.

Lemma 17 *Let $a \in \Xi$ and $a \to_{\lambda s} b_1 \to_{\lambda s} \cdots \to_{\lambda s} b_n \to_{\lambda s} \cdots$, an infinite λs-derivation. There exists N such that for $i \geq N$ all the reductions $b_i \to_{\lambda s} b_{i+1}$ are internal.*

Proof: The proof is almost the same as the proof of lemma 11. $\quad\square$

Proposition 3 *For every $a \in \Lambda s_t$, if $a \in \Xi$ then $a \in \lambda sg$-SN.*

Proof: Assume $a' \in \Xi$ and $a' \notin \lambda sg$-SN, then there exists a term a of minimal size such that $a \in \Xi$ and $a \notin \lambda sg$-SN. Let $\mathcal{D} : a \to a_1 \to \cdots \to a_n \to \cdots$ be a minimal infinite λsg-derivation and follow the proof of Theorem 4 to obtain:
$$\mathcal{D}' : a_N = C[(d\,\sigma^i)c] \xrightarrow{\text{int}}_{\lambda sg} C[(d_1\,\sigma^i)c] \xrightarrow{\text{int}}_{\lambda sg} \cdots \xrightarrow{\text{int}}_{\lambda sg} C[(d_n\,\sigma^i)c] \xrightarrow{\text{int}}_{\lambda sg} \cdots$$
Now three possibilities arise from lemma 9. Two of them have been considered in the proof of Theorem 4 and contradicted the minimality of $\mathcal{D}$. Take the third one: $a = C'[(d'\,\sigma^i)c']$ where $d' \twoheadrightarrow d$. Now we have $d' \twoheadrightarrow d \to d_1 \to \cdots \to d_n \to \cdots$. As d' is a subterm of a, $d' \in \Xi$, contradicting that a has minimal size. $\quad\square$

Therefore we conclude, using Propositions 2 and 3 and Corollary 3:

Theorem 5 *Well typed λs-term are strongly normalising in the λsg-calculus.*

Corollary 5 *Well typed λs-term are strongly normalising in the λs-calculus.*

6 Conclusion

In this paper, we started from the fact that generalised reduction and explicit substitution play a vital role in useful extensions of the λ-calculus but have never been combined together. We commented that the combination might indeed join both benefits and hence a λ-calculus extended with both needs to be studied. We presented such a calculus and showed that it possesses the important properties that have been the center of research for each concept on its own. In particular, we showed that the resulting calculus is confluent, sound and simulates β-reduction. We showed moreover that it preserves strong normalisation of the unextended λ-calculus and of the λ-calculus extended with each of the two concepts independently. We studied furthermore, the simply typed version of our calculus of explicit substitution and generalised reduction and showed that it has again the important properties such as subject reduction, soundness of subtyping, typing of subterms and strong normalisation of well typed terms.

Now that a calculus combining both concepts have been shown to be theoretically correct, it would be interesting to extend our calculus λsg to one that is confluent on open terms as is the tradition with calculi of explicit substitution.

It would be also interesting to study the polymorphically (rather than the simply) typed version of λsg. These are issues we are investigating at the moment. We are also investigating the correspondence of our calculus to methods that implement sharing and parallelism to test if the analysis of sharing given in [2] can be recast in an elegant fashion in our calculus.

References

1. M. Abadi, L. Cardelli, P.-L. Curien, and J.-J. Lévy. Explicit Substitutions. *Journal of Functional Programming*, 1(4):375–416, 1991.

2. Z.M. Ariola, M. Felleisen, J. Maraist, M. Odersky, and P. Wadler. A call by need lambda calculus. *Conf. Rec. 22nd Ann. ACM Symp. Princ. Program. Lang. ACM*, 1995.

3. H. Barendregt. λ-calculi with types. *Handbook of Logic in Computer Science*, II, 1992.

4. Z. Benaissa, D. Briaud, P. Lescanne, and J. Rouyer-Degli. λv, a calculus of explicit substitutions which preserves strong normalisation. *Personal communication*, 1995.

5. R. Bloo. Preservation of Strong Normalisation for Explicit Substitution. Technical Report 95-08, Department of Mathematics and Computing Science, Eindhoven University of Technology, 1995.

6. R. Bloo, F. Kamareddine, and R. Nederpelt. The Barendregt Cube with Definitions and Generalised Reduction. *Information and Computation*, 126 (2):123–143, 1996.

7. R. Constable et al. *Implementing Mathematics with the NUPRL Development System*. Prentice-Hall, 1986.

8. P.-L. Curien. *Categorical Combinators, Sequential Algorithms and Functional Programming*. Pitman, 1986. Revised edition : Birkhäuser (1993).

9. P.-L. Curien, T. Hardin, and J.-J. Lévy. Confluence properties of weak and strong calculi of explicit substitutions. Technical Report RR 1617, INRIA, Rocquencourt, 1992.

10. N. G. de Bruijn. A namefree lambda calculus with facilities for internal definition of expressions and segments. Technical Report TH-Report 78-WSK-03, Department of Mathematics, Eindhoven University of Technology, 1978.

11. P. de Groote. The conservation theorem revisited. *Int'l Conf. Typed Lambda Calculi and Applications LNCS*, 664, 1993.

12. G. Dowek et al. The coq proof assistant version 5.6, users guide. Technical Report 134, INRIA, 1991.

13. F. Kamareddine. A reduction relation for which postponement of k-contractions, conservation and preservation of strong normalisation hold. Technical report, Glasgow University, 1996.

14. F. Kamareddine and R. Nederpelt. A useful λ-notation. *Theoretical Computer Science*, 155:85–109, 1996.

15. F. Kamareddine and R. P. Nederpelt. On stepwise explicit substitution. *International Journal of Foundations of Computer Science*, 4(3):197–240, 1993.

16. F. Kamareddine and R. P. Nederpelt. Generalising reduction in the λ-calculus. *Journal of Functional Programming*, 5(4):637–651, 1995.

17. F. Kamareddine and A. Ríos. A λ-calculus à la de Bruijn with explicit substitutions. Proceedings of PLILP'95. *LNCS*, 982:45–62, 1995.

18. F. Kamareddine and A. Ríos. The λs-calculus: its typed and its extended versions. Technical report, Department of Computing Science, University of Glasgow, 1995.

19. F. Kamareddine and A. Ríos. Extending a λ-calculus with Explicit Substitution which preserves Strong Normalisation into a Confluent Calculus on Open Terms. *Journal of Functional Programming*, 1996. To appear.

20. F. Kamareddine and A. Ríos. Generalised β-reduction and explicit substitutions. Technical Report TR-1996-21, Department of Computing Science, University of Glasgow, 1996.

21. M. Karr. Delayability in proofs of strong normalizability in the typed λ-calculus. *Mathematical Foundations of Computer Software, LNCS*, 185, 1985.

22. A.J. Kfoury, J. Tiuryn, and P. Urzyczyn. An analysis of ML typability. *ACM*, 41(2):368–398, 1994.

23. A.J. Kfoury and J.B. Wells. A direct algorithm for type inference in the rank-2 fragment of the second order λ-calculus. *Proc. 1994 ACM Conf. LISP Funct. Program.*, 1994.

24. A.J. Kfoury and J.B. Wells. Addendum to new notions of reduction and non-semantic proofs of β-strong normalisation in typed λ-calculi. Technical report, Boston University, 1995.

25. A.J. Kfoury and J.B. Wells. New notions of reductions and non-semantic proofs of β-strong normalisation in typed λ-calculi. *LICS*, 1995.

26. Z. Khasidashvili. The longest perpetual reductions in orthogonal expression reduction systems. *Proc. of the 3rd International Conference on Logical Foundations of Computer Science, Logic at St Petersburg*, 813, 1994.

27. J. W. Klop. Combinatory Reduction Systems. *Mathematical Center Tracts*, 27, 1980.

28. P.-A. Melliès. Typed λ-calculi with explicit substitutions may not terminate in Proceedings of TLCA'95. *LNCS*, 902, 1995.

29. C. A. Muñoz Hurtado. Confluence and preservation of strong normalisation in an explicit substitutions calculus. Technical Report 2762, INRIA, Rocquencourt, December 1995.

30. R. P. Nederpelt, J. H. Geuvers, and R. C. de Vrijer. *Selected papers on Automath.* North-Holland, Amsterdam, 1994.

31. S.L. Peyton-Jones. *The Implementation of Functional Programming Languages.* Prentice-Hall, 1987.

32. L. Regnier. *Lambda calcul et réseaux.* PhD thesis, Paris 7, 1992.

33. L. Regnier. Une équivalence sur les lambda termes. *Theoretical Computer Science*, 126:281–292, 1994.

34. A. Ríos. *Contribution à l'étude des λ-calculs avec substitutions explicites.* PhD thesis, Université de Paris 7, 1993.

35. A. Sabry and M. Felleisen. Reasoning about programs in continuation-passing style. *Proc. 1992 ACM Conf. LISP Funct. Program.*, pages 288–298, 1992.

36. M. Sørensen. Strong normalisation from weak normalisation in typed λ-calculi. *Submitted.*

37. D. Vidal. *Nouvelles notions de réduction en lambda calcul.* PhD thesis, Université de Nancy 1, 1989.

38. H. Xi. On weak and strong normalisations. Technical Report 96-187, Carnegie Mellon University, 1996.

Modeling Sharing and Recursion
for Weak Reduction Strategies
Using Explicit Substitution

Zine-El-Abidine Benaissa,[1] Pierre Lescanne,[1] and Kristoffer H. Rose[2]

[1] INRIA Lorraine & CRIN, Nancy
[2] BRICS, Aarhus University

Abstract. We *present* the $\lambda\sigma_w^a$-calculus, a formal synthesis of the concepts of sharing and explicit substitution for weak reduction. We show how $\lambda\sigma_w^a$ can be used as a foundation of implementations of functional programming languages by modeling the essential ingredients of such implementations, namely *weak reduction strategies, recursion, space leaks, recursive data structures*, and *parallel evaluation*. We *use* $\lambda\sigma_w^a$ to give a unified model of several computational aspects. First, we give a precise account of the major reduction strategies used in functional programming and the consequences of choosing λ-graph-reduction vs. environment-based evaluation. Second, we show how to add *constructors and explicit recursion* to give a precise account of recursive functions and data structures even with respect to space complexity. Third, we formalize the notion of *space leaks* in $\lambda\sigma_w^a$ and use this to define a space leak free calculus; this suggests optimisations for call-by-need reduction that prevent space leaking and enables us to prove that the "trimming" performed by the STG machine does not leak space. In summary we give a formal account of several implementation techniques used by state of the art implementations of functional programming languages.

Keywords. Implementation of functional programming, lambda calculus, weak reduction, explicit substitution, sharing, recursion, space leaks.

1   Introduction

The aim of this paper is to present a framework for several forms of implementation of functional programming languages. It is often said that there are essentially two main classes of implementation, namely those based on *graph*

---

[1] INRIA-Lorraine & CRIN, Bâtiment LORIA, 615, rue du Jardin Botanique, BP 101, F–54602 Villers les Nancy Cedex (France). E-mail: {benaissa,lescanne}@loria.fr.

[2] Basic Research in Computer Science (Centre of the Danish National Research Foundation), Dept. of Computer Science, University of Aarhus, Ny Munkegade, DK–8000 Aarhus C (Denmark). E-mail: krisrose@brics.dk.

reduction and those based on *environments*. The first ones are efficient in that they optimize the code sharing, the second in that they allow a design of the implementation closer to the hardware. These two classes are traditionally split into subclasses according to the strategy which is used (evaluation of the value first, of the functional body first, or by need). However, in our approach a strategy is not an ingredient of a specific implementation, but something which is defined fully independently of the chosen form of implementation (graph reduction or environments). Our unifying framework is a calculus which describes faithfully and in detail all the mechanisms involved in weak reduction. Rather naturally we have chosen a weak calculus of explicit substitution (Curien, Hardin and Lévy 1992) as the basis, extending it with *global addresses*. This way, we can talk easily, and at a high level of detail, about addresses and sharing. At first, the calculus is not tied to any kind of implementation: the separation between graph reduction and environment-based evaluation emerges naturally when studying how to assign an address to the result of a successful variable lookup. Strategies come later as restrictions of the calculus. In this paper we study *call-by-value* and *call-by-name* of Plotkin (1975) as well as the not yet fully understood *call-by-need* strategy, and we show how parallel strategies can be devised. Finally we treat an important problem of implementation for which people propose ad-hoc solutions, namely *space leaking*: we propose a natural and efficient solution to prevent it (which we prove correct).

We start in Section 3 by combining sharing and explicit substitution for weak λ-calculi (reflecting that functional languages share the restriction that reduction never happens under a λ) into a calculus, $\lambda\sigma_w^a$, with explicit substitution, naming, and addresses. Moreover, it naturally permits two update principles that are readily identifiable as *graph reduction* (Wadsworth 1971) and *environment-based evaluation* (Curien 1991). In Section 4 we show how $\lambda\sigma_w^a$ adequately describes sharing with any (weak) reduction strategy; the proof is particularly simple because it can be tied directly to addresses; to illustrate this we prove that $\lambda\sigma_w^a$ includes the "λ_{let}" calculus of Ariola, Felleisen, Maraist, Odersky and Wadler (1995). In Section 5 we study how the usual extensions of *explicit recursion* and *data constructors* can be added to give the full expressive power of functional programming. Finally, in Section 6, we illustrate the generality of this calculus by defining the notion of a *space leaking*, and we study a class of *space leak free* subcalculi. As a corollary we get that the trimming used in the "STG" calculus of Peyton Jones (1992) is safe. Last we conclude.

2 Preliminaries

We commence by summarising certain standard concepts and notations that will prove convenient throughout.

Notation 1 (terms). We allow inductive definition of sets of terms using syntax productions. Furthermore, we write $C\{_-\}$ for a *context*.

Notation 2 (relations). We designate *binary relations* by arrows, following Klop (1992). Let $\rightarrow, \overrightarrow{_1}, \overrightarrow{_2} \subseteq \mathbf{A} \times \mathbf{A}$ be such relations and let $a, b \in \mathbf{A}$. $\overrightarrow{_{1+2}} = \overrightarrow{_1} \cup \overrightarrow{_2}$ and $\overrightarrow{_1} \cdot \overrightarrow{_2}$ denotes the composition of $\overrightarrow{_1}$ and $\overrightarrow{_2}$. $\twoheadrightarrow$ is the *transitive reflexive closure* of $\rightarrow$. $\rightarrow$ is *confluent* if $\twoheadleftarrow \cdot \twoheadrightarrow \subseteq \twoheadrightarrow \cdot \twoheadleftarrow$. The $\rightarrow$-*normal forms* are those a such that $\nexists b : a \rightarrow b$. $\twoheadrightarrow\!\!\!\mid$ is the *normal form restriction* of $\twoheadrightarrow$ that satisfies $a \twoheadrightarrow\!\!\!\mid b$ iff $a \twoheadrightarrow b$ and b is a $\rightarrow$-normal form.

Notation 3 (de Bruijn notation). We employ the "namefree" representation of λ-terms invented by de Bruijn (1972): Each occurrence of a variable in a λ-term is represented by a natural number, called the *index*, corresponding to the number of λ's traversed from its binding λ to it (so indices start at 0). The set of these terms is defined inductively by $M, N ::= \lambda M \mid MN \mid \underline{n}$. The *free indices* of a term correspond to the indices at the outermost level of what is usually known as the *free variables* and is given by $\mathrm{fi}(M) = \mathrm{fi}_0(M)$ where fi_i is again defined inductively by $\mathrm{fi}_i(MN) = \mathrm{fi}_i(M) \cup \mathrm{fi}_i(N)$, $\mathrm{fi}_i(\lambda M) = \mathrm{fi}_{i+1}(M)$, and $\mathrm{fi}_i(\underline{n}) = \{n - i\}$ when $n \geq i$ but $\{\}$ when $n < i$. We call this calculus λ_{NF} and when mixing it with other calculi we will refer to λ_{NF}-terms as *pure* terms.

3 Calculi for Weak Reduction with Sharing

In this section we generalize the weak explicit substitution calculus $\lambda\sigma_w$ defined by Curien et al. (1992) to include addresses in order to explicit pointer manipulations. Our starting point is reminiscent of the labeling used by Maranget (1991),[3] however, our notion of "address" is more abstract and allows us a better comprehension of implementations of machines for functional programming languages and their optimizations.

Figure 1 defines syntax and reduction rules of $\lambda\sigma_w^a$. Like $\lambda\sigma_w$ it forbids substitution in abstractions by never propagating explicit substitutions inside abstractions yet requiring that every redex must contain a substitution. This restriction gives a confluent weak calculus but necessitates using a term representation with lists of bindings as originally found in the $\lambda\rho$ calculus of Curien (1991).

$\lambda\sigma_w^a$ includes the special rule (Collect) which is meant to save useless computations and can be omitted: it collects "garbage" in the style of Bloo and Rose (1995), *i.e.*, terms in substitutions which are never substituted. Although computation in such useless terms can be avoided using specific strategies, the accumulation of useless terms in substitutions is a drawback w.r.t. the size of terms, and hence w.r.t. space complexity. In Section 6, we study this phenomenon well known for abstract machines as the *space leak problem*.

Furthermore, notice that the rules (FVarG) and (FVarE) have the same left hand side (LHS): the difference between these two rules is in the choice of the address in the right hand side (RHS) which is either b (FVarG) or a (FVarE). This conceptual choice has a direct correspondence to the duplication versus sharing problem of implementations: if the address is b, the RHS is a redirection of the pointer which refers to the address a (where the term $\underline{0}[E \cdot S]$

---

[3] In particular the use of developments and parallel reduction to model sharing.

Syntax. The *addressed preterms* are defined inductively by

$$T, U, V ::= E^a \mid \bot \qquad\qquad \text{(Addressed)}$$

$$E, F ::= M[s] \mid UV \qquad\qquad \text{(Evaluation Context)}$$

$$M, N ::= \lambda M \mid MN \mid \underline{n} \qquad\qquad \text{(Pure)}$$

$$s, t ::= \text{id} \mid U \cdot s \qquad\qquad \text{(Substitution)}$$

where everywhere a, b, c range over an infinite set $\mathbf{A}$ of *addresses*.

Weak β-introduction prereduction. $\xrightarrow[B_w]{}$ is defined by the rule

$$((\lambda M)[s]^b \, U)^a \rightarrow M[U \cdot s]^a \qquad\qquad (B_w)$$

Weak substitution elimination prereduction. $\xrightarrow{\sigma}$ is defined by the rules

$$(MN)[s]^a \rightarrow (M[s]^b \, N[s]^c)^a \qquad b, c \text{ fresh} \qquad \text{(App)}$$

$$\underline{0}\,[E^b \cdot s]^a \rightarrow E^b \qquad\qquad \text{(FVarG)}$$

$$\underline{0}\,[E^b \cdot s]^a \rightarrow E^a \qquad\qquad \text{(FVarE)}$$

$$\underline{n+1}\,[U \cdot s]^a \rightarrow \underline{n}\,[s]^a \qquad\qquad \text{(RVar)}$$

Collection prereduction. $\xrightarrow{C}$ is defined by the rule

$$M[s]^a \rightarrow M[s|_{\text{fi}(M)}]^a \qquad s \neq s|_{\text{fi}(M)} \qquad \text{(Collect)}$$

where *environment trimming* is defined by $s|_I = s|_I^0$ where $\text{id}|_I^i = \text{id}$ and $(U \cdot s)|_I^i = U \cdot s|_I^{i+1}$ when $i \in I$ but $\bot \cdot s|_I^{i+1}$ when $i \notin I$.

Fig. 1. Pre-$\lambda \sigma_w^a$: syntax and reduction rules.

is) to the address b (where the term E is). As a consequence, further (parallel) rewriting of this argument will be shared with all its other occurrences in the term. If the address is a, a copy of the term E at address b (or, to be precise, a copy of its root node because addresses of its subterms are not changed) is performed. Then the term $\underline{0}\,[E \cdot S]$ at address a is replaced by that copy and later rewriting of this argument will not be shared. Thus we see that the reduction $\xrightarrow{\sigma}$ contains two substitution elimination subreductions, $\xrightarrow{\sigma g}$ and $\xrightarrow{\sigma e}$. Let $\sigma_0 = \{(\text{App}), (\text{RVar}), (\text{VarId})\}$. Then $\sigma g = \sigma_0 \cup \{(\text{FVarG})\}$ and $\sigma e = \sigma_0 \cup \{(\text{FVarE})\}$. A consequence of mixing those two systems is the creation of a critical pair (non-determinism) and thus non-orthogonality. Fortunately, since this critical pair is at the root, the descendant redexs (residuals) (Barendregt 1984, Klop 1992) can be extended in a straight-forward way: We just observe that there is no residual redex of (FVarG) (resp. (FVarE)) after applying (FVarE) (resp. (FVarG)). We first establish that this is safe before we give the definition (Def. 8).

A *complete development* of a preterm T is a series of $\lambda\sigma^a_w$-rewrites that rewrite all redexes of T until no residuals remain.

Lemma 4. *Complete developments are fnite.*

Proof. Same proof as for λ-calculus (Barendregt 1984, p.290). $\square$

The nondeterministic choice between (FVarE) and (FVarG) makes complete development nondeterministic as illustrated by the following example (where we omit id and [id] for clarity):

$$(\underline{0}[\underline{n}^b]^c \; \underline{0}[\underline{n}^b]^d)^a \xrightarrow[\text{(FVarE)}]{\overset{\text{(FVarG)}}{}} \begin{array}{c} (\underline{n}^b \underline{0}[\underline{n}^b]^d)^a \xrightarrow[\text{(FVarE)}]{\overset{\text{(FVarG)}}{}} \begin{array}{c}(\underline{n}^b \underline{n}^b)^a \\ (\underline{n}^b \underline{n}^d)^a\end{array} \\ (\underline{n}^c \underline{0}[\underline{n}^b]^d)^a \xrightarrow[\text{(FVarE)}]{\overset{\text{(FVarG)}}{}} \begin{array}{c}(\underline{n}^c \underline{n}^b)^a \\ (\underline{n}^c \underline{n}^d)^a\end{array} \end{array}$$

We obtain four possible different resulting terms namely $(\underline{n}^b \underline{n}^b)^a$, $(\underline{n}^b \underline{n}^d)^a$, $(\underline{n}^c \underline{n}^b)^a$, and $(\underline{n}^c \underline{n}^d)^a$. It is clear that erasing the addresses of these four terms produces the same term, namely $\underline{n}\,\underline{n}$: the difference between them is the amount of sharing (or shapes of the associated graph) we obtain after a development. The use of (FVarG) increases sharing whenever (FVarE) decreases it. We will denote the set of preterms obtained by all possible complete developments of T by dev(T). Notice that these preterms depend on the fresh addresses introduced by (App) that the lower three are essentially the same term.

Lemma 5. dev(T) *is finite for any preterm T.*

Proof. If i is the number of (FVarG/E) redexes in T, then clearly #dev(T) $\leq 2^i$.

Definition 6 (sharing ordering). Let θ be a map on the set of addresses. The ordering $\unrhd_\theta$ is defined inductively by

- If for all i, $0 \leq i \leq n$ $T_i \unrhd_\theta T'_i$ then $M[T_0 \cdots T_n]^a \unrhd_\theta M[T'_0 \cdots T'_n]^{\theta(a)}$,
- $n^a \unrhd_\theta n^{\theta(a)}$, and
- if $T \unrhd_\theta T'$ and $U \unrhd_\theta U'$ then $(TU)^a \unrhd_\theta (T'U')^{\theta(a)}$.

we say that the addressed term T collapses in U, $T \unrhd U$ if there exists a map θ such that $U \unrhd_\theta (T)$.

Lemma 7. *Let T be a preterm.* (dev(T), $\unrhd$) *is a finite cpo.*

Proof. The lower bound of two preterms T_1 and T_2 belonging to dev(T) is the most general unifier of T_1 and T_2 where the addresses are interpreted as free variables (and the result of course considered modulo renaming). Moreover, $\unrhd$ is a partial ordering. $\square$

Now we can define the parallel extension $\twoheadmapsto_{R}$ of a rewrite system R which corresponds intuitively to the simultaneous (also known as *Gross-Knuth*) reduction of all R-redexes of a term T, *e.g.*, one $\twoheadmapsto_{B_w}$ step is the simultaneous reduction of all B_w-redexes.

Definition 8 (parallel extension). Let T and U be two terms. Then the parallel extension $\twoheadmapsto$ of the rewrite relation $\to$ is defined by $T \twoheadmapsto U$ iff $U \in \mathrm{dev}(T)$.

The next definition shows how to determine when an 'addressed term' corresponds to a 'directed acyclic graph:' this should be the case exactly when the 'sharing information' is non-ambiguous.

Definition 9 (addressing). Given some set of terms with a notion of *address* associated to some subterms. Assume $t \in \mathbf{T}$ is such a term and let $a, b \in \mathbf{A}$ range over the possible addresses.

1. The set of all addresses that occur in t is written $\mathrm{addr}(X)$.
2. The *outermost a-addressed subterms* of t is the set $t|a = \{t_1^a, \ldots, t_n^a\}$ with t_i those subterms of t for which an n-ary context $C\{\ldots\}$ exists such that $t = C\{t_1^a, \ldots, t_n^a\}$ and $a \notin \mathrm{addr}(C\{\})$.
3. t is *admissible* if for all $a \in \mathrm{addr}(t)$, $t|a$ is a singleton $\{t'\}$ where $a \notin \mathrm{addr}(t')$.
4. If $\to$ is a rewrite relation on $\mathbf{T}$ defined by a certain number of axioms, then for each address a, $\xrightarrow{a}$ is the *address restriction* of $\to$ to only those (proper) reductions where the redex has address a. This generalizes to any set of addresses $A = \{a_1, \ldots, a_n\}$: $\xrightarrow{A} = \bigcup_{a \in A} \xrightarrow{a}$.
5. $\twoheadmapsto^{a}$ (resp. $\twoheadmapsto^{A}$) is the parallel extension of $\xrightarrow{a}$ (resp. $\xrightarrow{A}$).
6. Parallel $\to$-reduction is $\twoheadmapsto^{\infty} = \bigcup_{A \subseteq \mathbf{A}} \twoheadmapsto^{A}$.

Parallel reduction $\twoheadmapsto^{\infty}$ expresses not only sharing but also parallel computation because at each step a parallel computer can reduce a set of addresses simultaneously. Notice that if $a \notin \mathrm{addr}(U)$ or $A \cap \mathrm{addr}(U) = \varnothing$ the reductions degenerate: $\{T \mid U \xrightarrow{a} T\} = \{T \mid U \twoheadmapsto^{a} T\} = \{T \mid U \xrightarrow{A} T\} = \{T \mid U \twoheadmapsto^{A} T\} = \varnothing$.

Proposition 10. $\twoheadmapsto^{\infty}_{B_w+\sigma+C}$ *preserves admissibility.*

Proof. By definition of parallel rewriting, one rewrite step rewrites all occurrences of an address a, hence admissibility is preserved. $\square$

Definition 11 ($\lambda\sigma_w^a$). Given the preterms and prereductions of Fig. 1.

1. The $\lambda\sigma_w^a$-*terms* are the admissible $\lambda\sigma_w^a$-preterms.
2. $\lambda\sigma_w^a$-*substitution* is $\twoheadmapsto^{\infty}_{\sigma}$,
3. $\lambda\sigma_w^a$-*reduction* is $\twoheadmapsto^{\infty}_{B_w+\sigma+C}$ (or just $\twoheadmapsto^{\infty}$ when confusion is unlikely).

As for $\lambda\sigma_w$ one associates with the pure term M the $\lambda\sigma_w^a$-term $M[\mathrm{id}]^a$ which will then reduce to weak normal form modulo substitution under abstraction. Normal forms V are of the form $(\lambda M)[V_1 \cdots V_n]$ or $\underline{n}\, V_1 \cdot V_m$. In the rest of the paper, we will only consider *closed* weak normal forms, called *values*, *i.e.*, $(\lambda M)[V_1 \cdots V_n]$, supposing that only closed terms are evaluated.

The last two lemmas of this section establish the connection between $\lambda\sigma_w^a$ and $\lambda\sigma_w$ and together show the *correctness* and *confluence modulo erasure* of $\lambda\sigma_w^a$. Both lemmas use the translation function "erase" which deletes all addresses of an addressed term, obviously resulting in a $\lambda\sigma_w$-term.

Lemma 12 (projection). *Let T and U be two addressed terms. If $T \Vvdash^{\infty}\!\!\!\!\to U$ then* $erase(T) \xrightarrow[\lambda\sigma_w]{}\!\!\!\!\twoheadrightarrow erase(U)$.

Proof. Easy induction on the structure of T. □

Lemma 13. *let W and W' be two $\lambda\sigma$-terms. If $W \xrightarrow[\lambda\sigma_w]{} W'$ then there exists two addressed terms T and U such that $W = erase(T)$, $W' = erase(U)$, and $T \Vvdash^{\infty}\!\!\!\!\to U$.*

Proof. Label each subterm of W by its access path to ensure that each subterm has a unique address and then rewrite using the redex's address. □

4 Reduction Strategies

In this section we show how conventional weak reduction strategies can be described through restrictions of the $\lambda\sigma_w^a$-calculus. First we formalize the classic sequential strategies call-by-name, call-by-value, and call-by-need. Second, we formalize two common parallel reduction strategies: spine parallelism and speculative parallelism.

The crucial difference from traditional expositions in both cases is that we can exploit that *all redexes have a unique address*. We will thus define a reduction with a strategy as a two-stage process (which can be merged in actual implementations, of course): we first give an inference system for "locating" a set of addresses where reduction can happen, and then we reduce using the original reduction constrained to just those addresses.

Definition 14 (strategy for addressed terms). Given a reduction $\xrightarrow[X]{}$ on a set of addressed terms.

1. A *strategy* S is a relation written $U \vdash_{\overline{S}} A$ from addressed terms U to sets of addresses A.
2. For a strategy S, *S-reduction* is the relation $\xrightarrow[X/S]{}$ defined by $U_1 \xrightarrow[X/S]{} U_2$ iff $U_1 \vdash_{\overline{S}} A$ and $U_1 \xrightarrow[X]{A} U_2$.

We begin with the possible *reduction in context* inference rules which make possible to restrict the addresses at which the rewrite rules can be applied.

Definition 15 (strategy rules). The $\lambda\sigma_w^a$-*strategy rules* are the following:

$$\frac{}{M[s]^a \vdash \{a\}} \text{ (Scl)} \qquad \frac{U \vdash A_1 \quad U \vdash A_2}{U \vdash A_1 \cup A_2} \text{ (Par)}$$

$$\frac{U \cdot s \vdash A}{M[U \cdot s]^a \vdash A} \text{ (Sub)} \qquad \frac{U \vdash A}{U \cdot s \vdash A} \text{ (Hd)} \qquad \frac{s \vdash A}{U \cdot s \vdash A} \text{ (Tl)}$$

$$\frac{}{(UV)^a \vdash \{a\}} \text{ (Sap)} \qquad \frac{U \vdash A}{(UV)^a \vdash A} \text{ (Lap)} \qquad \frac{V \vdash A}{(UV)^a \vdash A} \text{ (Rap)}$$

where we furthermore require for (Scl) and (Sap) that some $\lambda\sigma_w^a$-rule is, indeed, applicable. A $\lambda\sigma_w^a$-strategy S is specified by giving a list of conditions for application of each rule; this defines the relation $\vdash_{\overline{S}}$. Notice that the normal forms (or values) for some strategies are not $\lambda\sigma_w^a$-values, *i.e.*, closed weak normal forms. For instance, if (Rap) is disallowed then normal forms correspond to closed weak head normal forms (whnf) of shape $(\lambda M)[s]^a$.

Table 1 shows the conditions for several strategies. Notice that when (Sub) is disabled then (Hd) and (Tl) are not reachable.

Strategy	(FVar?)	(Scl)	(Par)	(Sub)	(Hd)	(Tl)	(Sap)	(Lap)	(Rap)
✓	E or G	✓	✓	✓	✓	✓	✓	✓	✓
CBN	E	✓	÷	÷			①	⊸①	÷
CBV	E	✓	÷	÷			②	⊸①	③
CBNeedE	E	④	÷	⊸④	✓	÷	①	⊸①	÷
CBNeedG	G	✓	÷	÷			①	⊸①	÷
Specul-$\|_n$	E	✓	⑤	✓	✓	✓	✓	✓	✓
Spine-$\|_n$	E	✓	⑤	✓	✓	✓	✓	✓	÷

✓: "always applicable;" ÷: "never applicable;" blank: "don't care;" ①: U is a value; ②: U and V are values; ③: U is a value and V is not; ④: if $s = U \cdot s'$ and $M = \underline{0}$ then U is a value; and ⑤: $\#A \leq n$.

Table 1. Strategies for $\lambda\sigma_w^a$.

For the remainder of the section we will discuss these strategies. Notice that there are two forms of nondeterminism. One is due to (Par), the only rule which contains the union operator and can yield more than one address for reduction. The other form of nondeterminism already mentioned in Section 3 (and here permitted only in the first strategy) is the choice between (FVarE) and (FVarG).

The first strategy, "✓," allows every rule and gives us the full $\lambda\sigma_w^a$-calculus.

Proposition 16. $\vdash_{\overline{X/\checkmark}} = \vdash_{\overline{X}}$.

Proof. An easy induction over $\lambda\sigma_w^a$-terms shows that $T \vdash_{\overline{\checkmark}} A$ if and only if $\varnothing \subset A \subseteq \text{addr}(U)$. □

Thus it is clear that all other strategies specified this way define reductions weaker than $\lambda\sigma_w^a$.

CBN and CBV are just the the call-by-name and call-by-value strategies of Plotkin (1975). In fact, they uses (FVarE) which does not share subterms.

The next two strategies are like CBN but add sharing in the way used by functional language implementation: CBNeedE is the call-by-need strategy (Launchbury 1993, Ariola et al. 1995); CBNeedG is an adaption of Wadsworth's (1971) "λ-graph reduction" to weak reduction.

The last two strategies realize *n-parallelism with sharing*. The *Speculative-$\|_n$* picks addresses everywhere in the term expecting that some reductions will be useful and the *Spine-$\|_n$* selects addresses in the head subterm disallowing (Rap) rule in order to compute the weak head normal form. The simple formulation we have found has promise for proving properties of parallel reduction, however, parallel reductions are otherwise outside the scope of this paper and the rest of this section focuses on sequential reduction. We will study these strategies. We start by focusing on the structural properties of terms preserved by these strategies. Then, we narrow our attention to just 'call-by-need-like' strategies.

Proposition 17. *Let $M[\mathrm{id}]^a \twoheadrightarrow_S T$. Then*

1. *If S disables (Rap) and enables (FVarE) only when E (in $\underline{0}[E^b \cdot s]^a$) is a value then T is of the form $(\cdots(N_0[s_0]^{a_0} N_1[s_1]^{a_1})^{b_1} \cdots N_n[s_n]^{a_n})^{b_n}$ where $n \geq 0$.*

2. *If S disables both (FVarG), (Sub), and (Rap) then all substitutions contained in T are of the form $[N_1[s_1]^{a_1} \cdot \ldots \cdot N_n[s_n]^{a_n}]$.*

Proof. Given T and $a, b \in \mathrm{addr}(T)$, we say that b is the *right-subaddress* of a if b occurs only in contexts $T = C\{(U\ E^b)^a\}$, and we say that T is *argument local* if all addresses b of such contexts are right-subaddresses of the correponding a. Since the freshness addresses condition of (App), and (FVarE) is disabled for terms of the form $\underline{0}[(T\ U)^b \cdot s]^a$, then rewriting preserves the argument local property. If we also disallow (Rap) then an argument local term has exactly the form of the first assertion which thus holds. The second assertion is easily checked by analysis of the possible rewrite steps. $\quad\square$

Figure 2 shows Ariola et al.'s (1995, Figure 3) "standard call-by-need λ_{let}-calculus." In λ_{let} substitution is represented by nested lets which means that sharing is tied to the term structure. This corresponds to machines with "shared environments" (*i.e.*, using a linked list of frames) hence λ_{let} must correspond to $\lambda\sigma_w^a$ with an environment-based evaluation strategy.

Proposition 18. *CBNeedE is sound and complete w.r.t. λ_{let}.*

Proof. The proof is based on constructing translations between the two calculi, proving the soundness and completeness diagrams

Syntax.

$$M, N ::= x \mid V \mid MN \mid \text{let } x = M \text{ in } N \qquad \text{(Terms)}$$
$$V ::= \lambda x.M \qquad \text{(Values)}$$
$$A ::= V \mid \text{let } x = M \text{ in } A \qquad \text{(Answers)}$$
$$E, F ::= [] \mid EM \mid \text{let } x = M \text{ in } E \mid \text{let } x = E \text{ in } F[x] \quad \text{(Eval. Contexts)}$$

Reduction. $\underset{\text{let}}{\rightarrow}$ is defined by the rules

$$(\lambda x.M)N \rightarrow \text{let } x = N \text{ in } M \qquad (\text{let}_s\text{-I})$$
$$\text{let } x = V \text{ in } E[x] \rightarrow \text{let } x = V \text{ in } E[V] \qquad (\text{let}_s\text{-V})$$
$$(\text{let } x = M \text{ in } A)N \rightarrow \text{let } x = M \text{ in } AN \qquad (\text{let}_s\text{-C})$$
$$\text{let } x = \text{let } y = M \text{ in } A \text{ in } E[x] \rightarrow \text{let } y = M \text{ in let } x = A \text{ in } E[x] \quad (\text{let}_s\text{-A})$$

Fig. 2. Ariola et al.'s call-by-need calculus, λ_{let}.

The only difficulty in the translations is to encode $\lambda\sigma_w^a$-substitutions as nested lets since substitutions may be distributed throughout the structure of terms whereas nested lets cannot. This makes it difficult to capture the sharing contained in the $\lambda\sigma_w^a$-term. Fortunately, the λ_{let}-calculus permits only call-by-need reduction which allows us to consider only terms of the form of Proposition 17.

$\square$

5 Constructors and Recursion

In this section we deal with two important features of pure functional programming languages, namely *algebraic data structures* in the form of constructors that can be investigated using a 'case' selector statement, and *recursion* in the form of an explicit fixed point operator.

Definition 19 (simple data structures). $\lambda\sigma c_w^a$ is the system obtained by extending the definition of $\lambda\sigma_w^a$ (pure) preterms to include

$$M, N ::= \cdots \mid C_{i,j} \mid \langle \cdots ; C_{i,j_i} : M_i; \cdots \rangle$$

where $C_{i,j}$ is a *constructor* with "identifier" i and rank j which means that in the selection component $C_{i,j} : M_i$, M_i binds the indices $\underline{0} \ldots j-1$ in M_i. Data values, possibly with arguments, can (only) be used to select one of these by the reduction

$$(C_{i,j}[T_0 \cdots T_{j-1} \cdot s]^b \langle \cdots ; C_{i,j} : M_i; \cdots \rangle [t]^c)^a \rightarrow M_i[T_0 \cdots T_{j-1} \cdot t]^a \quad \text{(Case)}$$

In order for constructors to behave as functions in programs and "consume" the appropriate number of arguments they should only be used inside the right number of abstractions, *i.e.*, we can encode lists as $\text{Nil} \equiv C_{0,0}$ and $\text{Cons} \equiv \lambda\lambda C_{1,2}$.

For recursion denoted by μM, where μ binds index $\underline{0}$ in M, we have two alternatives. $\lambda\sigma c\mu_w^a$ is what is obtained with the easy solution, which is to include the rule

$$(\mu M)[s]^a \rightarrow M[(\mu M)[s]^a \cdot s]^b \qquad b \text{ fresh} \qquad \text{(Unfold)}$$

(Unfold) must of course be applied lazily to avoid infinite unfolding.

Another solution consists in encoding unfolding such that it is always delayed until needed. The trick is to augment the explicit "horizontal" sharing that we have introduced in previous sections through addresses with explicit "vertical" sharing (using the terminology of Ariola and Klop 1994). We have chosen to do this using the $\bullet^a$ "backpointer" syntax (Felleisen and Friedman 1989, Rose 1996): reducing a fixed point operator places a $\bullet$ at the location where unfolding should happen when (if) it is needed.

The difference is illustrated to the right. Consider the initial term with a large (shaded) μ-redex containing a smaller (white) redex. Now, we wish to reduce the outer and then the inner redex. The top reduction shows what happens with (Unfold): the redex is duplicated before it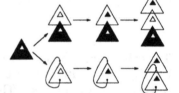
is reduced. In contrast using an explicit backpointer, illustrated at the bottom, makes it possible to share the redex by delaying the unfolding until the reduction has happened. The price we pay is that some potential redexes are lost, since backpointers are syntactic and thus can block specific redexes. Also, the admissibility definition becomes slightly more complicated.

Definition 20 (cyclic addressing). Given a set of addressed terms **T**.

1. The *cyclic addressed preterms*, $\mathbf{T}^\bullet$, allows subterms of the form $\bullet^a$. Preterms without $\bullet$ are called *acyclic*.
2. t is *cyclic admissible* if all addresses $a \in \text{addr}(t)$ satisfy either $t|a = \{\bullet^a\}$, or $t|a = \{F^a\}$ and $F|a \subseteq \{\bullet^a\}$. As before admissible preterms are called *terms*.
3. Given a rewrite relation $\rightarrow$ on (acyclic terms) **T**. The *cyclic extension*, $\twoheadrightarrow$, is the rewrite relation defined as follows. Assume the rule is $t \rightarrow u$. For each backpointer where admissiblity is violated: unfold the original definition for each possible C with $u = C\{\bullet^a\}$ and $a \notin \text{addr}(C\{\})$, *i.e.*, replace $C\{\bullet^a\}$ with $C\{t|a\}$ (which contains $\bullet^a$).

The cyclic extension of a set of rules is thus derived by inserting explicit unfolding *where an address is removed*.

Definition 21 ($\lambda\sigma c\mu_w^{a\bullet}$).

1. $\lambda\sigma c\mu_w^{a\bullet}$-*terms* are cyclic addressed $\lambda\sigma c_w^a$-terms extended with recursion μM.

2. $\lambda\sigma c\mu_w^{a\bullet}$-reduction, $\#^{\infty}\!\!\twoheadrightarrow$, is the cyclic extension of $\lambda\sigma c_w^a$-reduction and the rule

$$\mu M[s]^a \rightarrow M[\bullet^a \cdot s]^a \qquad\qquad \text{(Cycle)}$$

Let us briefly consider what the "cyclic extension" means. It is clear that (Cycle) preserves (cyclic) admissibility but not all rules do. Fortunately we can systematically reformulate the rules in order to insert the unfoldings which are needed explicitly. If we write $T\{\bullet^a := U\}$ for the operation which replaces each $\bullet^a$ in T by U, then the principle is simple: whenever an address a is *removed* from a subterm t then all occurrences of $\bullet^a$ *inside* t must be unfolded to the value of the entire subterm. This affects the $\lambda\sigma_w^a$-rules from Fig. 1 as follows:

$$((\lambda M)[s]^b\, U)^a \rightarrow M[U \cdot (s\{\bullet^b := \lambda M[s]^b\})]^a \qquad (\text{B}_w^\bullet)$$

$$\underline{0}[E^b \cdot s]^a \rightarrow (E\{\bullet^a := \underline{0}[E^b \cdot s]^a\})^b \qquad (\text{FvarG}^\bullet)$$

$$\underline{0}[E^b \cdot s]^a \rightarrow (E\{\bullet^b := E^b\})^a \qquad (\text{FvarE}^\bullet)$$

and (Case) from above changes as follows:

$$(C_{i,j}[T_0 \cdots T_{j-1} \cdot s]^b\ \langle \cdots ; C_{i,j} : M_i; \cdots \rangle\, [t]^c)^a \rightarrow M_i[T_0' \cdots T_{j-1}' \cdot t']^a \quad (\text{Case}^\bullet)$$

where $T_i' = T_i\{\bullet^b := C_{i,j}[T_0 \cdots T_{j-1}\cdot s]^b\}$ and $t' = t\{\bullet^c := \langle \cdots ; C_{i,j} : M_i; \cdots \rangle\, [t]^c\}$.

Theorem 22. $\lambda\sigma c\mu_w^{a\bullet}$ *is correct w.r.t.* $\lambda\sigma c\mu_w^a$.

Proof. The difficult point is to prove that delaying unfolding is safe. We do this by considering $\lambda\sigma c\mu_w^{a\bullet}\rho$ i.e., $\lambda\sigma c\mu_w^{a\bullet}$ annotated with the history of cyclic pointers $\bullet$. The rule (Cycle) becomes $\mu M[s]_\rho^a \rightarrow M[\bullet^a \cdot s]_{\{\bullet:=\mu M[s]^a\rho,\rho\}}^a$, whereas the other rules distribute the history into the term. Then we can show that if $M_\rho \,\#\!\!\xrightarrow[\lambda\sigma c\mu_w^{a\bullet}\rho]{\infty}\!\!\twoheadrightarrow\, N_\rho$ then $M\rho \,\#\!\!\xrightarrow[\lambda\sigma c\mu_w^a]{\infty}\!\!\twoheadrightarrow N\rho$. $\qquad\square$

6 Trim: A Space leak free calculus

A drawback of calculi such as $\lambda\sigma_w^a$ is that they leak space: not only can $\lambda\sigma_w^a$-terms contain unreachable subterms but these may never be removed by reduction.

For instance, consider the term $((\mu\lambda\underline{1}\,\underline{1})I)[\text{id}]^a$ reduces (with call-by-need) to a term of the form

$$\big(\, (\lambda\underline{1}\,\underline{1})[(\lambda\underline{1}\,\underline{1})[\bullet^b]^b]^d\ \underline{1}[\underline{1}[\cdots\underline{1}[I[\text{id}]^c \cdot (\lambda\underline{1}\,\underline{1})[\bullet^b]^b]^{d_n} \cdots]^{d_2}]^{d_1}\,\big)^a$$

with infinitely growing garbage (situations like these do, in fact, happen in real implementations).

In this section, we formalise the notion of garbage free terms and space leak free reduction. Then we present a calculus "Trim" which is space leak free for all strategies by ensuring that (Collect) is invoked sufficiently often that no garbage persists, essentially implementing a kind of run-time garbage collection. Finally, we show how the restriction of Trim to call-by-need reduction degenerates to the simple environment trimming used for this purpose by the STG-machine of Peyton Jones (1992).

Definition 23. *Garbage-free* terms are characterized by the requirement that for every subterm $M[s]^a$, $s = s|_{\text{fi}(M)}$.

Proposition 24. If $T \overset{\text{addr}(T)}{\underset{C}{\mapsto\!\!\!\rightarrow}} U$, then U is a garbage-free term.

Space leak freeness (first precisely formulated for a lazy abstract machine by Sestoft 1994) means that every (Collect)-redex will eventually disappear in a computation. In other words, no unreachable subterm stays indefinitely.

Definition 25 (space leak free reduction). Let D be a $\lambda\sigma_w^a$-reduction path starting at a garbage-free term T_0:

$$D : T_0 \overset{A_1}{\mapsto\!\!\!\rightarrow} T_1 \overset{A_2}{\mapsto\!\!\!\rightarrow} T_2 \overset{A_3}{\mapsto\!\!\!\rightarrow} \cdots$$

D is *space leak free* if $T_n = C\{E^b\}$ where E^b is garbage (meaning that $\underset{C}{\mapsto\!\!\!\rightarrow}$ can be used to replace it with $\perp$) implies that there exists $m > n$ such that E^b is collected in T_m. A reduction relation $\underset{R}{\twoheadrightarrow}$ (of $\lambda\sigma_w^a$) is space leak free if all its reduction paths starting at a garbage-free term are space leak free.

A naive way to provide space leak reduction consist in alternating between $B_w + \sigma$ reduction and a complete Collecting as stated in the folowing proposition.

Proposition 26. $\overset{}{\underset{B_w + \sigma}{\mapsto\!\!\!\twoheadrightarrow}} \cdot \underset{C}{\mapsto\!\!\!\rightarrow}$ is space leak free.

Proof. By proposition 24, it is clear that after each reduction step, there remain no addressed subterms which are garbage. $\square$

In the rest of this section, we present a calculus, Trim, that never introduces space leaks. The principle consist in analyzing the rules of $\lambda\sigma_w^a$. One notices that only (B_w), (App), and (Case), can produce unreachable terms. (App) introduces two new subaddressed terms of the form $\_[\_]^a$ (closures) on which an application of (Collect) might be necessary. (B_w) adds a new addressed term (argument) to the function's substitution; if we know that the B_w-redex is garbage free then it is necessary to check only whether the argument is reachable or not. (Case) can introduce unreachable terms in the substitution $T_1 \cdot \ldots \cdot T_m \cdot t$, hence, we need to apply (Collect). Thus, we replace these rules with the following (using the acyclic rules but can easily be generalised the cyclic calculus since neither (Unfold) nor (Cycle) introduces space leaks):

$$(\lambda M[s]^b T)^a \rightarrow \begin{cases} M[\perp \cdot s] & \underline{0} \notin \text{fi}(M) \\ M[T \cdot s] & \underline{0} \in \text{fi}(M) \end{cases} \qquad (\text{TB}_w)$$

$$(MN)[s]^a \rightarrow (M[s|_{\text{fi}(M)}]^b N[s|_{\text{fi}(N)}]^c)^a \quad b, c \text{ fresh} \qquad (\text{TApp})$$

$$(C_{i,j}[T_0 \cdots T_{j-1} \cdot s]^b \langle \cdots ; C_{i,j} : M_i; \cdots \rangle [t]^c)^a \rightarrow M_i[T_0 \cdots T_{j-1} \cdot t|_{\text{fi}(N_i)}]^a \qquad (\text{TCase})$$

Definition 27. The Trim-*calculus* is the calculus over addressed terms combining the original (FVarE), (FVarG), (RVar), and (Cycle) with the new (TB_w), (TApp), and (TCase). We write this reduction $\underset{T}{\mapsto\!\!\!\rightarrow}$.

Remark. Notice that $\xmapsto[\text{(TApp)}]{a} = \xmapsto[\text{(App)}]{a} \cdot \xmapsto{b} \cdot \xmapsto{c}$, and $\xmapsto[\text{(TCase)}]{a} = \xmapsto[\text{(Case)}]{a} \cdot \xmapsto[C]{d_1,\ldots d_m}$.

Theorem 28. *Let T be a garbage-free term. If $T \vmapsto{} U$ then U is a garbage-free term.*

Proof. By case analysis of each rule of $\vmapsto{}$. $\qquad\qquad\qquad\qquad\qquad\qquad$ □

Corollary 29. Trim *is space leak free.*

Since we cannot rewrite in unreachable terms, we can claim that Trim is isomorphic modulo substitution under λ to the weak version of Wadsworth's (1971) "λ-graph reduction." Trim ensures that all its strategies are space leak free. However, we remind the reader that collecting incurs an overhead, so it is desirable to minimize this task. One way is to exploit structural properties enforced by the used strategy. In the remainder of this section we study optimization provided by call-by-need w.r.t. space leak freeness, in particular, we show that a state of the art implementation, the STG-machine (Peyton Jones 1992), does not leak space.

One feature of call-by-need is that it always selects the leftmost outermost redex. If we apply (App) to the term $C\{(MN)[s]\}$ then we know that the left term $(M[s])$ will be evaluated first. Hence trimming this term is unnecessary since it cannot leak space. Similarly, a trimmed version of (B_w) and (Case) are not necessary. The only remaining rule, (App), becomes

$$(MN)[s]^a \xmapsto{a} (M[s]^b N[s|_{fi(N)}]^c)^a \quad b, c \text{ fresh} \qquad\qquad \text{(TAppN)}$$

Replacing (App) of the $\lambda\sigma_w^a$-calculus by (TAppN) forms Trim_N.

Theorem 30. Trim_N *is space leak free for call-by-name (CBN) and call-by-need (both CBNeedE and CBNeedG).*

Proof. Trim_N trims all terms where computations is forbiden, *i.e.*, right argument of applications. $\qquad\qquad\qquad\qquad\qquad\qquad\qquad\qquad\qquad\qquad$ □

Corollary 31. *Peyton Jones's (1992) STG-machine does not leak space.*

Proof. In the STG-machine, the arguments of applications and constructors must be variables which are bound by a *let* expression. Consider the term $MN_1 \ldots N_n$ which is written let $x_1 = N_1, \ldots x_n = N_n$ in $Mx_1 \ldots x_n$ where $N_1, \ldots, N_n$ are annotated with their free variables. The STG machine computes (see Peyton Jones 1992, section 5.3) that expression by placing the N_i's in the heap and trimming their associated environments. This obviously corresponds to n applications of (TAppN). $\qquad\qquad\qquad\qquad\qquad\qquad\qquad\qquad$ □

7 Conclusions

We have studied calculi of weak reduction with sharing, and proposed original solutions to several problems well-known from implementations, *e.g.*, understanding the consequences of sharing and cycles on correctness, proving an adequate model for call-by-need, and space leaking. In future works we will look at the consequence of this approach on a generic implementation design.

Acknowledgements. The authors would like to thank Eva Rose and Frédéric Lang for useful suggestions to the manuscript. Finally, the third author is grateful to INRIA Lorraine for funding while this work was undertaken.

References

Ariola, Z. M., Felleisen, M., Maraist, J., Odersky, M. and Wadler, P. (1995). A call-by-need lambda calculus. *22nd Principles of Programming Languages.* San Francisco, California. pp. 233–246.

Ariola, Z. M. and Klop, J. W. (1994). Cyclic lambda graph rewriting. *Logic in Computer Science.* IEEE Computer Society Press. Paris, France. pp. 416–425.

Barendregt, H. P. (1984). *The Lambda Calculus: Its Syntax and Semantics.* Revised edn. North-Holland.

Bloo, R. and Rose, K. H. (1995). Preservation of strong normalisation in named lambda calculi with explicit substitution and garbage collection. *CSN '95 – Computer Science in the Netherlands.* pp. 62–72. ⟨URL: *ftp://ftp.diku.dk/diku/semantics/papers/D-246.ps*⟩

Curien, P.-L. (1991). An abstract framework for environment machines. *Theor. Comp. Sci.* 82: 389–402.

Curien, P.-L., Hardin, T. and Lévy, J.-J. (1992). Confluence properties of weak and strong calculi of explicit substitutions. *RR 1617.* INRIA. To appear in J.ACM.

de Bruijn, N. G. (1972). Lambda calculus with nameless dummies, a tool for automatic formula manipulation, with application to the Church-Rosser theorem. *Proc. Koninkl. Nederl. Akademie van Wetenschappen* 75(5): 381–392.

Felleisen, M. and Friedman, D. P. (1989). A syntactic theory of sequential state. *Theor. Comp. Sci.* 69: 243–287.

Klop, J. W. (1992). Term rewriting systems. *In* Abramsky, S., Gabbay, D. M. and Maibaum, T. S. E. (eds), *Handbook of Logic in Computer Science.* Vol. 2. Oxford University Press. pp. 1–116.

Launchbury, J. (1993). A natural semantics for lazy evaluation. *20th Principles of Programming Languages.* pp. 144–154.

Maranget, L. (1991). Optimal derivations in weak lambda calculi and in orthogonal rewriting systems. *18th Principles of Programming Languages.* pp. 255–268.

Peyton Jones, S. L. (1992). Implementing lazy functional programming languages on stock hardware: the spineless tagless G-machine. *Journ. Funct. Progr.* 2(2): 127–202.

Plotkin, G. D. (1975). Call-by-name, call-by-value, and the λ-calculus. *Theor. Comp. Sci.* 1: 125–159.

Rose, K. H. (1996). *Operational Reduction Models for Functional Programming Languages.* PhD thesis. DIKU, Dept. of Computer Science, Univ. of Copenhagen. Universitetsparken 1, DK-2100 København Ø. DIKU report 96/1.

Sestoft, P. (1994). Deriving a lazy abstract machine. *Technical Report ID-TR 1994-146.* Dept. of Computer Science, Technical University of Denmark. ⟨URL: *ftp://ftp.dina.kvl.dk/pub/Staff/Peter.Sestoft/papers/amlazy4.dvi.gz*⟩

Wadsworth, C. (1971). *Semantics and pragmatics of the lambda calculus.* PhD thesis. Oxford.

Context-Sensitive Computations
in Confluent Programs*

Salvador Lucas

Departamento de Sistemas Informáticos y Computación
Universidad Politécnica de Valencia
Camino de Vera s/n, E-46071 Valencia, Spain.
e.mail: slucas@dsic.upv.es

Abstract. *Context-sensitive rewriting* is a refined form of rewriting which explores a smaller reduction space by imposing some fixed restrictions on the replacements. Any Term Rewriting System (TRS) can be given a context-sensitive rewrite relation. In this paper, we formulate conditions to guarantee the confluence of this relation. Moreover, for a confluent TRS, we are able to give sufficient conditions to ensure that the (eventually obtained) computed value of a given expression can be reached by using context-sensitive rewriting, thus leading to more efficient and still complete computations.

Keywords: confluence, functional programming, term rewriting systems.

1 Introduction

The operational semantics of functional languages is often given as term rewriting [3, 8]. A functional program is a set of equations that are interpreted as left-to-right rewrite rules [2, 14]. The execution of the program for any input data (term) consists of the evaluation of the term using the rewrite rules until it cannot be further reduced (i.e. until a *normal form* is reached).

In *context-sensitive rewriting* [9], for each function symbol in the signature Σ, we fix the set of *replacing* positions by means of a mapping $\mu : \Sigma \to \mathcal{P}(I\!N)$ (the *replacement map*) which specifies the set of positions which can eventually be reduced. Given a term t, the subterm of t at the occurrence u is a redex of the context-sensitive rewrite relation, if it is a redex [2] and the symbols in t which label the occurrences above u satisfy the particular *replacement* condition.

Context-sensitive rewriting has some strong connections with the lazy strategies of functional programming languages. Actually, the mechanism which allows us to prevent the evaluation of some expressions can also be used to declare that these reductions need not be done. Although giving support to lazy reduction techniques is not the main purpose of our work, context-sensitive rewriting does allow us to express fixed, meaningful restrictions on rewriting, similar to the

---

* This work has been partially supported by CICYT under grant TIC 95-0433-C03-03.

way that lazy reduction techniques approximate 'needed' reductions à la Huet et Lévy [6].

Example 1.1 *Let us consider the standard functional definition of the* if-then-else *operation:*

if(true, x, y) → x

if(false, x, y) → y

Given an input if(cond, t, s), *we are not interested in reducing either* t *or* s *until the condition* cond *has been computed. By defining a replacement map such as* $\mu(\text{if}) = \{1\}$, *the undesirable reductions are avoided with no extra control. This enforces the 'intended meaning' of the* if-then-else *operation.*

In executing functional programs, context-sensitive rewriting is a suitable, easy way to reduce the associated reduction space. The restrictions are specified on a purely syntactic basis and the optimization applies to any program.

Confluence and termination are the main computational properties of a TRS. In a terminating system, the existence of a normal form is ensured for all input term. In a confluent TRS, all (existing) normal forms of terms are unique. Confluent and terminating TRSs are called canonical. Context-sensitive rewriting always preserves termination and can sometimes be improved [10]. The problem of ensuring confluence is addressed in this paper. We define a class of TRSs whose induced context-sensitive rewrite relation can be proved to be confluent. Therefore, given a replacement map μ we would be able to obtain a μ-*canonical* behavior (confluent and terminating w.r.t. the context-sensitive rewrite relation), even if the TRS is not canonical.

On the other hand, when considering confluent (constructor-based) programs, we would like to use context-sensitive rewriting to improve evaluations without sacrificing completeness. Context-sensitive rewriting can compute different normal forms for a given expression, since the confluence and the length of the derivations might be modified by the replacement restrictions. However, even if the context-sensitive rewrite relation is proved to be confluent and terminating, it is essential to characterize conditions to guarantee that the value which is computed by standard rewriting and the evaluation performed by context-sensitive rewriting coincide. In this case it makes sense to use context-sensitive rewriting instead of using standard rewriting.

In this paper, we formalize the conditions ensuring all the above requirements. We prove that these restrictions are not too strong by showing that some well-known examples fulfill the conditions imposed here. Our results also suggest adequate definitions of the replacement maps leading to further improvements in (context-sensitive) computations.

Some approaches which are related to our work can be found in [7, 11], although the problems that they address are different. They introduce some similar syntactic replacement restrictions on the arguments of function symbols, but the corresponding reduction relations are intended to deal with lazy rewriting in an *eager* mode by means of a program transformation [7] and to deal with the implementation of lazy reductions by means of graph reduction techniques based on a class of labeled TRSs [11]. Thus the underlying reduction relations are different to context-sensitive rewriting and the computational behavior and properties differ.

This paper is organized as follows. In Section 2, we briefly review the technical concepts and results used in the remainder of the paper. In Section 3, we formulate some basic properties of the context-sensitive rewrite relation and we illustrate the usefulness of context-sensitive rewriting in functional programming. Section 4 deals with the definition of an adequate notion of critical pair in context-sensitive rewriting and gives a criterion to ensure confluence on a certain class of programs. Section 5 characterizes the preservation of normal forms when using context-sensitive rewriting.

2 Preliminaries

Let us first introduce the main notations used in the paper. For full definitions we refer to [2, 5, 8]. Throughout the paper, V denotes a countable infinite set of variables and Σ denotes a set of function symbols $\{f, g, \ldots\}$, each with a fixed arity given by a function $ar : \Sigma \to \mathbb{N}$. By $T(\Sigma, V)$ we denote the set of terms. A k-tuple $t_1, \ldots, t_k$ of terms is denoted as $\bar{t}$, where k will be clarified from the context. Given a term t, $Var(t)$ is the set of variable symbols in t.

Terms are viewed as labelled trees in the usual way. Occurrences $u, v, \ldots$ are represented by chains of positive natural numbers used to address subterms of t. Occurrences are ordered by the standard prefix ordering: $u \leq v$ iff there is a chain v' such that $v = u.v'$. $u \parallel v$ means that u, v are not comparable by means of $\leq$. $O(t)$ denotes the set of occurrences of a term t. A linear term is a term having no multiple occurrences of variables. $t|_u$ is the subterm at occurrence u of t. $O_s(t)$ denotes the set of occurrences of s in t, i.e., $u \in O_s(t)$ iff $t|_u = s$. $t[s]_u$ is the term t with the subterm at the occurrence u replaced with s. $t[u]$ is the symbol labelling the root of the subterm $t|_u$. We refer to any term C, which is the same as t everywhere except below u, i.e. there exists a term s such that $C[s]_u = t$, as the *context* within the replacement occurs. Roughly speaking, a context is a term C with a 'hole' (i.e., a lambda-bound variable) at a specific occurrence u.

Let us recall the main concepts and notations about the lattice of first order terms. A substitution is a mapping $\sigma : V \to T(\Sigma, V)$. The quasi-ordering of subsumption $\leq$ in $T(\Sigma, V)$, $t \leq t' \Leftrightarrow \exists \sigma \; t' = \sigma(t)$, induces an equivalence $\equiv$ on $T(\Sigma, V)$: $t \equiv t' \Leftrightarrow t \leq t' \wedge t' \leq t$. The ordering $>$ can be defined as $t > t' \Leftrightarrow t' \leq t \wedge t \not\leq t'$. Let $\hat{T}$ be the quotient set $T(\Sigma, V)/\equiv$ completed with a *maximum* element $\top$. $\hat{T}$ is a complete lattice. We denote the lub of two terms t, t' as $t \sqcup t'$. This term is unique modulo $\equiv$ and can be found (if it exists) by a unification algorithm. If this lub exists, we write $t =^? t'$ and say that t and t' are unifiable. A term s *overlaps* a term t if it can be unified with some non variable subterm of t. s and t are not overlapping, if neither s overlaps t nor t overlaps s.

A rewrite rule is an ordered pair (l, r), written $l \to r$, with $l, r \in T(\Sigma, V)$, $l \notin V$ and $Var(r) \subseteq Var(l)$. l is said to be the left-hand side (*lhs*) of the rule and r is the right-hand side (*rhs*). A TRS is a pair $\mathcal{R} = (\Sigma, R)$ where R is a set of rewrite rules. A TRS (Σ, R) is *left linear*, if all *lhs* of rules in R are linear terms.

For a given TRS $\mathcal{R} = (\Sigma, R)$, a term t rewrites to a term s (at the occurrence u), written $t \to_{\mathcal{R}} s$, if $t|_u = \sigma(l)$ and $s = t[\sigma(r)]_u$, for some rule $l \to r$ in R, occurrence u in t and substitution σ. $\to_{\mathcal{R}}$ is the one-step rewrite relation for $\mathcal{R}$.

N_k^+ is an initial segment $\{1, 2, \ldots k\}$ of the set of positive natural numbers N^+, where $N_0^+ = \emptyset$. $\mathcal{P}(N)$ is the powerset of natural numbers.

3 Context-sensitive rewriting

In context-sensitive rewriting [9], we impose a syntactic-based restriction which prevents performing some reductions. This is achieved by the replacement map.

Definition 3.1 (Replacement map) *Let Σ be a signature. A mapping μ : $\Sigma \to \mathcal{P}(N)$ is a replacement map (or Σ-map) for the signature Σ iff for all $f \in \Sigma$. $\mu(f) \subseteq N_{ar(f)}^+$.*

Definition 3.2 (Partial order on replacement maps) *Let Σ be a signature. Let M_Σ be the set of all Σ-maps and let $\mu, \mu' \in M_\Sigma$. We define a partial order $\sqsubseteq$ on M_Σ as follows: $\mu \sqsubseteq \mu' \Leftrightarrow \forall f \in \Sigma$. $\mu(f) \subseteq \mu'(f)$.*

It is clear that $(M_\Sigma, \sqsubseteq, \mu_\perp, \mu_\top)$ is a complete lattice. The (bottom) Σ-map $\mu_\perp$ is $\mu_\perp(f) = \emptyset$ for all $f \in \Sigma$. The (top) Σ-map $\mu_\top$ is $\mu(f) = N_{ar(f)}^+$ for all $f \in \Sigma$.

The replacement map determines the positions of the arguments which can be reduced for a given symbol of the signature. The replacement condition indicates the occurrences which can be rewritten.

Definition 3.3 (Replacement condition) *Let Σ be a signature and μ be a Σ-map. Let $t \in \mathcal{T}(\Sigma, V)$ be a term. The replacement condition is a relation $\gamma_{\mu,t}$ defined on the set of occurrences $O(t)$ as follows:*

$\gamma_{\mu,t}(\varepsilon)$

$\gamma_{\mu,f(t_1,\ldots,t_k)}(i.u) \Leftrightarrow (i \in \mu(f)) \wedge \gamma_{\mu,t_i}(u)$

We say that u is a μ-replacing occurrence of t or that $t|_u$ is a μ-replacing subterm iff $\gamma_{\mu,t}(u)$ holds.

We write $\gamma_t(u)$ when the replacement map is clear from the context. We also introduce the following notation derived from the concept of replacement condition: let us denote as $O^\mu(t)$ the set of *replacing* occurrences of a term t i.e. $u \in O^\mu(t) \Leftrightarrow u \in O(t) \wedge \gamma_t(u)$. $\bar{O}^\mu(t)$ is the set of nonvariable replacing occurrences, $u \in \bar{O}^\mu(t) \Leftrightarrow u \in O^\mu(t) \wedge t|_u \notin Var(t)$. $O_s^\mu(t)$ is the set of replacing occurrences of a subterm s of t, i.e. $u \in O_s^\mu(t) \Leftrightarrow u \in O^\mu(t) \wedge t|_u = s$. Denote as $Var^\mu(t)$ the set of *replacing variables* of a term t, i.e. $x \in Var^\mu(t) \Leftrightarrow O_x^\mu(t) \neq \emptyset$.

Now we introduce the one-step context-sensitive rewrite relation.

Definition 3.4 (One-step context-sensitive rewrite relation) *Let $\mathcal{R} = (\Sigma, R)$ be a TRS and μ be a Σ-map. A term t μ-rewrites to a term s, written $t \hookrightarrow_{\mathcal{R}(\mu)} s$, if $t \to_{\mathcal{R}} s$ at the replacing occurrence $u \in O^\mu(t)$. $\hookrightarrow_{\mathcal{R}(\mu)}$ is the one-step context-sensitive rewrite relation of $\mathcal{R}$ wrt μ. $\hookrightarrow_{\mathcal{R}(\mu)}^*$ is the context-sensitive rewrite relation of $\mathcal{R}$ wrt μ.*

In the sequel, when it is clear from the context, we drop references to the TRS $\mathcal{R} = (\Sigma, R)$ and Σ-map μ writing $\hookrightarrow$ instead of $\hookrightarrow_{\mathcal{R}(\mu)}$. Let us now consider a first example of context-sensitive rewriting.

Example 3.5 *Let us consider the TRS $\mathcal{R} = (\Sigma, R)$ with $\Sigma = \{0, \text{true}, \text{false}, \text{s}, +, \text{and}, \text{if}\}$ and rules:*

$$\text{if}(\text{true}, x, y) \rightarrow x \qquad \text{and}(\text{true}, x) \rightarrow x \qquad 0 + x \rightarrow x$$
$$\text{if}(\text{false}, x, y) \rightarrow y \qquad \text{and}(\text{false}, y) \rightarrow \text{false} \qquad \text{s}(x) + y \rightarrow \text{s}(x + y)$$

Assume the Σ-map μ to be $\mu(\text{if}) = \{1\}$, and $\mu(f) = \mathbb{N}^+_{ar(f)}$ for all $f \in \Sigma \setminus \{\text{if}\}$. Then, (redexes underlined)

$$\text{if}(\underline{\text{and}(\text{true}, \text{false})}, \text{s}(0) + \text{s}(0), 0) \hookrightarrow \text{if}(\text{false}, \underline{\text{s}(0) + \text{s}(0)}, 0) \hookrightarrow 0$$

since 1 and ϵ are μ-replacing occurrences of $\text{if}(\text{and}(\text{true}, \text{false}), \text{s}(0) + \text{s}(0), 0)$ and $\text{if}(\text{false}, \text{s}(0) + \text{s}(0), 0)$, respectively. However,

$$\text{if}(\text{and}(\text{true}, \text{false}), \underline{\text{s}(0) + \text{s}(0)}, 0) \not\hookrightarrow \text{if}(\text{and}(\text{true}, \text{false}), \text{s}(0 + \text{s}(0)), 0)$$

since 2 is not a μ-replacing occurrence of $\text{if}(\text{and}(\text{true}, \text{false}), \text{s}(0) + \text{s}(0), 0)$.

Remark 3.6 *Note that with the (top) Σ-map μ_T, $\gamma_{\mu_T, t}(u)$ holds for all term t and occurrence $u \in O(t)$. This is to say that, given a TRS $\mathcal{R}$, the context-sensitive rewrite relation for μ_T coincides with the standard rewrite relation, i.e. $\hookrightarrow_{\mathcal{R}(\mu_T)} = \rightarrow_{\mathcal{R}}$.*

The following proposition basically states that context-sensitive rewriting is closed under *replacing* context application, as standard term rewriting is.

Proposition 3.7 (Restricted context replacements) *Let $C \in \mathcal{T}(\Sigma, V)$. Let $u \in O^\mu(C)$. If $t \hookrightarrow^n s$ with $n > 0$, then $C[t]_u \hookrightarrow^n C[s]_u$.*

The following proposition shows how the context-sensitive relations induced by different replacement maps compare.

Proposition 3.8 (Monotonicity of $\hookrightarrow$ with respect to the order $\sqsubseteq$) *Let $\mathcal{R} = (\Sigma, R)$ be a TRS and μ, μ' be Σ-maps. Then $\mu \sqsubseteq \mu' \Rightarrow \hookrightarrow_{\mathcal{R}(\mu)} \subseteq \hookrightarrow_{\mathcal{R}(\mu')}$.*

From a computational point of view, this proposition mainly states that context-sensitive rewriting gives rise to a reduction space which is smaller than the one of standard term rewriting (consider the Remark 3.6). Context-sensitive rewriting is also proven stable under substitution.

Proposition 3.9 (Stability of $\hookrightarrow$) *Let $\mathcal{R} = (\Sigma, R)$ be a TRS, μ be a Σ-map and $\sigma : V \rightarrow \mathcal{T}(\Sigma, V)$ be a substitution. Then $t \hookrightarrow s \Rightarrow \sigma(t) \hookrightarrow \sigma(s)$.*

3.1 Applications

Improving the evaluation of expressions.

As we illustrated in Examples 1.1 and 3.5, in some cases it makes sense to evaluate some fixed argument up to its normal form whenever this outcome is necessary to determine which rule has to be applied to an outer occurrence. The following example further develops the advantages of this strategy.

Example 3.10 *Let us consider the rules which define the* short-cut *boolean operators and/or of Lisp:*

$$\text{and}(\text{true}, x) \to x \qquad\qquad \text{or}(\text{true}, x) \to \text{true}$$
$$\text{and}(\text{false}, x) \to \text{false} \qquad \text{or}(\text{false}, x) \to x$$

To evaluate a term and(t, s) *(*or(t, s)*), according to these rules, if the first argument reduces to* false *(*true*), any reduction performed on the second argument is useless, and does not contribute to computing the intended value.*

By imposing the replacement map $\mu(\text{and}) = \mu(\text{or}) = \{1\}$, *we avoid the evaluation of redexes which are different from the first argument of the input term.*

Another case of study arises in the realm of lists.

Example 3.11 *The following rules define the standard 'projection' operators* head *and* tail *on lists:*

$$\text{head}(x :: y) \to x$$
$$\text{tail}(x :: y) \to y$$

The first function only requires the evaluation of the head of the list and the second one evaluates the rest of the list. These points are only of interest if cons (i.e. '::') does not evaluate its arguments systematically. Therefore, programming languages have been conceived where cons does not evaluate all arguments (see [4, 8]). This is easily achieved, for example, by defining $\mu(::) = \emptyset$.

Manipulation of infinite data structures.

Lazy cons in Example 3.11 is a suitable tool for computing with infinite data structures, as we illustrate in the following.

Example 3.12 *Let us consider the following program which selects one element from an infinite list.*

$$\text{sel}(0, x :: y) \to x \qquad\qquad \text{from}(x) \to x :: \text{from}(\text{s}(x))$$
$$\text{sel}(\text{s}(x), y :: z) \to \text{sel}(x, z)$$

We define $\mu(::) = \emptyset$ *and* $\mu(f) = \mathbb{N}^+_{ar(f)}$ *for any other operator f. Let us consider the following derivation:*

$$\text{sel}(\text{s}(\text{s}(0)), \underline{\text{from}(0)}) \hookrightarrow \underline{\text{sel}(\text{s}(\text{s}(0)), 0 :: \text{from}(\text{s}(0)))} \hookrightarrow$$
$$\underline{\text{sel}(\text{s}(0), \text{from}(\text{s}(0)))} \hookrightarrow$$
$$\underline{\text{sel}(\text{s}(0), \text{s}(0) :: \text{from}(\text{s}(\text{s}(0))))} \hookrightarrow$$
$$\underline{\text{sel}(0, \text{from}(\text{s}(\text{s}(0))))} \hookrightarrow$$
$$\underline{\text{sel}(0, \text{s}(\text{s}(0)) :: \text{from}(\text{s}(\text{s}(\text{s}(0)))))} \hookrightarrow$$
$$\text{s}(\text{s}(0))$$

This avoids incurring in non termination even if the third rule is not terminating, thus achieving the same effect as in lazy reduction strategies.

Safe computations.

The concept of *safe computation* is the operational counterpart of the semantic concept of *strictness* [8, 16]. Given a Scott domain[2] D, a function $f : D^k \to D$

---

[2] Any Scott domain has a least element which we denote $\perp$, see [15].

is strict in the i-th argument if $f(x_1, \ldots, x_{i-1}, \bot, \ldots, x_k) = \bot$. By interpreting (as usual) the bottom elements of domains as a *non-terminating* computation, the strictness information can be used to define a computation strategy. If we evaluate a strict argument, then the *non-termination of that evaluation will not prevent a value from being produced* [8].

A reduction strategy which always evaluates on safe contexts is called a *safe* strategy. A context $C[\ ]_u$ is safe, if $C[\bot]_u = \bot$. By defining the replacement map $\mu(f)$ as the set of *strict* arguments of f, for all symbol f in the signature, it is immediate to see that any replacing context $C[\ ]_u$, $u \in O^\mu(C)$, is a safe context. Then any context-sensitive derivation turns into a safe derivation.

Strictness information for the functions can be eventually obtained from some kind of strictness analysis [12, 17].

4 Confluence of context-sensitive rewriting

A binary relation R on a set A is *confluent* [2, 5, 8] if, for every $a, b, c \in A$, whenever a R$^*b$ and a R$^*c$, there exists $d \in A$ such that b R$^*d$ and c R$^*d$. Analogously, R is said to be *locally confluent*, if, for every $a, b, c \in A$, whenever a R b and a R c, there exists $d \in A$ such that b R$^*d$ and c R$^*d$. An element $\bar{a}$ is said to be an R-normal form, if there exists no b such that $\bar{a}$ R b. $\bar{a}$ is an R-normal form of a if $\bar{a}$ is an R-normal form and a R$^*\bar{a}$.

A relation R is *terminating* [2, 5] iff there is no infinite sequence a_1 R $a_2 \cdots a_n$ R $a_{n+1} \cdots$. In a terminating relation, each element $a \in A$ has a normal form. In a confluent noetherian relation, the normal form exists and it is *unique*.

We need to distinguish the computational properties of the standard rewrite relation and the analogous ones in context-sensitive rewriting. Therefore we will speak of μ-confluence and μ-termination for the confluence and termination properties of μ-rewriting, i.e., the context-sensitive rewriting which uses the replacement map μ.

We can prove termination of context-sensitive rewriting by using standard methods in rewriting [10].

Theorem 4.1 ([10], Theorem 4.3) *Let* $\mathcal{R} = (\Sigma, R)$ *be a TRS and* μ *be a* Σ-map. If $\mathcal{R}$ terminates, then $\mathcal{R}$ μ-terminates.

For example, the TRSs in Examples 1.1, 3.5, 3.10 and 3.11 prove to be μ-terminating: the instances of these rules can be oriented from left to right by means of a simplification ordering [1]. Many other TRSs are μ-terminating despite the fact that this simple technique does not apply.

Example 4.2 *Let us consider the nonterminating TRS* $\mathcal{R} = (\{s, ::, \text{from}\}, \{\text{from}(x) \to x :: \text{from}(s(x))\})$. *If we fix* μ *to be* $\mu(::) = \{1\}$, *then it is easy to verify that any* μ-rewriting sequence from a given term t using $\mathcal{R}$ will eventually terminate. A formal proof of μ-termination of this TRS can be given by using standard methods also [10].

The *diamond lemma* (Newman, [6, 13]) establishes that any locally-confluent terminating relation is confluent. We centre our discussion on analyzing μ-confluence through the study of local μ-confluence of μ-terminating TRSs.

4.1 Local confluence

In standard rewriting, a terminating TRS with non overlapping rules is confluent [5]. In context-sensitive rewriting, the fact that the rules do not overlap does not imply μ-confluence as we show in the following example.

Example 4.3 *Let us consider the following non overlapping TRS $\mathcal{R}$.*

$$f(x) \rightarrow g(x, x)$$
$$h(0) \rightarrow 0$$

If we define $\mu(f) = \{1\}$ and $\mu(g) = \{1\}$, then we have the following μ-rewriting chains leading to two different $\hookrightarrow$-normal forms for the considered input term:

$$f(\underline{h(0)}) \hookrightarrow g(\underline{h(0)}, h(0)) \hookrightarrow g(0, h(0))$$
$$\underline{f(\underline{h(0)})} \hookrightarrow \underline{f(0)} \hookrightarrow g(0, 0)$$

The following definition formalizes the class of TRSs which we can guarantee to be locally μ-confluent. The main idea is that if there is any variable occurrence in the *lhs* of a rewrite rule which satisfies the replacement condition, then any other occurrence of this variable in the rule must be a replacing occurrence too.

Definition 4.4 (TRS with left homogeneous replacing variables) *Let $\mathcal{R} = (\Sigma, R)$ be a TRS and μ be a Σ-map. Let us consider a rule $\rho : l \rightarrow r \in R$. We say that ρ has left homogeneous μ-replacing variables, if, for all $x \in Var^\mu(l)$, $O_x(l) = O_x^\mu(l)$ and $O_x(r) = O_x^\mu(r)$. The TRS $\mathcal{R}$ has left homogeneous μ-replacing variables, if all rules in R have left homogeneous μ-replacing variables.*

As usual, we drop references to the replacement map μ when no confusion can arise. For example, the TRSs in Examples 1.1, 3.5, 3.10 and 3.11 have left homogeneous replacing variables.

This restriction constrains the canonical nature of a TRS. As a counterpart, it is more difficult for the rules to (μ-) overlap. First, we introduce the concept of μ-overlapping terms.

Definition 4.5 (μ-overlapping terms) *Let $t, s \in \mathcal{T}(\Sigma, V)$ and μ be a Σ-map. s μ-overlaps t at the occurrence u, if $u \in \bar{O}^\mu(t)$ and $t|_u =^? s$. Terms t, s are not μ-overlapping, if neither s μ-overlaps t nor t μ-overlaps s*

Now, a suitable notion of non μ-overlapping TRSs can be given.

Definition 4.6 (μ-overlapping TRS) *Let $\mathcal{R} = (\Sigma, R)$ be a TRS and μ be a Σ-map. Given two rules $\rho_1 : l_1 \rightarrow r_1, \rho_2 : l_2 \rightarrow r_2 \in R$ such that l_1, l_2 have no common variable (otherwise rename rules), ρ_1 μ-overlaps ρ_2, if l_1 μ-overlaps l_2. ρ_1 and ρ_2 are trivial μ-overlapping rules, if $\rho_1 = \rho_2$ and ρ_1, ρ_2 μ-overlap at ϵ. The TRS $\mathcal{R}$ is non μ-overlapping, if it does not contain (nontrivial) overlapping rules.*

Now we introduce the adequate notion of critical pair [5] regarding context-sensitive rewriting.

Definition 4.7 (μ-critical pair) *Let $\mathcal{R} = (\Sigma, R)$ be a TRS and μ be a Σ-map. Let $\rho_1 : l_1 \to r_1$ and $\rho_2 : l_2 \to r_2$ be rewrite rules nontrivially μ-overlapping at the occurrence $u \in \bar{O}^\mu(l_1)$. Let $t = l_1|_u$ and $t' \equiv t \sqcup l_2$, with $Var(t') \cap Var(l_1) = \emptyset$. The superposition of ρ_1 and ρ_2 determines a μ-critical pair $\langle t_1, t_2 \rangle$ defined by $t_1 = \sigma_1(l_1)[\sigma_2(r_2)]_u$ and $t_2 = \sigma_1(r_1)$, where σ_1 is the matching of t' and t ($t' = \sigma_1(t)$) and σ_2 is the matching of t' and l_2 ($t' = \sigma_2(l_2)$).*

Note that any μ-critical pair of the TRS is also a standard critical pair. The following example shows how the replacement restrictions can be used to avoid some overlaps which otherwise could lead to non convergent reductions.

Example 4.8 *Let us consider the following TRS:*

$\quad g(b, a) \to b$

$\quad a \to b$

and a replacement map μ such that $\mu(g) = \{1\}$. This TRS has overlapping rules. However, since 2 is not a replacing occurrence in $g(b, a)$, then there is no μ-critical pair in the program.

In the following theorem, we write $t \downarrow t'$ to denote the context-sensitive joinability, i.e. $t \downarrow t'$, if there exists s such that $t \hookrightarrow^* s$ and $t' \hookrightarrow^* s$. By lack of space, we omit the proof.

Theorem 4.9 *Let $\mathcal{R} = (\Sigma, R)$ be a TRS with left homogeneous replacing variables wrt a Σ-map μ. $\mathcal{R}$ is locally μ-confluent iff for every μ-critical pair $\langle t_1, t_2 \rangle$ we have $t_1 \downarrow t_2$.*

Corollary 4.10 *A non μ-overlapping TRS with left homogeneous replacing variables is locally μ-confluent.*

4.2 Confluence

The following corollary allows us to devise a method to check confluence in a terminating TRS with left homogeneous replacing variables.

Corollary 4.11 *Let $\mathcal{R} = (\Sigma, R)$ be a TRS with left homogeneous replacing variables wrt a Σ-map μ. If $\mathcal{R}$ is μ-terminating, let us denote by $\bar{t}$ an arbitrary $\hookrightarrow$-normal form of $t \in T(\Sigma, V)$. Then $\mathcal{R}$ is μ-confluent iff for every μ-critical pair $\langle t_1, t_2 \rangle$ of $\mathcal{R}$ we have $\bar{t}_1 = \bar{t}_2$.*

Example 4.12 *Let us consider the TRS $\mathcal{R}$ and replacement map μ of Example 4.8. This TRS is not confluent. For example: $g(b, \underline{a}) \to g(b, b)$ and $\underline{g(b, a)} \to b$. Nevertheless, since $\mathcal{R}$ is terminating, by Theorem 4.1, $\mathcal{R}$ is μ-terminating. Since $\mathcal{R}$ has left homogeneous replacing variables, by Corollary 4.10, $\mathcal{R}$ is locally μ-confluent. Now, by Corollary 4.11, $\mathcal{R}$ is μ-confluent.*

Given a TRS with left homogeneous replacing variables, Corollary 4.11 suggests an effective way to test the confluence of $\hookrightarrow$ provided that the number of μ-critical pairs $\langle t_1, t_2 \rangle$ is finite. If $\hookrightarrow$ is terminating, for any μ-critical pair $\langle t_1, t_2 \rangle$, we can finitely compute $\bar{t}_1$ and $\bar{t}_2$ and then check whether $\bar{t}_1 = \bar{t}_2$.

5 Preserving meaning in confluent constructor-based TRSs

We have characterized a kind of TRSs whose μ-confluence can be proved. We have also provided a suitable method to check μ-confluence in such TRSs. Now we focus on the question of coherence between standard evaluations in a TRS $\mathcal{R}$ and the corresponding context-sensitive computations for a given replacement map μ. The following example motivates the argument.

Example 5.1 *Let us consider the following (canonical) TRS $\mathcal{R}$:*

$$f(x, y) \to g(x, y)$$
$$g(b, b) \to b$$
$$a \to b$$

and a replacement map μ such that $\mu(f) = \mu(g) = \{1\}$. Then $\mathcal{R}$ has left homogeneous replacing variables, it is not μ-overlapping and it is terminating. By Theorem 4.1, Corollary 4.10 and Corollary 4.11, $\mathcal{R}$ is μ-confluent. However, we have:

1. $f(b, a) \hookrightarrow g(b, a)$ *and* $g(b, a)$ *is a* $\hookrightarrow$*-normal form, but it is not the* $\to$*-normal form of* $f(b, a)$ *since,*
2. $f(b, a) \to g(b, \underline{a}) \to \underline{g(b, b)} \to b.$

In other words, in spite of the fact that both relations $\hookrightarrow$ and $\to$ are terminating and confluent, the respective normal forms for the considered input term are different.

In this section, we centre our attention in *constructor based* TRSs. In the *constructor based* style of functional programming, the signature is the disjoint union $\Sigma = \mathcal{C} \uplus \mathcal{F}$ of two classes of symbols: symbols $c \in \mathcal{C}$, called *constructors*, that construct data terms, and symbols $f \in \mathcal{F}$, called *defined functions* or *operations*, that operate on data terms. Given a k-ary constructor symbol c, we also consider the set $\mathcal{H}_\Sigma(c) = \{c(t_1, \ldots, t_k) \mid t_i \in \mathcal{T}(\Sigma, V)\}$ of c - head normal forms (or just c-hnf).

Almost all TRSs in this paper are constructor based. Rules in such TRSs are as follows: $f(\tilde{\alpha}) \to r$, where $f \in \mathcal{F}$, $\tilde{\alpha} \in \mathcal{T}(\mathcal{C}, V)^{ar(f)}$ and $r \in \mathcal{T}(\Sigma, V)$. The constructor discipline is a usual practice in functional programming, and it is not considered to be too restrictive a framework to work in practice. In this section, all TRSs are assume to be *constructor based* unless we state otherwise.

In this setting, given a term t we distinguish between its *normal form* $\bar{t}$, which is a term, and its *evaluation* or *value* (its 'meaning') α, which is a *constructor term*. Computations not leading to values are considered to be failing. In the remainder of this paper, we are only concerned with succesful computations for contructor based TRSs.

5.1 Restrictions on the TRSs

Given a TRS, we are not only interested in reducing the computation space but also in computing the intended value (by context-sensitive rewriting) for a given term without losing completeness. In the evaluation of a term $t = f(\tilde{t})$, $f \in \mathcal{F}$, we can distinguish two kinds of steps:

1. Eventual reduction of the arguments $\tilde{t}$, i.e., application of the rewrite rules to some (subterm of) t_i, $1 \leq i \leq ar(f)$.
2. Reduction of t, i.e., a rewrite rule $f(\tilde{\alpha}) \to r$ (we call a f-rule) is applied to it (at the occurrence ϵ).

Note that the first kind of step can sometimes be avoided, while steps of the second kind must always be performed since the value of t is a constructor term. Therefore, at some stage of the computation, an f-rule should be applied. To do this, it could be necessary to evaluate the arguments.

Let us consider an outermost operation-rooted (proper) subterm s of t (i.e. $s = g(\tilde{s}) = t|_u$, $g \in \mathcal{F}$, and for all $v \in O(t)$, s.t. $\epsilon < v < u$, we have $t[v] \in \mathcal{C}$). We have the following cases to consider:

1. The rule does not demand evaluation of s, and s is a residual of t, i.e., s is a subterm of the *rhs* of the instantiated f-rule.
2. The rule does not demand evaluation of s, and s is *lost*, i.e., s does not occur in the *rhs* of the instantiation of the f-rule.
3. It is necessary to evaluate s before the application of the f-rule.

With these considerations in mind, we can find adequate restrictions on the rules of a TRS in order to safely improve the efficiency of the computations.

Firstly, if we delay the evaluation of an argument until the rule has been applied, in general, the constructor symbols (defined by no rule) should not restrict replacements.

Definition 5.2 ($\mathcal{C}$-replacing TRS) *Let $\mathcal{R} = (\Sigma, R)$ be a TRS and μ a Σ-map. We say that $\mathcal{R}$ is a $\mathcal{C}$-replacing TRS iff, for all $c \in \mathcal{C}$, $\mu(c) = \mathbb{N}_{ar(c)}^+$.*

TRSs in Examples 1.1, 3.5 and 3.10 are $\mathcal{C}$-replacing. TRSs in Examples 3.11 and 3.12 are *not* $\mathcal{C}$-replacing.

In order to be sure that the evaluation of an argument is not demanded by a rule, the *local matching* of a non replacing position should not depend on any previous reduction of the corresponding argument. This can be ensured by imposing the condition that non replacing occurrences of the *lhs* of the rules can only be variables. This restriction has to be strengthened to deal with the case when multiple occurrences of variables appear in the *lhs* of a rule.

Definition 5.3 (Replacing independent TRS) *Let $\mathcal{R} = (\Sigma, R)$ be a TRS and μ a Σ-map. We say that $\mathcal{R}$ is replacing independent if it is left-linear and the non replacing occurrences of the lhs of the rules of $\mathcal{R}$ are variables: for all $l \to r \in R$ and $u \in O(l)$, $\neg\gamma_l(u) \Rightarrow l|_u \in V$.*

For instance, TRSs in Examples 1.1, 3.5 and 3.10 are replacing independent. The TRS in Example 5.1 is *not* replacing independent.

Remark 5.4 *The twofold restriction of being a C-replacing and replacing independent TRS amounts to saying that, given any rule $f(\tilde{\alpha}) \rightarrow r$ of the TRS, the non replacing arguments α_j, $j \notin \mu(f)$ of the rule must be variables.*

The following lemma characterizes how C-replacing, replacing independent TRSs behave. Roughly speaking, under the imposed restrictions on the TRS, we just need to take into account (a subset of) the replacing arguments of f to apply a rule to an operation rooted term $t = f(\tilde{t})$.

Lemma 5.5 *Let $\mathcal{R} = (\Sigma, R)$ be a TRS and μ a Σ-map such that $\mathcal{R}$ is C-replacing and replacing independent. Let $t = f(\tilde{t})$ and $f(\tilde{\alpha}) \rightarrow r \in R$. Then t μ-rewrites at the occurrence ϵ iff for all $i \in \mu(f)$ such that $\alpha_i \notin V$ there is a substitution $\sigma' : V' \rightarrow T(\Sigma, V)$, where $V' = \bigcup_{\alpha \in \{\alpha_i \mid i \in \mu(f) \wedge \alpha_i \notin V\}} Var(\alpha)$, such that $\sigma'(\alpha_i) = t_i$.*

PROOF. The *only if* part is immediate. For the *if* part, since the non replacing arguments α_j, $j \notin \mu(f)$ of the rule are variables, we complete σ' to a substitution $\sigma : Var(t) \rightarrow T(\Sigma, V)$ by adding bindings α_j/t_j for these variables, and bindings α_i/t_i for arguments α_i, $i \in \mu(f)$ such that $\alpha_i \in V$. No clashes arise because $\mathcal{R}$ is left linear. Then $\sigma(f(\tilde{\alpha})) = f(\tilde{t})$ and the rule applies to the occurrence ϵ of t. $\square$

5.2 Preservation of evaluations

Before we are able to give the main result of this section, we need some preliminary results. The first lemma establishes that, whenever a rewriting derivation in a confluent TRS leads from a term to a head normal form, any other derivation starting from this same term can eventually reach a head normal form.

Lemma 5.6 *Let $\mathcal{R} = (\Sigma, R)$ be a confluent TRS. Let t and $t' \in \mathcal{H}_\Sigma(c)$ and $t \rightarrow^* t'$. Then, for any other derivation $t \rightarrow^* s$ starting from t, there is a term $t'' \in \mathcal{H}_\Sigma(c)$ such that $s \rightarrow^* t''$.*

PROOF. Since $\mathcal{R}$ is confluent, any other derivation $t \rightarrow^* s$ verifies that there exists t'' such that $t' \rightarrow^* t''$ and $s \rightarrow^* t''$. Since $t' = c(\tilde{t})$ and there are no rules defining c, t'' is a c-hnf. $\square$

The following lemma states that, in a C-replacing and replacing independent TRS, if there is a rewriting derivation from a term leading to a head normal form, then this term can be μ-rewritten.

Lemma 5.7 *Let $\mathcal{R} = (\Sigma, R)$ be a confluent TRS and μ a Σ-map such that $\mathcal{R}$ is C-replacing and replacing independent. Let $t = f(\tilde{t})$ for some $f \in \mathcal{F}$ and $t' \in \mathcal{H}_\Sigma(c)$, for some $c \in C$. If $t \rightarrow^+ t'$, then there exists some term $t'' \in T(\Sigma, V)$ such that $t \hookrightarrow t''$.*

PROOF. By structural induction on t. The case when t is a constant is immediate. Let us consider the induction case. Since t' is a c-hnf, some f-rule $f(\tilde{\alpha}) \rightarrow r$ must be applied in some step. By Lemma 5.6, any derivation starting from t can be completed to reach a c-hnf. Therefore, we fix a *lazy* strategy for the derivation and consider two cases:

1. The f-rule $f(\tilde{\alpha}) \to r$ can be used to reduce t at the occurrence ϵ with matching substitution σ. Then $t \to s \to^* t'$, with $s = \sigma(r)$. Therefore, $t \hookrightarrow t'$. Now, it suffices to take $t'' = s$ and the conclusion follows.

2. The evaluation of some arguments is demanded. By Lemma 5.5, we just need to evaluate the arguments t_i such that $i \in \mu(f)$ and $\alpha_i \notin V$. Let $s = t_i|_u = g(\tilde{s})$, $g \in \mathcal{F}$, be an outermost operation rooted subterm of t_i whose evaluation is needed. Since $\alpha_i|_u$ is a hnf (for example, a d-hnf for some $d \in C$), we have $s \to^+ s'$ and $s' \in \mathcal{H}_\Sigma(d)$. By I.H. $s \hookrightarrow s''$ for some term s''. Therefore, because $\mathcal{R}$ is C-replacing, $i.u \in O^\mu(t)$. By taking $t'' = f(t_1, \ldots, t_i[s'']_u, \ldots, t_k)$, where $k = ar(f)$, and by Proposition 3.7, $t \hookrightarrow t''$. Therefore the conclusion follows.

$\square$

The following theorem is the main result in this section. It formalizes the conditions which ensure that the evaluation of a term by term rewriting can be mimicked by context-sensitive rewriting.

Theorem 5.8 *Let $\mathcal{R} = (\Sigma, R)$ be a confluent TRS and μ a Σ-map such that $\mathcal{R}$ is C-replacing and replacing independent. Let $t \in T(\Sigma, V)$ and $\alpha \in T(C, V)$. $t \to^* \alpha$ iff $t \hookrightarrow^* \alpha$.*

PROOF. The *if* part is immediate, since $\hookrightarrow \subseteq \to$. For the *only if* part, we proceed by induction on the length n of the derivation $t \to^* \alpha$. The base case $(n = 0)$ is immediate. For the induction step $(n > 0)$, let us consider the derivation $t \to t' \to^* \alpha$. Let $u \in O(t)$ be an outermost occurrence of t such that $s = t|_u = f(\tilde{t})$. We must reduce s to a constructor term $\beta = c(\tilde{\beta})$ such that $\alpha|_u = \beta$. Therefore, $s \to^+ c(\tilde{s}) \to^* \beta$. By Lemma 5.7, $s \hookrightarrow s'$ for some term s'. Since $\mathcal{R}$ is confluent and $\hookrightarrow \subseteq \to$, we can take $t' = t[s']_u$. Now, since $\mathcal{R}$ is C-replacing, $u \in O^\mu(t)$. By Proposition 3.7, $t \hookrightarrow t'$. By I.H., $t' \hookrightarrow^* \alpha$, which proves the claim. $\square$

As an example, the TRSs in Examples 1.1, 3.5, 3.10 can be safely run using context-sensitive rewriting: standard rewriting and context-sensitive rewriting compute the same value for a given term and allows one to avoid many useless reduction steps.

It is not possible, in general, to extend this result to computing *normal forms* as the following example shows.

Example 5.9 *Let us consider the TRS:*

$$f(x) \to g(x, x)$$
$$g(0, x) \to 0$$
$$h(0) \to 0$$
$$h(s(0)) \to 0$$

Let us take $\mu(f) = \mu(g) = \mu(h) = \mu(s) = \{1\}$. This TRS fulfills the conditions in Theorem 5.8. Now $g(s(0), \underline{h(0)}) \to g(s(0), 0)$, which is a $\to$-normal form. However, $g(s(0), h(0))$ is already in $\hookrightarrow$-normal form. Note that $g(s(0), 0) \notin T(C, V)$.

From Theorem 5.8, even if the (confluent) TRS is *not* μ-confluent, the evaluations by means of $\hookrightarrow$ do converge.

As an additional consequence, it is worth noting that, by Theorem 5.8, having left homogeneous replacing variables is *not* a necessary condition to ensure μ-confluence, as the following example shows.

Example 5.10 *Let us consider the canonical TRS* $\mathcal{R}$:

$\mathbf{f}(x) \rightarrow \mathbf{g}(x, x)$

$\mathbf{g}(0, x) \rightarrow 0$

$\mathbf{h}(0) \rightarrow 0$

and replacement map $\mu(\mathbf{f}) = \mu(\mathbf{g}) = \mu(\mathbf{h}) = \{1\}$. *Note that all* $\rightarrow$-*normal forms are constructor terms. Therefore, by Theorem 5.8,* $\mathcal{R}$ *is also* μ-*confluent. But it does* not *have left homogeneous replacing variables.*

These results suggest an effective way to compute with context-sensitive rewriting instead of rewriting. By choosing a minimal replacement map satisfying the C-replacing and replacing independence restrictions of Definitions 5.2 and 5.3, we can obtain the greatest (complete) improvement. For instance, if we consider the program in the Example 3.5, we could still define $\mu(\text{and}) = \{1\}$ (and indeed $\mu(+) = \{1\}$) to further improve the efficiency without changing the semantics.

6 Conclusions

From the computational point of view, context-sensitive rewriting allows one to achieve more efficient computations in comparison with standard rewriting. Termination is preserved or enhanced by context-sensitive rewriting [10]. Confluence can sometimes be enhanced but could also be lost. We have established a class of TRS which prove to be confluent. We have also established some syntactic conditions to ensure that computations are kept under context-sensitive rewriting. This suggests a method for defining a suitable replacement map which enables efficient and complete context-sensitive computations.

The theory which was developed in the previous section only applies to C-replacing programs. For more general programs, the development can be more involved. For instance, the term $0 :: \mathbf{s}(0) :: \mathbf{tail}(0 :: \mathbf{nil})$ is not μ-evaluable by means of the TRS of Example 3.11. This is due to the restriction $\mu(::) = \emptyset$. Nevertheless, depending on the input term and TRS, we could even obtain complete evaluations. For instance, $\mathbf{sel}(\mathbf{s}(0), 0 :: \mathbf{s}(0) :: \mathbf{tail}(0 :: \mathbf{nil}))$ can be evaluated (to the value $\mathbf{s}(0)$ by the TRS in the Example 3.12, in spite of the fact that the operator $::$ has the same replacement restrictions.

The study of this more general kind of program is the subject of further work.

References

1. N. Dershowitz. Termination of rewriting. *Journal on Symbolic Computation* 3:69-115, 1987.

422

2. N. Dershowitz and J.P. Jouannaud. Rewrite Systems. In J. van Leeuwen, editor, *Handbook of Theoretical Computer Science*, volume B: Formal Models and Semantics, pages 243-320. Elsevier, Amsterdam and The MIT Press, Cambridge, MA, 1990.
3. H. Ehrig and B. Mahr. Fundamentals of Algebraic Specification. Volume 6 of *EATCS Monographs on Theoretical Computer Science*. Springer-Verlag, Berlin, 1985.
4. D.P. Friedman and D.S. Wise. CONS should not evaluate its arguments. In S. Michaelson and R. Milner, editors, *Automata, Languages and Programming*, pages 257-284, Edinburgh University Press, 1976.
5. G. Huet. Confluent reductions: abstract properties and applications to term rewriting systems. *Journal of the ACM* 27:797-821, 1980.
6. G. Huet and J.J. Lévy. Computations in orthogonal term rewriting systems. In J.L. Lassez and G. Plotkin, editors, *Computational logic: essays in honour of J. Alan Robinson*, MIT Press, Cambridge, MA, 1991.
7. J.F.Th. Kamperman and H.R. Walters. Lazy Rewriting and Eager Machinery. In J. Hsiang, editor, *Proc. of the 6th International Conference on Rewriting Techniques and Applications, RTA'95*, LNCS 914:147-162, Springer-Verlag, Berlin, 1995.
8. R. Lalement. Computation as Logic. Masson-Prentice Hall International, 1993.
9. S. Lucas. Fundamentals of context-sensitive rewriting. In M. Bartôsek, J. Staudek and J. Wiedermann, editors, *Proc. of XXII Seminar on Current Trends in Theory and Practice of Informatics, SOFSEM'95*, LNCS 1012:405-412, Springer-Verlag, Berlin, 1995.
10. S. Lucas. Termination of context-sensitive rewriting by rewriting. In F. Meyer auf der Heide and B. Monien, editors, *Proc. of 23rd. International Colloquium on Automata, Languages and Programming, ICALP'96*, LNCS 1099:122-133, Springer-Verlag, Berlin, 1996.
11. L. Maranget. Optimal Derivations in Weak Lambda-calculi and in Orthogonal Term Rewriting Systems In *Conference Record of the 18th ACM Symposium on Principles of Programming Languages*, pages 255-269, ACM Press, 1990.
12. A. Mycroft. The theory and practice of transforming call-by-need into call-by-value. In *Proc. of the fourth International Symposium on Programming*, LNCS 83:269-281, Springer-Verlag, Berlin, 1980.
13. M.H.A. Newman. On theories with a combinatorial definition of 'equivalence'. *Ann. Math.*, 43:223-243, 1942.
14. C. Reade. Elements of Functional Programming. Addison-Wesley Publishing Company, 1987.
15. J.E. Stoy. Denotational semantics: the Scott-Strachey approach to programming language theory. The MIT Press, Cambridge MA, 1977.
16. J. Vuillemin Correct and optimal implementation of recursion in a simple programming language. *JCSS* 9(3):332-354, 1974.
17. P. Wadler. Strictness Analysis on Non-Flat Domains (by Abstract Interpretation over Finite Domains). In S. Abramsky and C. Hankin, editors, *Abstract Interpretation of Declarative Languages*, Ellis Horwood Ltd., John Wiley and sons, pages 266-275, 1987.

Models for Using Stochastic Constraint Solvers in Constraint Logic Programming

Peter J. Stuckey and Vincent Tam

Dept. of Computer Science, The University of Melbourne, Parkville 3052, Australia.
{pjs,vtam}@cs.mu.oz.au

Abstract. This paper proposes a number of models for integrating stochastic constraint solvers into constraint logic programming systems in order to solve constraint satisfaction problems efficiently. Stochastic solvers can solve hard constraint satisfaction problems very efficiently, and constraint logic programming allows heuristics and problem breakdown to be encoded in the same language as the constraints. Hence their combination is attractive. Unfortunately there is a mismatch in the kind of information a stochastic solver provides, and that which a constraint logic programming system requires. We study the semantic properties of the various models of constraint logic programming systems that make use of stochastic solvers, and give soundness and completeness results for their use. We describe an example system we have implemented using a modified neural network simulator, GENET, as a constraint solver. We briefly compare the efficiency of these models against the propagation based solver approaches typically used in constraint logic programming.

1 Introduction

This paper proposes a general framework for integrating constraint logic programming (CLP) with a stochastic constraint solver to solve constraint satisfaction problems (CSP's) more efficiently. A CSP involves a set of variables, each of which has a domain of possible values, and a constraint formula, limiting the combination of values for a subset of variables. The task is to assign values to the variables so that the constraint formula is satisfied.

CSP's occur in a large number of applications, such as computer vision, planning, resource allocation, scheduling and temporal reasoning. But CSP's are, in general, NP-complete. Thus, a general algorithm designed to solve any CSP will necessarily require exponential time[1] in the worst case. Constraint logic programming systems have been successfully used to tackle a number of industrial CSP applications such as car sequencing [3], disjunctive scheduling [14] and firmware design [4]. Stochastic search methods have also had remarkable success in solving industrial CSP's [13] and constraint satisfaction optimisation problems (CSOPs) [1, 5].

Constraint logic programming systems use a constraint solver to direct a search for an answer to goal. When the constraint solver determines that the constraints collected on some derivation path are unsatisfiable, the CLP system

---

[1] Assuming $P \neq NP$.

backtracks and tries a different derivation path. Thus the key behaviour of the solver is its determining of unsatisfiability correctly. Typically, constraint solvers are incomplete, that is they do not answer for every constraint whether it is satisfiable or unsatisfiable. For example, many real number constraint solvers treat non-linear constraints incompletely, and integer constraint solvers are also typically incomplete. The major requirement of the incomplete solver in a CLP system is determining unsatisfiability, that is, as often as possible if a constraint C is unsatisfiable, then $solv(C) = false$.

Most constraint solvers in a CLP system used to solve CSP's employ the technique of constraint propagation to solve the set of constraints. Thus, they are algorithmic in nature. In order to guarantee finding a solution, these solvers are augmented with some form of enumerative search. When the CSP is tight,[2] this search may be very costly.

Many of the methods traditionally used in solving CSP's are not propagation based. A major class of CSP solving techniques are stochastic methods, for example: simulated annealing, neural networks and evolutionary algorithms. These algorithms are designed to find solutions to constraint problems, using a relaxation-based search. The methods are in general not guaranteed to find a solution, and typically involve a resource bound on the search which determines how long and how likely to find a solution the method will be. Such solvers do not usually ever determine when a constraint is unsatisfiable. But these kinds of solvers can be considerably more efficient than propagation based solvers on large or hard instance of CSP's. The problem we examine is how such solvers can be used efficiently in CLP systems.

Earlier approaches that considered incorporating stochastic solvers into CLP systems are restricted to one of the models we discuss. Lee and Tam [9] required the program to execute only a single derivation so that backtracking could never occur. At the end of the single derivation the stochastic solver (the GENET algorithm discussed later) determines a solution. Illera and Ortiz [6] use a genetic algorithm to search for a good solution to a constraint which is collected by a CLP system, hence using a stochastic method to tackle a CSOP. Both these papers show how using stochastic methods instead of enumeration methods traditional to CLP can lead to substantial benefits. Neither of these works use the stochastic constraint solver to control the search for a successful derivation; rather it is used only as a solution finder, hence most of the issues dealt with in this paper do not arise.

This paper is organised as follows. Section 2 briefly introduces some preliminaries for subsequent discussion. Section 3 describes various models for how a stochastic solver can be used within a CLP system, while Section 4 gives soundness and completeness results for these various models. In section 5, we briefly describe the GENET [13, 2] model which is a probabilistic artificial neural networks(ANN) used as the constraint solver to demonstrate the feasibility of our approach. We describe how we adopt the original model to support efficient incremental execution with backtracking on constraints. Section 6 gives our experimental results.

---

[2] A *tight* CSP has few solutions over a large search space.

2 Preliminaries

We briefly introduce constraint logic programming, for more details see [7]. A *constraint domain* $\mathcal{A}$ is a structure defining the meaning of the primitive constraints. A *primitive constraint* is of the form $r(t_1, \ldots, t_n)$ where r is a relation defined by $\mathcal{A}$ and $t_1, \ldots, t_n$ are terms over the constraint domain, e.g. $X > Y + 2$ is a primitive constraint over the domain of integer constraints. A *constraint* is of the form $c_1 \wedge \cdots \wedge c_n$ where $n \geq 0$ and $c_1, \cdots, c_n$ are primitive constraints. When $n = 0$, we shall usually write the constraint as *true*. A *valuation* θ for a set S of variables is an assignment of values from the domain of $\mathcal{A}$ to the variables in S. Suppose $S = \{X_1, \cdots, X_n\}$; then θ may be written $\{X_1 \mapsto a_1, \cdots, X_n \mapsto a_n\}$ indicating that each variable X_i is assigned the value a_i.

Let $vars(F)$ denote the set of variables occurring in a formula F. Let $\bar{\exists}_V F$ represent the formula $\exists w_1 \cdots \exists w_k F$ where $\{w_1, \ldots, w_k\} = vars(F) - V$. Let $\bar{\exists}F$ represent the formula $\bar{\exists}_\emptyset F$, the existential closure of F. If θ is a valuation for $S \supseteq vars(c)$, then it is a *solution* of c if the replacement of each variable by its value (as given by θ) yields a true statement, that is $\mathcal{A} \models_\theta c$.

A constraint c is *satisfiable* if there exists solution θ of c. Otherwise it is *unsatisfiable*. A *constraint solver*, *solv*, for a constraint domain $\mathcal{A}$ takes as input any constraint c in $\mathcal{A}$ and returns *true*, *false* or *unknown*. Whenever $solv(c)$ returns *true* the constraint c must be satisfiable, and whenever $solv(c)$ return *false* the constraint c must be unsatisfiable.

An *atom*, A, is of the form $p(t_1, \ldots, t_n)$ where p is a n-ary *predicate symbol* and $t_1, \ldots, t_n$ are terms. A *goal* G is a sequence of atoms and primitive constraints $L_1, \cdots, L_n$. A *rule*, R, is of the form $A\text{:-}B$ where A is an atom and B is a goal. A is called the *head* of R and B is called the *body* of R.

Execution proceeds by mapping one state to another. A *state* is a pair written $\langle G|c \rangle$ where c is a constraint and G is a goal.

$$L_1, \cdots, L_{i-1}, L_i, L_{i+1}, \cdots, L_m$$

where L_j, $1 \leq j \leq m$ are literals and L_i is the *selected literal*. There are two cases.

(a) L_i is a primitive constraint. Then c_1 is $c_0 \wedge L_i$ and, if $solv(c_1) = false$, G_1 is the empty goal written $\square$; otherwise G_1 is $L_1, \cdots, L_{i-1}, L_{i+1}, \cdots, L_m$.

(b) L_i is an atom $p(t_1, \cdots, t_n)$. Let R be a renamed version of a rule in P, sharing no variables with $\langle G_0|c_0 \rangle$ of the form

$$p(s_1, \cdots, s_n) \leftarrow B_1, \cdots, B_k.$$

Then c_1 is c_0 and G_1 is $L_1, \cdots, L_{i-1}, s_1 = t_1, \cdots, s_n = t_n, B_1, \cdots, B_k, L_{i+1}, \cdots, L_m$.

A *partial derivation* is a sequence of states $\langle G_0|c_0 \rangle \Rightarrow \langle G_1|c_1 \rangle \Rightarrow \cdots$ where at each stage $i \geq 0$ the selected literal is given by some *selection strategy* and $\langle G_i|c_i \rangle \Rightarrow \langle G_{i+1}|c_{i+1} \rangle$. A *derivation* is a maximal length partial derivation. A derivation is *successful* if it is finite and the last state $\langle \square|c_n \rangle$ is such that $solv(c_n) \neq false$. If $\langle G_0|true \rangle \Rightarrow \cdots \Rightarrow \langle \square|c_n \rangle$ is a successful derivation then $\bar{\exists}_{vars(G)} c_n$ is an *answer* to the goal G. A derivation is *finitely failed* if it is finite and at the last state $solv(c_n) = false$. Thus a derivation only terminates by success or the solver detecting an unsatisfiable constraint. Otherwise the derivation is infinite. A derivation is *fair* if it is finitely failed or each literal appearing in the derivation is eventually selected. A selection strategy is fair if it always produces fair derivations.

It will later be useful to refer to partial derivations where the last step is always a derivation step of type (a). Let $\langle G_0|c_0\rangle \overset{(a)}{\Rightarrow} \langle G_1|c_1\rangle$ represent a sequence of any number of type (b) derivation steps followed by a type (a) derivation step. Clearly for a partial derivation of the form $\langle G_0|c_0\rangle \overset{(a)}{\Rightarrow} \langle G_1|c_1\rangle \overset{(a)}{\Rightarrow} \cdots \overset{(a)}{\Rightarrow} \langle G_n|c_n\rangle$ the constraint solver is invoked on each of the constraints $c_1, c_2, \ldots, c_n$.

3 Using a Stochastic Solver

Consider the following simple example of a stochastic constraint solver for Boolean conjunctive normal form constraints (based on an algorithm by Wu and Tang [15]).

```
BOOL_SOLVE(c, ε)
Let m be the number of clauses in c
n := ln ε/ ln(1 − (1 − 1/m)^m)
for i := 1 to n
        generate a random truth assignment θ
        if cθ is true return true
endfor
return unknown
```

This algorithm is a randomised polynomial time algorithm for solving a Boolean constraint c. The second argument ϵ gives a bound on its incompleteness. Applied to a satisfiable constraint c, the algorithm[3] will return *true* with probability $1-\epsilon$ (this is quite deep result of [15]). So, ϵ is the probability that the solver returns *unknown* when the constraint c is satisfiable. All known complete solvers for this problem are exponential while this algorithm is polynomial. But this solver never returns *false* because it can never determine that constraint c is unsatisfiable. Hence it seems difficult to use it in the context of a CLP system where we need failure to prune the search space.

Because stochastic solvers in general can never determine unsatisfiability, when applied to an unsatisfiable constraint they will execute forever unless some limit is placed on them. Hence they usually have a resource limit, for example, the iteration limit n in BOOL_SOLVE. Thus, we define a stochastic constraint solver as a solver that takes two arguments, a constraint and a resource bound.

Definition 1. (Stochastic Solver) A stochastic solver *solv* takes a constraint c and resource limit n, and either returns

(a) *true*, a solution and the amount of resources used to find a solution, e.g. $solv(c, n) = \langle true, \theta, m \rangle$ where $m \leq n$,

---

[3] Assuming no individual clause is trivially false, or true.

(b) *unknown*, the empty valuation and the resource limit, e.g. $solv(c, n) = \langle unknown, \lambda, n \rangle$ where λ is an empty valuation.

We also define $res(\langle x_1, x_2, x_3 \rangle) = x_3$ and $truth(\langle x_1, x_2, x_3 \rangle) = x_1$.

Stochastic solvers are generally randomised algorithms hence they define a probability of finding a solution for some satisfiable constraint c. We assume if c is a satisfiable constraint, then $Pr(truth(solv(c, n)) = true) > 0$ if $n > 0$. That is the solver always has a chance of finding solution given some resources. We assume if c is an unsatisfiable constraint, $Pr(truth(solv(c, n)) = unknown) = 1$ whatever resource bound n is used. That is the solver is correct and never returns *false*[4]. We also assume for technical convenience that $Pr(truth(solv(c, -1)) = unknown) = 1$. That is given negative resources the solver always returns unknown.

Because of the mismatch in the type of information that a stochastic solver provides with that required by a CLP system several useful models arise for using a stochastic solver within a CLP system.

3.1 Model A

Stochastic solver as a constraint solver. The most obvious combination is to use the stochastic constraint solver to control the derivations. Clearly because a stochastic constraint solver only ever returns *true* or *unknown* it will never cause execution to backtrack if used directly. Hence at some stage, we must assume its failure to find a solution indeed indicates that the constraint is unsatisfiable. Thus we must sometimes treat the answer *unknown* as *false*. Clearly this will lead to incompleteness, but there are already a number of sources of incompleteness for CLP systems. For general CLP programs depth-first search and unfair literal selection lead to incompleteness. Many CLP programs to solve CSPs are guaranteed to only have finite derivations, so these problems cannot arise. But, even though guaranteed complete, the search for a solution may take too long, leading to a kind of "in practice" incompleteness. Hence we should be willing to accept the incompleteness of model A if it is not too great.

3.2 Model B

Stochastic constraint solver as a solution finder at the end of a derivation. The usual approach to solving CSP's in a CLP system is with a propagation solver. Propagation solvers are weak and do not detect many cases of unsatisfiability. Usually propagation solvers can only answer *false* or *unknown*, they can answer *true* when there is a unique value for each of the variables in the constraint (that is the solver can check that a valuation is a solution). Because of this CLP programs for solving CSPs typically have the following form:

```
goal(Vs) :- setupvars(Vs), constrain(Vs), labelling(Vs).
```

---

[4] It is not difficult to extend the presentation here to handle solvers that return *false*, but it is orthogonal to the problems we tackle.

First the variables are declared and then constrained, and finally the `labelling` predicate performs an enumerative search for a valuation, by setting each variable in turn to each of its possible values.

The enumerative search is usually where most of the computation time of the program is spent. Enumerative searches, even with clever heuristics to order the search well can perform very poorly, hence it is worth considering using a stochastic solver as a valuation finder. For Model B, the constraint check in a derivation is performed by a propagation solver during each derivation step of type (a), and then whenever a successful derivation is found, e.g. $\langle G_0 | true \rangle \Rightarrow \cdots \Rightarrow \langle \Box | c_n \rangle$ the stochastic solver is invoked on c_n to find a solution. In this way the `labelling` part of the program is not required.

3.3 Model C

Stochastic solver augmented by a propagation solver. This model is analogous to model A. At each derivation step the constraint is checked by the stochastic solver, and by a propagation solver. The role of the propagation solver is to detect unsatisfiability (which, when it is able to detect it, can be found much faster than the stochastic solver). In addition the propagation solver can communicate extra constraint information it derives to the stochastic constraint solver to improve its behaviour. The obvious example is communicating the domains of variables. Whenever the propagation solver can reduce the domain of a variable it can inform the stochastic solver of this reduced domain. This reduces the search space of the stochastic solver.

3.4 Model D

A stochastic solver is used in parallel with a propagation solver. The stochastic solver is used to give information about success — answering either *true* or *unknown*. The propagation solver is used to give information about failure, answering *false* or *unknown*. Constraints are sent to both solvers independently by the run-time engine. When the stochastic solver answers *true* the run-time engine continues the derivation immediately, without waiting for the propagation solver. When the propagation solver answers *false* the run-time engine backtracks immediately without waiting for the stochastic solver. Otherwise the run-time engine waits until both answer *unknown* before execution continues. A diagram of the interaction is given in Figure 1.

The combination of solvers working somewhat independently gives advantages to both: first the stochastic solver does not need to calculate every failure (as in model C), but additionally the propagation solver does not need to complete propagation of constraints for every satisfiable constraint store. Consider executing a goal $\langle c_1, c_2, c_3, c_4 | c \rangle$ where $c \wedge c_1 \wedge c_2 \wedge c_3$ is satisfiable, but $c \wedge c_1 \wedge c_2 \wedge c_3 \wedge c_4$ is not. Then suppose the stochastic solver quickly finds solutions for $c \wedge c_1$, $c \wedge c_1 \wedge c_2$ and $c \wedge c_1 \wedge c_2 \wedge c_3$ (for example if its solution for c is also a solution for these constraints). Before the propagation solver can finish propagation for $c \wedge c_1$ execution has continued adding the constraints c_2, c_3 and c_4. Now the propagation solver may be able to detect the unsatisfiability

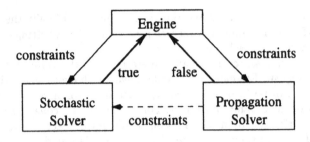

Fig. 1. A stochastic solver in parallel with a propagation solver

of $c \wedge c_1 \wedge c_2 \wedge c_3 \wedge c_4$ before it completes the propagation required for solving $c \wedge c_1 \wedge c_2 \wedge c_3$. Overall the failure of the derivation will then be detected faster.

Usage Strategies

When a stochastic constraint solver is required to communicate with the run-time engine, as in Models A, C and D we need a way of specifying at each derivation step of type (a) how many resources should be used. Similarly for model B we need a way of specifying how many resources are used at the end of each derivation. This is the role of a usage strategy. A *usage strategy* U is a function on derivations which determines how a stochastic solver is to be used. Given a partial derivation D ending in a derivation step of type (a), $\langle G|true \rangle \overset{(a)}{\Rightarrow}{}^* \langle G_n|c_n \rangle$ the usage strategy $U(D)$ gives

(a) a resource limit R to be used in solving c_n
(b) whether an *unknown* result is considered *unknown* or *false*.

Many usage strategies are possible, for example :

- Fixed Limit - the simplest usage strategy denoted $U_{fl(R)}$

$$U_{fl(R)}(D) = \langle R, false \rangle$$

where in each step R resources are allocated and failure to find a solution with R resources is considered to be "proof" that the constraint is unsatisfiable.
- Derivation Limit - a more complicated strategy denoted $U_{dl(R)}$

$$U_{dl(R)}(\langle G|true \rangle) = \langle R, false \rangle$$

$$U_{dl(R)}(D \overset{(a)}{\Rightarrow} \langle G_{n+1}|c_{n+1} \rangle) = \langle m, false \rangle$$

where $U_{dl(R)}(D) = \langle l, false \rangle$ and $m = l - res(solv(c_n, l))$. This encodes a strategy where in each derivation R resources are available for use. After each step in the derivation, the resources used $res(solv(c_n, l))$ are subtracted from the remaining resources.

Many other strategies are possible, for example where the fixed limit varies with the length of the derivation. Note that model B can be seen as a particular case of model C, given a usage strategy U_b for model B (which clearly only assigns resource for successful derivations) then the following usage strategy for model C yields equivalent derivations:

$$U_{c2b}(\langle G|true\rangle \overset{(a)}{\Rightarrow}{}^* \langle \square|c\rangle) = U_b(\langle G|true\rangle \overset{(a)}{\Rightarrow}{}^* \langle \square|c\rangle)$$

$$U_{c2b}(\langle G|true\rangle \overset{(a)}{\Rightarrow}{}^* \langle G_n|c_n\rangle) = \langle -1, unknown\rangle \quad \text{when } G_n \neq \square$$

4 Semantics

In this section we give theoretical results for the use of the various models.

4.1 Success

Regardless of which model and usage strategy U is used, we have the following soundness result for successful derivations. Note that the result is slightly stronger than the usual soundness result (see [7]) because stochastic solvers return solutions.

Theorem 2. *For models A, B, C or D if* $\langle G|true\rangle \Rightarrow^* \langle \square|c\rangle$ *is a derivation achieved using stochastic solver solv and usage strategy U then*

$$P \wedge \mathcal{A} \models c \rightarrow G$$

and if $solv(c, k) = \langle true, \theta, l\rangle$ *where* $U(\langle G|true\rangle \Rightarrow^* \langle \square|c\rangle) = \langle k, -\rangle$ *then* $P \wedge \mathcal{A} \models G\theta$.

Given we are using a probabilistic solver we cannot expect to have a strong completeness result. In practice CLP systems are already incomplete because of the fixed search strategy so completeness may not be seen as vital. But we would like to have some form of completeness.

Let us define $Prff(\langle G|true\rangle \overset{*}{\Rightarrow} \langle G_n|c_n\rangle, U)$ to be the probability that the solver applied to c_n using usage strategy U returns *false* when c_n is in fact satisfiable. Given the sequence

$$\langle G|true\rangle \overset{(a)}{\Rightarrow} \langle G_1|c_1\rangle \overset{(a)}{\Rightarrow} \cdots \overset{(a)}{\Rightarrow} \langle \square|c_n\rangle$$

where each c_i is satisfiable. The overall probability that this sequence succeeds using strategy U is

$$(1 - Prff(\langle G|true\rangle \overset{(a)}{\Rightarrow}{}^* \langle G_1|c_1\rangle, U)) \times \cdots \times (1 - Prff(\langle G|true\rangle \overset{(a)}{\Rightarrow}{}^* \langle \square|c_n\rangle, U))$$

Clearly as long as the probability of false failure never reaches 1 there is a finite probability that the sequence succeeds. We can guarantee this if the usage strategy provides enough resources so that the solver at each stage has a non-zero probability of finding a solution. We call such combinations of solvers and usage strategies *non-starving*. Because we assume for any satisfiable constraint c that $Pr(truth(solv(c,n)) = true) > 0$ if $n > 0$ any fixed limit strategy is non-starving.

Theorem 3. *Suppose program P is executed under model A, B or C using non-starving stochastic solver solv and usage strategy U. If $P \wedge A \models \bar{\exists}G$ then there is a non-zero probability that there is a successful derivation.*

For model D we have the usual completeness result for CLP because using model D we never assume the stochastic solver has determined unsatisfiability when this is not actually the case. For the other models we would like to ensure a greater degree of completeness. There exists usage strategies that can ensure this. Suppose

$$Prff(\langle G|true\rangle \stackrel{(a)}{\Rightarrow}^m \langle G_m|c_m\rangle, U) \le (\frac{1}{2})^{m+k}$$

for all derivations containing m derivation steps of type (a), where $k \ge 1$. Then the probability that a derivation with l steps of type (a) where all constraints are satisfiable is failed is less than

$$(\frac{1}{2})^{k+1} + (\frac{1}{2})^{k+2} + \cdots + (\frac{1}{2})^{k+l}$$

In other words the derivation will succeed using *solv* and usage strategy U with at least probability $1 - (\frac{1}{2})^k$.

Consider the following stochastic solver — based on that in the beginning of this section.

BOOL_SOLVE(c, n)
for $i := 1$ to n
    guess a truth assignment θ for c
    if $c\theta$ is true return $\langle true, \theta, i \rangle$
endfor
return $\langle unknown, \lambda, n \rangle$

For each constraint solve, the probability of an unknown answer for a satisfiable constraint is (from [15])

$$\epsilon = (1 - (1 - 1/m)^m)^n$$

where m is the size of c in terms of number of clauses. We will assume that each primitive constraint is a single clause, thus the size of constraint c_m is less than or equal to m. Now $0.25 \le (1-1/m)^m < 0.5$. Hence, $\epsilon < 0.75^n$. If usage strategy U chooses resources to be used at the mth step in a derivation as

$$n > (m + k)\ln(1/2)/\ln(3/4)$$
$$\text{e.g. } n > \qquad 2.5(m + k)$$

Then

$$Prff(\langle G|true\rangle \Rightarrow^m \langle G_m|c_m\rangle, U) \le (\frac{1}{2})^{m+k}$$

Thus we can expect[5] a probability of at least $1 - (\frac{1}{2})^k$ of finding any derivation that should succeed. Note that the overall resources used by a derivation is quadratic in its length using this strategy.

4.2 Finite Failure

Unfortunately because of the nature of the solvers we are unable to have any soundness result for finite failure for models A, B and C. This is because we cannot ensure that there is no *false failure*.

Definition 4. (False failure) A goal G is *falsely failed* for usage strategy U and solver *solv* if there is a sequence of states

$$\langle G|true \rangle \Rightarrow \cdots \Rightarrow \langle \Box|c_n \rangle$$

where each c_i is satisfiable, but the execution of this derivation using *solv* and U fails.

For model D of course we have the usual soundness of finite failure result for CLP. In contrast for models A and C we do have strong completeness results for finite failure provided the usage strategy satisfies a basic condition: A usage strategy is *eventually failing* if there is no infinite derivation D where $U(D_i) = \langle -, unknown \rangle$ for each finite prefix D_i of D. That is, eventually on every derivation the strategy will consider an *unknown* answer by the solver to be *false*. The theorem below make use of the program completion P^*, which is an *iff* version of the program that is required to have negative consequences, see [7] for details.

Theorem 5. *If $P^* \wedge \mathcal{A} \models \neg \bar{\exists} G$ then for models A and C if we use a fair selection strategy then any derivation for G using solver solv and eventually failing usage strategy U is finitely failed.*

Note that such a result does not usually hold for CLP systems using propagation solvers because these solvers are incomplete.

4.3 Iterative Deepening

For models A, B and C the possibility of false failure on all successful derivations means that a goal which has a solution may falsely fail. In particular given a derivation limit usage strategy for models A or C we may expect to falsely fail on all successful derivations if the limit is too small. This leads to the idea of re-executing the goal with more resources, to avoid the false failure and find a success. Thus we consider a form of iterative deepening approach.

Iterative deepening works by re-executing a finitely failed goal, using greater resources. For example, we can double the limits in the usage strategy. So when

---

[5] We have not taken into account the dependencies between successive constraint solves in this simplistic analysis.

a goal G fails using fixed limit strategy $U_{fl(1000)}$, we re-execute the goal using strategy $U_{fl(2000)}$. If that execution fails to find an answer then we re-execute usage strategy, $U_{fl(4000)}$, etc.

The aim of the approach is that a solution will be found quicker by automatically using the minimal number of resources required to avoid false failure. If we give too many resources to solve a problem, execution will be slowed because failure is determined by resource exhaustion. Hence too many resources slows execution. Iterative deepening automatically determines the (nearly) least number of resources required to find a solution. Clearly using an iterative deepening approach there is no possibility of finite failure since a goal with no solutions will run infinitely.

Technically we also need to ensure that no infinite derivations are possible, so that for example using strategy $U_{fl(R)}$ we never consider derivations of length greater than R, otherwise we cannot guarantee a goal will either succeed or fail. In practice the resource limits will usually manage this, but in theory we must use a *depth-bounded* usage strategy. A depth-bounded strategy is such that there exists number L such that for any derivation of length $m \geq L$, $U(\langle G|true \rangle \overset{m}{\Rightarrow} \langle G_m|c_m \rangle) = \langle -1, false \rangle$. In other words after some length of derivation the strategy allows only negative resources to the solver, ensuring it returns unknown, and this causes failure. For example, we can define a bounded depth fixed limit strategy as

$$U_{bdfl(R)}(\langle G|true \rangle \overset{(a)}{\Rightarrow^m} \langle G_m|c_m \rangle) = \langle R, false \rangle \quad \text{if } m < R$$
$$= \langle -1, false \rangle \quad \text{if } m \geq R$$

Thus any derivation of length $\geq R$ will be failed.

Using an iterative deepening approach we can ensure that eventually we will find a success if one exists. Note that iterative deepening does not make sense in the context of model D because it never falsely fails.

Theorem 6. *If $P \wedge \mathcal{A} \models \bar{\exists} G$ then executing goal G under models A or C using iterative deepening and a depth-bounded usage strategy U will find a successful derivation.*

5 A Constraint Solver : GENET

We have chosen the GENET [13, 2], a generic neural network simulator, to demonstrate the feasibility of our proposal. GENET can be used to solve binary CSP's with finite domains. A GENET network consists of a cluster of nodes for each domain variable in a CSP. Each node denotes a value(label) in the corresponding domain variable. And each constraint is represented by a set of inhibitory connections between nodes with incompatible values.

In the original GENET model, the entire network must be constructed before computation starts. However, a constraint solver in a CLP system must support efficient incremental execution since new primitive constraints are being added to an existing solvable constraint during a derivation. Therefore, an efficient incremental version of GENET is necessary. A naive but efficient incremental GENET, called I-GENET, adds new primitive constraints and variables to the network as they are collected. Its incrementality originates from the re-use of the connection weights which are computed using the heuristic learning rule in previous cycles. Thus, the network is *trained* while it is being built incrementally. A more detailed discussion of the incremental GENET is contained in [12].

6 Experimental Results

To compare the different models of using stochastic solvers, we have used ECLiPSe Version 3.5.1 and GNU C 2.6.3 running on a SPARCSTATION 1000, to build prototypes for the models A, B and C, using the backtrackable I-GENET as the stochastic constraint solver, and the ECLiPSe fd library as a propagation solver. Note that the first-fail principle (i.e. choose the variable with the smallest domain to be instantiated first) is used with forward checking to improve the performance of search in the ECLiPSe system. We also include another example of model A, using a version of GENET extended to use lazy arc-consistency [11] to reduce the domains of variables. Using this solver (denoted model A') has an effect similar to model C, where the reduction of domains comes from the propagation solver. Construction of a model D solver is not yet completed.

We give results of preliminary experiments comparing the different models using usage strategy $U_{fl}(1000)$ and compare our systems versus a traditional propagation-based CLP approach on a set of CSP's with and without disjunctive constraints. The Hamiltonian path calculation and disjunctive graph colouring are examples of CSP's with disjunctive constraints, while N-queens and permutations generation problems as examples of CSP's without disjunctive constraints. In all the test cases, the CPU time for the different models are the median over 10 successful runs to find a solution. All runs for the different models were terminated if the constraint solvers used 1000000 resources without finding a solution. And we aborted the execution of any ECLiPSe program if it took more than 10 hours. In any case, we use a "—" symbol to mean there were no successful runs and a "?" symbol to denote the execution took > 10 hours.

Hamiltonian Path Problems
Given a graph G of n vertices, the Hamiltonian path problem is to find the Hamiltonian path of G, in which *each* of n vertices in G is visited *once and only once* [10]. The Hamiltonian path problem is a practical CSP which is very similar to the route planning problems faced by many circus, travelling road company and travelling salesman. In any case, it can be regarded as an non-optimising version of the well-known travelling salesman problem, in which the salesman does not need to return to the original city.

The formulation of the program is the natural one for constraint programming, where each node i is associated with a variable V_i. A path is an assignment of an order of visiting the nodes (different values from 1 to n) to each variable, such that there is an edge from each node to its predecessor, and predecessors are chosen by disjunctive search. This formulation easily handles ad hoc constraints on the problem such as distance between two given nodes must be at least some distance k.

Problems	ECLiPSe	Model A	Model B	Model C	Model A'
10	0.040	4.195(11)	—	2.565(15.5)	0.460(11)
20	1090	58.27(21)	—	50.65(20)	31.75(20)
30	?	5493(46)	—	4287(46)	2687(46)

The table above show the execution time of ECLiPSe and the different models on Hamiltonian path problems using fixed limit strategies with the average number of backtracks in the search given in parentheses. The first two problems are coded from some interesting real-life examples in graph theory [10]. And the last one is a modified example obtained from [8].

In general, the stochastic models A and C outperform ECLiPSe and model B on all but the smallest example. This is because the search space for models A and C is much smaller than for the ECLiPSe because they determine unsatisfiability much earlier. Model B fails in all cases since the search space is so large, and it requires exhaustion of resources to initiate backtracking. For these problems Model C betters model A showing that the propagation solver can provide useful information for the stochastic solver during the search. And in these problems the improved stochastic solver (model A') finds useful domain reduction information without the overhead of communication with the propagation solver.

Disjunctive Graph-colouring Problems

The disjunctive graph-colouring problem is to colour a graph, possibly non-planar, with a number of hyper-arcs connecting nodes. A hyper-arc $\{(i_1, j_1), (i_2, j_2)\}$ specifies that at least one of the pairs of nodes (i_k, j_k) must be coloured differently. The disjunctive graph-colouring problem has wide applicability in time-tabling, scheduling and production planning.

Graph		CPU time				
Nodes	Colours	ECLiPSe	Model A	Model B	Model C	Model A'
10	3	19.96(6428)	1.580(4)	—	1.645(4)	1.820(4)
20	4	1362(65535)	0.690(1)	—	0.770(1)	0.770(1)
30	5	0.050(0)	0.115(0)	0.095(0)	0.210(0)	0.120(0)
40	5	0.070(0)	0.145(0)	0.105(0)	0.220(0)	0.155(0)
50	5	0.090(0)	0.200(0)	0.140(0)	0.345(0)	0.225(0)

The table above show results for ECLiPSe and the different models on a set of small-sized disjunctive graph-colouring problems. In general, each of the approaches where the stochastic solver controls the search (models A and C) outperforms ECLiPSe when the problem requires backtracking. This is because they do much less backtracking since they do not require a backtracking enumeration search. Here is an example when no useful domain reduction information is discovered by model C or model A'. Hence they do not improve on model A, and suffer some overhead.

N-queens Problem

The N-queens problem is to place N queens onto a $N \times N$ chess board so that no queens can be attacked. A queen can be attacked if it is on the same column, row or diagonal as any other queen. It is a standard benchmark for CSPs since the size N can be increased without limit.

No. of Queens	ECLiPSe	Model A	Model B	Model C	Model A'
10	0.040	0.200	0.195	0.320	0.290
20	0.220	3.665	2.195	4.200	4.020
30	0.880	23.79	10.11	27.43	23.91
40	0.810	93.12	33.58	96.04	95.82
50	63.42	253.3	73.09	268.8	257.1
60	3.580	594.0	146.4	625.5	605.8
70	66.67	1172	273.9	1242	1231

The above table shows the CPU time of ECLiPSe and the different models on a N-Queens problems where N ranges from 10 to 70. In general, ECLiPSe out-performs the stochastic approaches because the problems do not require backtracking on constraints and using the first-fail principle significantly improves the performance of the enumerative search strategy. Model B performs best among all the models since the problem does not involve any search on constraints and it does not need to expend resources on derivation steps except the last one. Again models A' and C do extra work without gaining any useful information for these problems. Thus, they are slower than model A.

Permutations Generation

Given a permutation f on the integers from 1 to n, we define the monotonies of f as a vector $(m_1, m_2, \cdots, m_{n-1})$, where m_i equals to one if the value of the $i + 1$-th element in the permutation is greater than that of the i-th element and zero otherwise, and the vector $(a_1, a_2, \cdots, a_{n-1})$ of advances of f such that $a_i = 1$ if the integer $f(i) + 1$ is placed in the permutation on the right of $f(i)$, and 0 otherwise. The problem is to construct all the permutations of a given range that admit a given vector of monotonies and a given vector of advances.

Length of List	ECLiPSe	Model A	Model B	Model C	Model A'
9	0.010	0.210	0.115	0.190	0.210
10	0.020	0.325	0.140	0.455	0.355
20	8.440	6.470	1.490	6.295	7.035
30	?	50.61	9.730	45.69	52.77

The table above shows the performance of ECLiPSe and the different models on the permutations generation given a number of vectors of different sizes for monotonies and advances. The first example is taken from [14] while the others are arbitrary examples of permutation lists with length from 10 to 30. For the first two test cases, ECLiPSe performs better than our models since the search space is relatively small. But when the length of the permutation list grows larger, the stochastic approaches out-performs ECLiPSe. In particular, model B performs best since the problems do not require backtracking on constraints. For these problems model C, in general, performs better than model A and A' since it gains useful information from the propagation solver, which cannot be deduced by model A'.

In conclusion, using a stochastic solver to control search (models A and C) is of benefit for disjunctive problems where the search space of constraints is large. For non-disjunctive problems model B is most effective and out performs enumerative search in many instances. Cooperating solvers (model C) can result in significant improvements, and usually do not add too much overhead. Improving underlying stochastic solvers (model A') is another worthwhile approach. No model is uniformly better — and the user should be prepared to experiment.

References

1. E.H.L. Aarts and J.H.M. Korst. Boltzmann machines for travelling salesman problems. *European Journal of Operational Research*, 39:79–95, 1989.
2. A. Davenport, E.P.K. Tsang, C.J. Wang, and K. Zhu. GENET: A connectionist architecture for solving constraint satisfaction problems by iterative improvement. In *Proceedings of AAAI'94*, 325-330, 1994.
3. M. Dincbas, H. Simonis, and P. Van Hentenryck. Solving the car-sequencing problem in constraint logic programming. In *Procs. of the European Conf. on Art. Int.*, 290–295, 1988.
4. M. Dincbas, H. Simonis, and P. Van Hentenryck. Solving large combinatorial problems in logic programming. *Journal of Logic Programming*, 8:75–93, 1990.
5. J.J. Hopfield and D. Tank. "Neural" computation of decisions in optimization problems. *Biological Cybernetics*, 52:141–152, 1985.
6. A.R-A. Illera and J. Ortiz. Labelling in CLP(FD) with evolutionary programming. In *Procs. of GULP-PRODE 95*, 569–590, 1995.
7. Joxan Jaffar and Michael J. Maher. Constraint logic programming: A survey. *Journal of Logic Programming*, Volume 19 / 20, May 1994.
8. J.H.M. Lee, H.F.Leung and H.W. Won. Extending GENET for Non-Binary CSP's. In *Proceedings of the Seventh IEEE International Conference on Tools with Artificial Intelligence*, 338–343, November 1995.
9. J.H.M. Lee and V.W.L. Tam. A Framework for Integrating Artificial Neural Networks and Logic Programming *International Journal on Artificial Intelligence Tools* 4(1&2), 3–32, June, 1995.
10. Ronald E. Prather *Discrete Mathematical Structures for Computer Science*. Houghton Mifflin,1976.
11. P. Stuckey and V. Tam, Extending GENET with lazy arc consistency. University of Melbourne, Department of Computer Science Tech. Report 96/8.
12. V.W.L. Tam. Integrating artificial neural networks and constraint logic programming. Master's thesis, Department of Computer Science, The Chinese University of Hong Kong, 1995.
13. E.P.K. Tsang and C.J. Wang. A generic neural network approach for constraint satisfaction problems. In G Taylor, editor, *Neural Network Applications*, 12–22. Springer-Verlag, 1992.
14. P. Van Hentenryck. *Constraint Satisfaction in Logic Programming*. The MIT Press, 1989.
15. L.C. Wu and C.Y. Tang. Solving the satisfiability problem by using randomized approach. In *Information Processing Letters* 41, 295–299, North-Holland, 1992.

Integrating Efficient Records into Concurrent Constraint Programming

Peter Van Roy[1], Michael Mehl[2], and Ralf Scheidhauer[2]

[1] Swedish Institute of Computer Science, Stockholm, Sweden
[2] Programming Systems Lab, DFKI, Saarbrücken, Germany

Abstract. We show how to implement efficient records in constraint logic programming (CLP) and its generalization concurrent constraint programming (CCP). Records can be naturally integrated into CCP as a new constraint domain. The implementation provides the added expressive power of concurrency and fine-grained constraints over records, yet does not pay for this expressivity when it is not used. In addition to traditional record operations, our implementation allows to compute with partially-known records. This fine granularity is useful for natural-language and knowledge-representation applications. The paper describes the implementation of records in the DFKI Oz system. Oz is a higher-order CCP language with encapsulated search. We show that the efficiency of records in CCP is competitive with modern Prolog implementation technology and that our implementation provides improved performance for natural-language applications.

Keywords. Concurrent Constraint, Record, Logic Programming, Implementation, Natural-Language Processing, Prolog

1 Introduction

Records are an important data structure with many advantages for program structuring and understandability. It has been shown that records can be naturally integrated into concurrent constraint programming (and therefore also into constraint logic programming) as a new constraint domain [19]. This gives a simple logical explanation of feature structures in natural-language processing (NLP). Erbach and Manandhar mention record constraints as a first requirement for future NLP systems [6].

This paper presents the implementation of records in the DFKI Oz system [16]. We evaluate the implementation according to its complexity as well as its space and time performance. Our implementation generalizes in two ways the compound structures (trees) of Prolog:

- *Concurrent constraints.* From the implementation viewpoint, the generalization of CLP(X) to CCP(X), where X is the constraint domain, requires two changes. First, the system is concurrent–there are multiple activities that evolve independently. Second, the system requires *two* basic operations on the constraint domain X, namely satisfiability and entailment checking (see Sect. 7). A CLP(X) language requires only a single operation on the domain X, namely a satisfiability check. We show that the two basic operations can be efficiently implemented for records.

– *Fine-grained record constraints.* Our implementation provides a solver over records that allows computing with partially-known records. Yet, its efficiency is comparable to that of modern high-performance Prolog implementations when the full power of the solver is not used.

This paper extends a WAM-like abstract machine to support record constraints and concurrency. The paper is structured into three main parts: definition of the constraint systems (Sect. 3), their efficient implementation (Sects. 4–7), and the evaluation of the implementation (Sect. 8).

For ease of understanding, we present and implement three constraint systems that progressively provide more powerful record-like operations: Prolog structures (finite or rational trees, Sect. 4), bound records (Prolog structures with named subfields, Sect. 5), and free records (that may be partially-known, Sect. 6). We implement the three constraint systems in a CLP framework based on a WAM-like abstract machine. We then extend the implementation to a CCP framework by showing how to generalize unification to perform an incremental entailment check (Sect. 7). Finally, we evaluate free records in DFKI Oz (Sect. 8).

2 Related Work

To our knowledge, this paper is the first work that explains from a practical viewpoint how to implement efficient records in a logic language. The paper is intended to complement the description of Amoz [10], an abstract machine for CCP languages that provides for deep guards, threads, and lexically-scoped higher-order procedures. The paper is based on foundational work on records [19] and ψ-terms [3] for logic programming. Most of the theoretical concepts were introduced by Aït-Kaci in the LIFE language [2]. The entailment checking algorithm, using the *scripting* idea, was used in early committed-choice systems and justified in [8].

Previous work with record-like structures was done as part of the work on LIFE compilation [5, 7, 12, 13, 14]. The main results of this work are the Beauty & Beast algorithm and the Half_Life system. These results give the first, albeit incomplete, indication that record-like structures can be added to CCP languages (and a fortiori to CLP languages) without loss of efficiency over records in imperative languages. The present work strengthens these results by presenting and analyzing an actual efficient implementation for DFKI Oz.

3 Constraints Over Trees

All constraints in this paper describe *rational feature trees*, i.e., rational trees with labeled edges and nodes. We use the short names *tree* and *record* interchangeably instead of rational feature tree in the following sections. We start the discussion of constraints by presenting a simple and general constraint system over trees. To obtain a practical system, we restrict the general system to three practical systems of successively increasing generality.

The rest of this paper shows how to efficiently implement the three restricted constraint systems. Section 4 sets the stage by briefly presenting the implementation of Prolog structures in CLP. Section 5 extends this to bound records and

Sect. 6 further extends it to free records. Section 7 shows how to do free records in CCP. We show how each stage can be implemented with the efficiency of the previous stage, when the new generality is not used.

3.1 General Constraints Over Trees

The underlying structure of our rational feature tree theory contains three domains, namely trees, sorts and features. Every domain has an infinite number of values. In a general formulation of tree constraints, we consider the following five basic constraints:

- A *sort constraint* $Sort(x, y)$ holds if and only y is a sort and the root of the tree x is labeled with y.
- A *feature constraint* $Feature(x, y, z)$ holds if and only if y is a feature and the tree x has the subtree z at the feature y.
- An *arity constraint* $Arity(x, F)$ holds if and only if F is a set of features and the tree x has subtrees exactly at the features appearing in F, and at no other features. We say that F is the *arity*[3] of x.
- An *equality constraint* $x = y$ holds if and only if x and y describe the same feature trees.
- A *record constraint* $Record(x)$ holds if and only if x is a tree.

In this general form, all arguments of the constraints are variables or values from the particular domains (trees, sorts, features, or sets of features). Little is known about the general form [20, 21].

3.2 Restricted Constraints Over Trees

To make these constraints practical, we restrict them. We present three progressively more powerful restricted versions: Prolog structures, bound records, and free records. We show how to implement all three systems efficiently.

The terminology "bound" and "free" records is chosen for its similarity to bound and free variables. Both bound and free record constraints describe rational feature trees. A *bound* record constraint entails both an arity and a sort constraint. Other record constraints are *free*.

Prolog Structures. Prolog structures are trees where the domain of features is limited to *positive integers*, i.e., for each node, the n edges of its subtrees are labeled with successive integers $1, ..., n$. There are three basic kinds of constraints:

1. A family of *functor* constraints $x = s(y_1, ..., y_n)$, for all values of s and nonnegative integers n. Each constraint is equivalent to:

$$Sort(x, s) \wedge Arity(x, \{1, ..., n\}) \wedge \bigwedge_{1 \leq i \leq n} Feature(x, i, y_i)$$

Both s (the *functor*) and n (the *width*) must be fixed. The Prolog built-in $functor(x, s, n)$ imposes this constraint with existentially quantified feature constraints, i.e., $Sort(x, s) \wedge Arity(x, \{1, ..., n\})$. [4]

---

[3] We call the number of arguments the *width*.

[4] Note that $Arity(x, \{1, ..., n\})$ implies $1 \leq \forall i \leq n \, \exists y \, Feature(x, i, y)$.

2. A family of *feature* constraints $Feature(x, i, y_i)$, for all integers $i > 0$. These constraints are written in Prolog as $arg(i, x, y_i)$. Imposing one when the arity and sort are not present gives a run-time error.

3. An *equality* constraint $x = y$.

In older Prolog systems, these constraints described a domain of finite trees. In modern Prolog systems they are based on a domain of rational trees (allowing cyclic structures).

Bound Records. Bound records generalize Prolog structures to have features (named fields) instead of successively-numbered fields. There are three basic kinds of constraints:

1. A family of *functor* constraints $x = s(f_1 : y_1, ..., f_n : y_n)$ for any sort s and distinct features $f_1, ..., f_n$. Each constraint is equivalent to:
$$Sort(x, s) \land Arity(x, \{f_1, ..., f_n\}) \land \bigwedge_{1 \le i \le n} Feature(x, f_i, y_i)$$
The integer $n \ge 0$ and arguments $s, f_1, ..., f_n$ must all be fixed.

2. A family of *feature* constraints $Feature(x, f, y)$ where f must be fixed. They can be imposed at any moment, but their resolution is delayed until the arity and sort are present.

3. An *equality* constraint $x = y$.

To create a new bound record, a functor constraint must be given. Since an arity constraint is always present, the set of features is fixed.

Free Records. Free records are described by more fine-grained constraints. It is possible to say that a free record has a particular feature without saying anything else. There are four basic kinds of constraints:

1. A family of *sort* constraints $Sort(x, s)$, for all different values of s. In each constraint s is fixed.

2. A family of *feature* constraints $Feature(x, f, y)$, for all different values of f. In each constraint f is fixed.

3. A family of *arity* constraints $Arity(x, F)$, for all different values of F. In each constraint F is a fixed set of features.

4. An *equality* constraint $x = y$.

Free records are provided as a logical data structure by the constraint system CFT [19]. CFT is a generalization of the rational tree system of Prolog II that provides finer-grained constraints and allows to identify subtrees by keywords rather than by position. There exists an efficient incremental decision procedure for CFT that decides entailment and disentailment between possibly existentially-quantified constraints.

As an example of what is described by CFT, consider the two records x and y given in the following Oz-like notation:
$$x = person(age : 25)$$
$$y = person(age : 25 ...)$$
This notation is an abbreviation for the two conjunctions:

$Sort(x, person) \land Feature(x, age, 25) \land Arity(x, \{age\})$

$Sort(y, person) \land Feature(y, age, 25)$

Because of the arity constraint, the record x may have no other features than age. The record y does not have this restriction.

4 Prolog Structures

This paper extends a WAM-like abstract machine to support record constraints and concurrency. To fix the notation, this section summarizes briefly the implementation of Prolog structures in the WAM. For more information about the WAM, the reader is advised to consult one of many works explaining Prolog implementation techniques [1, 9, 22]. All code fragments are given in a pseudocode closely resembling C++.

4.1 Representation of Prolog Structures

A Prolog structure is represented by functor and width fields, and an array of arguments (indexed from 0 to width-1):

```
enum Tag {REF, STR, ATOM, VAR};
class Term { Tag tag; switch (tag) {
case REF: Term *ref; case STR: Structure str;
case ATOM: Atom atom; case VAR: ... } };
class Structure { Atom *sort; int width; Term *args[]; };
```

The Term class is defined using a variant-record notation. Terms include variables (VAR), structures (STR), atoms (ATOM), and the reference (REF) which is used for binding and dereferencing. Using different tags for unbound variables and reference links is needed for the CCP implementation (see Sect. 7). The Atom type is used to represent sorts and features. Term uses a tag-on-data representation and the sort and width are stored as separate words. More optimized representations are straightforward modifications of this one.

4.2 Operations on Prolog Structures

Two operations are provided on Prolog structures: unification and access to a structure argument. Unification implements the functor and equality constraints and argument access implements the feature constraint.

Unification. If neither structure is known statically (i.e., at compile-time), then the following general rational-tree unification routine is called:

```
#define deref(t) { while (t→tag==REF) t=t→ref; }
#define bind(t,u) { t→tag=REF; t→ref=u; }
bool unify(Term *t1, *t2) {
    deref(t1); deref(t2); if (t1==t2) return TRUE;
    if (t1→tag==VAR || t2→tag==VAR) {
        if (t1→tag==VAR) bind(t1,t2); else bind(t2,t1);
        return TRUE;
    } else if (t1→tag==STR && t2→tag==STR) { ... } }
```

This routine handles terms that can be unbound variables, structures, and atoms. In the following sections we discuss extensions of the unification procedure, to handle bound and free records and to allow for speculative execution.

If one of the two structures is known statically, then the above unification routine can be statically decomposed into more primitive operations [22]. In the WAM, each functor constraint is independently decomposed into sort and feature constraints [1]. The unification $X = f(foo, bar)$ is compiled into the following abstract machine instructions:

```
get_structure X, f, 2
unify_constant foo
unify_constant bar
```

If foo or bar are of other types than atoms, then other specialized unify instructions will replace the unify_constant instructions. The get_structure instruction initializes two global variables called mode and s, which are used by the unify_constant instructions:

```
enum mode {READ, WRITE};
Term **s;
get_structure(Term *t, Atom *sort, int width) {
    deref(t); if (t→tag==VAR) {
        Term *nt=newStructure(sort,width); bind(t,nt);
        mode=WRITE; s=nt→args;
    } else if (t→tag==STR) {
        if (t→str.sort≠sort || t→str.width≠width) fail();
        mode=READ; s=t→str.args;
    } else fail(); }
```

We assume the fail() routine handles unification failure, e.g. in Prolog it restores the abstract machine state from the topmost choice point. The newStructure routine allocates a new structure with given sort and width on the heap. The unify_constant instructions use s to access the structure argument they are to unify with, and they use mode to decide whether to write a new value there or to read an existing value.

Argument Access. The arguments of a Prolog structure are numbered from 1 to the width. Accessing a structure is done with a single array indexing operation, augmented with the necessary type checks:

```
Term *access(Term *t, int i) {
    deref(t); if (t→tag≠STR) return error();
    if (i<1 || t→width<i) return fail();
    return t→str.args[i-1]; }
```

5 Bound Records

The representation of a bound record is closely related to that of a Prolog structure. Bound records are represented as arrays of terms. With this representation we can efficiently implement traditional record operations (record creation, argument access). The following sections describe how unification is modified for records.

5.1 Representation of Bound Records

To represent bound records, a term is modified to include the term type Record and its tag REC:

```
class Term { Tag tag; switch (tag) { case REC: Record rec; ... } };
class Record { Atom *sort; Arity *arity; Term *args[]; };
```

The type Record differs from Structure in that it replaces width by arity. The arity points to a hash table that maps features to offsets into the argument array args:

```
class Arity { class { Atom *feat; int index; } table[];
    int lookup(Atom *); int get_width(); ... };
```

Features are represented as atoms. All arities are kept in a single global table that is itself a hash table:

```
class AtomList { Atom *atom; AtomList *next; };
class ArityTable {
    class { AtomList *featlist; Arity *arity; } table[];
    Arity *insert(AtomList *); ... };
```

The procedure insert takes an arity given as list of features and searches for this arity in the table. If this is not found a new arity is created. ArityTable is needed to ensure that unification of two bound records is fast. Because arities are globally unique, equality between them can be determined by a single-word comparison.

5.2 Operations on Bound Records

Two operations are provided on bound records: unification of two records and access to a record argument. Unification implements the functor and equality constraints and argument access implements the feature constraint. We show how both of these operations can be done as efficiently for bound records as for Prolog structures.

Unification. Two records can be unified with no overhead compared to structure unification. There are two cases, namely if one of the records is statically known or not. If one is statically known, e.g., the unification is $X = f(a : foo\ b : bar)$, then the compiler determines the offsets of features a and b (for example, 1 and 0 in that order) and arranges the unify_constant instructions in order of increasing offset:

```
        get_record X, f, [a b]
        unify_constant bar
        unify_constant foo
```

The arity [a b] is statically inserted into ArityTable.

If neither record is statically known then the unification routine compares the sorts and arities. Since the arities are stored in the global ArityTable, this can be done in constant time by simple pointer comparison. Finally, the arguments are unified in pairs by traversing the two argument arrays in the same way as for Prolog structures. The only difference is that the width is given by t->arity->get_width() instead of t->width.

Argument Access. To access field feat of record rec requires looking up the field's offset in the record's hash table:

```
Term *access(Record *rec, Atom *feat)
{ return rec→args[rec→arity→lookup(feat)]; }
```

This requires a single hash table lookup. To make this almost as fast as indexed argument lookup, we use the *caching technique* pioneered in Smalltalk implementations [4] where the record's type, the feature, and the offset are stored in the instruction. If the feature feat is statically known then the following routine can be used:

```
Term *access_feat(Term *t) { // not in cache = -1
    static Arity *arCache=NULL; static int indCache= -1;
    deref(t); if (t→tag≠REC) return error();
    if (t→arity==arCache) return t→args[indCache];
    arCache=t→arity; indCache=arCache→lookup(feat);
    if (indCache ≠ -1) return t→args[indCache];
    else { arCache=NULL; return fail(); } }
```

If the feature is not statically known then an additional static variable featureCache is needed. In the case of a cache hit, both cases are as efficient as argument access to a Prolog structure. For DFKI Oz, we measure that the feature is known statically in 84% of argument accesses (with a run-time hit ratio of 95%), for a representative set of large programs totalling several tens of thousands of source lines.

5.3 Delayed Execution

In the above implementation, the access function fails if the record argument is a variable. In fact, we instead want to *delay* the functor and feature constraints until the argument is bound. The routines access and access_feat are easily extended to support delaying: it suffices to create a suspension, i.e. a delayed goal, if the first argument is unbound. This can be done without slowing down the common case. The code is extended as follows:

```
Term *access_feat(Term *t) { ... if (t→tag≠REC) {
    if (t→tag==VAR) { t→add_suspension(goal); return NULL; }
    return fail(); } ... }
```

We assume goal is a global variable pointing to the current goal being executed. We now briefly explain how add_suspension is implemented.

Delayed execution is implemented by the concept of a *suspension*. A suspension contains all the state necessary to reexecute a goal. We assume the following data structures to implement suspension handling:

```
class Term { Tag tag;
    switch (tag) { case VAR: SuspList *suspList; ... }
    add_suspension(Goal *); wake_suspensions(); };
class SuspList { Suspension *susp; SuspList *next; };
class Suspension { Goal *goal; ... };
```

We assume that Goal is defined elsewhere. A list of suspensions is attached to every term that can be constrained (e.g., an unbound variable, which can be bound). All the suspensions are executed ("woken up") when the term is constrained (e.g., the variable is bound). A term is extended with a suspension list and two basic operations: add_suspension adds a goal to the suspension list, and wake_suspensions empties the suspension list and executes all its goals. A new type of unbound variable can be added to optimize the common case when the variable has no suspensions. For more details see [11] (CLP) and [10] (CCP).

6 Free Records

Free records are provided by the constraint system CFT. The solved form of a free record constraint for x is summarized as follows (where $\{a_1, ..., a_n\} \subseteq F$):

$$Record(x) \wedge (\ Arity(x, F)\ |\ \top\ ) \wedge (\ Sort(x, s)\ |\ \top\ ) \wedge \bigwedge_{1 \leq i \leq n} Feature(x, a_i, y_i)$$

The constraint $Record(x)$ is mandatory. The other constraints are optional. This solved form is *variable-centered*, that is, all information about a variable can be represented locally at that variable.

For efficiency, free records have *two* internal representations. When the record is bound, we use the bound representation (see Sect. 5). When the record is free, we use the free representation. The transition from free to bound representation occurs when arity and sort constraints are imposed. This happens inside unification and is invisible to the programmer.

6.1 Representation of Free Records

The free representation must potentially allow an arbitrary number of features to be added. We implement the free representation by adding a new term type FreeRecord and its tag FREEREC:

```
enum Tag {FREEREC, ...};
class Term { Tag tag; switch (tag) {
    case FREEREC: FreeRecord frec; SuspList *suspList; ...}};
class FreeRecord { Atom *sort; DynamicTable *dyntab; };
```

Since the free representation can be further constrained, it must have a suspension list. The dynamic table contains a mapping from features to feature values:

```
class DynamicTable {
    int width, size; // current and maximum no. of elements
    class { Atom *feat; Term *value; } table[];
    Term *lookup(Atom *feat);
    void insert(Atom *feat, Term *value); int get_width();
    void iter_start(); Term *iter_next(Atom **feat); };
```

This mapping constitutes the solved form of the record constraints. The iter_start and iter_next operations are used to iterate through all elements of the table. The insert operation doubles the table size if it becomes too full, i.e., when width/size is greater than a given threshold. Thus insertion is done in constant amortized time. A threshold of 75% gives reasonable performance.

6.2 Operations on Free Records

Three operations are provided on free records: unification, argument access, and argument creation. The feature and sort constraints are implemented by accessing the sort or a feature value, instantiating the sort, or creating a new feature. The equality constraint is implemented by unification. The unifier of the free and bound representations is the bound representation. Therefore unification can be used to impose the arity constraint. We give no code for the sort operations since they are obvious simplifications of the feature operations.

Unification. Consider the unification of two free records x_1 and x_2 when both use the free representation and are statically unknown. The two dynamic tables must be merged. The new table contains the union of the elements of the original tables, and corresponding elements are unified. Merging table dt1 into dt2 can be done efficiently as follows:

```
class PairList {
    class Pair { Term *t1, *t2; Pair *next; } *list;
    PairList() { list=NULL; }
    void add(Term *, Term *); // add pair to the list
    bool next(Term **, Term **); }; // FALSE if empty
bool merge(DynamicTable*dt1,*dt2) { Atom *f1; Term *t1,*t2;
    PairList *pairs=new PairList(); dt1→iter_start();
    while (t1=dt1→iter_next(&f1)) { // next feature of dt1
        Term *t2=dt2→lookup(f1); // is it in dt2?
        if (t2) pairs→add(t1,t2); else dt2→insert(f1,t1); }
    while (pairs→next(&t1,&t2))
        if (!unify(t1,t2)) return FALSE;
    return TRUE; }
```

For correctness when unifying cyclic structures, the merging of the tables is separated from the unification of the pairs of feature values. The PairList temporarily stores the pairs. For efficiency, we merge the smallest table into the largest. Therefore the unification algorithm is extended as follows:

```
bool unify(Term *t1, *t2) { ... else if (t1→tag==FREEREC) {
    if (t2→tag==FREEREC) {
        DynamicTable *dt1=t1→frec→dyntab;
        DynamicTable *dt2=t2→frec→dyntab;
        if (dt1→get_width()<dt2→get_width())
            { bind(t1,t2); return (merge(dt1,dt2)); }
        else { bind(t2,t1); return (merge(dt2,dt1)); }
    } else if (t2→tag==REC) { ... // unify corresp. elements
        bind(t1,t2); return TRUE; // result is bound
    } else return FALSE; } ... }
```

Amortized time complexity is $O(min(|T_1|, |T_2|))$, where $|T|$ denotes the size of table T.

We extend the get_structure operation to unify with a static bound record:

```
get_structure(Term *t, Atom *sort, Arity *arity) { ...
    else if (t→tag==FREEREC) {
        Term *nt=newRecord(sort,arity); mode=READ;
        if (!unify(t,nt)) fail(); } ... }
```

In case the argument uses the free representation, a new bound record is created and the general unification routine is called. Unification of the arguments is done by the unify instructions as before. This is a simple way to extend get_structure to handle any number of new types.

Argument Access and Creation. Argument access and creation are done with the lookup and insert operations. With a reasonable hash function, these can be done in constant time.

7 Free Records in CCP

So far the record implementation has been presented as an instantiation of the CLP framework, giving the system CLP(Records), which requires an efficient incremental test for non-unifiability for CFT. We have presented a unification algorithm that implements this test. In this section, we extend the implementation to the CCP framework. See [8, 17, 18] for further information on CCP and its realization in Oz.

To extend our CLP record implementation to CCP, it is sufficient to support local computation spaces and to add an incremental entailment check for record constraints. Local computation spaces are CCP's counterpart to CLP's choice point segments, and can be implemented efficiently with a *scripting* technique. The entailment check is implemented as an extension to the unification algorithm.

7.1 Checking Entailment With Local Spaces

In theory, doing the entailment check is straightforward. To check whether the constraint store γ entails the constraint ϕ, create a local space and impose ϕ in it [8]. If imposing ϕ requires constraining variables in γ, then there exist bindings of these variables that conflict with ϕ. Hence the local space is not entailed. If the constraint store is later strengthened to $\gamma \wedge \gamma'$, then the entailment check is redone by reexecuting ϕ in the local space. For more details see [10].

For variable-centered constraints, *constraining* a global variable means *binding* it. Executing ϕ in the local space may bind global variables. We remove the bound pairs and store them in a *script* attached to the local space. If the script is empty, then γ entails ϕ. The script plays the role of a trail.

The local space has two operations: we can *enter* it (make it the current space) and *leave* it (make its parent space the current space). Entering a space is done by unifying the binding pairs in the script, thus emptying the script. Leaving a space means undoing the global variable bindings and saving them in the script.

Conceptually, whenever γ is strengthened, ϕ must be reexecuted in the local space. With the script we can make this reexecution incremental. When the constraint store γ is strengthened, we do not have to reexecute ϕ completely. It suffices to enter the local space and leave it again. This creates a new script, which may be smaller or larger than the original.

7.2 Representing Local Spaces

Extending unification to take local spaces into account requires unbound variables and records to know their home spaces:

```
class Space { class Script { Term *t1, *t2; } script[];
    add(Term *, Term *); leave(); enter(); ... };
Space *current;
class Term { Tag tag; switch (tag) {
  case VAR: Space *home; case REC: Space *home;
  case FREEREC: Space *home; ... } };
```

An unbound variable is represented as a term with tag VAR and space home. This can be encoded in a single word. All terms that can be bound (i.e., VAR, REC, and FREEREC) have a home space pointer. The bind routine is modified to take the term's space into account:

```
#define isGlobal(t) (t→home≠current)
#define isLocal(t) (t→home==current)
void bind(Term *t, *u) {
    if (isGlobal(t)) current→add(t,u); // trailing
    t→tag=REF; t→ref=u; }
```

All global bindings are stored in the script. The isGlobal test is similar to a trail condition.

7.3 Checking Entailment

Consider the unification of two free records x_1 and x_2 that both have the free representation. If one is local, then its representation is modified. If both are global, then a new local record is created and the globals are bound to it. In both cases the dynamic tables are merged. Depending on the sizes of the tables and the locality or globality of their spaces, design decisions need to be made how the tables are merged. There are three possible cases: x_1 and x_2 are both local, both global, or global and local. The case when both are local has been taken care of in Sect. 6.

If x_1 is local and x_2 is global, then the global variable is bound to the local variable,[5] and the global table is merged into the local table:

```
bool unify(Term *t1, *t2) { ...
    if (t1→tag==FREEREC && t2→tag==FREEREC) {
        if (isLocal(t1) && isGlobal(t2)) {
            DynamicTable *dt1=t1→frec→dyntab;
            DynamicTable *dt2=t2→frec→dyntab;
            bind(t2,t1); return (merge(dt2,dt1)); } ... } ... }
```

This requires looking through only the elements of the global table. It has amortized time complexity $O(|T_{global}|)$.

If both x_1 and x_2 are global, then a new local variable is created which contains the union of the global tables, and both global variables are bound to the local variable:

```
bool unify(Term *t1, *t2) { ...
    if (t1→tag==FREEREC && t2→tag==FREEREC) {
        if (isGlobal(t1) && isGlobal(t2)) {
            Term *t=newFreerec(); // make new local record
            DynamicTable *dt1=t1→frec→dyntab;
            DynamicTable *dt2=t2→frec→dyntab;
            bind(t1,t); bind(t2,t); merge(dt1,t→frec→dyntab);
            return (merge(dt2,t→frec→)dyntab)); } ... } ... }
```

This requires looking through the elements of both tables. It has time complexity $O(|T_1| + |T_2|)$.

---

[5] Binding must be done in this order, since merging into the global table is very expensive.

8 Evaluation and Measurements

The record implementation described above has been realized since DFKI Oz version 1.1 [16]. We provide measurements of the implementation's performance as well as its complexity. All benchmarks are run under Linux 2.0 on a single processor of an unloaded Pentium 133 MHz PC with 512 K second-level cache and 64 MB RAM. We compare DFKI Oz 1.9.13 (emulated) [16] with SICStus Prolog 3 (emulated) [15]. Garbage collection is turned off. In each benchmark, the basic operation is put in a tail-recursive loop and loop overhead is subtracted.

The evaluation is done in four parts. First, we evaluate the space cost of free records relative to bound records. Then we compare the time cost of Oz tuples (which are exactly Prolog structures) and Oz records (both bound and free) to structures in SICStus Prolog. Tuples are a subtype of bound records and use the same representation. Record features comprise atoms and integers (including bignums). Third, we do a more thorough comparison of bound records and free records from the NLP viewpoint. Finally, we summarize the implementation effort that was required to add records to DFKI Oz.

8.1 Space Evaluation

The memory usage of free records is within a small constant factor of bound records. The following numbers are taken from the DFKI Oz implementation. A bound record with f features takes $2 + f$ words of memory. It uses a tag-on-pointer representation. A free record with f features takes $7 + 2 \cdot 2^{\lceil \log_2 f \rceil}$ words if $f \leq 4$ and $7 + 2 \cdot 2^{\lceil \log_2(f/0.75) \rceil}$ words otherwise. This gives an average of $7 + 2f$ words if $f \leq 4$ and $7 + 3.6f$ words otherwise. That is, records with four features or less are particularly memory efficient. The parameters 4 and 0.75 can be adjusted for the best time/space trade-off.

The arity of a bound record is stored as an entry in the system's symbol table. The entry gives the mapping between feature names and offsets into the record. The entry's size is $8 + 6f$ words on average. This becomes significant only if there are few bound records with the same arity. Free records do not have an entry in the symbol table.

A free record is implemented as a resizable hash table that uses semi-quadratic probing. That is, probe number $i \geq 0$ is offset by $i(i+1)/2$ from the initial hash value. If the table size s is a power of two, then one can show that s successive probes will access all entries of the table. Therefore the hash table can be completely filled. The current system fills the table completely for $f \leq 4$ and to 75% otherwise.

System		Creation	Argument access	Unification
DFKI Oz 1.9.13	free records	7750	966	3975
	bound records	391	206	890
	tuples	395	207	869
SICStus 3	tuples	354	341	566

Table 1. Times for 600,000 basic operations (in ms)

8.2   Time Evaluation

Table 1 compares execution times for 600,000 basic operations. The times are accurate to within 5%. We define the three basic operations (term creation, argument access, term unification) as follows. Term creation builds a single term with three constant arguments. Argument access accesses a single constant argument three times. Term unification unifies two terms with three constant arguments each.

We see that the two emulators are competitive. These numbers confirm the result that records in CCP introduce no inefficiencies when used as Prolog structures. Tuples use the same representation as bound records without penalty. Argument access for bound records in Oz is fast because of caching (see Sect. 5.2). It is faster than SICStus because it is implemented as an emulator instruction, which has lower function-call overhead than a built-in operation. The time (but not the space) for creation of free records is large because creation is incremental. It is currently not possible to create a free record with a given set of features as a single operation. Doing so would require compile-time knowledge of the hash function, which is not yet implemented.

Operation	Time (ms)		Memory (KB)	
	1 feat	10 feat	1 feat	10 feat
Bound records (explicit suspensions)	2120	18200	16700	145000
Free records (solved form)	1100	7470	10900	29800

Table 2. Measurement of suspensions versus the solved form in DFKI Oz

8.3   Records for NLP

Free records are useful for NLP applications. For such applications, it is important to calculate with individual features without being obliged to create a bound record that contains all features. Consider for example a large parse tree. Free records allow one to efficiently express *paths* in this tree from the root to a leaf. Using bound records would require each node of such a path to contain *all possible* children, instead of just the child that is of current interest. A single path breaks even as a free record if there are at least 7 features at each node (i.e., $2 + f \geq 7 + 2 \cdot 1$).

A second example is the sample HPSG parser in the DFKI Oz release. This parser is 1.6 times faster and uses half the memory when using free records instead of bound records. This improved performance is not due to the efficient expression of paths in the parse tree. There is a second improvement that occurs when accessing features that do not yet exist. In a free record, the feature can be added directly, resulting in a CFT solved form. In a bound record, a suspension must be created to wait until the feature is added. We measure the difference between adding a feature and creating a suspension. Consider these two scenarios:

- **Bound records (explicit suspensions).** Access each feature of an unbound variable once, which creates a suspension for each feature.

– **Free records (solved form).** Incrementally create a free record by adding one feature at a time.

Table 2 compares the time and memory usage of 150,000 basic operations, for 1 feature and for 10 features. The solved form is from 1.9 (one feature) to 2.4 (ten features) times faster than a set of suspensions. The solved form uses from 1.5 (one feature) to 4.9 (ten features) times less memory than a set of suspensions.

8.4 Implementation Effort

The bound record implementation of DFKI Oz 1.0 was extended to free records. This required adding 2000 C++ lines to the emulator and 1000 Oz lines to the browser.[6] This is 10% of the basic emulator machinery and 5% of the browser. This required 10 man-weeks for the emulator and 2 man-weeks for the browser. The extension was simplified by using the emulator's support for constrained variables and scripting. Constrained variables are closely related to the attributed variables of ECLiPSe [11].

9 Conclusions and Further Work

We have shown how to extend CLP and CCP systems with efficient and flexible record constraints. We have demonstrated for DFKI Oz:

1. Bound records have the same time and space efficiency as structures in Prolog in a high-performance emulator implementation.
2. Free records have the same amortized time and space complexity as Prolog structures in a high-performance emulator implementation. Furthermore, the actual time needed is within a factor of five and the actual space needed is within a factor of four. The single exception to this conclusion in the current system is the time (not space) of free record creation, whose constant factor is larger since the record is created incrementally.
3. In addition to their additional constraint solving power, free records are more efficient than bound records for NLP in two ways. First, a feature constraint is at least twice as fast and uses less memory when represented in a CFT solved form than when represented as a suspension. Second, free records allow the efficient expression of paths in trees.
4. Adding a record constraint system to CCP is not much harder than adding a record constraint system to CLP. The CCP paradigm replaces choice points by local computation spaces and requires a single additional constraint operation, namely entailment. With local spaces, entailment can be implemented as an extension to unification.

Free records are a fully-integrated and robust part of DFKI Oz since version 1.1. They are being used by our group in a NLP project on concurrent grammar processing. Further refinements of the record implementation (including more optimizations, compile-time analysis, additional primitive operations, and more powerful constraints) must wait for experience from this project and other practical applications.

---

[6] The browser is a concurrent tool used to inspect Oz data structures.

Acknowledgements

Many thanks to the Programming Systems Lab of DFKI, to Richard Meyer and Ralf Treinen, and to DEC PRL once upon a time. This research has been supported by the Bundesminister für Bildung, Wissenschaft, Forschung und Technologie (PERDIO ITW 9601) the Esprit Project ACCLAIM (PE 7195) and the Esprit Working Group CCL (EP 6028). Peter Van Roy is supported by the ERCIM Fellowship Programme while on leave from DFKI. DFKI Oz and its documentation are available through WWW at http://ps-www.dfki.uni-sb.de/.

References

1. Hassan Aït-Kaci. *Warren's Abstract Machine, A Tutorial Reconstruction*. MIT Press, 1991.
2. Hassan Aït-Kaci and Pat Lincoln. LIFE: A natural language for natural language. Technical Report ACA-ST-074-88, MCC, Austin, TX, 1988.
3. Hassan Aït-Kaci, Andreas Podelski, and Gert Smolka. A feature-based constraint system for logic programming with entailment. In *5th FGCS*, pages 1012–1022, 1992.
4. L. Peter Deutsch. Efficient implementation of the Smalltalk-80 system. In *11th Principles of Programming Languages*, January 1984.
5. Gerard Ellis and Peter Van Roy. Compilation of matching in LIFE. *DEC PRL draft report*, May 1992.
6. Gregor Erbach and Suresh Manandhar. Visions for logic-based natural language processing. In *Workshop on the Future of Logic Programming, ILPS 95*, December 1995.
7. Seth Copen Goldstein. An abstract machine to implement functions in LIFE. *DEC PRL technical note 18*, January 1993.
8. Michael J. Maher. Logic semantics for a class of committed-choice programs. In Jean-Louis Lassez, editor, *Logic Programming, Proceedings of the Fourth International Conference*, pages 858–876. MIT Press, 1987.
9. David Maier and David Scott Warren. *Computing with Logic, Logic Programming with Prolog*. Benjamin Cummings, 1988.
10. Michael Mehl, Ralf Scheidhauer, and Christian Schulte. An Abstract Machine for Oz. In Manuel Hermenegildo and S. Doaitse Swierstra, editors, *Programming Languages: Implementations, Logics and Programs, 7th International Symposium, PLILP'95*, Lecture Notes in Computer Science, vol. 982, pages 151–168, Utrecht, The Netherlands, September 1995. Springer-Verlag.
11. Micha Meier. Better later than never. In *Implementation of Logic Programming Systems*, pages 151–165. Kluwer Academic Publishers, 1994.
12. Richard Meyer. Compiling LIFE. *DEA report, DEC PRL draft report*, September 1993.
13. Richard Meyer, Bruno Dumant, and Peter Van Roy. The Half-Life 0.1 system. *Available at* http://ps-www.dfki.uni-sb.de/˜vanroy/halflife.html, 1994.
14. Andreas Podelski and Peter Van Roy. The Beauty and the Beast algorithm: Quasi-linear incremental tests of entailment and disentailment over trees. In *11th ILPS*, pages 359–374, November 1994.
15. SICS Programming Systems Group. *SICStus Prolog User's Manual*. Swedish Institute of Computer Science, 1995.
16. DFKI Programming Systems Lab. *DFKI Oz System and Documentation*. German Research Center for Artificial Intelligence (DFKI), 1995.
17. Vijay A. Saraswat. *Concurrent Constraint Programming*. MIT Press, 1993.
18. Gert Smolka. The Oz programming model. In Jan van Leeuwen, editor, *Computer Science Today*, Lecture Notes in Computer Science, vol. 1000, pages 324–343. Springer-Verlag, Berlin, 1995.
19. Gert Smolka and Ralf Treinen. Records for logic programming. *Journal of Logic Programming*, 18(3):229–258, April 1994.
20. Ralf Treinen. Feature constraints with first-class features. In Andrzej M. Borzyszkowski and Stefan Sokołowski, editors, *Mathematical Foundations of Computer Science*, Lecture Notes in Computer Science, vol. 711, pages 734–743, Gdańsk, Poland, 30 August–3 September 1993. Springer-Verlag.
21. Ralf Treinen. Feature trees over arbitrary structures. Studies in Logic, Language and Information. 1995. To appear.
22. Peter Van Roy. 1983–1993: The wonder years of sequential Prolog implementation. *Journal of Logic Programming*, 19/20:385–441, May/July 1994.

The LOL Deductive Database Programming Language (Extended Abstract)

Mengchi Liu

Department of Computer Science
University of Regina
Regina, Saskatchewan
Canada S4S 0A2
mliu@cs.uregina.ca

Abstract. This paper presents a novel typed deductive database programming language LOL being developed at the University of Regina. This language effectively integrates important features in object-oriented data models, complex object data models, functional data models, and deductive query languages in a uniform framework. It supports object identity, structured values, complex objects, classes, class hierarchy, multiple inheritance as in object-oriented data models and complex object models. It treats atomic values, object identifiers, functor objects, tuples and sets uniformly so that functional dependencies can be represented directly and more generally than in functional data models. As a result, it subsumes most existing deductive database languages as special cases. The LOL language is given a well-defined declarative semantics that cleanly accounts for its object-oriented and complex object features.

1 Introduction

Two important extensions of traditional database technology are advanced data models and deductive query languages. Advanced data models are divided into two kinds: object-oriented data models and complex object data models. Both kinds of models support complex objects, class hierarchy and inheritance in different ways, which greatly enhance the modeling power of the traditional databases. In object-oriented data models [11, 15, 17], every object is represented by its object identifier which can be created or destroyed. Objects can have complex attribute values. The attribute values can be changed but such changes have no effect on the object's identity. Classes can have subclasses and attributes defined on superclasses are inherited by subclasses. Subclasses of a class must be declared explicitly. In complex object data models [7, 9, 22], objects are represented by structured values such as nested tuples and sets. There isn't a notion of object identity. Instances and subclasses of classes are inferred rather than asserted. On the other hand, deductive query languages such as Datalog [10] extend the expressive power of traditional databases by means of recursion and declarative querying with a firm logical foundation.

In the past few years, there has been a lot of research interest in combining object-oriented data models and complex object data models with deductive query languages respectively. The former provides a logic representation of object-oriented principles. Examples of this kind are O-logic[21], revised O-logic [14], IQL [2], F-logic [13], LOGRES[8], and ROL [19]. The latter extends Datalog with set and/or tuple constructors. Examples are COL [1], the calculus in [4], LDL [6], LPS [16], CORAL [24], and Relationlog [18].

Using object identifiers for every object is burdensome even in pure object-oriented databases and being able to use structured values as well is important as discussed in [2, 5, 17]. In deductive object-oriented databases, using object identifiers for every object is more problematic and pure value-oriented (i.e., complex object) approach is argued better in this regard [26].

In this paper, we combine deductive object-oriented approach with deductive value-oriented approach, especially Relationlog and ROL. We present a novel typed language called LOL (Logical Object Language). It effectively integrates important features in object-oriented data models, complex object data models, functional data models, and deductive query languages in a uniform framework. It allows information about real world objects to be specified partially or completely. It supports object identity, structured values, complex objects, classes, class hierarchy, multiple inheritance as in object-oriented data models and complex object models. It treats atomic values, object identifiers, functor objects, tuples, and sets uniformly and supports single-valued, functor-valued, tuple-valued, and set-valued attributes so that functional dependencies can be represented directly and more generally than in functional data models [12, 25]. As a result, it subsumes most existing deductive database languages, including Datalog, LDL, COL, Relationlog, O-logic, ROL as special cases. Indeed, LOL can be used as a pure object-oriented deductive database programming language, or as a pure value-oriented deductive database programming language. Most importantly, LOL allows both value-oriented and object-oriented features to be used together to take the advantages of both approaches.

LOL directly supports the notion of schema and is a typed language without using typed symbols such as typed variables syntactically as in [20, 23] and COL [1]. Instead, symbols of a LOL program are bound to certain types (called classes) based on the schema in the intended semantics of the program.

The LOL language is given a Herbrand minimal model semantics. A stratification in the spirit of several other researchers [1, 3, 6, 18] is used. Following the classical treatment of logic programming languages, we show that for a stratified program, a minimal and supported model when it exists can be computed bottom-up using a finite sequence of fixpoints, and used as the intended semantics of the program.

This paper is organized as follows. Section 2 introduces the syntax of LOL. Section 3 presents Herbrand semantics of LOL and introduces the notion of minimal model. Section 4 focuses on the stratification restriction on programs and bottom-up semantics. Section 5 concludes the paper.

Due to space limitations, the discussion is terse and proofs are omitted.

2 Syntax of LOL

We assume the existence of the following pairwise disjoint sets:

(1) a set of class names $\mathcal{C}$ including *int, real, string*;
(2) a set of function symbols $\mathcal{F}$ with arity $n > 0$;
(3) a set of attribute labels $\mathcal{A}$;
(4) a set of values $\mathcal{D}$ which is the union of the sets of integers $\mathcal{I}$, strings $\mathcal{S}$, and reals $\mathcal{R}$;
(5) a set of object identifiers $\mathcal{O}$;
(6) a set of variables $\mathcal{V}$.

A LOL database consists of two parts: a schema and a program. The schema contains information about classes, while the program contains information about objects. First we define schema.

Let C be a subset of $\mathcal{C}$, F a subset of $\mathcal{F}$, and A a subset of $\mathcal{A}$. Then the *classes* of LOL based on C, F, and A are defined as follows:

(1) if $p \in C$, then it called an *individual* class; if $p \in \{int, real, string\}$, then it is also called a *value* class; otherwise it is called an *object identifier* class;
(2) if f is a function symbol in F, $l_1, ..., l_n$ are attribute labels in A, and $p_1, ..., p_n$ are classes, then $f(l_1 \Rightarrow p_1, ..., l_n \Rightarrow p_n)$ is a class, called a *functor* class;
(3) if $p_1, ..., p_n$ are classes and $l_1, ..., l_n$ are attribute labels in A, then $(l_1 \Rightarrow p_1, ..., l_n \Rightarrow p_n)$ is a *tuple* class;
(4) if p is a class, then $\{p\}$ is a class, called a *set* class.

Classes of LOL are used to denote collections of objects that share common attributes. Based on the above definition, four kinds of classes are distinguished: individual classes, functor classes, tuple classes and set classes. Individual classes are further partitioned into two kinds: value classes and object identifier classes. The collections which value classes denote are fixed in LOL. In details, *int, real, string*, denote $\mathcal{I}$, $\mathcal{R}$, $\mathcal{S}$ respectively. The collections which object identifier and functor classes denote depend on the LOL program. The collections which tuple and set classes denote depend on the collections which the component classes denote.

The following are examples of classes:

Value classes:	*int, real, string*
Object identifier classes:	*person, part, basepart*
Functor classes:	*family(hus $\Rightarrow$ person, wife $\Rightarrow$ person)*,
	point(x $\Rightarrow$ int, y $\Rightarrow$ int)
Tuple classes:	*(city $\Rightarrow$ string, street $\Rightarrow$ string)*,
	(subpart $\Rightarrow$ part, qty $\Rightarrow$ int)
Set classes:	*{part}, {int}, {(city $\Rightarrow$ string, street $\Rightarrow$ string)}*,
	{(subpart $\Rightarrow$ string, qty $\Rightarrow$ int)}

Objects are described via attributes. Attributes are partial mappings from objects to objects. Attributes applicable to objects must be defined on their classes by attribute declarations.

If p and q are classes and l is an attribute label, then $p[l \Rightarrow q]$ declares an *attribute* l of p.

In a functor class $f(l \Rightarrow q, ...)$, or a tuple class $(l \Rightarrow q, ...)$, or in an attribute declaration $p[l \Rightarrow q]$, l is called either *single-valued*, *functor-valued*, *tuple-valued* or *set-valued* depending on q.

The attribute declarations of a class are used to constrain the attribute values of its instances as in traditional databases. Such typing constraints are built into the semantics of the LOL programs.

A class may have subclasses, and a subclass may have more than one superclass. A subclass inherits all attribute declarations from its superclasses, but may introduce extra attribute declarations local to itself.

If p and q are object identifier or functor classes, then p *isa* q declares p to be an *immediate subclass* of q and q to be an *immediate superclass* of p.

For example, we may use $point(x \Rightarrow int, y \Rightarrow int)$ *isa object* and *basepart isa part* to declare $point(x \Rightarrow int, y \Rightarrow int)$ and *basepart* as immediate subclasses of *object* and *part* respectively.

We use $p[l_1 \Rightarrow q_1, ..., l_n \Rightarrow q_n]$ *isa* $p_1, ..., p_m$ to stand for $p[l_1 \Rightarrow q_1]$, ..., $p[l_n \Rightarrow q_n]$, p *isa* p_1, ..., p *isa* p_m.

A *schema* is a tuple $K = (C, F, A, D_C, isa, D_A)$, where

(1) C is a finite subset of $\mathcal{C}$;
(2) F is a finite subset of $\mathcal{F}$;
(3) A is a finite subset of $\mathcal{A}$;
(4) D_C is a finite set of class definitions based on C, F and A.
(5) *isa* is a finite set of immediate subclass declarations;
(6) D_A is a finite set of attribute declarations such that all classes used are in D_C and all attribute names used are in A.

The above definition for schema is an abstract representation. In the following examples, we use a much more intuitive representation. The conversion from the abstract one to the intuitive one is straightforward.

Example 1. The following is a schema of LOL.

$part[name \Rightarrow string]$
$basepart[cost \Rightarrow int, mass \Rightarrow int]$ *isa part*
$compart[madefrom \Rightarrow \{(subpart \Rightarrow part, qty \Rightarrow int)\}$,
$\qquad\qquad assemblycost \Rightarrow int, massincrement \Rightarrow int]$ *isa part*
$\{(subpart \Rightarrow part, qty \Rightarrow int)\}[totalcost \Rightarrow int, totalmass \Rightarrow int]$

The *isa* binary relationship only applies to object identifier and functor classes. We extend it to set and tuple classes as follows.

For a given schema $K = (C, F, A, D_C, isa, D_A)$, *extended-isa* (abbreviated by *e-isa*) is a binary relationship, which satisfies the following:

(1) p *e-isa* q if p *isa* q.
(2) $(l_1 \Rightarrow p_1, ..., l_n \Rightarrow p_n, ..., l_{n+m} \Rightarrow p_{n+m})$ *e-isa* $(l_1 \Rightarrow q_1, ..., l_n \Rightarrow q_n)$, if p_i *e-isa* q_i for $i = 1, ..., n$ and $m \geq 0$.
(3) $\{p\}$ *e-isa* $\{q\}$ if p *e-isa* q.

We denote by *isa** and *e-isa** the reflexive and transitive closures of *isa* and *e-isa* respectively.

The notion *e-isa** captures the subclass relationship among all classes. For example, given *subpart isa part*, we have the following:

{*subpart*} *e-isa* {*part*}
$(l \Rightarrow \{subpart\})$ *e-isa* $(l \Rightarrow \{part\})$
$\{(l_1 \Rightarrow \{subpart\}, l_2 \Rightarrow string)\}$ *e-isa* $\{(l_1 \Rightarrow \{part\})\}$

We next introduce the following notion to capture the multiple inheritance from superclasses to subclasses as in both object-oriented data models and complex object data models.

$$D_A^* = \{p[l \Rightarrow q] \mid \exists p', p \ \textit{e-isa}^* \ p', \text{ and } p'[l \Rightarrow q] \in D_A\}$$

A schema $K = (C, F, A, D_C, isa, D_A)$ is *well-defined* iff

(1) there do not exist $p[l \Rightarrow q_1] \in D_A^*$ and $p[l \Rightarrow q_2] \in D_A^*$ such that $q_1 \neq q_2$,
(2) there do not exist distinct p and q such that p *e-isa** q and q *e-isa** p.

The schema in *Example 1* is well-defined by the definition.

For the rest of the paper, we assume the schema we discuss is well-defined.

Now we define terms and objects.

There are six kinds of terms in LOL: value terms, object identifier terms, functor terms, tuple terms, partial set terms, and complete set terms which are defined recursively as follows:

(1) a value is a *value* term;
(2) an object identifier is an *object identifier* term;
(3) a variable is either a *value* term, an *object identifier* term, a *functor* term, a *complete set* term, or a *tuple* term depending on the context;
(4) if f is an n-ary function symbol from $\mathcal{F}$, $l_1, ..., l_n$ are attribute labels from $\mathcal{A}$, and $O_1, ..., O_n, (n \geq 1)$ are terms, then $f(l_1 \rightarrow O_1, ..., l_n \rightarrow O_n)$ is a *functor* term;
(5) if $O_1, ..., O_n, (n \geq 1)$ are terms, $l_1, ..., l_n$ are attribute labels, then $(l_1 \rightarrow O_1, ..., l_n \rightarrow O_n)$ is a *tuple* term;
(6) if $O_1, ..., O_n, (n \geq 1)$ are terms, then $\langle O_1, ..., O_n \rangle$ is a *partial set* term;
(7) if $O_1, ..., O_n, (n \geq 0)$ are terms not involving partial set terms, then $\{O_1, ..., O_n\}$ is a *complete set* term.

Partial set terms and complete set terms are first introduced in Relationlog [18], which make the language more powerful. The definitions above are more general.

A term is *ground* if it has no variables. An *object* is a ground term. Six kinds of objects are distinguished: values, object identifiers, functor objects, tuples, partial sets, complete sets.

Example 2. The following are examples of objects:

Values:	20, 3.14, "Bob", "Mary"
Object identifiers:	$s_1, s_2, p_1, p_2, p_3, bob, mary$
Functor objects:	$point(x \rightarrow 100, y \rightarrow 200), family(hus \rightarrow bob, wife \rightarrow mary)$
Tuple:	$(city \rightarrow \text{"Toronto"}, street \rightarrow \text{"1, 2nd St."})$
Partial sets:	$\langle bob, mary \rangle, \langle (subpart \rightarrow p_2, qty \rightarrow 5) \rangle$
Complete sets:	$\{(subpart \rightarrow p_1, qty \rightarrow 20), (subpart \rightarrow p_2, qty \rightarrow 5)\}$

Partial sets and complete sets are homogeneous sets of objects, that is, objects of the same class but not necessarily of the same kind. They both are sets of objects but carry different meanings when they are related to other objects through attributes. A complete set means that the information it contains is complete, while a partial set means that the information it contains is partial, that is, part of a complete set. For example, for the partial set $\langle p_1, p_2 \rangle$, we can consider there is a corresponding complete set S such that $p_1 \in S$, $p_2 \in S$ and $cardinality(S) \geq 2$, which could be $\{p_1, p_2\}$, $\{p_1, p_2, p_2\}$, etc. depending on the program.

Follow the convention of Prolog, we use words starting with upper-case letters for variables. In our discussion, we will treat partial sets and complete sets as sets in the traditional sense so that it makes sense to have both $b \in \langle a, b, c \rangle$ and $b \in \{a, b, c\}$.

An *object expression* is defined as follows:

(1) If O is an object identifier or functor term and p is an object identifier or functor class, then $O : p$ is a *simple* object expression.

(2) If O is a functor term, then O is a *simple* object expression.

(3) If O and O' are terms, then $O[l \rightarrow O']$ is a *simple* object expression.

(4) If O, $O[l_1 \rightarrow O_1]$, ..., $O[l_n \rightarrow O_n]$ are simple object expressions, where $n > 0$, then $O[l_1 \rightarrow O_1, ..., l_n \rightarrow O_n]$ is an *composite* object expression, while O, $O[l_i \rightarrow O_i]$ for $i = 1, ..., n$ are called *constituent* object expressions.

(5) If $O : p$, $O[l_1 \rightarrow O_1]$, ..., $O[l_n \rightarrow O_n]$ are simple object expressions, where $n > 0$, then $O[l_1 \rightarrow O_1, ..., l_n \rightarrow O_n]$ and $O : p[l_1 \rightarrow O_1, ..., l_n \rightarrow O_n]$ are object expressions called *composite* object expressions, while $O : p$, $O[l_i \rightarrow O_i]$ for $i = 1, ..., n$ are called *constituent* object expressions of the corresponding composite object expressions.

(6) If ψ is an object expression, then $\neg \psi$ is a negative object expression.

An object expression is *ground* if it has no variables. A ground object expression is *compact* if it does not involve partial sets.

In a ground object expression $o[l \rightarrow o']$, o functions as a key which functionally determines o' as in the relational model. This functional dependency is built into the semantics of LOL. When o and o' involves partial sets, this expression represents information about real world objects partially, otherwise, completely.

Arithmetic and set *comparison* expressions are defined as in the standard arithmetic and set-theoretic theories.

We now define rules. A *rule* is of the form $A :- L_1, ..., L_n$, where the head A is a non-negative object expression and the body $L_1, .., L_n, n \geq 0$ is a sequence of object and comparison expressions. A *fact* is a rule with empty body, i.e., an object expression. A rule is *safe* if all variables in the head are limited and covered as defined in [6, 27].

Rules of LOL are used to infer instances of object identifier classes and functor classes as well as attribute values of objects. Instances of value classes such as *int*, *real* and *string* and the corresponding operations over them are built-in. Instances of set and tuple classes are automatically determined based on the instances of the corresponding component classes. Besides, instances of a subclass are also instances of its superclasses. We will discuss these issues in the section for semantics.

Let $K = (C, F, A, D_C, isa, D_A)$ be a schema. A *program* P based on K is a finite set of safe rules such that all class names, function symbols, and attribute labels used in P are in $C \cup F \cup A$.

Example 3. The following is a program based on the schema in *Example 1.*

p_1 : *basepart*[*cost* → 20, *mass* → 50]
p_2 : *basepart*[*cost* → 10, *mass* → 30]
p_3 : *basepart*[*cost* → 15, *mass* → 40]
p_4 : *compart*[*madefrom* → {(*subpart* → p_1, *qty* → 3),
                          (*subpart* → p_2, *qty* → 2)}]
p_5 : *compart*[*madefrom* → {(*subpart* → p_3, *qty* → 3),
                          (*subpart* → p_4, *qty* → 2)}]
{(*subpart* → P, *qty* → Q)}[*totalcost* → C, *totalmass* → M] :-
            P[*cost* → C_1, *mass* → M_1], $C = Q \times C_1, M = Q \times M_1$
{(*subpart* → P, *qty* → Q)}[*totalcost* → C, *totalmass* → M] :-
            P[*assemblycost* → C_1, *massincrement* → M_1],
            $C = Q \times C_1, M = Q \times M_1$
S[*totalcost* → C, *totalmass* → M] :-
            S_1[*totalcost* → C_1, *totalmass* → M_1], $S = S_1 \cup S_2$,
            S_2[*totalcost* → C_2, *totalmass* → M_2], $S_1 \cap S_2 = \{\}$,
            $C = C_1 + C_2, M = M_1 + M_2$
P[*assemblycost* → C, *massincrement* → M] :-
            P[*madefrom* → S], S[*totalcost* → C, *totalmass* → M]

As shown in the above example, traditional database aggregate operations such as *total*, *count*, etc. can be represented directly in LOL.

A *database* is a tuple $DB = (K, P)$, where K is a schema and P is a program based on K.

3   Semantics of LOL

This section defines the Herbrand interpretations and models for LOL programs.

We first define the universe so that various objects are elements of.

Let $K = (C, F, A, D_C, isa, D_A)$ be a schema. The *universe* U_K based on K is defined as follows:

$U_0 = \mathcal{O} \cup \mathcal{D}$
$U_i = U_{i-1} \cup \mathcal{F}(U_{i-1}) \cup \mathcal{T}(U_{i-1}) \cup \mathcal{C}(U_{i-1}) \cup \mathcal{P}(U_{i-1})$
$U = \cup_{i=0}^{\infty} U_i$

where

$\mathcal{F}(S) = \{f(l_1 \to o_1, ..., l_n \to o_n) \mid n \in \mathcal{N}, f \in F, l_i \in A, o_i \in S \text{ for } i = 1, ..., n\}$
$\mathcal{T}(S) = \{(l_1 \to o_1, ..., l_n \to o_n) \mid n \in \mathcal{N}, l_i \in A, \text{ and } o_i \in S \text{ for } i = 1, ..., n\}$
$\mathcal{P}(S) = \{\langle o_1, ..., o_n \rangle \mid n \in \mathcal{N} \text{ and } o_i \in S \text{ for } i = 1, ..., n\}$
$\mathcal{C}(S) = \{\{o_1, ..., o_n\} \mid n \in \mathcal{N} \text{ and } o_i \in S \text{ for } i = 1, ..., n\}$

Let $K = (C, F, A, D_C, isa, D_A)$ be a schema. The *Herbrand base* B_K based on K is the set of all ground simple object expressions which can be formed using objects in the universe U_K and class names and attribute labels in $C \cup A$.

A subset of B_K is *compact* if it doesn't contain any object expression that involves partial sets. A compact subset of B_K is *consistent* if it does not contain a pair of object expressions $o[l \rightarrow o_1]$ and $o[l \rightarrow o_2]$ such that $o_1 \neq o_2$.

An *interpretation* based on a schema K is a consistent subset of B_K.

It is our intention that in an interpretation, every object $p \in U$ is interpreted by itself; arithmetic, set and comparison operations are interpreted as in the standard arithmetic and set-theoretic interpretations; attributes are interpreted as partial mappings from compact objects to compact objects.

Before we define the notion of satisfaction of a rule, and thus of a program, we introduce several auxiliary notions.

Let S be a subset of B_K. An *instance* of a class in S is defined as follows:

(1) A value is an instance of a value class in S iff it is an element in the collection which the value class denotes.
(2) An object identifier or functor object o is an instance of an object identifier or functor class p in S iff $o : p \in$ S.
(3) A functor object $f(l_1 \rightarrow o_1, ..., l_n \rightarrow o_n)$ is an instance of a class $f(l_1 \Rightarrow p_1, ..., l_n \Rightarrow p_n)$ in S iff $f(l_1 \rightarrow o_1, ..., l_n \rightarrow o_n) \in S$ and o_i is an instance of p_i in S for $i = 1, ..., n$.
(4) A tuple $(l_1 \rightarrow o_1, ..., l_n \rightarrow o_n, ..., l_{n+m} \rightarrow o_{n+m})$ where $n > 0, m \geq 0$ is an instance of a tuple class $(l_1 \Rightarrow p_1, ..., l_n \Rightarrow p_n)$ in S iff o_i is an instance of p_i for $i = 1, ..., n$
(5) A partial or complete set s is an instance of a set class $\{p\}$ in S iff for every $o \in s$, o is an instance of p.

Let $K = (C, F, A, D_C, isa, D_A)$ be a schema, S a subset of B_K, and ψ a ground simple object expression. Then ψ is *well-typed* in S with respect to K if one of the following holds:

(1) ψ is $o : p$ and o is an instance of p in S.
(2) ψ is $f(l_1 \rightarrow o_1, ..., l_n \rightarrow o_n)$ and there exists a functor object class $f(l_1 \Rightarrow p_1, ..., l_n \Rightarrow p_n)$ in D_C of which ψ is an instance in S.
(3) ψ is $o_1[l \rightarrow o_2]$ and there exist classes p and q such that $p[l \Rightarrow q] \in D_A^*$ and o_1 and o_2 are instances of p and q in S respectively.

Let K be a schema and S a subset of B_K. Then S is said to be *well-typed* with respect to K iff every object expression in S is well-typed with respect to K. S is said to be a *well-typed interpretation* with respect to K iff S is well-typed w.r.t. K and is an interpretation.

A *ground substitution* θ is a finite mapping from $\mathcal{V}$ to $\mathcal{U}$. It is extended to terms, and expressions as follows:

(1) if $o \in \mathcal{O} \cup \mathcal{D}$ then $\theta o = o$
(2) if $X \in \mathcal{V}$ then $\theta X = \theta(X)$
(3) $\theta f(l_1 \rightarrow X_1, ..., l_n \rightarrow X_n) = f(l_1 \rightarrow \theta X_1, ..., l_n \rightarrow \theta X_n)$
(4) $\theta(l_1 \rightarrow X_1, ..., l_n \rightarrow X_n) = (l_1 \rightarrow \theta X_1, ..., l_n \rightarrow \theta X_n)$

(5) $\theta\langle X_1, ..., X_n\rangle = \langle\theta X_1, ..., \theta X_n\rangle$

(6) $\theta\{X_1, ..., X_n\} = \{\theta X_1, ..., \theta X_n\}$

(7) if E is an object or comparison expression, then θE results from E by applying θ to every term in E.

An object o is *part-of* a compact object o', denoted by $o \triangleleft o'$, iff

(1) $o = o'$;

(2) $o = f(l_1 \rightarrow o_1, ..., l_n \rightarrow o_n)$, $o' = f(l_1 \rightarrow o'_1, ..., l_n \rightarrow o'_n)$, such that $o_i \triangleleft o'_i$, for $i \in \{1..n\}$;

(3) $o = (l_1 \rightarrow o_1, ..., l_n \rightarrow o_n)$ and $o' = (l_1 \rightarrow o'_1, ..., l_n \rightarrow o'_n)$ such that $o_i \triangleleft o'_i$ for $i \in \{1..n\}$; or

(4) o is a partial set and for each $o_i \in o$ there exists $o'_i \in o'$ such that $o_i \triangleleft o'_i$.

A ground object expression $o_1[l \rightarrow o_2]$ is *part-of* a ground object expression $o'_1[l \rightarrow o'_2]$ denoted by $o_1[l \rightarrow o_2] \triangleleft o'_1[l \rightarrow o'_2]$, iff $o_1 \triangleleft o'_1$ and $o_2 \triangleleft o'_2$.

The following are several examples:

$a_1[l \rightarrow \langle b_1\rangle] \triangleleft a_1[l \rightarrow \{b_1\}]$

$f(l_1 \rightarrow a_1, l_2 \rightarrow \langle b_1\rangle))[l_3 \rightarrow \{c_1\}] \triangleleft f(l_1 \rightarrow a_1, l_2 \rightarrow \{b_1, b_2\})[l_3 \rightarrow \{c_1\}]$

$(l_1 \rightarrow \langle a_1\rangle))[l_2 \rightarrow a_1] \triangleleft (l_1 \rightarrow \{a_1\})[l_2 \rightarrow a_1]$

$\langle a_1\rangle[l \rightarrow \{b_1\}] \triangleleft \{a_1, a_2\}[l \rightarrow \{b_1\}]$

Let K be a schema and I a well-typed interpretation with respect to K. The notion of satisfaction (denoted by $\models$) and its negation (denoted by $\not\models$) are defined as follows:

(1) Let o be an object and p a class. Then $I \models o : p$ iff o is an instance of p in I and for every q such that p e-isa* q, o is also an instance of q in I.

(2) Let $f(l_1 \rightarrow o_1, ..., l_n \rightarrow o_n)$ be a functor object. Then $I \models f(l_1 \rightarrow o_1, ..., l_n \rightarrow o_n)$ iff $f(l_1 \rightarrow o_1, ..., l_n \rightarrow o_n) \in I$.

(3) For each ground simple object expression ψ of the form $o[l \rightarrow o']$, $I \models \psi$ iff there exists $\psi' \in I$ such that $\psi \triangleleft \psi'$.

(4) For each ground composite object expression ψ, $I \models \psi$ iff for every constituent object expression φ of ψ, $I \models \varphi$.

(5) For each ground negative object expression $\psi = \neg\varphi$, $I \models \psi$ iff $I \not\models \varphi$.

(6) For each ground comparison expression ψ, $I \models \psi$ iff ψ is true in the standard arithmetic and set-theoretic interpretation.

(7) Let r be a rule of the form $A :- L_1, ..., L_n$. Then $I \models r$ iff for each ground substitution θ, $I \models \theta L_1, ..., I \models \theta L_n$ implies $I \models \theta A$.

(8) For each program P, $I \models P$ iff for each rule $r \in P$, $I \models r$.

Let $DB = (K, P)$ be a database. A *model* M of P w.r.t. K is a well-typed interpretation w.r.t. K which satisfies P.

Because of the typing and functionality constraints, not all LOL programs have models. Besides, a program may have many different interpretations and models.

We intend to select a well-defined and well-justified minimal model if it exists as the intended semantics for an LOL program. We first define the orders on compact objects, compact object expressions, interpretations and models as in [18] so that we can properly define the notion of minimal model.

A compact object $o \in U$ is a *preferable sub-object* of a compact object $o' \in U$, denoted by $o \preceq_p o'$, iff:

(1) both are elements of U_0, and they are equal;
(2) both are functor objects: $o = f(l_1 \rightarrow o_1, ..., l_n \rightarrow o_n), o' = f(l_1 \rightarrow o'_1, ..., l_n \rightarrow o'_n)$, such that $o_i \preceq_p o'_i$, for $i = 1, ..., n$,
(3) both are tuples, $o = (l_1 \rightarrow o_1, ..., l_n \rightarrow o_n), o' = (l_1 \rightarrow o'_1, ..., l_n \rightarrow o'_n)$, such that $o_i \preceq_p o'_i$, for $i = 1, ..., n$.
(4) both are complete sets, and for each $o_i \in o - o'$, there exists $o'_i \in o' - o$, such that $o_i \preceq_p o'_i$.

The *preferable sub-object expression* relationship between compact object expressions of B_K, denoted by $\preceq_p$, is defined as follows:

(1) $o_1 : p \preceq_p o_2 : p$, if $o_1 \preceq_p o_2$.
(2) $f(l_1 \rightarrow o_1, ..., l_n \rightarrow o_n) \preceq_p f(l_1 \rightarrow o'_1, ..., l_n \rightarrow o'_n)$, if $o_i \preceq_p o'_i$ for $i = 1, ..., n$.
(3) $o_1[l \rightarrow o_2] \preceq_p o'_1[l \rightarrow o'_2]$, if $o_1 \preceq_p o'_1$ and $o'_1 \preceq_p o'_2$.

The following are several examples:

$$a_1[l \rightarrow \{b_1\}] \preceq_p a_1[l \rightarrow \{b_1, b_2\}]$$
$$f(l_1 \rightarrow \{\{b_1\}, \{b_1, b_2\}\})[l_2 \rightarrow \{c_1\}] \preceq_p f(l_1 \rightarrow \{\{b_1\}, \{b_2\}, \{b_1, b_2\}\})[l_2 \rightarrow \{c_1\}]$$

Let I_1 and I_2 be two interpretations. Then I_1 is a *preferable sub-interpretation* of I_2, or I_2 *contains* I_1, denoted by $I_1 \sqsubseteq_p I_2$ iff for every object expression $\psi_1 \in I_1 - I_2$, there exists an object expression $\psi_2 \in I_2 - I_1$ such that $\psi_1 \preceq_p \psi_2$.

The preferable sub-interpretation relationship has the following property.

Proposition 1. The preferable sub-interpretation relationship is a partial order.

A model M of P is *minimal* iff for each model N of P, if $N \sqsubseteq_p M$ then $N = M$.

4   Bottom-Up Semantics

In this section, we show that under a suitable syntactic restriction on the program, namely, stratification, a well-defined, justifiable minimal model, when it exists, can be computed using a sequence of fixpoint operators and used as the intended semantics of the program.

The notion of stratification has been used in several logical languages to give semantics to logic programs involving negation and sets [1, 3, 6, 18]. We present a similar notion here which takes instance inheritance into account.

Let $K = (C, F, A, D_C, isa, D_A)$ be a schema and P a program based on K. The set D_P of *defined symbols* of P is defined as $D_P = C \cup F \cup A$. The *defined symbols* of a rule is the defined symbols of the head of the rule. The relationships $>$ and $\geq$ on D_P are defined as follows:

(1) $x > y$ if there is a rule in which x is in the head, y in the body, and y is either in a negative object expression, or contains complete set terms.
(2) $x \geq y$ if y isa x or if there is a rule in which x is in the head, y is in the body, and $x > y$ is not true.

For each program P, the *dependency graph* G_P is a marked graph constructed as follows: (1) the set of nodes is D_P, (2) there is an edge from x to y if $x \geq y$, and (3) there is a marked edge from x to y if $x > y$.

A dependency graph of P represents the relationship *depend-on* between defined symbols of P.

A program P is *stratified* iff its dependency graph G_P has no cycle with a marked edge.

The stratification of the program induces an order of evaluation of the defined symbols as follows.

Proposition 2. Let P be a program, and D_P be the set of all defined symbols of P. Then P is stratified if and only if there is a partition $D_P = D_1 \dot{\cup} ... \dot{\cup} D_n$ such that

(1) if $x \in D_i$ and $x > y$, then there exists a j such that $i > j$ and $y \in D_j$.
(2) if $x \in D_i$ and $x \geq y$, then there exists a j such that $i \geq j$ and $y \in D_j$.

Unlike deductive value-oriented languages, the partition of the defined symbols may not imply a partition of the program as the defined symbols of rules may belong to several different layers.

This problem can be solved by rewriting each rule with defined symbols belonging to k different layers into k different rules such that the body of each generated rule is identical to the body of the original rule and the head contains only defined symbols of the same layer. For the rest of the paper, we assume the program we discuss has already been rewritten in this way.

Each partition of defined symbols induces a partition of the program into strata. For each $D_P = D_1 \dot{\cup} ... \dot{\cup} D_n$, let $P = P_1 \dot{\cup} ... \dot{\cup} P_n$, where for each i,

$$P_i = \{r \in P \mid \text{the defined symbols of } r \text{ is in } D_i\}$$

We now discuss how to define the semantics of stratified programs.

Let $DB = (K, P)$ be a database and I a well-typed interpretation w.r.t. K, the operator T_P over I is defined as follows.

$$T_P^1(I) = \{\theta B \mid A :\!- L_1, ..., L_n \in R, B \text{ is a constituent expression of } A, \text{ and}$$
$$\text{there exists a ground substitution } \theta \text{ such that } I \models \theta L_1, ...,$$
$$I \models \theta L_n\}$$
$$T_P^2(I) = \{o : q \mid o : p \in T_P^1(I) \text{ and } p \text{ } isa^* \text{ } q\}$$
$$T_P(I) = T_P^1(I) \cup T_P^2(I)$$

if $T_P(I) \cup I$ is well-typed with respect to K; otherwise T_P is undefined.

Here T_P^1 is similar to the traditional immediate consequence operator, while T_P^2 performs instance inheritance. That is, every object of a subclass is also an object of its superclasses. For example, if $p_1 : basepart \in T_P^1(I)$ and $basepart$ isa $part$, then, $p_1 : part \in T_P^2(I)$. Note that our notion of T_P incorporates typing constraints and $T_P(I)$ may not be compact.

Now we introduce the compaction operator C based on our earlier work on Relationlog [18]. It is used to integrate partial information spread among object expressions into complete information. We first introduce the following auxiliary notion.

A set S of objects is *homogeneous* if there exists a class c such that S is an instance of the set class $\{c\}$.

Let S be a homogeneous set of objects. Then S is *compatible* if for every pair $o \in S$ and $o' \in S$, we have

(1) $o = o'$;

(2) $o = f(l_1 \to o_1, ..., l_n \to o_n)$, $o' = f(l_1 \to o'_1, ..., l_n \to o'_n)$, and o_i and o'_i are compatible for $i \in \{1..n\}$;

(3) $o = (l_1 \to o_1, ..., l_n \to o_n)$, $o' = (l_1 \to o'_1, ..., l_n \to o'_n)$, o_i and o'_i are compatible for $i \in \{1..n\}$.

(4) both o and o' are partial sets;

(5) o is a partial set, o' is a complete set and $o \lhd o'$;

A set S of ground object expressions of the form $o : p$ is *compatible* if $S' = \{o \mid o : p \in S\}$ is compatible. A set S of ground object expressions of the form $f(l_1 \to o_1, ..., l_n \to o_n)$ is *compatible* if $S' = \{f(l_1 \to o_1, ..., l_n \to o_n) \mid f(l_1 \to o_1, ..., l_n \to o_n) \in S\}$ is compatible. A set S of ground object expressions of the form $o[l \to o']$ is *compatible* if $S' = \{o \mid o[l \to o'] \in S\}$ is compatible.

The *compaction* operator C is defined on a set S of objects recursively as follows:

(1) $C(\{o\}) = o$ if o is compact.

(2) Let S be a compatible set of objects of the form $f(l_1 \to o_1, ..., l_n \to o_n)$. Then $C(S) = f(l_1 \to C(S1), ..., l_n \to C(S_n))$ if C is defined on S_i, where $S_i = \{o_i \mid f(l_1 \to o_1, ..., l_i \to o_i, ..., l_n \to o_n) \in S\}$, for $1 \le i \le n$. Otherwise, C is undefined.

(3) Let S be a set of objects with a compact object $o \in S$. Then $C(S) = o$ if for every $o' \in S$, $o' \lhd o$. Otherwise $C(S)$ is undefined.

(4) Let S be a set of partial sets. Then $C(S) = \{C(S'') \mid S'' = \{O \mid O \in S' \text{ and } S' \in S\}$ is a compatible set and C is defined on $S''\}$. If C is not defined on S'', then C is undefined.

(5) Let S be a compatible set of tuples. Then $C(S) = (l_1 \to C(S_1), ..., l_n \to C(S_n))$ if C is defined on S_i, where $S_i = \{o_i \mid (l_1 \to p_1, ..., l_i \to o_i, ..., l_n \to o_n) \in S\}$, for $1 \le i \le n$. Otherwise, C is undefined.

(6) In any other cases, C is undefined.

Note that if $C(S)$ is defined, then $C(S)$ is a compact object. We incorporate the consistency checking in the definition of C.

We now define the *compaction* operator C on a set S of object expressions as follows:

(1) Let S be a compatible set of object expressions of the form $o : p$ and $S_1 = \{o \mid o : p \in S\}$. Then $C(S) = \{C(S_1) : p\}$ if $C(S_1)$ is defined.

(2) Let S be a compatible set of object expressions of the form $f(l_1 \to o_1, ..., l_n \to o_n)$ and $S_1 = \{f(l_1 \to o_1, ..., l_n \to o_n) \mid f(l_1 \to o_1, ..., l_n \to o_n) \in S\}$. Then $C(S) = \{C(S_1)\}$ if $C(S_1)$ is defined.

(3) Let S be a compatible set of object expressions of the form $o_1[l \to o_2]$, $S_1 = \{o_1 \mid o_1[l \to o_2] \in S\}$ and $S_2 = \{o_2 \mid o_1[l \to o_2] \in S\}$. Then $C(S) = \{C(S_1)[l \to C(S_2)]\}$ if $C(S_1)$ and $C(S_2)$ are defined. Otherwise, $C(S)$ is undefined.

(4) Let S be an arbitrary set of ground object expressions partitioned into compatible sets S_i, for $i \in N^+$. Then $C(S) = \bigcup_{i \in N^+} C(S_i)$ if C is defined on S_i and such obtained set is consistent. Otherwise, $C(S)$ is undefined.

Example 4. The following examples show how the compaction operator can be applied to objects and object expressions:

$$C(\{a_1, a_2\}) \qquad\qquad \text{undefined}$$
$$C(\{(l \rightarrow a_1), (l \rightarrow a_2)\}) \qquad\qquad \text{undefined}$$
$$C(\{\{a_1\}, \{a_1, a_2\}\}) \qquad\qquad \text{undefined}$$
$$C(\{\langle a_1 \rangle, \langle a_2 \rangle, \langle a_1, a_2 \rangle\}) = \{C(\{a_1\}), C(\{a_2\})\} = \{a_1, a_2\}$$
$$C(\{\langle\langle a_1 \rangle\rangle, \langle\langle a_2 \rangle\rangle, \langle\langle a_1, a_2 \rangle\rangle\}) = \{C(\{\langle a_1 \rangle, \langle a_2 \rangle, \langle a_1, a_2 \rangle\})\} = \{\{a_1, a_2\}\}$$
$$C(\{\langle a_1 \rangle, \langle a_2 \rangle, \{a_1, a_2, a_3\}\}) = \{a_1, a_2, a_3\}$$
$$C(\{f(l_1 \rightarrow \langle a_1 \rangle, l_2 \rightarrow \langle b_2 \rangle), f(l_1 \rightarrow \langle a_2 \rangle, l_2 \rightarrow \langle b_1, b_2 \rangle)\}) =$$
$$f(l_1 \rightarrow \{a_1, a_2\}, l_2 \rightarrow \{b_1, b_2\})$$
$$C(\{(l_1 \rightarrow \langle a_1 \rangle, l_2 \rightarrow \langle b_1 \rangle), (l_1 \rightarrow \langle a_2 \rangle, l_2 \rightarrow \{b_1\})\}) = (l_1 \rightarrow \{a_1, a_2\}, l_2 \rightarrow \{b_1\})$$
$$C(\{\langle\langle l \rightarrow \langle a_1 \rangle \rangle\rangle, \langle\langle l \rightarrow \langle a_2 \rangle \rangle\rangle\}) = \{(l \rightarrow \{a_1, a_2\})\}$$
$$C(\{a_1[l \rightarrow b_1], a_1[l \rightarrow b_2]\}) \qquad\qquad \text{undefined}$$
$$C(\{a_1[l \rightarrow \langle b_1 \rangle], a_1[l \rightarrow \langle b_2, b_3 \rangle]\}) = \{a_1[l \rightarrow \{b_1, b_2, b_3\}]\}$$
$$C(\{f(l_1 \rightarrow a_1, l_2 \rightarrow \langle b_1 \rangle)[l_3 \rightarrow \langle c_1 \rangle], f(l_1 \rightarrow a_1, l_2 \rightarrow \langle b_2 \rangle)[l_3 \rightarrow \{c_1, c_3\}]\}) =$$
$$\{f(l_1 \rightarrow a_1, l_2 \rightarrow \{b_1, b_2\})[l_3 \rightarrow \{c_1, c_3\}]\}$$
$$C(\{(l_1 \rightarrow \langle a_1 \rangle)[l \rightarrow \langle c_1 \rangle], (l_1 \rightarrow \langle a_2 \rangle)[l \rightarrow \langle c_2 \rangle]\}) =$$
$$\{(l_1 \rightarrow \{a_1, a_2\})[l \rightarrow \{c_1, c_2\}]\}$$
$$C(\{\langle a_1 \rangle[l \rightarrow \langle c_1 \rangle], \{a_1, a_2\}[l \rightarrow \langle c_2 \rangle]\}) = \{\{a_1, a_2\}[l \rightarrow \{c_1, c_2\}]\}$$
$$C(\{\langle a_1 \rangle[l \rightarrow \langle c_1 \rangle], \{a_1, a_2\}[l \rightarrow \{c_2\}]\}) \qquad\qquad \text{undefined}$$

As in Relationlog [18], partial set terms in LOL function in two different ways depending on whether they are in the head of rules or in the body of rules. When in the head, they are used to accumulate partial information for the corresponding complete sets. The conversion from partial sets to complete sets is done with the compaction operator C. When in the body, they are used to denote part of the corresponding complete sets. The conversion from complete sets to the corresponding partial sets is done by the part-of notion.

A well-typed interpretation I of P is *supported* iff $I \sqsubseteq_p C(T_P(I))$.

The powers of the operator T_P are defined using the compaction operator as follows:

$$T_P \uparrow 0(I) = I$$
$$T_P \uparrow n(I) = T_P(C(T_P \uparrow (n-1)(I))) \cup T_P \uparrow (n-1)(I) \qquad \text{if } C \text{ is defined}$$
$$T_P \uparrow \omega(I) = \bigcup_{n=0}^{\infty} T_P \uparrow n(I) \qquad \text{if } C \text{ is defined}$$

If C is not defined on $T_P \uparrow i(I)$, then $T_P \uparrow (i+1)(I)$ is undefined.

Let $T_{P_1}, ..., T_{P_n}$ be a sequence of operators. The *iterative powers* of the sequence are defined by

$$M_0 = \{\},$$
$$M_1 = C(T_{P_1} \uparrow \omega(M_0)) \qquad \text{if } C \text{ is defined}$$
$$M_2 = C(T_{P_2} \uparrow \omega(M_1)) \qquad \text{if } C \text{ is defined}$$
$$...$$
$$M_n = C(T_{P_n} \uparrow \omega(M_{n-1})) = M_P \qquad \text{if } C \text{ is defined}$$

Theorem 3. Let $P = P_1 \dot\cup ... \dot\cup P_n$ be a stratified program, and $T_{P_1}, ..., T_{P_n}$ the corresponding operators. If M_P is defined, then it is a minimal and supported model of P.

Given a program P, its *declarative semantics* is given by its minimal and supported model M_P evaluated as above if it exists.

There are two reasons why a program may not have a minimal and supported model. One is that the inferred collection of object expressions is not consistent, therefore the operator C is undefined. Another reason is that some inferred object expressions are not well-typed, therefore the operator T_P is undefined. These have to be checked at run time.

5 Conclusion

In this paper, we have presented a powerful deductive database programming language LOL which effectively integrates important features in object-oriented data models, complex object data models, functional data models, and deductive query languages in a uniform framework. We have developed a Herbrand minimal model semantics for the language and shown that it embodies in a natural and direct way the notions of object identity, structured values, complex object properties, classes, class hierarchy and multiple inheritance as in both object-oriented data models and complex object models. Under the stratification restriction, the semantics of a program is given by a minimal and supported model when it exists, which can be computed bottom-up and therefore used as the intended semantics of the program.

There are several issues which we still need to address. First, the multiple inheritance mechanism of LOL is simple, issues such as overriding are left to be dealt with. Besides, we intend to investigate how to incorporate update constructs within the language while maintaining the minimal model semantics. We are currently investigating how to effectively implement this language.

References

1. S. Abiteboul and S. Grumbach. COL: A logic-based language for complex objects. *ACM TODS*, 16(1):1–30, 1991.
2. S. Abiteboul and P. C. Kanellakis. Object identity as a query language primitive. In *Proc. ACM SIGMOD Intl. Conf. on Management of Data*, pages 159–173, 1989.
3. K.R. Apt, H.A. Blair, and A. Walker. Towards a theory of declarative knowledge. In J. Minker, editor, *Foundation of Deductive Databases and Logic Programming*, pages 89–148. Morgan Kaufmann Publishers, 1988.
4. F. Bancilhon and S. Khoshafian. A calculus for complex objects. *J. Computer and System Sciences*, 38:326–340, 1989.
5. C. Beeri. Formal models for object-oriented databases. In W. Kim, J.M. Nicolas, and S. Nishio, editors, *Deductive and Object-Oriented Databases*, pages 405–430, Kyoto, Japan, December 1989. North-Holland.
6. C. Beeri, S. Naqvi, O. Shmueli, and S. Tsur. Set construction in a logic database language. *J. Logic Programming*, 10(3,4):181–232, April/May 1991.

7. O. P. Buneman, S. B. Davidson, and A. Watters. A semantics for complex objects and approximate answers. *J. Computer and System Sciences*, 43:170–218, 1991.
8. F. Cacace, S. Ceri, S. Crepi-Reghizzi, L. Tanca, and R. Zicari. Integrating object-oriented data modelling with a rule-based programming paradigm. In *Proc. Intl. Conf. on Very Large Data Bases*, pages 251–261, 1990.
9. L. Cardelli. A semantics of multiple inheritance. In *Proc. Intl. Symp. on Semantics of Data Types*, pages 51–67. Springer-Verlag Lecture Notes in Computer Science 173, June 1984.
10. S. Ceri, G. Gottlob, and T. Tanca. *Logic Programming and Databases*. Springer-Verlag, 1990.
11. D. H. Fishman, B. B., H. P. Cate, E. C. Chow, T. Connors, J. W. Davis, N. Derrett, C. G. Hoch, W. Kent, P. Lyngbaek, B. Mahbod, M. A. Neimat, T. A. Ryan, and M. C. Shan. Iris: An object-oriented database management system. *ACM Trans. on Office Information Systems*, 5(1):48–69, January 1987.
12. B. C. Housel, V. Waddle, and S. B. Yao. The functional dependency model for logical database design. In *Proc. Intl. Conf. on Very Large Data Bases*, 1979.
13. M. Kifer, G. Lausen, and J. Wu. Logical foundations of object-oriented and frame-based languages. *Journal of ACM*, 42:741–843, 1995.
14. M. Kifer and J. Wu. A logic for programming with complex objects. *J. Computer and System Sciences*, 47:77–120, 1993.
15. W. Kim. A model of queries for object-oriented databases. In *Proc. Intl. Conf. on Very Large Data Bases*, Amsterdam, The Netherlands, 1989.
16. G. M. Kuper. Logic programming with sets. *J. Computer and System Sciences*, 41:44–64, 1990.
17. C. Lecluse and P. Richard. The O_2 database programming language. In *Proc. Intl. Conf. on Very Large Data Bases*, pages 411–422, Amsterdam, The Netherlands, 1989.
18. M. Liu. Relationlog: A typed extension to datalog with sets and tuples (extended abstract). In *Proc. Intl. Logic Programming Symp.*, pages 83–97, Portland, Oregon, U.S.A., December 1995. MIT Press.
19. M. Liu. ROL: A deductive object base language. *To Appear in Information Systems*, 1996.
20. J.W. Lloyd. *Foundations of Logic Programming*. Springer-Verlag, 2 edition, 1987.
21. D. Maier. A logic for objects. Technical Report CS/E-86-012, Oregon Graduate Center, Beaverton, Oregon, 1986.
22. A. Ohori. Semantics of types for database objects. *Theoretical Computer Science*, 76:53–91, 1990.
23. F. Pfenning, editor. *Types in Logic Programming*. MIT Press., 1992.
24. R. Ramakrishnan, D. Srivastava, and S. Sudarshan. CORAL: Control, relations and logic. In *Proc. Intl. Conf. on Very Large Data Bases*, pages 238–250, 1992.
25. D. W. Shipman. The functional extending the database relational model to capture more meaning. *ACM Trans. on Database Systems*, 4(4):297–434, December 1979.
26. J. Ullman. A comparison between deductive and object-oriented databases systems. In C. Delobel, M. Kifer, and Y. Masunaga, editors, *Deductive and Object-Oriented Databases*, pages 263 – 277, Munich, Germany, December 1991. Springer-Verlag Lecture Notes in Computer Science 566.
27. J.D. Ullman. *Principles of Database and Knowledge-Base Systems*, volume 1. Computer Science Press, 1988.

An Efficient and Precise Sharing Domain for Logic Programs

Christian Fecht

Universität des Saarlandes
66041 Saarbrücken
Tel.: +49–681–302–2464
fecht@cs.uni-sb.de

Introduction: Two variables X and Y *possibly share* in a set Θ of substitutions if there exists a substitution $\vartheta \in \Theta$ with $vars(X\vartheta) \cap vars(Y\vartheta) \neq \emptyset$. Many static analyses of logic programs heavily rely on accurate sharing information between variables: independence analysis for And-parallelism, freeness analysis, and occur check reduction to name a few. The well-known sharing domain **JL** of Jacobs and Langen [2] is considered as one of the most precise sharing domains. It represents concrete substitutions by sets of sets of variables. The abstract domain **JL** does not only express possible sharing, but is also able to express ground dependencies between variables. Since linearity information is useful to infer possible sharing, researchers enhanced **JL** with definite linearity information yielding the abstract domain **JL+LIN**. Unfortunately, **JL** and **JL+LIN** are inherently inefficient, because they have to deal with sets of sets of variables which can have exponential size. Often, **JL+LIN** is dramatically faster than **JL**, but there are many (even small) programs which cannot be analyzed by either **JL** and **JL+LIN**. Consequently, these sharing domains are not feasible in practice.

Downward Closed Sets: To remedy this situation, we propose to approximate an abstract substitution $S \in \mathbf{JL}$ by an abstract substitution $S' \in \mathbf{JL}$ with $S \subseteq S'$ which has a more compact representation. Sets which are downward closed have very compact representations, because they can be represented by their maximal elements. Recall that a set of sets S is downward closed if $A \in S$ implies that every subset of A is also a member of S. Our new sharing domain ↓**JL** is the downward closure of **JL**. The abstract unification procedure for ↓**JL** can be systematically derived from the abstract unification procedure in **JL**. The new domain ↓**JL** expresses possible sharing and definite groundness of variables, but it does not express ground dependencies between variables. In order to compensate this loss of precision, we add the groundness domain **POS** to ↓**JL**. The reduced product of ↓**JL** and **POS** is denoted by ↓**JL+POS**.

Experimental Evaluation: In order to practically compare the efficiency and the precision of **JL** and ↓**JL+POS**, we implemented analyzers based on these domains with the help of the Prolog analyzer generator GENA [1]. Table 1 shows the results of our experiments. The analyzers compute call modes for every predicate in the program. The precision of the analysis is the total number

program	efficiency			precision	
	↓JL+POS	JL	*ratio*	↓JL+POS	JL
action	12.70	∞	∞	41	?
ann	0.54	14.17	26.2	42	42
aqua–c	219.00	∞	∞	3879	?
b2	1.82	47.00	25.8	48	48
boyer	0.17	1.42	8.4	20	20
browse	0.13	5.79	44.5	6	6
chat	22.47	∞	∞	1152	?
chat-parser	7.71	∞	∞	439	?
chess	0.35	34.94	99.8	19	18
cs	0.18	1.82	10. 1	2	2
flatten	0.29	16.28	56.1	32	32
gabriel	0.16	0.28	1.8	11	11
life	0.11	0.12	1.0	1	1
nand	0.86	3.16	3.7	0	0
peep	0.22	0.15	0.7	0	0
press	0.95	15.20	16.0	50	50
read	0.79	5.04	6.4	30	30
readq	2.85	113.41	39.8	100	100
reducer	0.47	∞	∞	104	?
sdda	0.37	∞	∞	53	?
sendmore	0.18	0.31	1.72	1	1
serialise	0.11	2.76	25.1	10	10

Table 1. Experimental Evaluation of ↓JL+POS and JL

of sharing pairs between the arguments of predicates. Some of the programs are large real-world applications. For instance, *aqua-c* is the source code of Peter Van Roy's aquarius Prolog compiler (about 16000 lines of code).

- Programs *action*, *aqua-c*, *chat*, *chat-parser*, *reducer*, and *sdda* could not be analyzed by **JL**.
- *All* programs can be analyzed with ↓**JL+POS**. Most analysis times are very small or at least moderate. On most programs, ↓**JL+POS** is dramatically faster than **JL**.
- For most programs, ↓**JL+POS** infers the same number of sharing pairs as **JL**. There is only one program (*chess*) where ↓**JL+POS** is less precise than **JL** and infers one additional sharing pair.

References

1. Christian Fecht. GENA – a Tool for Generating Prolog Analyzers from Specifications. In Alan Mycroft, editor, *Second International Symposium on Static Analysis (SAS'95)*, pages 418–419. Springer Verlag, LNCS 983, 1995.
2. D. Jacobs and A. Langen. Static analysis of logic programs for independent and-parallelism. *Journal of Logic Programming*, 13:291–314, 1992.

Cheap Tupling in Calculational Form

Zhenjiang Hu[1], Hideya Iwasaki[2], Masato Takeichi[1]

[1] Department of Information Engineering, University of Tokyo
7-3-1 Hongo, Bunkyo-ku, Tokyo 113, Japan
Email: hu@ipl.t.u-tokyo.ac.jp and takeichi@u-tokyo.ac.jp
[2] Department of Computer Science, Faculty of Technology
Tokyo University of Agriculture and Technology
2-24-16 Naka-cho, Koganei, Tokyo 184, Japan
Email: hiwasaki@cc.tuat.ac.jp

Abstract

In functional programming, a program *prog* is usually expressed as compositions of transformations over data structures while each transformation is defined by a recursion $\mathcal{R}_i$ traversing over its input data structure, namely

$$prog = \mathcal{R}_1 \circ \cdots \circ \mathcal{R}_n.$$

This compositional style of programming allows clearer and more modular programs, but comes at a price of possibly high runtime overhead resulting mainly from the following two categories: (1) Unnecessary intermediate data structures passed between the composition of two recursions; (2) Inefficiency in a single recursion, such as redundant recursive calls, multiple traversals of the same data structures, and unnecessary traversals of intermediate data structures.

Although this paper is mainly concerned with elimination of the inefficiency in the latter case, these two kinds of inefficiency are much related, for which there are two known tactics, namely *Fusion* (or called *deforestation*) [Wad88] and *Tupling* [Chi93]. Fusion is to merge nested compositions of recursive functions in order to obtain new recursions without unnecessary intermediate data structures, while tupling is to remove redundant recursive calls and multiple traversals of the same data structure from recursions.

Different approaches are employed to formulate *fusion* and *tupling*. One, extensively studied by Chin [Chi93], is based on the so-called *fold/unfold transformation*. It, however, suffers from the high cost of keeping track of function calls and has to use clever control to avoid infinite unfolding, which prevents fusion and tupling being embedded in a real practical compiler of functional languages. To overcome this difficulty, quite a lot of studies have been devoted to another approach called *transformation in calculational form* [GLJ93, TM95, HIT96] based on the theory of *Constructive Algorithmics*. It makes use of the recursive structure information in some specific forms such as *catamorphisms* (or called *folds*), *anamorphisms* (or called *unfolds*) and *hylomorphisms* and finds how transformation can be performed over them.

The latter approach, being less general than the former, has been successfully applied to the fusion transformation. It is based on a quite simple *Acid Rain* calculational rule [TM95], an extension of the *shortcut deforestation* rule [GLJ93], and can be practically employed in a real compiler of functional languages (e.g., Glasgow Haskell Compiler). However, so far as we know, no attempt has been made to adapt this calculational approach to the tupling transformation for the improvement of recursive functions. We believe it is worth doing for two reasons. First, tupling and fusion are two most related transformation tactics, so they should be studied in the same framework. In fact, the roles of tupling and fusion are complementary; fusion merges compositions of recursions into one which then should be improved again by tupling in order to obtain a final efficient program. Second, with the same reason for the shortcut deforestation [GLJ93, TM95], tupling should be used practically in a real compiler. So far, we haven't seen a real practical compiler which performs tupling transformation.

In this paper, we propose the idea of *cheap tupling*[3] in a calculational way. Our main contributions are as follows.

First, we identify the importance of the relationship between tupling transformation and *structural* mutual recursions (not a simple mutual recursion) based on which we propose three simple but effective calculational rules for our cheap tupling transformation.

Second, as discussed above, our cheap tupling follows the approach of transformation in calculational form based on constructive algorithmics. This is in sharp contrast to the previous study based on fold/unfold transformation. Therefore, our cheap tupling preserves the advantages of transformation in calculational form, as we have seen in the discussion of shortcut deforestation in [GLJ93, TM95].

Third, our cheap tupling can coexist well with fusion in calculational form. In contrast, the previous study on this combination based on fold/unfold transformation is much more difficult because of complicated control of infinite unfoldings in the case where fusion and tupling are applied simultaneously.

References

[Chi93] W. Chin. Towards an automated tupling strategy. In *Proc. Conference on Partial Evaluation and Program Manipulation*, pages 119–132, Copenhagen, June 1993. ACM Press.

[GLJ93] A. Gill, J. Launchbury, and S.P. Jones. A short cut to deforestation. In *Proc. Conference on Functional Programming Languages and Computer Architecture*, pages 223–232, Copenhagen, June 1993.

[HIT96] Z. Hu, H. Iwasaki, and M. Takeichi. Deriving structural hylomorphisms from recursive definitions. In *ACM SIGPLAN International Conference on Functional Programming*, pages 73–82, Philadelphia, PA, May 1996. ACM Press.

[TM95] A. Takano and E. Meijer. Shortcut deforestation in calculational form. In *Proc. Conference on Functional Programming Languages and Computer Architecture*, pages 306–313, La Jolla, California, June 1995.

[Wad88] P. Wadler. Deforestation: Transforming programs to eliminate trees. In *Proc. ESOP (LNCS 300)*, pages 344–358, 1988.

---

[3] We call it *cheap* tupling after the name of *shortcut* deforestation.

Needed Narrowing in Prolog
(Extended Abstract)

Sergio Antoy

Portland State University

We discuss an implementation of *needed narrowing* deployed in an extension [4] of the Gödel compiler [6], which translates Gödel source code into Prolog source code. Our implementation is high-level, portable, and similar to, but more efficient than, [5] that in turn is an improvement of [7].

Needed narrowing [3] is a sound, complete, and optimal strategy for semantic unification in inductively sequential rewrite systems. Inductive sequentiality [1] amounts to the existence of a definitional tree $\mathcal{T}$ for each operation f, i.e., a set of patterns partially ordered by subsumption with the following properties up to renaming of variables.

- [root property] The minimum element, referred to as the *root*, of $\mathcal{T}$ is $f(X_1, \ldots, X_n)$, where $X_1, \ldots, X_n$ are distinct variables.
- [leaves property] The maximal elements, referred to as the *leaves*, of $\mathcal{T}$ are all and only (variants of) the left hand sides of the rules defining f. Non-maximal elements of $\mathcal{T}$ are referred to as *branches*.
- [parent property] If π is a pattern of $\mathcal{T}$ different from the root, there exists in $\mathcal{T}$ a unique pattern π' strictly preceding π such that there exists no other pattern strictly between π and π'. π' is referred to as the *parent* of π and π as a *child* of π'.
- [induction property] All the children of a same parent differ from each other only at the position of a variable, referred to as *inductive*, of their parent.

There exist operations with no definitional tree, and operations with more than one definitional tree, examples are in [1]. The existence of a definitional tree of a function f is decidable and simple to decide in most practical situations.

Our implementation of needed narrowing maps each operation f into a family of Prolog predicates $f_0, f_1, \ldots$ such that if $f_i(u_1, \ldots, u_n, u)$ succeeds, then u is a minimal head normal form of $f(u_1, \ldots, u_n)$. Like all modern approaches to the implementation of efficient narrowing, the predicates $f_0, f_1, \ldots$ are generated by a traversal of a definitional tree $\mathcal{T}$ of f. Clauses are generated when a each node of $\mathcal{T}$ is visited and depend on whether the node is a *branch* or a *leaf*. The latter case further considers whether the corresponding rule right hand side is a variable, a constructor-rooted term, or an operation-rooted term. Finally, half a dozen optimizations, some of which were originally proposed in [5], are applied to the generated code. A full account of the translation of $\mathcal{T}$ into $f_0, f_1, \ldots$ is in [2].

This work has been supported in part by the National Science Foundation under grant CCR-9406751. Author's address: Dept. of Computer Science, P.O. Box 751, Portland, OR 97207, antoy@cs.pdx.edu.

The semantic unification of terms t and u is computed by narrowing the equation $t \approx u$ to *true*, where "$\approx$" is defined by the equality rules of each sort [3]. Since these rules are inductively sequential, we obtain the Prolog predicates defining equality as for any other operation. We apply to this code a set of optimizations specialized for the relatively simple rules of "$\approx$". We use a definition of equality, referred to as *semi-strict*, that is more general than [5, 7], since throughout our implementation variables are substituted by constructor terms only — a property that also holds for Gödel, whose compiler has been extended with our implementation.

Our implementation differs from [5] in that we adopt a less strict notion of equality, which reduces the size of the search space in some cases; we perform more optimizations, which make better use of the built-in unification; and we take better advantage of mode information, which avoids the creation of some choice points and the execution of some unnecessary predicate calls.

We use the five equations proposed in [5, Sect. 7] to benchmark our implementation. The following table shows the computation time for finding the first solution of an equation as percent of the time required by Hanus's code. The comparison with several other implementations of narrowing in Prolog can be inferred using the benchmarks in [5], where it is shown that Hanus's code is the fastest.

Equation	E_1	E_2	E_3	E_4	E_5	Aver.
% time	64	44	68	44	41	50

The benchmark shows that our code is twice as fast as [5]. The amount of memory allocated by the two methods for computing the first solution of each equation is the same.

References

1. S. Antoy. Definitional trees. In *Proc. of the 4th Intl. Conf. on Algebraic and Logic programming*, pages 143–157. Springer LNCS 632, 1992.
2. S. Antoy. Needed narrowing in Prolog. Technical report TR 96-2, Portland State University, Portland, OR, May 1996. Full version of this abstract accessible via http://www.cs.pdx.edu/~antoy.
3. S. Antoy, R. Echahed, and M. Hanus. A needed narrowing strategy. In *Proc. 21st ACM Symposium on Principles of Programming Languages*, pages 268–279, Portland, 1994.
4. B. J. Barry. Needed narrowing as the computational strategy of evaluable functions in an extension of Gödel. Master's thesis, Portland State University, June 1996.
5. M. Hanus. Efficient translation of lazy functional logic programs into Prolog. In *Proc. Fifth International Workshop on Logic Program Synthesis and Transformation*, pages 252–266. Springer LNCS 1048, 1995.
6. P. M. Hill and J. W. Lloyd. *The Gödel Programming Language*. MIT Press, 1993.
7. R. Loogen, F. J. López-Fraguas, and M. Rodríguez-Artalejo. A demand driven computation strategy for lazy narrowing. In *PLILP'93*, pages 184–200, Tallinn, Estonia, August 1993. Springer LNCS 714.

Automatic Optimization of Dynamic Scheduling in Logic Programs

Germán Puebla and *Manuel Hermenegildo*

{german,herme}@fi.upm.es
Department of Artificial Intelligence
Technical University of Madrid (UPM)

(Abstract)

1 Dynamic Scheduling

Many modern logic programming languages provide more flexible scheduling than the Prolog traditional left-to-right computation rule. Computation generally also proceeds following some fixed scheduling rule but certain goals are dynamically "delayed" until their arguments are sufficiently instantiated to allow the call to run efficiently. This general form of scheduling is referred to as *dynamic scheduling*. Languages with dynamic scheduling also include constraint programming languages in which constraints which are "too hard" are delayed. In addition, most implementations of concurrent (constraint) programming languages essentially also follow a fixed left to right scheduling rule with suspension, where such suspension is controlled by the conditions in the *ask* guards. In fact, it has been shown that many such languages can be directly translated into (constraint) logic programs with dynamic scheduling with competitive efficiency. As a result, languages with dynamic scheduling are being seen more and more as very useful targets for prototyping or even implementing concurrent languages.

2 Optimization of Dynamic Scheduling

Dynamic scheduling increases the expressive power of (constraint) logic programs, but in most implementations it also introduces significant run-time overhead. The objective of our optimization is to reduce as much as possible this additional overhead by means of global analysis and program transformation, while preserving the semantics of the original programs. Previous work on optimization of dynamic scheduling has concentrated on detecting non-suspension (e.g., [4]) or on eliminating dynamic scheduling when it is not needed and/or producing reorderings in which dynamic scheduling is not needed any more (e.g., [1]). However, finding an order of literals in which no dynamic scheduling is needed does not guarantee that efficiency is improved. By this we do not mean to say that reordering should not be performed, but rather that it should only be performed when some conditions are met. In [7] we present optimization techniques which treat all the usual forms of delay declarations and are both correct and efficient in the sense of [5, 3], i.e., the observables are preserved and computation time is never increased (the *no slow-down* property is met). These optimizations include simplification of delay conditions in **when** meta-calls, and elimination of such meta-calls when not needed. Regarding **block** declarations, since they affect all the literals that call the corresponding predicate, they can in principle be simplified only if the simplification is allowed in *all* such literals. This is overcome by means of *multiple specialization* which involves the generation of several versions of a predicate for different uses.

3 Implementation and Experimental Results

The optimization techniques presented in [7] have been implemented in the CIAO compiler [6] using newly available analysis techniques [2]. This is, to the best of our knowledge, the first implementation and integration in a compiler of an optimizing technique for dynamic scheduling. A series of benchmark programs have been implemented in a reversible way, so that they can be used in two modes of operation, forwards and backwards, through the use of suspension declarations. Note that though the declarative meaning of these programs explains both modes of operation, the fixed left-to-right scheduling rule does not allow running them backwards. The results show that optimization times are comparable to the time that the SICStus compiler takes to compile the same benchmarks into compact-code. For forward execution, all delay declarations are eliminated, obtaining a program which is as efficient as the original program designed to work forwards. This means that it is possible to write programs that are reversible (either by using the delay declarations directly or by using a higher level language for which the compiler generates delay declarations automatically) without incurring any run-time overhead when executing forwards. For backward execution, many of the delay declarations are needed and thus are not always completely eliminated by the optimizer. However, even in this case some speed-up is obtained due to the optimizer simplifying the suspension conditions.

References

1. J. Boye. Avoiding dynamic delays in functional logic programs. In *Programming Language Implementation and Logic Programming*, number 714 in LNCS, pages 12–27, Estonia, August 1993. Springer-Verlag.
2. M. García de la Banda, K. Marriott, and P. Stuckey. Efficient Analysis of Constraint Logic Programs with Dynamic Scheduling. In *1995 International Logic Programming Symposium*, Portland, Oregon, December 1995. MIT Press.
3. María José García de la Banda García. *Independence, Global Analysis, and Parallelism in Dynamically Scheduled Constraint Logic Programming*. PhD thesis, Universidad Politécnica de Madrid (UPM), July 1994.
4. M. Hanus. Analysis of Nonlinear Constraints in CLP(R). In *Tenth International Conference on Logic Programming*, pages 83–99. MIT Press, June 1993.
5. M. Hermenegildo and F. Rossi. Strict and Non-Strict Independent And-Parallelism in Logic Programs: Correctness, Efficiency, and Compile-Time Conditions. *Journal of Logic Programming*, 22(1):1–45, 1995.
6. M. Hermenegildo, F. Bueno, M. García de la Banda, and G. Puebla. The CIAO Multi-Dialect Compiler and System: An Experimentation Workbench for Future (C)LP Systems. In *Proccedings of the ILPS'95 Workshop on Visions for the Future of Logic Programming*, Portland, Oregon, USA, December 1995.
7. G. Puebla and M. Hermenegildo. Automatic optimization of dynamic scheduling in logic programs. Technical report, Technical University of Madrid, 1996. Available from http://www.clip.dia.fi.upm.es/.

Oz Explorer: A Visual Constraint Programming Tool

Christian Schulte

Programming Systems Lab, German Research Center for AI (DFKI)
Stuhlsatzenhausweg 3, 66123 Saarbrücken, Germany
E-mail: schulte@dfki.uni-sb.de

Development of applications based on constraint programming proceeds in two steps. The first step is to design a principally working solution. This is followed by the much harder task to make this solution work for problems of real-world size. The latter task usually involves a high amount of experimentation to gain additional insights into the structure of the problem. Meier reports in [2] that a large part of the development process is spent on performance debugging. Therefore it is surprising that existing systems offer little support for the development of constraint programming applications (with the recent exception of [2]).

The Oz Explorer The Oz Explorer [3] is a visual constraint programming tool for Oz. Oz is a concurrent constraint language providing for functional, object-oriented, and constraint programming [5, 1, 4, 6]. It has a simple yet powerful computation model which extends the concurrent constraint model by first-class procedures, concurrent state and encapsulated search.

The Explorer uses the search tree of a constraint problem as its central metaphor. The Explorer implements a user-guided search strategy: The user can interactively explore the search tree which is visualised as it is explored. To the right a screen shot of the Explorer is shown with almost 14400 nodes, of which about 14300 do not correspond to solutions and are therefore hidden automatically.

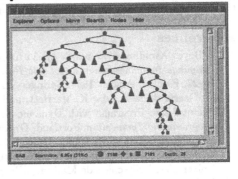

Nodes carry information on the corresponding constraints. The information can be accessed interactively by using predefined or user-defined display procedures. The Explorer can be used with any search problem. The problem need not be changed, annotated or modified in any way. In particular, the Explorer does not rely on a fixed constraint system.

First insights into the structure of the problem can be gained from the visualisation of the search tree: how are solutions distributed, how many solutions exist, how large are the parts of the tree explored before finding a solution. The insights can be deepened by displaying and analysing the constraints of nodes in the search tree: from this it can be deduced whether constraint propagation is sufficient and whether the heuristic suggests the right choices. User-defined display procedures allow to customise the Explorer such that analysing can be done by tools suited to a particular application (e.g., Gantt-charts for scheduling applications).

Interactive exploration allows to follow promising paths in the search tree without exploring irrelevant parts of it. This supports the design of new heuristics and search strategies.

Complex real world problems require that a tool is practical with respect to both efficiency and display economics. The amount of information displayed by the Explorer is variable: the search tree can be scaled and subtrees can be hidden. In particular, all subtrees that do not contain solutions can be hidden automatically. To deal with constraint problems that would use too much memory otherwise, the Explorer employs recomputation which trades space for time.

First-class Computation Spaces One reason that there are only so few tools for the development of constraint programs is that controlling search is hard in existing systems. Systems like CHIP, clp(FD), cc(FD), and ECLiPSe provide for a single fixed search strategy based on backtracking. In contrast to this, search strategies like single, all, and best solution search are not built-in in Oz, but are programmed using first-class computation spaces. The Explorer is one example of a user-guided interactive search strategy.

Acknowledgements The research reported in this paper has been supported by the Bundesminister für Bildung, Wissenschaft, Forschung und Technologie (FTZ-ITW-9105 and FTZ-ITW-9601), the Esprit Project ACCLAIM (PE 7195), and the Esprit Working Group CCL (EP 6028).

References

1. Martin Henz, Gert Smolka, and Jörg Würtz. Object-oriented concurrent constraint programming in Oz. In Vijay Saraswat and Pascal Van Hentenryck, editors, *Principles and Practice of Constraint Programming*, chapter 2, pages 29–48. The MIT Press, Cambridge, MA, 1995.
2. Micha Meier. Debugging constraint programs. In Ugo Montanari and Francesca Rossi, editors, *Proceedings of the First International Conference on Principles and Practice of Constraint Programming*, volume 976 of *Lecture Notes in Computer Science*, pages 204–221. Springer Verlag, Berlin, 1995.
3. Christian Schulte. Oz Explorer: A Visual Constraint Programming Tool. July 1996. Available from http://www.ps.uni-sb.de/~schulte/.
4. Christian Schulte, Gert Smolka, and Jörg Würtz. Encapsulated search and constraint programming in Oz. In Alan H. Borning, editor, *Second Workshop on Principles and Practice of Constraint Programming*, volume 874 of *Lecture Notes in Computer Science*, pages 134–150. Springer-Verlag, Berlin, 1994.
5. Gert Smolka. The Oz programming model. In Jan van Leeuwen, editor, *Computer Science Today*, volume 1000 of *Lecture Notes in Computer Science*, pages 324–343. Springer-Verlag, Berlin, 1995.
6. Gert Smolka and Ralf Treinen, editors. *DFKI Oz Documentation Series*. German Research Center for Artificial Intelligence (DFKI), Saarbrücken, Germany, 1995.

Author Index

Springer-Verlag
and the Environment

We at Springer-Verlag firmly believe that an international science publisher has a special obligation to the environment, and our corporate policies consistently reflect this conviction.

We also expect our business partners – paper mills, printers, packaging manufacturers, etc. – to commit themselves to using environmentally friendly materials and production processes.

The paper in this book is made from low- or no-chlorine pulp and is acid free, in conformance with international standards for paper permanency.

Lecture Notes in Computer Science

For information about Vols. 1–1075

please contact your bookseller or Springer-Verlag